AF184356

The Stakes of Regulation

ANTHEM OTHER CANON ECONOMICS

The *Anthem Other Canon Economics* series is a collaboration between Anthem Press and The Other Canon Foundation. The Other Canon – also described as 'reality economics' – studies the economy as a real object rather than as the behaviour of a model economy based on core axioms, assumptions and techniques. The series includes both classical and contemporary works in this tradition, spanning evolutionary, institutional and Post-Keynesian economics, the history of economic thought and economic policy, economic sociology and technology governance, and works on the theory of uneven development and in the tradition of the German historical school.

Editorial Board

Erik S. Reinert (series editor) – Chairman, The Other Canon Foundation, Norway and Tallinn University of Technology, Estonia
Rainer Kattel (series editor) – Tallinn University of Technology, Estonia
Wolfgang Drechsler (series editor) – Tallinn University of Technology, Estonia
Ha-Joon Chang – University of Cambridge, UK
Mario Cimoli – UN-ECLAC, Chile
Jayati Ghosh – Jawaharlal Nehru University, India
Steven Kaplan – Cornell University, USA & University of Versailles, France
Jan Kregel – University of Missouri, USA & Tallinn University of Technology, Estonia
Bengt-Åke Lundvall – Aalborg University, Denmark
Richard Nelson – Columbia University, USA
Keith Nurse – University of the West Indies, Barbados
Patrick O'Brien – London School of Economics and Political Science (LSE), UK
Carlota Perez – Judge Institute, University of Cambridge, UK
Alessandro Roncaglia – Sapienza University of Rome, Italy
Jomo Kwame Sundaram – Food and Agriculture Organization of the United Nations, Italy

The Stakes of Regulation

Perspectives on *Bread, Politics and Political Economy* Forty Years Later

Steven L. Kaplan

ANTHEM PRESS

Anthem Press
An imprint of Wimbledon Publishing Company
www.anthempress.com

This edition first published in UK and USA 2015
by ANTHEM PRESS
75–76 Blackfriars Road, London SE1 8HA, UK
or PO Box 9779, London SW19 7ZG, UK
and
244 Madison Ave. #116, New York, NY 10016, USA

Copyright © Steven L. Kaplan 2015

The author asserts the moral right to be identified as the author of this work.

All rights reserved. Without limiting the rights under copyright reserved above, no part of this publication may be reproduced, stored or introduced into a retrieval system, or transmitted, in any form or by any means (electronic, mechanical, photocopying, recording or otherwise), without the prior written permission of both the copyright owner and the above publisher of this book.

British Library Cataloguing-in-Publication Data
A catalogue record for this book is available from the British Library.

Library of Congress Cataloging-in-Publication Data
A catalog record for this book has been requested.

ISBN-13: 978 1 78308 476 0 (Hbk)
ISBN-10: 1 78308 476 6 (Hbk)

“La Porteuse de pain” by Jules-Félix Coutan (1882), Square St.-Jacques, Paris (destroyed by Vichy government, 1942) © Collection Roger-Viollet / Roger-Viollet

This title is also available as an ebook.

For Marie-Christine, *toujours complice*

CONTENTS

INTRODUCTION

All politics starts with a grain of wheat.—Mirabeau[1]
No bread, no politics.—Ange Goudard[2]
I like reality, it has the taste of bread.—Jean Anouilh[3]

I wrote *Bread, Politics and Political Economy in the Reign of Louis XV* as a doctoral dissertation at Yale. I had been studying the history of the American South with C. Vann Woodward, a wonderful teacher and splendid person whose deep social humanism and wise criticism I have never forgotten. My fascination with the South began at Princeton, a university deeply marked by its historical ties with the South. Princeton was still home to descendants of slaves manumitted by their student masters at graduation, some of whom worked in the eating clubs for which the university was (in-)famous. It also still attracted some of the South's best and brightest, as the formula put it, who were in search of an Ivy education in quasi-familiar terrain, a number of whom became my roommates and club mates. This was the more exotic component of a Brooklyn Jew's encounter with the wider Wasp world. If Princeton helped to incarnate a certain image of the South, my involvement in the civil rights movement had already drawn my interest to the southern experience. In retrospect, I suspect that my keen interest in the South, so deeply, emblematically and enigmatically an expression of America, had something to do with my own conflicted sense of needing or wanting to become more American, residue of a long-simmering feeling, not rare among the children of immigrants, especially early in their lives, that I did not belong.

1 "Toute la politique part d'un grain de blé." V. R. Mirabeau and F. Quesnay, *Lettres sur la dépravation et la restauration de l'ordre légal*, vol. 1 (London, 1769), 74.

2 "Point de pain, point de politique." Ange Goudard, *Les Intérêts de la France mal entendus, dans les branches de l'agriculture, de la population, des finances, du commerce, de la marine et de l'industrie*, vol. 1 (Amsterdam, 1757), 16.

3 Cited in Steven L. Kaplan, *Le Pain maudit: Retour sur la France des années oubliées, 1945–58* (Paris: Fayard, 2008), 1090.

I did not live this sentiment of unrootedness traumatically. On the contrary, it enhanced my curiosity for everything unfamiliar. I saw it as a sort of availability or receptivity. The burden of being an outsider had marked me indelibly, but I had begun to espy its advantages as well. I suspect that my French turn spoke to this quest to construct my "self." Perhaps in order to anchor one identity, I needed to acquire another. Indeed, I had nourished a long-standing flirtation with things French, begun in undergraduate courses taught by Charles Gillispie, Ira Wade, Albert Sonnenfeld and David Bien, kindled at work in a wine factory at Ivry-sur-Seine for three months (1962), and subsequently fostered by a Fulbright year at Poitiers (1963–64). I was not fully aware of the extent to which it had taken control of my *for intérieur* until the time of quasi-irrevocable choices came at Yale: selection of a thesis project and plans to undertake research in the field.

I had become engrossed by the symbolic and pragmatic vision of transforming the still inchoate nation by building a transcontinental railroad, some of whose investors were French. Woodward had brilliantly shown that the story of railroads (like that of grain) was not merely technological but quintessentially political and cultural.[4] A paper I wrote for Woodward on the Memphis, El Paso and Pacific Railroad seemed to open the path to an interesting dissertation project that could lead me in multiple directions, in the South and beyond. From what I was able to discern from afar, my major archival trove was situated in Paris, Texas—giving me a claim of moral anteriority to Wim Wenders. Later, the town erected a 65-foot replica of the Eiffel Tower, coiffed with a red cowboy hat, not quite a phrygian cap, yet an affirmation of liberty in northeast Texas. It seemed like a pleasant enough place, an opportunity to learn about (yet) another America. At the same time, psychologically and emblematically, it compelled me to confront the smoldering issue that I had repressed under Woodward's spell-binding aegis: was I really prepared to give up, more or less definitively, the other Paris? Though I remained strongly attracted to Woodward's (old/new) South—perhaps more to the tangled populist ideology of a Tom Watson and the People's Party, where a critique of unchained laissez-faire commingled with a strain of anti-Semitism and a resurgent racism that later engulfed him, than to the more irenic and sanguine message of Henry Grady—I knew in the end that, if I continued to do history, my work would be in France.[5]

---

4 See C. Vann Woodward, *Reunion and Reaction: The Compromise of 1877 and the End of Reconstruction* (Boston: Little, Brown and Company, 1951).

5 See the wonderful selection from Woodward's prolific correspondence, *The Letters of C. Vann Woodward*, ed. Michael O'Brien (New Haven, CT: Yale University Press, 2013).

Total History: Program and Conceit

I had already chosen my camp in France, within the fiercely contested terrain of French historiography, after having read every issue of the *Annales* in the Bloch-Febvre and then the Braudel incarnations. The notion of total history captivated me: at the age of 25, I had no critical perspective on it at all. Nor was there anyone at Yale in French history at that time to bridle my untainted, albeit jejune, ardor.

It seems strange, even implausible in retrospect, but in the 1960s, Fernand Braudel was not a classroom-word in the American academic community. Between the early, mixed reception of *La Méditerranée* at the beginning of the 1950s and its second coming in the early 1970s, Braudel commanded little scholarly press. Probably representative of the prevailing American point of view in the early years, Bernard Bailyn, at the dawn of a brilliant career, harshly reproached this sprawling, rambling book for failure to achieve "the integration of its parts that could result from the posing of proper historical questions." While Braudel is barely mentioned in the pages of the *American Historical Review* in the 1960s, Americans began to hear increasingly of the *Annales* and what cinephile (and Francophile) historian Eric Hobsbawm called "the French *nouvelle vague* in history." Yet even as Robert Forster, specialist of the French nobility, hailed Emmanuel Le Roy Ladurie's *Paysans de Languedoc* as a ground-breaking study in line with the pioneering work of "an entire school of French scholars" (that did not nominally include Braudel and that he christened elsewhere "the Labrousse school"), Richard Cobb unleashed anonymously in the *Times Literary Supplement* a savage and derisive onslaught against the supercilious and narcissistic "Nous des Annales."[6]

The *Méditerranée* of emergent American/Americanist social history was E. P. Thompson's *The Making of the English Working Class* (1963), despite its quite traditional methods. Its allure resided partly in his rejection of economism and his integration of culture as a social variable as well as in his ambition to cover "the total experience" of working-class life and to assay that experience from the perspective of the working class who lived it. Braudel's effort to rearticulate the link between economy and lived experience, adumbrated in the first edition of *Civilisation matérielle, économie et capitalisme (XVe–XVIIIe siècle)* in 1967 and favorably reviewed in the *American Historical Review* and the *Journal of Modern History* ("a resounding vindication of structuralism as a method of historical analysis"), did not have a weighty historiographical impact until the three volumes appeared together more than a decade later, though it

6 Reviews by R. Forster, *American Historical Review* 72 (Jan. 1967): 595 and 66: (July 1961): 1103–4; [R. Cobb], "Frères-ès-Conjoncture," *Times Literary Supplement*, 8 Sept. 1966.

convinced me that the long run was now incontrovertibly social. In the 1960s, Thompson and the *Annales* hive, along with Ernest Labrousse, Marc Bloch's successor at the chair of economic and social history at the Sorbonne, and his colleague in the chair of the history of the French Revolution, Georges Lefebvre, helped Americans to rescue social history from the archaic status of a residual hodge-podge enterprise devoted to manners and mores, voluntary associations, social events and *faits divers*. If definition continued to remain elusive, scholars who did social history fervently knew in their hearts who they were, even if others could not always identify them as such in reading their work. By 1968, in a review in which he discussed George Rudé and cited Albert Soboul and E. P. Thompson, Charles Tilly, one of America's trailblazers in this burgeoning field, cheerfully announced that "these are good years for European social history."[7]

During the 1960s, to study French social history, it made more sense to look to Labrousse, director of all the prodigious doctoral theses that made France's reputation in that domain, than to Braudel, whose scholarship did not target France and who believed that all history, especially across the long run, was perforce social without, however, specifically theorizing a social history beyond arguing for the intimate connection between history and the auxiliary (or lesser) social sciences. In a famous colloquium held at Saint-Cloud in 1965—the Poissy of social history—Labrousse proudly characterized the French historical corporation, a house with many mansions, for both the Communist Albert Soboul and the conservative Catholic Roland Mousnier (embodying the only non-Marxian social history alternative in the Sorbonne) attended this event, as "the most profoundly social of all the historical schools in the world." Grounding social history in a genealogy that comprised the human geographer Vidal de la Blache, Lucien Febvre and Marc Bloch, the *Annaliste* founding fathers, G. Lefebvre, the iconoclastic Belgian medievalist Henri Pirenne, and several French price historians, but not his contemporary Braudel, Labrousse defined it as the study of social groups and their relations, cast upon a three-tiered template redolent of the *Annales*' sesame.[8]

Braudel and Labrousse later collaborated in the joint editorship of the great economic and social history of France of our time, but at the outset, intellectual as well as institutional and probably ideological tensions put them at odds. Although quite bulimic in its appetite, the Labroussean exposition of social history was still too cramped for Braudel. Social history involved virtually all

7 Tilly, review, *Journal of Social History* 1 (Spring 1968): 296.

8 Labrousse, "Introduction," *L'Histoire sociale, sources et méthodes* (Colloque de l'Ecole Normale Supérieue de Saint-Cloud, 15–16 mai 1965) (Paris: Presses universitaires de France, 1967), 2, 4–5.

the dimensions of human reality and had to be projected in terms of a *histoire globale*—a dynamic point of view that is in mighty resurgence even as I write. Braudel acclaimed Labrousse's desire to uncover the *conjonctures sociales*, even social structures: it was imperative for the social actor to join the economic, though the champion of the long run questioned the temporal congruence of the two and the direction in which the social actor would be disposed to move. Braudel worried about the risk of Labrousse committing *lèse-science sociale*, as the pursuit of the *tout social* seemed to lead him in a regression toward the political time that Braudel abhorred. "Mediocre" at the end of the 1950s, Braudel judged the state of social history a few years later as progressing under the "magnificent leadership of E. Labrousse," but there was still a long way to go: "For, we must say it out loud: there is not yet a social history worthy of this fine name."[9]

Over time, my anxiety about scope, scale, space and time (Braudel's planetary gaze, his multi-century temporalities) and about the incongruity between my resources and the demands of a Braudelian project led me to shift imperceptibly in my pragmatic (but not my emotional) orientation from Braudel to Labrousse, though I never relinquished my preference for *La Méditerranée* and *Civilisation matérielle* over *L'Esquisse* and *La Crise*.[10] The *Méditerranée* gripped me because it was so deeply defamiliarizing. I relished the vast distances, the changes in speed and in rhythms, the rendezvous between the exotic and the ordinary, the play between continuity and change. Yet, it demoralized me even as it exalted me because I knew that I could not board Braudel's vessel. *Civilisation matérielle* thrust into relief aspects of the Braudel questionnaire that I thought might be accessible to me, in some form or other: systems of exchange, organization of markets, problems of supply, terms of trade and the banalities of everyday life. Nevertheless, broader Braudelian propositions continued to intrigue me. A "history swollen with all the other human sciences" had great allure for me, as did "histoire problème," which itself struck me as a powerful theoretical lever, as did the dizzying respiration of the long run, even if Braudel remained coy and ambivalent about theory. He shied away from theories because they were too constrictive or simply

9 Braudel: "Histoire et sciences sociales: la longue durée," *Ecrits sur l'histoire* (orig. 1958; repr. Paris: Flammarion, 1969), 49; "Histoire et sociologie," ibid., 107; "Introduction," *Annales: E.S.C.* 16 (May–June 1961): 12–13. Cf. Jean Boutier, "Fernand Braudel et les structures du social," in B. Arcangeli and G. Muto, eds., *Fernand Braudel: il mistiere di uno storico* (Naples: Edizioni Scientifiche Italiane, 1988), 91–109; and Jacques Revel's query: "Fernand Braudel a-t-il été un historien du social?" in Revel, ed. *Fernand Braudel et l'histoire* (Paris: Hachette, 1999) 18–19.

10 C.-E. Labrousse, *Esquisse du mouvement des prix et des revenus au XVIII*[e] *siècle* (Paris: Dalloz, 1933) and *La Crise de l'économie française à la fin de l'Ancien Régime et au début de la Révolution* (Paris: Presses universitaires de France, 1944).

erroneous; for intellectual and institutional reasons, he kept his distance from the grand theory of Marxism in particular. Yet, he suggested that every historian, in the manner of Molière, used theory whether she or he knew it or not, and then cited the German sociologist-economist Werner Sombart's famous "no theory, no history" in the preface to the 1967 edition of *Civilisation matérielle*.[11] And in the end, as at the outset, I thrilled to the foundational conceit: "total history," "the totality of the social" and "the total history of mankind." "Globality" was not hubris, Braudel tried to reassure me; it simply meant the desire, in confronting a problem, "to go beyond it systematically."

LSD: A Good Trip

Total history intoxicated me, but intellectually I would feast on LSD, the 1960s' *plat de non-résistance*.[12] This was the shorthand I used to define my framework to my jerry-built thesis committee at Yale: ***L**ongue durée*, **S**tructures**,** **D**aily Life. Braudel's articulation of time marked me indelibly. Although I never became a veritable long-runner, the concept has shaped all of my research for the last forty years; for just as long, first at Cornell, then in France, I devoted the first lecture in my Old-Regime–Revolution courses—the one meant to galvanize the students—to a Braudelian foray into time. If I had never reduced history to merely one damned thing after another, before Braudel, I had simply not thought much about time. The idea of time as multiple, multilayered, overlapping, textured, simultaneously continuous and discontinuous, remote and nearby, aloof and intimate, misanthropic and hospitable, hot and cold, orderly and chaotic, determined and contingent, dense and diffuse, prolix and pithy, colored by class and gender, represented differentially in colony and metropole, experienced differentially by dominant and dominated and by savant and popular—this was all revelation to me. If the plurality of time and the dialectic among the different velocities and cadences intrigued me, I made of the long run my personal golem, guide and ghost, "this cumbersome, complicated character," in Braudel's anthropomorphic and theatrical language.[13]

11 *Civilisation matérielle, économie et capitalisme (XVe–XVIIIe siècle)*, vol. 1 (Paris: Armand Colin, 1967), 9. In the 1979 edition (trans. into English two years later), obviously outside the purview of my reading in the 1960s, he claimed that "he set out to write outside the world of theory, of all theories." *Civilization and Capitalism, 15th–18th Century*, trans. S. Reynolds, vol. 1 (New York: Harper & Row, 1981), 23.

12 Wholly unexpectedly, I returned to LSD, the real thing—in fact, it was a synthetic compound, made from a chemical derived from ergot, a grain fungus—in my recent book *Le Pain maudit*.

13 Braudel, "Histoire et sciences sociales: la longue durée," *Ecrits sur l'histoire* (Paris, Flammarion, 1969) 41, 54.

If I did not explicitly practice the long run in my research—though my recent work has involved perspectives of three centuries—I was surely a *frère-ès-structure*. Yale was then awash in structuralism—literary, linguistic, anthropological. I remained persuaded that the diachronic was our *fonds de commerce*, but I did not apprehend the synchronic as an assault upon historicity. I followed attentively Braudel's debate with Lévi-Srauss on the one side and Sartre on the other, and was not wholly surprised to see the second edition of *La Méditerranée* doped with structuralism.[14] From the first to the second edition, there seemed to be double, convergent glissandi from geohistory to structure and from long run to structure. Increasingly indistinguishable, long run and structure stood in a reciprocally synecdochal relationship. Structures were both quasi-everlasting and manifestly impermanent, very constrictive and less so, prisons, to be sure, but not necessarily high-security prisons from which escape was unattainable. Braudel offered a loose definition of structure that augured for analytical latitude: assemblage, architecture, highly resistant relations that linger. I did not know what to make of his attack in 1958 on "an insidious, retrograde humanism" that initiated the discussion of the long run and its structural vocation.[15] Eight years later, Braudel seemed to point to a new, more capacious humanism, however ambiguous, or at least to a frontier between his and other disciplines:

> But the "structuralism" of an historian has nothing to do with the problématique that torments, under the same name, the other human sciences. It does not lead towards the mathematical abstraction of relations that are expressed as functions. It goes rather towards the very sources of life, in its most concrete, everyday, most indestructible and most anonymously human expression.

Far from a precocious apologist for agency, not yet a fighting word in the 1960s, I was nevertheless disconcerted, philosophically and pragmatically, by Braudel's stygian rendering of man "trapped in a destiny that he barely forged himself." Two years later in *Civilisation matérielle*, Braudel betrayed a certain ambivalence that intimated some small margin of maneuver (which later I would conceptualize through the Pascalian "cords of necessity and imagination" that could variously be clenched tightly or slackened significantly over time). First, the good news: "a rudimentary life which is nonetheless not entirely passively endured." Then, the bad news: "this life, more passively

---

14 Samuel Kinser counts 49 usages of the term "structure/structural" in the second edition as opposed to 11 in the first. "*Annaliste* Paradigm? The Geohistorical Structuralism of F. Braudel," *American Historical Review* 86 (Feb., 1981): 88n.

15 Braudel, "Histoire et sciences sociales: la longue durée," *Ecrits sur l'histoire*, 41, 50–51.

undergone than acted upon."[16] Braudel's intransigent disdain for the event and his cavalier attitude toward politics that, under the nascent influence of Foucault, we were beginning to think of in terms of power, aggravated my malaise. Structure seriously delimited human freedom, of that I was sure. But did that authorize or oblige historians to bypass the struggle in which women and men engaged against those constraints? Braudel inveighed against social-science abstractions, but if he refused to view daily life day by day, if he did not accept the "lived social"—*le social vécu*—as a valid terrain of observation, then didn't these interminable repetitions, reduced by moving averages to tedious sameness, merely congeal into a more or less mechanical abstraction? Nor did Braudel reassure me in his inaugural lecture at the Collège de France when he affirmed his humane concern for "each man grappling with his own life." The issue for me was methodology (later I would have said epistemology) rather than morality, and it concerned the collectivity rather than the individual. Why were historians to be dissuaded from contemplating the "deep movements of the life of men" in the short term when so much was at stake?[17] Did this not constitute the human flesh whose scent led Marc Bloch's ogre-historian to consider it his proper prey?

Crusty

Braudel's stigmatization of event-history did not shock me, but it loomed as gratuitously, even alarmingly overdrawn. The short run was indeed capricious and deceptive, but the event was not necessarily a trivial, vacant, surface agitation. If, under pressure from Sartre, Braudel conceded that the event could annex to itself layers of thicker significance, it was still the time of the journalist, of "the mediocre accidents of ordinary life," among which he included grain prices, crimes and theatrical performances. Labrousse, according to his *frère-ennemi*, managed the feat of connecting "an economic pathos [*pathétisme*] of the short run (new style)" to "a political pathos (very old style)."[18] If the *pathétisme*—the word is highly charged—is located in the event, in this case, the French Revolution, is it therefore too baroque, too exceptional and too irregular to be worth studying? If it is lodged, rather, in the historian's treatment, is this not an appreciation more aesthetic than scientific or scholarly?

16 Braudel, *Civilisation matérielle, économie et capitalisme (XVe–XVIIIe siècle)*, vol. 1 (Paris: Armand Colin, 1967), 10, 15.

17 Braudel, "Positions de l'histoire en 1950," *Ecrits sur l'histoire*, 35.

18 Braudel: "Préface à *La Méditerranée*," *Ecrits sur l'histoire*, 12 and "Histoire et sciences sociales: la longue durée," ibid., 46, 48–50.

This symbolic violence was all the more troubling to me because I read Labrousse as a piece, *Esquisse-cum-Crise*, and I construed his approach, in the context of my projected work on bread and the subsistence question, as inscribed in the long run, a procedure that for me ceded both to the teleological tyranny of the Revolution and to a contempt for day-to-day problems of survival (treated as wearisome accidents, spasms and outliers) that engendered, as I wrote in the introduction to *Bread, Politics and Political Economy*, "an abstract, homogenized social history devoid of flesh and blood and unconvincing despite its scientific cachet." Deploying an image that speaks to my deepest sensibility, years later, the fervent Labroussian Michel Vovelle, Soboul's successor in the chair of the French Revolution at the Sorbonne, affirmed what had become the *nouvelle histoire* doxa: that the short-run time of the event, which is also the quintessential time of politics, "only concerns a small superficial crust [*croûte*] of the history of man." In retrospect, it is clear to me that, as others were Trotskyist or Lambertist or Frankist in the 1960s, I was a (partial) *croûtiste*. I was much less certain than Vovelle, and *a fortiori* Braudel, "that true history, like true life, is elsewhere."[19] A passionate student of bread, equally enamored of crumb and crust—infrastructure and superstructure, I infer from Vovelle's choice of the image, not from his ideological itinerary—I know from having *mis la main à la pâte* that the crust, far from an accident or a décor or an illusion, is ultimately the expression of the same forces of fermentation and baking that construct the crumb and furnishes decisive clues concerning the state of the whole loaf—or should I say the *miche totale*?[20]

In any event, as I wrote my dissertation prospectus precisely on the multiple ways in which bread (and its antecedents) framed and indeed governed life in the Old Regime, I knew that, along with attentive scrutiny to numerous long-run *structures structurantes* and to "conjunctural" variables, I would have to look closely at politics, both from above and from below; at subtle and more brutal ways in which power was exercised, exchanged, resisted and reappropriated; at the structures as well as the protean features of everyday life; at the everyday

---

19 M. Vovelle, "L'Histoire et la longue durée," in J. Le Goff et al., eds., *La Nouvelle histoire* (Paris: Retz-CEPL, 1978), 330–31.

20 In my role as organoleptic militant and consultant, I have been leading the struggle in France, and elsewhere, to resist the eclipse of the crust—crustiness is the very essence of French bread-making tradition—in favor of a bun-like flaccidity that increasingly appeals to consumers, unaware of the full range of hedonic possibilities of the baguette. Only a proper baking—Maillard reaction and caramelization—can generate the production of aromas and the exchange of aromas between crust and crumb, thereby permitting the bread to attain its sensorial apogee. See my op-ed piece in *Le Monde* entitled "Sauvons la croûte," May, 2009 and my blog: http://lesommelierdupain.wordpress.com

order and how it was sustained and subverted; and at the way crises took root at the confluence of extremely long, middle-range and very short time. *Civilisation matérielle*, which appeared just at the right moment (1967), seemed less rigid and remote, despite its aerial gaze and its emphasis on "the frontier that marks the inflexible limits between the possible and the impossible." It was grand structural history that made everything appear intelligible and that made the reader feel intelligent; and its second chapter was propitiously entitled "The Bread of Each Day."[21] Everything seemed foreordained, yet uncertainty permeated the routines, occasional innovations had amplified consequences precisely because they were so rare, iterative contingencies were still contingencies despite their harrowing familiarity, the chronic tension between *vie matérielle* and *vie économique* created an arena of improvisation and negotiation, and the long run could not dilute the riveting drama of the human condition, even if it sternly refused the *pathétisme* of the daily struggle for survival and stability. While I worried that I was forsaking my masters, I continued to flatter myself that my inspiration and my thinking remained fundamentally *Annaliste*, deeply if deviantly Braudelian and elliptically Labroussian.

Wonder(ful) Bread

At Yale, I was a Pirandelloesque graduate student in search of an object, a notion, a practice or an institution that could serve as a totalizing metaphor, as a lever to penetrate into the whole range of human experience in past time: social, economic, religious, psychological, cultural, linguistic, technological and even political (allowing for the *Annales* allergy to skittish event-history). I thought about wine, given my recent hands-on experience (already heavily studied); police in its expansive, Platonic sense (I was already interested in regulation); love and fear (too elusive); catastrophe (tempting: a proto-ecological intuition); torture and the death penalty (darkly captivating); collective action (already under examination) and so on.

---

21 Braudel, *Civilisation matérielle, économie et capitalisme*, vol. 1 (Paris: Armand Colin, 1967), 9–15. Braudel's world was still a bit exotic in its quotidian, and he did not acknowledge the people-problem, let alone come to grips with it. The "ground-floor of everyday life," at least in French cities, was inhabited by the elites. The text was peopled with what Jack Hexter shrewdly and mischievously called "non-people persons": despite the fact that Braudel self-consciously opted for the "masses" over the "victors," he did not personify them. Hexter, "Fernand Braudel and the *Monde Braudelien*," *Journal of Modern History* 44 (Dec., 1972): 518. Aside from Roberto Lopez, an old friend of Braudel, Jack Hexter was the only person at Yale University with whom I talked at some length about this complex historian.

I don't recall how I came to bread: certainly not a Proustian connection to my Wonder Bread childhood[22], though we had an occasional, hand-baked ethnic "corn" bread whose moist, emollient texture, agreeable chewiness and nutty savor I can still discern somewhere in my cortex. Poised at the crossroads of the symbolic and the material, imperious daily necessity, powerful mobilizing force, all-purpose trope in everyday language, emblematic link between paternal/pastoral king and subject-children, expression of a complex economic nexus, an almost perfect candidate for a problematizing approach to historical investigation: bread seemed to have it all. Yet, I could not believe, for precisely these reasons, among others, that it had not been already deeply and widely explored. *Mais non*! For reasons that I cannot explain here, linked certainly both to the excruciatingly banal nature of the subject/object and to the extreme difficulty of locating it in the archives, very few scholars had seriously addressed it and no one "owned" it—in the sense that Lyon belonged to Maurice Garden, Caen to Jean-Claude Perrot, Beauvais to Pierre Goubert, Seville to Pierre Chaunu and children to Philippe Ariès.[23] Of course, since there was no one at Yale, or among the handful of French historians elsewhere whom I knew, to confirm or contest my reckoning of the historiographical situation and my "reading" of bread as a vector/vehicle/object/subject/problem, I knew I was gambling with high personal and professional stakes.

My wager initially took the form of a prospectus of about a hundred pages. My friends chided me mercilessly: a "total prospectus" for a "total thesis." I wanted to craft a coherent problématique, as thorough and probing a treatment as I could imagine of the bread question across the long eighteenth century; I realized, not from the start, but fairly quickly, that I would be able to complete only a portion of the program for my dissertation. Unwittingly,

---

22 An utterly tasteless, presliced, wrapped, hyper-white industrial loaf, larded with dubious additives whose presence was cognitively masked by the injection of reassuring vitamins and nutrients (whence the marketing claim to "build strong bodies"), Wonder Bread was delivered to our house three times a week during my childhood. I ate it toasted for breakfast and took it to school as the foundation of my lunch sandwich. An equivocal *frisson* traversed my now infinitely more sophisticated panivorous spirit when I read that Wonder Bread's parent company filed for bankruptcy in 2012. Yet nostalgics are to be reassured: purchased by a food conglomerate, Wonder Bread returned to American store shelves in 2013. For insights into this justly traduced, emblematic American food, see Aaron Bobrow-Strain's sprightly *White Bread: A Social History of the Store-Bought Loaf* (Boston: Beacon Press, 2012).

23 M. Garden, *Lyon et les Lyonnais au XVIIIe siècle* (Paris: Belles-Lettres, 1970); J.-C. Perrot, *Genèse d'une ville moderne. Caen au XVIIIe siècle*, 2 vols. (Paris: Mouton, 1975); P. Goubert, *Beauvais et le Beauvaisis de 1600 à 1730* (Paris: SEVPEN, 1960); and P. Ariès, *L'Enfant et la vie familiale sous l'Ancien Régime* (Paris: Plon, 1960).

I had in fact mapped out plans for a series of four books that I would eventually write over the following quarter century. After two years and several additional summers of research in all the Parisian archives and libraries and almost forty departmental depots, I spent a year again at Yale sorting my voluminous notes—still today, I do my research on individual paper notecards—and then went off to Cornell to take up my first post as an assistant professor, without a doctorate.

I envisioned studying first, as my dissertation, the elementary structures of the provisioning trade, whose protagonists were millers, brokers and merchant mealmen as much as grain dealers; the second work would target the bakery, its actors and its practices; the third would look at the decisive paradigm shift in the provisioning realm and in the conception of the social order, the cause and the expression of a deep sociopolitical crisis that jolted France, from the marketplaces, workshops and the *plat pays* to the salons and ministerial *bureaux*, as I already espied it; and, finally, a work devoted to what we used to call mentalities, a notion as beguiling then as it seems lame today, focusing on shared assumptions, expectations, apprehensions and attitudes of women and men of the eighteenth century, especially those who viewed themselves in the first instance as consumers, regarding subsistence and its claims on state and society.

To prepare myself to tackle the first phase in this immense enterprise, I spent the first two years at Cornell learning quantitative techniques, typing data into 80-column IBM cards and frequenting the computer center between 3 and 5 a.m., the time of abjection allotted to humanists toiling with numbers. I worked ceaselessly, but advanced barely inchmeal, the kilos of cross-tab and correlation print-out to the contrary notwithstanding. My department informed me at the beginning of my third year that if I did not submit my doctoral thesis within fifteen months, I would be fired. In desperation, I abandoned structures and statistical analysis in favor of a genre of history in which I felt methodologically comfortable and could progress rapidly—all the more so because I knew what I could demonstrate and thus what I would argue. This is how the sociopolitical section of the prospectus project became, first my dissertation, and then, *Bread, Politics, and Political Economy*, my first book, which appeared in 1976, year of a scorching heat wave that seriously damaged the grain harvest in France while engendering some exceptional wine, especially Pauillacs.

The Central Arguments

Given the discussion that follows, and the republication of *Bread, Politics* to which it is an introduction-*aggiornamento*, there is no point in rehearsing my arguments here and now. Two accomplished historians epitomized them deftly in their reviews. Keith M. Baker perceives the reform measures of the 1760s, inaugurating what I call liberalization, as "… indeed constitut[ing] a radical, even revolutionary break with traditional principles and practices." Louis XV embarked upon "a daring social policy … abolishing a system of controls with roots as old as the monarchy itself … extending the power of market forces over the distribution of a commodity hitherto regarded as too intimately bound up with the common good to constitute an object of mere exchange." This stark and sweeping deregulation struck at the hub of the system, aiming to unshackle its strengths without exacerbating its weaknesses, a process of sociopolitical and economic engineering that was at once delicate and brutal. "This radical social experiment, and the social and political upheaval that followed upon it," observes Baker, "laid bare the social and ideological foundations, the institutional strains and intellectual divisions, the administrative constraints and political limitations of the absolute monarchy."

Faced with the need for a composite and supple regulatory strategy necessary to deal with the pervasive particularism and a multiplicity of social interests "ultimately harmonized for the common good only through the exercise of royal justice, in its complex blending of liberty and constraint"—in light of the imbrication of grain policy and police with the very moral and mental structure of the monarchy—"why did the government break so radically, and with such determination, from that tradition?" asks Baker. While he invites the reader to find the answer in my book, he takes the trouble to emphasize that liberalization "was far more than a desperate strategy forced upon a politically bankrupt government by the desperation of fiscal exigencies or the misguided enthusiasm of a few physiocratic ideologues." To many of its proponents, liberalization offered "a new deal in the politics of the Old Regime: prosperity to the social and economic elites, legitimized by the promise of eventual abundance for the masses; fiscal relief for the government; and a new social compact, a new relationship between government and governed, that would substitute the harmony of the 'natural and essential order' of society for political confusion, institutional fragmentation, and constitutional strife."[24]

Daniel Roche characterizes *Bread, Politics* as a robust social history that "renews the old political history," and at the same time as an investigation of economy, collective psychology, mentalities and culture. Even as he places his emphasis on many complementary aspects of the grain/bread question, Roche concurs broadly with Keith Baker's reading of *Bread, Politics* by evoking

---

24 Keith Michael Baker, "State, Society, and Subsistence in the Eighteenth Century," *Journal of Modern History* 50 (December 1978): 701–4.

the radical change portended by liberalization, the "Copernican revolution" that the new way of thinking implied, the "decisive rupture" that the liberal reforms heralded in the structure and practice of monarchy, and "the rupture of the specific bond uniting the king—and his government—with the people." The French historian attaches special importance to the latter issue: "The relation people–king that dominated the police of subsistence changes in signification." The unavowed consensus that grain regulation was (always already) a political rather than an economic matter—"the *police des grains* is a policy/politics almost expressed as a mystical belief"—lost its once profound purchase. The economic was disembedded from the social, even as the market was naturalized.

In abandoning regulatory functions that had become political and moral obligations, "the corrupted government no longer respect[ed] the most sacred engagements" of the monarchy, remarks Roche. The result was twofold: the image of the king as a "nourishing father died a first death" in the revolts and market mutinies that often saw the consumers and the police in frank complicity, and the alliance between the government and the liberals crumpled. Despite ardent physiocratic propaganda, "the battle for liberty was lost for the people." Roche believes that "the failure of the reform can be read as the triumph of reality over theory," though the theory was not reducible to mere chimera or simple sectarian dogma. It was in part that, but also a serious reflection on how to extricate the kingdom from its overlapping impasses and how to recast it as a sort of community in which producers and consumers, the governors and the governed benefited from a dynamic of sustained growth and shared prosperity.[25]

Regulation: A Parenthesis

Stripped to its core, in cruder terms than Daniel Roche would have employed, the theory that capitulated (momentarily) to reality was an articulation of what is commonly dubbed in our time deregulation. The notion of regulation is, for very good reasons, much in fashion today, not in the rather pejorative sense of a glib and ephemeral mode, but as a function of intensely felt political, social, economic and moral imperatives, moored as much in deep structures as in passing business cycles. Of course, figured by other terms, what we ordinarily style regulation today has been the object of an intellectual, philosophical and ideological debate for centuries.

25 Daniel Roche, review of *Bread, Politics and Political Economy in the Reign of Louis XV*, *Annales: E.S.C.* 35 (1980): 1290–96.

The word itself is historically rare in incidence before quite recent times. There is trace of it in fourteenth-century France and Italy and in fifteenth-century England, where it derives from the Latin *regulare*, signifying to direct or control or rule.[26] In mid-to-late nineteenth-century France the word is attached to the science of mechanics and energy or to physiological matters. In France, jurists spoke of *réglementation* rather than regulation, virtually until the advent of what they call Reagan's "American conservative revolution."[27] By the time the fall of the Berlin wall had mightily discredited the notion of planification, the word "régulation" came to frame most questions concerning the relation of the French state to the economy. In the USA, the word already had a certain currency at the time of the Philadelphia (International) Centennial Exposition of 1876, in the midst of galloping industrialization. Subsequently, it surges in use during the Populist–Progressive era, until it entered its (first) golden age of application with the New Deal. The radical deregulation movement associated with Reagan generated a new kind of regulation, which has been styled post-modern, because of the shift in its methods and its anchoring, if not in its axiology. The word has taken on recently more precise general and sectorial connotations, but still refers to the early structuring ideas of rules or directions made and maintained by public authority; the control, adjustment or management of certain behaviors; and/or the bringing of order, implying the end of sundry disorders or the subjection to various kinds of governance.

It is almost irresistible, conceptually and analytically, to read regulation, say, into American constitutional debates in the late eighteenth century, or into French uprisings, popular and/or elite, resisting centralization in the seventeenth and eighteenth centuries. Tocqueville decried regulation, an expression in the end of despotism, associated with what increasingly partisan Americans in increasingly strident tones denounced as "Big Government," but he did not condemn all regulation. Socialists generally hailed regulation, but not without

---

26 In an English-language search, the Ngram Viewer on Google Books reveals a striking increase during the Enlightenment in the usage of the word regulation, with an unexpected dip around 1775, followed by a recovery. The curve surges again in the early twentieth century until the Second World War, loses ground in the 1950s and begins to climb again in the early 1970s. In French, there is an upward mini-blip during the Economic Enlightenment, followed by a virtual eclipse till the mid-nineteenth century, inaugurating a sustained ascending trend till roughly the last decade of the twentieth century. The survey data stop in 2000. The database ARTFL reveals that the entry "regulation" does not exist in the standard dictionaries of the eighteenth century—the Académie française, Trévoux, etc.

27 See the highly perspicacious and elegant piece of journalism by Guy Sorman, *La Révolution conservatrice américaine* (Paris: Fayard, 1983).

some nuances. The Reagan era engendered concepts such as the subsidiary state or the hollow state, terms that evoke for me my "lean or spectator" king/state of the liberalization moment during the Economic Enlightenment, the *Rex* repudiating his vocation of command and control. The American notion of public interest is less pregnant with social and political ambition than the French *res publica*, but neither is satisfied with the Coase theorem as a mode of operation. Critical in today's struggles for both social justice and equitable economic growth, regulation is shorthand for the debates, conflicts and compromises that attend state making, the construction of the social order, the promotion of development and the recourse to war and overseas expansion in European history, from the Middle Ages, more or less, to the present.[28]

Mingled Aromas of Archives and Bakery

That first book remained with me; in today's cultural lexicon, it was foundational. My own continuing work, and not merely a kind of narcissistic nostalgia for my youthhood, nourished my abiding interest in the questions that framed *Bread, Politics* and in the manner in which I treated them. During the last fifteen years of the twentieth century, I wandered off to research and write two substantial studies: one devoted to the world of work in eighteenth-century France, a logical counterpart to the corpus devoted to vital food supply issues; the second—I had been eager to poach on my own lived world for many years—an ethnography and critical historiography

28 On French use of the word and concept of regulation, with insightful reflections on American discourse and practice, see Elizabeth Zoller, "Droit et régulation," 27 Oct. 2008, available on the web site of the Académie des Sciences morales et politiques: http://www.asmp.fr/presentation/institution.htm. The American scholarly literature on the diverse treads of regulation/deregulation is enormous. *Inter alia*, see Thomas K. McCraw, "Regulation in America: A Review Article," *Business History Review* 49, no. 2 (Summer, 1975): 159–83; Barry Mitnick, *The Political Economy of Regulation: Creating, Designing and Removing Regulatory Forms* (New York: Columbia University Press, 1980); James Q. Wilson, ed., *The Politics of Regulation* (New York: Basic Books, 1980); George Stigler, *The Citizen and the State: Essays on Regulation* (Chicago: University of Chicago Press, 1982); Thomas K. McCraw, *Prophets of Regulation* (Cambridge, MA: Harvard University Press, 1986); Martha Derthick and Paul Quirk, *The Politics of Deregulation* (Washington: Brookings Institution Press, 1985); Kenneth J. Meier, *Regulation: Politics, Bureaucracy, and Economics* (New York: St. Martin's, 1985); Cass Sunstein, *After the Rights Revolution: Reconceiving the Regulatory State* (Cambridge, MA: Harvard University Press, 1990) and *Free Markets and Social Justice* (Oxford: Oxford University Press, 1997); Ian Ayres and John Braithwaite, *Responsive Regulation: Transcending the Deregulation Debate* (Oxford: Oxford University Press, 1992); Richard H. K. Vietor, *Contrived Competition: Regulation and Deregulation in America* (Cambridge, MA: Harvard University Press, 1994).

of the bicentennial of the French Revolution (in which bread and liberty played crucial roles), a rare opportunity in which past and present intersected organically and clamored for cross-reflection.[29]

During the first decade of the third millennium, however, I returned to the fold, as one reviewer commented. In a sense, I had never really left it. Ever since I started preparing the CAP in baking in 1969, I began regularly to visit bakeshops and evaluate bread quality.[30] I never presented for the exam: though I was excellent in theory—after all, I was a pupil of Parmentier—my technical/manual skills were insufficiently developed, despite two rigorous months of apprenticeship in two bake rooms with remarkably adept and generous senior baker-workers. If I were to be able to write convincingly and perhaps evocatively about Old-Regime bread, I felt that I needed to learn how bread was made in French baking rooms that perpetuated certain of the practices and much of the ambience of eighteenth-century *fournils*. I never regretted that impulse: my work is suffused with the combined aromas of the archives and the bake room. As a result of my apprenticeship and the contacts I initially made, I began to network with diverse actors in the grain–flour–bread complex, including millers, brokers and regulators as well as bakers and their wives, the latter still playing a crucial role in many shops, despite changing business and family models in the profession.

Even when I studied issues that had little or nothing to do with the bread nexus, I kept assessing bread virtually every week that I was in France, and I sustained and deepened my quasi-embeddedness by exchanges with the actors of the circuit. I gave talks to large groups of bakers, often under the patronage of their millers, and I became immersed in their concerns, some of which were mine for *Bread, Politics*, the *Provisioning of Paris*, and *The Bakers of Paris*: the price of wheat, the miller and baking qualities of the cereal varieties chosen as preferred or recommended, the relative merits of different agents of fermentation, the deterioration of the sensorial characteristics of the baguette (viewed as the "bread of common consumption," the standard loaf), the proliferation of the so-called special breads (in the wake of Poilâne, one of my baking mentors), the price of bread, the recruitment and formation of apprentices, the long phase of artisanal anomie in the train of ceaseless decline in per capita bread consumption and the rise of the jolting competition of industrial baking along with big box stores.

---

29 *La Fin des corporations* (Paris: Fayard, 2001); *Farewell, Revolution: Disputed Legacies, France, 1789/1989* and *Farewell, Revolution: The Historians' Feud, France, 1789/1989* (Ithaca, NY: Cornell University Press, 1995). The French edition, *Adieu, 1789* (Paris: Fayard, 1993), appeared in a single volume two years earlier.

30 *Certificat d'aptitude professionnelle*, a career-entry diploma that qualifies one for the exercise of the métier.

So I operated in parallel universes that I was determined one day to find a pretext to mingle. I had sketched out some ways in which the dialogue between present and past molded and (I hope) enriched my analysis in *The Bakers of Paris*, more forthrightly in the introduction to the French edition. In 2004, I crossed the Rubicon into the commercial nether-world, propelled by a passion for bread and a critical spirit nurtured by a long career as a historian: with my wife, after six months of herculean, daily toil (fetching, then tasting the bread of 600 bakeries, half of the intramural Parisian stock), I published *Cherchez le pain: Guide des meilleures boulangeries de Paris.* I gave away my origins, and probably troubled a certain number of readers, when I referred, in the introduction, to "the epistemological fragility" of the entire endeavor of comparative evaluation. Still, it was at once a fascinating transgression and a return to my roots as a historian, not quite a latter-day contribution to the *Annales* series on *enquêtes sur la vie matérielle* in the Braudelian vein, but an undertaking that seemed consistent with my trajectory.

Bread in Our Epoch

Next came another sort of prism for apprehending in retrospect *Bread, Politics*, a study launched 30 years later, but that seemed to emerge logically—I am tempted to say congenitally, or at least constitutionally—from my doctoral thesis. Entitled *Le Pain maudit: Retour sur la France des années oubliées, 1945–58*, it was the fruit of eight years of research in numerous public and private archives, undertaken with the zeal of a dour graduate student. In its broadest ambition, *Le Pain maudit* was the adumbration of a social history of the post-war period that the narrow political historiography of the Fourth Republic, hegemonic, had never called for, and, more specifically, a study of the mechanisms and shortcomings of regulation, statist and corporatist, bureaucratic and professional, national and regional, of the grain–flour–bread complex or circuit (or *filière*).

The protagonist of the story was bread itself, whose resurgence as a major actor was highly improbable (if not for war) and utterly decisive (in working out the complex post-war compromises between liberalism and interventionism, or regulation): between the Liberation and De Gaulle, as during the Old Regime, nothing connected the daily lived reality more staunchly to public administration than bread. The bakers and millers of the twentieth century, under immense pressure to adjust to a cereals market now officially "organized," had much in common with their eighteenth-century counterparts, despite mechanized kneading and steel-roller grinding; the "police des grains" found significant echoes in the renascent regulatory debate; and the riots of 1947—*taxation populaire*, mutinies to resist "nocturnal removals," hostility to exports, visions of a famine plot and complicity between authorities and members of the community—were strikingly redolent of those of the 1760s and 1770s. For me, this long-run perspective was a heady whiff of the *histoire totale* conceit of my apprenticeship years as a historian.

As a matter of good intellectual hygiene, as I worked on, first, *Cherchez le pain*, and then *Le Pain maudit*, I looked every day at the prices of wheat at Rouen and Chicago, I read systematically the professional press, degraded heirs to the exceptionally thoughtful and probing publications of the immediate pre- and post-war periods, such as *L'Ami du Boulanger* and *Le Petit meunier*. I scrutinized the tensions between Brussels and Paris on agricultural, especially cereal-growing and bread-making policy and prescription. I followed with avid interest the grain situation on the word stage, where the stakes were still located in the tyranny of the vital staples, not the debonair quest for the organoleptic champion among elite bakers. I wrote an op-ed piece in *Le Monde* entitled "Mauvais pain, mauvais gouvernement," after the jolting wave of food/grain revolts that erupted all over the world in 2007–2008 when the price of cereals soared (wheat reached its historic apex at $482 per metric ton in March 2008, almost three times above the level of July 2005).[31] The vertiginous upsurge in food prices aggravated an already tenuous financial situation occasioned by a global speculative bubble in real estate and equities, fed by subprime loan losses and the toxic calamity of credit default swaps. I was moved to reflect on the sociopolitical significance of both increasingly inaccessible prices and increasingly unacceptable quality of bread—historically, the two factors are inextricably linked—after reading about demonstrations/riots in Sénégal denouncing expensive loaves "unfit to enter the human body," reminiscent of so many scenes of Jacquerie in France, symbolically consistent from 1358 to 1768 to 1952 (in the elegant office of Antoine Pinay, président du Conseil), in which protesters brandished blackened, fetid loaves as a marker of misery and subordination, and of the failure of governance, the abjuring of responsibility, the violation of trust.

Bad harvests and subsistence anxiety were indirect causes of the Arab spring.[32] Egypt suffered disproportionately because it remains the world's biggest wheat importer: subsidized bread provides a third of Egyptian calories; consumers spend only a slightly lower portion of their income (almost 40%) on their survival ration than had their counterparts in pre-Revolutionary France. Global food prices peaked in March 2011, shortly after Mubarak's defenestration. As in 1977 and 2008, bread riots erupted, but this time there

---

31 *Le Monde*, 11–12 May 2008.

32 See Thomas Friedman's interesting column, *New York Times*, 4 March 2013.

seemed to be a real prospect of transforming them into a durable political movement—as in contemporary Tunisia where bread also played a catalytic role in launching the Jasmine Revolution. Demonstrators in Cairo shouted a slogan well known to French historians, among others, demanding "Bread and Liberty!" I wrote an op-ed paper where I recounted a soccer match held at the epicenter of the movement of insurgency, Place Tahrir, rebaptized Liberation Square. One team took the name "Bread" and the other "Liberty."[33] In their first encounter, a Sunday night in late January, Bread triumphed.[34]

My research for *Bread, Politics* had long before taught me that bread did not always win in a combat against liberty. "The poor prefer bread to liberty," wrote Rousseau, but he hinted at the paradox that risked engulfing the Egyptians. On the one hand, bread was not enough even when it was cheap and abundant: the raïs could achieve that. As in 1789, liberty seemed to be the precondition for and guarantee not only of a formal right written into the law, but also of an equality of opportunity etched into the social reality of everyday life, the promise of a concrete sort of justice. On the other hand, history warned that too much liberty, in its promethean eruption, with its totalizing ambitions, outside the safety zone of a customary moral economy or of a democratically decided regulation, could deprive the ordinary citizen, first of her ration of bread and eventually of her liberty. I treated the foundational paradox in *Bread, Politics*: the audacity of the liberals of the Economic Enlightenment, in their program of regeneration, was to begin with the most difficult, the most dramatic and the most perilous—bread. Bread was the occasion for demolishing both the first ideological Bastille and the last bastion of social contractualism of the Old Regime: the liberalization of the grain trade in 1763–64 inaugurated a long battle over social and political legitimacy and justice that continues today.[35]

---

33 *Le Monde*, 8 Feb. 2011.

34 Cf. the remark/question of Albert Camus, born in Algeria, where bread also figured in the repertory of necessity: "Who do you prefer, the person who wants to deprive you of bread in the name of liberty, or the one who wants to take away your liberty in order to guarantee you your bread?" *Actuelles II. Chroniques 1948–53* (Paris: Gallimard, 1953).

35 To convey a sense of the extreme tension that enveloped the liberalization debate, I cited this extract of a remonstrance that the Rouen Parlement addressed to Louis XV in my piece in *Le Monde*, 11–12 May 2008: "In suppressing all the regulations, and thus affording liberty an unlimited scope, one destroys the inner workings and resilience of societies; the peoples are mixed [without reference to their socio-juridical roots], sovereigns become mere grandees that some luster distinguishes, but that is accompanied by no [social] utility; thus this system that seems to found and establish everything tends in fact to jostle and destroy everything."

The Mystique of Bread in France

Infinitely more prosperous and stable than the cereal-dependent countries staggered by riots, France felt the impact of world price volatility at this very moment (2008–12). Although wheat accounts for only a bit more than 5 per cent in the cost of the baguette, and flour 15%, bakers passed on price increases—never price decreases—to consumers, who grumbled audibly. Freed definitively of the last remnants of Pascal's "cords of necessity," for the past half century the French remain bound to bread by his "cords of the imagination": even when it was no longer a true necessity, one could not imagine a veritable meal without bread, and bread should always remain cheap, no matter what. This is what the bakers denounced as "the mystique of bread," a deleterious and anachronistic symbolics to which the government deferred long after the eclipse of any objective justification, for it maintained price controls on the daily loaf until the end of 1986. Several decades after the suppression of bread-price regulation, at the very moment of the Egyptian revolution, the millers of France, for the last half century on a liberal trajectory after an almost equally long dirigiste-corporative phase, demanded national, European and, ideally, international regulation of the cereals market(s) in order to put a halt to speculation, vehemently denounced, especially in its American incarnation (pension and hedge funds buying grain as parts of structured products deals).[36] Others fulminated against Russian

36 On the surge in wheat and other cereal prices in the spring and summer of 2012, caused in large part by droughts in the United States and "agro-meteorological" disturbances in Ukraine and Russia, among other sites of production, see *Le Monde*, 8–9 July 2012, 31 July 2012 and 13–14 July 2013, and *Le Figaro*, 15 Nov. 2012. Cf. the FAO call for regulatory measures, and the discussion of the South Korean undertaking to tax certain transactions in an effort to curtail speculation. *Le Monde*, 28 Aug. 2012. The FAO also predicted that the planet was entering a long phase—at least a decade—of high cereal prices. Even as the French millers complained about the "volatility" of grain prices in 2012, two events/markers of that same year underlined the historical ambivalence of the behavior and attitudes of millers and other grain traders toward regulatory issues. First, the abolition of the official/authorized monopoly of the Canadian Wheat Board, the largest agency for the commercialization of wheat in the world, whose export policy weighed heavily on world markets. Partisans of the measure hailed it for the new entrepreneurial opportunities and spaces of tonic competition that it would make available. Critics, including French millers, denounced the decision as certain to aggravate price volatility and promote the opacity of transactions. Second, regulatory authorities imposed a record-breaking collective fine of almost a quarter billion euros on a consortium-trust of French and German millers who engaged in illicit price-setting arrangements to limit competition and enhance profits. *Le Petit Meunier-La Dépêche*, 6 Jan. 2012 and *Le Monde*, 14 March 2012. The price story is more complex than the so-called King-Davenant law allows. See Richard Stone, *Some British*

embargoes on exports that nourished speculation. How could the tandem speculation-export not strike a hospitable chord for me, just as the Egyptian allegory on the articulation of liberty and regulation (or equality)?

Return to America by the Grain Route

I long nurtured the hope—vain for lack of time—that my grain interests would take me full circle back to my American history origins. Perhaps my earliest scholarly encounter with the question of flour production occurred during my research for my senior thesis at Princeton on the Philadelphia Centennial Exposition of 1876. Several Central European exhibitors presented, probably for the first time on the American side of the ocean, the newly developed process of roller-milling that would shortly revolutionize the industry. I did not return to this question for many decades, until I became interested, from the European side, in the ebbing of stone grinding, also featured in several world's fairs, including one in which the Hungarians operated a trial roller mill in Paris wearing spotless black tuxedos to demonstrate their industrial mastery, a quasi-antiseptic environment, far from the cramped space impregnated with white powder, erotically dispersed by pounding stones in Chaucer's mill. Later, I desired to write about eighteenth-century inventor Oliver Evans, a pioneer in the application of steam power and automation to grain milling, in the spirit of the gradual reduction technology and rationalized integration of "economic milling," a crucial innovation in the French subsistence nexus of the Economic Enlightenment that I had studied in depth.

I wanted to work on the extraordinary effort of Joseph Leiter, son of a co-founder of the Marshall Field retail empire, to corner the world wheat market in 1897–98. This was the sort of larger-than-life, Paul-Bunyonesque American speculation, well before the specter of Goldman Sachs or J. P. Morgan began to haunt Europeans, that inspired Jean Jaurès in the late 1880s, followed by others, to propose *dirigiste* systems to regulate grain imports and exports precisely to combat volatility and egregious profiteering. The blend of acute rationality and megalomania, figured by the Leiter endeavor,

Empiricists in the Social Sciences 1650–1900 (Cambridge: Cambridge University Press, 1996). This law argues that, given the relative immutability of demand for cereals, a deficit or surplus in supply generates variations in prices much more significant than the variations in actual volumes of goods produced. Prices spike in a shortfall, and they plunge in a burst of abundance. Moreover, the current discussion needs to take into account effects of substitution and other types of evolution that adumbrate structural modifications in the allocation of arable (the increasingly keen demand for animal protein in places such as China, the allure of biofuels and so on).

which resulted in millions in losses, inspired the novel *The Pit: A Story of Chicago* (1903) by Frank Norris, a Zola-esque naturalist, with a vivid lyrical intonation.[37] Norris pondered the impact of prodigious and ambiguous forces such as wheat or capitalism on individual behavior. He evoked the sort of hoarding and monopoly that I studied in *Bread, Politics*, antisocial maneuvers and manipulations and market dysfunctions on a planetary scale that underlined, for the author, the absurdity and futility of the discreet gesticulations of the invisible hand in the absence of a structure of public regulation and of a shared ethical code. The prior volume in his series, *The Octopus: A Story of California* (1901), took me back to my "populist" years with Woodward: it depicted, in terms self-consciously resisting the Manichean reductionism to which the subject inclined him, the acrimonious clash between farmers (whom Norris favored) and a railroad (muscular and corrupt). The novelist was unable to complete the final volume in which he passed from production and distribution to consumption, a problématique at once complementary and antinomic. Entitled *The Wolf*, this novel intended to cast into relief the horrors of famine in a village or region, perhaps European. I mused about doing a critical edition of the almost trilogy that Norris had called *The Epic of Wheat*, for whose translation into French I lobbied.

In the spirit of intersecting kindred American and European concerns, I looked briefly at the idea of pondering the similarities and differences between FDR's regulatory approaches to agriculture (the successive Agricultural Adjustment Acts and the ever-normal-granary idea), on the one hand, and the Popular Front/proto-corporatist efforts to organize the wheat market in France, along with Mussolini's more precocious "Battle for Wheat," on the other hand. Finally, throughout these years, and not just when I trembled about obtaining my doctorate in time, I fantasized about becoming an international grain trader, a more interesting alternative than law school, it seemed to me, where one had to be cosmopolitan as well as clever and (sometimes) flinty. I don't know why I never sent a CV to Cargill or Continental.[38]

---

37 I will leave it to Sophus Reinert to reflect on the significance of the formal first and middle names of Norris: Benjamin Franklin. See his fascinating "*The Way to Wealth* Around the World: Benjamin Franklin and the Globalization of American Capitalism," *The American Historical Review* 120, no. 1 (2015), forthcoming.

38 My intellectual and venal interests in the grain trade profession were quickened by the so-called Great Grain Robbery of 1972. See James Trager, *Amber Waves of Grain* (New York: Arthur Fields Books, 1973) on the background and the excellent piece of investigative journalism, targeting the seven hyper-discreet families, the hapless, interest-conflicted or corrupt American regulators, and the cunning Russians, by Dan Morgan, *Merchants of Grain* (New York: Viking Press, 1979). Though it is now gravely

A Second Edition of *Bread, Politics and Political Economy*

It seemed to me a good idea to republish *Bread, Politics* because it had been so long out of print, and because I (and others!) believed that it was still a fruitful scholarly object, pertinent to debates not only regarding the Old Regime/Revolution but also the subsequent centuries, including our own world. It seems to me that it has held up rather well during the past forty years. We are no longer in the hyperbolic age of total history, but, in retrospect, the study of bread as a Maussian "total social fact"—methodological tool and concept—seems to have been reasonable and advantageous. As a quasi-all-encompassing lever and metaphor, bread has permitted me to infiltrate and probe a host of discrete domains whose specific connections would not have spontaneously surged forth.

The main claims of *Bread, Politics*, as Keith Baker and Daniel Roche considered them, have not been seriously challenged. Some of my arguments, findings and suggestions have helped shape the unfolding historiographical agenda over the years. They concern the rehabilitation of the event and the necessary central place of politics in the social; the coding of the material as cultural and vice versa, underlining the salience of "things" and the relevance and richness of banality; the relations between state and society, mediated by manifold forms of regulation; the fundamental connections between technology and politics; the deeply cleft and strikingly variegated character of the Enlightenment, no longer possible to view globally as the party of humanity, even if one can locate multiple threads of unity within its diversity and division; among philosophes, *sensu lato*, the deep fault line on the question of laissez-faire rights and the claims of capitalism to serve the general interest; the relations between politics and political economy; the polysemy of "police" as institution, as ideology, as noun and verb; the urgency of abandoning the canonic Manichean readings of the eighteenth century, fashioned in part by revolutionary teleologies, partitioned into putative good guys (king, philosophes) and bad guys (parlements, church, guilds and the entire corporative structure); more specifically, the imperative of revising the way we apprehend and interpret parlements and the behavior of their magistrates, taking special note of the significant ideological and political cleavages among and between parlements; the persistent tensions between the center and the periphery, and the ever-ambiguous role of intendants and *gens du roi* in the centralizing process; the need to rethink the relationship between

out of date, I have reverently kept the text I acquired in a second-hand bookshop in the early 1970s, the vade mecum of my apprenticeship in grain trading practices, James S. Schonberg, *The Grain Trade: How It Works* (New York: Exposition Press, 1956).

kingship, the Enlightenment and various proxies for so-called modernization; the tensions and synergies between parlementary and ministerial systems of law enforcement and regulation; the functioning of the contrôle-général and the bureaux in its orbit, relations between the contrôle-général and local authorities and the broader issue of the nascent proto-bureaucratic aspects of the administrative monarchy; the discourse of paternalism and the struggle to appropriate it; the particularities of popular culture and its relations with dominant/savant culture; the strikingly wide and deep diffusion of the famine plot persuasion throughout French society, from bottom to top, an expression of a certain paranoid style of ideation that is hard to view as pathological, given its pervasiveness; the shifting nature of political legitimacy, generally and in rapport with popular attitudes toward kingship; representations of the people; the structures, repertories, ideologies and dynamics of collective action concerning food issues; the role of women in food *émotions* and revolts; the organization, operation and objectives of grain, flour and bread markets; the question of mills and millers, virtually unstudied heretofore; the extent to which grain crises (*chertés* and dearths) must be viewed as functions of the vast and tortuous distance between the postharvest farms and consumer tables as much as statistical outcomes of the crop magnitude and quality (and the specific nature of the flour crisis, wholly independent of harvest results); the recruitment, organization and operations of political and economic lobbies and pressure groups; the meaning of reform in the Enlightenment context, the role of reformers within the government and their relations with reformers in civil society; and the mechanisms of state intervention on the supply side: from army victualers (*munitionnaires*) to generic royal investors (*gens intéressés dans les affaires du roi*), from Protestant and/or court bankers to Atlantic shippers and international traders, from subsistence specialists to main-chance speculators.

Shortcomings

Bread, Politics has shortcomings, to be sure, some of which are clear to me, while others doubtless lurk in the penumbra of my core of critical self-consciousness. If I raised significant questions, I did not always resolve them or answer them well; I address a certain number of them in chapters that follow. For example, I did not articulate, in a compelling fashion, the question of liberalization in particular and liberty in general with the other major issues that constituted politics during the Enlightenment, especially in the second half of the century. *Inter alia*, I should have found a better strategy for making the connections between fiscality and the liberalization project. I regret that I did not embark into the daunting space of religious thought and lobbying in order to see the extent to which economic and social questions elicited attention and/or engagement. This sort of work will flower in the future, I suspect, as scholars of political economy examine the spell of Jansenism, for example, or reassess the legacy of Malebranche or assay the significance of the divine in physiocracy. I barely began the huge task of mapping out the ways in which ideas concretely influence or shape policy and politics, a cartographical venture that raises epistemological issues as well as analytical ones. I did not do a good job of defining and analyzing public opinion, either in sociological or historical terms; I remain doubtful that the public sphere generation and its epigones, summoning Habermas to do the heavy lifting for them, have found the solution. Transparent and/or luminous in the eyes of many scholars, public opinion abides, in my view, as both a blind spot and a black hole in Enlightenment/eighteenth-century studies. More promising is recent work devoted to the so-called people-problem that I identified and discussed, but did not sufficiently problematize and probe. Apropos, I would have made a less timid argument today about popular political consciousness, notably in food mutinies, than I attempted in the early 1970s.

Despite first-hand research in a large number of departmental archives and numerous municipal depots, I was unable to restitute complete agency to provincial actors: that requires full-time commitment. A number of other frustrations stem from this sort of barrier: basically a lack of time to exploit fully identified sources or to track down propitious leads. For example, I could not amass sufficient data on the contentious export question, quantitative (real and feigned transports abroad; plots or maneuvers to manipulate the ceiling price established to cutoff traffic and so on) or qualitative (stories of enterprising traders, old hands or opportunistic neophytes, *négociants* or petty upstarts).

There are other issues that I would have liked to explore, or that I should have not failed to investigate. One of them is *not*, as a somewhat querulous reviewer (animated by a wholly naïve conception of nitty-gritty archival research) suggested, a study of the demographic repercussions of the crisis of 1765–75. Work on parish registers, an exigent and onerous assignment, is an enterprise unto itself, far beyond the arguably ambitious boundaries of the study as it stands. Moreover, while the question of the impact of severe dearth on mortality, nuptiality and fertility is intrinsically interesting and important, I do not believe that the primary and most germane gauge of a subsistence crisis in the eighteenth century is demographic.[39] In the realm of the socioeconomic consequences of liberalization, had I disposed of unlimited

39 Cissie Fairchilds, review of *Bread, Politics and Political Economy* in *Journal of Interdisciplinary History* 8 (Winter 1978): 571–72.

time and resources, I would have been more immediately motivated to look at the possible effects of the reality or the prospects of liberty on the decision making of cereal cultivators: for instance, the movement of lease prices (hard to capture in the very short-term), modifications in technology (how rapid are such reactions?), land reclamation, sowing strategies, extension of conservation capacity and so on. An often dated, incomplete and uneven fund of scholarship on agriculture, in particular on production, productivity, managerial and technical innovation and the quality and flow of information, hampered me in the upstream phase of my work, where primary research was materially impossible for me to conduct. Given the centrality of agricultural regeneration in the debates over liberalization—turning on assumptions about the harrowing lethargy of agriculture as well as its nimble aptitude for rapid revival—it would have been extremely enriching to dispose of more data and analysis on this pilot sector in the economy.

Home Remedies

Some of the imperfections of *Bread, Politics*—generally overlooked by reviewers—I myself subsequently remedied. They derived from the (dis-) order in which the agenda of research, thickly outlined in my Yale prospectus, unfolded. *Bread, Politics* should have been the final or perhaps the penultimate study in my series, not the first. I knew a lot, but not enough, as far as I was concerned, about the architecture and organization of the grain and flour trade, about merchants, millers and brokers, and about bread, bread making and bakers (and bakers' wives) when I wrote *Bread, Politics*. I was much stronger on the eighteenth-century conjunctures than on the centuries-old structures that undergirded this study, but remained embryonic in elaboration. Markets constituted the very marrow of my analysis; years of research had made me familiar with them, but I did not have a real command of their morphological complexity and, at bottom, of how they worked, day to day, and under different degrees of stress or serenity. That took much more time and toil to crystallize. I had to anticipate, conjecture or dodge in certain places. Had I written *Bread, Politics* after *Provisioning Paris*, *The Famine Plot Persuasion* and *The Bakers of Paris*, it would have been in some ways a different book: not in the central sociopolitical analysis of liberalization and its conditions, but in the framing context of the supply trade, its highly variable practices and its ambivalent yet generally adaptive police. The book would have had a different organization—narrative analysis interspersed with structural analysis—and a different rhythm.

Ironically, one of the reasons that *Bread, Politics*, and, *a fortiori*, its suite, did not provoke scholarly work dealing directly with these cardinal social, political, economic and cultural questions may have been the perceived sense that I had a corner on the market, as it were. Of course, I am naturally (and culturally) not a hoarder, though I am an inveterate speculator. I would have welcomed *frères-ès-meule, pétrin et marché.* There were other possible explanations for the lack of appetite for this kind of research. First, let us note matters of craft. Work on the grain–flour–bread complex was extremely aleatory, since sources were elusive, scattered and usually indirect, and highly labor intensive. As jobs and resources began to dry up in the late 1970s, as time abroad became harder to wrench and to subsidize, as the loss of nerve of many scholarly presses favored a new economy of research, as jobs within history departments shifted toward the culturalist pole and reward systems evolved as a function of the new priorities, the allure of my kind of work dimmed sharply. Perhaps, even more significant were matters of mode and method. I mean, first, the decline and fall (and, in some precincts, the discredit) of social history. Then, concomitantly, the rise, affirmation and apotheosis of a broadband culturalism, sometimes as amorphous as it was ambitious, which defined itself in opposition to social history rather than as an opportunity to reappropriate and recast the social in fresh manner. "Political culture" seemed logical and comfortable; a "social culture" analogue gained no traction.

Two Score Years

Still, it goes without saying that, during the past four decades, much has been written on many of the themes or concerns of *Bread, Politics* that has taught me a great deal. During that same period, a debate of uneven quality, fervor and impact has raged about how we do history. Were I to recast *Bread, Politics* today, the latter influence would probably bear more heavily upon me than the former. I began reading philosopher Jacques Derrida and the Frankfurt school just as I was finishing my dissertation. I discovered the literary criticism, semiology, historiography and sociology of Roland Barthes, Michel de Certeau and Pierre Bourdieu shortly afterward. Then I came upon anthropology, a marvelously enriching and durable encounter. Claude Lévi-Strauss and Mary Douglas, to be sure, but the roster was heavily American: Sidney Mintz, Eric Wolf, Clifford Geertz, Victor Turner, Terry Turner and *tutti quanti.* On the way, before the *Annales* abjured its secular neo-Marxism by abandoning the subtitle *Economies, Sociétés, Civilisations* in favor of a more irenic and open-ended *Histoire, Sciences Sociales*, I was marked by *Geschichte und Gesellschaft* and by *Quaderni storici*, each of which promoted specific ways of conceiving the historiographical enterprise, in an interdisciplinary, theoretically inflected, reflexive spirit.

These readings, these rendezvous and the reflections they inspired deeply conditioned the ways I thought about the past. I did not, for instance, renounce my interest in structures in light of the interrogations of post-structuralism, but I refined my manner of construing them as objects and concepts. I did not repudiate my sympathy for quantification, despite reservations about the Galilean paradigm that I had already avowed in *Bread, Politics*, but my engagement with certain approaches in cultural history and with micro-history invited me to think about problematization, argument and evidence in fresh ways. Despite the extravagances and absurdities that accompanied or infested them, I found the linguistic turn to be a tonic experience, and the jagged post-modern campaign to be stimulating. Nonreferentiality never struck me as a viable intellectual or philosophical option (there is a there, there), yet the questioning of foundational concepts and canonic taxonomies and of inherited and sometimes disguised forms of domination/subordination seemed to me to promote rewarding, if occasionally febrile, exchange. I never believed that the social or political could be reduced to discourse (still less, to language games), but the post-modern moment enjoined me to remember that the social was not natural and that the conditions of production of discourse needed to take into account the mediation of language and, more generally, of sign systems.

The admonition/exhortation to think hard about the work of language, its uses and its relation to other kinds of practice and the discussion concerning the instability of meaning I found all the more helpful because I continued to believe in the priceless benefits of archival research, conducted not like a fact harvest, but as an interrogation, driven by an even-handed or symmetrical skepticism; archival research not as the only road to salvation, but as an extraordinary opportunity for historians in all branches who relish close reading and the hermeneutics of suspicion, deconstruction and the play between the producer (of the document in question) and the acts of production accomplished by the historian as a consumer. The experience of these 40 years has not diminished my conviction that one can accede to and in part reconstitute and reconstruct the past, that all such reconstitutions and reconstructions are not equal in value and validity, that the clichéd devil is often in the detail and that the administration of proof is one of the most fundamental obligations of the historian. Across those four decades, I have become more self-conscious about epistemological issues, pragmatically sacrificed to (sometimes trying) methodological issues in my formative years. I have also come to see much more acutely the utility as well as the cost of engaging in one's self-analysis as a sort of ego-analogue to disciplinary reflexivity.

Companion Tome

The text that you are now reading is the introduction to the companion volume to the second edition of *Bread, Politics and Political Economy in the Reign of Louis XV*. The body of the latter remains basically unchanged. The chapters that follow are meant to speak to the 40 years that have elapsed since its initial publication. They reveal how I have evolved in reaction both to the changing intellectual/epistemological/historiographical/sociopolitical environment and to some of the significant scholarship that has been accomplished. This companion volume is conceived as a commentary on and a dialogue with *Bread, Politics* and with fellow researchers who have written in and around the concerns of that book.

All of the authors with whom I deal are serious and talented scholars; if I did not think so, I would not have bothered to allocate energy and space to their work. Because I esteem that such a strategy is ultimately the most constructive in invigorating and renewing the agenda, I focus on areas of contention between us: in epistemological assumptions, in methods, in the use of sources, in demonstration, in interpretation, in the assignment of weight and significance to variables and so on. I believe strongly in the value of critical debate: not one-liner barbs or precipitate executions or stealthy lynchings, but reasoned address, criticism that is argued, elaborated, buttressed, documented and overt. I consider that there is a deficit of critical debate in this age of winsome uptalk and political correctness; I think that this reluctance to engage is impoverishing. We are social creatures, and sociability matters to us, structures our interactions and enriches us. In my view, however, it is rendered artificial and fragile when, in the professional domain, it is founded squarely on indulgence, accommodation, circumvention and/or palliation. In my eyes such a demarche constitutes less an expression of respect than a strain of unavowed paternalism, masked as civility. This is not an appeal for a return to the bellicose virtues of a Hobbesian state of nature, or a naïve denunciation of ordinary protectionist practices within networks, chapels or other relationships. It is a plea for the fostering of frank, vigorous exchange, not subject to the moral censure of a subterranean collective superego, proof that certain forms of regulation can be deleterious.

The chapters that follow deal with themes with which readers of my first book are conversant: regulation, the matrix motif; agriculture; markets; collective action and the moral economy; the people; order and disorder; the parlements in the age of the Economic Enlightenment; the king and kingship; the monarch and his ministers in the elaboration and execution of public policy; the new historiography of political economy; and the old, persistent tragedy of famine, understood as the problem of food insecurity in its less virulent incarnations. I engage them all with keen interest, albeit with unequal intensity, reflecting less a sense of hierarchy than my own passions and idiosyncrasies.

My discussion is "problem"-oriented. I deal with numerous scholarly studies that have appeared since the publication of *Bread, Politics*, but not in the vein of canonical book reviews. I focus largely on the questions that I considered, or failed to raise or resolve, in *Bread, Politics.* In many cases, I touch on only a small part of a given scholar's contribution, in the hope of clarifying issues that I deem fundamental, but that I do not claim to be the only major matters that the author treats. I am deeply preoccupied with how markets work, for instance, and how the grain and flour (or provisioning) trades are organized, managed and regulated (I theorize my view in distinguishing what I call marketplace from market principle). I mine the book (or article) in question for information and interpretations relevant to these affairs, without pretending to appraise the rest of the work, save to the extent that it frames or affects the themes I privilege. In kindred manner, I treat several studies dealing with political economy in terms of their pertinence to the liberalization movement that profoundly marked the Economic Enlightenment (and French society more generally). My quarrel with their treatment of the liberal reforms of the 1760s, the liberal lobby that prepared the grounds for change, the forces of resistance to it, and so on or with their reading of certain sources or with their articulation of the relations between the social, the political and the cultural has no bearing on my admiration for the powerful and cogent arguments they make concerning subjects outside my purview.

There is no organic link between the disparate studies I scrutinize, merely an overlapping or intersection or kinship of concerns. The unity of outlook derives from the triangulation between the *Bread, Politics* of 1976, a selection of the scholarship of the past four decades, and the critical gaze that I direct toward both. That gaze is hedged by strong convictions, surely marked by biases, of which I am either conscious or unaware, but convictions in favor of which I try to present arguments and evidence. Certain themes recur frequently, within a given chapter and in successive chapters, because they are pervasive. If I did not judge them to be particularly interesting and significant, I would not insist upon them, despite their prevalence; and, if they continue to capture my attention, it is because we, yours truly included, have not yet dealt with them in a truly stimulating and/or compelling manner. So, for example, I evoke repeatedly the people-problem: from Michelet's oceanic-messianic wave to Pierre Goubert's 20 million of resilient Frenchmen (or even to Victor Hugo's "Il te ressemble; il est terrible et pacifique… il a le movement, il a l'immensité… ."), the often undifferentiated masses we discreetly call "people" remain elusive in terms of sociology, psychology, culture and behavior. We often take them for granted, as a staunch point of reference, without any real grounding. We talk about them as one and as many, as homogeneous or unitary on some matters and motley or cacophonous on others. We treat the people alternately as "it" or "the," we extrapolate from the microcosm to the macrocosm and we generalize on the basis of few cases. We impute to "a" or "the" people aptitudes (a capacity for strategic thinking, for example, or for collective self-discipline, or a comprehension of natural rights) that sometimes seem to bespeak ideological and sentimental projection rather than an empirically verifiable foundation. Still, whether fascinating or nettlesome, the people remain, massive, imposing and problematic. In a different yet analogous register, the question of public opinion reverts incessantly, also because it looms at once as absolutely decisive and extremely refractory to close, cogent analysis or coherent theorization.

I remain faithful to the premise of *Bread, Politics* that the subsistence question, broadly construed, is at the core of eighteenth-century history, and that the issues joined by the struggle over liberalization have marked French (and European/Atlantic) history ever since, and continue to shape our destiny today: the bristling tension between liberty and equality, and the debate over the necessity, legitimacy and character of regulation. I write these words barely a year after reading Thomas Picketty's already celebrated/notorious *Le Capital*, and a few hours after examining the just-released updated report of the Organization for Economic Cooperation and Development on income inequality and poverty. The latter argues that economic growth has not been fairly shared and that the economic crisis has only "widened the gap between rich and poor." Among other matters, it "assesses the effectiveness of social and labor market policies in tackling poverty and high inequalities." I would not pretend that there is a straight line that leads from the nourishing prince and the social contract of subsistence to the modern welfare state. Yet, the relation between the mission of regulation and the attenuation of inequalities, resulting in enhanced social justice, seems to me to be virtually linear.[40]

* * * * *

Nota Bene: May I use this occasion to express my gratitude to Fernanda, Erik and Sophus Reinert for their precious assistance in this project and, more generally, for their unfailing wisdom in counsel and fidelity in friendship.

40 Shortly after completing this text, I read the humane and pragmatic piece by Joseph E. Stiglitz that suggests that one of the missions of regulation, broadly conceived, is to attenuate inequality. *International New York Times*, 28–29 June 2014.

Chapter I

(RE-)THINKING REGULATION: POLICE, PRICES, MARKETS

During the past forty years, very few studies have appeared dealing with the provisioning trade. This dearth of production is especially striking in the 1970s and '80s when social history still rode its quasi-hegemonic tide, barely challenged until the run-up to the bicentennial of the French Revolution.[1] Long before the relatively recent globalizing turn, foreign trade, largely focused on colonial relations, commanded substantial interest. Commerce within France, dominated by cereals, in terms of magnitude and significance, elicited hardly any curiosity. It seems hard to impute this situation to the considerable older literature, scholarly and "antiquarian," denser in its concern for the regions than for the capital, which was very often badly dated. Nor did the great "urban" theses, under the aegis or influence of Ernest Labrousse of the Sorbonne, former secretary to Léon Blum, champion of an incipient quantitative socioeconomic approach, more or less in the spirit of the *Annales*, devote keen attention to the subsistence question. Labrousse himself seemed to have exhausted the arena of price studies; and the uncertainty regarding the discreet, herculean labors of Jean Meuvret, another pioneer in the socioeconomic realm, specialized in agricultural, especially grain-related issues—how much of what was bruited had he completed and when, if ever, would it come out?—doubtless had a dissuasive effect. My *Provisioning Paris: Merchants and Millers in the Grain and Flour Trade During the Eighteenth Century* (Ithaca, 1984), the first probing research into the elementary structures of the grain and flour trade in the greater Paris area, a socioeconomic and cultural study blending quantitative and qualitative analyses, did not spur any vocations, notwithstanding its efforts to recast notions of markets and of regulation. I was especially disappointed that no one explored further the milling trade/industry, still a largely virgin domain of inquiry, despite its crucial place in the French industrial and social economy, and despite the transformative impact

1 Some of the signs of disaffection are pondered in the two volumes of my *Farewell, Revolution*: I: *Disputed Legacies, France, 1789–1989*, and II: *The Historians' Feud, France, 1789–1989* (Ithaca, NY: Cornell University Press, 1995).

of its technological innovation and business practices. Indeed, generally speaking, all remained quiet on the historiographical front of what was called the grain–flour–bread circuit: no wheels turning, stones grinding or dough fermenting.

As far as the market was concerned—as concept, ideology, institution, set of practices—we seemed to have reached the end of historiography, if not of history: no one problematized it; it was what it was supposed to be by those who fully elaborated its code and destiny during the nineteenth century. Nor did the question of regulation, so sensitive today in myriad theaters, call forth scrutiny, no more on the administrative or political plane than in a social or economic register. The highly promising recent renewal of "police" studies concentrated on matters other than provisioning issues.

Fortunately, a number of scholars eddied against this trend. I examine some of that work in this chapter (and other portions elsewhere in this book). I also consider some of the stimulating work in the social sciences that can help us understand markets, in particular a rejuvenated/reinvented economic sociology and a noncanonical analysis from economists, some of whom draw substantially on sociological and anthropological insights.

Ode to the State

Judith A. Miller's *Mastering the Market: the State and the Grain Trade in Northern France, 1700–1860* (Cambridge, 1998) aspires, in the daunting wake of Charles Tilly, to construe the subsistence issue as the critical variable in the "reformulation of the French state" across 150 years. In other words, as she puts it somewhat quaintly, "What is striking about the period is less the disruptive effect of food shortages on the French state"—she has little to say on their impact on French society—"in the Old Regime, the Revolution, and after than the forces that restored order" (1–2). A sometimes rapturous ode to the state, the book is inscribed in a Whiggish trajectory, resolutely moving forward despite epiphenomenal setbacks, that ushers in an "increasingly skillful" management of public affairs. In the unfolding teleology that casts into relief the "growing competence and authority" of administrators, the welfare state is precociously at work already in the Old Regime where the "charge" of local officials is to "feed [the people]", a significant step beyond the benchmark agenda of the *prince nourricier* and his *police des grains* (5).

The representation of a state, more or less crippled, presumably by "wars, shortages and revolutions," mired in "confusion" yet moving inexorably toward "assurance" through "consolid[ation]" of its power, strikes me as a straw man (2, 6). The *doloriste* pole of this itinerary draws inspiration from and is reinforced by a sort of protracted apocalyptic dawn: "How was stability to be wrested from turmoil?" (25). But the default quality of the social ecology was not unremitting tumult or upheaval; public administration did not face a daily dose of "anarchy" (2). The construction of order was the unremitting challenge for the authorities, but they did not launch the process everyday from the brink of chaos. Everyday order was a consensual social objective, mobilizing as a rule both the attic garrets and the ground floor of the *hôtel particulier*. In dealing with disorder, Miller is tempted by what Tilly called the "hydraulic model," a mechanistic and reductionist etiology. Uncertainty was endemic and unsettling, shortages were frequent, yet riots were relatively uncommon. Consumers did not characteristically mutiny "at the slightest rumor of failure," though it would have been fruitful for Miller to explore the repertory, recruitment and objectives of the uprisings she encountered (1).[2] Even the (physical) marketplace, figuring both the ravenous stomach and the throbbing heart of city, town or hamlet, was only exceptionally a place of the portentous "turbulence" to which Miller alludes (64). If *chertés*, of highly uneven acuity, struck often, and dearths more than occasionally, "famines" did not occur in France after 1709 (44, 195).

If the structuring tale of valiant state self-rehabilitation strikes me as wobbly, Miller's decision to extend her gaze through the mid-nineteenth century infuses her project with a salutary respiration, though her relegation of the Revolution to merely "one episode in the gradual evolution of the French state and economy" verges on caricature. She declares the persistently amorphous "market" to be "mastered" by the last third of the nineteenth century and the provisioning issue no longer a threat (296). In fact, the grain question does not recede into oblivion, although producers now become as central in state reckoning as consumers and surpluses often elicit as much fretfulness as penuries: a tepid physiocratic revenge?[3] Tariff policies fail to bring stability, and the Popular Front instantiates an "organization" of the wheat (later the generic cereals) market that eclipses the most utopian (or dystopian) reveries of the Enlightenment. Before and *after* the Second World War, the management of the so-called "filière blé-farine-pain" is a paramount concern for the state, which establishes a specific, sprawling administration to deal with it until the European Union induces it to inflect its thinking and refit its bureaucracy with the advent of the first Common Agricultural Policy (1957–62).[4]

2 "The trials of the 1817 food rioters yield a sense that these disturbances, while troubling, were no longer viewed as containing politically subversive undertones," J. Miller writes, in the passive voice that blurs issues of agency and causality throughout her book (294). Nicolas Bourguinat contests this "sense" in his excellent *Les Grains du désordre. L'État face aux violences frumentaires dans la première moitié du XIX*[e] *siècle* (Paris: Editions de l'Ecole des Hautes Etudes en Sciences Sociales, 2002), discussed below.

3 I allude here to the physiocrats' fervent advocacy of the primacy of the producer and their stark warnings against the crippling economic costs of (over-)abundance.

4 For this paragraph and the next, see S. L. Kaplan, *Le Pain maudit: Retour sur la France des années oubliées, 1945–58* (Paris: Fayard, 2008).

In the twentieth century, bread resurfaces as a major actor and a critical sociopolitical problem, not only in wartime, fertile terrain for subsistence atavism, but also afterward, for example, in the decade after the Liberation when the state toiled energetically, often brutally, and not always responsibly and efficiently, to assure the nourishment of the population. In the midst of a protracted dearth that lasted till the mid-1950s—one reason to assess prudently the takeoff and the impact of the *Trente Glorieuses*—the bread question once again crystallized the debate between partisans of varying degrees of regulation, of interventionism and even of *dirigisme* (a structured sector, to be guided and buffered by lasting state action) and proponents of a neo-Turgotian-style laissez-faire (the sweeping liberation of the grain–flour–bread industry, allowed to work out its own destiny "commercially," that is, according to the unbridled play of supply and demand in a genuinely competitive arena).[5]

In an enlarged horizon, from Louis XIV through François Mitterrand (under whose presidency the state finally relinquished the fixation of the price of bread, a project promoted as eagerly by the socialist head of state as by his rightist prime minister, Jacques Chirac), it appears plain that it is rash to affirm, as Miller does, that by the nineteenth century (where consumers require on the average significantly more than the pound of bread she accords them) "bread, not grain, became the commodity of contention" (7). Bread does not grow under the paving stones of the cities, the physiocrats mercilessly taunted the "urbicoles";[6] yet urban consumers hardly needed this lesson, which explains why the CGT—the massive labor union close to the Communist Party—organized sentinels to prevent "removals of grain" (especially at night) on the Norman Seine in 1947, a year marked by myriad subsistence revolts/food riots—even as inhabitants of cities on or near the river did the same two hundred years earlier.

5 I am struck by the robust presence of a *dirigiste* inclination in the debates that followed the suppression of rationing and of the Ministry of Food Supply, during the agonizingly prolonged post-Liberation dearth. This reflection, built on the specificities of the "organization" of the grain market and of the milling industry, drew its inspiration less from collectivist experiences in the Soviet sphere than from the ideas of the more or less centrist strain in the "X-Crise-Group" of Polytechniciens and other technicians with a planifying agenda who accepted a market economy so long as it accommodated a statist orientation that obviously attenuated the latitude of the actors. See Kaplan, *Le Pain maudit* and Olivier Dard, "Voyage à l'intérieur d'X-Crise," *Vingtième siècle* 47 (July–Sept. 1995): 132–47.

6 *De bonne guerre*, and with plausibility, critics taunted the physiocrats as "fireside quibblers" who knew very little about the countryside, a charge that is not globally true when one looks at the trajectories of many individuals, beginning with Quesnay and Mirabeau.

Taming an Elusive Market and an Absent Grain Trade

Mastering the Market is a study of markets that divulges stunningly little about them. Instead of problematizing the market as a concept and as an institution, this monograph takes its existence for granted as an ageless system of allocation that operates according to anachronistic neoclassical logic and language. Apparently, the "market forces" and "market mechanisms"—never spelled out—operate in the period Miller investigates more or less as they do today (25, 43, 52, 72, 76, 112, 143, 258, passim). She evokes the "workings of the market," but takes it to be a transparent template and process that requires no historical or theoretical scrutiny (243, 282). She casts her work as the story of the "taming" of the grain trade, but this commerce also escapes sustained, probing examination: we learn virtually nothing about its structure, its personnel and their recruitment, or its practices. It looms as a salient absent presence, branded with a timeless, static quality, despite the deep changes wrought by the commercialization and later the partial industrialization and incipient concentration of the *puissance d'écrasement* of the milling world, and the displacement of grain by flour as the central currency of exchange. Bakers (frequently seconded by factors or brokers who provided credit, stockage/conservation and other transactional facilities) played a critical role in this mutation, but their buying and bolting habits, their shifting relations with suppliers and their methods of fabrication linger in the shadows. "Merchant" is as fuzzy and generic a title/status in the provisioning sphere as *fonctionnaire* will become in the state bureaucracy. Vital institutions, such as the grain merchants' guild of Rouen—so contentious in eighteenth century debates, so crucial in administrative calculations—remain shrouded in mystery. J. Miller tells us that the shock of liberalization had no significant effect on the players in the grain trade, though we know that a throng of new faces entered their rank in the capital and several of its sprawling supply crowns (81).

Indeed, the profound rupture of liberalization set in motion in the 1760s, with violently disruptive consequences, reiterated in the 1770s with similar results, does not bulk large on Miller's radar. She refuses to acknowledge its radicality, either in political or social terms, or more narrowly as an administrative revolution: whereas the laws of 1763–64 in fact totally dismantled the regulatory/police apparatus and tied the hands of the local authorities of all categories, she strangely concedes the "lifting of a number of controls on the grain trade" (43, 194), and the "strip[ping]" of local officials "of a number of their tactics for countering shortages" (93). Physiocracy, which helped engender the only project of the Economic Enlightenment that became the unequivocal law of the land, registered by the parlements, and that subverted myriad moral, economic and political covenants and conventions, is treated as an abstraction (113), while Turgot, not a physiocrat, but no less intransigent on the total inviolability of the foundational natural rights of property and liberty in the grain trade (and beyond), is depicted as a relativist applying "stricter guidelines" in the governance of commerce in cereals, an aporia in both his thought and action (109). In Miller's calculus, at best, the liberalization movement and moments accelerate a process etched in the unfolding of history, coterminous with the advent of modernity.

Central government policy elicits little more interest because the monarchy, too, unravels with its policies, in this teleological narrative.[7] "When the Crown faltered," the local and regional authorities "carried on" and saved the day, the decade and perhaps even the century, as a result of their astute management of human and material resources and their capacity for accommodation within continuity. Naturally, Miller credits them neither with the sabotage of royal (not physiocratic)[8] policy nor with the undermining of royal authority, thus casting into relief both the limits of (corrosive yet coherent) liberalism and of (an insufficiently absolute) absolutism. Despite the sometimes abyssal gap between elite and workaday administrative culture, it is regrettable that Miller chose not to "read" the doctrine and the ideological implications of the increasingly muscular sphere of political economy, from Gournay/Quesnay through the stark revolutionary confrontation between liberal and moral-economic voices, from the ideologues to the sociologizing and modernizing coterie around Napoléon III.[9] Such an exploration would have helped make sense of the trickle-down liberalism that percolates into the minds of local (and sometimes regional) administrators and magistrates, whose quintessential

7 In the story of state "reformulation" that structures Miller's monograph, it is hard to situate her clearly on the Tocquevillean statist grid. She acknowledges readily "the centuries-long process of centralization" (64). On the one hand, it seems to have imposed a certain tentacular dominion in the realm. On the other hand, globally, cumulatively, this concentration of power proves relatively ineffectual in many crucial domains. On the one side, the historian rejects the depiction of a tottering state mired in miscalculation. On the other side, the state urgently needs to be reformulated in order to accomplish some of its most important missions. Miller hedges her bets. The "stormy moments" in the exercise of monarchical/state power were "only way stations in a longer process of growing competence and authority" (5).

8 Though they celebrated the laws of 1763–64 as a momentous breakthrough, the physiocrats regarded them as insufficient and in the end blamed their failure as much on their deficit of radicality as on the resistance to their implementation, especially at the local level. See Steven L. Kaplan. *Bread, Politics and Political Economy during the Reign of Louis XV* (The Hague: Martinus Nijhoff, 1976).

9 Riven by structural tensions between ethnographic ambitions and ideological assumptions, the "enquêtes" on cereals (with penetrating excursions in the grain and flour trade) and on the bakery (the latter in particular bearing Le Play's mark) could

pragmatism seems to be informed, in Miller's treatment, not only by the adaptive and flexible police heritage, but also by the ambient intellectual currents and policy debates.

In light of "the growing acceptance of market forces even before 1763," Miller blithely asserts, "the distinction between the physiocratic market and contemporary practices was not necessarily clear" (76). What is unclear is what she means by this putative consensus crystallized by "market forces." What is patently clear is that there was a prodigious chasm, fathomed by all the actors, between "contemporary practices" that tolerated provisionally variable degrees of liberty (of transgression of the law, until it changed dramatically in 1763) in periods free of subsistence stress and the infinitely more exigent and ominous physiocratic "market" that demanded a total freedom for the merchant (no registration or surveillance; freedom to buy and sell anywhere, at whatever price one wished, on sample or in the fields or barns, and to use agents and form associations to effect these transactions; authorization to hoard and keep secret stocks; sacralization of property in grain, upon which neither state nor society could exercise any legitimate claims; absolute immunity from any intrusion by authorities on any pretext in the disposition of their property by dealers and any other possessors of grain). The physiocratic project, parts of which the authorities allegedly appropriated, was not about the lubrication of exchange; it was about the annihilation of regulation and entitlement, about national renaissance through the rejuvenation of agriculture doped by a high-price policy, about the transformation of the commonly held ideas of market and of kingship itself. Flight from the physical market site in post-1763 France should not surprise Miller (nor did it stun most local officials, whom she characterized as already socialized into the "marketplace" practice of "free trade") (79, 81–82). This was the proper vocation (and the ironic emblem) of free trade, inherently immoderate.

Free Trade as Simulation and as Regulation

Miller takes as a given what she must demonstrate: that an "emerging definition of marketplace free trade" flourished widely in the eighteenth century. Ever nebulous, this labile concept enabled "skillful" officials to intercede in behalf of buyers, and even to coerce growers or owners to supply markets, that is to say, to do what the police habitually had done, especially in difficult periods.

have proved valuable to Miller. See Conseil d'Etat, *Enquête sur la révision de la législation des céréales*, 2 vols. (Paris: Imprimerie Impériale, 1859); and Conseil d'Etat, *Enquête sur la boulangerie du département de la Seine* (Paris: Imprimerie Impériale, 1860).

Apparently, the historian discerns no tension between the (unproven) "deep commitment to free trade" of magistrates and their undiminished willingness to manipulate grain commerce. There seems to be a double litmus of a free trade administrative conscience: intervention that is conducted "discreetly," "quietly," and/or "secretly"—difficult to achieve in a marketplace site rife with suspicion, anxiety and rumor—somehow does not infringe on commercial liberty; and abstention from imposing prices as a general albeit not hallowed rule[10] (67–70, 85–91). The historian herself acknowledges the "numerous variations on the market place definition of free trade." I have written extensively about the police (broadly construed) across the past forty-five years, in daily urban life and in rural areas, in labor and product markets, in the guilds, in multiple areas of public policy and administration, in the twentieth and in the eighteenth centuries. I share much of Miller's sympathy for the "local officials," though her apotheosis of their collective deftness and cunning strikes me as overdrawn (112–13, 292, 297, passim). Yet, it seems to me as much a distortion of reality to refer to Miller's marketplace practices as a form of free trade as to represent New York City's "stop and frisk" drill as part of the emerging definition of civil liberties.

Since a preoccupation with grain leads us close to the soil, why not call a spade a spade? To the extent that it compromised the provisioning of their jurisdictions, many of her officials contested and undermined, stealthily and/or brutally, the free-trade mandate accorded by the liberalization of 1763–64[11]; to the extent that it facilitated that task, many agreed, artfully and imaginatively, to "avert their eyes" and tolerate a significant but limited dose of free trading during noncrisis years before and after the liberalization episodes. Why indulge the mystification of characterizing classical supply-side state/administrative intervention as an instrument in the service of free trade, apparently through its cryptic capacity to resolve the "contradictions in prevailing policies." The author rebaptizes government-backed or -designed or -financed selling operations as "simulated" sales in the hope of making them pass for contrivances favoring free trade because they are presumptively located "halfway" between conventional "*grains d'ordonnance*" campaigns and a projected ideal type called "the market economy." Manifestly manipulative, these "simulated" sales were real, not feigned, transactions. If they required a new label, "dissimulated" might have been more apposite and limpid because

10 Miller oscillates between the ideal of operations conducted "invisibly" and the reality of endeavors "somewhat concealed" (70).

11 What Miller calls, without irony, in reference to Turgot's liberalization, "deft implementation" (93).

they were meant to be concealed. In any event, it seems to me highly unlikely that "simulated sales" could have "sustained fragile trade networks" precisely because they were artificial, stage-managed, sporadic and constantly menaced with the risk of exposure (56, 70–71).

One would not fundamentally change the sense of Miller's treatment (and even her overarching argument/telos, which is less about a free-trade state than a pragmatic, flexible, opportunistic victualing state whose ultimate mission is to wither away) if one substituted the word "regulation" every time she uses the formula "free trade." She is surely talking about regulation when she writes, for example, that officials "reshaped free trade to accommodate the needs of their towns" or that consumers "drew the very clear conclusion that free trade was to be tempered and adapted to their needs" (106). A century later, it was not free trade that "guarantee[d] most bakers a modest security and fairly stable profits"—assuming for the moment that this proposition is valid—but administrative *encadrement*, that is to say, regulation.

Why cling to a hazy, homeopathic, often frankly degraded or vestigial notion of free trade which, in the end, resembles a sediment of diverse "lite" proto-liberal ingredients composing the police elixir, the canonic potion at least since the time of Delamare, who theorized an unevenly constrained commerce that tended always naturally and sometimes perilously toward liberty? It would be disingenuous to portray the "police of grains" as a sort of chrysalis for the slowly maturing free trade butterfly. But the police of grains—the system of regulation—that I have studied for decades furiously resembles the assumptions and operations of Miller's free-trade officials. J. Miller herself is not wholly comfortable with her free-trade *doctrine*. She offers a quasi-concession and finds some solace in the adjective "moderate." It seems to apply with equal pertinence to the interventionist and the liberal polices of what I call regulation. She prizes prefects who followed a "moderate, but still interventionist, approach" and who grafted a "moderate" exegesis on regulatory decrees even as she appreciates a Restoration Commission that toiled to maintain grain prices at "moderate levels"[12] (231–32, 242). Two centuries of civil and military administration generated "a moderate form of free trade" (297) even as the French state created "a moderate free trade in the 19th century" (300). Egregious oxymoron for serious liberals, "moderate free trade" made sense to those whom the latter stigmatized as "restricteurs" and "réglementaires."

12 In the same vein, Miller hails the "gentle" measures of a prefect in 1812 and underlines the lessons from the *dirigiste* experience of the first Napoléon that led later administrators to favor the efficacy of "subtle pressure on the grain trade." She has little use for brutality and boorishness of "wrathful magistrates" or "intemperate parlementary presidents" (64, 233).

Certainly the state did not "create free trade", as Miller contends. She frames her case with a specious dichotomy opposing state intervention, about which she tells us a great deal, and the ever elusive "market," about which she tells us virtually nothing. But, as scores of political economists (from the most precocious to the most mature, the most *dirigiste* to the most liberal) have reminded us, the state, directly and indirectly, deliberately and inadvertently, has played (and continues to play) a major role in the development and comportment of capitalism and its institutions, including the market, both in its early modern incarnations and in its neoclassical guise. As far as "free trade" is concerned, in the weak sense in which J. Miller uses it, it seems to me that the state stimulates, husbands, regulates, deregulates, obstructs, facilitates, punishes and pardons, but does little creating. In this instance, rather than begetting, it codified, a task that it took up seriously with Louis XIV and abandoned twice during the Economic Enlightenment with two daring (even rash) attempts to reinvent itself (and its relations with a society whose foundations it also shook). After absolutism proved insufficiently powerful to engender liberalism, the state returned, in the aftermath of the Revolution, to the more prosaic labors of mediating, arranging, collecting, classifying and synthesizing. It codified, in this broad sense of the term, the multiple, disparate (and sometimes contradictory) practices of free trade that arose from the "comptoir" (Gournay) and the "charrue" (Quesnay, Mirabeau), from top-down reform and bottom-up resistance to it, from local re-appropriation of central fiat, from infinite individual negotiations and collective compromises, from focused commercial lobbies and diffuse social movements, from international economic pressure and regional economic preference.[13]

The *Braconnier*: Seduction and Disillusion

Like Judith Miller, Bernard F. Harcourt links police and liberty in the grain and bread markets of eighteenth-century France. He writes much less knowledgeably than does Miller about the grain trade and the bakery business (craft and commerce), and much more knowledgeably than she does about markets, especially in the neoclassical mold. Miller would have profited

13 See the heuristically provocative remarks on markets (inherently dynamic) that will habitually seek ways to skirt the regulations (putatively static): regulation is socially useful to the extent it brings private costs in line with social costs. Allan Metzger, *Why Capitalism?* (Oxford: Oxford University Press, 2012). To situate Metzger's ideological engagement, note that he served as the president of the ultraliberal (European sense) Mont Pelerin Society for the term 2012–14, preceded, among others, by F. A. Hayek, Milton Friedman and Gary Becker.

considerably from Harcourt's deconstruction of the antinomy market/discipline (or, as I prefer to formulate it, liberty/regulation).

It was a pleasure to read Harcourt's *The Illusion of the Free Market* (Cambridge, MA, 2011). Intellectually poised and pugnacious, it is imaginatively conceived and nimbly written, and it treats matters of exceptional importance to us both as citizens and as scholars. A fiercely "American" story with universal implications, it is framed in deeply cosmopolitan terms. I concur warmly with the author's strong, central argument, riveted in the final line of the book: "It will not be possible to break the hold of our excessively punitive carceral state unless we first free ourselves from the very language of 'free' markets."

It was also exasperating to read this work because the author appropriates historical arguments in a manner that is often cavalier and deeply flawed. As a matter of principle if not etiquette, it would be curmudgeonly to tax this professor of political science, law and criminology for his lack of familiarity with old-regime political, social, economic and institutional history, some of which is quite specialized.[14] In the end, however, as a result of his own construction, his thesis that the free-market myth has gravely warped American politics and punishment policies depends on the cogency of his historical analysis. Harcourt plunges into the history with zest, self-assurance and a certain audacity (I am thinking particularly of his vertiginous apprenticeship in the "Y" series of the French National Archives). In this role, he must assume all the responsibilities (risks and benefits) of Michel de Certeau's *braconnier* (poacher). I take him to task all the more reluctantly because I don't relish playing the role of de Certeau's *propriétaire* (landowner) and because I resonate with much of Harcourt's polemical and militant agenda. Yet, both the historical demonstration and the arguments that he claims to draw from it are absolutely crucial to his entire project, an intellectual genealogy of the notion

14 Though he ought to have found out that grain traders did not live in castles; that an "esclave marron" was not a "brown slave" but a fugitive slave; that the "galères" referred first to condemnation to rowing in naval vessels and later to hard labor, not to transportation; and that "laborer" does not do as a translation for *laboureur*, a word that in the Paris region generally meant a peasant (we would say farmer) who owned a certain amount of land and sometimes rented supplementary parcels, generally to grow cereals. Sometimes, contemporaries conflate *laboureur* and *fermier*, the latter habitually a renter of land, in his physiocratic guise a veritable agricultural entrepreneur, ready to invest, attuned to price movements, "commercial." See Jean-Marc Moriceau et Gilles Postel-Vinay, *Ferme, entreprise, famille: grande exploitation et changements agricoles: les Chartier: XVIIe–XIXe siècles* (Paris: Ecole des Hautes Etudes en Sciences Sociales, 1992); Moriceau, *Les fermiers de l'Île-de-France. L'ascension d'un patronat agricole (XVe–XVIIIe siècle)* (Paris: Fayard, 1994); and Moriceau, *La Terre et les paysans aux XVIIe et XVIIIe siècles* (Rennes: Presses Universitaires de Rennes, 1999).

of natural order framed by a parallel between the eighteenth century and our contemporary world which are said to share a certain ideological consonance.

Original Sin

The foundational defect in Harcourt's work is his deep lack of understanding of the provisioning trade—its organization, its composition and its functions—and, *a fortiori*, of the *police des grains*, the formula commonly used by contemporaries to describe the regulation of this commerce, widely considered to be a quasi-public service.[15] The latter point is salient; Harcourt does not ponder its significance. Grain was the ration of survival of the vast majority of French women and men, the source of the bulk of their calories (and in many cases of their proteins as well). No issue preoccupied authorities more relentlessly than the subsistence question, even as no task mobilized the energy of the *menu peuple* more urgently than the quest for their daily bread. A social contract (of subsistence) bound the monarch, *prince nourricier*, to his subjects, the children to whom he played the role of symbolic father. This link

15 Closer to his Chicago base than to Paris, Harcourt might have gleaned an intimation of the sheer power of the provisioning question by reading the work of one of the Board of Trade's fictional chroniclers, Frank Norris, situated mid-way between French naturalism and Sinclairean muckraking (let us leave his anti-Semitic proclivities in parentheses). In his writing, wheat is stronger than man who does not succeed in taming it, despite all his cunning and all his maneuvers. A quasi-supernatural force, wheat triumphs, enriching, intoxicating and then spoliating the dominant groups, while terrorizing, starving and then finally assisting the masses. *The Pit* is the story of hoarding, of those antisocial crimes denounced as far back as the dawn of time, prominent in the preoccupations of the *police des grains* in eighteenth-century France whose agents had not yet to worry about monopoly on the planetary scale. But it is perhaps the next to last paragraph of the second novel in a projected trilogy, *The Octopus*, that most succinctly evokes the implacable, sometimes merciless fury of grain: "BUT THE WHEAT REMAINED. Untouched, unassailable, undefiled, that mighty world-force, that nourisher of nations, wrapped in Nirvanic calm, indifferent to the human swarm, gigantic, resistless, moved onward in its appointed grooves. Through the welter of blood at the irrigation ditch, through the sham charity and shallow philanthropy of famine relief committees, the great harvest of Los Muertos rolled like a flood from the Sierras to the Himalayas to feed thousands of starving scarecrows on the barren plains of India." Cf. Jean Jaurès' almost contemporaneous reminder that it is man who makes wheat, not the inverse, that production of it is not "the spontaneous work of nature" and that "nature itself is a marvelous human artifice," a posture inimical to physiocrats and to melancholic leftists such as Norris. Concluded the combative French socialist: "The union of the earth and the sun is not sufficient to beget wheat. It required the intervention of man, of his restless thinking and his patient will." *La Petite République*, 31 July 1901, cited by Jacques Potus in *Industries des céréales*, 35th year (Apr.–May, 2014).

constituted both an attribute and a sacred responsibility of kingship; his (or the state's) capacity to fulfill this trust/duty remained the paramount measure of political legitimacy well beyond the French Revolution.

It followed that cereals supply was simply too important to be left exclusively to traders, whose reputation, shaped by a gloomy anthropology derived from classical tradition and scholastic admonition, aroused permanent suspicion, not only on the part of the consumer-people but also from the perspective of the police, the great "tremblers" of the Old Regime. As it pertained to grain, police did not mean primarily law enforcement and repression, or evoke men in uniform (20); contrary to Harcourt's exegesis, those were not the signal traits of the lieutenance générale de police of Paris. Police embraced a grander horizon, the Platonic notion of the sage administration of the community: as noun, verb and adjective, police was used to describe the ways in which social and civic life should be organized to foster "the public good." From Colbert to Necker, from Bossuet to Montesquieu and from Mably to Robespierre, the conviction prevailed that provisioning was the highest priority of each government, as much to assure its longevity as to protect the public, and that the king's subjects had some sort of claim on the grain supply as the guarantee of their existence. Save during the "physiocratic" or liberal decade inaugurated in 1763, the subsistence question—what Harcourt calls the *police des grains*—was a highly political but nonpartisan issue. The *police des grains* was, first and foremost, a *structure structurante*, a defining framework of governance and social relations, not, as the author maintains, a fugitive political response to popular panic in crisis moments (albeit, it was that, too). It was a *policy* matter, a sort of administrative ethos, not merely a short-term mechanism of appeasement or social control.

The Trade and the Police

This contextualization casts into relief both the fallacy of Harcourt's remorseless trivialization of the *police des grains* and the double blunder of site/sight, that is, his location/identification of the *police des grains* and his choice of a specific archival lever to get at it. One can neither "see" the *police des grains* from the Châtelet, the Parisian mega-court, housing the police, among other jurisdictions, nor can one apprehend it from an intramural Parisian vantage point. Paris commanded exceptional attention, but given its sprawling supply hinterland (or crowns), it must be inscribed in a kingdom-wide template. The contours of global (and Parisian) subsistence regulatory policy fall under the generally assertive direction of the controller-general, a sort of superminister of the economy and public order, the king's chief deputy for matters of provisioning, who supervised an embryonic bureaucracy—a "grain department" and a mini-council mobilizing the energies of several intendants of commerce and finance. The secretary of state for the royal household, whose jurisdiction included Paris, collaborated with the contrôle-général. Since the subsistence question was at once a "national" (or central) priority and a primordially local affair, the controller-general relied upon regional and grassroots officials to furnish information on harvests (prospects and outcomes), commercial activity, prices and so on; to implement government policy (at times provoking frictions and requiring negotiations); and to respond to shifting circumstances on their own initiative, more or less within the royal regulatory design, depending upon their judgment, their taste for risk, and their jurisdictional competition in the field.

The parlements—thirteen sovereign law courts with political pretensions and quasi-legislative authority—exercised the "grande police." It featured a responsibility for provisioning and grain and flour trade affairs, undertaken sometimes in concert, sometimes in competition, with the intendants. The grande police took form through the office of the procurator general, whose largely autonomous judicial administration gave him a deeper reach into *la France profonde* than the royal agents in the parallel state administration.

The grain and, increasingly, the flour trade (Harcourt, like Miller, is oblivious to the nascent structural mutations in victualing commerce) depended on jurisdictions outside the city of Paris. As we shall see, the Parisian lieutenant of police exerted considerable influence, as he dispatched agents throughout the supply crowns, exercised a *droit de suite* that enabled him to intrude into myriad local collector markets despite resistance and collaborated with or challenged the authority of the prévôt des marchands, the head of the Parisian municipality who policed all water-borne grain traffic, still a considerable segment of the Parisian supply. Under the tutelage of the first president and the procurator general of the Paris parlement, who convoked other officials as well as specialists as the need arose, the prévôt joined the lieutenant of police in the weekly assembly of police that assessed the subsistence situation and fixed short- and middle-term policy. In other words, Harcourt could not possibly have apprehended *any* of the basic attitudes or decisions of the lieutenant in the domain of the *police des grains*—or evaluated the relative fecklessness and futility of his actions—from his narrow and highly restricted archival perch and his choice of secondary sources. Nor did the lieutenant enjoy, in his sole jurisdiction, anything resembling full sway over the *police des grains* concerning the capital.

Given the stakes of subsistence policy, the agonizing insecurity and chronic poverty in which the mass of consumers lived and the constant threat of shortages attributed to nature (harvest shortfalls) or to human contrivance (administrative blockages, logistical obstructions caused by deficient communication and transportation, and speculative manipulations on a petty or ambitious scale), the authorities embedded the *police des grains* in the organization and the ordinary operations of the grain and flour trade: it was institutionally built-in. It was very difficult for traders to escape the structures of the grain police that identified them; traced their itineraries and their frequentations; limited and/or monitored their capacity to stock; generally choreographed their activities, with more or less latitude depending on the time, place and conditions; imposed passports and/or safe-conduct passes for circulation (sometimes open-ended, often destination-specific, frequently mandating written confirmation of delivery); sanctified the marketplace as the exclusive place of exchange, an injunction variably enforced, but never repudiated as the default requirement and the implacable conceptual framework of the *police des grains*, until the liberal experiment(s). This was the ordinary *police des grains*, the regulatory paradigm well known to all actors.

The authorities applied the rules unevenly, depending on supply and stock levels and harvest prospects or results, but also as a function of their own temperaments, their relations both with dealers (traders and grower-sellers) and with their "constituents" and their "hierarchy," the system of command and accountability in which they operated. Sometimes senior officials, such as the procurator general or intendant, dispatched detailed orders (not always rigorously followed) and general guidelines on other occasions (for instance, "close your eyes upon violations" as long as supply and price conditions do not generate stress); at still other moments, because he was particularly well entrenched or merely neglected by his superiors, a local official improvised on his own reckoning of the situation.

Harcourt seems unacquainted with this police apparatus. He is content to conclude that the "*police des grains* was a political response to crisis moments of unrest and hunger," a variation on the hydraulic model that Tilly decried (169). I was among the first to insist upon the flexibility and the pragmatism in the discourse and especially in the practice of a significant number of agents in the police of provisioning. Sufferance for transgression, however, was not a programmatic posture; rather, even when protracted, it was understood to be not merely conditional, but exceptional.[16] A pragmatic and opportunistic manner in which to fluidify exchange and nourish an ample supply, this

16 Small dealers managed to adjust to the waxing and waning of these uneven rhythms of indulgence and sternness. More muscular merchants, however, found this climate detestable because of the nagging uncertainty; and liberals throughout the eighteenth century excoriated this sham play of leniency and severity, expression of the same vice. In addition to my *Bread, Politics and Political Economy* that treats the early denunciations by the Gournay circle, close to the "comptoir" in spirit, see Claude-Jacques Herbert,

way of doing—a practice rather than a policy—was, by definition, erratic. Indulgence of this sort was predicated upon two separate but often overlapping premises: first, that the dealers had internalized durably the elementary structures of control that could be activated at any time; and second, that a tacit, asymmetrical covenant or understanding between the authorities and the traders/suppliers operating habitually in their zone governed conduct and empowered the former to summon the latter into full compliance when they deemed fit. This amounted to a system of prophylaxis that, in the eyes of the police, endowed the trade, even left on its own, with a certain stability and that gave reassuring expression to the state's commitment to the consumer-people. Without these basic structures of reciprocity, of forbearance and acquiescence, it would have been extremely hard for the authorities to move into emergency or crisis mode. In any event, given the intense cereal dependence of Old-Regime society, and the shared inability to master the environment, the frontier between crisis and "normal" times was irremediably blurred.

Paris: A Provincializing Vantage Point

Given Harcourt's appetite to seize the *police des grains*, it was a serious mistake to choose the vantage point of Paris; within the Parisian police archives, narrowly construed as the "Y" series, few sources could have occluded his view more thoroughly than the documents from the *chambre de police* (of the 18,000 bundles and registers that compose the kilometers of the Y, his study examines four cartons from the *chambre de police* and one from the petit criminel). The lieutenant convenes the *chambre de police* on Fridays and judges usually on the basis of written reports of the 48 police commissaires, purely mechanical formulas or richly enthnographic observations. The court's mission is confined to questions involving the "public order" (hygiene, sanitation, security, fire prevention, prostitution, drunkenness, mendicancy and so on), aspects of the regulation of the guild world[17] and the "police de l'approvisionnement": this formal title may have misled the researcher, for in fact this rubric touches quite intentionally on minor matters concerning food markets (bread, wine and meat). A hint that the author was unlikely to find substantial issues here is the fact that the lieutenant of police could

Essai sur la police générale des grains (London, 1755); Gustave Schelle, *Vincent de Gournay* (Paris: Guillaumin et Cie, 1897); T. Tsuda, *Mémoires et Lettres de Vincent de Gournay* (Tokyo: Kinokuniya Company Ltd, 1993); Loïc Charles, Frédéric Lefebvre et Christine Théré, eds., *Le Cercle de Vincent de Gournay. Savoirs économiques et pratiques administratives en France au milieu du XVIIIe siècle* (Paris: INED, 2011).

17 On this question, see S. L. Kaplan, *La Fin des corporations* (Paris: Fayard, 2001).

not pronounce "peines afflictives," bodily punishments or penalties inflicting privation of personal freedom. The *chambre*'s protocol confined the judge to imposing fines, court costs and damage-plus-interest claims.

In general, judicial penalties tell us very little about the *police des grains*. This police is commonly extrajudicial, given its objectives. The point is to find modes of sanction, sometimes informal, that chastise errant conduct, but reinsert the actor as rapidly as possible into the commercial circuit. Officials resort to the courts to make an example, to settle a score, to placate consumers and far less frequently to punish a wayward merchant or grower-supplier. Egregious cases of "manipulations" or "maneuvers," often dubbed "monopoly," frequently issue in administrative rather than judicial resolution. Judicial penalties are a small part of the regulatory arsenal that includes threats, exhortations, negotiations, public stigmatization, administrative confiscation or requisition or disbarment from commercial activity in extreme cases, material incentives or rewards or compensations. The penalties pronounced in the *chambre de police* are quite modest (a tremulously relative notion in the universe of the laboring poor) because they punish modest offenses.

The Trivialization of the *Police Des Grains*

Viewed upon this background, Harcourt's assumptions about the nature of his material turn out to be fatally erroneous. He wrongly believes that his cartons reveal the daily policing program of the commissaires. In fact, they bespeak only a very small portion of a commissaire's police activities, the most routine, predictable and repetitive segment—a "trivial" part, to use the author's lexicon. The bulk of a commissaire's work—the most interesting part, involving all manner of complaints, denunciations, reports on various kinds of transgression (verbal and physical, financial and moral, individual and collective, public and private), interrogations, investigations, minutes of meetings, correspondence with the sindics of the company of commissaires or with the bureau of the lieutenance and so on—are to be found in the papers of the commissaires, attached to an office and usually passed down to successors. These consist of thousands of bundles or cartons, from Y 10719 through 17623: this is the material from which Arlette Farge has drawn the bulk of the rich data for her pioneering studies of Paris life, viewed and lived from below;[18] these are the papers that enabled me, in *Provisioning Paris* and *The*

18 Among her myriad studies, see *Dire et mal dire, l'opinion publique au XVIIIe siècle* (Paris: Seuil, 1992); *La Vie fragile: Violence, pouvoirs et solidarités à Paris au XVIIIe siècle* (Paris: Hachette, 1986); *Le Goût de l'archive* (Paris: Seuil, 1997).

Bakers of Paris, to uncover a vast amount of information concerning the baker grain and flour trade, relations between bakers and suppliers (millers and factors as well as grain merchants), the grain and flour trade at the Halles (land-based traffic), behavior at the formal and informal bread markets as well as in the shops and a whole range of policing activities that concerned more often bread than raw materials, but that also revealed how the police tried to inflect exchange practices by changing the organization of the Halles, recasting the facilities (a new building for grain and primarily flour sales) and coordinating the work of the measurers and porters who were police auxiliaries rather than manual laborers (Harcourt confuses the porters and the *forts des Halles* who did the heavy lifting) and who monitored entries into the city and markets, verified quality, maneuvered to obtain bargaining and lower prices and recorded the price transactions in the celebrated and precious registers called *mercuriales*.[19]

There were inspectors and commissaires specialized in the bakery or in the flour or grain trades: Poussot, de Courcy and Demachurin, for example, dealt with matters that touched directly upon provisioning policy as well as personnel and practice. Harcourt cites Demachurin, in passing, for an affair involving a fraudulent egg sale, for him a wholly marginal area of professional concern. It is simply impossible to extrapolate the full nature of what the author breezily calls the "beat" of the commissaire from the humdrum reports in the *chambre de police*. All senior commissaires and many of their junior colleagues had "transversal" as well as territorial competences—in provisioning or wet nursing or gambling or debauchery or Lutherans or seasonal migrants or nuns and monks or precious metals and money or the book trade or cabaret and inn-keeping or prisons or hospitals or in scores of other domains. The secretariat of the lieutenance générale coordinated these attributions through a number of departments, one of which focused on victualing matters. Although the Châtelet, institutional base of the Paris Lieutenant's operations, was certainly not the best locus from which to scrutinize the *police des grains*, certain of its archives could yield pertinent data, but *not* the handful of cartons in the category that Harcourt "closely" examined.

It follows that Harcourt's conclusions, uttered in triumphal and absolute tones, lose their luster. Persuaded that he is looking at the *police des grains*, he affirms that "a close examination of the archives from the police of the Châtelet of Paris at the National Archives, the famous *Série Y*, reveals the trivial

19 See Steven L. Kaplan, *Provisioning Paris: Merchants and Millers in the Grain and Flour Trade During the Eighteenth Century* (Ithaca, NY: Cornell University Press, 1984) and *The Bakers of Paris and the Bread Question, 1700–1775* (Durham, NC: Duke University Press, 1996). Neither of these works appears in Harcourt's bibliography. Two of Farge's prolific *oeuvre* are in his bibliography.

and sporadic nature of the policing," that "the police regulations concerned trivial matters" and that "the violations themselves were trifling and involved fines only." There is neither rigor nor reserve in Harcourt's scholarly self-representation: his work in a few cartons drawn exclusively from the *chambre de police* morphs imperceptibly into "the contemporaneous police records from the Châtelet"—a claim I would not dare make after having worked for decades in the Y series—which "exude the absolutely trivial nature of the daily routine of a *commissaire*..." (154). Harcourt oscillates between two poles: the first, a dispiriting positivist tantrum (his cartons are "representative" and "extremely relevant for our purpose," his review of the material is as "careful" as his reading is "close," his peremptory conclusions are irrefragable because they are based on overwhelming evidence drawn from documents he deems of singular "exhaustiveness," despite his ignorance of their producers and their protocol of production, and his science immunizes him against the risk of "perceptions of grain regulations that may well be distorted by the personal biases of the historians and narrators of the field"); and the second, an engaging eroticization of the archive that many of us have experienced, a sort of rite of passage, an exuberant, reciprocal *dépucelage* ("After the sewn thread in the corner of the yellowing papers is unfastened to unfold them—for what seems to be the very first time—these elaborate documents, some neater and more legible than others but all meticulously transcribed, reveal the world of the Paris streets circa 1758") (23, 25, 154, 158).

The Fecalization of the Police

On the basis of this incipient archival limerence, "it appears" to the author "that street cleaning was practically all the police cared about." After unswept streets, "the next most common violation," and the one that Harcourt seems to relish most, "involved fecal matter on the sidewalk" (23–24). Symbolically and tactically, is there any more incisive manner to disparage the significance of putative police undertakings, not only in Paris but also implicitly throughout the realm and throughout the Old Regime? The fecalization of the police reaches its incontinent apogee in the work of one of the corps' most accomplished agents, commissaire Lemaire, for whom the 21st of February 1758 "seemed to be a particularly bad day," for on his patrol through his district, he encounters five instances of fecal matter left in front of buildings on the rue neuve St. Médard and two in the rue Mouffetard. Apparently here and elsewhere, Lemaire had evidence not only of the deposit of the feces, but of the act of inhabitants throwing the waste matter from their rooms to the street. A few days earlier, commissaire Chénon reported "a lot of fecal matter." In early March, commissaire Dubuisson recorded four incidents of forsaken excrement[20] (159–60, 164). If Harcourt had not been so stubbornly determined to "prove" his thesis empirically, he would have realized, after these forays, that he was in deep shit, that is to say, in the wrong place to do what he wanted to do, to test the hypothesis that had already congealed in his mind into a (putatively revisionist) historical fact.[21]

Lemaire, incidentally, like his entire company, spent much more time on matters other than fecal, though I hasten to remark that the young historians in France (and elsewhere) who have energetically and astutely renewed the historiography of the police would argue that matters of sanitation, public health, air pollution, urban waste removal and neighborly sociability, among others, speak to larger questions of the social tissue, the forging of concepts of order and well-being, the evolving view of an urban aesthetic and the like.[22] Harcourt characterizes the important text that Lemaire wrote, ostensibly for the court of Vienna, under the aegis of the celebrated Paris police chief Sartine, as a "report on police enforcement … that reflects the sporadic enforcement of these police regulations and that [*sic*] any enforcement coincided with moments of food shortages."[23]

---

20 In the tables on pages 164 and 165, the archival references should read Y 9459 A and B rather than Y 9495 A and B.

21 It is an irony and a symptom of Harcourt's debacle in the "Y" series and his self-inflicted bibliographical handicap that he records the rounds of the commissaire Dubuisson on the rue de la Mortellerie, unaware that this was the street of the "barons" of the water-borne grain trade, among the biggest and most highly scrutinized actors in the provisioning of Paris (157). While the Bureau de la Ville exercised primary jurisdiction over these merchants, the lieutenance encroached on its dominion both from within the city and from the supply zones where it could exert leverage on the *commissionnaires*, or buying agents, of the Mortellerie and other port-attached suppliers.

22 I am thinking of P. Brouillet, J. Berlière, Vincent Denis, Catherine Denys, J.-L. Laffont, Brigitte Marin and Vincent Milliot, among others, none of whom is cited in this book. For them, the kinds of police/policing activities that Harcourt evokes are far from "child's play" (24).

23 J.-B.-C Lemaire, "Mémoire sur l'administration de la police de Paris", 1770, Bibliothèque historique de la Ville de Paris, s. CP 5178, and the copy on which Lenoir commented, Médiathèque d'Orléans, fonds ancien, ms. 1402. A. Gazier published a version entitled *La Police de Paris en 1770. Mémoire inédit composé par ordre de G. de Sartine, sur la demande de Marie-Thérèse*, in *Mémoires de la Société de l'histoire de Paris et de l'Ile-de-France* (1879): V.

I do not have the space here to contest Harcourt's symmetrical contention that "the same is true of letters written by the lieutenant De Marville to the minister Maurepas during the period 1742–1747," which should be read in tandem with Marville's manuscript letters in the *Bibliothèque historique de la Ville de Paris*. See an adumbration of my argument in my "Provisioning Paris: The Crisis of 1738–1741," in J. L. McClain, J. M. Merriman and U. Kaoru, eds., *Edo and Paris: Urban Life and the State in the Early Modern Era* (Ithaca, NY: Cornell University Press, 1994), 175–210.

I believe that this is an inaccurate reading. The "mémoire" is a "didactic treatise of police," as Lenoir, Sartine's successor, observed, but it raises questions about the objectives and the methods of the police in the wake of brisk population growth, enhanced mobility and the continuing debates of the Economic Enlightenment concerning the ways to spur and manage economic development and articulate it with social cohesion and moral fortitude. Lemaire wrote at the zenith of the acute subsistence crisis, culminating in a deep social and economic crisis, provoked by the confluence of protracted dearth and the dismantling and paralysis of the *police des grains* in 1763–64. Marked by this tsunami of disorder, the commissaire links the necessity "to maintain order" with the imperative "to keep a watchful eye on the common needs of the citizens." Ambivalent concerning the reliability of commerce, strongly inclined to view grain as consubstantial to the sphere of police rather than the orbit of commerce, Lemaire is nevertheless not a megalomaniacal interventionist. Day to day, commerce had responsibility for victualing, and its driving force was a regimented liberty that required registration of merchants and their storehouses, transparent exchanges on the physical marketplace and so on. The trade enjoyed a cautious and intermittent toleration for transgression, largely confined to periods of subsistence ease and geared to facilitate the commercial plunder of the provinces for the benefit of the capital, emblematic "maker" of the price throughout the kingdom. But the market remained above all a space of regulation—of discipline in Harcourto-Foucauldian language—of a permanent orchestration of supply and demand. To the physiocratic dogma of the inviolability of the natural right of the grain owner to dispose of his property with total liberty, Lemaire opposed a vision of grain, "commodity of first necessity," as a "[form of] collective wealth to which the subjects of the State have a natural and equal right, because it pertains essentially to their subsistence and their tranquility." The *police des grains* thus cannot be construed as an accessory, diluted, desultory, occasional administrative preoccupation.[24]

The "Truth": A Hoard of Error and Misunderstanding

In the "Y" series, Harcourt thought he had come across the real thing, the "truth" as he sometimes calls it: that the *police des grains* barely mattered. But the work that he (needlessly) slighted as trivial and trifling was in fact the

24 See Steven L. Kaplan and Vincent Milliot, "La Police de Paris, une 'révolution permanente'? Du commissaire Lemaire au lieutenant de police Lenoir, les tribulations du *Mémoire sur l'administration de la police (1770–1792)*," in Catherine Denis, Brigitte Marin and V. Milliot, eds., *Réformer la police: les mémoires policiers en Europe au XVIIIe siècle* (Rennes: Presses Universitaires de Rennes, 2009), 69–115.

work of what contemporaries often denominated, without pejorative hue, the "petite police." His "careful review of the more significant sentences meted out by the police chamber" (Y 9488 and 9499) reveals that "the *police des grains* constituted a minor function of the chamber's jurisdiction" (166). The author had no idea just how right he was. His finding is useless precisely because the jurisdiction he surveyed had virtually nothing to do with the *police des grains*. The *police des grains* is not reducible to a courtroom of any kind in Paris or elsewhere, or to a more or less swollen catalog of regulations, not all of which, incidentally, bear the same weight. Harcourt's exultation in the news that "the most egregious and heavily policed offense was illicit gambling" does not, alas, constitute proof of the "epiphenomenal" character of the of the *police des grains*[25] (167).

Nor does "it turn out that the *police des grains* represents only a small fraction of the business of the lieutenant de police, all of which is essentially trivial" (169). If the author had looked in the right places (I'm referring not to prohibitively labor-intensive work in multiple archives and libraries located in various places in France; he could have done this in Hyde Park through the scholarly literature), he would have found that the provisioning of Paris represented an imposing fraction of his business even in good times: weekly policy assemblies with other leading officials; daily reports from his own subsistence bureau, manned by a secretary centralizing all data on grain, flour and bread in the city and faubourgs as well as in the partially decommercialized zone that extended to a radius of up to 40 kilometers around the capital; coordination between the grain bureau of the lieutenance and the grain department of the contrôleur-général; frequent conferences and other exchanges with his specialists among the commissaires and inspectors; correspondence with itinerant agents in the hinterland; correspondence with authorities in the marketplace towns of the supply crowns; daily reports on prices from the measurers; reports on twice weekly bread markets; supervision

25 To buttress this argument, Harcourt cites a work by museum curator A. Babeau published 140 years ago, and utterly superseded by numerous studies, like G. Afanassiev's, another cornerstone (but the Russian scholar does double service as scholar and ideologue) (167). Harcourt prefers the nineteenth century for his brief discussion of the feudal legacy, a choice that can only astound an historian working today in this field that has been dramatically renewed in the past quarter century (174). The bibliography on the history of economic thought, especially the various eighteenth-century French liberal movements, is extremely uneven. The quasi-obligatory point of departure in this domain is Jean-Claude Perrot's stunningly brilliant *Une histoire intellectuelle de l'économie politique, XVIIe–XVIIIe siècles* (Paris: Editions de l'Ecole des Hautes Etudes en Sciences Sociales, 1992).

of yield trials on conversion of grain into flour and flour into bread in order to gauge reasonable profit margins for bakers and establish parameters for emergency price maxima; and the enumeration could continue.[26]

To fortify his case, Harcourt uses the standard normative sources and does not always resist the temptation to extrapolate from the rules putative data about actual practice, information that not even sentences yield reliably for lack of adequate contextualization. The rules "have come down to us as pure discipline"—whatever this neo-Foucauldian code means—"but in truth, they were not vigorously enforced—or rarely so" (153). Once again, the author simply has no basis to sustain this claim; "in truth," he has no evidence. Moreover, he deploys a dubious method of guilt by association or proximity to impugn the testimony of the writers of police manuals. First, he invokes for no compelling reason a diabolical information-gathering machine—not yet the NSA, yet as fascinating as it was extravagant in its time—devised by J.-F. Guillauté, an officer in the regional mounted constabulary, to track millions of royal subjects (152). Then Harcourt links gratuitously Guillauté's fanciful project with the grain police codifiers whose picture of the *police des grains* "was somewhat fantastic" (153). Somewhat fantastic? Has the author demonstrated the chimerical inclinations of Delamare and the others? No: their view is "fantastic" because it does not fit well with certain parts of his thesis. The codifiers and manual composers were not merely fanciful: they were also obsessive, if not frankly neurotic. They spent their time "desperately tracking and reiterating any proof that they had that these ordinances [concerning the *police des grains*] were enforced. But these proceedings were few and far between, and involved only trivial matters" (170).

These writers were joined in trivial pursuit by "the historians of the Parisian grain and bread markets" who could not then profit from Harcourt's archival discoveries ("a disproportionate number of terribly minor infractions and a relatively small place for the *police des grains*"). Who were these forlorn historians? Harcourt names "predominantly liberal opponents of the regulations such as Fréminville and Afanassiev." The first was a minor eighteenth-century magistrate, author of a treatise on the police, bereft of any liberal vocation (hardly an "opponent of the regulations") and the second a late nineteenth-century Russian scholar of liberal affinities whose work is cruelly dated. Harcourt represents them as cherry pickers, though he rightly clings to the cereal metaphor (they root up sentences "related to the *police des grains* from the haystack of police records") (169). They apparently exercised a far greater influence on Harcourt's genealogy than any other

26 See Kaplan, *Provisioning Paris* and *The Bakers of Paris*.

historian working in the field has imagined. Thus "we should be wary of having so much of our understanding of the *police des grains* filtered through the lens of these opponents, who apparently had a morbid fascination with regimentation" (170).

Why would the so-called adversaries of regulation nourish a "morbid fascination" for the object of their obloquy? Manifestly not because illustrations were hard to unearth or spectacular (rather than banal) in character. Moreover, Harcourt presents absolutely no evidence that they have so significantly conditioned "our" understanding of the *police des grains*. If he had wanted to find "opponents of the regulations" who genuinely influenced the long-term historical comprehension, he could have turned logically to the physiocrats. No one in the eighteenth century assailed the *police des grains* with more withering, uncompromising and indignant criticism than these *économistes*, as they were known. To be sure, they did not refrain from polemical hyperbole in the propagation of the principles of their new science, but it is interesting to note that the burgeoning voice of anti-physiocracy—in the parlements or in the Republic of Letters, for example—rarely took issue with the physiocratic characterization of the police per se as infringing upon rights of property and liberty, forcing grain and flour to the marketplace, espousing the cause of consumers against producers, deterring robust, well-capitalized, risk-taking merchants (*négociants*) from entering the grain trade as a result of a climate of unremitting uncertainty and so on. (They disagreed on whether these actions were justifiable or legitimate, occasional or systematic, collateral damage or deliberate spoliation.) The examination of the discourse on the *police des grains* tells us nothing directly about the practice of police, but in terms of refraction—Harcourt's "filtering"—it reminds us that the defenders of the police (a much less monolithic group than their adversaries) and their enemies agreed that the authorities exercising the *police des grains*, especially at the local level, never left the stage, even if they played different roles at different moments.

The Phases of Sophistry

In the service of his overriding thesis and his deeply legitimate contemporary concerns, Harcourt spells out his global argument on police in a series of glissandi whose motor is fervor rather than logic or evidence. Phase one begins with what I called the fecalization of the *police des grains*, that is to say a systematic belittling of its significance as an activity of the authorities. In phase two, Harcourt reinscribes himself, at least partly, in the social reality of the eighteenth century. Piddling in action, shallow in purview, unnecessary in everyday economic (and social) transactions, presumably unhoned in skills for lack of operational experience, the *police des grains* nevertheless rises to the occasion when it is enjoined suddenly to cope with a shortage and contain the people. Here we move smoothly from structural fecklessness to spasmodic efficacy.

In phase three, Harcourt slides from depreciation and trivialization, modulated by a latent capacity for crisis management, to a sort of draconian exaltation of the *police des grains*. The focus here is ideational rather than performative, but, as we shall note, the boundary is not always clearly demarcated. "To our modern eyes," Harcourt affirms, "the Parisian *police des grains* … has come to symbolize excessive government control and intervention" (6). Who are these "modern eyes?" What is the case for this stereotype that recent scholarship has done so much to dissipate, this alleged consensus? Even today, he persists, "most commentators and historians"—unnamed—"continue to characterize the ancien régime administration as excessive, overregulated, and frenzied in its minute management of the most trivial infractions" (7). This claim is untenable. For sole support, the author solicits Michel Foucault, but the philosopher can provide little more than cover and cachet, for his interest in "la police disciplinaire des grains" is more conceptual and heuristic than analytical, and his chief source in this instance is Delamare, the norm-codifier (and Paris police commissaire) whom Harcourt reads in an ambivalent way.[27]

"The Paris markets of the eighteenth-century," the author reiterates, "signify the epitome of excessive regulation—of government intervention gone awry, of authoritarian control of the economy, of pure discipline" (16). The physiocrats—passionately invested in the campaign against police practice and the police ideology that reached well beyond its sphere of direct action—are among the rare observers of the police who subscribed to something resembling this bloated, distorted, histrionic perception of the *police des grains*.[28] Physiocratic discourse was referential: it bespoke a view of documented practice in the eyes of the *économistes*. Harcourt deals with both aspects, but in ways that are sometimes cryptic. Indeed, a tension between a history of ideas and a history of actions traverses his entire book. In reference

27 Certainly Foucault did not impute to the *police des grains* the dystopian disciplinary fantasy of "eradicate[ing] all disorder" (7).

28 Apparently in part based on physiocratic press releases, Beccaria embraced this foundational category that Harcourt quite rightly labels as illusory, despite his malaise in identifying the paternity of the phantasm. The Italian's template for punishment was "the economic logic of minute governmental administration of every aspect of economics and exchange … the economic model of 'police' typified by the *police des grains*" (59).

to extravagant regulation, for example, it appears—though the phrasing is foggy—that representation mutates discreetly into practice: "… the intricate and extensive web of royal decrees and ordinances that governed absolutely every aspect of the commerce of grain under the ancien régime, the tangled snare of regulation that gave rise to the very 'grain wars of the eighteenth-century'… " (6).

From a phase emphasizing the inordinately harsh character of the *police des grains*, Harcourt sidles into a stage of mitigation and revision. In the fourth phase, where we appear to be staunchly moored in the realm of action rather than representation, his investigation "reveals that the *police des grains* of eighteenth-century France was far less disciplinary than it has been made out to be" (152). He reminds us that "actual reports from long-ago Paris *commissaires* belie the claims of overbearing discipline in the eighteenth-century" (171). Ever more implausibly, Harcourt slides, or rather swerves, into the final stage: rudimentary dialectic or urbane casuistry? Here he maintains that police is, despite its glowering mask, fundamentally "liberty enhancing." Liberty is a polysemic and/or protean notion about which the author does not overly fret. Deploying a passive voice that comfortably obscures identity/agency, he writes: "Indeed, we impose the category of discipline too easily, too reflexively, on the eighteenth century, forgetting that, in the early decades of the century, the *police des grains* was perceived by many, if not most (and certainly by the dominant political elite at the time) as liberty enhancing" (18). Yet who are the "many," "most" and "the dominant political elite," and what is the evidence for their supposed position?[29]

29 The mysterious, nameless "political elites" appear again on p. 27. However one defines them—high-level administrative personnel and magistrates, for example—it would be impossible to pretend to characterize their collective thinking on policy issues, even if we can claim to discern or infer certain dispositions. In Harcourt's terms, at once nebulous and procrustean, it is hard to fit in, say, Pierre le Pesant de Boisguilbert, a middling provincial magistrate in the "early" period of which Harcourt is so fond (late seventeenth–early eighteenth centuries) who ardently pressed the liberal cause, rehabilitating egocentricity and fulminating against the *police des grains* as brutalizing, stultifying, inimical to nature's dictates and wholly incompatible with liberty, its antithesis. See his *Traité de la nature, culture, commerce et intérêt des grains* (1707) and in particular *Le Detail de la France* (Brussels, 1712). Or, Jacques Necker, in the second half of the century, a successful banker (and erstwhile grain speculator) and powerful minister of the economy who believed in a sort of *troisième voie* that reconciled certain commercial imperatives of liberty without debilitating the sociopolitical, moral and economic vocation of a police that was both activist and discerning. But there is no indication that Necker ever imagined the police as "liberty-enhancing." See his *Eloge de Jean-Baptiste Colbert* (Paris: J. B. Brunet, 1773) and especially his *Sur la Législation et le commerce des grains*, 4th edition (Paris: Pissot, 1776).

Delamare, whom Harcourt calls to testify on his behalf, considered liberty to be "the soul of commerce." This appreciation was not mere cant, but the commissaire hedged and conditioned it in so many ways that it requires contortions to see his police as "liberty-enhancing"—whatever the author means precisely by this formula (cf. 173).[30] Without any demonstration, Harcourt simply affirms that "police and liberty formed a coherent whole," the only way to assure cheap and abundant bread (20–21). Unnamed eighteenth-century "thinkers *perceived* the *police des grains* as liberty enhancing" and the real market, in a refrain with which we are now quite familiar, was "far more free" than "we" are willing to admit today (22). Liberty, in Harcourt's sense, seems to me to be as integral to the *police des grains* in Old-Regime France as rehabilitation is to the carceral policies of most American prisons today.

Every step in this final glissando is more flabbergasting than the previous one. "Truth be told," intones the author, "there was far more liberty under the *police des grains* of early eighteenth-century France than the codebooks and manuals might suggest" (153). But this is an epiphanic truth, for there is no documentation to sustain it. Beyond rhetorical patronizing, who in France believed that "'police' was supposed to protect and promote liberty, not infringe upon it?" (171). Now we toboggan into epistemological free fall, for in this climactic skid we are free to reinvent the meaning that contemporaries attached to words and concepts. The notion of liberty that the author reads into the normative texts "was the liberty of consumers from the manipulation of the merchants" (173). Isn't this a strained, tortuous way to talk about regulation that holds dealers in check? Here Harcourt joins Miller in a sort of intellectual/conceptual malapropism. There's more: "It was a more paternalistic or protectionist freedom." Are protectionism and paternalism the basic constituents of the idea and practice of liberty in the trenchant debates of eighteenth-century France? (173).

30 It is simply absurd to claim that "... the discourse of liberty at the heart of Beccaria's and Delamare's writings was as strong and robust as that of the Physiocrats" (171). The physiocratic case for total, complete, entire, full, indefinite and unencumbered liberty—these are some of the adjectives that they habitually employ—imbricated with an equally intransigent notion of property, is utterly remote, epistemologically, politically and economically, from anything Delamare envisaged. See my forthcoming *Raisonner sur les blés* (Paris: Fayard, 2015).

Misconstruing Physiocracy: The Colonial Pitfall

This is a "different" conception of liberty from that of the physiocrats, avows Harcourt (173). These *économistes* pose problems for the author: perforce, given the magnitude of the corpus, he has read them partially and selectively.[31] He exaggerates Quesnay's influence on some matters and underestimates it on others (27, 29, 31). The so-called severing of "police" from public economy occurred well before Quesnay began to receive in his famous *entresol.* Intellectually, and theoretically, Harcourt is right to connect the physiocratic vision of liberty with the "notion of orderliness." Historically, in lived experience, however, he thoroughly ignores the chaos that liberty introduced into the grain and flour markets in the 1760s and 1770s, and the proliferating disorder it ignited throughout the kingdom, abetted by a series of harvest shortfalls. The first liberalization, set in motion by the measures of 1763–64—in my view the most radical reforms undertaken before the Revolution—constituted the only real test, a partial one at best, of the application of certain core tenets in physiocratic doctrine.

This episode is of no interest to Harcourt. He wants to situate the test in the (colonial/Atlantic) new world—this is ultrafashionable historiography today—in Martinique, port of entry for another series of misapprehensions, but necessary detour for his argument. Lemercier de la Rivière, a zealous physiocrat, served two truncated terms as intendant of the island.[32] Despite Harcourt's insistence, he did not and could not transform Martinique into a laboratory for physiocracy. He held office during the Seven Years' War and its immediate aftermath, an extremely delicate time in geopolitical, economic, social and psychological terms; he shared power with an influential governor who did not espouse his ideology (about whose degree of development we

---

31 The author would have benefitted from looking in particular at the work of Loïc Charles. First, his thesis, *La Liberté du commerce des grains et l'économie politique française (1750–1770)* (Université Paris 1, 1999); then the edition of Quesnay that he prepared with J.-C. Perrot and Christine Théré, *Œuvres économiques complètes de François Quesnay et autres textes*, 2 vols. (Paris: INED, 2005); an article that he signed by himself: "A Visual History of the *Tableau économique*," *European Journal of the History of Economic Thought* 10, no. 4 (winter, 2003): 527–49; and two articles that he wrote with C. Théré: "Les textes économiques parlent-ils d'eux-mêmes? Quelques réflexions sur le bilan et les enjeux de l'édition INED 2005 des œuvres de Quesnay," *Cahiers d'Economie Politique,* no. 57 (2009): 47–80; and "The Writing Workshop of François Quesnay and the Making of Physiocracy (1757–1764)," *History of Political Economy* 40, no. 1 (Spring, 2008): 1–42.

32 Lemercier was a magistrate in the Paris Parlement, not an adviser. His supposedly "highly publicized dispute with the abbé Galiani on the *police des grains*" refers to the *économiste*'s refutation (not cited) of the Italian's *Dialogues*, but Harcourt seems unaware of the latter's caustic and hilarious rebuttal (97–98). See S. L. Kaplan, ed., *The Bagarre: Galiani's "Lost" Parody* (The Hague: Martinus Nijhoff, 1979).

know quite little, since Lemercier did not publish his first "physiocratic" piece until after he left service[33]); he received orders from Versailles that constrained his freedom of action without denying him real latitude, but his own career ambitions—he aspired quite early on to become nothing less than controller-general—made him loathe to take undue risks (34, 100).

Harcourt associates gratuitously Lemercier's operational "severity" as field administrator with physiocratic canon, even as he wrongly asserts that "faith in the free market emerged, hand in hand, with a theory of legal despotism…" (148, 151). The physiocratic campaign in the 1760s aimed at the regeneration of agriculture (and thus of France). It was predicated upon the formal recognition of the inviolability of the natural rights of property and liberty, in conjunction with untrammeled competition which would issue in the quasi-institutionalization of the *bon prix*, the right or natural price, the generation of a national market attuned to the "common" or European market, the equalization of prices across the realm, the promotion of abundance and the attenuation of the acuity and incidence of dearths.

This policy—the absolute negation of the *police des grains*—implemented in 1763–64, was in no way contingent upon the notion of legal despotism, even if it did sketch out a new political relation between a voluntarily lean king, constrained by natural law, and parlements induced to cooperate by the monarch's very rejection of the high-handed and arbitrary rule associated with the epithet despotic. Lemercier's "highly interventionist" administration in the Antilles was not a parable for a physiocratic future: it had no kinship with Quesnay's doctrine. In his writings, about "legal despotism" as well as the natural order, the magistrate-*économiste* never deviated from his school's precept that the least government was invariably the best. Legal despotism was never an administrative (or an executive–legislative) blank check. It was not very despotic, by metaphorical and historical indicators current in eighteenth-century writings; on the contrary, it aimed at subjecting executive authority to the stringent limits that natural law imposed on state action. Nor was its vocation confined to sanction deviance—Harcourt's *déréglés*: the repressive function was far less salient in physiocracy than the author imagines.[34] Legal despotism allowed a place for a host of standard "regalian" functions (minting coin, making war, according grace) and other public services (education, infrastructure) (34, 51,

33 His position on slavery might have kindled friction within the Quesnay's chapel, since several *économistes* abhorred this institution.

34 Arnaud Orain reminds me that the physiocrats viewed the *contrebandiers* brilliantly delineated by Michael Kwass in his new book—his *déréglés*—as merchants like any others. In this sense, the *économistes* are much more interested in "guiding" the "animal liberty" of individuals than repressing it. Orain, personal communication. See Kwass, *Contraband: Louis Mandrin and the Making of a Global Underground* (Cambridge, MA: Harvard University Press, 2014).

78–79, 234). Legal despotism is certainly more indispensable to Harcourt than to post-Quesnay followers of physiocracy or sympathizers such as Turgot.

Price Volatilty and Markets; Regulation and State Making

Straddling 400 years and venturing broad European comparison beyond the ken of most of us, Scandinavian economic historian Karl Gunnar Persson, with mastery and modesty, renews considerably our understanding of grain markets. He crafts a neo-modernization argument, with a double inflection, functionalist in methodology and Whiggish in mood. Emphatically, however, he does not map out a simplistic or linear itinerary. On this Braudelian journey, prices are his principal lodestar. Price volatility, driven largely by nature (harvest outcomes), but also by culture (commerce and police, with their respective uses and abuses), undermines stability, and in a sense maintains states in a protracted infancy. The promethean Enlightenment—what I call the Economic Enlightenment—strained against these limits: its "intuition" was that market integration would lead to price stability and thereby create the conditions for a general emancipation, beginning with the abandonment of regulation, only necessary when markets could not deliver[35] (xvii).

The contingent necessity of regulation did not make it any less consubstantial to state making. Regulation is construed both as an institution and a policy, the first as an unwavering *idée-force* incarnate, the second as a variable tool of control. Assuming various forms, from the management of public granaries to the repression of what Persson calls "insider trading," a powerfully evocative anachronism, the *police des grains* remains a major instrument of governance. Even in the larvated guise of benign neglect, it cannot be mistaken as a Trojan horse for liberalization, but rather its inveterate, albeit pragmatic, foe. The author reasons vigorously that regulation cannot wilt (and presumably perish) until market performance demonstrates its superfluousness. I would have liked for him to problematize the notion of market failure (and, *a fortiori*, of *the* market, in ordinary operation and in success, if the latter is not a pleonastic formulation). Market failure presumes, ontologically, that markets are construed to "work"; as much as it may shock economists and economic historians, there are some

35 Abandonment or attenuation? It is not clear from this text whether the emancipation could occur in stadial terms, beginning with a diminution of regulation. The pragmatism of the French authorities already fulfilled this criterion and, while it may have improved market performance on occasion (or even more often), it certainly did not foster market integration. Nor am I sure that Persson (as a cliometrician) would subscribe to Bernard Harcourt's quite reasonable contention that there is no such thing as a free market. Persson, *Grain Markets in Europe, 1500–1900: Integration and Deregulation* (Cambridge: Cambridge University Press, 1999).

of us, uncomfortable with such presumptions of temporal transcendence and conceptual transparency, who would very much like to see the discourse/practice of "market" subjected to more rigorous definition and historicization. Though one can imagine that "market power," for example, means very much what the French connoted when they fulminated against "monopoly" (perhaps from both the liberal and the police side) in the eighteenth century, I would have welcomed an unpacking of the archetype, across time and space (74–75). In any event, the author addresses crucial questions concerning market behavior, and the relations between markets on the one hand, and ideas, politics and social dynamics on the other.

Though Persson clearly believes that the *police des grains* was destined to wither away eventually, he does not demonize it, in echo of the liberal lobbyists and ideologues, nor does he postulate its intrinsic fecklessness and futility. He has both thoughtful and perplexing observations to make about regulation (in the latter category, for example, the wholly implausible "centralized system of food provision" in Colbertist France) (1). Yet, he claims to be much less interested in "the political game that generated observed policies"—one of the areas upon which I have toiled—than in asking "if the nature of public intervention conformed to the expectations provided by the economic theory of market failure"—a domain more remote from my competence. The latter focus is rich in insights that obviously shift the protocol of demonstration to which I am accustomed. Persson shows, through this method, how the "carrots and sticks," as he styles them, coexist, as the theory predicts (but cannot explain): thus, on the one hand, subsidies compensate grain merchants for social gains they engendered and, on the other hand, the threat of unleashed "market power" justifies police vigilance or control. The provisional conclusion is fascinating in light of the usual Manichean binaries: though the question should not "be disposed of lightly," he finds in the end that the political interventions themselves were not "the *real* cause of the poor performance of the markets" (73).

A Pragmatic *Police des Grains*: Efficiency, Moralty and Famine

Hovering, drone-like, far above the markets, Persson discerns factors that elude terrestrial historians and, occasionally, misconstrues others that bear on the issues on the ground. In France, he overemphasizes the weight of accredited merchants (a small minority), fails to explain the structural reasons for the serious underdevelopment of the grain merchant profession, underestimates the presence of price fixing in both grain and bread and fails to take into account the differential regulatory practices in rural and urban loci (77). Yet, he is right to note a less intrusive and more selective eighteenth-century *police des grains* and to direct attention to the (occasional) public "crowding out" of private commerce (even if the public–private divide is not always luminously denoted) (75, 86–87). He avows the difficulty of assessing the *net* impact of regulation in quantitative terms. His evaluation of the utility of public intervention is prudent and nuanced, remote from the mechanistic and reductionist conclusions deplored by the critics of the "Galilean" paradigm in historiography. If Persson credits public provisioning with the capacity to preempt speculative excesses, if it replaced private supply, "one should not rush to the conclusion that the policies were misguided [provided] a constant supply could be obtained at a lower price level." The litmus here is not being Pareto-efficient, the author stresses, but attaining "equitable distribution of scarce resources, generating social gains"—these terms are cryptic—and lower crisis mortality—an insufficiently pertinent and/or capacious measure of crippling social disarray.

Still, I endorse fully the author's appreciation of the *police des grains*, predicated on the fact that efficiency was an insufficient ambition for public policy:

> On moral grounds and more importantly for understanding actual policies[,] a 'fair' distribution—in the sense that the worst consequences of subsistence crises were to be avoided—helped to preserve social order and was therefore also in the interest of an élite eager to remain so. While it is easy to see motivation for these policies as a short-term remedy and in the midst of a subsistence crisis it is more doubtful whether regulation is tolerable if it leads to *permanent* negative effects in the volume of trade and stifles the development of trading networks [*sic*]. However, there is no firm evidence that this actually was the case. (86–87)

Indeed, Persson finds a certain amount of evidence that public intervention contributed to price stability (88).

When I wrote *Bread, Politics and Political Economy*, to orient myself and engage in the sort of dialogue between past and present that I believe enriches historiography, I turned to current or relatively recent events—such as famines in India, China and the African continent—that offered certain parallels with Old-Regime subsistence questions. In his consideration of the welfare effects of price instability, Persson turns to modern inquiries on famine and poverty, notably to the highly suggestive work of Amartya Sen—discussed below—which underlines the political responsibility for much apparent food penury and the utility of the concept of entitlement for reflecting on causes, effects and remedies. Juxtaposed to a "moral economy" approach, entitlement, with an emphasis on generating a capability to function and fulfill personal goals and participate in social life, suggests Persson, may be a more telling way to think about the struggle for enhancing "survival chances" and attaining a capacity that permits normal "doings and beings" (23).

If the moral economy framework is to be fruitful, the economic historian argues that it must not be viewed as an "expression of contempt towards markets in general." Rather, he postulates it to be a targeting of "market *failure* and poor market performance" (23). He does not discuss the allocation of responsibility for that failure, though it would seem to be significant, in terms of collective ideation and comportment, to distinguish between the malevolence of cupiditous suppliers and the ineptitude, brutality and/or corruption of local officials. Deviation from "expectations of what life should be like," he contends, building implicitly on certain of James Scott's insights,[36] became the benchmark of the unacceptable, though this normative formulation sounds a loftier tonality than the riot discourses that Jean Nicolas, Cynthia Bouton, John Bohstedt or I have generally uncovered.[37] The bottom line for Persson, however, always is the price: in its "social" setting, at stake is the "fair" price. He envisages collective action premised on the moral economy as shaped by a notion of "relative deprivation," which he does not develop with sufficient precision.

Connecting the Social and the Economic

It seems to me that Persson is not wholly successful in his articulation of the economic with the social. Not a simple task, it recalls to mind Jean Bouvier's astute contention that the word and concept of capitalism draw reflection as much toward the social as to the economic: "Because the social is *la manière d'être* of the economic. It is men and women (individuals, groups, milieus, classes, masses) who make this history, labeled, for reasons of disciplinary classification and not without a certain naiveté, economic."[38] Persson does not

---

36 J. C. Scott, *Weapons of the Weak: Everyday Forms of Peasant Resistance* (New Haven, CT: Yale University Press, 1985) and *The Moral Economy of the Peasant: Rebellion and Subsistence in Southeast Asia* (New Haven, CT: Yale University Press, 1979).

37 See, for example, Jean Nicolas, *La Rébellion française, mouvements populaires et conscience sociale (1661–1789)* (Paris: Seuil, 2002); Cynthia Bouton, *The Flour War: Gender, Class and Community in Late Ancien Regime France* (University Park: Pennsylvania State University Press, 1993); John Bohstedt, "The Moral Economy and the Discipline of Historical Context," *Journal of Social History* 26 (1992): 265–84; and *Riots and Community Politics in England and Wales, 1790–1810* (Cambridge, MA: Harvard University Press, 1983). I examine these texts below.

38 Jean Bouvier, "Le capitalisme et l'État en France," *Recherches et travaux. Bulletin de l'institut d'histoire économique et sociale de l'université Paris* 1, no. 15 (Dec. 1986): 48, cited by Corine Maitte, Philippe Minard and Matthieu de Oliveira, eds., *La Gloire de l'industrie. Faire de l'histoire avec Gérard Gayot* (Rennes: Presses Universitaires de Rennes, 2012), 11.

seem at ease in evoking the popular culture. Highly sensitive to injustice and privation, he is equally intolerant of behavior that he judges as irrational and/or obstructionist. I am thinking, for instance, of his implicit censure of the *menu people* who share a "long-standing suspicion of grain merchants which biased the interpretation of daily events." The bias bespeaks the author's sometimes technocratic calculus: these popular representations, deeply rooted in experience, memory and customary exegesis—the physiocrats reviled them as "prejudices"—impede "the efficiency-enhancing properties" of the economic reforms tending toward the realization of price stability, the "desirability" of which the author sees as the object of a broad social consensus (134).

The discussion of the social actors themselves is sometimes foggy: who are "typical cultivators"? What is the concrete evidence that peasants, as a rule, did not bother to harvest when the price incentives were incommensurate with the costs involved? This question joins a larger debate about the economic reckoning and behavior of cultivators—from the entrepreneurial *fermiers* whom the *économistes* lionized to the simplest *laboureurs* with modest holdings: did they refuse to sow when price projections were unexalting? (11, 12, 23). The author's claim that there were "no conflicting interests among producers and consumers as to the desirability of price stability" strikes me as a hybrid of normative projection and wishful thinking. Consumers in both towns/cities and in the countryside (peasant day workers and others who bought rather than sold in the marketplace) shared an objective common interest of which most were probably oblivious. The level of price stability separated these consumers, fixated on a just price for their daily bread (or equivalent), from peasant growers who sold surpluses, in particular the entrepreneurial cultivators, who endorsed the liberal goal of the *bon prix*, the right or natural price that reached the "general" European market standard. Even if we granted, for the sake of argument, a consensus on the (somewhat abstract/subjective) goal of price stability, there would certainly be socially marked differences on how to achieve it, for example, by hastening state withdrawal from the arenas or by enhancing state engagement (134). In any event, the notion of equilibrium was at the heart of many of the Enlightenment debates on political economy.

Liberalization and Political Authoritarianism

Persson treats the question of disengagement—liberalization and deregulation—in a stimulating final chapter cast in comparative terms. The eighteenth century persists as the watershed for reform rightly ascribed in many cases to physiocratic inspiration, but to the neglect of liberal thinkers hostile to much of the *économiste* program and to pressure groups composed of commercial and/or agricultural interests drawing on their "business" experience that remained largely untheorized. "Enlightened despotism"—the concept is worn and largely bereft of carrying capacity—is the vector of the "political authoritarianism" that Persson, in the wake of others, considers necessary to realize liberalization. If he is correct to insist that the liberal credo embodied a minority point of view, he is surely wrong, at least in France, to see it as "sometimes shared only by the entourage of enlightened despots." Moreover, under self-imposed teleological coercion, he dismisses too readily the resistance to liberalization, reduced murkily to "the forces of traditionalism," identified in the early period as "vested interests" in the grain administration and throughout as consumer reticence to acknowledge the improvements in market performance.[39] Other scholars, deploying other sources, will have to scrutinize Persson's hypothesis that the eclipse of the food riot—perhaps not so completely at the mid-point of the nineteenth century as he suggests—resulted from improved market performance, in demonstrable fact and in popular collective representation. Cheaper transport was the decisive variable, along with better information flows and curtailed storage costs, in Persson's plausible scheme, where technological change obviated the recourse to regulation by reducing price volatility through a more or less fully integrated national market.[40] What is more elusive in this problématique is the way in which the economic shapes or even determines the political and the cultural, that is to say, the process by which the mass or at least a majority of consumers embraced the "new pro-market ideology" and found alternatives to "the efficient means of political resources" that food-rioting had constituted (91, 103, 106–7, 132–33, 135–37, 142).

Economic Sociology

In the years since I wrote *Provisioning Paris*, under the bracing influence of a rich anthropological literature on formal and informal market formation, operation and reproduction, a relatively recent current of economic sociology

39 Here, again, Persson is too nebulous in discussing the social forces and voices at play: "government élites" and "public opinion" both require definition (132). Cf. the changes to which he refers in the equally amorphous "public mind" (147).

40 Persson characterizes price volatility as being "to a great extent technologically determined" (107). He also addresses in passing another major controversy in French historiography: the question of agricultural production and productivity. Since technological progress in farming was "slow," he suggests that changes in yields—"the pattern of harvest disturbances"—did not play a major role in the long-term decline of price volatility. He concludes: "The fact that market integration increased, and in the absence of any other obvious cause, makes it probable that the decline in price volatility was the product of market integration and not a gift of Nature" (113).

has generated a stimulating avalanche of research on market questions.[41] Here I can address only in passing the quasi-foundational note sounded in Harrison C. White's seminal article "Where Do Markets Come From."[42] One of his students, Mark Granovetter, has exercised considerable influence on social historians with his discussion of embeddedness, a notion I first encountered in eighteenth-century anti-physiocracy and then in Karl Polanyi.[43] Along with the sociology of networks, there developed a robust neo-institutionalist school of the sociology of organizations, perhaps best epitomized by the work of Walter W. Powell and Paul J. DiMaggio.[44] I came across the culturalist approach of Charles W. Smith only recently, though his analysis did not fulfill for me the alluring and portentous promise of his title, *The Mind of the Market.*[45] No work, empirically and analytically, has intrigued and engaged

41 For the general grounding of the field of economic sociology, see Neil. J. Smelser and Richard Swedberg, eds., *The Handbook of Economic Sociology* (Princeton, NJ: Princeton University Press, 1994) and Richard Swedberg, *Principles of Economic Sociology* (Princeton, NJ: Princeton University Press, 2003).

42 *American Journal of Sociology* 87 (Nov. 1981): 517–47. Cf. his synthetic *Markets from Networks: Socioeconomic Models of Production* (Princeton, NJ: Princeton University Press, 2001).

43 "Economic Action and Social Structure: The Problem of Embeddedness," *American Journal of Sociology* 91 (1985): 481–510. Jens Beckert has renewed the debate in "What is Sociological About Economic Sociology? Uncertainty and Embeddedness in Economic Action," *Theory and Society* 25 (1996): 803–40.

44 *The New Institutionalism in Organizational Analysis* (Chicago: University of Chicago Press, 1991). It is probably reasonable to place in this lineage the highly suggestive and ambitious book of Neil Fligstein, *The Architecture of Markets: An Economic Sociology of Twenty-First-Century Capitalist Societies* (Princeton, NJ: Princeton University Press, 2002). See also his thoughtful "Markets as Politics: A Political–Cultural Approach of Market Institutions," *American Sociological Review* 61 (1996): 656–73. I regret that I lack the space to take a look at the contributions of the institutionalist school, inspired by Thorstein Veblen and later developed in his own manner by John R. Commons. Within a broad framework of institutions that in some ways prefigure the "conventions" of today, institutional economics construes markets as the product of intricate interactions of sundry institutions including individuals pursuing divergent interests, enterprises, governments, rules and norms. Veblen challenges the neoclassical assumption that capitalism is efficient and Commons suggests that it cannot avoid debilitating impasses without various mediations, usually undertaken by the public sector. See, as a point of departure, Walton H. Hamilton, "The Institutional Approach to Economic Theory," *American Economic Review* 9 (March 1919): 309–18; and K. William Kapp, *The Foundations of Institutional Economics*, eds., S. Berger and R. Steppacher (Oxford: Routledge, 2011).

45 The subtitle is somewhat deflationary for the poacher-historian: *A Study of Stock Market Philosophies, Their Uses, and Their Implications* (Totowa: Rowman and Littlefield, 1981).

me more than the investigations of Viviana A. Zelizer, though they are somewhat difficult for the historian to appropriate even on the theoretical plane.[46] I have been closer to some strands of the French scholarship in this area, particularly the theoretical and empirical efforts of Pierre Bourdieu and his students to articulate economics with sociology.[47] I have not profited optimally from the extremely interesting work of the (quite heterogeneous yet still) so-called schools of regulation and of the economy of conventions. And I am embarrassed to avouch that I knew and appreciated the Philippe Steiner who studied political economy and historical market theory, but not the scholar of economic sociology, whose recent field work calls to mind the commodification studies of Zelizer.[48]

Everything Is Market, Nothing Is Market

In an astute, epistemologically self-conscious book, at once synthetic and innovative, Pierre François looks at the market through the prism of a sprightly and nonhomogeneous economic sociology, founded on the "sciences de l'enquête"—the sciences of investigation—rather than on those of the model[49] (18–19). Viewing the market both as concept and as object, he assumes an embeddedness, not strictly in Polanyi's idiom of the economic subordinated to the social, but in terms of a more general embedding of economic operations in chains of social interactions that constitute a social world that is highly differentiated and heterogeneous rather than a seamless web. Morphology preoccupies the sociologist as much as dynamism: as the individual navigates between constraint and opportunity in the web of economic interactions, the market is one of the "forms" that can stabilize the chains of interplay (12–14).

46 For example, *The Social Meaning of Money: Pin Money, Paychecks, Poor Relief, and Other Currencies* (Princeton, NJ: Princeton University Press, 1994), *Pricing the Priceless Child: The Changing Social Value of Children* (Princeton, NJ: Princeton University Press, 1985) and *Morals and Markets: The Development of Life Insurance in the United States* (New York: Columbia University Press, 1979). More directly pertinent to my reflection is perhaps her "Beyond the Polemics of the Market: Establishing a Theoretical and Empirical Agenda," *Sociological Forum* 3 (1988): 614–34, which I discovered too late to use in this essay.

47 Among much else, see Bourdieu's "Le Champ économique," *Actes de la Recherche en Sciences Sociales* 119 (Sept., 1997) and *Les Structures sociales de l'économie* (Paris: Seuil, 2000).

48 For example, (with Jean-Jacques Gislain), *La Sociologie économique (1890–1920): Durkheim, Pareto, Schumpeter, Simiand, Veblen, et Weber* (Paris: Presses Universitaires de France, 1995), *La Sociologie économique* (Paris: La Découverte, 1999) and *La Transplantation d'organes: un commerce nouveau entre les êtres humains* (Paris: Gallimard, 2010).

49 Pierre François, *Sociologie des marchés* (Paris: Armand Colin, 2008).

The organization of stabilized interactions among actors constitutes the beginning of a definition of market that must also take into account the practices of actors that issue in "regularities" that François calls "mechanisms," the social workings that explain how relations come about (22). Extrapolating from anthropologist Claude Lévi-Strauss' celebrated formula that a society can be described by a combination of exchanges of words, goods and women, one is tempted to suggest that "everything is market," the ensemble of human interactions, alimenting economist–sociologist Gary Becker's desire to make of the "economic market" the "absolute model of [all] social functioning." François poses a number of compelling objections, in particular the blurring of all distinctions in situations of interaction that render exchange possible (or not) and the denial of the differentiation of economic and social forms. (23–25) The polar alternative—"nothing is market"—is no more satisfying, for it leads, in its neoclassical morphing, from a concrete reality (of the sort that I recognize in the grain and/or flour markets of Brie-Comte-Robert or Pontoise or Sens or Etampes) to "an abstract mechanism, fleshless and mathematized" (27). In the wake of this transformation, two characteristics seem susceptible to theorists as defining factors: the role of price, which restricts the range of interactions that can be subsumed under the market tag, and the idea, not of the traits of the so-called market, but of the conditions of its perfection, which depend largely on "forms of competition." François has no difficulty in showing that a perfect market (implying atomicity of actors, homogeneity of goods, divisibility of goods and perfection of information) is, to say the least, exceptional (if one allows for its conditions of possibility) and of little use to sociologists (save perhaps in exposing the fragility of the naturalist argument of the liberal vulgate that pretends that the elimination of rules that hobble it would suffice to bring it into existence) (29–30).

Weber

The sociologist's reading of Max Weber issues in an assumption that irrigates the entire subsequent discussion. Market for Weber is no more opposed to society than it is outside of it: the market is on the contrary "a manner of making society [*faire societé*]," an ambiguous albeit propitious formula that seems to epitomize pithily the project of economic sociology. Making society is stabilizing relations: it is as important for François, and Weber, as coordination is for economists. In putting to work actions in society, the social actors stabilize the social forms that the German sociologist calls "societization." The market depends on this stabilization (captured by Weber's notion of "community"); more precisely, it is a "form" that is built upon the arrangement of two sorts of relations, one of competition and the other of exchange. Exchange generates a social order dependent on the articulation of interests, but exchange itself does not make a market for lack of formalized competition. Even with relations of competition, however, exchange must be more or less continuous, framed by codes assuring the honoring of property transfers, by a series of understandings (that resemble "conventions") which make what Weber sees as a "community," indeed "a market community." The "social activity" of the market presupposes competition, which means a Simmelesque "struggle," whose irenic disposition Weber underlines, that reinforces rather than saps the community.[50] Yet, one has to wonder about the pacific threshold of a space of conflict whose nonegalitarian features are patent—in fact, egregious on the eighteenth-century labor market, for example, but also in bread, grain and flour markets, especially in times of subsistence stress. The Weberian market makes society, yet it breaks with traditional solidarities (of the Durkheimian sort[51]), it begets community based in part on impersonal relations and pregnant with conflict: François should have unpacked this conceptualization more carefully, building in other Weberian components of capitalism, such as rationality and (self-)interest (38–54).

From the Gift to The State

I will not dwell on the excellent discussion of alternative modes of coordination to the market that have been proposed, including the gift, in its classical anthropological formulation, and its modern (militant) exegesis, in both cases instantiating the social bond. The historian of the Old Regime is especially interested in the argument that while the gift retains the trace of anterior relations, the market "is a place without memory" (61–65, 69). Yet, it is precisely the resistance to amnesia that marks both the ordinary operations of grain, flour and bread markets, and the market breakdowns that sometimes result in violent collective action. The marketplace (as I construe a market defined as a regulatory bastion) and the moral economy both rely on memory to structure relations, prompt remonstrances, inaugurate negotiations, justify

50 Struggle or conflict is an integral part of Georg Simmel's highly imaginative sociology. Conflict is a form of socialization to the extent that it issues from multiple interactions. Conflict is the resolution of tensions as much as their source. Competition in a market is also, in this manner, a struggle. See Simmel,"Soziologie der Konkurrenz," *Neue Deutsche Rundschau* 14 (1903): 1009–29; "Das Ende des Streits," ibid., 16 (1905): 746–53; "The Sociology of Conflict," *The American Journal of Sociology* 9 (1903–1904): 490–525, 672–89, 798–811.

51 See perhaps the best known work of the French sociologist Emile Durkheim, *De la division du travail social* (Paris: Presses Universitaires de France, 2007; orig. ed. 1893).

sanctions and so on. Among the most striking differences between "my" markets and those of modern times is the predicate that the parties to an exchange in a market tooled as a mechanism of spontaneous coordination, based on the rationality of self-interested players, are connected in a limited or particular commercial exchange "free of any engagement for the future" (87).[52] Though eighteenth-century markets allow for variability as a function of circumstance, the ordinary perimeter and practice of exchange implies, on the contrary, a more or less sustained relationship hereafter, an understanding and acknowledgment of some sort of link, of an embryonic—potential if not ineluctable—reciprocity. Merchant practice, as seen in the consular courts, or echoed in business failure statements of accounts or probate inventories, in certain occasions recognized as legitimate a sort of coercion of custom founded on repeated and remembered exchange relations rather than contract or even expressed oral accord.

François treats, in part as a coordination question, the casting of the state in opposition to the market. In the manner of the Austrian liberal school (notably, Ludwig von Mises and Friedrich A. Hayek), for instance, one can note the "epistemic" deficiencies of the state to promote the virtues of the market. In opposing market and state in quasi-symmetrical manner, one can invoke Marxists and others who summon the latter to correct/combat the rampant commodification of social relations generated by the former. For historians plunged further in the past, the opposition of market and state is not in any way foundational or even habitual, at least until the Economic Enlightenment. The market is a tool of state making, of fiscality, of the expropriation of grain surpluses, of the rationalization of local administration and of the regulation (and transformation) of myriad behaviors. Should one see it as ironical or merely logical that the market (or, rather, markets) only acquire the competence to contest certain aspects of stateness or state regulation (impossible to construe from the very start as *intervention*, since state and market were in so many ways imbricated) once the state has nourished them to a certain maturity? If it is perhaps reasonable, for the sake of debate, to accord Hayek's premise, it is difficult for the state or its agent to amass the knowledge of infinite numbers of singular facts necessary to justify intervention in modern markets (governmental omniscience opposed to the rationality of countless individual economic actors); and it certainly makes no sense to speak of vampiric "social engineering" in the context of Old-Regime

52 Cf. "Commercial exchange [*échange marchand*, often translated as market transaction, but in our discussion such a rendering would be tantamount to begging the question], because it supposes the placing in parentheses of personal relations, is, in its ideal-type form, an amnesic exchange" (103; cf. 106).

regulatory ideology and practice (73–74). François argues that it is no longer tenable to suppose a "frontal opposition" between market and state.

In ways redolent of the Old Regime, the sociologist describes a state intervention that is not tantamount to the wholesale supplanting of "market mechanisms." Rather, the state's role is merely one of several elements at play in a "complex and necessarily heterogeneous dynamic." Twentieth-century governments found it increasingly difficult to intervene at will: the "implementation problem" thwarted or disturbed the introduction of regulation; various groups contested the legitimacy of this intervention; the regulation did not always proceed from an astute and refined appreciation of the relations of means to ends; and the government did not always have the tools, juridical and political, to effectuate its regulatory mission. Certain observers even evince an "effacement of the political" as a consequence of the syncretic ways in which public policy is often carried out: composite or hybrid forms of public action, with private-sector participation, "government by the market" and so on (110–12, 116). This conflation of the market and political regulation is reminiscent of the argument adumbrated by Foucault, evocative as usual, but difficult to work out historically *in situ* (for example, in examining the labor market, the guilds, the subsistence question and the operation of both collector and final-user markets, and the commercialization of flour and the rise of commercial milling), that liberalism, in the eighteenth-century sense, needs to be seen itself as a mode of governance, as a conscious technique for administering and managing social and economic relations. Liberalism in this instance is irretrievably corrosive of the state and the social contract that underpinned it; it does not make of the market (or of markets) a proxy for a mixed economy in which various entitlements of embeddedness can be salvaged. It does not propose a joint coordination of the allocation of resources. In some ways, it amounts to a more radical version of the old notion of a bourgeois revolution in the mode of *Germinal.*

Return to a (Nonprocrustean) Embeddedness

The "deconstruction" of the notion of market that François attributes to contemporary sociology in some ways seems atavistic if not wistful. I am thinking in particular of the return to a certain embeddedness, the idea that commercial practices—*pratiques marchandes*—are wholly traversed by and invested with social and/or cultural contents, indeed even with moral and/or religious substance. In the re-embeddedness frame, there is an imbrication or entanglement rather than an opposition of the commercial and noncommercial dimensions. This intermingling tacitly or explicitly returns to the Old-Regime subordination of the economic to the social

(80–84). François discusses the place of "organizations" in exchange, more or less bureaucratized, routinized and hierarchical: even in rudimentary form, one encounters these in very few sectors in the Old-Regime economy. Much more common are network relations, in part because "networks are lighter on their feet" than organizations. Network exchanges derive from and generate the sorts of reciprocities that flourish in the Old Regime, even as they do in many sites today. The network is a form of coordination of economic activities especially apt when circumstances require a dense and reliable information in order to guide exchange (86–88).

Neil Fligstein construes "markets as politics": François deals sympathetically with his sociology, but does not sufficiently explore what this political nexus signifies. The American sociologist asks what rules must exist in order for markets to function and what kinds of social structures are required to produce stable markets. He distinguishes in terms that François leaves cryptic between the "social" conception of what actors intend to do in a market vis-à-vis their "economic" conception, a distinction that speaks to the deconstruction adduced above. Despite his contemporary focus—his "firms" are not like mine—Fligstein asks the same sort of questions that animated my investigation: by what processes or dynamics are markets created, maintain their stability, change over time and how are different markets related to each other? He regards markets as stable and structured exchanges: the market is not "the spontaneous emanation of interactions of human actors returned to the state of nature," and its stability does not stem from its labile, impalpable, amnesic and ephemeral situation, though it would have been useful to indicate the role that "rules" play in the engendering and reproduction of this stability. This market, insists François, "is very much a certain way of making society," fostering the social, as Weber indicated (96–97).

Making Society

Without intending it, Pierre François makes a very strong case for historians to pay attention to historical sociology, in this instance especially historians seeking to make sense of markets in the age before Ricardo. The profession of epistemological faith at the outset flatters the social historian's sense of priorities: "The first action that founds the sociological undertaking is a return to the field [*terrain*] and to the realm of the empirical [*empirie*]."[53] Whereas the market of economists is a "theoretical construction," the sociologist commits to studying "concrete markets." The dramatis personae in the market theater

53 It would be onerous, even for a scholar as austere as I, to resist the formula: "the *empirie* strikes back!"

are not limited to suppliers and demanders, but include a host of other actors, for example, diverse intermediaries (not all of them profit-driven or parasitical middlemen, but others with mixed functions not reducible to commercial calculus) and *prescripteurs*, players undertaking various institutional, cultural, moral or political roles, including different kinds of regulation. François emphasizes the "symbolico-material" mechanisms and arrangements that operate in the market, providing suitable tool-kits and giving voice to rules, norms, labels, brands, reputations and so on. The sociologist does not presume that calculating, optimizing, egocentric, rationally driven behavior is a "natural necessity." Her or his gaze must take into account the heterogeneity of manners of doing and seeing. Nor is the market a privileged site for the reign of impersonal relations; on the contrary, it relies on interpersonal relations forged by the actors on or in the market. Yet, it must be stable and rely on prices of goods and services in order to frame exchanges. In what stands in part as a correction of Polanyi-ish (but not Pollyanna-ish) excesses or misappropriations by epigones, François affirms that the market is not a disruptive force that destroys social relations: "on the contrary, it is a way of making society" (281–82).

Conventions: No Pure Economy

Predisposed by my own research and my conceptual assumptions, where the notion of conventions played an undertheorized albeit significant role, my interest for the "economy of conventions" stemmed in part from my understanding of its desire to accord the social a certain autonomy.[54] As

54 The most useful introduction, in my opinion, is André Orléan, one of the founding fathers of this ambitious project to rethink social science. See his "L'Economie des conventions: définitions et résultats," postface to the re-publication of *Analyse économique des conventions* (Paris: Presses Universitaires de France, 2004), 9–48. Equally valuable, with a more self-conscious historical perspective, is Rainer Diaz-Bone and Laurent Thévenot, "La sociologie des conventions. La théorie des conventions, élément central des nouvelles sciences sociales françaises," *Trivium* [online], 5 | 2010, placed online on 10 Jan 2010, accessed 17 August 2014 online: http://trivium.revues.org/3626. Arguing that the concept of convention has a "strategic importance" in the understanding of the "new French social sciences," they warn against an excessively narrow, or insufficiently ambitious, construction of convention. It is neither, in the Weberian humor, a custom, a habit or a usage nor, in Durkheimian disposition, a "social fact" whose nonobservation by the members of a collectivity issues in negative sanctions on this group. "More complex," the notion in the economy of conventions is a "complete paradigm for the sociological and socioeconomic analysis of organizations and social institutions, of social cognition, of action, interaction, and coordination, as well as of the social construction of entities and of their qualities."

André Orléan put it, one of the driving ideas was to contest the "unilateral vision" of a hegemonic/exclusive "pure commercial transaction" in favor of taking into account diverse institutional forms and "structures of governance" framing economic relations in a social setting and proposing multiple ways of fulfilling the "coordinating" vocation of the market as economists generally—tropismatically—apprehend it.[55] In rejecting the contention that an economic analysis can have as its object "the market of pure competition on its own," the conventionalists also place into question "the pure logic of strategic rationality." The convention offers me an analytical lever because of its social predicate: it can be reduced neither to the pooling of individual rationalities nor to utility calculation or the selection of an equilibrium in the evolutionist approach. The famous efficient stabilized coordination is not automatically the product of the rationality of the actors. The macro-economy is "embedded in a society," maintains this economist, and, as a result, its efficacy depends closely on the values to which the society adheres: "In other words, there exists no pure economy."

The convention proceeds often from an engagement generating "obligations and duties" among the members of a community. Orléan enumerates the "key words" of the economy of conventions: accords, common points of reference, beliefs, collective representations, justification, symbolic power and legitimacy—almost all of them notions that I deploy in *Bread, Politics* and that social and cultural historians have used during the past quarter century. For the economist, this "narrow" conventionalist exegesis issues in "a theory of collective action" geared to overcome the contradictions ("aporias") of rational choice theory. But he seems to prefer a grander respiration, citing the brilliant treatise of Luc Boltanski and Laurent Thévenot on "economies of worth" as "a veritable theory of the social and economic world," a work that I find immensely fruitful (especially if one situates it beyond the polemic with Bourdieu).[56] Still, for the profane reader I am, there abides a tension in Orléan

---

55 Cf. The claim that "the reference to the market as the sole mode of coordination is a mystification."Gérard Duménil and Dominique Lévy, 'Des économies 'avec marchés.' Un point de vue marxiste," special issue of *L'Economie politique* 37 (Jan. 2008): 52–55, devoted to the theme "Qu'est-ce-que l'économie de marché?" The article underlines the limits of the market's mission and aptitude ("the market, as such, does not determine comportment") even as it acknowledges what the market can do, or at least is believed to do (e.g., obliging agents to verify the soundness or accuracy of their behavior, concerning, say, production or investment). The discussion of commodification is less edifying.

56 Luc Boltanski and Laurent Thévenot, *De la Justification. Les économies de la grandeur* (Paris: Galliard, 1991), wonderfully rendered in English by Catherine Porter as *On Justification: Economies of Worth* (Princeton, NJ: Princeton University Press, 2005).

between a social that aspires to a certain autonomy and the idea that, in the end, only individuals can act and shoulder collective ambitions; between the convention as a solution to the problem of coordination and the convention as a (supple and/or pluralistic) response to a series of other questions; between the convention and other rules of the game or rules of behavior allowing actors to coordinate their comportment resulting in different sorts of social interaction. Virtually all of these positions/inflections, along with a theory of institutions as rules of the game leading to still other forms of coordination, invite us to imagine the morphology and operation of markets in fresh ways, certainly in a more inchoate manner for the Old Regime than for the world of banks too big to fail.

Denaturing the Market and a Constitutive Convention

Another of the moving forces in the program of the economy of conventions, François Eymard-Duvernay, stresses the reevaluation of the role of the rationality of the actors for whom the question of coordination, dear to economists, is merely one of myriad preoccupations, of which the market is only one expression, in the framework of various institutions and conventions. The embeddedness that Orléan seems to take as a given, he disputes on the grounds that an economic sociology embracing it "runs the risk of producing an excessively straitened 'sociology of the social'."[57] No embeddedness perhaps, but the market is not outside the society.[58] Without developing the promising idea of the "political roots" of the economy, Eymard-Duvernay emphasizes that mercantile (or commercial or capitalist) society is in permanent rivalry with other social forms. If the concept of convention enters economic theory, it is because of the unfulfilled promises of a "pure commercial logic" or a logic of "strategic rationality" (21).

57 F. Eymard-Duvernay, "Du Marché généralisé à la pluralité des conventions constitutives," in Bernard Convert, ed., *Repenser le marché* (Paris, 2003), 15–32. See also two important volumes edited by Eymard-Duvernay containing rich and surprisingly disparate pieces: *L'Economie des conventions. Méthodes et résultat,* 2 vols. (Paris: La Découverte, 2006).

58 On the putative autonomy of the market and its capacity to settle the social question, see Nicolas Potel, "Marché et autonomie des acteurs: histoire d'une illusion," special issue of *L'Economie politique* 37 (Jan. 2008): 25. The goal of this piece is "to demonstrate that the very concept of an autonomous market, enabling the accord of individuals outside of any collective perspective and of any other mode of social bond, is illusory … no one can pretend that the market resolves on its own the question of social harmony."

Proposing the idea of "a constitutive convention" that does not depend on individual rational choice and implies social hierarchies grounded, not on individual preferences, but shared ideation and/or values that economists view as market disturbances, the economist quite self-consciously challenges the putative "universalism of the market, by considering it to be an institution (or convention), among others." This decentering of the market is tantamount to its "denaturalization": it results or derives from "a constitutive convention," the sort of institution that describes the market of the Old Regime, from my point of view, as well as the ones that will displace it over time (22). In his typology, reinforcing my own interpretation of the marketplace, Eymard-Duvernay views "the market, a political construction, [as] a society of consumers," and anticipates the ways in which producers will question its legitimacy (23). Here the situation complexifies—as it did in the Economic Enlightenment—because "the consumer is not the sole appraiser of what it is good to do"[59] (24). In this fresh conceptual approach, the market is "a conception of society on which persons depend in order to justify their actions." In other words, in this new epistemology, the market is no longer "a state of nature, it is a political construction" (28–29). Eymard-Duvernay focuses on contemporary cases, yet his template—mobilizing questions of coordination, values and justice—offers the historian pertinent perspectives.[60]

Conventions: The Possibility of History

Robert Salais is another cofounder of the conventionalist group, perhaps the most historically oriented, whose work I encountered in my studies on labor markets and the guilds in the eighteenth century. He deployed theoretical arguments reinforcing my own disposition to problematize the realization of the product in the study of work as a social enterprise. He invoked the notion

59 For an excellent case study that deals, in part, with the deep tension between producers and consumers, with issues of contingent determination of quality and with the ways of forging an accord that is at once political, social and moral, see Philippe Minard (with special attention to the idea/system of "the regulated convention" attributed to Colbert), "Economie de marché et Etat en France: mythes et légendes du colbertisme," special issue of *L'Economie politique* 37 (January 2008): 77–93. See also his *La Fortune du colbertisme. Etat et Industrie dans la France des Lumières* (Paris: Fayard, 1998).

60 Still, it would have been worthwhile developing the political side more fully, including the role that the state might play in various kinds of mediation/intervention. On the role of the state as guarantor of the atomicity of the market so that no actor can modify the price to his/her advantage and, more generally, to the state's coordinating functions, see Jean-Marc Daniel, "L'Economie de marché: liberté et concurrence," special issue of *L'Economie politique* 37 (Jan. 2008): 48.

of a "mystery" in the activity of work that I found extremely interesting: a mystery founded on multiple contingencies and uncertainties issuing from what he called "human liberty" and requiring various forms of coordination, through conventions, themselves bespeaking certain shared assumptions and values about production, exchange, equivalence, anticipation and so on. More broadly, this approach questions the objectivity, universality and obligation of the "moral rule," in the neoclassical case, "the rule of the market." The neoclassical market does not exhaust the possibilities for economic exchange: there are "mixed configurations between the convention of the market and other conventions of the social bond."[61]

Salais turns to the other ("noneconomic") social sciences in order to escape the handicap represented by "the strategy of reduction to which economic theory has constant recourse." He looks to the economy of conventions as a possible avenue to move beyond the incessant balancing between "subjectivism" and "objectivism" in the social sciences. A convention is a "regularity" anchored in social actions, but which is presented to actors as "an objectivized form." That signifies, on the one hand, that objects and rules are presented to the members of a community in terms of long-standing social conditions whose origins are forgotten (in this instance, the convention becomes in a sense "inexpressible" to the participants) and, on the other hand, as products of a human activity, the "objectivity" and the "form" of whose conventions cannot be completely estranged from the "intentionalities" and actions that governed their creation. This makes the social tooling or orchestration of the convention—the rules, the objects, the knowledge—accessible to scholarly research, indeed specifically to empirical research. The heart of the epistemology of the economy of conventions must be, for Salais, "work on the notion of historicity." One aim is to avoid the pitfalls of a (relativistic) society that ceaselessly (re-)negotiates the terms of the conventions and a (rigid or immobile) society based on a conception of structural concordance between the object and the ways of thinking of

61 R. Salais, "Approches économiques et historiques récentes du marché," *Genèses* 1 (1990): 163, 166. In this piece, Salais rehearses elegantly an argument that has been widely made in the past two decades on Adam Smith's refusal to see the economy in isolation and his keen concern for linking the harmony of society and of exchange with his notion of "sympathy" in a project aiming at forging the social bond, a sort of proto-conventionist perspective that L. Thévenot develops elsewhere: "The project of Adam Smith was not to extract the economic outside the field of society (and of the social sciences), but to link it to a political philosophy, to a conception of the social bond and a science of the government of men" (164). See also the special issue of *Revue économique* 40 (March 1988) devoted to the economy of conventions with thought-provoking contributions by Salais, Orléan, Thévenot, Eymard-Duvernay, Jean-Pierre Dupuy and Olivier Favereau.

actors. Since the hypothesis of crisis through rupture of the convention persists, the economist argues that "the possibility of a history" is preserved.[62] Through a historical approach—that remains frankly amorphous albeit inviting—"the renewal of the theory of the market could thus render necessary … the renewal of the debates on methods within the social sciences."[63]

Regulationists

The theory of regulation, often associated with Michel Aglietta (a sometime collaborator of André Orléan) and Robert Boyer, introduces a dose of agency into a conception of structurally conflictual social relations whose contradictions mobilize various modes of regulation. The regulationists share certain similarities with the conventionalists, including a lively interest in institutional forms (among them, competition and state intervention) and modes of coordination and stabilization. Given its accent on capital accumulation (its shifting modalities and consequences) and on post-Industrial Revolution economies, regulationist theory per se is less germane to historians than that of the conventionalists, though its preoccupation with crises evokes the work of Ernest Labrousse for whom "each society has the crises of its structures."[64] Taken at its most superficial level, the hypothesis that big crises demand an adjustment or a more sweeping revision of the mode of regulation—institutional alteration—seems to fit the experience of the Old Regime, at least in certain cases, though a conceptual stretch is required. This institutional modification presupposes social conflict that, while possible in a conventionalist logic, is consubstantial to regulationist assumptions about evolution. There seems to be some uncertainty about the dénouement of crisis in the regulationist scenario: while a satisfactory solution seems necessarily political, an apparent institutional remodeling does not necessarily provide an acceptable or durable resolution.

---

62 For a possible "historical" example of such a rupture, see the business community studied so masterfully by Jean-Pierre Hirsch which remains utterly unconvinced, as a whole, that competition is the indispensable prod and precondition to innovation. "La Concurrence: discours et pratiques, hier et aujourd'hui," special issue of *L'Economie politique* 37 (Jan. 2008): 67. See also his *Les Deux Rêves du commerce. Entreprise et institution dans la région lilloise (1780–1860)* (Paris: Editions de l'Ecole des Hautes Etudes en Sciences Sociales, 1991).

63 R. Salais, "Approches économiques et historiques récentes du marché," 169–70.

64 See, for example, Michel Aglietta, *Régulation et Crises du capitalisme* (Paris: Calmann-Lévy, 1976); Robert Boyer, *Théorie de la régulation. Une analyse critique* (Paris: La Découverte, 1986); Boyer, *Théorie de la régulation, 1. Les fondamentaux* (Paris: La Découverte, 2004); Boyer and Yves Saillard, eds., *Théorie de la régulation. L'état des savoirs* (Paris: La Découverte, 1995).

Like the conventionalists, the regulationists refuse to reduce the actor to a sediment of calculating rationality. The regulationist operates, across time, within or through various sociocultural institutions and interactions that recall the fashioning of a Bourdieusian habitus. Endowed with multiple partial identities or inclinations within a relatively stable, cumulative framework of seeing and being, the actor is not destined to embrace this or that choice. Here a more vigorous articulation of the social and the political, within the context of what is called an economic dynamics, would be helpful. If there is no more "pure economy" for the regulationists than for the conventionalists, the former do not seem to decenter the market as starkly as the latter. The regulationists whom I have read, despite an often cursory interest in the nonusable past, appear neither to project their representation of economic life into the economies they study nor format the market instead of scrutinizing how it works, reproaches that Michel Callon directs to certain practitioners of the (sometimes) dismal science.[65]

A Political and Social Imperative

"The subsistence of the people is the most essential object that must occupy the administration," wrote Jacques Necker, minister, *philosophe*, banker and grain speculator.[66] Save for two brief interludes, this commitment to the consumer-people of France was the uncontested tenet of public policy during the Old Regime. It was founded on the conviction that social stability could be guaranteed only by guaranteeing the food supply. History seemed to prove beyond a doubt that hunger and dearth had "preceded, prepared and caused" grave, sometimes fatal disorders in Rome, Constantinople and China. Without order, government could not endure and society could not hold together.[67] The prerequisite for order, in the words of an eighteenth-century administrator, "was to provide for the subsistence of the people, without which there is neither law nor force which can contain them."[68]

---

65 M. Callon, ed., *The Laws of Markets* (London: Blackwell, 1998). Cf. different conceptions of markets as ideological paradigms rather than empirical frameworks for observing and assessing economic activity: Roy Dilley, ed., *Contesting Markets: Analyses of Ideology, Discourse and Practice* (Edinburgh: Edinburgh University Press, 1992) and James Carrier, *The Meanings of the Market: The Free Market in Western Culture* (Oxford: Berg, 1997).

66 Necker to Sartine, 14 February 1778, Archives Nationales (hereafter cited as AN), F 11* 1, fol. 258.

67 Nicolas Delamare, *Traité de la police* (Paris, 1705–38); *Journal de l'agriculture, du commerce des arts et des finances* (January 1772): 48; Jacques Necker, *Sur la législation et le commerce des grains.*

68 Bertier de Sauvigny, "Observations sur le commerce des grains," Bibliothèque Nationale de France (hereafter BNF), manuscrits français (hereafter cited as ms. fr.) 1134, fol. 228.

To assure an adequate food supply was not only in the interest of the government but was also its obligation, according to the doctrine (or covenant: the social contract of subsistence) that gradually developed to define relations between governors and governed. The people would "submit" provided their existence was safeguarded. This obligation became a responsibility and an attribute of paternal kingship: what more solemn duty could a father have than to enable his children to enjoy their daily bread? It was something the monarch was expected, even required, to carry out.[69]

All (consumer-) subjects were theoretically equally dear to the King, but the mission to provision the capital had primacy over all others, because of the government's conviction that "outcries of need there would be more dangerous than anywhere else and would set a fatal and contagious example."[70] Political experience had demonstrated well before the eighteenth century that it was cheaper to take a risk with food supply in the provinces than in Paris. The capital's population was immense, between 600,000 and 700,000 around mid-century, and the vast majority of its inhabitants led extremely arduous and uncertain lives. They were more likely to react collectively and violently to threats to their subsistence than to any other danger. A Parisian uprising, it was believed, could overturn the government. Thus, Paris was permitted to "devour" a substantial chunk of the kingdom because, as an author of a treatise on the police observed, without the special administrative advantages that the capital enjoyed "one would have trouble imagining that there are sources capable of meeting the needs of this vast pit."[71]

Market Principle

Even for Paris, however, the King was supposed to be only the victualer (or, as the revolutionaries put it, the baker) of last resort. It was not the government's intention actually to furnish consumers with grain or bread, nor indeed did the public expect it to. The government was not equipped to take over the primary food supply; it intervened through regulation. The burden of public authority was not to feed the people, but to make sure they would be fed. This distinction implied a fairly simple division of social labor. Producers grew the grain; theirs was the task, aided by a host of intermediaries, to distribute it. The government had to make sure that it reached the public in "due time," in good

69 Kaplan, *Bread, Politics and Political Economy*, introd. and chap. 1.

70 Louis-Sebastien Mercier, *Tableau de Paris*, vol. 4 (Amsterdam, 1783), 203; Delamare, *Traité de la police*, 2: 828; Regnaud, "Histoire des évènements arrivés en France depuis 1772," BNF, ms. fr. 13747; anonymous memorandum to controller-general (1784), AN, F [11] 294–95.

71 N.-T.-L. Des Essarts, *Dictionnaire universel de police*, vol. 1 (Paris: Moutard, 1786–90), 329.

condition and a price accessible to the bulk of consumers. Authorities tracked grain from the time it was seed until bakers made it into bread, watching its movement from hand to hand and trying to keep it optimally visible and reassuringly ubiquitous by enforcing certain rules of conduct and exchange. This surveillance and regulation was called the police of provisioning. But the actual task of provisioning was left to commerce.

Commerce drew its power and derived its rationale from the *market principle.*[72] The market principle signified a system of relations in which prices were determined by the impersonal forces of supply and demand, regardless of the site of transaction, and in which these prices allocated resources, income and outputs. Predicated upon a global scheme of endless self-adjustment, the market principle demanded an untrammeled freedom of action for commerce. Interference of any sort would shatter its coherence and jeopardize its mission. Commerce thus required a quasi-institutional independence vis-à-vis the basic structures of social control. Its eighteenth-century partisans, of whom the physiocrats were the most vociferous, justified this autonomy on the grounds that the market principle, consisting of the "holy" and "imprescriptible" rights of property and liberty, sanctified by nature's law, was anterior to all forms of social organization. Less sophisticated eighteenth-century exponents of commercial liberty, such as grain growers and merchants, understood the market principle more or less viscerally in terms of their right to dispose sovereignly of what they owned without regard to social or political or moral predicates and constraints. Since the sum of all interests was ineluctably congenial and since the outcome of their interplay was necessarily socially beneficent, the perspective was reassuring.[73]

---

72 My reading of market principle and marketplace in the context of the eighteenth century is inspired by Karl Polanyi, *The Great Transformation* (New York: Farrar and Rinehart, 1944); Karl Polanyi, "The Economy as an Instituted Process," in Karl Polanyi, Conrad M. Arensberg and Harry W. Pearson, eds., *Trade and Market in the Early Empires* (Chicago: University of Chicago Press, 1957); Karl Polanyi, *Primitive, Archaic and Modern Economies,* ed. George Dalton (Garden City, NY: Doubleday,1968); Karl Polanyi, *The Livelihood of Man,* ed. Harry W. Pearson (New York: Academic Press,1977); Paul Bohannan and George Dalton, eds., *Markets in Africa* (Evanston: Northwestern University Press, 1962). An earlier version of this argument appeared in *Provisioning Paris,* chap. 1.

73 See Claude-Jacques Herbert, *Essai sur la police générale des grains, sur leurs prix et sur les effets de l'agriculture* (London, 1755) in E. Depitre, ed., *Collection des économistes et des réformateurs sociaux de la France* (Paris: Geuthner, 1910), 7, 21, 57, 95; Pierre-Joseph-André Roubaud, *Représentations aux magistrats* (London, 1769), 398–401; Nicolas Baudeau, *Avis au peuple sur son premier besoin* (Amsterdam and Paris, 1768), 72–73; Pierre-Paul Lemercier de la Rivière, *L'Intérêt général de l'Etat* (Paris, 1770), 64–65; Pierre-Samuel Dupont de Nemours, "Vrais principes du droit naturel, *Ephémérides du citoyen* 3, première partie no. 2 (1767): 102–3 and deuxième partie, no. 2: 131–33, 160–61,167; J. P. L. Luchet, *Examen d'un livre qui a pour titre: "Sur la législation et le commerce des bleds"* (n.p., 1775), 40–41.

The police by and large grasped the logic of the market principle, but recoiled from it because it alarmed and unnerved them. They worried about its apotheosis of and dependence upon selfishness and its lack of social accountability. They were suspicious of its animus against public authority. To some extent they may have shared the ageless and widely held belief that there was something odious about the merchant. If the provisioning trade were left strictly to commerce, they were convinced, society would live in constant peril. Frequently, commerce discharged its task of distribution proficiently. At any moment, however, it was capable of provoking disarray and panic. Prompted only by "amour-propre and immoderate cupidity for a sordid profit," merchants time and again offered grain "only when they wished." They did not hesitate to use their enormous leverage to "promote public misfortune" in order to profit from it. They caused artificial dearths or aggravated real ones by hiding and hoarding, by purchasing futures, by recklessly outbidding all rivals and by spreading news that was at once incendiary and demoralizing. The police classified all these practices under the rubric "monopoly". There was no more serious antisocial crime, for it struck down thousands of innocent people. Monopoly was the fruit of liberty run amok, of the illusion of the beneficent effect of legitimated egocentricity. Yet, in the police view, it was not at bottom a distortion of the market principle but its most complete expression.[74]

The police did not blame commerce for this behavior, for it was "in the very nature" of the trade. In some kinds of exchange, it was tolerable and even advantageous to allow the market principle, with all its risks, free reign. In most types of trade, shortage, tardiness, fraud and other defects or vices caused harm or inconvenience only to individuals, and never in mortal doses. The police were unwilling to permit the business of provisioning to become just another business, however. Grain was an item of "first necessity," ultimately a matter of life or death, for millions of consumers, whereas other goods merely complemented subsistence or enhanced pleasure. In the provisioning trade, "the least error almost always affected the public," menacing the whole community at its most vulnerable point.

The police attitude toward commerce and toward merchants was deeply ambivalent. On the one hand, provisioning was fundamentally a commercial operation and traders were absolutely necessary to do the job. On the other hand, the market principle was dangerous and unreliable, and the grain

74 For this paragraph and the next two, see Kaplan, *Bread, Politics and Political Economy*, chap. 2.

trader was somehow even more rapacious and untrustworthy than any other merchant, for who but vicious men could choose to speculate on the subsistence of their fellows? Provisioning could be confided to commerce only ambiguously, conditionally and incompletely. Since society depended on it for survival, the police conceived of grain commerce as a kind of public service and imposed restrictions upon grain traders that other merchants escaped. The grain merchant's obligations to the public would sometimes require him to set aside his self-interest. In echo of the remote yet lingering Scholastic ethic, he had to be satisfied with a "just and legitimate gain" (even as he had to respect, on occasion, the imperative of the just price). Implicit in the police vision of the grain trade was the notion that the grain held by a merchant (or producer) was not perfectly and exclusively his own to dispose of as he saw fit. As the primary source of subsistence, grain was a "common good" upon which society had certain claims. Since the police had no reason to believe that the merchants would honor those claims voluntarily, they elaborated a set of rules that defined the way in which the trade was to be practiced.

Marketplace

To the market principle, the police opposed the *marketplace* as a physical location and as a congeries of prescriptions that were rooted in (but not necessarily confined to) the market as a designated site. The market principle implied no sacrosanct place of exchange; the marketplace demanded physical concentration of goods and actors at a fixed place. The market principle required freedom from control and constraint, whereas the marketplace imposed surveillance and regulation. The one celebrated improvisation, the other routinization. The market principle was fundamentally private in ethos and operation, the marketplace quintessentially public. Transactions according to the market principle were closed (or covert) and occurred in open social space, while marketplace exchange was open and occurred in (en)closed space. The market principle measured success in terms of profits; the test of marketplace success was public tranquility.

Defined as a principle, the market was elusive: it was at once everywhere and nowhere; it was threatening because it was in some sense untouchable, unclassifiable and mobile. Defined as a place, the market was something that the police could invest and control. In a concrete, functional sense, the marketplace as a physical site served as the linchpin of the regulatory apparatus. In a more general way, the marketplace as an *idée force* and as a symbol of engagement embodied the police ideology. There was no single more important regulation concerning the provisioning trade than the requirement that all transactions occur in the marketplace.[75] This was the best guarantee of honesty and efficiency, not only in the view of the police, but also in that of Old-Regime (and revolutionary and postrevolutionary) consumers, for whom market participation was the supreme test of civism. By concentrating the supply and rendering it visible and by making transactions transparent, the marketplace satisfied the deepest expectations of the consumer-people. Even the (constantly revocable) derogation accorded to registered Paris merchants, permitting them to operate outside the marketplaces of the designated "supply crowns," was conceived as part of a larger marketplace strategy that aimed at giving the edge to metropolitan traders over their local competitors (just as it enabled Parisian authority to supersede local authority) and at guaranteeing the hegemony of the central or final marketplace of the capital over the subordinate collector-marketplaces. Other regulations, for example, those dealing with licenses for merchants and passports for grain and flour, emanated from the marketplace, even if they were meant to govern the space outside it. In some way or another, everything pertaining to the police of provisioning revolved around the marketplace.

The marketplace, as I construe it, was the consecrated space of neither capitalism nor carnival. No Smithian invisible hand ministered providentially to the needs of the parties involved. The marketplace bore the unmistakable imprint of the hands of the police (although the authorities placed a high premium on discretion). Unlike Bakhtin's "free place", the marketplace of the police was a preeminently official venue, structured, organized and regulated (at least in theory). Bakhtin's marketplace, infused "with unofficial spirit," was a post of subversion, derision and laughter. It defied both cooptation and control: "It enjoyed a certain extraterritoriality in a world of official order and official ideology." The marketplace of the police was devised precisely to refuse extraterritorial privilege and to enshrine the official worldview. Yet, the official spirit of the marketplace

75 Royal declaration of 19 April 1723, BNF, Collection Joly de Fleury (hereafter cited as Coll. Joly), 1829, fols. 302–3; Archives de Paris, D5Z carton 9; Des Essarts, *Dictionnaire*, 1:19, 330, 402; Delamare, *Traité de la police*, 2: 790–97; Edme de la Poix de Fréminville, *Dictionnaire, ou Traité de la police générale des villes, bourgs, paroisses et seigneuries de la campagne* (Paris: Gissey, 1758), 72; Duchesne, *Code de la police, ou Analyse des règlements de police* (Paris: Prault Père, 1767), 99; William Mildmay, *The Police of France* (London, 1763), 99; BNF, Coll. Joly 1312, fol. 117.

was no less "with the people" than the unofficial marketplace that Bakhtin so brilliantly evoked.[76]

The police intended the marketplace not to throttle commerce, but to domesticate it and moralize it, not to obliterate the market principle, but to correct it. The police designed the marketplace as a way of articulating the requirements of trade with the needs of state and society. They tried to incorporate certain features of the market principle, while excluding or tempering others—a gesture denounced as futile and hollow by the advocates of the market principle, who insisted that it had to be taken as an indivisible whole. For them, liberty was entirely incompatible with the marketplace of the police. If the authorities engineered the marketplace to prevent monopoly (i.e., to prevent liberty from degenerating into license and libertinage), the proponents of the market principle contended that it was precisely the marketplace (i.e., too little liberty) that caused or nurtured monopoly. Unalloyed, the market principle was utterly corrosive of the marketplace as a physical site, as a worldview and as an apparatus of control. It made the marketplace superfluous, save as an occasional matter of convenience. If the marketplace was erected as a dike to contain the burgeoning tide of the market principle, its adversaries scorned it because that tide was irresistible. Goods tended to flee the marketplace as the market principle attempted to assert itself. Thus, the *pays de cocagne* of certain grain and flour merchants—those capable of profiting from this kind of freedom—was the space outside or between the established marketplaces.

Embeddedness and Rationality

In theory, the more pervasive the market principle, the less the economic importance of the marketplace as a site of transactions and the less its political and ideological importance as a concept and institution of social organization. In part, viewed from today's vantage point, the market principle was underdeveloped in eighteenth-century France because the economy was underdeveloped. Yet, it was also underdeveloped because it was self-consciously resisted, and the marketplace loomed large as one of the vehicles of this resistance. The marketplace was the sign of a certain kind of backwardness (to the extent that the market principle was on the side that we conventionally call "progress") and the mark of a certain kind of vitality (to the extent that the French were trying to grapple with one of the most agonizing problems of modernization).

76 Mikhail Bakhtin, *Rabelais and His World*, trans. H. Iswolsky (Cambridge, MA: Harvard University Press, 1968), 153–54. On the noneconomic functions of the marketplace, see also Bohannan and Dalton, eds., *Markets in Africa*, 15–19.

In Old-Regime France, the social organization was not submerged in the market principle, as it is in most "market" societies today. Rather, the distribution of certain goods—in particular grain and flour—was determined by the social organization. Embedded in the social and political institutions, the provisioning trade could not escape certain rules and controls that expressed values to which Frenchmen by and large subscribed. The marketplace stood for the priorities resulting from this type of governing code. When, on several occasions, liberalizing reformers sought to disembed the grain and flour trade from the traditional social organization (or free the promethean market principle from the chains of the marketplace), the immediate consequences were catastrophic.[77]

Marketplace exchange was the police (and the popular or consumer) norm: this was the way the provisioning trade was supposed to work, according to regulatory theory. Market principle exchange was the way the merchants wanted the provisioning market to work, and the way the police (and the consumer-people) feared that it would indeed work, if the official rules were not obeyed (or not enforced). How in fact did the provisioning trade work?

A twentieth-century economist might suggest that the forbidden practices were neither evil nor dangerous, but rational and beneficial—that, more efficiently than the police methods, they got grain and flour into the hands of those most able to make effective use of them, and that they passed the risks of holding stocks in unstable markets to those most willing to bear them. The economist might be tempted to argue that the market, following the market principle, functioned much better than the police believed, and that the main culprit in the story was not the libertine merchant or liberty run amok, but the authorities, whose actions undermined confidence and generated insecurity and who failed to make a pretty good market even better by providing more complete information, better public goods (notably in transportation) and uniformity in weights and measures. The police and the people, the economist might add, believed that they lived in a (market) world of combinations in restraint of trade and of monopoly prices and monopoly profits, but in fact their world was quite competitive, with relative ease of entry and other conditions that usually obtain in the neoclassical model.

Our economist might very well conclude that there were two worlds in the eighteenth century: a world of self-indulgent myth and delusion, associated with what I have called the marketplace, or the regulatory ideology ("phantoms," said the physiocrats, archenemies of the police), and a world of hard-nosed, self-adjusting reality, associated with the market principle or with unfettered commerce.[78] I am inclined to acknowledge the existence of

---

77 See Kaplan, *Bread, Politics and Political Economy*, chaps. 4, 5, 7, 9, 10 and 12.

78 Herbert, *Essai sur la police générale des grains*, 4; speech of Creuzé Latouche, 8 December 1792, in *Archives Parlementaires*, vol. 54 (Paris, 1879–94), 682.

multiple, often rival, and contradictory realities. The way in which the police, and the consumer-people, represented the world to themselves constituted a powerful reality that shaped every aspect of the provisioning process, including price making. From this perspective, it is of little consequence that what the police perceived as a "monopoly" price may have at bottom been nothing more than a modern economist's equilibrium price. The interesting question is not whether the police were right or wrong, but why they saw things as they did. Yet, I do not want to suggest that the police reality was somehow inferior to the economist's because it was essentially psychological or "subjective" as opposed to "objective." The police framework was not necessarily fatally flawed. Many of their doubts and fears about provisioning were the fruit of distortion and exaggeration: perceptions refracted by ideology (a combination of "prejudices" and "ignorance", observed the physiocrats).[79] Many others, however, were warranted by the structural conditions of the grain and flour trade in the eighteenth century. Nor should we assume that the neoclassical outlook was or is a value-free recipe for universally desirable development or "progress." In physiocracy, its early expression, and its later, more refined avatars, neoclassical economics is as much an ideology as an analytical tool, and in this sense is flawed in some of the same ways as the police view. It is perhaps futile to apply the same categories of analysis to the police and neoclassical models—while the latter sees the issues in economic terms, the former regards them above all in social and political terms. We return to the point of departure of the police: provisioning was too delicate and too imperious a task to relegate to the economic domain, that is, to entrust to the market principle.

Marketplace and Market Principle: Tension and Dosage

The story of the grain and flour trade is to a large extent the narrative of the tension between the marketplace and the market principle, the account not of a battle between the forces of Darkness and the forces of Light, but of the shifting relationship between two theories and two (or more) realities. It would be a mistake to infer either from the timeless and merciless strictures of the

79 Controller-General L'Averdy to procurator general, 4 December 1765, BNF, Coll. Joly 1131, fol. 9; L'Averdy to same, 23 October 1766, BNF, Coll. Joly 1109, fols. 145–46; Turgot to intendant of Alençon, 19 September 1774, Archives Départementales (hereafter cited as AD) Orne, C 89; Roubaud, *Représentations*, 39, 80, 93; "Avis du Parlement du Dauphiné," *Ephémérides du citoyen* 7 (1769): 156; Turgot, "Lettre circulaire aux officiers de police dans les lieux où il y a des marchés de grains," 15 Feb. 1766, AD Haute -Vienne, C 479.

police regulations or from the self-serving propaganda of the physiocrats that the police operated in a mindlessly and mechanically rigid and oppressive fashion. The authorities themselves understood the need to reconcile regulation and liberty, which they recognized as "the soul of commerce."[80] They knew that the cost of over-policing was sometimes as onerous as the cost of overlaxness. Even as they anguished over the dangers of allowing the merchants too much freedom, they worried about "disgusting" them and stifling commerce. The officials responsible for provisioning internalized the tension between marketplace and market principle.

The problem was to find the proper dosage. In theory, the police never veered from their commitment to the marketplace; in practice, their position was often temperate, tolerant and flexible. Delamare, the celebrated police theorist, who drew on his long experience as a field agent, recommended a differential police of provisioning: one police for periods of abundance, another for intermediate years, still another for dearth and a fourth style of police for famine.[81] During "normal" years—most of the period with which we are concerned—the Paris authorities practiced benign neglect. They neither repudiated procedures that had been fully assimilated by the trade nor condoned blatantly illicit activities, and they refrained from rigorously executing many of the regulations and permitted others to lapse into virtual desuetude. The traditional controls, especially the mosaic of rules fixing all transactions at the official market sites, the procurator general of the Paris Parlement, one of the highest judicial and administrative officials in the realm, informed the provincial and local authorities "are not to be strictly executed when there is no dearth to fear." He openly avowed that these regulations "hamper the grain trade" and should only be used with extreme discretion. In everyday practice, he urged officials to avoid "authoritarian ways" and to "close your eyes" when they encountered violations of the marketplace code that did not threaten the public interest.[82] Often, the police abstained from coercive measures, not out of indulgence for the merchants, but rather to avoid provoking "alarms" and "anxieties" among consumers. The authorities were sufficiently self-critical to ask themselves whether the classical remedy would not, in the specific circumstances at hand, prove worse than the disease.[83]

80 Delamare, *Traité de la police*, 2: 775.

81 Ibid.,794.

82 Procurator-general to fiscal procurator of Charly, 23 November 1757, BNF, Coll. Joly 1107, fols. 6, 7; BNF, Coll. Joly 1130, fols. 156–57 and 2418, fol. 177.

83 Kaplan, *Bread, Politics and Political Economy*, chaps. 2 and 3.

The evidence indicates that officials very often followed this remarkably subdued and supple line throughout the kingdom. Trading practices deemed monopolistic in periods of stress frequently passed for reasonable commercial operations in more tranquil times; an action only became monopolistic to the extent that it maimed the public interest. The police in the Paris region generally rebuffed price fixing, not from scruples about violating the property rights of dealers—the physiocrats branded *taxation* "theft"—but because they felt that it did more harm than good. Although they had no sympathy for merchant "abuses," along with their mentor Delamare, they had no interest in running "a forced commerce."[84] Merchants enjoyed a real albeit circumscribed liberty. This liberty, however, was not a right derived from nature, but a concession granted conditionally by society. It remained contingent on the good faith of the merchants and on supply conditions.[85]

In theory—perhaps even more tellingly in rhetoric—the marketplace and the market principle were at antipodes. In practice, the opposition was less harsh and unremitting. The tension between them was partly resolved in time (merchants were allowed much more freedom in good periods than in bad) and partly in space (certain areas were more hospitable to liberty than others). In some ways, the marketplace and the market principle adjusted to and accommodated one another. Merchants and authorities shared in a kind of complicity. The merchants learned never to attempt certain transgressions and when to venture others, and incorporated numerous controls into their daily practice. The police were surprisingly opportunistic and elastic—doubtless in part because the marketplace arsenal they held in reserve gave them a sense of deep strength. They were also divided among themselves on a number of major issues. There was no consensus, for instance, on dispensation accorded to Paris dealers to operate outside the market sites.[86] The merchants appreciated and profited from the distinctions made between law and usage.

---

84 Delamare, *Traité de la police*, 2: 922–34; BNF, ms. fr. 21647, fols. 64–74; Duplessis to procurator general, 2, 5 January, 21 September 1726, BNF, Coll. Joly 1118, fols. 5, 8–9, 206–7; Jacques St.-Germain, *La Vie quotidienne en France à la fin du grand siècle d'après les archives du lieutenant général de police Marc-René d'Argenson* (Paris: Hachette, 1965), 208–9; *Ephémérides du citoyen* (August 1767), cited by Georges Weulersse, *Le Mouvement physiocratique en France de 1756 à 1770*, vol. 1 (Paris: Félix Alcan, 1910), 538.

85 *Journal économique* (May 1752); AN, K 908. Cf. Louis Viala, *La Question des grains et leur commerce à Toulouse au dix-huitième siècle* (Toulouse; E. Privat, 1909), 29–30.

86 "Mémoire contre la Déclaration du 9 Septembre 1737," BNF, ms. fr. 21635, fols. 168–69; Missonnet to procurator general, 31 July, 30 October 1752 and 2 April 1753, BNF, Coll. Joly 1112, fols. 114, 192–93; Foucaud to procurator general, April 1757, BNF, Coll. Joly 1113, fols. 240–41.

Nevertheless, the police of provisioning remained, in many ways, a forbidding system. The market principle never operated beyond the shadow of the marketplace. Dealers still had to live in great uncertainty about the future, comply with many vexatious rules and face inconsistencies in police attitudes in different places as well as at different times. Even though officials frequently overlooked the rules in easy periods, they often enforced them vengefully in hard times, as if to atone for their indulgence. Even in times called normal, the prospect of dearth, the dread of tomorrow, preoccupied everyone.

* * * * *

The provisioning question, according to a widely shared Old-Regime persuasion, was basically about culture rather than nature. To be sure, "meteorological accidents" occurred, resulting in harvest shortfalls. But they tended to be quite localized and seldom severe, rarely capable of jeopardizing supply without distortions wrought by conspiracy, speculation or simple greed. For the regnant representation portrayed France as the granary of Europe, a land of blessed bounty, where surpluses were naturally far more common than penuries—the latter perceived as the fruit of human vice rather than divine spleen. Thus, the intense focus, administrative and popular, on the distribution side—the *police des grains*—rather than the production side.

The liberty lobby challenged the assumptions underpinning this optimism, denounced, not as mere naiveté, but as benighted (mis)understanding called "prejudices," a myopic, consumerist fixation that failed to appreciate the realities of the economy, in particular the chronic stagnation of agriculture and the distortions in the market caused, not by grain owners and merchants, but by regulators. Whatever their attitude toward physiocracy and its fellow travelers, historians, notably during the past half-century, have evinced a more Malthusian point of view and/or have problematized the questions of agricultural (essentially cereal) productivity and production. The following chapter takes us upstream in the supply chain.

Chapter II

AGRICULTURE AND THE FRENCH ECONOMY OF THE OLD REGIME

The publication of *Bread, Politics and Political Economy* coincided with the eclipse of the grand doctoral thesis in France, the onerous yet fecund apprenticeship, sometimes extended till midlife or beyond, often marked by a provincial exile (or *retour aux sources*: it depended on one's frame of mind and ambition), which generated massive works, occasionally as prodigious in their influence and prestige as in their size. In particular, the age of the magnificent regional peasant studies was over. These were the studies most likely to touch directly on agricultural production/productivity. In this domain, they yielded highly disparate results, in part because of differences in the quality and quantity of sources and in methods of analysis and interpretation. And, in any event, they spoke to regional specificities that did not necessarily result in fruitful comparisons or findings that could be extrapolated to a broader scale (as the English are more willing to venture). Scholars such as E. Le Roy Ladurie, P. Goubert, G. Lefebvre, P. de Saint-Jacob, P. Bois, R. Baehrel and others dazzled us with the vivid reconstitution of rural life and the "structures and conjunctures" of the countryside, but did not resolve the question of agricultural output.[1] Nor did the less numerous yet immensely informative theses on the nobility—joining, in extremely variable relations, seigneurs and peasant, both highly diverse—fill this gap.

The synthetic works that followed often took as their framework the "ni-ni" formula that flourished in French politics: neither demographic nor agricultural revolution. It was reassuring to know that there was no demographic revolution, whatever that signified precisely (though we learned

---

1 Emmanuel Le Roy Ladurie, *Les Paysans de Languedoc* (Paris: SEVPEN, 1966); Pierre Goubert, *Beauvais et le Beauvaisis de 1600 à 1730* (Paris: SEVPEN, 1960); Georges Lefebvre, *Les Paysans du Nord pendant la Révolution française* (1924), new ed. (Bari: Editori Laterza, 1959); Pierre de Saint-Jacob, *Les Paysans de la Bourgogne du Nord au dernier siècle de l'Ancien Régime* (Paris: Les Belles-Lettres, 1960); Paul Bois, *Paysans de l'Ouest* (Le Mans: Vilaire, 1960); René Baehrel, *Une Croissance, la Basse-Provence rurale (fin du XVIe siècle à 1789)* (Paris: SEVPEN, 1961).

rather quickly that population growth was nevertheless quite brisk during the eighteenth century) because it would have proved challenging to explain how the society nourished this (implicitly) huge human surplus. The absence (or, rather, exasperating tardiness) of an agricultural revolution led scholars to focus on the negatives: obstacles, barriers, blockages, bottlenecks, contradictions, and incoherences of a social, psychological, ideological, political, juridical or administrative as well as an economic nature that penalized (or mutilated) the primary sector. Scholars discussed notions of an immobile ecosystem spanning several centuries, of an extremely fragmented agricultural map that revealed a handful of regional champions and a host of dwarves, and of agronomic innovation on the margin (or in the salons and experimental cabinets). One of the last great collective historical investigations targeting rural France during the Old Regime looked at the tithe as a surrogate for measuring agricultural production and productivity. A team leader in the latter, E. Le Roy Ladurie, advanced further upstream in his work on the etiology of harvest outcomes.[2]

"Go to Heaven for the Climate, to Hell for the Company"

For reasons of specific training, intellectual disposition, the sources that are available and readily usable and the state of historiography, most of us who study the subsistence question, in the broadest sense, focus much more on the structuring processes and the consequences than on the triggering causes, particularly agricultural and climatological. One of the most creative and eclectic historians of the second half of the twentieth century, Emmanuel Le Roy Ladurie, played a pioneering role in both these fields. His earliest research touches upon agricultural production and productivity in the regional context, with national implications, and deals with the problem of historicizing the climate long before such a topic became fashionable or urgent.[3]

It was not easy to study the climate as a historical and social-scientific object in the 1950s and 1960s when most of his colleagues, as Le Roy Ladurie reports—Braudel was a crucial exception—regarded it with irony. Best known for his work on peasants, his blockbuster (I believe the word is appropriate)

---

2 Though much more discreet than in previous epochs, agricultural/rural historiography is neither irremediably atrophied nor immobile today, thanks in particular to the work and intellectual inspiration of G. Postel-Vinay, the extraordinary energy and achievement of J.-M. Moriceau and the contributions of Gérard Béaur.

3 One year after the appearance of his mammoth and enormously influential thesis *Les Paysans de Languedoc*, marked by a Marxo-Malthusian theoretical framework, Le Roy published, under Braudel's auspices, *Histoire du climat depuis l'an mil* (Paris: Flammarion, 1967).

Montaillou, and myriad other works in historical anthropology and the history of the Ancien Régime, Le Roy Ladurie acquired a primitive version of the Swedish incremental borer for measuring tree rings even before he finished his thesis research, and when he came to Cornell as A. D. White Professor-at-Large in 1980, his first professional visit was neither to the Lavoisier papers nor to the French Revolution Collection, but to a specialist in dendrochronology housed in our Classics Department. On the morrow of the killing heat wave of 2003 in France that brutally underscored the violence of climactic phenomena, and on the eve of his 75th birthday, he published the first of three volumes treating the history of the climate from the thirteenth to the early twenty-first centuries.

For obvious reasons, it is the second volume of the trilogy that concerns us here, *Histoire humaine et comparée du Climat, vol. II: Disettes et Révolutions, 1740–1860* (Paris, 2006). It is a book that is at once chatty and polemical, garrulous and trenchant.[4] It is occasionally, deliciously self-indulgent, gallicizing English words directly incorporated into the prose ("affluent," "relevant") (86, 135) and forging neologisms for the task at hand (*millésimes crisiques, années subsistanciellement difficiles* or *anti-subsistancielles, trimestres traumatiques anti-blé*) (12, 13, 95, 133, 134, 144, passim). Hostile to a monocausal account of past happenings and unwilling to deny a, or the, major role to agency, Le Roy Ladurie appears obliged in the end, like Braudel, to acknowledge the relatively

4 The major polemical operation here is a symbolical parricide, another in a series of serious critical interrogations of the work of Ernest Labrousse, launched many years ago by David Landes, recently renewed by David Weir (but these critiques focus on the mechanism of the grain crisis, in particular the relationship between prices, income and demand for nonsubsistence goods, rather than on the object of Le Roy's ire here). The dominant and domineering figure in postwar economic (and social) history in France, director of some of the most significant doctoral theses of the epoch, including *Les Paysans de Languedoc*, Labrousse created the template for price studies, displacing numerous predecessors and marginalizing contemporary rivals. Le Roy Ladurie contests here his famous "intercycle de crise," 1778–87, a sustained period of depression that allegedly destabilized the kingdom, making it ripe for the detonating subsistence crises on the eve of 1789 and thus contributing mightily to the causation of the French Revolution. For Le Roy Ladurie, Labrousse's emphasis on the intercyclical crisis betrays his obsession with "the bad inflation of 1919 and the 1930s." On the contrary, he maintains, this was a period of "good inflation," an "intercyclical phase of persistent and sometimes splendid economic growth, the key indicators all enjoying a green light at least until 1787 (consumption of the masses, landed income, wool industry, foreign trade)" (87–88). He goes on to devote to this critique a whole chapter entitled "The Myth of the Labroussean Crisis of Ten Years, 1778–1787," in which he engages in a bit of overkill on his mentor's "schizophrenic demi-masterpiece." He insists again on the positive indicators that

limited latitude of human intervention.[5] For the eighteenth and nineteenth centuries—the waning of the little ice age—the book is an agro-meteorological primer that explains harvest shortfalls (through seasonal cadences such as the *douche-sauna-douche* effect, a picturesquely described meteorological disaster) and their consequences (political, regulatory—the *police fromentale*—social, symbolic and especially demographic). For this neo-Malthusian, perhaps also

undermine "Labrousse's construct," including a series of generally quite ample harvests, resilient real wages, mounting land leases and a general "prosperity of French agriculture." In other words, Le Roy Ladurie reduces the purchase of climate on Revolutionary etiology: it plays a "late" role in the run-up to the Revolution that turned basically on matters he enumerates as "political, budgetary, fiscal, parlementary, religious." He concludes that the relevant optic here is a history "that is properly and strictly *political* in the best sense of this adjective." Yet, after having apparently joined the sometimes bitter "revisionist" quarrel squarely in favor of the Anglo-American "antisocial" interpretation, represented in France (and subsequently everywhere else) by F. Furet, he points immediately to a handful of historians whom he describes as sharing or at least converging in this politicalist point of view: Georges Lefebvre, Albert Soboul, François Furet, Jean Egret and Mona Ozouf in that order. Is this Le Roy Ladurie's puckish sense of irony, placing Furet-Ozouf in the same basket as the objects of their virulent criticism, Lefebvre and Soboul? Or an incongruous irenic amalgamation? Or, as I suspect, a lack of intimate familiarity with the historiographical debates on the Revolution, ignited in France by Furet's merciless *Penser la Révolution française* (Paris: Gallimard, 1978) (132–42, and the long footnote 466–67). For the critique of various aspects of the Labrousse enterprise and heritage, see David S. Landes "The Statistical Study of French Crises," *Journal of Economic History* 10, no. 2 (Nov. 1950): 195–211; David R. Weir, "Family Income, Mortality, and Fertility on the Eve of the Demographic Transition: A Case Study of Rosny-sous-Bois," *Journal of Economic History* 55 (Mar. 1995): 1–26; Weir, "'Les Crises économiques de la Révolution française," *Annales E.S.C.* 46 (1991): 917–47; Weir, "Markets and Mortality in France, 1600–1789," in Roger Schofield and John Walter, eds., *Famine, Disease, and the Social Order in Early Modern Society* (Cambridge: Cambridge University Press, 1989); François Caron, "Introduction générale," *Histoire sociale, histoire globale?* (colloquium of Jan., 1989), ed. Christophe Charle (Paris: Editions de la Maison des Sciences de l'Homme, 1993); Philip T. Hoffman and Jean-Laurent Rosenthal, "New Work in French Economic History," *French Historical Studies* 23 (Summer, 2000): 439–453; Michel Margairaz, "Histoire économique et sciences sociales: alliance, cohabitation, confrontation ? *L'Économie politique* 57 (2013): 72–90. Though only indirectly germane, see the penetrating commentary of M. Aymard, "Autoconsommation et marchés: Chayanov, Labrousse ou Le Roy Ladurie ?" *Annales E.S.C.* 38 (1983): 1392–1410. For an overview of many of the issues directly concerning Labrousse, see Maria Novella Borghetti, *L'œuvre d'Ernest Labrousse. Genèse d'un modèle d'histoire économique* (Paris: Editions de l'Ecole des Hautes Etudes en Sciences Sociales, 2006).

5 There is no simple or simplistic nature/culture divide, but "nature" seems to trump politics quite regularly (22).

marked by the scholarship of Jean Meuvret,[6] the inescapable test of the acuity and even the sense of a subsistence crisis was demographic: mortality (the Grim Reaper sustaining the harvest image), morbidity, marriages and births: the first two escalate or skyrocket, while the second two dwindle or collapse. I argue below that this measure is too restrictive; a mortality crisis, as the demographers say, denotes, very often, but not always, a subsistence crisis; a subsistence crisis, with enormous, cascading social, economic, political and psychological disruption, can occur without necessarily generating a substantial yield in death. Le Roy Ladurie observes that 1770 was a year of significantly enhanced mortality, on the one hand similar to 1740, which bore "some traits of the crucifying misery of the age of Louis XIV," and on the other hand was nothing like the hecatombs of the worst crises of that king's reign (1663–64, 1709–10) (19, 50). Yet he recognizes—the narrative is a bit disjointed—that other years of acute dearth—1767–68, 1774–75—generated grave crises[7] of the kind I just evoked without cataclysmic demographic disarray (39–51).

The Politicization of the Weather; or "Climate is What we Expect, Weather is What we Get"

Despite his enormous appetite for all sorts of variables, Le Roy Ladurie's temptation to reduce the subsistence to a demographic affair does not spare him some contradictions and inconsistencies. The crisis of 1770–71—"an anti-subsistence, weather crisis"—is in fact "a *pure* climatic-grain crisis, the ideal for the historian of the climate," all the more so because there is no war involved (48). But the historian knows very well that no crisis is pure in any sense, emic or etic, metaphorical or analytical, that politics is involved from the get-go, that the "sociopsychological" effects are confined neither to mortality nor to nuptiality (48, 70–71), but touch deep fears about hunger, misery, unemployment, inaccessible prices, market manipulation, profiteering, conspiracy, administrative corruption, royal abjuration of responsibility or blindness and transgression of deeply rooted customary understandings. He understands clearly that riots and disorder of other kinds, which define crises as much as postponed marriages, outbreaks of amenorrhea, depressed

6 I'm thinking of his seminal article "Les crises de subsistances et la démographie de la France d'ancien régime," *Population* 1 (1946): 643–50.

7 I agree with Le Roy Ladurie that crisis "is a much overused word" (35) that he and I and others continue to use, as a sort of Pavlovian shorthand. Here the agonies of the past and present nourish and reinforce each other. France, for example, has been in some sort of (more or less serious) crisis or other since I began frequenting the hexagon in the 1960s. It is the learned equivalent of "peoplisation": without a crisis, it seems hard to pitch a book, maybe even an article. Still, collectively, we need to do better in conceptualizing and "theorizing" crises.

sperm counts, gastrointestinal diseases or even deaths, are not the unmediated result of too much or too little rain, too much or too little warmth.

Hearing the tocsin of the abandonment of liberalization sounded by Terray (though with more nuance than he allows) in 1770, Le Roy Ladurie himself evokes "the politicization of the weather," alternately baptized "politicization of the climate," though he does not succeed in articulating the play of climate and politics in a cogent manner. His reading of the end of liberalization is not very solid (Terray's measure in December 1770 has little to do with "flattering the masses, passionately fond of the police"), yet he raises broader issues that exercise all historians of the eighteenth century, such as the alleged "ungovernability of an Ancien Régime society"—evocative of the refrain on the supposed unreformability of Fifth-Republic France—even as he reverts steadfastly to his claim, which no longer seems relevant, as he might say, that the liberal debacle was "a matter of pure climate, of weather *pur et dur*, as in 1461 as in 1661" (55, 57, 58).[8] He seems to suggest that the age-old policies of "royal dirigisme" drew legitimacy and force from a keen climate sensitivity, a certain eco-realism. The 1760s was the very first time that ministers dared defy nature, embodied by a sort of meteo-memory: "even if it meant for them to be quickly disavowed when the torrential rains and the cold returned at top speed" (69).[9] The agro-meteo chronicle takes on a life of its own, unfolds mechanically and generates implausible zigzags: for example, after the terrible perturbations of 1770–71, as early as 1772 a "post-depression 'recovery'," signaled by a road-building boom, for Le

---

8 His boundless erudition and enthusiasm (almost) allow Le Roy Ladurie to have it both ways. On the one hand, "the cold-cool fluctuation of 1766–1771, producer of mass poverty, was incidentally the cause of diverse political changes in France." Then, on the other hand, after raising the hypothesis of a deficit of solar irradiation, he writes, without any segue anxiety: "These volcanic–atmospheric disturbances, reducing the delivery of solar radiation, and thus damaging the crops, render quite futile the theorems of the physiocrats and Turgot on the ultra-rational and absolute necessity of the freedom of the grain trade, with the 'bon prix' as part of the deal. They [the disturbances] reveal as much more reasonable the solidly grounded principles of a Terray, then a Necker, partisans of liberty when the crop is sufficient, and of regulation when it is more or less short" (59).

I regret that I have never asked Le Roy Ladurie, preoccupied with the pragmatic outcomes of governance and the resistance to it, whether he had the occasion to dialogue with M. Foucault, his colleague at the Collège de France, focused on the theoretical tools, or technologies, of governmentality.

9 Choiseul in 1770, like Necker in 1789, "were both victims, in certain ways, of bad cereal news, product of an extreme winter or of soaking rains that recently struck the Paris Basin, or of some other climate-grain catastrophe, the scorching of grain (1788) or some other complication. . ." (70).

Roy Ladurie "oxygen after asphyxiation," for me a fragmented and highly uneven effort to create public-works jobs to attenuate the still burgeoning misery (73).

In much the same mood, Le Roy Ladurie explains the Flour War as basically an agro-meteo story. Despite "a thousand other grounds," including "the dogmatism of a hyper-distinguished *économiste*" called Turgot, a "certain growing *conscientisation* [*sic*]" of the "popular masses" (whose spontaneous uprising was "à la Rosa Luxembourg") and a cumulative "weakening"—a quasi-mutilation—of absolutism, in the end the climate did the deed: "How to explain the Flour War (spring 1775)? Quite simply by the rain," a "rotten year" breaking all records for the number of days of drenching humidity (77–85). Snared by his own fervor, this ex-partisan of "total history," in whom the culturalist had long eclipsed the materialist, lapses into a sort of climate determinism which, despite its peremptory and hyperbolic claims, fruitfully reminds us what, as students of the Old Regime, we have learned as citizens of the twenty-first century: the enormous influence of weather uncertainty, caprice and catastrophe—in the modern instance, partly of human origin.

A Global Approach to the Economy: Uncertainty, Temporality and Exchange

Emmanuel Le Roy Ladurie borrowed his agro-meteo formula from Jean-Yves Grenier's important book, *L'économie d'Ancien Régime: Un monde de l'échange et de l'incertitude* (Paris, 1996). It is the product of a dissertation written under the direction of Jean-Claude Perrot, whose elegance of mind and pen his student has inherited. This is a book that is as thoughtful as it is challenging for the reader neither trained in economic theory nor accustomed to the ways in which it inflects historical epistemology. There is a great deal that I admire in this highly original and exigent study, perhaps above all its ambition: "a global approach to the economy of the Ancien Régime" (9). The theoretical, taxonomic and analytical inadequacies of the historiography, particularly in its incidence on what the French call modern history (sixteenth to eighteenth centuries), have led Grenier to venture "a new orientation … to identify the principal formal characteristics of the economy of the Ancien Régime and to deduce from it a model that accounts for and explains the essential empirical and observable data" (10). His angle of attack, pivoting on"the couple value-price" in the context of a reflection on exchange, enables him to formulate hypotheses "on the economy in its entirety" that are largely beyond my competence to assess with confidence (11). I am somewhat awed by Grenier's capacity to align in a single paragraph the authority of Etienne Bonnot de Condillac, sensationist epistemologist and liberal economist, and of Kenneth

Arrow, perhaps the major theorist of modern neoclassical economic theory and Nobel Prize winner (371).[10]

There are numerous areas where I learned much from Grenier.[11] My own work resonates with the idea that the uncertainty of the world of the eighteenth century shapes the economy pervasively, if one can impute a sort of state of mind or mood to it. It finds expression in unstable markets, anemic financial institutions, generally unpredictable behavior, and what the author calls, much more problematically for me, an absence of real regulation. Yet, he qualifies his remark immediately by referring to a mode of functioning of constant readjustments, a defining characteristic of the economy whose context (and in some ways whose text, or pragmatic vulgate) is "a temporality marked by the aleatory." By aleatory, I understand here the chronically adventitious, usually unintended, sometimes spontaneous: unplanned, to be sure, and contingent, but in some sense conditioned, if not framed, by certain institutions, *sensu lato*, such as assumptions, customs, relations (agonistic or irenic), administrations of various genres (vertical and horizontal) and mental universes (historiographically and epistemologically, the most dubious of his categories in this discussion) (420).

This brilliant reflection on temporality—a complex notion marked by rhythms and respirations that evoke Cantillon and Turgot, Verri and Vico, Say and Sismondi, J. S. Mill and Hicks, Kondratiev and Kuznets, Simiand and Labrousse—traverses the whole book. Grenier betrays an impressive mastery of

10 Arnaud Orain chastises Grenier and me for failing to take into sufficient account the "classical republican" inflexion of Condillac's world view, locating his ideal in the "simple life" limiting the progress of the arts and stanching luxury, in an eschatology close to that of Mably, Condillac's brother, in *Des Droits et des devoirs du citoyen* (1758, published 1789). The Condillac case also questions the Pocock–Skinner separation of the liberal and classical republican discourses. See the article Orain cowrote with Julie Ferrand, "The Natural Law of Equality at the Heart of the Controversy between Mably and the Physiocrats," in S. L. Kaplan and Sophus Reinert, eds., *The Economic Turn: Recasting Political Economy in Eighteenth-Century Europe*, forthcoming.

11 Among the myriad debts I have contracted to Jean-Yves Grenier is the knowledge that the stressful, compensatory comportment of bread eaters amidst the *menu peuple* during price surges that I have described discursively has been theorized as the Giffen effect (also known as Giffen goods: ordinarily, as the price of goods augments, the substitution effect induces consumers to purchase less of it, and more of substitute goods; in the circumstances generating Giffen goods, the income effect prevails, impelling people to buy more of the goods, even as its price increases). I suppose that each of us, in her/his discipline, has Monsieur Jourdain moments in which we are delighted to learn that we have been speaking prose all our life without knowing it. In the same Jourdainian vein, however, I would surely have made a fool of myself if I pretended to understand, say, the workings of the mathematical analytical tool called Cobweb that Grenier uses so fruitfully (387–90).

the architecture of the temporalities that enables him to give the "cycle of the Ancien Régime" an extremely compelling global account, even if certain of the evidence-based arguments strike me as incommensurate with the modelization—contemporary (Economic Enlightenment) or retrospective (today's neoclassical theory)—that frames them. Exchange, the fulcrum of the author's approach, is insightfully examined in its multiple avatars: the tools developed by actors to enhance their leverage through capital and information, the instrumentalization of time for speculative ends, the impact of exchange on types and levels of activity as well as on revenues, the primordial role of exchange in the formation of prices and wages (stamped by Grenier's recurrent warnings—is it presumptuous for me to see myself as one of the targets?—against an excessive anthropologization of the subsistence–wage nexus in particular).

The Social and the State

The "social" is not an emphatically salient object of concern in *L'Economie d'Ancien Régime*. I am not sure that Grenier would agree with Jean Bouvier's understanding of the intimate relation between them, cited above, that "the social is the way of being of the economic."[12] Yet he clearly sees exchange as a social as well as an economic act. He evokes this quite nicely—"the very composite social formation" of the Old-Regime economy—by taking the case of price making where the grain's extremely heterogeneous social provenance comes into play: tithes, *rentes*, lease payments, sharecropping fees and seigneurial dues, each of which bespeaks specific costs of production and commercial strategies (420). Grenier shows how other variables are inscribed in the social (and political) fabric: wage making (in which I believe he exaggerates the intervention of public or judicial administration) and the fixation of interest rates, where supply and demand, socially embodied, summon or are subjected to the mediation of the market, with its rules and constraints, which stands in the ponderous shadow of the monarchy, not only guarantor of the public good, but also the principal borrower in the kingdom. Profit is also socially as well as economically differential: on the one hand, a stabilized rate (denoting a patrimonial conception of wealth); on the other hand, a speculative rate that reflects economic uncertainties and exchange practices. Comparing the (social) "quality" of persons with the quality of merchandise, the economic historian makes an argument that interests me and that I have advanced elsewhere; he thickens it by articulating social classification and concepts of usage value (101–3).

12 Jean Bouvier, "Le capitalisme et l'État en France", *Recherches et travaux. Bulletin de l'institut d'histoire économique et sociale de l'université Paris 1*, 15 (Dec. 1986): 48. (Bouvier's full citation is in chap. I.)

Though I wish he had developed this theme much more fully, Grenier insists on the role of the state in the economy, apart from any ideological or strategic engagement and beyond a more or less predatory fiscal vocation. I like his formula: the state "expresses the unity of contradictory interests, beginning with its own" (422). Of course, the state operates frequently without a mask or rather with unequivocal cues concerning its disposition: thus Colbert pressurizes major financiers to invest in commercial or industrial companies or allocates grants and privileges to private entrepreneurs, a mission of "the modern State" for Grenier as opposed to an expression of sclerotic court-society ethos, following A. Skornicki (92).[13] A subsidy in this environment looms less as a form of assistance than as a necessary condition for productive investment. The economic historian argues that monarchical institutions were indispensable for "the valorization of capital," necessary in light of the "aleatory" factors that are the leitmotifs of this study: unstable economic environment, irregular demand, wars, sundry risk factors and so on. Yet their intervention occurs "on the margin," allowing capital to do its work, through various established apparatuses such as "market mechanisms," presumably in the (neo-)classical mold, through the fabrication of norms by the "unitary monarchical principle" itself—apparently Grenier's way of thinking about what others call absolutism or administrative monarchy or even enlightened despotism—and through the corporative system (96–98).

These and other institutions—from parlements to family networks—accompany and nourish the development of capital during its entire life cycle (91). If the accumulation of capital is the role of individual entrepreneurs, the state's "fiscal economy" both obstructs and fosters the process, sometimes in the same gesture (92–95). One's relationship to the state—and not more narrowly to the court—and with the world of capital determines whether one is "in credit" or "in discredit" (89).[14] This credit, reinforced and amplified by personal ties, opens opportunities for contracting loans, for example, and frames the stages of capital's life cycle: formation, utilization and valorization (96).[15]

---

13 Arnault Skornicki, *L'Economie, la cour et la patrie* (Paris: CNRS Editions, 2011), discussed below in chap. VI.

14 See the expansive yet highly nuanced sense of credit that Clare Haru Crowston forges in her wonderful new book *Credit, Fashion, Sex: Economies of Regard in Old Regime France* (Durham, NC: Duke University Press, 2013).

15 Here and throughout the book, one senses the intellectual presence of Gilles Postel-Vinay, who has taught a seminar with Grenier for years. See, for example, on the issue of credit, lending and borrowing that preoccupies Grenier, Philip T. Hoffman, Gilles Postel-Vinay and Jean-Laurent Rosenthal, *Priceless Markets: The Political Economy of Credit in Paris, 1660–1870* (Chicago: University of Chicago Press, 2000).

Agriculture, Peasants and Rational Decision Making

Grenier could have not only navigated comfortably in the Gournay circle, but also attended Quesnay in his *entresol* and frequented both Necker's salon and Mirabeau's Tuesdays, because he is as keenly interested in agriculture as he is in commerce and industry. His study contains a richly textured discussion of the supply side of this cereal-dominated economy, with which I have failed to deal methodically, despite excellent training by Jean Meuvret. I have viewed the subsistence question largely from a neo-Malthusian angle: a constantly problematic, even Sisyphean effort to marshal a ration of survival for a growing population—no demographic revolution, we were told, but no agricultural revolution either—pressing against an ever-strained carrying capacity. By training, inclination, historiographical formation and (archival) experience, I viewed the subsistence issue as first of all a social and political question: cereals dominated the economy, but in this context of structural precariousness and chronic shortage, the economic problematic was in some sense overdetermined. As an independent variable, the economy was implacable; as a dependent variable, it was merciless. Under a relentlessly doloristic cloud, it did not leave much space either for the mass of contemporary actors or for the coterie of latter-day historians who followed their plight.

Economistic, Grenier's treatment of cereal farming is not economystifying. On the contrary, he lays out clearly the various conditions for (rational) decision making in an area where I believed—and am still inclined to believe—that the bulk of peasants had, objectively, little freedom of action and, subjectively, still less. I extrapolated not from a landscape of "immobile history" but from a host of excellent regional theses devoted to the peasantry. These were peasants who, confronted with multiple imperatives—personal, familial, seigneurial, ecclesiastical, royal, and juridical—tended, *bon an, mal an*, to do the same thing, assuming they had the seed, the means and the authorization to plant. Short-term price movements seemed to have little purchase on their behavior. The vast majority of peasants seemed more or less immune to market adjustments. A surge of abundance did not induce them to plant less the following year; a stinging penury, crippling many, enriching few, did not and could not result in a strategy of expansion. Only a very small number of peasants—the brawny, physiocratic type, entrepreneurial *fermiers* or the robust, calculating *laboureurs* who published pieces in the "economic" press of the day—and managerially oriented, generally better-off noble and bourgeois landowners could make immediate business judgments affecting ongoing operations, investment or sowing plans. Jean-Marc Moriceau's probing long-run study of Ile-de-France cultivators, taking into account a range of players, often hale, but not cut of the same cloth, and diverse scenarios, did not encourage me to forswear my (rudimentary) assumptions; nor did the splendid monograph on the Chartier family that he wrote in collaboration with Postel-Vinay.[16]

By the force of his argument—not of his documentation, which depends heavily on speculative, salon-style agronomy—Grenier has convinced me, at the very least, that the question requires much further investigation. Postulating the lack of a sharp discontinuity between lands permanently cultivated and those that were rarely, occasionally or never sown, he follows Boisguilbert, the *économistes*, and Jean Meuvret, in the wake of *homo economicus*, in emphasizing that the short-term economic (and agro-meteorological) environment, figured by price reports and prospects, largely determined how much land was seeded. He also explores the influence of prices on investment; the impact of the latter on production and productivity; the significance of the size of farms, the quality of the soil, the kinds of agronomic techniques employed, all of which enable the historian to propose a "typology of marketed supply" that shows how "the regular production of grain for commercial purposes is confined to

16 Jean-Marc Moriceau, *Les Fermiers de l'Île-de-France. L'ascension d'un patronat agricole (XVe–XVIIIe siècle)* (Paris: Fayard, 1994); Moriceau and G. Postel-Vinay, *Ferme, entreprise, famille: grande exploitation et changements agricoles. Les Chartier, XVIIe–XIXe siècles* (Paris: Editions de l'Ecole des Hautes Etudes en Sciences Sociales, 1992). The protagonists in these studies are a minority finely attuned to the market. René Baehrel's peasants do seem to respond to market incentives, in a segmented and circumstantial manner. See his *Une croissance: La Basse-Provence rurale,* 150, 162–63. Jean Meuvret took an ambivalent position on the reaction of peasant grain growers to price changes. He did not exclude price effects on planting and productivity, yet he found several structural factors, as well as fluctuating "conjunctural" influences, which militated against this sort of adjustment. Whereas the "bon prix" could have proved to be "the most effective of stimulants" to a small group of vigorous *laboureurs*, the vast majority of peasants suffered from a "moral paralysis" of which neither excessively low prices could be considered the principal cause nor high prices the specific remedy. Short-term price fluctuations were baneful, yet not determinate in terms of the decision to plant per se: "On the one hand, there was hardly any question about limiting cultivation … on the other, this farming was practiced in a deficient manner." In the last of the posthumously published volumes, the historian writes: "Very few producers consulted the mercuriales [price register] before fixing the nature and extent of their sowing. But the extreme values of price rises or declines, by causing selling at a loss or penury, led quite frequently some of them to abandon planting entirely." J. Meuvret, *Le Problème des subsistances à l'époque de Louis XIV: La production des céréales dans la France du XVIIe et XVIIIe siècle*, vol. 1 (Paris: Mouton, 1977), 101; *Le Problème des subsistances à l'époque de Louis XIV: La production des céréales et la société rurale,* vol. 1 (Paris: Editions de l'Ecole des Hautes Etudes en Sciences Sociales, 1987), 215; *Le Problème des subsistances à l'époque de Louis XIV: Le commerce des grains et la conjoncture,* vol. 1 (Paris: Editions de l'Ecole des Hautes Etudes en Sciences Sociales, 1988), 178–79.

a small group of operators"[17]; the weight of noncereal farming; and the role of labor in the equation. The economic historian is much more skeptical than Le Roy Ladurie about the explanatory capacity of the agro-meteo, especially in annual rhythm, Le Roy's preferred observational cadence. He questions the lag time between weather events, on the one hand, and prices and production on the other hand, and suggests the "short term"—by which he seems to mean something like three years or so—as a more reliable reference point (a sort of *aggiornamento* of the quinquennial model in Quesnay's *Encyclopédie* articles), though only the long movement can generate a real autonomy of production and the middling term a genuinely random ("*aléatoire*") weather behavior. After hinting that the major producers were indeed capable of quite rapid reaction and readjustment to prices, a bit later Grenier concludes more cautiously, apparently in light of the internal logic of the process, that a "production strategy" is in fact implausible: "in the short term (up to three years), the intentional variation of production is limited, production imposes its [own] inertia … above all, the perception of economic data that could modify the production intentions is difficult in the short term" (270–92).[18]

Divergent Ways of Doing

None of this discussion is accompanied by the administration of proof, as the French call it. Rather, we have a confident general narrative punctuated by occasional examples, here and there: a subdelegate who comments that there is no unused arable in his purview; an article in the *Ephémérides du citoyen*; a citation

17 This angle leads Grenier to make interesting remarks on the psychosocial and political motivations of these "gros exploitants" as well as their maximizing impulse (289).

18 In the end, Grenier firmly shifts the focus from the short-term relation, evoked by numerous economists in the eighteenth century, between prices, levels of investment, reduction of planted arable land and decline in production, to the longer term. Yet, the text of the Gournayian Claude-Jacques Herbert (aligned here between Boisguilbert and Quesnay) seems to argue, in liberal-apocalyptic terms, for a very short-term impact that constrains the "laboureur"—an actor one does not know where to insert in Grenier's grid—to cut back on the next year's sowing (296). Moreover, the economic historian raises another fascinating question: the extent to which, in the midst of the relative fixity of global supply at a given moment, an actor enjoys "the possibility of varying the distribution of sales thanks to storage" (292). Is the three-year threshold suggested a viable one? Requiring what sort of housing, aeration, conditioning, treatment and so on? Here we could use evidence on the realities of conservation technology, coming not from Intieri, Galiani, Duhamel du Monceau or even Mathieu Tillet, perhaps closer to the ground than the others, but the account books or other testimonies of cultivators.

from François Véron de Forbonnais, a percipient critic of the physiocrats; an undocumented and vaporous claim—surprising to me, for agro-meteo reasons and for the massive evidence of dearth throughout the kingdom north of the Loire—that "production takes off again, according to the circumstances, towards 1766–68"; the enigmatic assertion of a "continuous increase in prices" during the period 1758–68, whereas the evidence suggests that prices remained quite low through 1765, lubricating the passage of the liberal legislation, notably parlementary registration (281, 284, 285). These remarks point to a broader gap between our respective ways of doing history, based, in the end, more on differences of style and temperament than on some sort of foundational epistemological rupture. By no means indifferent to demonstration, Grenier seems nevertheless much more focused on interpretation. I find it hard to follow him as he moves seamlessly from a formal model to a contemporary intuition (say, Necker's or Condillac's, acclaimed for its perspicacity and its putative fidelity to real-world practices), which in turn is taken as a sort of ethnographic key to market (in this instance, speculative) behavior that is evoked with a single archival citation, in this case undated and of unidentified voice (372).

I have written about certain parallels between the grain police and the police of the labor market. In a similar vein, Grenier notes that "the similarity is strong between the order of work and the order of goods, both stemming from the framework of corporate regulations" (98). What surprises me is the extent to which he appears to infer social (and economic) reality from normative sources, in particular guilds statutes. As a result, he subscribes to the liberal stereotype (codified by the Gournay circle) of the extreme rigidity of the labor market (113). In practice, if you will indulge me this formulation, it cannot be said that the rules prevailed as a rule. The labor market was a site of intense conflict, and of occasional brutal repression that worked very unevenly at best. It was also a space of improvisation, negotiation and compromise: masters and journeymen found solutions, as frequently outside the corporate framework as within.[19] The historian takes the journeymen printers, a closely supervised profession, as examples of regulatory rigidity that hems in tightly entry and exit within "the strict corporate framework" (246). Yet this is to overlook the role of *alloués*, journeymen surrogates, functioning outside the corporate orbit in a parallel universe directly connected to print shops.[20] I would be more

19 See Kaplan, "La lutte pour le marché du travail à Paris au 18e siècle," *Revue d' histoire moderne et contemporaine* 36 (July–Sept. 1989): 361–412. For some bracing insights into conflict in the context of the affirmation of a "common identity" among workers, see Samuel Guicheteau, *La Révolution des ouvriers nantais. Mutation économique, identité sociale et dynamique révolutionnaire (1740–1815)* (Rennes: Presses Universitaires de Rennes, 2008).

20 See Kaplan, *La Fin des corporations.*

skeptical than the author about the capacity of a parlement to effectively ban an association of workers or of royal institutions at various levels to impose wage standards that serve as a functioning referential template (114–15). With ingenuity, he defines the laboring poor—the exposed little people—as those without any protection from competition (246). Still, *gagne-deniers, porte-faix* and other urban dayworkers, on the Paris ports and central markets as well as elsewhere in the realm, often constituted more informal groups that operated in ways mimicking the corporate sphere. Normative texts are not a reliable guide to actual practice, especially in hiring, firing and voluntary departure [*congé*]. They do not trace a cartography of control over a world much less static than he suggests, where actors outside the corporate system—the swarms of the so-called "false workers" or *sans qualités, chambrelans* (often protected by masters), and workers moored in "privileged places"—outnumber officially identified and legitimate agents, at least in the big cities (247–48, 255–54).[21]

In an analogous manner, while Baudeau, Galiani and Necker (less plausibly Condorcet) can help us understand collective behavior in situations of severe subsistence stress, discursive sources tell us little that is reliable about the operations of the grain and flour trades. No one who has scrutinized the changes in personnel and practices in the eighteenth century, and particularly in the 1760s, can affirm, as Grenier does, that "liberalization of the trade in 1763 and 1764 alters nothing" (370). On the issue of liberty, I strain to fathom the precise meaning of the following sentence, which I presume requires an economist's parsing: "The period of liberalization between 1763 and 1776 does not inaugurate, moreover, any major change in the short-term evolution of prices." Obviously, this is a "Galilean" gaze, as Carlo Ginzburg might say, founded, apparently, on a citation from Labrousse, the kind that seems to estrange us from lived experience and common-sense reckoning.[22] Closer to the ground, it is manifest that virtually all of France felt and reacted to jolting spikes in prices between 1766 and 1770 (in the south somewhat later, but prices in the north remained volatile, upwardly disposed and onerous through the early 1770s), and, of course, again in 1775. Hailed by numerous interest groups, public and private, the price rise generated by the first liberalization and the protracted dearth that amplified its effects, provoked anxiety, panic and proliferating disorder. Is Grenier's point that it did not inflect prices in

21 See Kaplan, "Les Corporations, les faux-ouvriers, et le faubourg St.-Antoine," *Annales E.S.C.* 43 (March–April 1988): 253–78, and *La Fin des corporations*.

22 Grenier seems to shift the focus from the short term to a longer span in his note in which he writes that Labrousse's analysis led him to observe "that the liberty of the grain trade had no influence on the periodic movement or on the long-term movement of prices" (468n).

a way sufficient to meet the physiocratic criterion for the regeneration of agriculture? Perhaps.[23]

At the outset of his book, Jean-Yves Grenier acknowledges the "*pertinence*" of the structuring distinction that I make between "market place" and "market principle," but finds it conceptually wanting (10).[24] I am flattered that this example, among others, illustrates for him the necessity of his own enterprise. His "new orientation" has not received the careful attention from Old-Regime scholars that it richly merits in part because of its extremely hybrid nature—economic and econometric theory and method, Perrot-like (often luminous) history of ideas, sporadic plunges into the archives, a tension between an ideal-type and a socio-realistic analysis and a prose at once graceful and (for many readers frequently) recondite. For reasons that overlap to some degree, we agree that a "liberty–regulatory" opposition cannot account for the most significant aspects of the provisioning question in an economy of exchange of heterogeneous characteristics (373 and passim). One of Grenier's signal achievements is to oblige us to reexamine the nature of the market. In the end, he rejects both the self-regulating market of the economists and the world of hyperanthropologized and fragmented transactions governed by customs and rules: "Neither the market principle by itself nor the focus on the sole marketplace, but the two together" (423). *D'accord.* But we need to map out the terms of exchange in the concrete markets rather than the abstract ones.

A More Sanguine View of Agricultural Growth

Today, in France, we speak about the sector of activity, or complex, labeled grain-flour-bread (*blé-farine-pain*). Since *Bread, Politics*, I have continued to write extensively about flour, mills and millers, bread, bakeries and bakers, from the end of the seventeenth to the early twenty-first century. In none of my work, however, have I paid *close* attention to the first component/stage: the production of grain, despite the (urban-dwelling) physiocrats'

23 If regulatory practices are more supple, uneven and uncertain than Grenier supposes (extrapolating them from legislation and/or police codes), is his elegant model showing the operation of different types of speculation in the context of market provisioning imperiled? (373–74). Moreover, it seems reasonable to maintain that regulatory practices that the French historian deems economically destabilizing are socially and psychologically reassuring.

24 See Kaplan, *Provisioning Paris.*

sardonic prod, addressed to urban-dwellers like myself, that it did not grow under the paving stones of city streets (where my generation looked for the beach). The major reason is that the subject, inherently sprawling and complicated, is beyond my reach. The variable that concerned me directly, cereal production, remained very hard to get at, in the age before sophisticated and efficient tools of data collection and analysis, before farmer's unions, the dense network of grain cooperatives and diverse state institutions such as the Office national interprofessionnel des céréales, despite the precocious statistical appetite of certain ministries in the second half of the eighteenth century. I relied in 1970, as I do in 2014, on the secondary literature, uneven in quality, as in all fields of inquiry, but far more active in the twentieth century than today, when Jean-Marc Moriceau and a handful of others valiantly resist the tide of scholarly indifference to the rural world, ironic counterpoint, and reaction against the long phase of postwar vogue for peasant studies.

The big question at the outset of my research was the Malthusian challenge: did France, the most populous nation in Europe, expanding by around 30 per cent in the course of the eighteenth century,[25] produce a sufficient amount of grain to feed its inhabitants, most of whom derived most of their calories, and in many cases, a significant dose of their protein intake, from these cereals, generally, but not exclusively, consumed in the form of bread. Implicitly, the answer seemed to be clear, since the kingdom suffered no famine, *sensu stricto*, after 1709, no kingdom-wide assault of plague, only occasional thrusts of mortality and morbidity usually, but not always, closely correlated with substantial harvest shortfalls, which cruelly penalized sizable segments of the laboring and idle poor, without, however, decimating the population of the realm. The scholarly literature was vacillating, testimony at once to its vitality and its inability to make a durably convincing demonstration. Students witnessed the rise and fall of two revolutions, one labeled agricultural and the other dubbed demographic, intuitively connected, at first energetically affirmed and then more or less frankly abandoned. Then, even as research seemed clearly to show a quite considerable, if not revolutionary, increase in population, a deeply pessimistic cast continued to mark the rural economy, if not fully "immobile," then stickily refractory to development from the thirteenth

25 From 21.5 to 28.5 million inhabitants. See Jacques Dupâquier, ed., *Histoire de la population française*, vol. 2 (Paris: Presses Universitaires de France, 1988), 61–68 and 438–68 (the latter section drafted by J.-Y. Grenier).

to the eighteenth centuries (subsistence agriculture, collective constraints, archaic techniques, generic allergy to change and so on).[26]

Some recent work, building in part on the pioneering dissidence of Jean Meuvret, has argued strongly in favor of a more positive appreciation of the agriculture of the Enlightenment, as it were. Cautious, calling for further investigation on numerous issues, J.-M. Moriceau is nevertheless resolute, and globally convincing, in his conviction that eighteenth-century agriculture moved ahead on several key fronts. Perhaps, there was no revolution before chemical fertilization and the beginning of mechanization, but the eighteenth century experienced a decisive "agricultural transition." Beyond clear-cut signs of higher cereal yield in the second half of the century, myriad innovations constituted a "break" with the past and an anticipation, even delineation, of the transformation of farming methods and of productivity that would bear full fruit by the Second Empire. On the basis of recent research, much of it his own, using heretofore untapped archival sources, mobilizing technical criteria often ignored by historians, such as the specific weight of grain (kilograms per hectoliter), Moriceau presents an agriculture that is increasingly effervescent well before the exhortation of the physiocrats (whose portrayal of agricultural decadence was vigorously contested by François Véron de Forbonnais, a major economic thinker, close to Gournay, who has not yet captured the attention he merits).[27] For Moriceau, the progress of this agriculture is much less usefully measured in the salons than in the fields, whose protagonists are remarkably

---

26 See E. Le Roy Ladurie, *Les Paysans de Languedoc*; "L'histoire immobile," *Annales E.S.C* 29 (1974): 673–92; "De la crise ultime à la vraie croissance, 1690–1789," in *Histoire de la France rurale*, eds. G. Duby and H. Wallon, vol. 2 (Paris: Seuil, 1975–76), 359–599; *Histoire des paysans français, de la peste noire à la Révolution* (Paris: Seuil, 2002); and, with J. Goy, "Première esquisse d'une conjoncture du produit décimal et domanial: Fin du Moyen-Age-XVIIIe siècle," in their *Les Fluctuations du produit de la dîme: Conjoncture décimale et domaniale de la fin du Moyen Age au XVIIIe siècle* (Paris: Mouton, 1972): 335–74. Pierre Goubert, *Beauvais et le Beauvaisis de 1600 à 1730* and "Les paysans et la terre: seigneurie, tenure, exploitation," in *Histoire économique et sociale de la France*, eds. F. Braudel and E. Labrousse, vol. 2 (Paris: Presses Universitaires de France, 1970), 119–58. Michel Morineau, "Y a-t-il eu une révolution agricole en France au XVIIIe siècle?" *Revue historique* 486 (Apr.–June 1968): 288–336; *Les Faux-semblants d'un démarrage économique: agriculture et démographie en France au XVIIIe siècle* (Paris: Armand Colin, 1971), where he denies a rupture in agricultural production and productivity, yet rejects a static view of rural France; "Révolution agricole, révolution alimentaire, révolution démographique," *Annales de Démographie historique* (1974): 335–371.

27 A good place to begin pondering the necessary reassessment of Forbonnais is Loïc Charles and Arnaud Orain, "François Véron de Forbonnais and the Invention of Antiphysiocracy," in Kaplan and Reinert, eds., *The Economic Turn in the Eighteenth Century*, forthcoming.

inventive, almost as much in the way in which they use the regnant norms/rules/laws in their region as in their application of new instruments and procedures.

With important territorial variations, the arable surface increased as a result of land clearing, a marked decline in fallow (much less rigidly and much more imaginatively integrated into rotations than supposed)[28] and the encroachment of wheat on the space heretofore consecrated to other (so-called secondary) cereals. New or more refined techniques for planting, harvesting and transporting improved efficiency and work productivity (including revamped ploughs with double-blading and deeper traction; better harnessing and more effective management of draft animals; increasing recourse to artificial meadows as well as the recovery of human and other waste for fertilization; revised methods and/or new tools for reaping, threshing, winnowing, sifting, outdoor hay-stacking and indoor storage). It is not clear to what extent the quite active societies of agriculture and the agronomist chapels in the provincial estates contributed concretely to this renewal.[29] Moriceau maintains that the weight of peasant autarchy has been overestimated, the penetration of commercial practices underestimated, the differences in incidence of innovation between small-scale and large-scale (physiocratic-style *grande culture*) exaggerated and the often-rehearsed gap between theoretical agronomy and practical cultivation overstated.[30]

A More Slashing Revision

On another scale, in a different style, mingling econometric analysis (undergirded by unexamined assumptions about how markets worked), targeted archival research and extremely thoughtful analysis, Philip Hoffman

28 See the provocative piece by Jacques Mulliez casting wheat as a necessary evil. Without ignoring its centrality, he deplores the tyrannical template of the wheat-centric agronomists of the Economic Enlightenment (generally followed by historians), who regarded corn as an affront (certainly not as a grain), detested the potato despite its socio-nutritional and economic qualities, and misunderstood the significance and practices of fallowing. The suppression of fallow was no more a mark of enlightened, rational agronomy than taking the Beauce as the paradigm of agricultural France. Mulliez concludes, quite cogently, that France was a country, not of agriculture, but of several concurrent, complementary and sometimes rival agricultures. "Du blé, 'mal nécessaire.' Réflexions sur les progrès de l'agriculture de 1750 à 1850," *Revue d'histoire économique et sociale* 26 (Jan.–Mar. 1979): 3–47.

29 In terms of its hemmed-in problématiques, in some ways the information-rich study of André J. Bourde is quite dated: *Agronomie et agronomes en France au XVIIIe siècle* (Paris: SEVPEN, 1967).

30 J.-M. Moriceau, "Au rendez-vous de la 'Révolution agricole' dans la France du XVIIIe siècle. A propos des régions de grande culture," *Annales. Histoire, Sciences Sociales*, 49th year (1994): 27–63.

reaches conclusions largely congruous with those of Moriceau in his engaging long-run tableau entitled *Growth in a Traditional Society: The French Countryside, 1450–1815* (Princeton, 1996). Strategically, he aims to demolish what he calls the consensus view (the *Annaliste* sediment of a more homogeneous and linear historiographical trajectory than the one Moriceau chronicles), to fathom scholarship's "astounding" inability to explain economic growth despite the "extraordinary attention" devoted to it since the epoch of Adam Smith, and to boost the claim for the utility of an "economics" approach to both old and new societies (3–20).[31]

So Hoffman rejects Marxo-Malthusian ideas, repackaged by numerous *Annales* researchers, of agrarian stagnation and structural inertia, Bloch's thesis that small farms and resistance to enclosure and individualistic enterprise occluded development, the cultural arguments of Weber and Polanyi that cast peasants as immanently uneconomic actors and the general characterization of France as a (predominantly) subsistence economy at least until the Revolution.[32] Self-sufficiency proved to be largely a myth, especially in the Paris area, as did tropismatic village community opposition to change (33, 37, 81, 94, 198). A luminous and original study deeply renews our understanding of the rural labor and rental markets, of the dynamic role of credit and thus of the very choreography of socially differential agrarian economic activity (including mobility, clientelism, wage formation, supposed land hunger and the reciprocal advantages of much-maligned sharecropping) (41–80).[33]

31 In the case of the Old Regime, Hoffman's rhetoric is sober and even understated, save the following somewhat mawkish and pious plea, meant to echo Thompson's bracing call for posthumous reparation, that to deny the benefits of economic analysis (implicitly to ordinary people) "… does a terrible injustice to the dead, by denying that they were capable of strategic behavior" (8).

32 Hoffman reminds us once again of the positive (emulation) and perverse (distortion) effects of obsessive comparison with England, conducted by contemporaries and, in retrospect, by historians, which merits, in my view, a global (revisionist) synthesis, perhaps in the manner of Renaud Morieux's *Une mer pour deux royaumes. La Manche, frontière franco-anglaise XVII*[e]*–XVIII*[e] *siècles* (Rennes: Presses Universitaires de Rennes, 2008), without forgetting the trailblazing template of François Crouzet focused on the economy from a quasi-institutionalist perspective, "Angleterre et France au XVIIIe siècle: essai d'analyse comparée de deux croissances économiques," *Annales E.S.C.* 21 (1966): 254–91. The American historian might have paid more attention to the *other* obsession that exercised parasitic effects on French historiography from the 1930s, through the putative *Trente Glorieuses*, and perhaps beyond: the riveting, perhaps sometimes overawing preoccupation with *croissance*, Hoffman's very own theme.

33 The only element I missed here was an energetic problematization of the cliché of the "seigneurial reaction" (64, 103).

Deploying his "total factor productivity" indices, the practitioner of Carlyle's dismal science claims that the overall picture in the eighteenth century was decidedly less dismal than generally portrayed, albeit Malthusian tensions persisted, that growth was manifest, particularly after 1750, and especially, if erratically, in the Paris basin, among other areas, unevenly favored: temporal and regional differences alienate Hoffman from the consensus view (132–33, 136). Neither enclosures nor technological change explains the growth in the Parisian basin; instead, Hoffman underscores opportunities stemming from the heady development of the Paris market (145, 171). Yields increased for some of the same reasons that Moriceau adduced (e.g., soil penetration, seed selection, and fertilization) (150–51).

Productivity gains and higher yields, *pace* the physiocrats and Marc Bloch, were independent of farm size; before the age of chemical fertilization and mechanization, what drove agricultural productivity, for Hoffman, was nothing in the usual refrain along with farm size (such as demography, class structure, landlord–tenant relations or the "obstacles raised by peasant mentalities," a quaint and opaque formula[34]): "rather it was taxes and prices, and even more so, peace, demand from large cities, and access to trade" (162, 190–91, 205). Like Karl Gunnar Persson, another "new" economic historian whom we have discussed, Hoffman places considerable emphasis on declining transport costs as a powerful growth stimulus (96, 102, 184–85, 204). The exculpation of French landlords I find cogent, and the minimization of the influence of collective constraints in farming an interesting yet less convincing proposition (187, 189).

Culture and Agriculture

Far from being parochial or clannish in his way of thinking and doing history, Hoffman evinces nevertheless some ambivalence on the significance of cultural variables. Evoking "a cultural shift from an ideal of reciprocity to one of individual gain," he contends that when one scrutinizes it closely in two regions in the eighteenth century, "it bore no relationship to economic activity." More broadly, in the same discussion, he warns against "confus[ing] culture and the economy, which, at least in early modern Europe, were two largely independent spheres" (189).[35] I have never found evidence of this sharp estrangement. I construe the economy as a simultaneously material

34 Hoffman summons the largely discredited, hyper-unproblematized concept of "mentalities" elsewhere (88, 144, 189).

35 The "it"—the deep cultural shift evoked here—is hard to follow in its implicit permutations across time in this woolly paragraph (189).

and symbolical phenomenon; save in "Galilean" (and occasionally cliometric) terms, I cannot imagine an economy that is not subject to constant cultural intervention, at every level of perception and representation, decision making and action; and culture, never in a heteronomous relationship with the economy, depends on it every day in one way or another, particularly for matters of production and reproduction, exchange and diffusion, access and (re-)appropriation, institutionalization and so on. Even issues such as moral hazard, on which the economic historian insists in a very fruitful manner, are permeated with decisive cultural conditioners (41, 78–79, 198–200, 205). The same might be said for notions of honor and reputation in reference to the search for and allocation of credit (73–74). Hoffman himself points to "important social and cultural implications" that engagement in the local market elicits and acknowledges that, to get at certain questions concerning the economy, "we must know all the details of local life," many of which are cultural, and I don't think he codes "details" here pejoratively (198–99). In the last two paragraphs of this fine book, the author still seems more comfortable with the idea of a disjunction between the cultural and the economic, but he notes that, at least in traditional societies, economic predictions are "indeterminate", for the outcome—the equilibrium?—depends on "the indigenous culture." It is not clear, however, why he assigns culture to local (subordinate? passive?) status, while the "economic and political forces" are somehow above or at least devoid of other cultural influence: "And it was these outside forces, not the peculiarities of local customs, that ultimately explained growth" (205). It does not seem to require a hermeneutic leap to imagine a "market," driven by powerful "outside" (disembedded) forces, ostensibly free of cultural taint, which is in the end utterly corrosive of the so-called indigenous culture.

A Legend in the Field

Jean-Marc Moriceau and Philip T. Hoffman, like everyone who writes about agricultural growth (and subsistence issues), cite the herculean (and deeply insightful) labors of Jean Meuvret, a self-effacing pioneer whose massive thesis (and postdoctoral work) did not appear until well after his death, thanks to the energy of his wife, colleagues and students. On the basis of a few published articles and what was not yet called a buzz traversing the corporation of early-modern historians, he was the scholar I wanted to meet when I began working on my thesis in the late 1960s. Thanks to Old-Regime-style networking through the masonry of *normaliens* that stretched from Yale to the rue d'Ulm, I benefited immensely from his counsel and encouragement from the very start of my two-year thesis sojourn in France. In his eulogy, Richard Cobb, *le plus français des historiens anglais*, remarked that Meuvret "did not have much esteem for American historians."[36] I did not detect this bias or suffer from it. He was unremittingly affable and mightily voluble: he not only responded with precision to all my queries, but also launched into enthralling, improvised *cours magistraux*, on the mode: "everything you ever wanted to know about provisioning [or about agricultural technology, or about archival research], but never dared to ask." These lectures usually began at the end of his seminar, held in the Sorbonne, during our deliciously protracted, dawdling walk up the boul'Mich (in the day of cafés galore and bookstores rather than numbingly formulaic clothing shops) to the Luxembourg RER Station, whence he returned to Sceaux. Still, it would have been of great

36 The most telling evocation of, and homage to, Meuvret, in my view, comes from the beguiling pen of Cobb, as different a personality from the French historian as I can imagine, yet a close friend. In deference to both exceptional scholars, archival rats and frères-ès-froment, I maintain the French: "Mais où justement n'est-il pas allé, cet infatigable voyageur-ès-archives? Y a-t-il une commune de France qui n'ait pas vu son passage? Existe-t-il un dépôt d'archives, soit départemental, soit communal, qui n'ait pas eu sa visite, en quête d'une mercuriale de plus, d'un terrier jusque-là inconnu? Je me rappelle une occasion, il y a une quinzaine d'années, quand, dînant chez les Meuvret, quai de l'Horloge, je lui ai dit que, travaillant dans le grenier de la mairie de Brie-Comte-Robert, me servant d'une dizaine d'Almanachs du Département de Seine –et-Marne en guise de table, j'ai vu au passage des terriers datant de la fin du XVIIe siècle. Inutile d'ajouter que, la même semaine, M. Meuvret a pris le car de Brie, à la porte de Vincennes. Ses passages à Rouen, ses aventures, rue de Crosne et dans les ruines du Palais de Justice, ses montées à la maternité du Mont-Saint-Aignan, endroit que se disputaient les filles-mères rouennaises et les archives de la Seine-Inférieure, les habitudes quelque peu balzaciennes de l'archiviste en chef de l'époque, les bizarreries de l'archiviste adjoint, les exercices de gymnastique du chat de ce dernier, appelé *Boufflers*, comme M. Meuvret grand amateur des papiers jaunis et quelque peu rognés par les rats, tous les épisodes rouennais font partie de cette riche encyclopédie d'anecdotes et de souvenirs qui constituent l'essentiel de ce que j'appellerai la littérature meuvretiste… Mais il y a eu encore les récits au sujet de Beauvais, de Chartres, d'Avignon (dont l'archiviste de l'époque portait le sobriquet de *Tête de Veau*—il était en effet peu aimable, c'est le moins qu'on puisse dire), de Langres, de Marseille, il y a eu les excursions dans *le plat pays*, par les Routiers de Normandie et les Cars Renault. Il y a eu les patientes explorations des fonds de certains châteaux … S'il avait *écrit*, au lieu d'avoir *parlé* ses souvenirs, ils auraient constitué un récit de voyage aussi riche, aussi picaresque que *Gil Blas*."

Cobb then described exactly the experience I enjoyed many years later, following a modified itinerary, consequence of Meuvret's departure from Paris for the southern suburbs: "A 6 heures, nous sortons ensemble [from the National Archives]. Combien d'entre nous ont connu ce cheminement long, parfois périlleux, aux méandres aussi imprévisibles que ceux de sa conversation, de la rue des Francs-Bourgeois jusqu'au quai de l'Horloge, passage pour lequel il fallait compter au minimum trois quarts d'heure. On marche fort lentement, M. Meuvret parlant, faisant d'un bras un geste circulatoire. Premier arrêt devant l'église des Billettes. M. Meuvret me fait face, il

advantage to me had these six masterful volumes appeared at the outset of my scholarly odyssey.[37]

Cobb lamented Meuvret's lack of ambition for himself rather than for others. Yet it is difficult to imagine a project more ambitious than Meuvret's, at least as it was posthumously reconstituted. He envisioned his enterprise as an undertaking in three parts, "complementary and solidary": the first, a volume on French cereal production during the Old Regime, focused on the "technical and social milieu"; the second, a study of the grain trade and price movements; and the final installment, the "police of grain" and the monarchical administration, as well as the repercussions of subsistence crises on the political and policy spheres (1977, 1: 14). It would be temerarious to attempt to summarize the six volumes, which in fact cover only the first two parts; instead, I shall comment on features I find particularly salient, astute or controversial. Reflecting on the apparent tensions between political and economic temporalities, and introducing as primordial the spatial dimension that eluded Labrousse, Meuvret quite self-consciously, yet often only implicitly, adumbrates a specific epistemology for the study of the economic in past time.[38] This compulsive archival hunter–gatherer reproaches historians who have worked in his area with a lack of theoretical musing, of critical self-examination and of comparativist disposition, the

tourne sur lui-même, pour souligner un point capital. On re-démarre. Deuxième arrêt, devant *La Bière*, parfois devant le kiosque à journaux; achat du *Monde*, et de nouveau, on arrive à l'essentiel. Traversée précipitée et terrifiante de la rue de Rivoli, au moment même où les feux se mettent au vert. Troisième arrêt au bas de la statue d'Etienne Marcel. Puis, fuite en avant encore plus périlleuse, au milieu de bruits de frein, pour traverser le quai. On atteint tout de même l'autre bord. Je transpire. Quatrième arrêt devant les bouquinistes. Cinquième arrêt sous l'Horloge. Sixième arrêt devant un antiquaire qui expose de la faïence chinoise. Septième arrêt devant la porte du 39. 'Montez un moment.' Le moment se prolonge, fort heureux, toute la soirée." R. Cobb, "Hommage à Jean Meuvret," *Bulletin de la Société d'histoire moderne*, 71st year, 15th series, no. 3 (1972): 5–9.

37 J. Meuvret, *Le Problème des subsistances à l'époque de Louis XIV: La production des céréales dans la France du XVIIe et XVIIIe siècle* (Paris, 1977), 2 vols.; *Le Problème des subsistances à l'époque de Louis XIV: La production des céréales et la société rurale* (Paris, 1987), 2 vols.; *Le Problème des subsistances à l'époque de Louis XIV: Le commerce des grains et la conjoncture* (Paris, 1988), 2 vols. See full citations above, n. 16.

38 Or as George Grantham elegantly describes his quest: to craft "economic history as a scientific discipline—how time-specific conditions interact with timeless economizing to produce an economic *history*." "Jean Meuvret and the Subsistence Problem in Early Modern France," *The Journal of Economic History* 49 (Mar. 1989): 187. The notion of "timeless economizing"—is it an anthropological constant? a (neo?-)classical postulate?—invites debate.

absence of which allows ideology a free reign. Faithful to his demographic interests, he contrasts his privileged period of Louis XIV's long ascendancy, when "the excessive rise in the price of cereals was a sign of death," to an eighteenth century when it announced "cyclical storms" heralding grave social and psychological disruption, but the distancing of "tragedy," a claim for which—as he well understood—one could find locally thousands of exceptions (1977, 1: 13, 15, 17, 26–27, 104–07, 143).

Crises and Prices, Structures and Conjunctures

He asserts—without working out—the case for a stark discontinuity between the Ludovican hecatombs and an eighteenth century where crises are of palpably lesser gravity, the litmus being exclusively demographic. His optimistic evaluation is as unconvincing as his contextualization is intriguing and somewhat peremptory: "the revolution of subsistence manifested symptoms and developed its effects in an unchanged technical framework in which there still held sway the old ways of farming, the old modes of soil utilization, to which we can add the old rural custom, the old regime of privileges, and a largely unaltered distribution of landed property." Rather surprisingly, he places "the critical point of the subsistence revolution" before 1750, without elaborating his argument, save to place the emphasis quite plausibly on the attenuation of annual price fluctuations, notably the "spike points," capable of "prompting panics" and, in their wake, "lethal dearths" (1987, 1: 215–16).[39]

Prices beguile Meuvret; they seem to bear a burden far more portentous than a (mere) marker.[40] As I suggested, I find that sometimes he does not

39 I find Meuvret *slightly* more persuasive—despite the lack of demonstration—when he abandons "subsistence revolution" in favor of the postulate of "a suppression of food risk, at least in the acute form in which it always had been [heretofore] known," and again extremely thought-provoking when he links this notion, not in the first instance to urban provisioning—not really his direct concern—but to the attitudes and behavior of "the peasant masses" who, he argues, undergo a transformation, resulting in an amorphous (but apparently decisive) "new psychology" that frees them from certain "fears" about their own survival that affected their inclination to work their land (owned or rented) with care and to enter the commercial circuit (1987, 1: 215–16).

40 See his methodological cogitations on price history, including a critique of Simiand and an un-Labroussean interest in the representation of prices (and wages) on the part of contemporaries. *Inter alia*: "The price thermometer is that of the physician: one must learn how to read it. The fever that it measures is an indispensable symptom to discern, but it must be brought into perspective with other indicators and interpreted as a function of the general condition of the sick person. It is quantitative, but must allow a closer connection with the qualitative" (1977, 1: 32–41).

articulate the relation between the *conjoncture*—crucial concept for him, Labrousse and the whole Braudelian generation—and the structure(s) that he reconstitutes patiently, almost piece by piece. It should be noted in passing that he does not disdain the "event"—the anathematized "événementiel" of the *Annales*—especially from the perspective of the actors in his richly textured, nonlinear story, and he sustains some interest in the political, especially state making, not dismissed for the nervous cadence imputed to the political or for its putatively anecdotal or mostly ephemeral impact on what matters most. He also sketches a vision of the study of political economy that must take account of "the realities"—he means social, "technological," economic—in order to be credible, a position that would place him in agonistic relation to some of the recent work that we are discussing in this book (1977, 1: 15–16, 19–31, 45).[41] Shaped by the totalizing aspirations of the *Annales* milieu—thus his inclination to treat "French agriculture considered as a whole, even French society taken in its entirety"—Meuvret knows nevertheless that "France's name is diversity," as Lucien Febvre put it, and that the study of (agricultural) rurality is inseparable from the growth of gargantuan urban markets such as Paris. Yet he believes that it is "probable that a certain unity reigned in the agricultural economy," for reasons linked to technological and structural constraints (social, mental, logistical and so on). Still, he rejects the notion of immobility that seduced certain of his colleagues. Concretely, in relation to the growth issue, he postulates the very strong likelihood of an increase in yields from the end of the seventeenth to the end of the nineteenth century (1977, 1: 46–53, 211–15).[42]

---

41 Meuvret emphasized the generally neglected role of the *technique* (that I rendered in the case above "technological"), a concept that he cast in broad terms, but that he analyzed, concretely and with acuity, in the text (see 1977, 1: 24, 41, 51, 103–82 for example), and especially throughout the notes, three volumes that merit consideration in their own account. He also intimates a dualism "realities"-mentalities (or "états d'esprit") that demands elucidation (1977, 1: 45).

42 Arguably, one could make the case that Meuvret waffled on the issue of inertia, or looked at it with ambivalence. He evokes in the next volume "the structural fixity, at least relatively, not only of the agricultural system, but of the whole of the rural economy that reacted around it." He enumerates various obstacles to English- or Dutch-style innovation in farming practice, which he did not see as prodigiously difficult to achieve: congealed customs and fossilized institutions, privileges (fiscal in the first instance, then hunting, among others) and, above all, land distribution, geographically fragmented and apportioned in a socially unequal and "often anti-economic" manner. Yet Meuvret refuses arrant pessimism: the operations of diverse farming enterprises on the ground "prove the possibility of multiple adaptations."

Technology, Innovation and Growth

No one has written more compellingly about Old-Regime agronomic/agricultural techniques than Meuvret.[43] Space remains crucial for him: he underlines the geographical distribution of different plowing tools and modalities, of (notoriously insufficient yet differential) fertilization practices, of hay shortages and so on (1977, 1: 103–10, 121–27). From my experience as a consultant to French mills, I can affirm that he possesses a better command of the *valeur boulangère* of seventeenth- and eighteenth-century varieties of wheat than most modern millers today have of the limited array of authorized bread-making types of grain they use. Still, I regret that he has so little to say specifically about flour (1977, 1: 145–47). He recounts sowing—decision making, soil preparation, passage to action—in a sprightly idiom between a cautionary tale and the farmer's almanac, including the requisite proverb ("It is better to have sowed densely than sparsely, in order to preempt harvest damage"), advice conditional in real life on economic means, soil type, the pressure of time and weather and the "extremely thin margin of security" left by various other pitfalls in the process (1977, 1: 145–63). Agronomy flourished in what I call the Economic Enlightenment, according to Meuvret, because of the interpenetration of agro-reformist, experimental-scientific, salono-academic, practical farming and public-administrative milieus. The people who got France's veritable agricultural prospects wrong were the urban writers, without a clue to farming, and the physiocrats, familiar with the rural universe, but quixotic in their overestimation of the promise of agricultural regeneration (1977, 1: 58–65, 68–69, 85).

Here the reader must be attentive to his own prejudices (1987: 1: 9–10, 47–54, 58–65). Somewhat more enigmatic, and problematic, is Meuvret's desire to give the study of cereal trade and grain markets "its natural foundations that the state of agricultural productivity imposes" (1977, 1: 47). Why natural? As opposed to cultural? What does natural signify? Is this formula a neo-Malthusian credo? A whiff of early structuralism? Or a technologically driven aesthetic of realism in the manner of Sigfried Giedion, *Mechanization Takes Command: A Contribution to Anonymous History* (Oxford: Oxford University Press, 1948)?

43 Meuvret also has interesting views on the sociocultural, political and juridical framework for (and/or embedding of) the massively, inherently technical character of farming. He calls attention to the primacy of *la coutume*—the codification of traditional usages—which enjoyed more day-to-day local traction than royal legislation. Yet he does not sufficiently develop the ways in which customary practices (concerning behavior, interaction, informal dispute resolution and so on) condition agricultural life and in the end suggests that the lack of a veritable, promulgated code penalized the rural world (1977, 1: 77–82). In the last analysis, in case of deep conflict between the social and the technological, on the one hand, and the juridical on the other hand, the latter inexorably cedes: "Men do not always have the laws they wish, but in the long run, they keep only those that they tolerate" (1987: 1, 69).

Meuvret, as we have seen, is not wholly consistent on the question of the obstructive capacity of agricultural practices in the question of growth. By and large, however, he maintains that it is too easy to condemn globally the ensemble of "old agrarian ways" as an "essential obstacle to agricultural growth."[44] The old technology was not a monolithic block, not without practical utility and thus not an inexorable barrier to change. For example, collective obligations, and communal regulations more generally, did not systematically constrain peasant behavior (certain crucial collective practices, such as pasturing, benefited the well-off minority, and often invited transgression), and peasants rejected "forced rotation schedules." In the quaint idiom of nineteenth-century prefects and twentieth-century agents of the Renseignements géneraux, the rural historian contended that the "esprit public" did not resist the suppression of fallow per se, but feared the diminution of land planted in grain: "arable land was everywhere… a sacred thing," whence the hostility to the encroachment of animals and the modernizing schemes of certain reformers (enclosures, starkly individualistic ethos).[45] In the end, the "major resistance to agricultural progress" resided less in this or that traditional practice, but in "a totality of collective representations"—modern translation of *esprit public*. He never elaborates, but collective psychological factors, perhaps more in the vein of Febvre than Bloch, weigh heavily in Meuvret's analysis, as does the moral climate that seems intimately related. His peasant—when he generalizes, social differentiation within this massive population fades into the background—is not La Bruyere's, to be sure, but this actor is inveterately frightened, as "he is less a businessman than a man of fear." If he has grain in surplus, he worries about not having enough should the next year be unfavorable, and he is inclined to hold on to it, to the profit of rats and weevils, and, of course, if he does not have enough right now, he is convulsed with apprehension (1987, 1: 12, 14–15, 22, 30–31, 38–43, 45, 208, 211–12, 215; 1988, 1: 19, 146–47).

Grain Trade, Transportation and Psychology

Jean Meuvret's final posthumous volume, concerned largely with the grain trade and its backward and forward linkages, is the least finished, yet far from

44 Cf.: "the initial factor in this decisive change [the eclipse of 'great dearths'] could not be plausibly located in the domain of agricultural production whose fundamental conditions remained for a long time without any essential alterations" (1987, 1: 216).

45 Cf. Meuvret's percipient remarks on "the contradiction between the concern for food and the concern for money," which touches not only on the issue of subsistence and market penetration, and price behavior, but also on the broad "monetary" problematic that interested the author (1987, 1: 208).

the least accomplished. It abounds with rich, original analyses that cause me at once joy and melancholy, because they remind me most directly of our conversations, of his passing and of my apprenticeship. His chapter on storing and granary formation, developing the notion of "spontaneous stockage," is the finest study of the question, albeit incomplete. If various leaseholders and *fermiers* amassed the most significant "recurrent stocks" and if stored grain played a crucial role as a bank and a credit vector ("lending grain, means of prestige, means of power, means of exploitation"), Meuvret's demonstration of the role of the regular clergy in the provisioning circuit is among his richest insights.[46] Once again, the constraints that fix limits are psychological as well as social, technological and economic (the political vein is unmined): "Eat one's grain, or sell it?" The historian of agriculture reminds us, as Bruno Latour recently put it, that "rationality is woven from more than one thread."[47] He cautions us that "selling grain at the highest possible price" is not the only rational decision that an actor could make and that ostensible hoarders are as often as not "distributors of food" rather than "bull speculators." Here it would have been useful to reflect on the articulation of rural capitalism with the network of reciprocities (Meuvret's favored trope of "solidarities and complementarities"), conceptions of equilibrium and notions of the moral economy (perhaps more in the direct line of James Scott than of E. P. Thompson (risk-averse, subsistence-first peasants, a socially undifferentiated image that clashes at least implicitly with Hoffman's peasants operating increasingly in an economy of active exchange rather than "of subsistence").[48] The grain merchants in this rural environment are nonspecialists, and they are often involved with seigneurs (noble, bourgeois and, in a loose sense, ecclesiastical) and with their collecting agents (1988, 1: 13–46).

The granular treatment of transportation scrutinizes conditions of production as well as outcomes. Meuvret maps out the advantages and limits, natural and man-made, of water vis-à-vis land (the state's role is more manifest here, yet still not fully developed) and the cost–benefit calculus that must take into account,

---

46 This line of investigation led me to undertake my first published article: "Lean years, Fat Years: The Community Granary System and the Search for Abundance in Eighteenth Century Paris," *French Historical Studies* 10 (Fall, 1977): 197–230. Later, in the spirit of his broader concern about stockage, I wrote: "Grain and Flour Conservation in Eighteenth-Century France," in Marcel Gast et al., eds., *La Conservation des grains à long terme*, vol. 3 (Paris: CNRS, 1984).

47 Bruno Latour, *Enquête sur les modes d'existence. Une anthropologie des Modernes* (Paris: La Découverte, 2012).

48 James C. Scott, *The Moral Economy of the Peasant: Rebellion and Subsistence in Southeast Asia* (New Haven, CT: Yale University Press, 1977).

beyond just price, the (relative) certainties as well as the (chronic) uncertainties of the weather, the durability of capital equipment, the extent and reliability of human capital (a highly fragmented system, an infinity of small actors, rarely specialized, full-time and part-time, occasional robust shippers, numerous "boutiquiers de la navigation"), the speed/time factor, the reckoning of risks of accident, the security of merchandise in transit (possibilities of conditioning, likelihood of deterioration and so on) and the various modes for coastal navigation including boats, barges and vessels, beasts of burden and carts of manifold sorts (he works out dexterously, for example, the strengths and weaknesses of the hauling wagons: their capacity, their wheel and axle assemblage, the braking mechanisms, the energy or draught animal requirements, maintenance and so on; and the need to factor in the expenses of dismembering boats at the end of certain voyages or replacing animals working with water carriage). Once again, Meuvret casts into relief the immense weight of space in all its diversity and in multiple registers, the "tyranny of physical geography," to be sure, but also changing fiscal, juridical, administrative and customary (usages including weights and measures) regimes.[49] Peerless on description and taxonomy, the historian did not have time to work out the implications of the transportation situation for the provisioning of markets, in particular urban centers (47–96).

Meuvret discusses the late seventeenth-century grain trade in extremely general terms; here it is hard not to feel, with real intensity, the sketchy nature of a scholarly project under construction. This is a commerce highly uneven in rhythm of activity, recruiting from a wide social spectrum, expanding and contracting according to the harvest and the business cycles, undercapitalized, unattractive because of the unfavorable risk/profit ratio, but not especially perturbed by the police, often indulgent. Fragmented economically, highly dispersed spatially, Meuvret's grain trade had a hard nucleus of regulars, especially in the cities and their hinterland, and a shifting periphery of "occasionals," opportunists and/or part-timers exercising several occupations at once. Certain types, evoked in passing, interested him particularly: the "plebeians," the "blatiers," moving grain on the back of a mule from one place to another, yet profiting from their mastery of "les trucs du métier" that gave them a "specialist's" advantage in the microcosm; transporters, engaged incidentally in the trade, on a wholly different scale from *négociants*, who filled the hold of a cargo ship when the opportunity beckoned; inn- and tavern-keepers, who served as correspondents ("commissionnaires") for urban-based traders, sometimes stored grain or facilitated illicit sales on

49 Note his intriguing reminder that there were monetary change-rate differentials even within the realm, disappearing quite slowly despite the standardizing appetite of the administrative monarchy, which gave rise to "complex speculations from one place to another, despite their unification by the link of a national currency" (1988, 1: 178).

sample off the market; *maîtres de postes*, privileged transporters of people, goods and mail, who used the leverage of information—a sort of precocious insider-trading—to engage sporadically in grain business; certain market officials and even administrative or judicial officers, using their authority to undertake deals that were illegal and meant to be sub rosa. He introduces figures such as factors, about whom we have learned a great deal since, and hints at the protean role of credit, which we have come to understand as both highly variegated, ubiquitous at every stage, and decisive in terms of assuring circulation and transactions. He intimates how family networks (or firms) reduced business costs by assuring trust and connection (1988, 1: 97–143; 2: 83, 94).

The "circuit of cereals" depends above all on harvest outcomes, but it is also mortgaged to the anxiety of peasant growers, whose typology is barely spelled out. They retain the bulk of their harvest: fearing risk, they restrict sales, which increases instability and, in turn, thus aggravates risk, especially in the (structural) absence of "sufficient inter-regional and international compensations." With regard to instability not only of supply but also of demand, Meuvret probably exaggerates "the important fraction of the urban population," a sprawling, motley bourgeoisie that stretches from "officers of finance and justice" to physicians, lawyers, certain shopkeepers and even archers of the constabulary, which drew its food supplies, including grain, from rural properties of diverse size and yield that they owned. This analysis leads him to provocative suggestions—not fleshed out—about demand elasticity on grain markets, especially in good times, and the quasi-uncommercial character of local markets that do not seem to have a collector vocation in some central-place cartography. The moral economy insinuates itself again, without pronouncing its name: the rural population in particular shared the expectation that, in a world governed justly, prices should remain more or less immobile. This "psychological atmosphere hostile to any change" crept into the fully commercialized grain markets. Given the heterogeneity of practices, weights and measures, application of regulations and the psychological climate just elicited, Meuvret asked his characteristically trenchant question: how were "professional merchants" to behave? Save in Paris and a handful of big cities, they had little interest in declaring themselves openly; various kinds of camouflage protected them (1988, 1: 145–58).[50]

50 For perspicacious remarks on the characteristics of "marketed and nonmarketed corn" by an excellent economic historian operating from a vantage point quite different from mine, see G. Grantham, "Jean Meuvret and the Subsistence Problem," 187–88, and passim. Grantham insists much more than I on the functioning of monetary circuits in price formation, in shaping grain circulation and in generating (in part) subsistence crises. Ibid., 196–97. I note in passing that I think he misreads Meuvret on the impact of moral economy values on peasant comportment ("unvarnished fantasy," he scoffs). Ibid., 198.

Meuvret goes on to sketch succinct portraits of some of the players who enter into the market, directly by selling or through credit relations, including more or less entrepreneurial *laboureurs* and *fermiers* (and *fermiers–laboureurs*), various seigneurs and seigneurial agents, certain officials and perhaps the elite of millers, whose trajectory he only begins to outline. If he claims that most wholesale transactions occurred off-market—a somewhat rash generalization—he adds that, in any event, they were not wholly insulated from the market. The French historian brings his exceptional familiarity with the rural world to bear in arguing that the relative immunity enjoyed by many wholesalers was directly linked to their role as collectors of dues and fees of various sorts in kind, which enabled them to summon the patronage of powerful interests to obtain police tolerance. In kindred manner, army and navy victualers—provisioning oligarchs—about whom we know astonishing little, reaped the benefits of the same regulatory leverage. Meuvret reiterates how transportation was crucial in shaping the character of the trade in grain, a cumbersome merchandise of low unit value. It discouraged what he calls centrifugal traffic moving toward the ports and frontiers, and did not facilitate centripetal circulation toward Paris and other urban agglomerations, especially north of the Loire. He notes, but barely begins to account for, the "common" phenomenon, as much in periods of calm as in phases of agitation, of significant price differentials for the same merchandise, at the same moment, in different sites: the deeply destabilizing problem that the physiocrats and other liberals promised to remedy. Yet he maintains, without bringing proof to bear, that in the absence of a national cereals market, one can speak nevertheless "in the very least of a quasi-national system of prices," an opaque system that he does not unpack (1988, 1: 158–87).

* * * * *

It is no easy matter to imagine, let alone determine, the (possible) impact of agricultural growth on contemporary representations of supply, from popular as well as administrative and elite perspectives. Shortages provoked anxiety; but inquietude was consubstantial to the uncertainty that dominated the world of the Old Regime. Given their structural character, neither anxiety nor shortage issued necessarily in collective action—either the best known sort that we call popular or another kind that I associate with local police behavior. There is no mechanical threshold after which police indulgence cedes to severity or popular consternation spasms into violence. Ideologically, the people and the police expect little variation in harvest outcome, measured by grain availability and price at the marketplaces; practically, they are accustomed to a certain dose of it. Neither is particularly forgiving when hard times strike; the behavior of neither is readily predictable. Beyond the (exogenous, portentous) specter of famine that contests the (normative, soothing) vision of Cockaigne, there are many other factors that come into play in structuring and triggering collective action. I discuss some of them in the next chapter.

Chapter III

COLLECTIVE ACTION AND ITS ACTORS: THE MORAL ECONOMY AND THE MARKET, THE PEOPLE AND THE ELITES, DISORDER AND ORDER

The social order, especially in the towns and cities, was always a work in progress, a daily construction. It was framed and constrained, but not irrevocably determined and articulated by royal, parlementary and municipal law. The law enforced and reinforced it, but could not on its own produce and reproduce it. By social order, I mean a system of relatively stable relations among groups and individuals founded on certain implicit reciprocities (such as respect for each others' vital interests and customary rights) and on open-ended negotiations concerning respective claims upon the community and the polity whose urgency varied according to shifting circumstances. The understandings that undergirded this process of forging order did not by any means preclude frictions and even frank conflict. These counterpoints did not, however, ordinarily compromise the state of public tranquility that constituted the collective objective. Despite fundamental socio-economic, psychological and cultural cleavages, by and large no one had reason to subvert this order, if the integrating mechanisms functioned. They included built-in forms of recourse, institutional and informal, local and central, for dispute settlement, and for compensations and sanctions that obtained general approbation (allowing for protest at the margin).

Everyone concurred that a reliable system of provisioning was the sine qua non for the maintenance of social peace and a modicum of social cohesion, and for the fruitful operation of the economy on which everyone depended, directly or indirectly. That meant, at least in urban locus, a regular supply of grain and flour, almost exclusively for bakers, and of bread in sufficient quantity, of satisfactory quality and at accessible prices for the final consumers. The quest for daily bread was the cardinal preoccupation of the vast majority of inhabitants. At this social moment, norms and expectations had to be fulfilled: it was the litmus of success, not only for the authorities of all stripes but also for the community as a whole. Save for the usual number of cynics, misanthropes and proto-anarchists, no one had an interest in seeing it explode or implode. The rich and the poor, the dominant and the dominated all shared a stake in sustaining tranquility, for disorder, in its various avatars, menaced them all (while opening opportunities for a small number at various places in the social hierarchy). They all lived under the tyranny of grain, even if the elites enjoyed a diet that did not confine them to cereal dependence in a strictly nutritional way. No threat was more deeply destabilizing (and mobilizing) than manifest shortage, though the dread of hunger itself could place great strain on the system: in the end, no one ever became fully adjusted or inured to the corroding uncertainty of daily life in an environment that could not be mastered.

The passage to action was rarely mechanical, the knee-jerk response to the price register or to some other, always fatal stimulus. The crowd-in-the-making was inherently combustible, but it rarely erupted at the first provocation or summons. The stewards of the public order had some chance to act or react. Habitually, the administrative and/or judicial authorities—the police—practiced a sort of subsistence prophylaxis. In case of breakdown, however, they did not have fail–safe protection. The situation became imminently calamitous once the shared assessment of the community loomed as irretrievably bleak and propelled it to the point of panic. When consumers began to clamor that they would "rather be hanged than starved," the recourse to instrumentalized disorder seemed to be the only way to bring about a restoration of order. It took multiple expressions: demonstrations, assemblies ("mobbing"), *émotions* (which were to riots what *cherté* was to dearth), riots, rebellions, uprisings and so on. The operation could be relatively pacific or extremely violent; self-consciously disciplined or chaotic; highly focused on specific goals (such as blocking or seizing grain or flour) or more diffusely driven by anger and rancor; undertaken with the overt or more usually tacit approval (sometimes complicity) of authorities, or launched without consultation or "diplomatic" calculation. According to many historians, collective action often took the form of what E. P. Thompson, the distinguished British scholar, famously baptized the "moral economy." This chapter discusses some of the debates generated by attempts to account for the behavior of that abyssal entity known (or unknown) as "the people."

The Flour War as a Window on Change: Capitalism and Feudalism

In *The Flour War: Gender, Class and Community in Late Ancien Régime French Society*, Cynthia Bouton has written a deft and provocative book on the most famous single subsistence uprising (1775)—in fact, a cluster of cascading riots—in the eighteenth century.[1] She is most persuasive in her anatomy of the events: social recruitment of the insurgents, types of collective behavior, ideological templates, genesis of conditions and relations that help account for the dynamics of interaction and outcomes. She is less cogent when she ventures to make of the Flour War "a unique window" (xxi) on prerevolutionary France, when she casts it as a marker of cumulative change rooted in a more or less extended chronology and a harbinger of what will unfold (xxix); in a word when she overloads its conceptual and analytical carrying capacity. Bouton is right to be ambitious, although I think she could have built directly on her elegant internal analysis. The problem is her ability to sustain more sweeping (and sometimes woollier) claims—for example, that "the Flour War reflected the larger processes of transition within Ancien Régime society by containing within itself changes both of scale and scope," (251) or that through the Flour War "we can see that by the late eighteenth century the pace of change in France had accelerated, with multiple consequences" (260). On a more delimited register, there are many intellectual and sociopolitical forces anterior to the Flour War that account for the hardening of the conception of property rights more compellingly than the outburst of 1775.

Though I regard as excessively sanguine (and impossible to substantiate) the claim that "by the late eighteenth-century, France had mastered … the subsistence question," I concur with Bouton that the foreboding of hunger persists remorselessly.[2] She argues that it both finds expression in and strains the framework of the moral economy configuration. Rather than reifying an intemporal and static moral economy, she tries to build in changing socioeconomic and political structures (despite problems with fixing chronology), the specificity of the often perfunctorily treated rural experience (more or less palpably marked by the quasi-colonial relationship with Paris, alternately symbiotic and predatory), and the complexity of gender relations (turning on an exemplary problematization of the supposedly predominant role of women in gate keeping and riot comportment) in order to recast its functioning.

One of the most original parts of the book is the chapter devoted to the (Tilly-esque) idea of uneven development of capitalism and centralization, broad categories of activity that condition such phenomena of change and resistance to change as market penetration, shifts in land usage and allocation,

1 C. Bouton, *The Flour War: Gender, Class and Community in Late Ancien Régime French Society* (University Park: Pennsylvania State University Press, 1993).

2 Cf. the intense political and social fear in England of hunger-driven "infuriated mobs." Christian Petersen, *Bread and the British Economy, c. 1770–1870*, ed. A. Jenkins (Aldershot, UK: Scolar Press, 1995), 97.

as well as agricultural technology, bearing collectively on production and productivity, on commercial patterns and practices, and on relations of domination and subordination. Capitalism looms ominously throughout the book: the author does not come to grips with it in a methodical fashion. We know that it is at work, in various loci, in overt and in subterranean fashion, but it escapes a probing examination in terms of its means and ends, save in its implacable "proletarianization," or its unexamined engendering of the so-called national market (26, 47, 182, 229, 249, 252).[3]

The dialectical (yet not necessarily social) antithesis of capitalism with feudalism—a term that appears to be used interchangeably with "seigneurialism"—also enjoys a foggy prosperity in this study.[4] Inscribed in ineluctable transformative/transitional processes that hark back to the days of Sweezy and Dobb, feudalism is never unmasked in an analytical fashion that reveals concretely its social and economic (and surely also political) role.[5] Acutely and fruitfully critical in her assessment of the historiography of many important questions—this is one of the great strengths of the book—Bouton's heuristic skepticism suddenly turns asymmetrical when dealing with

3 Statements such as the following cry out for unpacking: "Capitalism—commercial, agricultural, and industrial (or proto-industrial)—had made significant progress over the course of the century" (219). And, apart from the pertinence of the term, with its strong ideological charge, and its capacity to do rigorous sociological work across time, "proletarianization" raises a major structuring question: a century after Jean Jaurès, both a major historiographical influence and a leading political figure, and a long half-century after Ernest Labrousse, in broad ideological sympathy with him, are we any closer to understanding how to articulate, and weigh, the narratives of growing prosperity (recently boosted by the application of the "consumer revolution" argument to France) and of growing pauperization? Does it suffice merely to characterize this tension as the founding ambivalence of the eighteenth century?

4 See the symptomatic allusion to "the specific historical conjuncture of the development of capitalism in the context of a still-dynamic feudal structure. . . ." (251). Or the even more assertive and peremptory: "There tends to be an almost universal neglect of the fact that, in France, the emerging market economy and the centralizing state were developing within the context of a still dynamic feudal/seigneurial society" (27). I believe that the issues of capitalism (in particular, with priority) and feudalism (even more for the powerful imaginary it orchestrates at least till the end of the eighteenth century as for its alleged socioeconomic vitality) merit serious scrutiny. Yet these notions will, I fear, be dismissed as mere cant unless they are developed. In the context of the Flour War, the question remains whether Bouton can, in fact, discern as much as she claims about widening social and economic inequality, for example, in these few weeks of intense turbulence (251).

5 The original debate, which appeared in the pages of *Science and Society*, was reprinted as P. M. Sweezy, et al., *The Transition from Feudalism to Capitalism. A Symposium* (New York: Science & Society, 1963). A much expanded collection of essays was published as

the arguments of Guy-Robert Ikni and Florence Gauthier, who postulate a resurgent "feudalism" that bears directly and indirectly on (rural) subsistence insurgency which, in the late eighteenth century, betrays a neo-millenarian character—"an essentially egalitarian program"—that repulses feudalism and capitalism, a thesis that, in my view, they fail to sustain in their writings (xiv, 26, 39).[6] If most historians prudentially keep their distance from C/capitalism, hydra-headed snare, it appears that "feudalism" is enjoying a certain comeback, as a protean conceptual vector rather than a category of social analysis—regression or reversion?—especially among historians of economic thought, perhaps because it has serious implications only for how we see the (relatively remote) past, not the present or the future.[7]

Politics and Populism, Conservatism and Progressivism, Liberalism

When I characterized grain riots as "primitive" political gestures 45 years ago, I was reacting against the Marxizing tendency to deny them political agency for lack of necessary prerequisites, among them class consciousness. In a way that, retrospectively, seems timid and oblique, I wanted to affirm the political voice of the participants, and their desire and capacity to make claims upon the stewards of power and the owners of property. I think Cynthia Bouton gets this right, not because of, but despite, the various teleologies that tempt her. I resonate emotionally, though not intellectually, with the populism that traverses her study and congeals in crescendo at the end—populism as the counterpoint to miserabilism, as these notions are mapped out by Claude Grignon and Jean-Claude Passeron.[8] I find Bouton's sociology too hazy, lodged in unexamined assumptions about social structure and dynamics. When she writes about "the class basis for participation" in 1775, I am

---

R. H. Hilton, ed., *The Transition from Feudalism to Capitalism* (London: New Left Books, 1976). A generation later, Brenner reopened some of these dossiers, but focused initially on why capitalism generated so little allure to land-owning peasants. Robert Brenner, "Agrarian Class Structure and Economic Development in Pre-Industrial Europe", *Past and Present* 70 (1976): 30–74.

6 See F. Gauthier and G.-R. Ikni, "Introduction" and "Le Mouvement paysan en Picardie: meneurs, pratiques, maturation et signification historique d'un programme (1775–94)," in their jointly edited volume *La Guerre du blé au XVIII*e *siècle. La critique populaire contre le libéralisme économique* (Montreuil: Editions de la Passion, 1988), 7–30, 187–204.

7 See my remarks in chapter six, devoted to the "new political economy" in history.

8 *Le Savant et le populaire, misérabilisme et populisme en sociologie et en littérature* (Paris: Seuil, 1989).

not sure what she means, any more than I am when she evokes "a middle-class consciousness around the idea of property" (221, 231). Given her own emphasis on the extreme "diversity among the common people," I don't see the point of superimposing anachronistic taxonomies (29).[9] She knows the personnel of the rioters better than any previous scholar, and on this as well as on other points, she understandably wants to distinguish the Flour War, her *fond de commerce.* Yet I do not see the evidence, given the scale and range of description that her proposal implies, that those who formed the rank and file of the Flour War battalions came more frequently from the lower ranks of the common people than the rioters who were their predecessors, presumably as a result of accelerated proletarianization (249).

Aside from the epistemological futility of such essentializing, I do not see the utility of viewing food riots in terms of a dichotomy between "an essentially conservative" vision of an ideal society (a point of view ascribed to most historians who have looked at the question) and a presumably progressive perspective espoused by a narrower cadre of percipient commentators (28). Depending upon discursive tools, prior experience and shared memory, specific circumstances, evolving commercial and social structures, and so on, the affirmation of certain rights or the demands for guarantees, for vengeance and/or retribution or for simple assistance can be construed as backward or forward looking, or perhaps as simultaneously nostalgic and anticipatory (to use a Marxizing formula with a visionary hue) or at once wistful and lucid (anchored in the ongoing task of community construction); or the historian could resist the binary summons and instead focus on the ambiguities, the tensions and the ways in which the several tendencies subvert each other.

To cast into relief the significance of the Flour War moment, Bouton deploys a before-and-after contrast on a number of issues. Such a comparison, as I suggested, is often hard to uphold. I think that she could have strengthened her case had she clarified the relationship between the first liberalization, sketchily evoked, and the second, Turgot's. "To Louis XVI's ministry, which was intent on implementing massive changes in the process of provisioning in particular and mobilizing the country's resources for greater wealth in general," she writes, "the Flour War appeared to signal danger" (248). Did

9 I am struck by the implicitly magical and teleological character of the reasoning that makes of the Revolution a transmogrifying agent: "On the one hand, only the force of Revolutionary experience transformed the common people into the politically radical *sans-culottes*" (29). In fact, beyond the invocation of the vulgate (incarnated by Albert Soboul's *Les Sans-Culottes parisiens en l'An II. Mouvement populaire et gouvernement révolutionnaire: 2 juin 1793–9 thermidor an II* (Paris: Librairie Clavreuil, 1958)), we have only the very vaguest notion of the "making" of the *sans-culottes* and an extremely uncertain purchase on their sociology. See Kaplan, *La Fin des corporations* (Paris: Fayard, 2001).

this ministry—Turgot's—learn nothing from the previous liberalization experience? If so, why? If they did draw lessons, what were they? Why the cautious understatement on the augur of the Flour War? Aside from apparent changes in the social recruitment of rioters, set in the context of the very recent and vivid memory of the hundreds of riots of the 1760s, it bellowed danger because Paris was critically involved.[10] Bouton accords little attention to the ideological (and political) setting. She assimilates Turgot to physiocracy in ways contested by many historians. Thus, she discerns "a clash of two world views—one the popular 'moral economy' and the other the up-and-coming physiocratic vision of laissez faire…" (256).[11] Can one reduce Turgot's conception of market principle and practice and his anthropology of man to "the physiocratic vision of free trade?" (199). Indeed, in the aftermath of the physiocratic debacle of the early 1770s, can one serenely refer to the physiocratic brand of laissez-faire as "up-and-coming?" The intellectual lineage, say, of a fervent Revolutionary liberal such as Roland de la Platière, passes through Turgot to connect, not to Quesnay, but with Gournay.[12]

Stalinism, Neo-Liberalism and a Popular Political Economy

Cynthia Bouton contributed a chapter rehearsing her argument on the moral economy to a collective work entitled *La Guerre du blé au XVIIIe siècle* (Paris, 1988), edited by F. Gauthier and G.-R. Ikni.[13] As in her book, the strengths lie in the ways in which she elicits the distinctive features of rural insurgency and the capacity of the crowds to channel older forms of the protest repertory in the service of "a much broader critique of society" (110). The weaknesses

10 The deficit of attention to memory in this study is conspicuous—all the more so because it invites problematization in the context of the so-called moral-economy studies where it often occupies a significant, albeit sometimes silent, place. I wonder, for instance, about the (apparent) utter absence of trace of the famine plot persuasion (172) in 1775, extremely widespread through the Terray period, and very much on Turgot's mind when he went after Sorin and Doumerc, grand public victualers, and negotiated with the Leleu, prospective government suppliers.

11 Since Bouton situates her vantage point unequivocally from below rather than from above, it is fair to ask her to explain what she means, for instance, when she refers to "practices associated with free trade" that provoked popular discontent (83).

12 The ideogenetic issues involving influence, transmission and (re-)appropriation remain among the major challenges of an intellectual history that wants to be sociocultural. The "Gournay" of Turgot, for example, is not Mably's Gournay in *Du commerce des grains* (1775).

13 The book showcases a French translation of E. P. Thompson's famous article on the moral economy, long before there was even a viable project afoot to translate *The Making of the English Working Class,* hardly testimony to French scholarly cosmopolitanism.

reside in her failure to make more explicit the attributes of this critique and its relation to the spectacular mutation of royal subsistence policy, to the structural changes in the provisioning trade and to the politicization of social and economic relations on the ground. In a rambling, impassioned and often cryptic introductory essay, the editors of the volume seek to cast preoccupations such as Bouton's (and presumably E. P. Thompson's) into a larger context/agenda, featuring an avenging moral populism. Even as it settles certain ideological and quasi-epistemological scores on the eve of the bicentennial of the (still radioactive) French Revolution,[14] this Introduction denounces the "economism" that nourishes both neo-liberalism (in its inchoate stage in the eighteenth century and its Thatchero-Reagan juncture in the late twentieth century) and a certain neo-Stalinism, reductionist, objectively complicit with liberalism, and historically programmed to disdain and to obliterate the "retrograde" popular movements on which it fed (7, 8, 11, 15).

Paradoxically, joined at the hip by an economic materialism that steers them, Fukuyama-like, to the end of history, the "Stalinist and neo-liberal versions of the French Revolution" reject "universal natural rights and the political," the terrain that Gauthier and Ikni believe leads to a profound rereading of the past, from below and from above, in the last quarter of the eighteenth century, predicated on the unyielding imbrication of liberty and equality, rather than their fatal antagonism (15, 16). A reflection on Thompson's moral economy prompts the authors to call for a moralization of the economy—an ethical urgency today perhaps even more pressing than it was during the Enlightenment and the Revolution (18). In opposition to the pitilessness of physiocratic natural law that privileges the rights of property and liberty over the right to exist, a posture canonized by successive phases of capitalism, and in opposition to a historiography that united Marxists and *Annalistes* in a Galilean embrace ("the imperialism of the theory of demographico-economic determinism" (21)), Gauthier and Ikni appeal for a (more or less militant, civic and humanist) rehabilitation of the sociocultural (curiously, but symptomatically, without taking into account either the swelling wave of postmodernism or the so-called new cultural history, already flourishing in many places in Europe and in the USA) (21).

This is not the place to engage in the polemic embodied in a text that is jeremiad-manifest as much as historical monograph/historiographical inventory. Gauthier and Ikni attempt to corner the market on fraternal, communitarian and ethical sentiment in the service of a populist vision of history, expressed in a "popular political economy" or a "popular moral economy" that is no more

14 See Steven L. Kaplan, *Farewell, Revolution*, 2 vols. (Ithaca, NY: Cornell University Press, 1995).

reducible to the "old monarchical paternalism" than it is to the "new political economy" (25). This popular political economy is founded on a universal right to exist and on a rejection of domination, exploitation, bellicosity and accumulation committed in the name of the putatively inviolable right of property or of the claims of arbitrary authority of any sort. This popular political economy will venture to realize its normative conception—redolent in certain ways of the *police des grains*—in the French Revolution (27–29).[15]

Florence Gauthier develops her position on the project "for economic democracy" that Robesierre styled "popular political economy" in a chapter christened "From Mably to Robespierre. From the Critique of the Economic to the Critique of the Political, 1775–1793." There are many puzzling aspects to this piece, most already adumbrated in my evocation of the Introduction, including the decision to begin with Turgot in utter obliviousness to the first liberalization, which did not fail to mobilize her protagonist Mably, who wrote his first, mordant critique of physiocratic liberalism in 1767.[16] The discussion of the (second) Mably suffers from a lack of probing scrutiny of certain pivotal notions, such as market, trade, "commercial capital" and even property (the latter right destined to be constricted, yet in ways and with justifications that need to be examined) (114–21). A severe critic of "economism," Gauthier herself seems to presume that markets work like markets (within her particular taxonomy, opposing habitually overlapping wholesale and retail vocations and postulating a public–private discontinuity): in fact, market functioning, linked inextricably with regulatory practices, requires problematization in at least three periods, preliberalization, the more or less evanescent liberal phases of the Old Regime and of the class-based early Revolution ("liberal economist terror") (122, 127) and the halcyon Robespierrist years.[17] Though beyond our purview, the Manichean treatment of predatory capitalist grain traders plundering the

---

15 It is hard to penetrate undefined notions such as "the logic of the private retail market," devoid of historical contexualization and analytical precision (29).

16 Gabriel Bonnot de Mably, *Doutes proposés aux philosophes économistes sur l'Ordre naturel et essentiel des sociétés politiques*, written in 1767 (not 1768, as commonly supposed), but not published till considerably later. See the recent edition edited by Eliane Martin-Haag, collection *Philosophica* (Toulouse: Presses Universitaires du Mirail, 2012). For a fresh and cogent treatment of Mably's grain politics and philosophy, see Julie Ferrand and Arnaud Orain, "The Natural Law of Equality at the Heart of the Controversy between Mably and the Physiocrats," in S. L. Kaplan and Sophus Reinert, eds., *The Economic Turn: Recasting Political Economy in Eighteenth-Century Europe*, forthcoming.

17 It is staggering to read Gauthier's judgment that V. Ljublinski's extremely dated and tendentious book, *La Guerre des farines* (Grenoble: Presses Universitaires de Grenoble, 1979), "remains the best study of the formation of the private wholesale subsistence market in France in the 18th century" (121–22n).

poor requires a double deconstruction: as discursive archetypes or tropes and as alleged forms of practice (125). The supposed opposition of the natural/private to the political cries out for searching exploration (137). So does the contention that the notion of the maximum itself places into question the distribution of the means of production, issuing logically in "a critique of the bourgeois right of property" (127n).[18] Robespierre, following Mably, subordinated "the right of property to the right to exist" (131), but so did Galiani, Necker, Linguet, Briatte, Hume and, in their manner, Bossuet and Montesquieu, all of whom, like the Incorruptible, "refuse the autonomy of the economic" (134). Moreover, a repudiation of unlimited liberty in the grain trade does not necessarily suppose a rejection of economic liberalism in other domains.

Moral Economy, "Market Forces" and Price Fixation

In an imaginative and ambitious study that sweeps across two centuries, Dominique Margairaz and Philippe Minard use price fixation—local and national, popular and official, spontaneous and carefully designed—as a device to interrogate the moral economy as it emerged and evolved in many different sociopolitical and economic ecologies.[19] They offer a probing reading of the Thompsonian paradigm, epitomized in four rubrics of collective ideation and action: the affirmation of the community's right to dispose of its (own) resources, the latter notion more or less intentionally cast in amorphous terms albeit invested with absolute priority; the sanctuarization of the "just price" for consumers, understood in terms of a threshold of universal accessibility; the will to punish those who prey on the misery of the people; and the demand that the authorities furnish guarantees for the realization of these objectives (61).

The two historians lament a "dilution" and then a muddling of the meaning and precision of the Thompsonian moral economy in recent historiography, a corruption due to promiscuous, unrefined and/or unfounded usage. This is a thoughtful and fecund exercise, though I wish the authors had proffered a definition of the "market" (and "market forces"), a taxonomical term and marker in several different registers—institutional, social, ideological, moral and even political—that frames their entire discussion. Their reading of Thompson's conception is encomiastic and exigent. They challenge the

18 I do not find persuasive Dominique Margairaz's acrobatic effort to read the law of the Maximum as an expression of liberal predicates, but her discussion of the origins and application of this governing tool is much more enlightening than the treatment accorded by Gauthier. See note 19.

19 Margairaz and Minard, "Marché des subsistances et économie morale: ce que 'taxer' veut dire," *Annales historiques de la Révolution française* (2008), no. 2: 53–99.

temptation to reduce or distill it excessively: thus, the critique of C. Bouton for focusing narrowly on the "nourishing paternalism" at the expense of the idea of justice deeply rooted in community membership (59). Deploying my distinction/tension between marketplace and market principle, Margairaz and Minard argue for a popular consciousness of operating within a market structure, but the latter is not delineated beyond vague commercializing functions. We are more or less convinced that the members of the community understand their moral economy, but we do not know what they construe as a market, and I do not see the grounds for insisting that popular behavior—presumably in times of subsistence stress—does not constitute a rejection of liberalism: the question remains open. Yet I concur with the two authors that there is no necessary correspondence between the logic from above (based on Thomistic or *salus populi* postulates) and the crowd's sense of the moral economy (60–61).

I would contest the historians' suggestion that the price schedule (the *taxe*) bespoke a tightly normative approach, conveying the authorities' "conception of equity," apparently divorced from any empirical basis. Without abjuring their ultimate authority to impose socially and politically the most useful price solution, police officials at various levels, sometimes assisted by subsistence scientists and/or academicians, conducted hosts of tests (*essais*), some of them hinged upon dubious assumptions or sabotaged by interested parties, but others often reflecting reasonable estimates of the costs involved in bread making (from field, barn or mill to bakers).[20] Margairaz and Minard characterize the multiple social, moral and political stakes of the construction of a price schedule quite perceptively: its participation in a comprehensive vision of the hierarchical social order, the moral obligations consubstantial to that order

20 I know that it is crotchety, but I must note that the remarks of the two historians on the bread-making process do not inspire confidence. The yield of wheat into flour not only depends upon the specific weight of the former but also depends, crucially, on the milling diagram, in particular the targeted extraction rate. Flour quality is a highly complex notion that does not vary mechanically with the extraction rate; a darker flour does absorb more water than a whiter one, yet hydration and dough stiffness depend in important ways on the recipe, the age of the flour and its floor time, the season, the weather conditions and the use of improvers or stabilizers such as fava bean flour, which affects both color and amylasic action and so on. The humidity of bread refers to the amount of water it contains after baking, and is linked to staling; the authors probably meant hydration of the flour, or the dough-in-the-making (65). In the historical account properly speaking, it would have been extremely useful to explain the composition, if not the diagram, of the contemporary loaves, for example, the *pain à tout* (are we literally at 100% extraction without any envelope removal? Doubtful…) and the *pain miche* (67).

and the socially differential distributive justice that reinforced its coherence. I would have liked an unpacking of the *rapports de force* that they invoke, especially in terms of the conflict between bakers and millers, in particular reforming millers committed to the process called economic milling, and the more subtle yet acute strife generated by the deeper changes in the structure and practice of the provisioning trade that are not addressed here, especially the displacement of grain (and its increasingly defensive agents) by flour (and its increasingly aggressive agents). It would also have been helpful to glance at the larger debate over *taxation* at all levels, grain, flour and bread, and in particular the reluctance of many administrators of interventionist proclivity to have recourse to price-fixing because of unintended consequences and perverse effects (on the most obvious plane), driving away actors, but also in terms of the feedback mechanisms, i.e., the way in which a bread *taxe* constrained the price of grain (where the latter was formally allowed to fluctuate) (68).

Maximum, Liberalism and the Eclipse of the "Moral Economy of the Crowd"

The treatment of the maximum, as it traversed the Revolution's most intensely social phase, hinges on reasoning that is generally robust, but not always convincing and consistent with the earlier argument.[21] I find the distinctions between political economy (and perhaps economic policy) and a strictly political or moral approach (and the distancing of police from all of the above) to be woolly. Robespierre's chilling yet familiar (one could say traditional) reference to "the homicidal hand of the monopolist" invites comparison with this very theme that traversed the eighteenth century and attained an apogee of scrutiny during the phases of liberalization.[22] The claim that the inaugural maximum was in the first instance a measure of circumstance that followed the pattern of the "moral economy of the crowd" strikes me as very plausible, as does the proposition that the latter draws upon a "background of

21 Dominique Margairaz has already made the case that informs this study. See: "Le Maximum: une grande illusion libérale, ou de la vanité des politiques économiques," in *Etat, finances et économie pendant la Révolution française*, Comité pour l'histoire économique et financière de la France (Paris: Librairie de l'Imprimerie nationale, 1991), 399–428, and "Le Maximum, politique économique ou politique sociale?" in J.-P. Jessenne, G. Deregnaucourt, J.-P. Hirsch and H. Leuwers, eds., *Robespierre: de la nation artésienne à la République et aux nations*. Actes du colloque d'Arras (Villeneuve d'Ascq: Centre d'histoire de la Région du Nord et de l'Europe du Nord-Ouest, 1994), 263–78.

22 Monopoly as epithet and sociopolitical instrument remained important throughout the nineteenth century, spiking at several moments in the public and popular consciousness, at mid-century and—as noted here—toward the end of the century (97).

economic culture" (that the authors unfortunately characterize as a "common mental equipment," an outdated concept with no explanatory potency used repeatedly in their article). Much more problematic is the contention that the specific economic culture in question was the Gournayian current that Simone Meyssonnier audaciously baptized "egalitarian liberalism," but whose purchase in French society—Old Regime or Revolution—remains undemonstrated.[23] They make no case for this allegedly authentic liberalism as an operative ideological force (70–72; cf. 69 and 78).

Margairaz and Minard maintain arguably that the notion of the moral economy of the crowd no longer makes any sense once the maximum—the *taxe*—is generalized and all goods are treated equally. It is not clear to me, however, that this authorizes one to impute a theory of general equilibrium to Barère, a Jacobin who rehearses the Delamarist aphorism that circulation and *a fortiori* liberty are "the soul of commerce," and to affirm, with the discreet rhetorical abetment of Meyssonnier, the existence of a liberal continuity embodied by the maximum, allegedly a nondirigiste program, figured as mimicking the still undefined and unproblematized entity called market (74–75).[24] Is it sufficient to declare Barère a more or less quixotic utopian to shelter him from the charge of envisioning the existence of a popular right to existence or other rudimentary entitlements (an argument that does not depend on F. Gauthier's idiosyncratic spin)?

It strikes me, at best, as rash to make of the battle against hoarding the pillar of liberal policy—or rather the so-called "matrix of liberal political economy"—especially if one recalls that the ardent liberals, who toiled to implement liberalization (including Turgot), rehabilitated hoarding as a normal, fruitful commercial practice and ceaselessly denounced a putative popular right to existence as a benighted prejudice and a pretext for the most baleful kinds of arbitrary state intervention.[25] My position does not, incidentally, require me to view the maximums as a class program, to embrace certain Montagnards as proto-socialists, or to associate Robespierre with a

---

23 Simone Meyssonnier, *La Balance et l'Horloge, La genèse de la pensée libérale en France au 18ème siècle* (Montreuil: Editions de la Passion, 1989).

24 In an élan of casuistical voluptuousness, I suppose that I could propose that the *police des grains*, in its/their manner, also mimicked the market. I note in passing that, throughout this chapter, there is a strong, unspoken analytical embrace of classical/neoclassical notions of the market, market forces, and the laws of the economy (95).

25 Is it plausible to argue that hoarding, to the extent that it is less the expression of perfect competition than its antagonist, is inimical to liberal doctrine? In a stretch, perhaps theoretically; practically, during the eighteenth century and then in much of the nineteenth century, liberals refused to allow hoarding to be vilified and disqualified from the arena of normal commercial transactions.

putative popular political economy (though, again, I strain to discern the pointed distinction that the authors posit between a moral argument and political stand on the one side and the sphere of political economy on the other). The authors do not seem to serve their own cause in conceding that Robespierre was morally and politically willing to sacrifice the foundational liberal rights of property and liberty, at least situationally, as we have come to say. In the service of their polemical ends, the authors end up making implicit claims that verge on the extravagant, notably the notion of a full-fledged Robespierrist embrace of economic egocentricity (76–78).[26]

The Anatomy of "Rebellion"

In turning to Jean Nicolas' monumental *La Rébellion française. Mouvements populaires et conscience sociale (1661–1789)*, the scale of apprehension and anatomy shifts from several score to thousands of *émotions*, riots, movements, risings and so on, consolidated in 13 categories: subsistence unrest joins other rubrics of protest, some intimately linked to it (work conflict, for instance) and others focused on issues that bear unevenly, occasionally or rarely upon it (resistance to fiscality or to the military, judicial and police apparatus of the state or to its reform initiatives; acts of hostility to the nobility and its privileges, to the seigneurial system, to the church and/or religion, to claims of notables and to municipal authority).[27] The author proposes a series of typologies that take into

26 Along with Napoleon, Robespierre remains the great enigmatic figure of the Revolution. A steady stream of scholarship illuminates his itinerary, his thought and his action, without providing the quantum leap in understanding that seems requisite. Ruth Scurr's Robespierre-as-priest is an interesting take. *Fatal Purity: Robespierre and the French Revolution* (New York: H. Holt, 2007). Quite recently, Peter McPhee has offered a sympathetic account, attentive and rigorous. *Robespierre: A Revolutionary Life* (New Haven, CT: Yale University Press, 2012). In his insightful and somewhat mixed review of the latter, David Bell evokes François Furet's notion that the "best way of all to understand Robespierre may simply be as a pure unalloyed conductor of revolutionary ideology." This cryptic phrase, epitomizing an idealist epistemology that, in my view, leads to a historiographical cul-de-sac, desperately clamors for unpacking. D. A. Bell, "The Conductor," *The New Republic*, 5 April 2012. A radicalized version of that perspective, springing from a very different worldview, albeit with a similar presentist tonality, ventures an articulation of the ideological with the social, neither pure nor unalloyed. It is not the work of a revolutionary scholar, but strikes me as quite stimulating, in its critique of a conceptual and political "decaffeination" of the Revolution, its exegesis of "divine violence" and its empathetic portrait of The Incorruptible. See Slavoj Zizek's "Introduction" to *Robespierre: Virtue and Terror* (London: Verso, 2007).

27 Jean Nicolas, *La Rébellion française. Mouvements populaires et conscience sociale, 1661–1789* (Paris: Seuil, 2002).

account complementary and/or intersecting factors such as space and time (from the broadest purview: a regional geography of social turbulence and its seasonal rhythms; through a narrower gauge: the disparate and overlapping characteristics on the urban–rural spectrum, propinquity to power and to merchandise, relation to sites of exchange, storage and/or transshipment), modalities of action and targets of remonstrance and/or retribution, social recruitment/composition and gender (where Bouton's nuances cede to the enormous quantitative weight of women's presence, strategic and tactical (403–04)). The historian then traces a highly useful chronology of rebellion, habitually preceded by dearths issuing from more or less severe meteorological disruption, occasionally aggravated by war and often amplified by popular fear or panic, from the calamitous phases of Louis XIV's reign to the beginning of the Revolution before engaging in an exploration of recurrent themes and unresolved questions concerning the practices and meanings of collective action in the subsistence arena.

Even as I pay homage to this encyclopedic endeavor, I will raise several minor and a few more significant questions. I regret that Nicolas did not pursue the problématique of the "two Frances" which, in fact, is not a north–south story, with exceptions, save in crude term of seditious incidence, but one of a host of two Frances that are woven in the fabric of countless regions and subregions where there is what Bouton, following Tilly, calls uneven development and what Nicolas himself characterizes, in a shorthand that requires unpacking, as a differential hospitality to capitalism, a relative openness or closedness (343–46). An increase in the bread price of one sou per pound, in 1664 or a century later, is never "a slight augmentation" (350). Given the size of the pool, it would be churlish to expect a rigorous sociology of the actors, but it certainly is not enlightening to learn that "the people" of Saint-Lô, or elsewhere, join the fray, or that various "bourgeoisies" intervened at other times and places (391, 422). In the same vein, the timid rebuke to Bouton on proletarianization does not clarify the debate (403). Nicolas' partial and lucid test of one aspect of E. P. Thompson's (original) version of the moral economy argument in quantitative terms struck me as imaginative, though I would have liked to see him confront the model in full conceptual dress (411–12).

The Character of Eighteenth-Century Grain Riots

I cannot follow Nicolas in his characterization of the grain police as a largely unpredictable, if not fickle, undertaking (and this apart from the incongruities between various levels and jurisdictions of administrative action). At the risk of pushing the argument too far, I would espouse the antithetical position in affirming that there was indeed a police doctrine that structured both enforcement and indulgence until the liberal rupture: it was the institutionalization of the marketplace as a site of mandatory, regulated exchange (with some consensual exceptions) (411). This doctrine did not preclude pragmatic adjustment—on the contrary—yet it did not generate the sort of vertiginous uncertainty at which the French historian hints, in the wake of the physiocrats. The nature and organization of the provisioning trade evolve across the century, especially in large cities and their hinterlands, but this does not capture his interest. Nor does he take on the historiographical debate on market maturation and integration (here in the neoclassical sense of the notion of market operation).

On the impact of liberalization, Nicolas does not give full vent to the psychosocial approach that he says he wants to privilege (336). And on the still controversial question of popular politics, after a nuanced discussion, in the end he seems to come out more nearly on the side of the "primal scream" (368) as the expression of subsistence protest in the densely tumultuous 1760s than on the line of a more articulated political consciousness (long embryonic, but not necessarily archaic, old but not axiomatically obsolete), born of disappointment, indignation, disaffection and a sense of betrayal. In the 1760s an awareness of the king's unwonted emancipation (or disavowal) of his children-subjects may not have reached deeply into popular consciousness in this idiom, but there is considerable evidence for a widely resented feeling of abandonment by the government, at all levels, of its responsibility for the collective daily bread, echoed by consumers, and not exclusively in the hyperbolic expression of the famine plot persuasion or in the ritualized language of overheated and fugitive alienation (the *mauvais discours*).[28] Popular attitudes moved beyond fury against grain owners and traders and rancor at local officials. Scores of riots that I scrutinized denounced injustice, not just hoarding or monopoly or other discrete manifestations of antisocial crime. That injustice bespoke claims on the regnant order—political and social claims. I take very seriously Nicolas' sensible warning against succumbing to the populist siren; but it seems to me that he risks disposing of the proverbial baby with the bath water (423–29, 434–35).

The double process of the desacralization of kingship and of bread is initiated from above, not from below; in this light, Nicolas' reproach of my position as extreme strikes me as neither germane nor founded (432). Liberalization heralded a new politics grounded on a new relation between king and people, state and society. Standing in egregious violation of the laws of nature, the sacred

28 See Arlette Farge, *Dire et mal dire. L'opinion publique au XVIII*^e^ *siècle* (Paris: Seuil, 1992) and Lisa J. Graham, *If the King only Knew: Seditious Speech in the Reign of Louis XV* (Charlottesville: University of Virginia Press, 2000).

social contract of subsistence no longer possessed purchase, constitutional, juridical or moral. Corrosive of the monarch's traditional paternalistic role as "nourishing prince," the market principle embodied by the liberal reforms deprived bread of its residual sacred status, echo of the holy in the profane communion of ingesting shared daily fare. How could this dramatic recasting of responsibilities and relations not provoke a political reaction? That seismic shock elicited political responses from the people and the police that took the form, not of a precocious and implausible rejection of monarchy, but of a supplication and a summons addressed to Louis XV to assume the full burden and authority of kingship. I do not see why one has to "seek the political, if it exists [in *La rébellion française*] in the emergence of a collective will that goes beyond the subsistence problem" (435). To set the bar at this level of relative sophistication (does it imply a predicate of class consciousness?[29]) is once again to relegate subsistence insurgency to the realm of the primal scream and to assimilate politics to the ascension to citizenship in the Revolution.

Order

In his excellent *Grains de Désordre: l'Etat face aux violences frumentaires dans la première moitié du XIXe siècle*,[30] Nicolas Bourguinat shows how egregiously vain it is to imagine that regulation (the police of grain and, he rightly notes, of flour, of millers who are merchants[31]) gives way to a self-adjusting free trade (or the widely recognized efficacy of the free market) in the wake of the Revolutionary/imperial upheavals. He casts his problématique in terms of the ever tense and rarely static relations between state and society, of the ways in which a self-consciously political voice attempts to articulate economic behavior, driven by both creative dynamism (capitalism, a nascent industrial revolution) and venerable egocentrism (self-interest), with a notion of social order, a no less dynamic, protean and elusive work in progress. Order, the historian argues, was not reducible to legislation; far from determining it, law shaped the social order more elliptically, through processes of variable application issuing

29 Nicolas seems to outstrip (or transcend) here what he calls "les formes suraiguës de conscience de groupe" (429).

30 Nicolas Bourguinat, *Grains de Désordre: l'Etat face aux violences frumentaires dans la première moitié du XIXe siècle* (Paris: Editions de l'Ecole des Hautes Etudes en Sciences Sociales, 2002).

31 I think that the author could have seriously enriched his study had he looked more closely at what he calls on several occasions industrial milling, at the Darblay family which plays a crucial role in the transformation of the milling world, and more broadly, at the commercialization that preceded the industrialization of milling.

from confrontation, negotiation and compromise, as characteristic of the nineteenth century as of the eighteenth. Order depended equally on parallel processes that generated a system of social classification bespeaking pragmatic arrangements subject to acts of redress or rectification when it seemed to tolerate excessive injustice. Collective action or contestation, in particular the "violences frumentaires" that Bourguinat considers his "laboratory," are not necessarily or irrefragably subversive of the social order. Part of the play of confrontation and negotiation, quasi-institutionalized, they constitute a sort of "established disorder" that is dialectically engaged with the quest for order—the construction of the everyday order that I have conceptualized elsewhere (12–14, 345).[32]

Economism, and the Juggernaut of State-Making Capitalism

Bourguinat laments that nineteenth-century grain movements have heretofore been treated in a cramped "economistic and Labroussean perspective"—ironically and regrettably, the long taboo on subjecting the Labroussean approach to critical scrutiny, notably in France, has conferred upon it an ontologically pejorative cast. Bourguinat shares the culturalist antipathy for Ginzburg's Galilean paradigm: at numerous junctures, he deplores the blind spots and reductionisms of attempts to treat collective action in a purely quantitative way ("serial or sequential"), a disputable reproach that requires both richer elaboration and nuance (15–18, 351).[33] His target here

32 See Steven L. Kaplan, *The Bakers of Paris and the Bread Question, 1700–1775* (Durham, NC: Duke University Press, 1996), "Introduction." I would have liked for Bourguinat to elaborate concretely on the various ways, discursive and behavioral, in which "public order remained a floating and precarious" notion in both the Old Regime and the nineteenth century (337).

33 Cf: "Now, the typologies constituted by historians of grain violence, particularly with a view toward computer-based or cartographic treatments, have very rarely bothered to take into account these problems, which could invalidate the interpretations [of these historians]." Perhaps Bouguinat wishes to spare his targets or supposes, in the manner in which the French "microcosm" often operates, that we all know the incriminated parties ("Des noms! Des noms!"). It is not, however, fair play to cast aspersion without citing examples. Perhaps in part for generational reasons, I resonate more sympathetically with the revolt led by Roger Chartier against imposing a quantitative template on intellectual history (later cast as cultural history)—treating the (putatively superstructural) "C" in the same fashion as the E and the S in the paradigm embodied by the *Annales: Economies, Sociétés, Civilisations*—than with the more or less visceral antipathy to quantification of those who, though not quite digital natives, arrive on the scene just a step before the "millenials." After-shocks of post-modernism? In any event, the case for quantification made by Bourguinat's own generation is clearly much more

is the master of this field of study, Charles Tilly, in my view one of the great innovator-practitioners of social history and historical sociology.[34] Allergic to Tilly's long-run appetite, despite the fact that it is patently less noxious to lived experience than Labrousse's, Bourguinat taxes him, not without certain grounds, for a gaze blemished by a double teleology, the high-powered linkage of state-making and capitalist development that supposedly pigeonholes and distorts the nature, play and impact of grain movements, diminishes the weight of politics as an independent variable and blurs generally the role of agency (thus obscuring the logic and motivations of grain movements), first in the Revolution (to which Bourguinat wants to restitute a creative role, despite important continuities with the Old Regime) and then in the nineteenth century (not the triumphant, linear advent of market-driven modernity).[35]

Bourguinat rebuffs the idea, imputed to, if not strictly derived from, the Tillys (Louise joining Charles at several junctures) that subsistence-based collective action is basically a form and frame of the Old Regime, an emblem of archaism (the futile resistance of peasants to incorporation in a market-world). He suggests that nineteenth-century grain movements cannot be fruitfully understood as largely about the rejection of agrarian and commercial capitalism; nor can it be confidently assumed that public authorities usually embraced a laissez-faire point of view and exercised a generally effective mode of governance: at best deregulation was "a hesitant undertaking, accomplished in small steps, spread out over time." Finally—on this point I am in ardent accord—the Tillys' claim that a national market emerged roughly in mid-eighteenth century is at least a full century premature (15–20).

A Critique of Thompson's Moral Economy

In multiple forms, the theme of the moral economy infuses this book; Edward Thompson's pioneering work, which continues to generate debate, crystallizes

sensitive to both cultural history and to the broader taxonomic and epistemological issues to which he points—vaguely. See Claire Lemercier and Claire Zalc, *Méthodes quantitatives pour l'historien* (Paris: La Découverte, 2008).

34 Tilly's bibliography is a gargantuan treasure. Besides the well-known *The Contentious French* (Cambridge, MA: Harvard University Press, 1986), see the pioneering study "Food Supply and Public Order in Modern Europe," in *The Formation of National States un Western Europe*, ed. C. Tilly (Princeton, NJ: Princeton University Press, 1975), 380–455, and his elegant, synthetic essay, *The Politics of Collective Violence* (Cambridge: Cambridge University Press, 2003).

35 The following quotation conveys the author's malaise: "Because, at bottom, the rapid development of capitalism functions as a sort of monolithic specter always in the background, never in the full light of day" (17).

many of the issues that Bourguinat deems crucial, even as he recasts in part the focus, emphasis and analysis. He pays homage to the rich Anglo-American historiography inspired by Thompson, in which he is the object of both criticism (constructive and hostile) and reappropriation. In the latter realm, Bourguinat distances himself equally from the narrow usage of a moral economy restricted largely to the paternalism of prince and gentry, and from its dilatation that endows the laboring poor with rights to assistance and/or a living wage. He esteems that Thompson operates within a relatively static model based upon a crabbed bipolarity "patrician–plebeian"; accords too little place to the role of gender; fails to account for the ways in which the breakdown of consensual or contractual arrangements regarding subsistence, especially in big cities, results in violence; does not explain the processes through which cleavages of interest, profession and status are reconciled with the exigencies of community cohesion required for collective action; does not show how specifically the stakes of subsistence shape those divisions; and does not give full expression to the "plurality of relations of power or conflict" in such a way as to place into relief what Bourguinat calls the politics or the political (21–22).

Less militantly and with less ingrained panache than Thompson, Bourguinat identifies with the plight and aspirations of the crowd, though he enters the debate at a point where rescue and rehabilitation are no longer urgent requirements. The crowds—the de-essentialized plural is important—do not dazzle him, but impress him with their capacity to update and in some sense rebrand their way, first, of apprehending their concrete circumstances (in an implicitly comparative context inscribed in their collective memory) and, then, of affirming values, often expressed as denunciations and demands, concerning their role in and claims upon the community (or on multiple communities, vertically or horizontally connected). They view the world *politically*, through a double prism, normative and empirical, in which their quasi-contractual expectations coexist, often uneasily, with their perception of "sordid calculations and the play of interests" in their evaluation of the subsistence situation. Following William Beik, and my own arguments about the subsistence syndrome and the famine plot persuasion, Bourguinat considers numerous beliefs, such as the permanent horizon of a golden-age abundance, the subversion of princely beneficence and/or the planning and practice of monopoly and hoarding, not as myths, but as the collective popular recollection of past perfidies and the lucid intuition of maneuvers by various groups outside and inside public administration.[36] This complex subsistence politics calls for

36 William Beik, *Urban Protest in Seventeenth-Century France: the Culture of Retribution* (Cambridge: Cambridge University Press,, 1997); S. L. Kaplan, "The Famine Plot Persuasion in Eighteenth-Century France," in *Transactions of the American Philosophical Society* 72, no. 3 (1982).

a reexamination of the precarious social, economic and symbolic order built around grain, flour and bread (22–23).

Rejection of a Popular Political Economy

Even as Bourguinat reads the moral economy as "the play of the convergences and divergences" between the legislative/regulatory apparatuses and the demands for a form of "redistributive food 'justice' that underpins the founding arrangements and compromises of a communitarian order," he rejects the contention, ideologically and teleologically driven, that a popular political economy, sanctified by the burgeoning social movement of the Revolution, delivered the moral economy from a certain institutional co-optation and cognitive torpor (53, 92–94, 312, 355). Galvanized by a populist, sometimes lyrical vision of the affirmation of an expansive right to existence, heralding even more subversive sociopolitical and economic ambitions, the partisans of this argument pay little attention to the heterogeneous sociology of their actors; to the political divisions and resistance from within the so-called advanced revolutionary groups; to persistent tensions between hinterland and towns/cities, and between shop-workers and farmers; and to the structures and practices of the grain and flour trade and the processes of provisioning that shaped daily life as well as transformational and regenerative ideals.

Even as they posit a political mutation in the repertory and social eschatology of contestation from below, the stalwarts of the populist thesis postulate a vague nexus of affinities and linkages between the price-fixers and egalitarians of 1792–93 and "the first great social confrontations, contemporaneous with the physiocratic reforms." Allusion to the protracted and widespread trauma of the first liberalization—the dramatic rupture that constituted a veritable political mutation—of the 1760s? No, a historical truncation and abbreviation, an unrefined cut to the chase: the Flour War eclipses the far more dense socio-geography of eruptions of the prior decade, in part because it touched Paris and in part, paradoxically, because it involved, not a proto-Robespierre, but the iconic pioneer of liberalism in the eyes of today's true believers, Turgot, both more and less than a garden-variety physiocrat (373–81).[37]

Moreover, Bourguinat rightly observes that the command economy of the Mountain was not "in complete breach with the discourse of the traditional

37 On the wholly unconvincing case for a popular political economy, see Guy-Robert Ikni, "La Critique paysanne radicale et le libéralisme économique pendant la Révolution française: droit social, économie morale, ou économie politique populaire?" in *La Révolution française et le monde rural* (Paris: Editions du CTHS, 1989); Ikni and Florence Gauthier, "Le Mouvement paysan en Picardie: meneurs, pratiques, maturation et

subsistence riot." In his exploration of the continuities and discontinuities between the crowds that mobilized during the Old Regime, the Revolution and the nineteenth century, he notes a persistent legalism, a stubborn localism, a flexible arsenal for action, a relentlessly complex play between Power and the People (reciprocity, collusion, betrayal, revenge, submission, repression, rehabilitation, symbolic and material exchange) and a more ambiguous and subtle role for women than I have suggested that requires a sort of triangulation between the women, the authorities and the male protestors (311–16, 323–28, 332–35).[38] In what is globally an extremely insightful study, I would have liked a more robust explanation of the dynamic that transforms a crowd into a community (and vice versa); and I remain skeptical that the nineteenth-century crowds differ from their eighteenth-century counterparts by appealing more frequently to the authorities than to (Thompsonian?) notables (312–14).

Liberty and Regulation, the Strong and the Weak

Bourguinat ventures to work out the ways in which the discourse and appetite for liberty accommodated a dogged desire for regulation (from commercial and administrative actors, with merchants sometimes finding the same solace in the blocking of an outward-bound shipment and grain-owners in the *taxation populaire* of their merchandise as the baker derived from the published price schedule or ceiling).[39] On the one hand, the specter of a persistently shadowy entity called the free market invests the period Revolution/Empire and affirms its pretentions with increasing confidence in the course of the nineteenth

signification historique d'un programme (1775–1794)," in Jean Nicolas, ed., *Mouvements populaires et conscience sociale* (Paris: Maloine, n.d.); Gauthier, "De Mably à Robespierre. De la critique de l'économique à la critique du politique, 1775–1793," in Gauthier and Ikni, eds., *La Guerre du blé au XVIIIe siècle*; Cythia Bouton, "Les mouvements de subsistance et le problème de l'économie morale sous l'Ancien Régime et la Révolution française," *Annales historiques de la Révolution française* 68 (2000): 71–100.

38 Bourguinat has induced me to rethink my position on the role of women, which was closer to the interpretation of Cynthia Bouton, "Gendered Behavior in Subsistence Riots: the French Flour War of 1775," *Journal of Social History* 23 (1990): 735–54. Cf. the standard reflection on women in the front-lines of subsistence insurgency and on the alleged inclination of the government not to take women's participation very seriously, save in the case of food contestation. Roger Dupuy, *La Politique du peuple: Racines, permamences et ambiguïtés du populisme* (Paris: Albin Michel, 2002), 60, 108.

39 Here (355) and elsewhere (87–88, passim), Bourguinat tests the limits of his methodology on two registers: first, he never deals frankly with the extent to which he is hostage to various hues of official reality (dependence upon administrative correspondence in his efforts to attain what he construes as social reality—"le réel"); second, he extrapolates readily (perhaps imprudently) from administrative discourse to the logic or perception or

century. On the other hand, stubbornly local and chronic difficulties reinforce the hesitations of the state's superego, torn between the postulate that modernity/rationality require its withdrawal from the subsistence domain, assimilated to the economic field, henceforth severed from its traditional sociopolitical vocation, and the gluttonous anxiety that such a renunciation would imperil its stability, if not its legitimacy. Neither state nor society seems able to escape, night or day, an ever enthralling (albeit increasingly nuanced) version of J.-P. Hirsch's two dreams, in this instance, for example, "a known liberty and a hidden surveillance" (92). Extremely astute in his appreciation of this foundational dilemma, Bourguinat is nevertheless too parsimonious in his analysis of the process of separating the Jacobin (and neo-Jacobin) vision of an authoritarian regeneration of society from a nineteenth-century proto-technocratic understanding that social and economic progress were inextricably linked, the one with the other, and both with the state (94).

Beyond harnessing and canalizing a promethean developmental energy, at stake was the idea and practice of public order, which strikes me as a notion "less floating and precarious" for the eighteenth century than for the nineteenth century, though the Economic Enlightenment formalized the idea of a natural economic order that necessarily preceded (according to the *économistes*) the routinized, quasi-mechanical concept of public order. The rethinking of fundamental relations between state and society, police and people and—in Necker's almost incendiary terms—between property rights and popular rights (the claims of the strong vis-à-vis the claims of the weak) demanded a reordering of priorities, methods and legacies.[40] Two lines of analysis tempt Bourguinat. First, the question, already present in larvated state in the preliberal Old Regime, of orchestrating the coexistence of regulation and liberty, of private property and mandatory market transactions and so

thought of myriad social actors. For instance, to stay with a case I just invoked, the "tactical" acquiescence of grain growers to *taxation* (355) or the more sweeping (albeit somewhat oblique) conclusion concerning the established disorder (357): "It is thus not to be excluded that a large proportion of the actors, magistrates, protesters and even victims saw here a sort of established disorder, the expression of a communitarian moral code in the end preferable to the spectacle of injustice." Finally, if he rightly criticizes the implicit conceit of certain quantifiers that counting in some sense takes the place of a theoretical framing of problems in order to make possible various exegeses and interpretations, it is possible to read this reproach, at certain junctures, as a sort of defense mechanism for his own failure to reach a sufficient threshold of proof, for he bases extremely insightful analyses on few cases.

40 See the lamentably neglected text of Jacques Necker, far more than a pamphlet of circumstance, as the French say: *Sur la Législation et le commerce des grains* (Paris: Pissot, 1776).

on. I have no doubt of the concurrence of these apparently antagonistic ways in both police discourse and practice: this is where the constitutive ambiguity was lodged. For lack of demonstration, however, this historian does not convince me that "the idea of regulation had never been truly absent from liberal economic thinking of the second half of the 18th century." To make the case for "this principle of the non-contradiction between liberty and regulation," it would have been more rewarding to show where it was *truly present*: certainly not in the corpus of the grain-riveted physiocracy of the 1760s and early 1770s. In liberal practice, it certainly strains credulity to conceive of Turgot's quixotic plan "to pass on the cost of the average price-rise of cereals" to the bakers as an example of a regulatory surrogate or safeguard (87).[41]

The People and Established Disorder

The other, more problematic, but heuristically tonic, hypothesis posits a collapsing of the notion of regulation into the lived (and acted) moral economy, of assimilating state intervention—not to discredit or stigmatize it, but to situate it, socially and politically—to collective action, conceptualized as the necessity for the police "to show why the rationality of laissez-faire was superior to that of contestatory behavior," a variation of K. G. Persson's argument that efficient market operations obviate regulation (and implicitly render popular insurgency consensually superfluous) (337). Without illusion about educating the people, and with highly variable degrees of enthusiasm for venturing it, the physiocrats affirmed that, in any event, change (driven by *évidence* and natural law) would constrain them to abandon their prejudices; reading these prejudices as pragmatic ideology-forged-by-life, Galiani and

41 Nor is it at all clear in what manner Turgot deployed the "vigilance of the State" or how it acted in 1774–75 to prevent the public from viewing liberalization as a "noble or fiscal plot." The notorious famine plot persuasion mobilized considerable audiences in 1775: the nobility played no role, and fiscality was a subordinate theme. In 1846, Bourguinat points to a noble-driven famine plot rumor (167).

While I disagree that "the pre-revolutionary liberal doctrines were originally organized and limited"—the notion "liberal" here is far too nebulous to be helpful–I concur with Bourguinat's reasoned rejection of Dominique Margairaz's thesis that the Maximum of the Revolution was "derived from the very sources of French liberalism" (88). See Margairaz, "Le maximum général ou la logique des interdépendances économiques," in *Etat, finances et économie sous la Révolution française* (Paris: Librairie de l'Imprimerie Nationale, 1991) and "Nouvelles approches pour une vieille question: le maximum," in M. Vovelle and A. de Baecque, eds., *Recherches sur la Révolution. Un bilan des travaux scientifiques du Bicentenaire* (Paris: La Découverte, 1991).

Necker (the latter more sanguine than the former on the people's capacity for reason) postulated that the people would never abandon their claims upon property-in-grain and their solemn expectation of royal protection/intervention when necessary. At least through the Second Empire, officials remained exasperated at the unwillingness or incapacity of the people to understand the advantages of unfettered free trade.[42]

Bourguinat does not attempt to define the ubiquitous, ever-worrisome and always elusive "people," though they are major actors in his story: the task is simply intractable. In a somewhat scattered manner, he deals with various representations of the "people," never quite nailing the shifting relationships between various sorts of work (first urban vis-à-vis rural, then distinctions between different sorts of productivity in primarily city shops) and the taxonomic categories, inflected by ostensibly very different moral judgments (filth, crudeness and ignorance did not signify the same qualities or elicit the same reactions in the sixteenth and the nineteenth centuries) and by variable criteria of segmentation (compare Condorcet's purge of the "people" with Orléanist classification, or the sundry species of dangerous classes, marked as much by stereotyped origins as stereotyped actions) (279, 282, 284–97, 301, 304). The effort to salvage the people, as it were, by recasting their composition probably was tantamount to the exclusion of those who most readily fell victim to intense moments of ravaging hunger: though succinct, Bourguinat's portrayal of the savage and widespread reality of hunger, notably during the three great crises of the first half of the nineteenth century, is compelling, and he connects it cogently to the sense of outrage and the call for justice associated with the moral economy, which remains a coherent discourse at least till mid-century (240, 319).

The "riot" was the generic popular riposte to the proposition that the "harmonious play of exchange" could achieve the social concord that obsessed thinkers (and actors) such as Necker, who believed that only the state—through shifting policies of action and inaction—could assure this outcome (339). Nevertheless, everyone seemed to agree, from the rioters (said to work scrupulously to distinguish their comportment from any behavior

42 Cf. Adam Smith's comparison of religion and (regulatory) prejudice. Though both would presumably wilt under the impact of education, in chapter 5 of *An Inquiry into the Nature and Causes of the Wealth of Nations*, ed. Edwin Cannan (1776; repr. New York: The Modern Library, 1937), the philosopher underlines their symmetrically procrustean nature: "The laws concerning corn may everywhere be compared to the laws concerning religion. The people feel themselves so much interested in what relates either to their subsistence in this life, or to their happiness in the life to come, that government must yield to their prejudices… ."

smacking of criminality, a hyper-clean depiction that would have left Richard Cobb incredulous[43]) to those authorities who encouraged, tolerated or covered them and to those officials who excoriated the "unsettled" or "dissolute" climate, that regulations which the administration (at whatever level) tried to impose were "only applicable to the extent that opinion approved them," in the instance, the opinion, primordially, of consumers (342). It is in this sense that it seems fruitful to me to characterize subsistence violence as a "form of established disorder" (345).

The "People Problem" and Its Epistemology

Remarkably self-assured and commensurately brilliant, often highly imaginative, sometimes derivative, now and again quirky, *La Nature du people*, published by Déborah Cohen in 2010, heralds the arrival of a major new force on the French historiographical scene.[44] The title is promising, given the salience and stubborn elusiveness of the people as actor and category, and in light of the polysemy and ambiguity of the heavily solicited notion of nature. The subtitle is somewhat misleading, since the book barely deals with the nineteenth and twentieth centuries, and enters the twenty-first century only briefly, albeit tellingly, deploying bold comparisons in a militant agenda that generates unexpected dividends for the more narrowly construed historical project. Cohen does not resolve the people problem, as I have described it. Yet, amidst dozens of books that have ventured, in some way or other, to address the issue in the past three decades[45], hers is unequivocally the freshest and most

43 See R. C. Cobb, *The Police and the People: French Popular Protest, 1789–1820* (Oxford: Oxford University Press, 1970).

44 Cohen, *La Nature du peuple: Les formes de l'imaginaire social (XVIIIe–XXIe siècles)* (Seyssel:Champ Vallon, 2010).

45 I regret that the author did not conduct a critical inventory of this stock of works, either in the text itself or in an essay in annex in the vein of Peter Gay's dazzling bibliographical essays: *The Enlightenment: An Interpretation* (New York: Alfred A. Knopf, 1966–69), 1: 423–552 and 2: 571–705. (A second lament: absence of an index, a veritable plague in the French publishing world, out of phase with the modern epistémè).

For a very recent, highly un-Foucauldian reflection on one aspect of the notion and practice of the people, viewed largely from the perspective of the people, see Yves-Marie Bercé's engaging and incisive *La Dernière Chance: histoire des suppliques* (Paris: Perrin, 2014). Often perfunctory in its analysis (on the people as nature and nation, on the unfitness of the people to enjoy liberty, on sedition as the sole voice of people and so on) and cast in traditional history-of-ideas manner ("the movement of ideas"), Gérard Fritz's *L'Idée de peuple en France du XVIIe au XIXe siècle* (Strasbourg: Presses Universitaires de Strasbourg, 1988) nevertheless offers many telling insights (on the question of inequality, on the invisibility of the people—a theme that Cohen develops—and its ambiguous unity, and on the relation of people and king). Drawing on his excellent command of the

Revolution (and the anti-Revolution), Roger Dupuy has written a more sophisticated book—a series of short essays—that explores the equivocal notion of the political in popular and "populist" context in a globally familiar historiographical framework, leavened by sporadic polemical exegeses, reprimands and insights (on the salience of class and class consciousness in old and more recent debates, allegedly "archaic" comportment, an unproblematized gender issue, a fruitfully problematized rural/urban nexus, the religious fiber of revolt, the "strategic" popular choices constituting an "everyday" politics that somehow escapes the shadow of food preoccupations (P. Sorokin's "food *taxis*"), "localism" and community solidarity, and the tenacious dodginess of public/popular opinion). Dupuy, *La Politique du peuple.* Note, also, a collection of short essays, entited "Peuple, Plèbe, Populace: Idées, représentations, quotidien de l'Ancien Régime au temps des Girondins," several of which are quite suggestive, especially on the shifting representations of the people in the Revolution, albeit surprisingly indifferent to methodological issues. They appear in a special issue of the *Revue française de l'histoire du livre*, 59th year (1990). Globally, the contributions are strongest on discursive analysis (notably, J. Boutier, "Discours sur le peuple en révolte. Les lendemains d'Allassac" (22–27 janvier 1790) (185–202)) and weakest on sociology (notions of class within broader taxonomical systems). Daniel Roche's agile introduction is replete with insights on the paradox of the (perceived) strident voice of "mute" people, on the difficulties of definition of a protean and refractory category, on the people as beast and as child, on the fear of the conflation of ranks, on the matter of the educability of the people and on what he calls "Christian political economy," a notion upon which I would have liked for him to elaborate (17, 19, 20, 27, 29). In an imaginative and thoughtful book with a strong thesis that merited debate instead of quasi-universal neglect regardless of one's appreciation of its interpretation, Benoît Garnot explored the resistance of the "peuple," construed as the mass of the dominated and the vulnerable, to the efforts of a panoply of elites to regulate and domesticate them. It seems marked less by the seal of a Foucauldian disciplinary perspective than by a certain populism in the sense of Grignon–Passeron. See Garnot, *Le Peuple au siècle des Lumières: Echec d'un dressage culturel* (Paris: Editions Imago, 1990). Philippe Guignet organized a useful, comparative reflection on the urban "people." See Guignet, ed., *Le peuple des villes dans l'Europe du Nord-Ouest (fin du Moyen Age–1945)*, 2 vols. (Lille: Centre de Recherches sur l'Histoire de l'Europe du Nord-Ouest, Université Lille III, 2002–2003) (in epitome, this historian reports: "le peuple des villes existe, nous l'avons rencontré"). In his recent doctoral thesis, Vincent Danet has subjected the Guignet enterprise to critical scrutiny and, more broadly, has conducted an intelligent, refreshing, pugnacious and sometimes quite peremptory assessment of a vast swath of historiographical literature dealing with the conceptualization, definition and demonstration of the existence of (various avatars of) the "people." (Incidentally, he conducts an interesting, testy and uneven discussion of the evolution and tribulations of social history (with a special focus on its urban incarnation in the *Annales* manner), the strengths and frailties of the Galilean moment and the tensions between microhistory and canonic social history). Vincent Danet, "Le second peuple de Nantes au XVIIIe siècle: environnements du quotidien et interactions sociales", 3 vols., doctoral dissertation, Université de Nantes, 2011 (accessed through HAL: archives-ouvertes), I, 22–68. Danet has forged a conception of what he calls the "second people," by which he refers to the urban laboring population outside the corporate universe (though not necessarily outside its gravitational purchase). He fashions this view/category perhaps

provocative, even if she occasionally falls into the miserabilist/populist trap[46] that she herself denounces or remints familiar notions into more highly prized conceptual coin. Since I regard the people problem as one of the paramount issues in the history of the Old Regime and the Revolution (and beyond…), I will comment on certain general matters of conceptualization and analysis in Cohen's book, though I will pay particular attention to the points that intersect with the subsistence question, and its forward and backward linkages.

La Nature du peuple is a rich compound of several kindred historiographical genres and influences. It is a dexterous foray into a supple intellectual history rather than a more formalistic history of ideas, less the reification of doctrine as in Lovejoy than concern for the speech acts in the manner of Skinner via Austin ("how to do things with words").[47] Markedly influenced by Foucault, this intellectual history is constantly tempted by the siren of archeology, the allure of discontinuity and the fecund "conditions of possibility" proffered by the framework of the epistémè, the foundation of a system of order, of discourse and, ultimately, of knowledge (in this instance, the naturalizing epistémè that shapes the elite representation of the people in the first half of the eighteenth century). Largely based on the conventional type of discursive sources that nourish intellectual history, the book boasts as well an important section that hearkens back to what was once (optimistically, amorphously and ephemerally) dubbed the social history of ideas. The latter, in its broadest rendering, aspired to treat not only the conditions of production of texts but also the ideas or representations of the least lettered part of the population,

---

in part in reaction to historians, ranging from eminent elders such as François Furet to his fellow doctoral student at Nantes, Samuel Guicheteau, who are tempted to include in the category "people" virtually the entire world of work, including the whole range of corporate masters, and in the case of Furet, an apparently wide selection of merchants and shopkeepers. See Furet, "Pour une définition des classes inférieures à l'époque moderne," *Annales E.S.C.* 18 (1963): 459–74, and Guicheteau, *La Révolution des ouvriers nantais: Mutation économique, identité sociale et dynamique révolutionnaire (1740–1815)* (Rennes: Presses Universitaires de Rennes, 2008). Danet's second people is closer to Daniel Roche's rich and discerning notion, elaborated in *Le Peuple de Paris* (Paris: Aubier, 1981).

46 I am referring (once again) to the analytical framework of C. Grignon and J.-C. Passeron, *Le Savant et le populaire, misérabilisme et populisme en sociologie et en littérature* (Paris: Seuil, 1989).

47 For purposes of general orientation, see Arthur Lovejoy: *The Great Chain of Being: A Study of the History of an Idea* (1936; repr. New York: Harper & Row 2005) and *Essays in the History of Ideas* (1948; repr. Baltimore: Johns Hopkins University Press, 1978); Quentin Skinner, "Meaning and Understanding in the History of Ideas," *History and Theory* 8, no. 1 (1969): 3–53 and *The Foundations of Modern Political Thought*, 2 vols. (Cambridge: Cambridge University Press, 1978); J. L. Austin, *How to Do Things with Words: The William James Lectures Delivered at Harvard University in 1955* (Oxford: Oxford University Press, 1955).

its (sometimes not so) silent majority. Here the inspiration is double (triple if one takes into account Cohen's ideological engagement in her own social and political universe): first the capacious sensibility for the world "from below" of Arlette Farge, without the lyricism and the intensity of her communion with the (police) archives, and then E. P. Thompson's rethinking of class in sociocultural terms (Cohen appropriating less the relational dimension than the focus on experience), which required the displacement, yet not the raw nullification, of canonic Marxist economism (the ontological priority of relations to the means of production).

Representations and the Social Imaginary

If the new cultural history most touched by postmodernism disdains foundational categories, it privileges a foundational tool and concept: representation(s). Cohen's book turns to a great extent on elite representations of the people, the ways in which the latter internalize or contest them, and the capacity of the people to generate representations of themselves, more or less stained by the repertory of elite stigma. These representations, and the values, institutions and symbols they embody or signify, presumably map a large part of the social imaginary, formula consecrated in the subtitle. Like the once quasi-magical notion of mentalities, that dispensed historians from doing so much (socio-archeological) work, the concept of social imaginary, marked incidentally by Lacan (where it operates the paradox of an unreality that generates very real effects), developed adroitly by Castoriadis (who viewed it as a crucible for forging social ties and representations of contingent realities) and substantially refined by Charles Taylor (who casts it as a central mechanism in the constructing of social life, linking individual and community in mutually beneficial exchanges), often seems to serve as a convenient *auberge espagnole* in historical analysis.[48]

Cohen treats the discursive forms of the social imaginary with verve and acuity. Her register of predilection is hermeneutic; the administration of proof

48 The work of the two decades cast in terms of representation(s) and the social imaginary is strangely redolent in some ways of the panoply of social studies orchestrated long ago by Roland Mousnier dealing with perceptions of hierarchy, assumptions about rank and status, legitimating and stigmatizing images of the other. They have been consigned to oblivion for good reasons (flawed methodology and sociology) and bad (ideology and temperament), but they were pioneering in many ways, even as they were controversial. Perhaps, it is time to reexamine them in terms of the tools that the new cultural history (or is it now the "*new* new") has honed.

is rarely a major concern.[49] Although Cohen is certainly a new-wave culturalist, sometimes she seems to read culture as the reflection of some infrastructural factor(s). I am a bit surprised that she is intellectually so comfortable with the relation between discursive constructions and what is conventionally called the real world: in other words, that referentiality is so unproblematic. She assumes, quite rightly in my view, that all theorizations have a social impact (the social being a sprawling and protean space refractory to demarcation[50]), yet has little to say about the impact that the social and political spheres exercise on the production of theory. For abbé Coyer, pastor Briatte, commissaire Chenon, Madame Leprince de Beaumont and Necker, does "people" figure the social, and thus some fundamental dimension of reality, in the same manner? Or, are there not only significant differences in representation and linkage among the observers, but also discordances between the people and the social, between the people and reality?

---

49 In the archive, the culturalist reveals a surprisingly positivist appetite. In a strikingly original discussion of subjectivity and access to emotion (with its bodily sedimentation), leading to the claims for the people's unfitness for political affirmation, Cohen makes the case, in the context of the catastrophe occasioned by the marriage of the dauphin in 1770 that left 130 persons dead (mostly "people") and hundreds wounded, that sadness is beyond popular reach because this feeling presupposes the attribution of responsibility for the event, which, upon examination, proved to be accidental: "*this belief is inscribed in the facts*… " (71–77; my emphasis). In the service of this argument, she cites some pertinent archival material and leaves out other (contravening) data, for example, the investigation that incriminates the recklessness and bluster of the Prévôté des marchands or the woeful denunciation of the incongruity of a prodigal celebration in the midst of the misery of protracted dearth. See S. L. Kaplan, ed., *The Bagarre: Galiani's "Lost" Parody* (The Hague: Martinus Nijhoff, 1979). More than an admirable avowal of humility, the eschewing of "exhaustivity" in archival research (especially in the inexhaustible "Y" series) is a hygienic reality check. But, in its place, can "several nodal examples" do the job of generating the evidence necessary for demonstration (161)? How does one determine the threshold required to "attest the existence of this pragmatic popular culture," the point at which the affirmation becomes credible, if not provable, rather than remaining just interesting or suggestive (361)? Humility morphs into jaw-dropping imprudence when, in the course of this same, thoughtful discussion of an alleged pragmatic popular culture, Cohen writes, with staggering reach, that "*the documents of the last part of the century*" suggest a modification in the behavior of the "guilty persons" (363–64; my italics). Talented and resourceful, the historian can work from both microhistorical and far more "massive" archival perspectives, but she leaves me the impression that she prefers the fragmentary "cas singuliers" (14). She faces the recurrent problem of reconciling her flair for tantalizing generalization with the exigencies of demonstration.

50 Cohen's work is replete with spatial imagery that merits examination (see, for example, 6, 8, 9, 10, 12, 77, 161, 417, passim). The question of course transcends this particular study: why and how has the notion of space (with spin-offs such as "site") gained such wide currency to denote features or phenomena or relationships or groups that have not habitually been associated with area, volume, distance, expanse and so on?

Invisibility and Reality

Essentialist, naturalized elite representations of the people require a certain amount of (psychological) repression, but are not subject to a reality check, save in moments of severe collective stress—such as a subsistence crisis or a riot—when (exogenous) reality erupts into the lives of the elite, bound in so many more or less unobtrusive—trivial or routinized—ways to the people, and into the (chronically vulnerable, precarious) lives of the populace/plebs/multitude. Otherwise, by and large, Cohen contends that the people remain invisible; the elites don't see them because they are already fixed in their minds as abstractions (77). How far can one push this interpretive insight? The servant is imperceptible because ubiquitous and banal? He or she bears a large part of the responsibility for shielding the people from the eyes of the elites, though the domestics are instructed fairly often to allow certain agents of the people to pass. The bread *porteuse* whom the magistrate enjoys trying to seduce; the carter because he has first-hand news about storm damage in a country home or château; the wig boy/hairdresser who enters the boudoir of Madame is indiscernible for the same reasons, despite the fact that he—figured conventionally as (lower) body—touches her socially undefiled elite body; and the *marchande de mode* or perhaps even the dressmaker passes inconspicuously, despite the need to demonstrate wares, discuss and/or haggle over price. Can the people remain unseen in the village assembly following mass? In the church, town or country?

Cohen's point is not only elegant and suggestive, but also seems to verge on a sort of conceit, an affectation or a form of mannered mystification. In the second half of the century, the situation changes: elites, taken with a "taste for facts" and observation or touched by spasms of sentimentality, no longer want to rely on what the inner gaze (or the innate idea) is said to have already identified, evaluated and classified. Yet the people enjoy a rhetorical existence in which they escape coagulation and immobilization as a metaphor for the changing state of mind and action of certain (wayward) members of the elite who lose their sangfroid and their principles and "become people," as Dupont and Mirabeau, among others, suggested. So, "the people is always people and must not have an impact on you," the curé of the parish of Bonne-nouvelle cautions the lieutenant of police Sartine in 1770 (74), but it is a more portentous situation when the police become people.

It is not always easy for Cohen to articulate the multiple registers of reality with which she is concerned, in particular the reality of representation(s) that clearly mold behavior and thinking within the elites and among the "people" and the social reality in which the people exist, not as clotted abstractions, but as actors in the everyday order of things. In the first register—and to varying degrees in the second—membership in the people is determined by poverty. It can be construed less as a social phenomenon than as an expression of nature or providence. Or it can be portrayed as a lived social identity/experience that has a range of gradations and incarnations. They designate, *inter alia*, the insufficiently differentiated, vast residual category of the laboring poor, which is not reducible strictly to the unskilled or status-less [*sans qualités*], can include both masters and journeymen along with agricultural dayworkers, sometimes capable of wielding a scythe, and former leaseholders or current (Lilliputian) landowners; is often heavily gendered feminine and stratified age-wise to expose especially the very young and the old; depends on contingent, or conjunctural, as well as structural factors, allowing actors to move in and out of indigence. The range extends to those who are irretrievably down and out, through an intrication of choice, handicap, constraint, and bad luck, running the gamut from professional beggars, paying taxes in some instances, to criminals, floaters, the mentally ill and the denizens of sundry *cours des miracles*. If the *hobereau's* sword and habitus make it impossible to assimilate his poverty to the popular template, the barrier is less systematically insurmountable for manure-shoveling vicars. The matter of sources put aside, it is probably because the elites, despite their manifest multiplicity, are, nevertheless, comparatively much less heterogeneous than the people, that Cohen is more successful in exploring their representations of the people than in analyzing the ways in which the people see and project images of themselves.

Identity, Representation and Action

In some ways, the people are no less intractable to historians today than they were to the eighteenth-century police (and more generally to public administration, bottom and top). Is it sufficient to fix upon a generic representation? A universal people? Immutable and immobile, despite the observable (gratifying or worrisome) phenomena of taxonomical and socio-spatial movement? Do rural and urban "people" see themselves in the same way, read elite characterizations (or caricatures) in kindred fashion? Conversely, do elites represent all the peasants in the manner of the moralist Jean de La Bruyère or the traveling agronomist Arthur Young, or are they inclined to view them differentially, more or less in terms of their relations to the means of production, if I may be playful, as did Mme de Sévigné or Mirabeau, Molière or Marivaux? Is the *homme sylvestre*, who terrified so many (fellow) peasants, cut of the same (essential) cloth as Millet's gleaners, dim-witted perhaps, but in any case not savage? Elites may have amalgamated the broad spectrum of urban people into a stereotypical unity, but urban people certainly saw themselves in the plural. The very act of quitting the countryside, as writer-observer Restif de la Bretonne testified, figures a caesura, not for all, but for many decidedly ex-peasants, who learned quickly to relish wheaten-white loaves, fabricated daily by urban bakers. In the cities, actors moved not only in and out of poverty and in and out of jobs, but also in and out of stereotypical ranks: a fallen guild master, former *juré* in the corporation, going to work as a journeyman; unlicensed workers setting up as surrogate masters in "privileged" urban territories; insurgent journeyman, contesting the domination of their masters, by taking them to court and brandishing swords, as if they were their equals.[51] Elements of the urban poor imperiled the everyday order to which others clung fiercely.

Cohen rightly notes that the proliferation of singular acts, often contradictory, can only thwart generalization, presumably for the contemporary actors as well as historians. She rejects any crude determinism from representation to act: "to interpret these actions, one thus needs to understand from what social logics they derive," with what "tools" the actors themselves make sense of their actions. The question is whether the representations that construct, and are constructed by, the imaginary do (or can do) the work that Cohen assigns to them, in particular whether they are a reliable guide to the lived social life in which all the actors participate and whether they offer access to "the concrete of the everyday." Do these representations "describe the social world" or evoke its broad, normative contours in a quite general way? Do they enable the actors to negotiate the social world with a view toward accomplishing specific tasks and not merely not getting lost? A comprehension of "the logics of the imaginary at work" presumably informs actors of what they are authorized (or not) to do, but does it instruct them how to do? Beyond a very approximate orientation that sets up reference points, landmarks and perhaps benchmarks, what is the bearing of the categories constructed by the actors themselves on their action? Can the actors as well as historians "read the social world," by deploying, in particular, the category of the people? At what level of specificity? With what degree of navigational autonomy? (8–11)

Through these representations one reads more a narrative (or a congeries of cautionary tales) than a map. It seems credible to me to postulate that the elites "express by their daily speech and their acts a social ethos"; given the cartographical woolliness of their social imaginary, I am much less convinced that "they act as a function of their representations of the world."[52] It seems reasonable to me to hold that the text (from the multiplicity of which the

51 It would be worth scrutinizing the term "garçon," conjuring up permanent subaltern status, used interchangeably in many trades with the appellation journeyman, whose French rendition, *compagnon,* does not figure the *man* as opposed to the *boy.*

52 Cohen readily concedes that "the realities can begin to diverge from the cultural model," but rightly observes that these divergences make no sense unless one first identifies the model (12).

historian skillfully draws her material) "stabilizes a vision," but it is not clear to me how it "rationalizes practice": it is not only that there persists a (more or less familiar) gap between discourse and practice, but also that the relationship between them, analytically elided, remains enigmatic. The fiction of an all-embracing people—un-gendered, undifferentiated, unidentified and vaguely incarnate—was less profitable to the (patently fragmented) dominated than to the dominant. The question of the utility, as well as the fatality, of this representation of the people remains open (8–11, 17).

Work

Given the primacy of work in the political elite's conception of the people, inherently volatile and brutal, especially menacing in the context of dense urban concentrations, I would have imagined it as one of the structuring essences of the dominant representation of the people-as-horde (analogies with certain animals drafted to generate energy or do other work might have permitted a simultaneous naturalization of people-as-work in the depiction). After all, numerous elite voices considered work as the first line of police, as the rampart of social control, as the only route to salvation and, gradually, as a source of wealth creation and not merely an emblem of protracted Christian expiation. Perhaps, Cohen devotes less attention to work than I would have expected because she believes that it has lost some of its "explanatory power," as historians have turned from the shop-floor (atelier or, later, factory) to the discourses that allegedly construct worker identity. Cohen notes physiocratic reluctance to accord value added—in terms of net product—to work, though their posture is deeply ambiguous. She credits Adam Smith, reacting against the physiocratic conception, with reevaluating and revalorizing work in the eyes of part of the savant milieu (217). Yet Turgot's abolition of the guilds, in the name of the natural right of everyone (almost) to undertake work as he (and sometimes she) desired, conveyed a very positive image of work on the eve of the publication of the *Wealth of Nations*. And *Philosophie rurale*, a physiocratic manifesto, jointly composed by Dr. Quesnay and Mirabeau, deploys biblical maxims and flattering metaphors to underline the centrality of work without which neither the net product nor the *bon prix* would be possible.[53]

53 *Philosophie rurale ou Économie générale et particulière de l'agriculture, réduite à l'ordre immuable des lois physiques et morales qui assurent la prospérité des empires* (Amsterdam: Libraires associés, 1763).

Cohen embroiders a neo-populist argument for the perception and actions of sundry workers on the basis of a supposedly widespread use of the notion of natural law. I do not find her demonstration any more persuasive than I did Mike Sonenscher's, from whose (otherwise) superlative book on *Work and Wages* she elicits the idea.[54] With precious little evidence, she strains to anchor a range of claims, affirming customary rights, in a natural-rights repertory far more familiar to the lawyers drafting briefs than to the journeymen or false workers seeking justice as they construed it. I concur with her that "popular reasoning issues in action more than in discourse," but rather than passing from "theory to practice," as she writes, I believe that the workers pass from practice to practice. To contend that the popular "knowledge about natural law is above all a matter of implementation" is for me to beg the question (403).[55]

It is not clear in Cohen's classification system, as she moves imperceptibly from abstract representation to concrete behavior, how to stratify the guild universe, part of which seems assimilable to the lower or even middle branches of elite arborescence, though the frontier does not only separate the *sanior pars* from the lower-order communities, but also traverses many corporations through the interior, separating an elite nucleus of actors we might have called

54 Michael Sonenscher, *Work & Wages: Natural Law, Politics, and the Eighteenth-Century French Trades* (Cambridge: Cambridge University Press, 1989). I have not yet seen the new edition (2012) with a preface presumably repositioning his argument in the context of recent scholarship and his own quickened evolution toward a more textually oriented approach in the framework of a creative history of ideas.

55 I think that Cohen relies more on rhetoric of special pleading than on evidence in her forced effort to make the case: "Of course, as one finds it in the mouths of unlicensed workers or the crowd that rushes to their defense, the argument has neither the precision nor the complexity of the traditional discourse of natural right developed from Thomas Aquinas through Locke. If our demonstration is therefore not based on long and well formulated declarations, but on the striking recurrence of a little word, of a descriptor, 'thief,' it is not by error but for structural reasons. That which one could designate as popular discourse on natural right is not of the same nature as the learned *jusnaturalist* discourse; that said, from the learned discourse to the people, there is not an absolute discontinuity" (403). Cf. p. 405 where Cohen contends that the invocation of a nebulous natural rights argument—often familiar claims of usage and necessity to which she ascribes a theoretical genealogy—is "relatively frequent." As part of the same construction, she (mis)characterizes the guild statutes as embodying special privilege (a deprecatory "droit particulier" as opposed to a laudatory "droit naturel"), following the polemical liberal line of Clicquot de Blervache and the Gournayites, rather than taking into account, beyond the (often ambiguous) monopoly attribution, the multiple policing, administrative and socializing functions with which the authorities charged the communities (399, 407).

embryonic bourgeois (if this terminology were still politically correct and historiographically admitted) from a larger and far more variegated periphery of lesser masters, some of whom toiled as subcontractors for their more dynamic colleagues, or barely got by on their own. An informal stratifying mechanism differentiated the ranks of the illicit, underground or sanctuarized world of work—far larger than Cohen intimates—not all of whom would qualify as "people," according to emic criteria, and would perhaps also trouble elite representation of the people (for example, some of the well-off associates of Réveillon, whose factory in the faubourg St.-Antoine was the target of prerevolutionary rioting to which the author alludes).

It is hard not to be struck by the density and intensity of conflict within the category of "people" during the eighteenth century: inside the guilds; in the parallel universe of often semiorganized but unincorporated work; in the labor market where workers, including future masters, frequently organized (in *compagnonnages, confréries* or trade-specific associations levying membership fees and conducting collective business) to face up to masters in bitter, intermittent and occasionally prolonged conflict (aggravated dramatically in the first few years of the Revolution); in the sometimes violent confrontation of workers among themselves in their organizations; and, beyond the minority urban universe, in the vast and kaleidoscopic countryside, marked by endemic disputes over common rights and constraints, resistance of the dispossessed to better-off peasants, jealousies among rival harvesting teams, competition for access to various employments, rejection of outsiders (foreigners) of all stripes and so on.

There is a strong tension in Cohen's writing between an unequivocal acknowledgment of diversity and heterogeneity (though not necessarily strife) within or among the "people" and a desire to underscore certain unifying factors, such as a common logic embodied in an applied pragmatism (opposed to an inaccessible abstract thought), that remains so open-ended, so adaptable and so accommodating as to attenuate its mobilizing capacity. More powerful, in the end, seems to be the classical form of (fluid) union wrought by subjection to domination and common anathema. So, the coherence of the notion or category of people is to be located, in large measure, in shared, stouthearted struggle. Writing during the protracted thermidor following the postmodern insurgency, Cohen clings, after all, to a foundational category, though in the framework of a political-discursive strategy, in the manner, say, of a Stedman Jones, rather than a social structural approach of the "marxizing" or *Annales*, version E.S.C ("1.0").[56] When all is said and done, because the "said" and

56 See, for instance, Gareth Stedman Jones, *Languages of Class: Studies in English Working Class History, 1832–1982* (Cambridge: Cambridge University Press, 1983).

the "done" are not habitually synchronized, it seems difficult not to give precedence to the one over the other. In Cohen's view of the people (as well as her view of the view of the people), discourse seems finally to trump "the open corpus of possible behaviors" in identifying this group (416–17).

Speech, *Émotion*, Violence

The "people," as we shall see shortly, express themselves, in the eyes of certain observers, primordially in collective action: the riot, the uprising or the wonderfully apt French locution, *émotion*. Cohen rejects the idea that "violence is the distinctive language" of workers—and by extension, of the "people"—who have no other manner of affirming an existence that is not recognized. I think that she is right to suggest that, despite powerful constraints, there are numerous cases of "popular attempts to seize a possible equality as a speaking being" (341). The availability or temptation or challenge of speech is the vector that leads her to forge her argument for popular pragmatism as another way to articulate judgments and to "think" social and political relations. The historian overlooks nevertheless the many institutional structures in which elements of the people are socialized into the practice of speech and of politics: in the guilds (where combat in electoral and business assemblies is a veritable apprenticeship in the conquest and uses of power) and in the *confréries* and the *compagnnonages* where workers are initiated into the practice of speech for the purpose of making claims, defending putative rights, attacking or thwarting the assaults of adversaries.

Cohen correctly emphasizes the centrality of the problematic of "speaking with the king." The corporate system—Séguier's famous chain, composed of multiple rings, each representing a corps or corporation, from the village assembly and the guild to the judicial companies, academies and universities, leads directly to the monarch—is founded in part on the promise of one's voice reaching the crown, with the reciprocal obligation of a royal response. Cohen dexterously uses the Damiens affair in 1757—the attempt to assassinate the king that may have been planned to fail—as an illustration at once of the internalized (she uses, interestingly, the French word *incorporation*) taboo on "popular political thought" and the attempt to transmit such thinking to the king "by means of the body [*corps*]." It was not a question of killing the king, but of "touching him" (338–39). I would suggest that Damiens' act—touching the king with his knife, as he put it—figured a seditious (insolent but well-meaning) reappropriation of the canonic thaumaturgical gesture by which the newly crowned king adduces his divine nature by touching scores of persons afflicted with scrofula in order to impart a providential cure. By his "touch,"

Damiens aspires to cure the king of the infirmities that prevent him from being a good father to his children-people.[57]

In collective as well as individual action, the people utilize symbolic language as well as verbal speech and violence. Cohen presents an inventory of representations of people as rioters that at times strikes me as procrustean. The liberals were not the only elite actors who regarded the people as incapable of looking after their own interests (75). Yet the police, on the labor market(s), and local authorities, in markets operating in metropolitan collector zones, often testified to surprisingly adroit (albeit sometimes illegal) management of their interests by workers and consumers. The effacement of individuality in elite representation seems quite plausible, but Cohen carries it over into social practice where she exaggerates its prevalence, in my opinion (56). The elites viewed the mutinous people as an aggregate, not in individual terms. Cohen's argument, however, that leaders of these rebellions, habitually singled out and often harassed and/or arrested, were not perceived as individuals but as "part of the people," seems to me cryptic and unconvincing (52–53).

Nor have I encountered a systematic tendency to treat riots as "simple problems of the maintenance of order"—in fact, restoring the conditions for order, like creating them in the first place, was never a simple matter—rather than as expressions of protest, as "an ensemble of signs to interpret" (58). On the contrary, the police often "read" the riots with keen discernment, enabling them to decode popular action, inducing them to indulge certain excesses (or not) and disposing them to engage or spurn negotiations. If the people were "essentially" violent—violent in their essence, according to the representation Cohen imputes to her elites—then how could a society function day to day (beyond the confines of its imaginary)? The elites would be essentially terrified or in a posture of paralyzing uncertainty; or they would demand a sort of permanent, preemptive repression by the state. Surely, the stereotypical ferocious and sanguinary butcher, so evocatively portrayed by L.-S. Mercier, did not figure the mass of people, either in discourse or in practice (59).[58]

Riots and Liberalization

Given the immense handicap that Cohen ascribes to the people (in active riot or in the state of structural volatility that makes them potentially explosive at

57 One of the anonymous scholars that the publisher commissioned to read this manuscript suggests an interesting, alternative exegesis: that Damiens "contaminated" the king by touching him.

58 Mercier, *Tableau de Paris*, vol. 1 (Paris: Société typographique, 1782).

any moment), it is hard to fathom how they manage to erupt "in the moment of 1770" (incidentally, "an epistemic moment" for Cohen), to take part "in the debate." She cites Tocqueville as support for her point of view, but his observations bespeak more nearly her pluralism than his pertinence. Why and how did the consumer suddenly surface as capable of engaging in a debate on policy and philosophy? As I myself have argued, this debate aimed, as Cohen writes, to "define in a radical way what a good government would be." But she does not explain why and how the "consumer" could suddenly spring up from "the mass," how this persona could command attention in the "1770 moment," given the postulate "that there is never a specific context for the people, because it is inconceivable that they can fall within the framework of an event-based dimension… " (51, 55, 161).

Furthermore, why date the "birth of political economy in its liberal form" at the end of the 1760s, when in fact it began to crystallize in the 1750s and then impinged mightily on the political and policy scene in the early 1760s? (162).[59] Why accord paradigmatic status to the Flour War and make it the vector of the rendezvous between the newly "erupted" consumer and the physiocrats on the eve of their debacle, when in fact it was an aftershock, despite its prominence (linked more to the ascension of Turgot than to the replay of part of the radical liberal reforms) after hundreds of subsistence revolts during the previous decade? (197, 331, 412).

In the real riots of 1775 (and, as Cohen herself acknowledges, of the 1760s) rather than the posed, stilted riot of elite representation, the people betray the qualities that many of us have identified: rationality, calculation and deliberation. This is what Cohen elegantly dubs "une émeute diserte," phrasing that I am inclined, if I read her correctly, to render as "an eloquent riot," an action that speaks, even if it remains hard

59 Notions of genesis obviously invite worthwhile but often interminable debate, require nuances and exceptions. Obviously, the liberalism of Gournay and his circle differed significantly from that of Quesnay's school, and strong spirits such as Turgot draw on both, unevenly and not always avowedly. On certain important issues, the Gournay circle fractures: Gournay–Forbonnais–Plumard do not share the same ideas as Abeille–Morellet–Turgot. And the liberalism of the first trio diverges from some of the fundamental doctrines that shape physiocratic liberalism: no natural order, no intransigently unlimited liberty, no sacred and inviolable law/right of property as a pillar of the system. As Arnaud Orain put it, in a personal communication, Gournayian liberalism is not "moderate"; it is just not a "transcendent" notion. Instead, it draws pragmatically on the experiences of both *négociants* and public administrators, center and periphery. See the revisionist collection devoted to Gournay: Loïc Charles, Frédéric Lefebvre and Christine Théré, eds., *Le Cercle de Vincent de Gournay: Savoirs économiques et pratiques administratives en France au milieu du XVIIIe siècle* (Paris: INED, 2011).

for the people to accede to speech, the expression, through various acts on the public stage, of a sentiment of injustice and of specific grievances, which nevertheless may not be sufficient to constitute a popular "political thought" (318, 324–25).[60] In the same sense, given the barriers to popular appropriation of speech, I would have liked for Cohen to elaborate on the somewhat casual formulation, "from a situation and a few words, a riot happens," and to explain the surprising permeability of popular milieus to learned culture (409).[61]

A number of issues concerning liberalization invite clarification.[62] By and large, Cohen's treatment of physiocracy is remarkably fresh, both in terms of its flight from facts to a less capricious theoretical mooring and in terms of its confrontation with some of the writers whose originality and significance are

60 Cohen's discussion of the play and meaning of violence is extremely suggestive, but too cursory. She needs to unpack such intriguing statements as "Violence is thus not to be understood as an incapacity to accede to speech, but as the sign of its powerlessness" (331). It might have been worthwhile here for Cohen to enlarge upon her critique of L. Tilly and the broader question of popular political consciousness (at the risk that the latter term's highly charged connotation takes us on a detour) (325).

61 Is she thinking here of classical populist visions of (re-)appropriation that Roger Chartier has splendidly inventoried or of trickle-down models that sometimes seem to tempt Robert Darnton or of dialogic modes that Aaron Gourevich, Carlo Ginzburg and David Sabean work out in quite different ways? R. Chartier, *The Cultural Origins of the French Revolution*, trans. L. Cochran (Durham, NC: Duke University Press, 1991); Robert Darnton, *The Great Cat Massacre and Other Episodes in French Cultural History* (New York: Basic Books, 1984) and *The Kiss of Lamourette: Reflections in Cultural History* (New York: Norton, 1990); Aron J. Gurevich, *Categories of Medieval Culture*, trans. G. L. Campbell (London: Routledge & Kegan Paul, 1985) and *Medieval Popular Culture: Problems of Belief and Perception*, trans. János M. Bak and Paul A. Hollingsworth (Cambridge: Cambridge University Press, 1990); David W. Sabean, *Power in the Blood: Popular Culture and Village Discourse in Early Modern Germany* (Cambridge: Cambridge University Press, 1987); Carlo Ginzburg, *The Cheese and the Worms: The Cosmos of a Sixteenth Century Miller* (Baltimore, MD: Johns Hopkins University Press, 1980). Might Cohen find some affinity with Slavoj Zizek's effort to move beyond false consciousness (that prevents "people" from seeing "how things really are") in understanding the access of "people" to ideas/ideology and then to "reality"? *The Sublime Object of Ideology* (London: Verso, 1989)

62 At the outset, Cohen characterizes the experience in terms so narrow as to miss, or deform, the significance of these radical reforms: "the debate on the liberalization of the price of grain." Liberalization was about fundamental social, political, economic and psychological transformation, of which the grain price was only one of many important elements. It was first of all a liberalization of attitudes and institutions, customary political conceptions and administrative practice, notions of exchange and equilibrium, social relations and social cohesion (16).

diminished by the very name we give them: the anti-physiocrats.[63] I wonder, however, for what reasons—given all that Cohen has told us about the moral ostracization and symbolic lobotomization of the people, and their implicit lack of aptitude for evolution—the *économistes* "sincerely believed that the people would open their mind to the new regulations" (the latter term, used without irony, denoting, I presume, the suppression of the entire regulatory apparatus, save, provisionally, for Paris) (181). After having miscalculated on the popular capacity for and willingness to embrace deep change, Cohen's physiocrats manage nevertheless to inflect the conventional representation of the people, beyond their own chapel, among unnamed portions of the elites, in ways that I wish she had explained. The debates they ignited "contributed to the abandonment of a discourse on popular categories, functioning according to a stereotypical psychology: men and women of the people are henceforth conceived first and foremost as economic variables, as producers and consumers among others on a market." She postulates a profound mutation. The *économistes* prompted precisely which groups to abandon their earlier assumptions? Which parts of the elites embraced their economistic ideas? How long did it require to effect the transformation? Did the trauma of liberalization serve as midwife to the birth of the new representation(s)? What is the market to which Cohen refers? A single market for goods and labor, suited to both city and country? A universal market principle? (217).[64]

---

63 Cohen might have enriched the discussion by making more explicit the connections and discontinuities between the earlier liberal currents and the affirmation of the physiocratic school/sect. The Gournay line merits more attention, especially given its interest in social classification, and the thesis of "egalitarian" liberalism demands a critical assessment (172). On political physiocracy in the narrow sense, I find Cohen less convincing. Legal despotism is not an analogue to Linguet's "good tyranny," or a recipe for an "all powerful government." On the contrary, it is conceived expressly as a mechanism to constrain royal power, to oblige it to cede to natural law, to "free it" from the obligation to intervene according to traditional expectations, to renounce the very means to be "all powerful" on its own account (199, 202).

64 Cohen notes that "the chronology is important here." But the reader does not easily follow the trajectory of the physiocrats' social imaginary. Before the enterprise of liberalization, they apparently shared the prevailing representation of the people as prisoners of age-old prejudices. After the failure of liberalization, they turned their reflection back upon the question of "why the crowd is not accessible to physiocratic 'evidence,' despite the campaign of explanation and propaganda." Cohen needs to make clear whether the physiocratic view of the people's opinion on the subsistence question as stemming from "the order of instinct" (driven by "passions" resulting from "ignorance" and "blindness") is a return to a representation held prior to liberalization or is the product of frustration with an unrealized or thwarted liberalization (180–83).

Necker's People

Like Déborah Cohen, Jacques Necker, Genevan, Protestant, banker, philosophe and future minister—this chain of qualifiers strikes a quasi-pleonastic chord in the French eighteenth century—was galvanized by the Flour War, to the extent that, in his case, it confirmed the diagnosis that he had just elaborated in *Sur la Législation et le commerce des grains* (1775), which appeared almost simultaneously with those popular subsistence eruptions. Given his analysis of the first liberalization, and his assessment of the liberalizing law echoing the measures of the 1760s that Turgot promulgated shortly after his ascension to the contrôle-général, in 1774, the banker-philosophe could not have been wholly astonished by these uprisings. For the Genevan, as for the French historian, "the people" was one of the major protagonists of his book. His view of them stems from an understanding of society as composed of starkly antagonistic elements. The struggle for subsistence morphs into what he tremulously (and anachronistically) styles a class struggle, an unending confrontation in which the propertied subjugate the impoverished, "the strong oppress the weak."[65]

Necker's self-consciously schematic social stratification opposes those without property (save in themselves) to those who have it (in a wide range of degree and type, though land is its most significant single embodiment, according rural folk logical primacy over their urban counterparts).[66] Yet, he is perfectly aware of the considerable difficulty of "fixing the limits of the word peuple." One cannot include under this rubric everyone *born* without property, because there are those who acquire it through talent and/or special situations. Nor can one exclude all those who own some property, because it can be too small to spare them from misery. Still, given their centrality in his

65 *Sur la Législation et le commerce des grains* (Paris: Pissot, 1775), 87. Characteristically dual, Necker's class system is occasionally expanded in a tripartite system that blends the social and the political/paternal/familial. Thus, his allusion to the ideal of "a sound harmony between the respective rights of the very big classes of society, the Proprietors, the industrious Men, and the Sovereign." *Législation*, 79. Another tripartite version convokes "Seigneurs of the land," merchants, and the people. Ibid., 8. Cf. Graslin's quite similar dichotomy between "proprietors," boasting various forms of property that others envy or require, and "workers," with merely "work" as a possession. J.-J. Louis Graslin, *Essai analytique sur la richesse et sur l'impôt* (London, 1767), 177.

66 Though Necker privileges the rural/agricultural people for reasons that are both demographic and symbolic, throughout the *Législation* he resists the effort that he attributes to the physiocrats to separate the urban from the rural folk: they have more in common as a result of the structuring fact that they are both consumers, the vast bulk of the peasants being buyers rather than sellers of staples.

story, he knows he must impose a working definition: "Under this name, in this work, I refer only to that part of the Nation born without property, of parents more or less in the same situation, and who, not having been able to receive from them an education, are reduced to their natural faculties, and have no other possession than their physical strength or some easy and unrefined craft." The "people" are the most numerous and the most poverty-stricken class of society, their wretchedness deriving directly from the tyrannical power that proprietors exercise over them.[67]

While he defends at numerous junctures the dignity and humanity of the people, he tends to essentialize them, in (dolorist) terms of basal needs and actions, which emphasize their helplessness and subservience by juvenilizing them and likening them, not only implicitly but also explicitly, to animals, the latter comparison occasionally applied both to the dominant and to the subordinate social groups in play. The people are children who need to be allowed regular access to nourishment; the people are a certain threshold of calories that can be counted, at least approximately, albeit for them the term "subsistence" also bespoke the part of their survivalist income that they had to devote to "some clothing" and "a hut," which is to say, "all the needs of absolute necessity," the accouterments and markers of their misery. "Survive today, work to live tomorrow," notes the writer, "that is the sole interest of the most numerous class of Citizens." Psychologically, they are accorded no respite: each day begins with "the same fear" and also "the same hope": that, in exchange for their services, they will be able to wrench "a modest share of the surplus of the rich." Since the people are utterly excluded from political life which presumably could instill them with a sense of responsibility for their destiny—"since they are not involved in the [making of] the laws or [the conduct of] business, it is difficult to reason with them, and dangerous to give them orders without showing consideration towards them"—the

67 *Législation*, 165–66. For examples of popular indigence, see *De l'Administration des finances de la France*, in *Oeuvres Complètes*, ed. Baron de Staël, vol. 4 (Paris: Treuttet & Würtz, 1821), 319, 326, 356. The experience of the Revolution, especially after the declaration of the republic, leads Necker not to abandon completely the paternal and political affinity he had evinced for the people, notably in 1775, but to warn, not so much against their idealization, as against their instrumentalization. The people was a "fiction," it embodied "an abuse of the idea attached to a collective name [by which] these adulators of the multitude attempt to mislead us." By casting the "people" as "the general will personified," these Rousseauian revolutionaries claimed that it could never be "a tyrant." Yet Necker espied in this "abstract" construction of the people an apology for an absolute equality that slid easily into "a tyrannical democracy." *Réflexions philosophiques sur l'égalité* (1793; Paris: Institut Coppet, 2012), 28–29.

people must be treated dexterously, habituated rather than constrained: "they must be led like a sensitive child." This child becomes extremely anxious "when he is seized with alarm, well-founded or not, concerning his means of attaining his subsistence." When he is fully aroused and energized, he becomes a feline who bellows in a different voice from the proprietor-lions in whose predatory space he lives: "this people-child, whom one leads on a leash, in the midst of the inequality of property, and across a thousand objects of privation and envy is nothing but a lion who roars when he fears for the basic necessities of life."[68]

Clamor, Denunciation, Justice and Force

Because the "people" are concerned about nothing "beyond the price of bread," Necker circumscribes rather narrowly their political socialization.[69] "When one sees them joining together in a commotion regarding public events," he observes, "it is not that they understand what is happening." Oblivious to any "abstract cause," they merely use any opportunity that arises to express their sense of injustice, a highly concrete and political act. Their political idiom is less rebellion, which is merely a modality, than denunciation, which is a way to affirm their existence and to protest its inherently oppressive and unfair conditions. The denunciation is not abstract: though not always nominally precise, it is meant to call to account those whom they consider responsible, a changing panoply of actors including specific proprietors or employers, traders, millers or government officials. Necker situates the impulse

68 *Législation,* 82–83n, 153, 397. Elsewhere in his text, the Genevan deploys the same image of savage beasts: "These are lions and defenseless animals who live together." Ibid., 80–81, 87, 385, 400, 409. The abbé Morellet severely castigated his erstwhile friend Necker for his great error in treating proprietors as voracious lions. Morellet, *Mémoires de l'abbé Morellet,* ed. Lemontey, vol. 1 (Paris: Librairie Française de Ladvocat, 1831), 156–57. Cf. a deeply pessimistic appreciation of the prospects for the evolution of the "people" in France, notably as long as they remained subsistence-dependent. *Législation,* 158. Throughout the 1760s and 1770s, in the great grain debates and in other arenas, the English case loomed large. For reasons the Genevan enumerates, the English people are significantly "less people" than their French counterparts (the English enjoyed a higher general wage level, fewer holidays, a lower population density, more institutional opportunities to express themselves and, finally, were closer to their sovereign). Ibid., 158–60.

69 Pertaining to the "people," Necker writes elsewhere in *Législation*: "The bread that nourishes them, the Religion that consoles them, these are their only ideas." Here he pushes the bread obsession as far as he can, but introduces the solace of religion about which he has little to say in the work. Ibid., 152.

somewhere between selective scapegoating and a sort of shaming indictment: "It's rather that, carrying continually within themselves the feeling of their misery, [the people] profit from all opportunities to broadcast it widely and to impute their misfortune to someone else." The "people's" other(s) cannot escape, or pretend not to know. Necker does not depict the "people" as characteristically combustible or methodically inclined to mutiny, though he surely overestimates the efficacy of laws prohibiting assembly. Distress and its pathos seem to undermine or postpone the will to insurgency: "Thus misery, death and disease annihilated numerous families before the People dare to rise." Violent outbursts are sometimes spontaneous, but more often the product of a certain gestation.

Paradoxically, the relative lack of popular clamor, or its very sporadic character, reinforces the insensitivity of the administrative class and the socioeconomic elites, the latter in particular who remain disinclined to peer too closely into the daily life of the "people" and ready to avert their eyes till a crisis erupts.[70] This willful "ignorance" of "the most essential relations of humanity" presents "bizarre contradictions," especially in the cities. Necker takes the example of the canonic and reiterative ban on gambling and the "general scandal" that ensues, which the government is already poised to prevent or repress. Is safeguarding the morality of the people more urgent than their vital well-being? "Justice," argues the philosophe, means hearing their "sufferings" and averting them: "It is a fine idea for a Sovereign to be watchful of the misfortune of his People, as a result of the powerlessness of their complaints and of the ease with which he could oppress them." Theoretically, even under subsistence duress, justice also implies a recourse to force "if the People do not listen to reason." Yet, Necker maintains, this kind of force is no longer a reasonable or just force when "it must clash with a general feeling," in this instant, a collective sense of injustice as a result of penury. Indeed, this collective action, an error, must still be considered an expression of reason when it derives from "human nature." *Cherté* and dearth break down not only

70 Cf. on the averted gaze and the delayed popular reaction: "We quiet down about these [dearth-related] calamities, as long as they are obscure and domestic, because one would have to follow them in one's mind right into the disgusting lodging of the indigent, an ordeal which we do not want even for a moment to afflict upon our imagination; it is only after the outcries of distress, only after the tumultuous sounds of the moaning and complaining, that our compassion awakes; but a prolonged suffering had preceded these public clamors, and more than one family head, impatient over his misfortune, had ceded, perhaps in secret, to the counsels of misery." *Législation*, 373. Surely, Necker allows for Tocquevillean cases where relations between "people" and proprietors are (feudally) reciprocal, if not openly cordial, but he does not cite any.

habitual patterns of provisioning, but also habitual patterns of behaving, and the good administrator will understand this, in 1789–90 as in 1775.[71]

The moral economy that Necker adumbrates is quite complex. Though he denies the "people" a right to revolt, under extreme pressure he accords them extenuating circumstances and does not stigmatize collective action. Repressive force may prove necessary, but he does not regard it as (always already) inherently judicious. And implicit throughout the discussion is the claim that sanctuarizes the "people," that recognizes their humanity and elevates them decisively from the status of animality or protracted infancy. It is in some sense the final word on the subsistence question from a social and political as well as a moral point of view in the grand scheme of things, over against the imperious right of property, "this multitude of men, who have nothing to exchange, who want only bread for the price of their labor … they, also, have their claims and titles." What Linguet had identified with the stomach (or hunger) of the people, Necker located in their very birth, by which they "have acquired the right to exist."[72]

Prejudices, Anxieties, Passions and Social Laws

Perhaps, because he knows that it will be badly received and most likely ineffective, Necker generally avoids deploying fear as an argument to threaten or motivate or evenly simply admonish the powerful on the risks of managing the powerless. He wants his readers to understand how the people are, ontologically, how they react emotionally, with what possible consequences politically. There is no need to be frightened by the "prejudices of the People," because, in fact, they will not make the laws that frame social relations, even if those prejudices will constrain the law sometimes. Indeed, that will happen on only one specific occasion: "The People will always have only one powerful

71 *Législation*, 54, 153, 160–62. Necker is sympathetic to consumers' "murmurs" during subsistence stress, even as he notes their "incapacity for remembering and expressing gratitude," which I read as reference to the collective forgetfulness of past royal largesse and the abiding suspicion of mixed royal motives (the worst case embodied in the famine plot persuasion). *Législation*, 288, 290. Cf. Necker's insightful remarks regarding the cascading insularity of perceptions of subsistence difficulties in the early years of the Revolution: "Moreover, nothing could destroy personal feelings, in the moment when the risk of a dearth seems quite likely; at that instant, the homeland narrows in scope and, step by step, it becomes embodied for everyone by his Province, then his Canton, his City, his Community [in the corporate order of things], and finally, sometimes, in his Household or in his Family." *Sur l'Administration de M. Necker par lui-même* (Paris, 1791), 418.

72 *Eloge de Colbert*, in *Oeuvres Complètes*, vol. 15, ed. Staël, 37–38.

and energetic emotion, the only one that the Administration is not capable of vanquishing: the one that concerns their subsistence." They have become inured, over time, to minor bumps, to imperceptible increases in the grain price, because wages gradually bridge the relatively innocuous gap.[73] What is socially and politically dangerous as well as intolerable to the people—this is one of the policy leitmotifs of the book—is "a sudden and considerable rise in prices [which] will always inflame them: thus the Government must avert these sorts of price movements, as much as the laws can prevent them".[74]

The stakes are so substantial that the Genevan ventures an oblique critique of a physiocratic-based liberalization and a deft commentary on law making in which utilitarian ends are hedged in psychological and political terms. Laws ordinarily are meant to serve "the greatest advantage of the Society." Yet, they might also prove to be wise even if they appeared to be contrary to the principles adopted as most apt to promote the prosperity of the realm, because the latter can be founded only on public well-being, "and this felicity can never depend exclusively on a system, because the essential condition of Happiness is the idea that one has of it; thus, if each time that the goal is to work for the good of the State, it is necessary to fuel the worries of the majority of Citizens, this good is no longer a good." The psychological and the material spheres overlap. Anxiety is painful; mushrooming in the subsistence theater, it undermines the happiness of the majority. Certainly thinking about both 1763–64 and 1774, the banker-philosophe concluded that "any purely abstract discussion on the *affaires* of Administration is always insufficient [:] thus, when one seeks to subject the dominant passion of the People to a general system, one stops and corrects oneself; it is on the contrary the system that must be in conformity with this passion." Necker's conception of governance is close to Galiani's: one must take into account all the factors, all the circumstances and all the particularities at a given moment. A system is useful only to the extent that it considers all of these elements, including the shifting psychological state

73 Necker's word for imperceptible is *insensible*; given his way of understanding the psychology of the "people," this (paradoxical) choice of diction may bespeak his interest in sensationism, closer to Condillac's radically empirical account of the workings of the mind than to Locke's well-known view. See Hans Aarsleff, *From Locke to Saussure: Essays on the Study of Language and Intellectual History* (Minneapolis: University of Minnesota Press, 1982); Isabel F. Knight, *The Geometric Spirit: The Abbé de Condillac and the French Enlightenment* (New Haven, CT: Yale University Press, 1968); Arnaud Orain, "Choix individuels, Morale et Théorie de la valeur dans l'œuvre de l'abbé de Condillac (1714–1780)," (doctoral dissertation, University of Paris I, 2004); Lorne Falkenstein, "Étienne Bonnot de Condillac," *The Stanford Encyclopedia of Philosophy* (Fall 2010 Edition), online.

74 *Législation*, 154–55.

of the people. The Genevan could pass for the Neapolitan when he writes, concerning the administration, that "it is the force of the ocean's waves that must be calculated in erecting a dike on the shore."[75]

Necker's material miserabilism carried over into a certain moral miserabilism. The "people" were cramped emotionally and intellectually. Unlike the physiocrats, he never questioned that they understood their interests, albeit they were enlightened not by reflection, but by instinct. They had only two inexorable passions, situated clearly on the instinctual register, for food and for sex, for survival and reproduction. Unable to conquer the intelligentsia fully, "évidence" was a vast distance from touching the "people," as the physiocrats envisioned. Caringly disposed toward them, the Genevan nevertheless saw no reason for optimism concerning their evolution "because their roughness, their blindness, and their ignorance result from the social laws and will never change".[76]

These social laws give expression to a rigid, withering social reality and underline the abyss that separates the banker-philosophe from the physiocrats. For the latter, the rural and urban masses are mired in prejudices, certainly the qualifier that occurs most frequently when the *économistes* write about the consumer-people (or, for that matter, about the subaltern administration, and by extension anyone else not touched by the *évidence* that makes it impossible not to recognize the imperatives of natural law or the transformative advantages of liberalization). The "people" are cognitively impaired, in a quasi-mechanical fashion; intellectual and emotional obstructions make them subject to flawed assumptions, erroneous interpretations and psychological affectations, that is to say, according to the physiocrats, to the tyranny of prejudices. Their own logic obliges these thinkers to be sanguine: over time—they are almost always vague about temporalities—the "people" can overcome these prejudices as they become enlightened, through processes barely intimated. Necker does not deny that the "people" are intellectually handicapped, but he anchors this issue in the social question, not in the first instance in the minds of the actors. The "people" act in the ways that the physiocrats often describe more or less faithfully, not because they are coarse or stupid or uninitiated in certain mysteries, but because they are dispossessed and oppressed. This brutalization may generate attitudes that can be likened to what the physiocrats christen prejudices. For the Genevan, however, they bespeak the defense of legitimate interests of persons inscribed in an asymmetrical struggle not of their choosing in which their survival is at stake. People are not prejudiced because they are

75 Ibid., 154–55.
76 Ibid., 5, 155–56.

unenlightened; rather, it is because they are property-less and powerless. This perspective of social realism, which the physiocrats refuse to engage, gives depth and coherence to Necker's analysis. This proximity to lived experienced is not compatible with what he calls their "system"; their "abstract ideas" are impervious to the "combat obscur" that the future minister believes to be at the core of the social process.

Imagination, Education and Inequality

Influenced by Locke and Condillac, the banker-philosophe believed that their senses moved and shaped the ways that the "people" apprehended and decoded their world. To fathom this inchoate epistemology, he relies on an often cryptic notion of imagination that merits a separate treatment.[77] This imagination seems to fit neither in the magical intermediation between thought and being of the Renaissance (though Necker's concept is sometimes redolent of Paracelsus' "internal sun") nor in the Enlightenment tension between lucidity and dream. Necker's imagination appears to be closely linked to sensation, both in Plato's sense of a "combination of sensation and of opinion" and in Malebranche's suggestion of a psycho-physiological theory of association linking things and the self, a "sympathy" connecting oneself to the surrounding world. Imagination here seems to crystallize as a cognitive force during the complex process in which an individual attends to his sensory impressions. This imagination, in Voltaire's terms, is "active," because it combines received images. It has an ambiguous relation to external reality, occasionally morphing into what we call representation, yet it participates in an inner reality to which outsiders have only indirect access. It operates sometimes in synergy, but sometimes in antagonism, with what Necker calls opinion: they collaborate, for example, in the making of prices. Imagination does not appear any more volatile than opinion, though it is less susceptible to manipulation because it is better sheltered; yet, if it is in some ways more personal/individual, it also participates in framing collective representations. While this argument requires much more scrutiny, it seems that imagination

---

77 I counted, for example, fifteen pages in the Staël edition of *Législation* where Necker deploys the term at least once and almost sixty mentions in his later study on religious opinion. *Sur la Législation et le commerce des grains, Oeuvres Complètes*, ed. Staël, vol. 1 (Paris, 1821), 34, 56, 110, 165, 166, 203, 229, 230, 253, 255, 260, 301, 306, 323, 332. *De l'Importance des opinions religieuses* (Liège, 1988), 10, 16, 37, 40, 43, 44, 48, 57–58, 84, 108, 109, 133, 137, 140, 151, 161, 209, 219, 227, 230, 234, 255, 262–63, 274, 299, 309, 312, 314, 321, 328, 330, 333, 337–39, 348, 351, 355, 363, 368, 371, 375, 378, 393, 395, 405, 412, 417, 434, 437, 441, 453, 455.

must recede in order to make place for "the authority of reason," and this progression does not seem to be programmable or predictable.[78] Doubtless, it is related to formal education, which is beyond the reach of the "people," given the socioeconomic constraints that govern their lives.[79]

If—counterfactually—the "people" were not compelled to renounce instruction for socioeconomic reasons, were they in fact educable? Here and there, Necker seems to entertain this thought experiment, though he does not explore the question thoroughly in *Législation*, and never clearly concludes. The most pertinent paragraph takes cynical aim at the physiocrats in particular (wondering whether they could reach the masses "by the force of *évidence*, effect of modern science") and at the Enlightenment in general (content to speculate on the impact of progress, yet still, *grosso modo*, attached to the traditional social order that political reforms in the sense of reducing arbitrary rule would not necessarily modify, certainly not in depth). What no one seemed to have taken into account in speculations about the gradual enlightenment of the "people" was its potential for profoundly destabilizing society.[80] Or did this issue remain unspoken precisely as a result of its incendiary implications? Would not an

78 *Opinions religieuses*, 417.

79 For the treatment of imagination, see note 72 above and especially Jacques Marx, "Le Concept d'imagination au XVIIIe siècle," in Raymond Trousson, ed., *Thèmes et figures du siècle des Lumières* (Geneva: Librairie Droz, 1980), 147–59. I am grateful to Arnaud Orain for this reference. To take the measure of the Condillacian affinity with Necker's conceptions, see Orain's articles: "Decline and Progress: The Economic Agent in Condillac's Theory of History," *European Journal of Economic Thought* 10 (Autumn 2003): 379–407; "Directing or Reforming Behavior: A Discussion of Condillac's Theory of *Vrai Prix*," *History of Political Economy* 38 (2006): 497–530; and "The Moral Theory of Condillac: A Path toward Utilitarianism," *Revue de philosophie économique* 13 (2012): 95–120. Cf. Necker's rueful assessment of the way the (nameless early) revolutionaries viewed their countrymen, throughout the social spectrum, in a manner that betrays residual physiocratic influence as well as an indifference to the force of imagination: "Take note as well how, in imitation of their nature, they seek to make of us abstract beings. How they leave to the side everything that pertains to the imagination, to this active motive of many things, at the point of intersection of so many opinions and sentiments." *Sur l'Administration de M. Necker par lui-même*, 378. Two years later, the ex-minister refers to imagination as "this continual agitator," capable of engendering not only political ideas but also "phantoms" that inhabit the "people," nourished by existential anxieties. *Réflexions sur l'inégalité*, 52, 53, 62. Still later, in his *Cours de morale religieuse* (1800), he expresses pessimism about the imaginative aptitude of the "people": "None of the resources, just as none of the restlessness of the imagination, belongs habitually to the last classes of the people." Cited by Henri Grange, *Les Idées de Necker* (Paris: Klincksieck, 1974), 117.

80 One thinks of the remarks—between *boutade* and embryonic social analysis—of Rétif de la Bretonne and Louis-Sébastien Mercier on the perils of teaching (urban) workers to read. See Kaplan, *La Fin des corporations*.

educated class of workers place into question the asymmetries and injustices on which the Old Regime was founded? "Is it really so sure that the spread of enlightenment was to the advantage of the Proprietors?" asked Necker, at once provocative and fretful.

> If the People were capable of heeding abstract truths, wouldn't they, at the same time, have the capacity to reflect on the origin of ranks, on the source of private property, and on all the institutions that are inimical to them? Is it so certain, after all, that this inequality of knowledge has not become necessary to the preservation of all the social inequalities that brought it into being?

The Genevan's take is in the end pessimistic: he favors a sort of ordered movement or evolution, but foresees enormous structural inertia and enhanced resistance as the risks of change become more conspicuous. "But all these inequalities will never cease," he anticipates, "and the People of all times will always be the same; they never listened to reason concerning the dearness of bread, and they will never listen to it".[81]

For Necker, the people are intrinsically important—morally and materially—as citizens who constitute, sustain and enrich society and state, along with others, to be sure, albeit in the end they are more indispensable. Their role, then, is not merely tragic; beyond suffering, they contribute mightily to the wealth and power of the nation.[82] Necker's vigorous populationist posture shaped his attitude both toward the "people" and the ways in which the state and the powerful (formerly known as the ruling classes) treated them. Guarantor of a muscular state and a durable prosperity, a sturdy, gradually expanding population presupposed a constant pushback against what we would later know as the Malthusian obstructions. Here was another compelling reason to support the consumer quest for a reliable grain supply. For the future minister, one of the major arguments justifying "the obstacles imposed upon the free exportation of grain" and other "prohibitive laws" is their efficacy in "the fostering of national work and the upkeep of the population."[83] Foreigners subsidize their well-being by buying their labor (not only in finished industrial goods but also in the form of flour rather than grain) and refraining from

81 *Législation*, 158.

82 I do not follow Grange on the distinction between a physiocratic emphasis on wealth (implying a demographic optimum) and a Necker more interested in population-as-power than in wealth creation per se. In my view, the banker-philosophe regarded the two as inextricably linked. See Grange, *Idées de Necker*, 91 (but also his remarks on the religious dimension of Necker's populationism, 517–87).

83 Cf.: "A country that would harvest a great deal of grain, and that would sell constantly to foreigners, would have an imperfect population." *Législation*, 34.

appropriating their food. This policy was as political as it was paternal: "The population becomes, in political economy, the surest guarantee of the union of Happiness and of strength."[84]

The Protocol of Riots in England and Wales

The people problem, as we have seen, has long exercised historians of England, from E. P. Thompson, Eric Hobsbawm and George Rudé to the generation of John Bohstedt, an American long immersed in British archives. Bohstedt has written with imagination and acuity about the English provisioning experience, largely from a political or sociopolitical perspective, in ways that have helped me better grasp certain aspects of the French case(s). In *Riots and Community Politics*, he argues that the riot was "a kind of informal give-and-take that shared several characteristics of institutional politics."[85] Extra- rather than anti-institutional, this social politics implicated police and people in a "protocol of riot" that affected policy, but did not jeopardize the organization of local power (4–5). The English common people, like the French, were accustomed to acting collectively, and "rough convention" governed both nonviolent and more raucous demonstrations. While recognizing the important task of rehabilitation that George Rudé and others undertook in casting riots as rational responses to grievances rather than paroxysms of impetuous, destructive behavior, like Richard Cobb, who chides Rudé's crowd for being "altogether too respectable," Bohstedt resists a new doxa (or stereotype) that romanticizes the crowd.[86] The antidote is a more rigorous historical contexualization that eschews psychologizing (human nature is not on the agenda), that is less selective, that attempts to explain the incidence of uprisings and, above all, that accounts for the behavior of the crowd (it is a kind of tautology to propose that their grievances created the riotous crowd) (11).

It turns out that most grievances did not generate riots as mechanically as the rational response paradigm intimates, and that the connection between hardship and collective action is empirically weak as well as theoretically hobbled. Like C. Tilly, Bohstedt rebuffs the hydraulic model; as we have found in France, the *mercuriale*, or price register, does not secrete collective violence in any predictable manner (15–19). Of course, prices mattered, but an understanding of their mediation requires a much more

---

84 *Législation*, 17–18, 124–25; *De l'Administration des finances*, ed. Staël, vol. 4, 266, 292, 524.

85 J. Bohstedt, *Riots and Community Politics in England and Wales, 1790–1810* (Cambridge, MA: Harvard University Press, 1983).

86 See R. C. Cobb, *The Police and the People: French Popular Protest, 1789–1820*, 89.

complete tableau of local social politics, predicated in large measure on the sodalities and arrangements of the community, its shared expectations and the "red lines" that it draws (e.g., exportation as an alien threat to its well-being). The qualities of familiarity and interaction among members of a community (evidenced through networks born of work, play, worship, exchange or association of various sorts) that Bohstedt finds in England also appear to exist in French communities that have similar itineraries, yet they are hard to discern and demonstrate (22–23). It is worth noting that English magistrates, like their French counterparts, construe property rights in foodstuffs as imperfect and in some sense conditional—in the English case, even after the old statutes against forestalling, engrossing and regrating, for example, had been abrogated, just as in the French case, after liberalization cleansed and redeemed these "crimes" as legitimate and socially beneficial commercial practices (24–25). This common ambiguity permitted a wider appeal to shared, age-old assumptions that constituted an ideology to which people and police could subscribe with uneven or asymmetrical engagement, setting the ground for what Bohstedt calls "local political bargaining" (26).

Golden Ages, Markets and Mentalities

In France, as in England and Wales, vertical, reciprocal relations between police and people induced both sides to respect a "protocol" in riots that we label spontaneous at the risk of slighting their structural roots (202). Like Bohstedt, I do not view food riots as backward-looking, according to some teleological template impatient to see consumers become labor in proper class choreography or to embrace the pursuit of change through electoral politics that, in France, would have no relevance till well into the nineteenth century, after the lush albeit fraught opportunities that the Revolution briefly proffered. Eighteenth-century food rioters did not erupt in pursuit of a golden age, though in France there are myriad cases during the two liberalizations and the Revolution when the crowd affirms regulatory values that hearken back to a covenant between prince and people and that are compatible both with paternalism and sundry notions of rights, lodged variously in custom, nature, contract and collectivity, interpreted in multiple, sometimes discordant ways. Bohstedt stresses that the decline in food riots, in the English case, does not represent a shift from "traditionalist to progressive ideology" (211–12).

In sympathy again with Bohstedt, as I indicate elsewhere in this work, I do not believe that food riots can be understood as local reactions against the growth of a national market system, though such a position by no means presupposes that, locally, the penetration of capitalism, in its myriad forms, notably agrarian, commercial and industrial, did not provoke collective riposte. Bohstedt concurs with Karl Gunnar Persson: far from fostering food upheavals, the (slow, uneven) growth of the (inchoate) national market was beginning to make them obsolete by 1800 (in France, almost a half century later). I will not rehearse the American scholar's argument, important in the English case, on the shift to a certain radicalism in the trajectory of the nineteenth-century crowd, albeit the historiography of the sans-culottes, in some ways much less sophisticated, faces similar questions of transition and transformation (211–12).

It does seem useful to recall Charles Tilly's insistence that collective violence was not intrinsically archaic, but that it stemmed regularly from everyday social and political processes across the long run (220). For reasons that elude me, Bohstedt seems wedded to the idea of extrapolating a sense of "mentality" from the quotidian milieu of the concrete, particular and local in which rioters are immersed. It seems to me more fruitful to concentrate on the hypothesis that riots are part of a complex relation inscribed in "the system of property and power"—a relation that I can recognize in France as well. And I endorse his rejection of the theory of hegemony as an explanation for the lack of massive insurgency in England. In France, as in England, we see considerable evidence of the autonomy of a robust plebeian culture, which E. P. Thompson maps out. Bohstedt perhaps underestimates the subtle ways in which ideology and various symbolic constructions shape popular representations and practices, albeit I tend to agree with him that, in the end, politics—the articulation and enforcement of claims—depends on *rapports de force*, as riots habitually showed (222–23).

The Politics of Provisions

More than a quarter century after the publication of *Riots and Community Politics*, John Bohstedt returned to the question of food supply in another important study in which he rethought certain assumptions about the relation of the past to the present, about the formation and operation of ideology, about vertical and horizontal social relations and about the articulation and exercise of power. This recent work is a broader study, at once more exacting in terms of demonstration and more synthetic in its analysis, targeting what he calls "the politics of provisions."[87] I construe the politics of provisioning in France as a struggle over the legitimacy of claims and frequently for their implementation that takes place at multiple levels in disparate ways. It occurs within the

87 J. Bohstedt, *The Politics of Provisions: Food Riots, Moral Economy and Market Transition in England, c. 1550–1850* (Burlington, VT: Ashgate, 2010).

central government itself and within and among competing (theoretically complementary) administrative and judicial organs; among intellectuals and within a press that is censored yet finds space for a certain plurality of views; sometimes between the governors and the governed, sometimes between a common front of the local police and the people against higher authorities and various economic actors; between a variegated albeit robust liberal lobby and partisans of a generally supple yet structuring regulatory persuasion; and finally between consumers and producers (more often obliquely than directly) and between haves and have-nots (in a diffuse yet framing manner). Wisely, Bohstedt opts for a less sprawling, tidier definition, at once precise and elastic, emphasizing initiatives from below in the combat for the daily bread that is widely assumed to be a right, an entitlement and an imperious necessity that justifies, in the not notoriously indulgent mind of Hobbes, transgressions against the law, notably procuring food by force or stealth: "Provision politics could be summed up as common people's collective actions to avert acute hunger and their rulers' responses." Casting the question over the long run—700 food riots between 1550 and 1820—the American historian is interested in both the rise and the fall of this politics (1–3, 10).

Dearth recurred frequently; given the preponderance of bread or grain in the family budget, "cherté" precipitated alarm, below and above, as well as "acute social tension." While the English rioted over a panoply of issues, from excise taxes and enclosures to military conscription and the selection of prayer books, the food insurgency was the most common. Rioters had no illusions about the gravity of the stakes: in England as in France, they did not shrink from the rallying cry: "We'd rather be hanged than starved."[88] The movement from (ordinary) anxiety to panic, from (everyday) order to chaos, from (normative) submission to insurrection, and then the restoration of tranquility and the reaffirmation of quasi-contractual bonds constituted an oft-repeated cycle as common to France as to England. I am not at all sure that the French resorted to repression by physical force nearly as frequently as the English did in Ireland. Perhaps Bohstedt underestimates the role of vertical solidarities, the claims of reciprocity and the exercise of negotiation across the channel, but he is probably right, in echo of Tocqueville's caustic deploration, that local, gentlemanly paternalism, embedded in (once) traditional social relations rather than (relatively recent) institutions of the usurpatory central administration, "lubricated political authority" and took

88 Bohstedt identifies the readiness to rebel sooner than starve as a "mentality" (23), a concept familiar to readers of his *Riots and Community Politics*, liminally situated between the psychological and the sociological, which seems to me to lack efficacy either as description or in explanation.

responsibility for furnishing relief much less often in France than in England. Yet the description of food markets as "not simply functions of supply and demand," but institutions "politically constructed, permeated by power and normative judgments, high and low, and modified by social contestations," resonated with the French experience (1–3).

In Bohstedt's tableau, the people are actors, partners and collaborators even as they move in and out of what on the other side of the channel we would call rebellions. Operating with a model that parallels my distinction between marketplace and market principle, he shows how the marketplace in some sense belongs to and in any case is recognized as the privileged space of the people. Still, if the women and men willing to remonstrate or mutiny hold center stage, Bohstedt stresses their symbiotic and synergistic relation with the authorities, riveting a theme on which I, too, have placed emphasis. "The interaction of rioters' and rulers' expectations and actions on the economic, moral or cultural, and the political plane is what I mean by the politics of provision," he writes. This was a politics predicated on the permanent tension between consensus and conflict, involving "struggles" over food, private property that could not elude public claims in certain circumstances. Widely held norms governed its distribution in these times, but they were "contested" and intrinsically equivocal and parlous.

The settlement of issues turning on food allocation in times of scarcity almost always turned on "struggles" whose orchestration and denouement Bohstedt vividly evokes. They were "sanctioned ultimately on both sides by physical force: the power of crowds vs. the power of muskets and gallows"—the confrontation of two agonistic understandings or projects of order and disorder. This researcher also fathoms, it seems to me, in ways that sometimes escape historians inured to demographic analysis or remote from the lived experience of the laboring poor and the destitute, the sheer savagery of hunger, the predatory character of extreme penury, the thing in itself and its specter, whose lacerating stress is both psychological and physical.[89] Dearth elicited the perpetual threat of consumer intervention in the marketplace: "the story of provisioning politics was to end when armed state power excluded popular interference." That would not be till the nineteenth century: In the interim, the historian believes in the efficacy of the politics of provisions, which may

89 With manifestly fewer constraints, novelists have done a better job dealing with this than historians, frustrated by insufficiently loquacious or intimate sources. See, for instance, the classic work of Knut Hamsun, *Hunger* (1890), trans. Sverre Lyngstad (New York: Penguin, 1996). On a far less lofty literary plane, albeit with evocative moments, see Piers Paul Read, *Alive: The Story of the Andes Survivors* (London: Secker & Warburg 1974). See chapter 7 for other leads.

very well have mitigated the risk of "famine" and/or its consequences, and contributed to the task of state making, a hypothesis that is only paradoxical if one sees riot making in reductionist manner (4, 6, 12, 21, 23, 120).

A Critique of Thompson's Moral Economy

No historian who specializes in collective action, especially in England, can avoid a reckoning with E. P. Thompson's moral economy. I sympathize with Bohstedt's approach: a vibrant homage to the pioneering, insightful work of this exceptional scholar, followed by a searching critique of certain shortcomings in his conception and analysis a half-century after their elaboration, based in large measure on research that his work stimulated. Bohstedt challenges the specifically Tudor–Stuart genesis of the moral economy, positing in its stead a "praxis of provision politics" that waxed and waned over three centuries as a function of a dialectic between the atemporal "law of necessity" and ever-changing conditions (11). Given Thompson's assumptions about shared political–cultural–communitarian values and about the motor of severe hardship, asks Bohstedt, "why did hungry people sometimes not riot?" He upholds that other factors are required to complete the explanation of why and how people rioted for food, "since economic causation and moral outrage were not enough."[90] However hungry, he argues, reasonably, it seems to me, people were disposed to "calculate their political prospects," assay what we would call opportunity costs: a consciousness of their political assets shaped their comportment as much as or more than their deprivations (12–13). The historian quite pertinently posits that Thompson's view of the workings of the moral economy was marred by a lack of familiarity with the structure and operation of the grain and flour trade, the hidden part of the iceberg in many studies that deal with "subsistence" collective action (14).

---

90 "I have argued elsewhere that the economic 'causation' of food riots is even weaker than Thompson supposed," writes Bohstedt (12). Later in this study, it seems to me that he strains to distance his rioters from any referential relation (through memory, legend or inherited customary norms) with "old regulations and paternalist texts about 'forestallers, regraters and engrossers'." Yet, like their French counterparts—we are in eighteenth century England, dubbed the "golden age" of food riots—they did denounce and attack grain owners or traders who hoarded, engrossed and so on. According more emphasis to material determination than he previously claimed was his wont, the American researcher observes: "But it was need, not simply moral offense, that found voice in their words and actions" (105). He is aiming at Thompson's remark that "an outrage to these moral assumptions, quite as much as actual deprivation, was the usual occasion for direct action." "The Moral Economy of the English Crowd in the Eighteenth Century," *Past & Present* 50 (1971): 79.

Bohstedt further reproaches the British historian with a practice that also permeates his *Making of the English Working Class*: inferring popular attitudes and collective norms from the discourse of elites. His examination of the words of rioters, though imperfect, persuades him that "a *popular*" moral economy was not simply "derived from the 'old paternalist moral economy'." Thus, the need to examine the whole range of rioters' "motivations and calculations" beyond the framework of a moral economy, to reconstitute "a whole ecology of provision politics" that takes into account, along with pressing necessity and paternalism, the "relationships, resources and recourses" of the rioters as well as their representations of the world at the moment they faced dire choices (14–15). Finally, without an excess of positivist zeal or revanchism, Bohstedt makes the case for a conjoined quantitative and qualitative examination of riots instead of reducing (or bloating) a relatively small number of them to sacrosanct anecdotal status, susceptible to unrepresentative extrapolation. At the margin, this is a double indictment of a variant of *histoire événementielle*, long after its rehabilitation, and of a certain kind of smug micro-history, though our historian is really more interested in pragmatic issues of methodology ("So I count riots" and "I mean here to examine what people said and did") than in epistemological debate (15–20).

Exports, Monopolies and the Violence of Popular Vengeance

England suffered a phase of intense subsistence turbulence in the 1760s, at the very time that dearth-cum-liberalization convulsed France. Exportation, as a detested principle charged with toxic memory and as a deleterious fact of life, shaped the English unrest in ways similar to the French experience. Despite a major industrial slump following the Seven Years' War, burgeoning unemployment, decline in real wages and an impaired harvest in 1766 that resulted in proliferating *cherté*, a six-month parliamentary ban on exports, which had not only been permitted for some time but also encouraged, expired, and just as a cereal crisis began to crystallize, even as farmers were threshing, traders once again could ship abroad without limits and obtain *bounties* for so doing. There followed, one is tempted to say predictably, an "explosion of riots" aiming to halt the cascading tide of grain surging toward the ports. Though bereft of spectacular reform issues to polarize attitudes as in France, the government re-promulgated the old (long-repudiated) statutes against forestallers, regraters and engrossers—what one called the *police des grains* across the channel—but, according to certain press reports, magistrates hesitated to execute them for fear of aggravating the dearth by interfering with the transactions and speculations of grain holders and traders. Finally, before the new parliamentary session, the government, facing swelling exports and proliferating riots, overcame its constitutional scruples, in the name of the *salus populi*, and banned exports (111–12).

Bohstedt insists that halting exports rather than "regulating marketplaces" was the core of eighteenth-century provision politics. During riots in the 1740s and 1750s, worried consumers attacked mainly exporters, often bolting mills, the centers of commercialized milling applying an integrated, mechanized technology, highly suggestive of certain aspects of French economic milling. While these mills in France had no notorious connection with export networks, their operators stood accused on occasion, like the English millers, of organizing monopoly—the word resonates in similar ways in both monarchies—and practicing adulteration, among other questionable activities. I was astonished to learn that in all three rioting periods, the millers—apparently not organized corporatively—took out newspaper advertisements "to assure the public" that they were not using whiting, chopped straw, dung, bones, or other adulterants or bleaches, and to deny that they were exporting. This suggests a considerable "opinion/media" lag between the two countries: in France, there is virtually no applied nexus of exchange between commercial and cultural realms. Though I can imagine other explanations, according to Bohstedt, "these ads evidently assumed their readers were either among the rioters or in contact with them; they did not cast rioters as the marginal poor or outsiders" (113–15).

Pursuing his refutation of/polemic against the Thompson model, Bohstedt underlines that rioters who destroyed mills were not reacting against "market innovations"; his crowds were far more precociously accustomed, generally, to what he vaguely calls commercialization (which was "neither new nor a target for resistance" in the eighteenth century) and, more specifically, to off-market trading, by sample, in the field or in barns, than would-be French rioters. And while English rioters readily believed bolt-millers, flour factors and other export-oriented intermediaries to be hoarders and "monopolizers" who found sundry ways to keep grain away from marketplaces, "those grievances are common to many times and places, hardly redolent of particular market codes." Yet, his besetting need to deny the efficacy of Thompson's old codes seems, at least in part, undermined by his own assertive emphasis on the power of memory ("memory banks" accumulating the capital of riot experiences that nourished successive waves of collective actors in their appraisal of opportunities): is it not plausible that there lodged in the collective memories, legends and customs of the English rioters, community by community, something resembling what I would call a Delamarist sediment, the distillation or precipitation of compilations of regulations and norms articulated and transmitted over the decades and centuries? (112, 119, 129–131, 140, 143, 163).

I am inclined to align myself with Bohstedt in his skepticism of the squeaky-clean image that early rehabilitating historians of the crowd, Rudé hand-in-hand with Thompson, assigned to the crowd-in-action: habitually restrained, disciplined and programmed to pay a just price for seized grain or flour, to eschew (gratuitous) theft, to endorse, at least implicitly, the canon of the inviolability of private property. He notes that rioters "typically used violence to seize food and valuables," plundered goods and stole money in numerous cases, beat up victims and by no means systematically made payment for (confiscated) food sold on the market, improvised or official.[91] From my French perspective, this mixed picture seems more familiar, if perhaps somewhat overdrawn in the name of reestablishing a balance, reading empirical data without a certain idealizing (or *angélisant*) refraction; I recognize disorder, bacchanal and cruelty as well as abnegation, decency and self-control in the crowd: a mix of Lefebvre and Cobb, with a firm rejection of the caricature-anathema stereotypes of Le Bon at the end of the nineteenth century, or Eric Rohmer at the beginning of the twenty-first century (in his beautiful and nastily tendentious film *L'Anglaise et le Duc*) (119–21).

Morality and the Market

In a richly textured, thoughtful and engaging book, the Belfast-based historian James Davis gives us a long-run perspective on the moral economy, coupled inextricably, in his view, with a real-life, functioning market.[92] In historiographical terms, in terms of the spillover from medieval to early modern times, one of his tasks appears to be, in some sense, to rescue the market from its morality (even as he argues consistently for their intermeshing). Deeply marked by E. P. Thompson, many, if most, historians privilege the moral economy over the market, or the morality over the economy in their conceptualization, research and analysis. Embedded in the social, the economic seems no longer to merit dedicated, holistic attention: devoid of autonomy, its intrinsic dynamism registers only sporadically; the economy endures a segmentation that postulates an implicit break between the commerce of goods of first necessity and the trade in all the rest. Davis contends, often cogently, that this perspective is not supported by the evidence, medieval or early modern, and that it is futile to oppose starkly the economic to the sociocultural (the political is, alas, largely outside his purview).

91 Yet Bohstedt allows that "rioters' actions were often disciplined, *when* they were disciplined by the praxis of patronage" (142).

92 *Medieval Market Morality: Life, Law and Ethics in the English Marketplace, 1200–1500* (Cambridge: Cambridge University Press, 2012).

Yet his lapidary empiricism seems in part driven by dauntless economistic assumptions. I am thinking specifically of the claim, a leitmotif in his lexicon, that there are "market forces" (sometimes called market mechanisms or "market laws" or "free-market forces") that are both foundational and transparent, that is, sheltered from any need for problematization (21, 23, 25, 29, 418, 443, 444, 448). I feel uncomfortable (free?) riding on the misty albeit telic wave of an "increasingly market-oriented" society, while, from an anthropological perspective, it is no more reassuring to face "growing capitalist instincts," for I do not construe capitalism as natural, innate or unlearned (32, 375, 411, 448). Nor have I ever encountered a "free market" outside theory class, a handicap that hampers my ability to measure, with Davis, the extent to which "noneconomic forces," which are manifestly legion, "distort" such putative free places (26, 60, 445). I would be disinclined to invoke market efficiency as a near universal, transcendental criterion for success, rather than handling the question of efficiency as a time-specific, culturally and situationally fashioned and economically shaped variable (27, 412, 450, 453–55).[93]

Still, even if it seems to begin with certain aprioris or Walrasian sempiternal verities, the great (and uncommon) strength of Davis' work is the care, detail and critical prowess with which he treats the operations of the concrete, not the abstractly paradigmatic, market. Mobilizing an impressive range of data—literary, ecclesiastic, administrative, quantitative and comparative—he shows us how a medieval market worked; the various expressions of its regulation; how contemporaries (not always socially differentiated) represented economic actors and practices, in particular the motives and comportment of merchants; and how in fact traders actually behaved (where the distinction between retailers and middlemen tends to blur, the nomenclature and the boundaries rendering difficult comparison with French dealers).[94] Aside from its intrinsic *maestria*, the discussion serves as an implicit reproach to historians of the moral economy in particular, extendable to students of collective action, among others, both those who revile and those who admire neoclassical models of exchange, but

---

93 In the same vein, whether in the Smithian or Beckerian idiom, I doubt that the discussion of whether individuals were habitually "economically rational" or whether irrationality dominated their behavior is useful, in terms of Davis' own argument (26, 447, 451). Cast in terms of a more generic strategic rationality, the question might have more traction and pertinence.

94 Davis pays opulent attention to retail trades, but is obviously also interested in middlemen, who appear as badgers, traders, merchants without specific qualification or, in some instances, as engrossers. I would have liked a clearer articulation of the levels and relations among them, and of the extent to which the popular knowledge of the market on which the historian insists covers the wholesale or semiwholesale side as well as the retail camp (83–120, 233–41, 253–63, 311–14, 391–407, 420–26, 413, 429).

seldom bother to impose a reality check on their suppositions; and perhaps especially those, generally found among the revilers, who presume that because an economy, and *a fortiori* a market, are embedded, and thus deeply constrained by social and/or ethical conventions, there is no need to wonder about how the processes of selling and buying worked, since the outcomes are more or less predictable, if not foreordained, notably where subsistence issues prevail.

The Medieval Roots of the Moral Economy

Even if he only addresses it directly in the last part of his book, Davis is implicitly preoccupied with the Thompsonian template: How can you put the words "market morality" in the title of a book, especially one devoted to English history, without having to deal with the historian who owns the issue, however much his property claim has been contested over the years. Thompson's notion of paternalism derived in part from assumptions about a medieval worldview that Davis clarifies, criticizes and nuances. I have no competence to assess, as a medieval scholar would, the "upstream" case that Davis makes: to my unschooled eyes, with some reservations about his conceptualization, already intimated, and his demonstration, I find his argument and evidence to be globally quite compelling. I have rarely read a more sprightly and concrete description of exchanges at the market. In epitome, Davis' medieval markets work pretty much the way markets functioned in the late eighteenth century—and perhaps beyond (this massive structuring continuity at once reinforces and saps Thompson's reasoning). Indeed, if one accepts the premise, certainly compatible rhetorically with Smithian language, that "a practical, moral basis is important for any economic system," one can, with Davis, describe his markets in quasi-neoclassical idiom.

As we shall see, the historian categorically spurns a stark dichotomy severing *homo economicus* from *homo ethicus* [*sic*]. His markets evince a quasi-naturalized blend of "market forces" and of market morality. His market bears limited and/or superficial resemblance to my marketplace, which I see as a regulatory bulwark, programmed to operate with considerable flexibility and variable countenances (or masks), or rather, *not* programmed at all—the image is too robotic—but designed to adapt to changing circumstances. The trajectory of the Davis market is not *un long fleuve tranquille*, yet it proves to be remarkably robust and resilient, a felicitous composite of (pursuit of) self-interest and (attentiveness to the) general interest, the latter apparently understood here as the concern for the commonwealth and the poor. Mutually antagonistic on one level, economy and morality, in Davis' scenario, are mutually dependent in practice, socially, albeit not organically, symbiotic. Between the thirteenth and eighteenth centuries, the market changes in morphology and in ambition, but not basically in behavior, apart from modifications in scale, contingent upon regional development and shifting factors of production. Increasingly, the famous market forces seem to swell in brawn and gluttony, as if they were on anabolic steroids; but there is no breakaway moment, as the geostrategists and sports announcers say, because the moral configuration manifests unrelentingly what Davis calls, not without a whiff of resigned wonderment, "belligerency". Tit for tat, bespeaking equivalent retaliation? No: more like tit and tat in complicity to achieve ends that generally meet, more or less, everyone's needs, in Davis' underlying Whiggish tenor.

The historian enumerates not only the multiple regulations enunciated for the market, especially the retail side, but also the exchanges involving middlemen that are at least as sensitive, especially in stressful times. Yet, his narrative creates the strong impression that these more or less exogenous or formal or translated kinds of regulation are obviated in practice, or at least reduced to a sort of rhetorical redundancy, by the internalized ethos of buyers and sellers alike (451). This code draws on custom, on inherited or remembered or perceived notions of justice (commutative, distributional and social), on expected reciprocities, perhaps on ideas of entitlement (this question is not worked out) and on the keenly felt presence of God, in some voice or other (25, 455) (a God whose tenacious influence we, scholars of the eighteenth century, tend to underestimate greatly or dismiss because of the blows, often self-inflicted, sustained by the church and because of a mix of Enlightenment aprioris and teleologies). Though he sometimes seems ready to take his chance on human nature, incarnated by the Smithian self-interest that is much more likely than sweet benevolence to put dinner on the table, Davis remarks in the end that men cannot be fully trusted, and thus that the formal regulations must remain in place, at least in the social dynamics prevalent before the Industrial Revolution.[95] Even so, he suggests that regulation is truly

95 "People might have internalized norms of behavior and had a disposition to obey such norms, but no society could rely exclusively on such a disposition. There remained an important role for enforcement and punishment, particularly in markets where there were more impersonal dealings" (455). Although there were outsider and free rider problems in French markets, I do not think that the inclination to regulate correlated negatively with familiarity of the actors (sellers and buyers) to the authorities. The historian also takes note of the issue that became so contentious among the thinkers of the Economic Enlightenment: a compelling reason to regulate stemmed from the fact that society was not naturally harmonious, the postulate of virtually all the anti-physiocrats (452). Yet, in the end, Davis concludes that a "market morality" is more tellingly forged by informal than formal constraints.

effective only if the values it is designed to enforce are already embedded in the society (451).[96]

In etic terms, Davis leaves me convinced and envious; I wish we had an array of studies of markets of this caliber for France. On the emic side, he is less persuasive, despite his framing interventions. Obliquely and by extrapolation/interpolation—but without a genuine demonstration—he affirms that ordinary people were fully attuned to the mechanisms and the workings of the market. They fathomed its operations, presumably, because the "markets had been part of people's lives" for so long (444). We don't learn precisely how poorer consumers, apparently urban, acquired "a substantive knowledge about how markets worked day-to-day" (445). Nor was there a city–countryside gap in this cognitive domain, because "the peasantry [as well as their lords] understood market mechanisms very clearly," an observation the historian ostensibly infers from the pervasive role of money and credit in the rural milieu (21). Yet, Davis avers that there are serious doubts regarding popular command of realities (underappreciation of the positive role of cornmongers, for instance) and about the extent to which popular fears, presumably about monopoly, manipulation, and dearth-exploitation were indeed founded (for me, an interesting yet secondary question in the study of subsistence issues, and, arguably, also an impertinent question in the double sense of the word, for I am uneasy about tacitly chiding consumers for being anxious when they allegedly had no reason to be, especially consumers who are said to be quite familiar with how the market works; I surmise that Davis would not subject moral anxieties to the same reality check (445)). I do not suppose that Davis' market-knowledgeable people were sophisticated enough to interpret forestalling and regrating as Schumpeterian entrepreneurial initiatives (372); it took the radicalizing liberalization measures in France in the 1760s to rehabilitate these activities in this flattering, efficiency-enhancing and modernizing manner. Is Davis sympathetic with Adam Smith's well-known observation that "the popular fear of engrossing and forestalling may be compared to the popular terrors and suspicions of witchcraft?"[97] If this were to be the case, it would then be hard to take seriously the sundry apprehensions and anxieties of the benighted (yet market-knowledgeable

96 In discussing internalization, Davis clings on occasion to worn concepts that have lost their carrying capacity, such as "mentalities," "mental climate" and "mindset" (22, 23, 31, 416).

97 Smith, *An Inquiry into the Nature and Causes of the Wealth of Nations*, ed. E. Cannan (London, 1937), IV-5-65. The citation continues: "The unfortunate wretches accused of this latter crime were not more innocent of the misfortunes imputed to them than those who have been accused of the former. The law which put an end to all

and, thus, socioculturally schizophrenic) "people." Still, along with the intimation that fear cannot be considered a rational (or strategic) act, one senses in Davis' treatment a hierarchy or value gradient of concurrent or competitive realities, with the etic submerging the emic.

Perhaps, I am guilty of asymmetrical skepticism, or the Gallican bias of my own experience, because I find it much less problematic to conceive of the way in which this same people manifest cultural beliefs that shape market institutions or to embrace Craig Muldrew's exhortation to "take into account the cultural meanings which economic phenomena have for everyday people," which will help us better understand, beyond regulatory prompts, why people make "ethical decisions *within the market*" (26, 27).[98] The cultural context is bewildering because it involves so many disparate elements—memory, tradition, religion and the primacy of one's salvation, endogenous notions of justice, law, the writings of commentators that are often contradictory and regulatory doctrine and application (which themselves involve a tension between the practical and the ethical, between (say) encouraging economic exchanges and promoting social cohesion, between (say) preventing social unrest and sheltering elite commercial privileges) (29–30). Davis portrays his people as cognitively alert, active rather than passive in the market. Yet the cultural context is so much a part of shared experience and so pervasively appropriated and transmitted by the actors that I infer that one could learn and perform ethical behavior in the market a bit in the manner of Monsieur Jourdain's acculturation: *sans le savoir* (451).

The audacious liberalization experiment in France cast into stark relief the enormous weight of this cultural patrimony in shaping behavior and the egregiousness of the royal political calculation that a substitute culture—and a new way of daily life—could be imposed literally by decree. The reformers

prosecutions against witchcraft, which put it out of any man's power to gratify his own malice by accusing his neighbor of that imaginary crime, seems effectually to have put an end to those fears and suspicions by taking away the great cause which encouraged and supported them. The law which should restore entire freedom to the inland trade of corn would probably prove as effectual to put an end to the popular fears of engrossing and forestalling." Apart from seeming to blame hunger on the hungry, the Smith remedy failed in France twice, during the two episodes of liberalization that he watched closely.

98 My emphasis. C. Muldrew, "Interpreting the Market: the Ethics of Credit and Community Relations in Early Modern England," *Social History* 18 (1993): 168. Cf. Richard R. Wilk's reminder that "moral issues are never far from economic life." *Economies and Cultures: Foundations of Economic Anthropology* (Boulder, CO: Westview Press, 1996), 106. Note also his noncanonic insights in "Taking Gender to Market: A Comment on the Markets Debate." *Feminist Economics* 2, no. 1: 90–93.

believed they could overcome by sheer force of neutral science and political will the "belligerence" that many authorities and commentators knew full well undergirded popular conceptions of subsistence rights. The implications of the crisis were so fraught that it seems inconceivable that they could have been resolved *within the market* (or even within the marketplace). The market principle, which denied any legitimacy to the moral economy, tenebrous relic of a discredited past, did not take into consideration that part of the vocation of the laissez-faire market was to lower the transaction costs of sustaining a modicum of social peace and cohesion as well as the costs of search, negotiation and enforcement.[99]

The Pragmatic Moral Economy

The upshot of this entire discussion—at least for nonmedievalists—is to reject the Thompsonian opposition between the moral economy and the market economy. More intimately familiar with the "medieval concepts of the economy" that E. P. Thompson drew upon, Davis argues that the two practices, to use a Bourdieusian locution of reconciliation, coexisted, that the basic moral principles had not significantly altered since the Middle Ages and that the moral economy did not erode when confronted by an increasingly vital economy in the eighteenth century. His moral economy is supple and adaptive. The market was not subordinated to moral imperatives. Though Davis does not map out the grounds for a veritable synergy, he maintains that the moral economy was "not necessarily incompatible with market values" and that its rhetoric had permeated the vocabulary of everyday marketing.

Proverbial bastion of the stigmatization of unfettered self-interest, avidity and the rapacity for gain, the Middle Ages were in fact highly commercialized and its actors keenly aware of the utility of markets and conversant with the users' manual (411–12, 417–18, 442). The people and elites of the early modern period had the same consideration for the legitimacy of a "reasonable" profit as the medieval counterparts, even as they shared the same opprobrium for the trader, the "popular odium" evoked by Adam Smith

99 Cf. the remark of Douglass North, whose institutional theory nourishes Davis' analysis: "Informal constraints that are culturally derived will not change immediately in reaction to changes in the formal rules. As a result the tension between altered formal rules and the persisting informal constraints produces outcomes that have important implications for the way economies change." Douglass North, *Institutions, Institutional Change and Economic Performance* (Cambridge: Cambridge University Press, 1990), 45.

enjoying a wider purchase than he imagined (427–28).[100] Overregulation suited no one, in the thirteenth or the eighteenth century; as long as the players respected notions of community needs and obligations and the just price (theoretically, the unencumbered fruit of the encounter of supply and demand, yet subjected to certain normative corrections that became more militant in the sixteenth century), no one favored inhibiting trade (433, 448). Dubious himself about the efficacy of regulation, Davis seems to want to stem any renewed regulatory impulse by reminding the actors retrospectively that middlemen were "important cogs in the commercial system," a fact of economic life recognized more readily by certain (unspecified) regulations and by certain (unnamed) "advocates of the new political economics" than by the (equally anonymous) "adherents to the ideals of the moral economy" (434–35, 437, 439).

Nevertheless, the historian remains faithful to his composite line of persistence of basic, framing notions and actions, their conciliation in practice and a permanent and sometimes subconscious balancing act, the core of this Sisyphean, acrobatic labor realized by a deft and dynamic "medieval Church and ideology."[101] In comparison, the moral economy of the early modern period was "stagnant and conservative and increasingly detached from economic change and new mercantile ethics." But it *was*. It existed, and indeed "may have actually gained in strength among consumers" during the English Old Regime. The postmedieval moral economy, contends Davis, was a "pragmatic compromise between the forces of economics, laws and morals"—a "triologic" configuration whose components he alternately baptizes as "morals, law and reality," or "ideology, laws and behaviour" or "morals, law and practice" or "religion, literature and law," or "trade, law and ideology" (30, 32, 33, 438, 457).

The basic alchemy is the same, an uneven but incessant exchange between three competences or influences or perhaps dispositions of pressure that act both in the very short and in the very long run: first, the cultural context, as Davis sometimes calls it, or the ideology, or the congealed and internalized

100 Smith, *Wealth of Nations*, IV-5-48. It is a drastic shortcut for the moral philosopher to attribute this attitude to "ignorance." Ibid., IV-5-63. Committed to accentuating continuity and consensus, Davis does not explore likely tensions between elite and popular culture.

101 "Ultimately, the market required a balance of acquisitiveness and probity for its success and stability" (447). The acquisitiveness is ingrained/internalized: for certain commentators learned, for others innate. I pass on this debate. Whence the probity? Presumably, it is from the cultural side, one of many of the values internalized by the people, as important to the market economy as the moral economy. If this reading is plausible, there is no space or role for regulation: it is already architecturally superfluous.

notions of custom, norms and values, including or accompanied by various manifestations of religion and sundry doses of a sacred and profane literature that addresses these issues, all of which constitute the armature of market morality and forge the compass of *homo ethicus*;[102] then the law, a pillar unto itself, the base of the triangle, at once source and consequence of ideology, norms and values, the law that also figures regulation, control, implementation, enforcement and punishment; and, finally, the "forces of economics," destined one day to eclipse and recast the two other components, described simply (in emic terms) as trade, with more sophistication (in etic terms) as practice or behavior, or in the language that, I suspect, bespeaks Davis' deep take on the question, "reality," the way things are or are becoming, the inexorable facts on the ground, quintessentially economic in character. The triangle is relatively stable, but not immutable, as the weight of the three components shifts over time and across space. Thus, moral commentary and the law lag—predictably, given the force field in which the three factors are situated—behind the "reality of economic circumstances" (30).[103]

According to the "pragmatic moral economy," the people did not, however, express their "moral rights," unspecified "traditional customs" that held powerful sway, "in anti-market terms." Thompson's moral economy "was not an ideology that was in conflict with the market, but it was a belligerent popular ethic that could not [or would not?] adapt to the new *laissez-faire* policies of the late eighteenth century that sought to erode traditional paternal notions" (446–48, 457). A posture that fit the thirteenth century had become objectively anachronistic, according to Davis, even as it continued to mobilize

102 Davis wants us to understand that the formulaic inscription should not mislead us into thinking that the shared cultural baggage is tantamount to a dominant ideology (or mentality) to which everyone subscribes or adheres. He sees, on the contrary, myriad signs of contestation and conflict in the discourse on markets and on ethics (30).

103 In some sense, the pragmatic moral economy, or at least the Bourdieusian field in which it operates, persists even today, for it remains imperative to make capitalism work in an acceptable fashion: it is too bad that Davis devotes only a paragraph to its contemporary relevance. He notes that the "stock figures" of the "accumulative trader and the vulnerable consumer" flourish still in the twentieth century. Is there no stereotype of the regulator to accompany them, to work toward the need for reconciliation on which the author insists? Does the absence of the figure of the regulator not dilute his conviction that "trade, law and ideology, inseparable and yet contradictory bedfellows," remain relevant in our world? "Despite suggestions that modern market ethics lack scruples and morality," Davis observes, "it is clear that such issues cause hand-wringing and consternation." Presuming that the latter formula is not designed to be ironic, I wonder if Davis means to say that hand-wringing and consternation are the most muscular response commonly available these days to perceived ethical flaccidity and that they are, indeed, capable of overcoming the ethical deficit (458)?

popular support, apparently on a wide scale. In the end, the balance underlined by Davis seems very much out of equilibrium. Finally, the argument for the imbrication of market and morality seems more compelling for the Middle Ages, when the market was more welcoming and forgiving because still in so many ways embryonic, than during the Enlightenment, which announces the crossing of the (capitalist) market Rubicon.[104] Belligerence has pathos, but not efficacy, considerable nuisance power but not durable capacity to resist, and in the age that celebrates the *doux commerce*, it seems vulgar and out of place, embodying a lower-order Rabelaisian, popular virility, not the elegance of exalting, emancipating and potent egocentricity.[105]

Rereading Thompson: Moral or Economic?

In an agile and provocative reassessment of the multiple notions of moral economy that have emerged in the wake of E. P. Thompson's pioneering labors, the sociologist (also anthropologist and physician) Didier Fassin reminds us of several points that may have eluded us.[106] First, Thompson himself did not cling tenaciously to the term "moral" and, implicitly, to the moral component, in the exalted sense commonly attached to this word, in his account of the functioning of English society at the community level in more or less ordinary times and, particularly, in stressful moments. In his own revisiting of his seminal article, the English scholar seemed willing to trade moral (somewhat bizarrely) for sociological or political (1237–38). Second, that researchers in sundry disciplines have reappropriated the locution "moral economy," sometimes in rather direct anthropological filiation with the original version, while in other cases at considerable remove. Scores of studies pay homage to Thompson's formula, even as they criticize it, reconfigure it or move beyond it—investigations not only of hunger riots, poverty and labor unrest in various parts of the planet, more often than not in our contemporary

104 Davis oscillates temperamentally between adventurousness and circumspection. On the medieval "fit" I evoked, he cautions that medieval theory and practice were not in complete alignment. To accommodate divergence, tensions and antagonisms, he summons complexity, an irenic and not unreasonable device for casting the interplay between moral and economic practice (32–33).

105 Bakhtin strikes me as more useful here than Hirschman. Of course, I am referring to Mikhaïl Bakhtin, *L'œuvre de François Rabelais et la culture populaire au Moyen Âge et sous la Renaissance*, trans. A. Robel (Paris: Gallimard, 1970) and Albert Hirschman, *The Passions and the Interests: Political Arguments for Capitalism Before its Triumph* (Princeton: Princeton University Press, 1977).

106 Fassin, "Les Economies morales revisitées," *Annales. Histoire, Sciences Sociales*, 64th year (2009/6): 1237–66.

world, but also of immigration, morbidity and epidemiology (HIV-AIDS, alcoholism), entrepreneurship, corruption, stem-cell research and bioethics, racism, ancestor worship and so on. Having himself deployed the moral-economy template, whose heuristic value he celebrates, Fassin believes the time has come to reflect on its banalization and its debilitation: the attenuation of its analytical acuity (1239–40).

For Fassin, Thompson's turn to the moral economy bespoke, *inter alia*, a conviction that quantitative/materialist explanations could not account for crucial parts of the social experience. If, as the social scientist puts it, Thompson wanted to move beyond the objectification of the working class to the process of its subjectification in his celebrated *The Making of the English Working Class*, in the case of hunger riots, his protagonists tended to be peasants rather than workers whose actions could not be understood in mechanistic, Pavlovian or "spasmodic" terms. Fassin sees Thompson's challenge as introducing anthropological thinking into the historical discipline by acknowledging that the poor—presumably largely rural in this instance—possess the same social skills, in particular the aptitude to produce norms, rights and obligations, as the so-called primitive peoples (1241–42).

Fassin argues that most commentators have failed to distinguish adequately two "very distinct levels of analysis" in the moral economy. In the first, the moral economy corresponds to a system of exchanges of goods and services that characterize societies before the market epoch, which I take to mean the period of market domination in the neoclassical sense, and which the sociologist notes is often seen in Polyanian terms (the passage of moral economy to political economy dovetailing with the shift from the embedded economy lodged in social organization to the disembedded or market economy). In the second, densely present in Thompson but overlooked by "most" scholars, the moral economy embodies a "system of norms and obligations."

I wonder whether Fassin's strictures are not overdrawn, precisely because the two parts of Thompson's template—the economic and the moral (or the social against the market) overlap and nourish each other. The sociologist contends that Thompson prods his readers to favor the first, to which he accords much more space, though the second is never absent. In his revisiting article,[107] the English historian clearly situates the center of gravity in the dearth-shrouded market, where the emotion of rage and injustice gives a "moral" charge to the protests and criticisms of consumers, an articulation that displaces, according to Fassin, the salience of norms and obligations:

107 See Thompson, "The Moral Economy Reviewed," in his *Customs in Common* (London: Merlin Press, 1991), 259–351.

"Reading E. P. Thompson carefully (and even if he does not himself establish this distinction), one might wonder if the moral economy that interests him is not in the end more concerned with mores [*moeurs*] than with moralities [*valeurs*], which is, at bottom, the manner by which the social sciences, and anthropology in particular, have for a long time considered the moral question." I am not sure whether historians will find this differentiation/difference to be either luminous or compelling (1243–45).

Scott vs. Thompson, Values vs. Norms

In the ramification of the concept/notion of moral economy from its source to the social sciences, Fassin identifies political scientist James Scott as playing the paramount role. Yet he toils to show how little Scott ascribes overtly to Thompson's inspiration and how much he diverges from the historian's way of thinking. Situating the latter squarely in the riot (as in the marketplace), the sociologist argues that revolt looms much less large in the political scientist's purview than multiple forms of daily resistance, much of it codified and even choreographed, some of it improvised or idiosyncratic: this resistance does not strike me as fundamentally different from the "tricks" played by historian Carlo Poni's Italian peasants against their masters[108] and, in a slightly different mode, it traverses *The Making of the Working Class*. Scott's resistance, which gives expression to and is framed by a safety-first subsistence ethic and an expectation of justice that allows nevertheless for a "tolerable" dose of exploitation, does not constitute a sharp break with what we find in early modern Europe, even if the grammar of its reciprocities and covenants has a particular intonation.

The second difference that separates the (American) political scientist from the (English) historian, according to the (French) sociologist, and which seems to me strained, turns on the contention that Scott reintroduces values into the moral economy: he "speaks of the values that link the peasants at once to the big landlords and to the other members of their community," treating the exploitation by the landlords and the reciprocities among the peasants as belonging to the same "moral universe" whose values are tied to the survival ethic. Fassin argues that Scott's actors somehow constitute a more organic and functional community than Thompson's company of elites and common folk, where apparently the idioms of clientelism,

---

108 C. Poni, "Peasant Tricks and Landlord Strategies in the Bolognese Countryside," unpublished manuscript. All of Poni's friends and admirers hope that this brilliant article, completed in February 1980, will appear soon in a book tentatively entitled *Worlds of Work: Peasants and Artisans, Engineers and Theorists.*

deference, assistance, benevolence and mutual obligation in all the realms of interaction and activity are less consensual and thus less binding. "It is in this way a local world of values that defines the moral economy" in the case of Scott, concludes Fassin, adding, with a wisp of censure, that "we are far from the confrontation on the market around the fixing of the grain price."

My first reaction is that we are less far than the sociologist indicates. My second reaction is to question the distinction—on which Thompson's relegation is based—between a lower-order realm of "norms and obligation" associated with (mere, mundane, structuring) "usages and customs" where Thompson operates and "the space of values and of affects, and singularly of a sentiment of justice" where Scott takes his place. The latter deals with the "evaluative" (i.e., that which is tolerable and that which is not), while Fassin construes Thompson's normative universe as simply "understanding that which is done and that which is not done." The latter formula describes a degraded normativity, a shared way of doing, perhaps, but not a principle of right action regulating behavior in a group. In the context of early modern Europe, and perhaps more generally, I would view norms as inculcating shared values that constitute both social structure and social cohesion. In the Old Regime, norms and obligations and even usages and customs contained and conveyed values.[109] Thompson's marketplace confrontation is a manifestation of a form of reprisal for treachery, for an assault on values and a violation of norms (1246–50).[110] The lack of exacting definition of these analytical categories does not facilitate a fluid dialogue between writer and reader. This is one of those junctures where even a historian with strong social-science inclinations has to wonder whether the sociologist's remoteness from the field (or *terrain*) in question—especially eighteenth century England, but also twentieth century Southeast Asia—refracts his perceptions and hampers his ability to test the theoretical assumptions that undergird and drive his critical appraisal.

---

109 Later in this article, Fassin appears to acknowledge the imbrication of norms, values and emotions (1257; cf. 1265 as well).

110 Fassin (1249n) asks Thompson to support his cause in a citation from "The Moral Economy Reviewed" (341): but the English historian gives credit to Scott for going further than he did in his description of values and moral attitudes. He did not avow that values and moral attitudes did not weigh heavily in his analysis. Fassin may have an interesting line of argument concerning the role of values in the articulation of various moral economies, but he does not map it out (for example, 1247, 1251).

The Moral Economies in Social Science: Privileging the Moral, Sacrificing the Political

After paying (critical) homage to the first-generation theorists/practitioners of the moral economy approach (Thompson the inventor, Scott the promoter), Fassin passes to the second generation, figured by Lorraine Daston, who introduces the concept into the history of science (and more broadly into the social sciences) in the mid-1990s, without much regard for or recognition of the founding fathers. She interests the French social scientist keenly, for he enthuses, in the register of the grandiose, that she "opens the concept to a possible general theory of moral economies." The shift she engages, enlarging or displacing the concept beyond the universe of the "dominated"—sometimes referred to here as "the poor"—to a larger world, which starts with the savant milieu (her special interest), and opens myriad vistas, is not without a price: the historian of science amputates the concept of "this political dimension that gave to the approaches of E. P. Thompson and J. C. Scott their power of social analysis," the capacity to enrich our "intelligence of the social," as Fassin felicitously remarks elsewhere in the text (1255, 1261, 1265).

In the locution-concept moral economy, there is the moral, which, Fassin argues, is the terrain that Daston appropriates, and there is the economic, where he anchors Thompson, attaching, in my view, far too much weight to the latter's willingness to renounce the term moral in a paragraph of his critical reflection on the idea of moral economy in 1991, and far too little to the huge bulk of his *oeuvre* where the moral is imbricated in the economic, where the economic is cast as simultaneously symbolic and material and where it is virtually impossible to think about the economy without taking into account norms, obligations and values. Moreover, the political is implicit in the moral; the moral requires the political, for it is its domain of public expression. The moral—at least in an eighteenth century/Old Regime context—depends on the midwifery of the political in order to result in action, to move from the *dire* to the *faire* (1256; cf. 1259).

Nor am I comfortable with the polarity that Fassin ascribes to Thompson, opposing, on the one hand, a political economy (defined in cramped terms as "relations of production and relations of class," a neoclassical distillation that does not respect the imperative for "historically situated" analysis that the sociologist repeatedly stresses (1261, 1264)) which, left to itself, "proposes a perspective from the outside that objectifies situations, but frequently delegitimizes the experience of the actors" and positing, on the other hand, moral economies whose introduction "re-estabishes a point of view from the outside and recognizes a political subjectivity." I suspect that Thompson would consider this dichotomy as factitious, even as he would contest Fassin's implication, which advances his own theorization quite effectively, that the English historian did not genuinely "take seriously the moral dimension," which appears to have fallen victim to "a strictly economic reading." The social scientist is surely right that the moral economies of French or Palestinian adolescents—fascinating case studies of collective action—"are not principally ethics of material subsistence." Yet it might be argued that the moral economies of English food rioting or of French *taxation populaire*—I relish Fassin's plural—were not narrowly "ethics of material subsistence." It would be absurd to reduce them to arrogation of complex carbohydrates and vegetable proteins, without taking into (central) account the reaffirmation of rights, the articulation of customary claims and the summons to honor the "social contract" (that Fassin incorrectly limits to a relationship between consumers and merchants and/or big landlords instead of extending it to a covenant between the people and the prince/state) (1264–65).[111]

In the end, despite the force of his own powerful critical momentum, Fassin embraces a surprisingly irenic posture: he rejects the supposed antagonism between political economy and moral economy: they must be "conceived/worked out [*penser*] together," situated historically and theorized coherently, albeit asymmetrically. Today's scholarly objects are neither English nor Southeast Asian revolts or resistance, but the sociologist suggests that their analysis has been impoverished by the amnesia that has removed Thompson and Scott from the radar of many researchers. Fassin reassures us: his peroration is not an encomium to the conceptual begetters. He espouses a cause hard not to admire: the cultivation of "a constantly evolving concept." If this article cast into relief hesitations and contradictions in the usage of the moral economy, it also underlines its analytical potential and critical vivacity. Daston opened a new path, called to prosper, but at a serious cost: "the depoliticization of the concept." If one imagines the array of moral economies at once in terms of whole societies and of specific social groups, then one must be vigilant about the tensions and conflicts between them in order to take the measure of the significance(s) of one's analysis. Fassin's concluding sentence is more than a *clin d'oeil* to the devisers and developers of the concept; it is a particular social scientist's profession of faith: "For, at bottom, as of the moment that it takes its

111 In the juxtaposition between objectivities and subjectivities, the outside and the inside, the material economy and other economies ostensibly less susceptible to measurement, I detect a whiff of Carlo Ginzburg's warnings about the pertinence and the perils of the so-called Galilean paradigm, embodied at a certain epoch by the *Annales E.S.C.*, among others. See Carlo Ginzburg, "Signes, traces, pistes. Racines d'un paradigme de l'indice," *Le Débat* (Nov. 1980): 3–44; Carlo Ginzburg and Carlo Poni, "La micro-histoire," *Le Débat* (Dec. 1981), 133–36.

place in the framework of social relations, morality is also a political matter" (1259, 1264–65).

Collective Bargaining by Riot

In the wake of a reconstruction of global capitalism, generating policies of "liberalization and austerity," John Walton and David Seddon argue that we witnessed, during the last several decades of the twentieth century, a reappearance of food riots and kindred forms of popular protest, almost all of them in developing countries around the world (4–5, 21–23).[112] Reminiscent of the earlier European experience, albeit "historically unprecedented," these movements are "fundamentally a product of the international political economy." The authors find both disciplined and coherent direct popular action of a familiar pedigree, as well as fresh forms of protest which they liken to "an intra-national strike wave" (23). They uncover in most of these food riots "processes analogous to economic liberalization policies that produce food riots [in the past]," but emphasize the international context: neo-liberalism perturbs the Third World in "much the same fashion" as laissez-faire policies in Europe dislocated towns and regions socially and economically (24). Exploring what Eric Hobsbawm neatly styled "collective bargaining by riot," Walton and Seddon review the repertory of European unrest (*taxation populaire*, diminished to the generic status of "price riot"; resistance to removal of grain and flour; agrarian demonstration, the didactic destruction of merchandise virtually never seen in Old-Regime France; and the market riot subjecting merchants, millers and public officials to retribution). In the nineteenth century, rioting tended to be better organized and often to integrate labor contention with food demands (25–26). If hard times set the stage for unrest, following C. Tilly and others, the authors argue that vociferous contestation stemmed not so much from hunger as from the conviction that malevolent forces deprived the people of food to which they had "a moral and political right" (27). I would suggest that it is extremely difficult to make a clean distinction, in terms of motivation and mobilization, between hunger, a psychosomatic phenomenon, and the acute sense of moral outrage and outcry for justice that drives uprisings.

Riots bespoke popular defiance vis-à-vis changes both in state and in market behavior. In France, they were neither as uncommon in "agricultural regions" as the authors indicate nor significantly denser in industrial

---

112 John Walton and David Seddon, *Free Markets & Food Riots: The Politics of Global Adjustment* (Oxford: Blackwell, 1994).

localities than elsewhere, though they probably erupted more often in distribution centers such as ports and collector markets than in other towns. The discordances between practices in England and France are interesting, though the actors are similar, especially women (but not necessarily because they were "better acquainted with the marketing practices of food dealers" or "more apt to detect unjustified shortages and food prices") and younger workers and apprentices (28). Usually, rioters selected their targets carefully (storehouses of alleged speculators, mills, religious communities, more rarely bakers and other retailers moored in their neighborhoods) and they revealed limited, rather modest objectives (a return to good order, as consumers represented it) (29).

Four Theories

Walton and Seddon examine four theories that historians have deployed to account for the morphology and conduct of food riots. The first, dubbed "rational response," postulating a proportional reaction of threatened consumers to various levels of privation (and, presumably, though this merits articulation, anxiety), "is no theory at all," according to the authors, because it fails to explain the process by which people decide when and how to act and because it is based on empirically feeble assumptions (the core predicate linking unrest with degrees of suffering is quite often unfounded) (31). E. P. Thompson's moral economy is deemed more viable theoretically and empirically, yet it suffers from some serious limitations (sentimentalization of popular life and behavior, an inadvertent yet palpable neglect of real desperation and deprivation, misrepresentation of collective action as a backward-looking response that slights popular engagement in "modernity" and so on) (31–32). The community-oriented theory taxes the moral-economy approach as narrowly focusing on working class agency (exaggerating class coherence and efficacy as a political voice, while excluding artisans and small farmers, among others), whereas political movements derived their vitality from "traditional communities," cohesive and proud, roiled by disruptions to a way of life, often occasioned by capitalism, yet not reducible to class interests (32–33). Walton and Seddon sympathize with the community theory, fine-grained in its explanation of how rioting operates. Yet they reproach this view, perhaps somewhat peremptorily, with failing to articulate the local with the broader state/market factors, with "national and international forces," experienced here as mere "external threat[s]" (33).

The logical extension of the community theory is the fourth model, pivoted on state and market influences at the national level. Yet, given the absence of a national market in eighteenth-century France, it is impossible to explain food riots largely as local reactions against market intrusion, or to link the hypothesis of a national market to the transition from paternalistic to laissez-faire policies.[113] In my view, the emphasis on state expansion rather than state disengagement in critical sectors is equally misplaced. Walton and Seddon criticize this fourth theory for its culturalist deficit, according too little attention to "the meanings and processes that animate protest action" (34–35). Globally, despite or because of their discrete imperfections, the authors see these theories as "complementary rather than opposed," felicitously operating on different levels of social organization, proposing a mix of causal factors and concurring on the important question of the gradual eclipse of the food riot in the nineteenth century.

On the waning of food riots, less nuanced than Thompson, Hobsbawm announces the transmogrification of the *menu peuple* into the "industrial working class", endowed with new priorities and fresh repertories of action. Bohstedt's structural argument for fewer dearths and less price volatility provides a more solid case for the ebbing of food riots—earlier and more pronounced in England than in France. In the community idiom, he notes an unraveling of "patronage politics", which cedes ground to "class politics". At the risk of underestimating the urban attachment to customary rights, often inimical to market forces, C. Tilly cites as decisive the definitive victory of the state over the peasantry after centuries of struggle: the dissolution of the peasant community, which lingered nevertheless well into the nineteenth century, removed the last of bastion of the defense of traditional rights and claims that resisted capitalist penetration (36).

Walton and Seddon forge a synthesis, attributing the disappearance of "classical food riots" to a combination of improvement in agricultural production and distribution, an attenuation of the risk and fear of dire hunger (based on extrapolation rather than demonstration), the tentacular penetration of the state that weakens local political influence and quickens the abandonment of (vestigial) paternalism, more effective modes of repression, an accelerating industrialization (with disparities in configuration and time-table between England and France) and a consequent congealing of a national class-struggle-based politics. Walton and Seddon maintain that the theories of Hobsbawm and Tilly result inexorably in the eclipse of "primitive forms" of protest such as "the bread riot" as a result of

113 As we have seen, John Bohstedt rejects the national market thesis in England where "the chronologies of food riots and of capitalist market development do not match." *Riots and Community Politics in England and Wales, 1770–1810*, 211–12. *Grosso modo*, the French trajectory is quite similar.

the combined impact of industrialization and state centralization. Yet, the authors contend that from the mid-1970s "austerity protests" in the guise of price riots and popular risings swept across the "development" landscape, including Latin America (Brazil and Argentina), Eastern Europe (Poland) and Africa (Zambia), places that rank among the "world's most industrialized economies" and boast both labor organization experience and forms of centralized and bureaucratized (sometimes authoritarian) states (36–37).

Resurgence of Food Riots: Liberalization and Austerity in the Twentieth Century

After a protracted period during which food riots were virtually absent from the world stage, ask Walton and Seddon, how can one account for the resurgence of the last decades of the twentieth century? Modern austerity protests, defined as large-scale collective action provoked by grievances over state policies of economic liberalization initiated in response to the debt crisis and market reforms urged by international agencies, began in the mid-1970s. Often denounced as the "IMF riots," these manifestations frequently began in the wake of worldwide recession, aggravated by successive oil-price jolts and declining commodity prices that together threatened or generated insolvency.[114] The shock treatment, administered in the name of austerity, miracle nostrum guaranteed to lead to economic stabilization, occasioned portentous distributional problems (reduction of subsidies and wages, on the one hand, and increases in prices on the other). The authors compile an inventory of riots and other mass demonstrations in 39 of 80 debtor countries, with 146 incidents between 1976 and 1992. Overwhelmingly urban, these protests ranged in nature from "classic food riots" (Morocco, Brazil and Haiti) to general strikes and spasms of violence, most of which expressed demands for lower prices, restoration of subsidies, jobs and even debt repudiation. "Overurbanization" seems to have been a common framing condition, in part because it spawned well-developed organizational infrastructure capable of mobilizing political actors. "Welfare policies" fashioned to respond to these disturbances created the "bases for a new [urban] middle class" in certain

114 The process leading to plans for structural adjustment is obviously much more complex than I have space to suggest, with the petrodollar largesse resulting from the vertiginous oil price increases of the 1970s inundating western banks, which disbursed it as loans to developing nations that found themselves unable to repay as the prices of raw materials plummeted in the 1980s. The ensuing debt crisis heralded the arrival of the IMF and austerity policies.

countries, notably in Latin America, where Hobsbawm's view of a tradition of long-term social quiescence proved untrue (39–43, 45–46).

The bargain between the state and the urban poor sealed in many "developmentalist" regimes obviously recalls the priorities of regulatory/paternalist regimes in France; the reciprocities governing these covenants conveyed claims to "rights" redolent of insurgent Old-Regime consumers. If one strains to detect Thomistic relics in the Old-Regime vision of rightful expectations and economic justice, the voice of liberation theology in favor of the needs of the poor is stentorian. In Africa, the moral economy drew upon tribal and ethnic linkages retooled for the urban setting and on colonial forms of indigenous self-government, issuing in organizations similar to those present in Latin America. Walton and Seddon posit the existence of a "traditional moral economy" along the lines of the shared vision that drove Islamist collective action. It is not clear, however, how it evolves across time, whether it was ever deeply entrenched outside urban areas in an earlier time, and the extent to which it connects, more or less seamlessly, with the developmentalist moral economy (or "the developmental social contract") of the second half of the twentieth century. In the French (and English) cases, from the seventeenth to the nineteenth centuries, the claims of the social contract of subsistence preceded and ultimately undermined liberalization. In the examples that the authors adduce, targeting austerity riots, it is not certain if it is liberalization, never rigorously defined but figured by IMF-style reforms, that crystallizes the formation of a *new* ideology of rights (a moral-economic logic challenging the juggernaut of international capitalist political economy) or if it just revitalizes a customary stock of claims for justice. In any event, in the eyes of crowds from Rio to Rabat fulminating against the IMF, the state has betrayed its commitments, even as it had in the eyes of French consumers, both rural and urban, during the liberalization of the eighteenth century (48–50, 52).

With sharp insight, Walton and Seddon note the parallels and differences between classical food riots and modern austerity protest that we cannot detail here. They convincingly stress a common thread that moves collective action beyond simple cost-of-living paroxysms of discontent: riots constituted rejection of the abandonment of paternalistic protection, construed as legitimate and more or less irrevocable rights. Perhaps, the most striking change in the confrontations is the role played in the eighteenth century by global economic factors and actors (limpid) and the salience of "an essential class struggle" (cryptic). Less persuasive is the claim that "it is not the availability of goods—a slippery notion, at least in the eighteenth century—that is at issue in austerity protests, but their price. Certainly distributional inequalities played a framing role in the Old-Regime riots, yet "famine" was not a characteristic condition, and price was almost always the ever ambiguous proxy for shortage, "real" or imagined, "natural" or artificial. Other putative distinctions are overdrawn: the authors maintain that authorities today are targets of crowd ire, "but now as perpetrators of hunger rather than as protectors of the people too slow to act in their expected capacity." Yet, as the famine plot syndrome reminds us, consumers in eighteenth century France also suspected the authorities of deliberately fabricating hunger (50–53). This bracing essay in comparative historical sociology across space and time makes me regret once again my use of the word "primitive" to describe the profoundly political character of early modern food riots whose very political nature—as a strategy of empowerment—I was clumsily seeking to salvage. Another manifestation of the "people problem," this is the sort of disabling reticence that often afflicts young researchers unsure of the articulation between the conceptual and the empirical, more mature historians trying to navigate between the Scylla of populism and the Charybdis of miserabilism or, among others, scholars trying to reconcile their findings with the ideological assumptions that shape their analysis, knowingly or not.[115]

* * * * *

Among the most important authorities tasked with the maintenance, and sometimes with the construction, of public order in Old-Regime France were the parlements. Sovereign courts of justice, these parlements exercised simultaneously other functions, administrative and political. Charged with the "grande police," they had indubitable responsibility (shared with intendants and the ministry) for regulating the provisioning trade and repressing disorder. Emanations of the royal council, the parlements exercised quasi-regalian functions when they participated both in the feeding of the people/subjects and in their discipline. These were not the only domains in which the magistrates contested the monarch's paternal exclusivity: they, too, claimed to be the "fathers of the people."

The clash over the affection (and implicitly the fidelity) of the people bespoke a larger field of confrontation that opposed king and parlements across the eighteenth century. Bitter disputes over financial management and accountability, religious doctrine and its institutional ramifications and the

115 In the latter category, I was probably influenced by Marxist historians with whom I had personal contacts such as Eric Hobsbawm and Jeffry Kaplow. I am thinking—in deep retrospect—in the first instance, of *Social Bandits and Primitive Rebels* (New York: Free Press, 1960) and *Bandits* (London: Weidenfeld & Nicolson, 1969); and, in the second, *The Names of Kings: The Parisian Laboring Poor in the Eighteenth Century* (New York: Basic Books, 1972).

supposed constitutional obligations and limitations on monarchy envenomed relations between the king and the courts. Politics, generally viewed as the struggle over the exercise of power at the center and apex, was defined by parlementary contestation of royal prerogative. The sole giver of laws—*de pleine puissance, de certaine science, d'autorité royale*—the king found his legislative monopoly encroached upon by the parlements' use of regulatory decrees (*arrêts de règlement*) to craft and interpret law in their jurisdictions, by their manipulation of the right to register laws in order to modify their contents and meaning, and by their vast network for the enforcement of royal law, executed as the procurator general of each court saw it. Hedged by the so-called fundamental laws, by Christian scruples and by the social contract of subsistence, absolutism, the dogma and creed of Old-Regime kingship, theorized as governance free of any restriction, elicited a virulent, relentless critique from the parlements, torturers and executioners of Calas and La Barre, following the codes of the time, but ardent enemies of the "arbitrary". Inherently controversial, given their ambiguous institutional position and their behavior, construed by some observers as a self-conscious political opposition, the parlements have long been the object of intense historiographical controversy. I explore some of those issues in the next chapter.

Chapter IV

THE PARLEMENTS IN THE AGE OF ECONOMIC ENLIGHTENMENT

When I launched my research for *Bread, Politics and Political Economy*, I began with a number of regnant historiographical assumptions concerning the eighteenth century that framed my questions and were likely to condition as well the answers I would find. One of the most important concerned the parlements, from Voltaire to Michel Antoine, distinguished historian of the monarchy and its institutions, portrayed collectively as benighted enemies of "progress," archaic and scheming obstructionists, self-regarding and self-aggrandizing defenders of privilege and position and so on. One of my teachers, R. R. Palmer, in his lecture course and his writings, castigated the sovereign courts for paralyzing the monarchy and undermining reform and derided them for their inability to distinguish significant from petty issues (in the latter instance, denigrating their opposition to Turgot's recasting of the *corvée* as a quasi-universal fiscal obligation, a point of view that I have since come to view as a fundamental misreading of the ways in which parlementaires viewed the social order).[1] Based on robust research and reflection—I will not raise here the crucial question of ideological refraction—the secondary literature, globally hostile to the parlements, was quite convincing. After several years in the archives, however, some of it spent in the X series in Paris and parallel parlementary archives in the provinces featuring debate reported in the *Conseil secret* and the process of drafting remonstrances, supplemented by correspondence and memoirs of numerous magistrates, I could no longer subscribe to the prevalent interpretation.

The point of view with which I emerged was not a logic of rehabilitation, but the need to reexamine the governing stereotypes, in part by reassessing the motives, intentions and behavior of the parlements and their magistrates in

1 See R. R. Palmer, *The Age of the Democratic Revolution: A Political History of Europe and America, 1760–1800*, 2 vols. (Princeton, NJ: Princeton University Press, 1959–64). On my reading of the stakes of the corvée debate and the way in which a majority of parlementaires construed the relation between the system of social classification and the political order, see Kaplan, *La Fin des corporations* (Paris: Fayard, 2001).

virtually all domains of their activity, and in part by deconstructing the binary system that casts the eighteenth century in terms of white hats and black hats, heroes and villains, patriots and egoists and so on. In the white corner stands the modernizing and rationalizing monarch, relooked version of the frayed figure of the enlightened despot, comforted by progressive ministers and buoyed by forward-looking intellectuals called philosophes. In the black corner, a Montesquieuian medley of retrograde, parochial, intolerant and intransigent defenders of the status quo and guardians of their specific claims to honors, advantages, immunities and liberties, including, *inter alia,* the parlements stage center, various other sovereign courts (aides, comptes), the church (a sometimes embarrassing companion) and the guilds, among others. The deconstruction is not geared to issue in fifty shades of soothing grey, but to extricate us from the reduction and occlusion of a framework disposed in a stubbornly Manichean sense. This is not the place for a global revision; it took me a decade to work out (in part) the story of the guilds (or corporations), and I would not presume to do the same for the multiple actors and institutions in the two camps.[2] I would argue for reappraisals, not only between the two sides, but also within each of the alignments.

My concern here is with the parlements. Remember that these institutions, 13 "sovereign courts" operating in jurisdictions of extremely uneven size across the realm, disposed of immense political influence through their prerogative of registering royal laws and exercised quasi-legislative power as a result of their regulatory authority, in addition to the exertion of crucial judicial functions, primarily on the appeals level. My research, undertaken more than four decades ago, persuaded me that we were getting it wrong both ways: we weren't seeing the forest for the trees (identifying various evidence-based patterns or big pictures) and we weren't seeing the trees for the forest (grand received ideas shrouded important and multiple variants). So many years later, it seems jejune to plea for complexity or complexification. Yet in my studies, parlement after parlement, I was surprised to uncover so much disparity among companies and so much diversity and division within them. The "union-des-classes" template that so many historians borrowed from the parlements themselves did not get at the reality of their political cultures, their ways of doing and their clashes of habitus in a milieu ostensibly homogeneous. My work on liberalization revealed striking clashes among different parlements and bitter quarrels *within* them that are not reducible to a neo-Beardian analysis of interest, but require us to construe interest in a more capacious, nuanced and labile manner. They are perhaps better accounted for by a

2 See Kaplan, *La Fin des corporations.*

neo-Althusserian analysis of ideology, but it, too, requires supplementation in order to allow for differences in apprehension, appreciation and exegesis. The liberalization experience is corrosive of many clichés, because it revealed not only cleavages within and among the parlements, but also deep fissures in the world of philosophes, the putative "party of humanity" that was supposed to speak with one voice on decisive issues.

One can subject a parlement—less often *the* parlements as if they were one—to pungent or passionate criticism (say, Toulouse on the Calas horror), subsequently laud or revile it for embracing hyper-liberal positions on questions of political economy and then praise it for forging a critique of royal prodigality, fiscal irresponsibility, administrative abuse and political arbitrariness in a mode that has credible claims on the designation "reformist." Viewed across the century, the parlements were generally hostile to the crown's actions, but not inveterately. The spaces and mechanisms of collaboration, if not complicity, often informal, had not been thoroughly explored. Center–periphery tensions framed relations not only between king and courts, but also between the Paris Parlement, bloated in jurisdiction and pretention, and its provincial counterparts. In any event, it was clear to me in 1970 that the so-called reputation of the parlement(s) demanded a searching reconsideration.

Scholars have devoted a substantial amount of research to the parlements in the past several decades, much of it revisionist in the polysemic sense of the word. One powerful source of rethinking emanated from pioneering studies on Jansenism, driven in large part by Dale Van Kley.[3] Another stems from a revived and reburnished political history, which had suffered far more in France than elsewhere. A veritable rehabilitationist school has emerged, largely Anglo-American in inspiration, today dominated by a group of "younger" French historians, dispersed throughout the hexagon. They exchange frequently in colloquia and manifestly find nourishment in each other's work. Their common cause has framed their interrogations: to judge from their analyses and conclusions, it is not unfair to characterize them as kindred in their thinking. To some extent, their reclamation of the parlement(s), albeit sometimes quite nuanced, has reinforced the older historiographical cleavages. In any event, in my opinion, their tendency to remain not only within their

3 Dale Van Kley, *The Jansenists and the Expulsion of the Jesuits from France* (New Haven, CT: Yale University Press, 1975); *The Damiens Affair and the Unraveling of the Old Regime* (Princeton, NJ: Princeton University Press, 1984); *The Religious Origins of the French Revolution* (New Haven, CT: Yale University Press, 1996). See also Catherine Maire, *De la cause de Dieu à la cause de la Nation. Le Jansénisme au XVIIIe siècle* (Paris: Gallimard, 1998), many of whose positions Van Kley cogently questions.

own historiographical niche, but also within the milieu of the courts and the magistrates has imprinted their scholarship with a certain insularity. It has isolated them from other currents, historiographical and historical, notably in the social, economic and cultural spheres. Even their bread-and-butter subject—politics—suffers conceptually from the narrow prism through which they apprehend it. The "they" must, of course, be specified and relativized. I try to do this in the following discussion, which begins with a precursor, if not a founding father, William Doyle, the most cosmopolitan in his perception and practice of political history.

It's the Constitution, Stupid!

Perhaps the foremost (and wisest) British scholar in this domain, William Doyle published his elegant study of the Parlement of Bordeaux in 1974, slightly too late for me to use in *Bread, Politics and Political Economy*. It treats an assertive, combative court, buoyed by the surging tide of prosperity that maritime commerce had afforded this dynamic regional capital. The very title of Doyle's inaugural book—situating the Parlement at the end of the Old Regime—seems to announce his impatience to get to the French Revolution, the study of which would become his specialty. The teleological risks do not daunt him: he embraces them, making his focus the role played by the sovereign court in the crisis that engulfed the last decade of the eighteenth century. The sharp emphasis on the process of unraveling, issuing in a crisis that would prove apocalyptical for the parlement and the social order it embodied, shapes Doyle's analysis at every turn, depriving it, in my view, of the revisionist edge sorely lacking in the historiography of the Old Regime per se, at the time that he crafted this monograph, and still today.

The issues about which the Aquitaine magistrates "felt most passionately" were "personal ones." Unlike their Toulouse counterparts, heavily invested in cereal production, the Bordeaux judges had "little personal stake in the great debate" over the grain trade—"the most burning economic issue"—in the 1760s, according to Doyle, whose "personal stakes" gauge strikes me as a reductionist instrument for taking the measure of ideology as well as interest in the public domain. Still, he corrects his own somewhat desultory characterization of the grain question as basically one of "agricultural policy"—public order ("social stability and subordination") depended on a successful provisioning policy. He passes too summarily across the 1760s: "extreme suspicion for free trade in grain" does not adequately capture the position of a court seriously divided, yet solidary with the sister courts that welcomed the radical reforms of 1763–64.The acute penury and proliferating riots of the early 1770s mobilized the parlement of Bordeaux far more earnestly than earlier. Doyle does a good job of recounting the ways, often quite muscular, in which the magistrates responded to speculation, burgeoning misery and popular restlessness, but he eschews broader and deeper examination of the social, economic, cultural and political assumptions that fashion their thinking and their action.

The parlement seems riven by a largely unexplored tension between a case-by-case pragmatism, sanctioning a host of interventionist measures devised by the court, and a loftier belief in the virtues of liberty that Doyle sees as the framing perspective of the court. "The magistrates in general," asserts Doyle, much to my surprise, "were not interested in economic arguments except insofar as they bore on the political problem of public order." In a fundamental sense, this begs the question, since virtually no one thinking about political economy, not even febrile liberals, could dispense with a concern for public order. It is still more puzzling, given the fickle public posture of the court, including the circumstantial indulgence of the magistrates for various sorts of *dirigisme*, to read that "free trade in grain seemed to them the best way of assuring this [public tranquility]." Given the parlement's self-regarding use of the notion of public order—I'm thinking of the manner in which the magistrates deployed it to try to sanctuarize various wine privileges—it would have been helpful had Doyle subjected this lever and locution to critical scrutiny (203–6, 209).[4]

Was the influential President de Gascq among this putatively majoritarian current? Apparently, he joined in the criticism of Terray's centralization of supply-side intervention: it is regrettable that Doyle did not pursue this question, for it fanned the ever-smoldering flame of the famine plot persuasion, with the ministry cast as monopolist. Yet this posture did not foreclose intervention undertaken locally. One wonders equally how many magistrates would have sympathized with Gascq's (wholly private?) conviction that, in the midst of the dearth and disarray if 1773, "the people is not wrong to complain." After all, he observed, evoking a trope echoed in anxiety-ridden marketplaces throughout Europe-in-scarcity, "the people is unable to pay for its bread ... their ordinary expression is to say that we would prefer to die on the gallows than to die of hunger... " (205–6).

Like the Bordeaux magistrates, Doyle believes that "the basic issue behind their altercations with the government was not so much economic as constitutional": it is in this historiography that he is most at home. I would argue that the grand questions of the Economic Enlightenment, many of which issued in brisk policy debates, concerned both the (re-)construction of the social order and all aspects of the question of governance, touching almost certainly on matters that parlementaires generally deemed constitutional.

4 Nor did the liberal spirit fashion the parlement's attitude toward colonial trade policy, qualified here as "Colbertian" (210–11).

The conventional constitutional conception, as regards the parlements, seems to me to be excessively narrow, driven by the well-known religious and financial clashes, which reduce politics to the *portion congrue*, in terms of its social incidence. Doyle is surely right to advance that "the central constitutional problem of eighteenth-century France, at least until 1788, was that of governmental responsibility." One could argue that this was also the core (political) issue in the debate over liberalization. How broadly do this historian, and the younger parlementary scholars who have emerged in his wake, construe this idea of responsibility? How strict a construction do they give to a constitution that is not fleshed out in writing and cast in bronze? The subsistence question is certainly a bridge in my eyes between the socioeconomic/cultural and the political–constitutional (214, 217).

The segregation of the former, as if it would pollute or distort the latter, strikes me as a sterile approach. The historian must articulate them in a common framework, work out their relations and explore subtle and overt connections. The liberalization experience bears directly both on fiscality—Doyle himself notes the parlement's view that onerous taxation cripples agriculture—and on royal prerogative and obligation, the proper relations between king and intermediary bodies and other matters on the politico-constitutionalist agenda. It seems impoverishing to me to cite 1763 as a crucial year in terms of royal–parlementary exchanges on fiscal issues, as Doyle does, without calling attention to the fact that this is the inaugural year of liberalization; or to invoke Maynon d'Invault's desire to prolong the second twentieth tax in December 1768 without observing that this very year and month mark the apogee of subsistence turbulence; or to invoke the ambivalent reception that the sovereign courts gave to Terray's first steps upon his advent to the contrôle-général (partial bankruptcy, followed by tax increases), without noting the dramatic transformation of political economy of grain, flour and bread that he announced at the same time. As I argue below, it makes no sense to me to discuss the Brittany affair—an eruption of violent parlementary resistance in the early 1760s in a historically refractory province to royal fiscal demands specifically and to the legitimacy of royal authority more generally, complicated by bitter personal and clientelist rivalries, an episode that numerous skillful historians regard as the pinnacle of constitutional confrontation—in isolation from liberalization, whose social, economic and political implications are certainly more tectonic (222–23).

Soft Revisionism, Slippery Politics

Already a scholar of considerable nuance, the Doyle of 1974 does not fit inexorably and completely into the Manichean scheme of parlementary historiography. By today's standards, his revisionism is quite tempered. There is little heroic about the magistrates of Bordeaux, either in the beginning or at the end of the tale. The English historian views the parlements generally as "passive" agents who react to events rather than taking significant political or policy initiatives. They were neither original nor remarkable in their combat to resist or arrest the development of absolutism. They played their most distinctive public role as defenders of the province; and all social groups benefited from this stewardship. Doyle reserves no tolerance for at least one vein of the antiparlementary indictment: "It is not only crude and unsubtle to see the parlement as the narrow defender of the interests of one social group; it does not fit the facts either." Nevertheless, if they were not single-mindedly egotistical or self-indulgently obstructionist, the magistrates were greatly absorbed by personal quarrels, rarely united whatever the gravity of the challenge facing their body, and betrayed "utter indifference to public responsibilities," allowing "private circumstances" quite often to determine their public conduct. Though "one of the keys to the power of the parlements," the ever slippery and intangible force called public opinion failed to jolt the magistrates into lucid self-analysis.

Yet if rehabilitation is hardly an obsessive preoccupation in Doyle's treatment of the courts, his precise take is not always clear. If "the spirit of party" epitomized their "most obvious characteristic," their "internal quarrels" undermined, at least in part, the nurture of "their personal interests." The categories here are not sharply demarcated: if one discerns readily a harsh appreciation of their quasi-suicidal inability to apprehend "where their own interests lay," beyond the Gironde, it is much more difficult to fathom what exactly the historian denotes when he writes, in quasi-conclusion, that "when the paths of politics and vested interest crossed, politics usually claimed the right of way" (309–11). My major disappointment with this engaging monograph is precisely its failure to theorize—as one says more commonly on the Continent than in the United Kingdom—the meaning of politics.

What Makes Government Work?

Julian Swann's *Politics and the Parlement of Paris under Louis XV, 1754–1774* (Cambridge, 1995) is one of the finest rehabilitationist studies. It does the best job of characterizing the historiographical debate.[5] It is generally equable in

5 Swann, *Politics and the Parlement of Paris under Louis XV, 1754*–1774 (Cambridge: Cambridge University Press, 1995). He is less reliable when venturing beyond the parlementary political milieu, for example, in placing Roger Chartier under the inspirational aegis of François Furet (38–39n).

tone—I dare not say judicious—reserving harsh strictures for the Antoine-royalist-reformer line, censured as extremist, yet not sparing William Doyle, esteemed pioneer, for pushing his functionalist revisionism too systematically.[6] Swann rejects repeatedly the Manichean formulation in all of its avatars (canonically: the vested, corporate self-interests subverting modernist monarchical reform). If he believes that the parlements are historically and institutionally disposed to collaborate with the crown and mobilize their resources far more effectively than the monarch, he acknowledges that the king, albeit submerged by an engulfing, quasi-structural weakness (never explained, save circumstantially), is not wholly inept, is sometimes willing to listen patiently and is compelled to expend too much governing energy on the management of parlementary mutiny (47, 71–72, 192–93, 201). In the end, however, even if Swann casts his *problématique* as the need to account for the disintegration of a political relationship constructed over several generations and "conducted according to tacitly recognized rules"—presupposing an irenic, consensual, mutually beneficial political environment, hailed as the new vulgate—it is clear that the king will bear the onus of failure and the stigma of responsibility (44, 236, passim). Still, in the wake of J. H. Shennan[7] and others, Swann's interest in the second revisionist line—the articulation of "the unwritten codes and conventions that made government work"—is fecund, and it restores a certain balance of inquiry, although it remains an investigation *à charge*, unmasking royal "mishandling," "mismanaging" and pig-headedness (40, 184–85).

Judicial Politics, Eviscerated Politics?

My major reproach concerns not Swann's conclusion, but his method, which betrays a lack of epistemological reflexivity. The languid argument for founding the study on an ever-larger "contextualization" is wholly incommensurate with the sophistication of numerous points of his analysis (39, 80, 123, 198, 212–13). Even in its lustiest expression, this hyper-contextualization

---

6 William Doyle did not convince me in his case against Maupeou as an ambitious opportunist without a genuine reformist agenda in the article he published more than four decades ago. "The Parlements of France and the Breakdown of the Old Regime," *French Historical Studies* VI (1970): 415–58. Nor do I subscribe to his more recent argument, rightly criticized by Swann, postulating a "stable" political system, in some ways nurtured by controversy, but in the end sapped by the toxicities of the Brittany affair. See his "The Parlements" in Keith M. Baker, ed., *The French Revolution and the Creation of Modern Political Culture*, vol. 1: *The Political Culture of the Old Regime* (Oxford: Pergamon, 1987), 157–68.

7 J. H. Shennan, *The Parlement of Paris* (Ithaca, NY: Cornell University Press, 1968).

remains confined to "the prevailing political climate" (162). This historian's view of politics bespeaks less a conceptualization of the notion that (for me) necessarily integrates social, economic, psychological and cultural variables than a chronicle of strife as the two major actors lived and recounted it. Curiously, the "judicial politics" that characterizes interaction indoors, in the microcosm, appears less hermetic than the larger purchase of politics outdoors, in the society of the Old Regime (56–81). Swann emphasizes its "complexity" (58, 201). The panoply of remonstrance, registration and *lit de justice* merely constituted "the public façade of politics." Behind it burgeoned an intricate world of "unofficial contacts, debates, and factional intrigue." The latter pullulates with quasi-Namierite appetite and dexterity, generated spontaneously in the Palais or infiltrated from Versailles, less smothering than in the work of John Rogister,[8] yet placing a premium on tactics, maneuverings and "cabalist" activities that issue in a sort of tautology, a "politicization" of judicial affairs (58, 60, 65–66, 75–78). The proliferation of intrigue that seems both to eddy against *and* accompany the resolute search for "consensus" that is said to drive the parlementary engine calls for explanation (66).

Given Swann's approach, the vigorous campaign for liberalization, the crystallization of political economy, the negotiations preceding the liberal laws, their promulgation, the serial harvest shortfalls and the ensuing sociopolitical maelstrom, resulting in the most socially turbulent decade of the reign, barely appear on the author's radar screen, despite the parlements' deep implication in much of this experience. Among other things, liberalization was a project for a joint royal–parlementary extrication from the chronic impasses that paralyzed politics. Can one account for the momentous decision to repudiate the social contract of subsistence by evoking a putative "reform fever" that the monarch "caught?" (220–21). The 1760s, for Swann, is about the fiscal confrontation, the Brittany affair, the fronde-like parlementary comportment and their political and constitutional impact. Liberalization, though it roiled the lives of millions of French women and men, did not fit into the rehabilitationist template. Yet, in principle, the king could not afford to be indifferent to the way in which he represented himself to his subjects. "Unable to govern," the scholar of parlement observes, "Louis was incapable of projecting a positive image of royalty." But did the king "produc[er] of bastards" do more damage to his reputation and the moral capital of kingship than the king as grain trader rather than baker, the prince as vampire rather than nourisher, the monarch as hoarder, speculator and patron of the hideous *pacte de famine*? (236). In this domain, Swann does no better in his treatment of

8 John Rogister, *Louis XV and the Parlement of Paris 1737–1755* (Cambridge: Cambridge University Press, 1995).

"public opinion" than elsewhere in the book, the habitually nebulous force (or *idée-force*) for which, on occasion, he makes complacent, undocumented claims (thus, for instance, in the serious "crises" associated with judicial strikes or exiles "the magistrates received support from all social levels, stretching from the princes of the blood to domestic servants") (83; cf. 82, 170).[9]

Parlementary Appetite and Doctrinal *Bricolage*

In recent years, a veritable school of younger scholars in France has focused on the study of parlements from sundry perspectives, the bulk of which cast these multitasked institutions in positive terms, with more or less critical reserve, depending on particular issues and polemical contexts. Frédéric Bidouze's treatment of the remonstrances of the Parlement of Navarre illustrates this vigorous historiographical current, inspired in part by Jean Egret's adumbration of the theme of a "culture of opposition" (22).[10] Without clasping the *thèse nobiliaire*, he rejects decisively the *thèse royale*, voiced in its most brutal form by Voltaire's apotheosis of the lion, categorically superior to less noble predatory animals, modernized by Michel Antoine's incisive formula–hypothesis: "monarchy or anarchy" (218).

This is the terrain where Bidouze is at his best, underscoring the parlement's claims on a certain sharing of power, and the arguable though not wholly unambiguous legitimacy of its appetite to exercise some legislative and political prerogatives—all this without denying the "permanent coup d'état" that the collective parlementary insurgency seemed to signal, if not embody. In so doing, the parlement of Navarre, along with the others, forges a new political culture, through a sort of spasmodic *bricolage* rather than by systematic construction. The author refuses to regard parlementary engagement—frequently it resembles combat—as narrowly self-centered and self-interested resistance. Without denying a tension between impulses of "sincerity" and of "egoism," he characterizes parlementary politics as a sprightly participation in a healthy public debate and exchange. Bidouze intimates, for instance,

9 "Public support, broadly defined, reinforced the Parlement's political authority," Swann contends, undoubtedly quite plausibly (84). But the methodological problem is that it is in fact public support, broadly *undefined*.

10 *Les Remontrances du Parlement de Navarre au XVIIIe siècle* (Biarritz: Atlantica, 2000). F. Bidouze identifies with Jean Egret, whom he describes, in somewhat stilted language, as "ayant sa dialectique sur la compréhension" (22). I had the good fortune of taking a course with Egret at Poitiers in 1964, my first "lived" antidote to Palmer's line. See J. Egret, *Le Parlement de Dauphiné et les affaires publiques dans la deuxième moitié du XVIIIe siècle*, 2 vols. (1942, Roanne: Horvath, 1988) and *Louis XV et l'opposition parlementaire* (Paris: Armand Colin, 1970).

that the view of (new) taxes as war-time exceptions is not unreasonable (or in some meta-sense unconstitutional), and that the fiscal issue is much less often about how much than about how collection can and should take place—this is the core question of provincial liberty, a matter of fundamental right rooted in history and law, not to be dismissed as insular narcissism. He maintains that the remonstrance system is passably efficient, that it generates invaluable exchange of information and perspective and time and again results in conciliation and accord, not irresistibly in confrontation and conflict.

All Political Culture Is Local

In the end, the parlement's ultimate pragmatic sanction for its actions is directly connected to its mooring in "the local reality" that is sometimes too remote for the central power (or the sister courts) to apprehend (208). Teaching at Pau, published at Biarritz, studying a Navarre that is often relegated to folkloric status in our rhetoric ("France and Navarre"), even as he shows mastery of the (anachronistic) "national," Bidouze resonates with the local, which he declines to stigmatize as particularistic, if by the latter one means a vocation to take seriously the concerns of a kind of "Navarreness." Nevertheless, if he speaks on occasion in the voice of the institution he investigates, that voice sometimes figures metonymically the tone and words of all the parlements when the incentives for solidarity outweigh the temptations of autonomy (12, 22, 102, 112–14, 205, 207–8, 216).

There are a few areas where Bidouze is less compelling. Predicated on an extremely muted reflexivity, his lofty "epistemological" promises remain largely unfulfilled. He never really takes us into the "specifically linguistic and poetic domain"; his reading of the remonstrances, for example, is insightful in the canonic mode established more than a century ago by Jules Flammermont (216, 226–29).[11] With a long board that seems to be his "dialectic," he surfs on the culturalist wave with insufficient preparation. His guides, in the succession to Tocqueville and Daniel Mornet,[12] are an unlikely trio, François Furet, Keith Baker and Roger Chartier (221–22). Each is a remarkably accomplished historian, but they hardly constitute a "school", even if they all address questions of language and discourse. Furet returns to an idealist style of historiography closely linked with late nineteenth-century philosophy and

11 J. Flammermont, ed., *Remontrances du Parlement de Paris au dix-huitième siècle*, 3 vols. (Paris: Imprimerie nationale, 1888–98).

12 A pioneer in the modern scholarly study of the intellectual origins of the French Revolution: Daniel Mornet, *Les origines intellectuelles de la Révolution française, 1715–1787* (Paris: Armand Colin, 1933).

Baker verges on nonreferentiality, postures that distance them radically from Chartier, who forged a robust cultural analysis that remains anchored in the social.[13] If it is fair to ascribe to them (in part) the paternity of a renewed notion of political culture, it seems to me fanciful to pretend that they have resolved the question of public opinion. Their alleged "proclamation of the sovereign rights of public opinion" thus dispenses Bidouze from problematizing the concept/phenomenon and subjecting it to critical interrogation (21–23, 51, 222, 311, 402).

In the same vein, the author does not look closely at the fascinating play between "people" and parlement(s) that traverses the century and that intensifies in repercussion at each episode of political crisis when the magistrates openly contest the royal monopoly to the title of father of the people (41, 49, 353). A final unintended consequence of the apprenticeship with this school of political culture "defining the types of discourse that shaped the prerevolutionary confrontations" is the ensnaring of the author in a sturdy teleological web, contrary to his explicit intention to avoid this sort of deference to the denouement of 1789. The will to resist this inclination seems further to have been sapped by the author's desire to contest the alleged backwardness of the Navarre region in the development of a political culture commensurate with the substance and pace of the rest of the realm (207, 219, 223, 225, 234, 239, 261–62, 264, 288, 308, 312, 334, 338, 350, 384, 398).[14]

Toward a More Open, Inclusive Politics?

Celebrating the resurgence of a muscular political history, in his introduction to a collective volume consecrated to the "parlementary world" of the eighteenth century, Alain J. Lemaître writes in the same spirit as F. Bidouze,

13 See Furet's savaging of Chartier in his review of *Les Origines culturelles de la Révolution française* in *Le Nouvel Observateur*, 25–31 October 1990. On the differences between Chartier and Baker, no less profound, albeit more civil in expression, see the exchange between them: "Dialogue sur l'espace public," *Politix*, no. 26 (1994): 5–22. On the historiographical context of the clash that separated Chartier and Furet in particular, see Kaplan, *Farewell, Revolution: The Historians' Feud, France, 1789/1989* (Ithaca, NY: Cornell University Press, 1995).

14 A certain defensiveness concerning the articulation between the region and the kingdom in the revolutionary run-up sometimes renders the author's prose as fustian as it is obscure: "Mais nous pouvons également avancer que le caractère particulier de la Pré-révolution en Béarn, dont l'hésitation à députer aux Etats Généraux est une illustration majeure comme la tiédeur rencontrée par l'épisode révolutionnaire, prend une dimension problématique pour qui veut éclairer le discours politique sous l'Ancien Regime et l'insérer dans une vision totalisante implicitement annonciatrice de l'ébranlement national" (225).

who also participated in the colloquium that gave rise to this volume.[15] He calls for a recontextualization of the parlements in "the history of the Ancien Regime and of the *res publica*" in order to escape the ossifying effects of the classical historiographical template pitting the devotees of royal authority against the partisans of a "liberal," English-like political opposition (11). The epistemological menu is frugal and woolly: the binary "French tradition" has trouble overcoming ideology and emotion in order to attain "an objective view" (12). Political economy (as an enterprise in intellectual history) and capitalism (as a driving social and economic force with forward and backward linkages to politics) appear to be absent from the agenda. A renascent and obdurately undefined feudalism is present here, as in many other recent studies: it would be worthwhile reflecting on the cause and significance of this unanticipated comeback (14).

Julian Swann's essay, perhaps the most broadly cast in this anthology, reminds us that many Anglo-American scholars avoided the procrustean polarization "crown–parlements" by crafting the concept of "judicial politics," presupposing "a series of unwritten rules and conventions through which the relations between government and parlements were organized" (17, 24). This disposition echoes an important current in sociology that refuses to see conflict as the relentless framework for everyday life.[16] Negotiation and bargaining loom larger than ideas and policies in relations between king and courts, not infrequently marked by collaboration, as F. Bidouze hinted, while public opinion enjoys, here as elsewhere, a sort of disincarnated extraterritorial existence (24–26, 29, 31, 33). Later in this book, Catherine Maire makes the same case, thematic mantra of the rejuvenated political history of the parlements: behind the scenes consultations "show the extent to which 'absolutism,' by its search for compromise and conciliation, is a more moderate system than historiographical tradition generally supposes" (171).

Without traducing his camp to espouse Dale Van Kley's mordant critique of the notion of judicial politics, Swann shares nevertheless his rejection of the alembicated approach of John Rogister, who cultivates a blinkered view of a politics confined to cramped elite spaces (28–29).[17] Swann believes that one can fortify the concept of judicial politics by enlarging its scope to take into

15 Alain J. Lemaître, ed., *Le Monde parlementaire au XVIIIe siècle: L'Invention d'un discours politique* (Rennes: Presses Universitaires de Rennes, 2010).

16 See Luc Boltanski and Laurent Thévenot, *On Justification: Economies of Worth*, trans. C. Porter (Princeton, NJ: Princeton University Press, 2006).

17 See D. Van Kley, "Pure Politics in Absolute Space: The English Angle on the Political History of Pre-Revolutionary France," *Journal of Modern History* 69 (1997): 754–84; David Bell, "How (and How Not) to Write *Histoire Evénementielle*: Recent Books on Eighteenth-Century French Politics," *French Historical Studies* 19 (1996): 1169–79

account "a social, cultural and intellectual context," but the nostrum is vague and the method of application unspecified (29). In any event, his analysis points toward complexity: divisions within the parlements and a multiplicity of parlementary discourses (31, 33–34). Yet the space for Jansenism contracts: the author insists that it is a marginal influence in many provinces. Swann's conclusion is disappointing: a somewhat complaisant, even angelic, depiction of the renewal of parlementary studies, without asperities or frictions. The old stigmatizing interpretation of globally reactionary and egotistical parlementary world is rightly laid to rest. What remains to contemplate? "The intellectual and cultural richness of the parlements… a great variety of opinions on all the great economic, political and constitutional questions of the time" (37).

It's the King's Fault

A companion study focused on the Paris parlement by Joël M. Félix underlines monarchical responsibility for the polarization (and sometimes the maiming): Louis XV tainted any form of opposition to his will as "republican," an epithet of overwrought ostracism. Cast against a royal posture more unyielding in principle than in practice, this historian characterizes parlementary behavior as intrinsically more supple, the product of debates on policy issues that "never" elicited unanimity, even if the plurality vote compelled adhesion. (42, 44). Félix argues that the sovereign court did not seek to attack frontally the political foundation of the monarchy, but "to apply certain correctives to the manifestation of royal authority…," a view that fits well with the structuring themes of the "new" community of parlementary scholarship (48). Yet I wonder if there is not an unwarranted rush to erect as canon a kind of sapient parlementary self-restraint that excludes peremptorily the desire to subject the king to a certain political wardship or supervision. Nor am I convinced by the irenic casuistry that presents the affirmation of parlementary appetite as directed not at "reducing royal authority, but on the contrary reinforcing it" (54). Astutely, Félix underlines the centrality for the parlementaires of the right of property in their demarcation of the frontier separating absolutism from despotism (49, 55). What a shame, however, not to insert the parlementary perspective in the broader debate on property that galvanized philosophes and political economists, for many of whom property was *the* foundational category, anterior to any form of political or social organization. If Swann's call for broadening the scope of parlementary history, in particular with an opening to the social and the cultural, is more than *voeux pieux*, it seems to me necessary to integrate the trajectory of this institution into a nonteleological reflection on the construction of the Old Regime.

In a piece that is at once rambling and elliptical, F. Bidouze rivets here again his persuasive critique of "a partial, partisan and tragic vision of the parlementary opposition" (58). Engrossed by an obstinately amorphous concept of public opinion that he believes he has mastered, he seems little interested in ways to embody it, giving it a social content and articulating the political with the social, as Swann suggests. Why not relate Malesherbes' evocation of "the misfortunes of the people," in this instance perhaps less incantatory than ethnographic, with the real ambience of proliferating popular misery in 1771 (76–77)?). This segmentation of gaze highlights the risk of re-enclosing the new parlementary history in a largely open-field landscape. Author of the most elegant essay in Lemaître's collection, Peter Campbell proposes an intellectual history focusing on the 1780s that does not necessarily move in the direction of *désenclavement* that I advocate. Yet his object is what he calls political life, which seems to allow for more openings than political culture or even politics. It appears to me that he would deepen his own examination of such richly ambiguous and protean notions as *patrie*/patriotism and despotism by looking at their social and economic origins and/or linkages as well as their linguistic genesis and political–cultural incubation. Such an integrated approach might lead to a more compelling grasp of the operation of public opinion, one of Campbell's unproblematized concepts/agents (200, 204, 218, 220).[18]

Magistrates and Ideology in the Republic of Letters

In the volume he edited entitled *Les Parlementaires, les lettres et l'histoire au siècle des Lumières*, Frédéric Bidouze energetically pursues the rehabilitative task.[19] In this phase, a group of historians redeem numerous magistrates, whose parlementary stigmata sometimes barred them full recognition as citizens in the Republic of Letters (what the editor calls "the community of the eighteenth century") (4). Though this republic of philosophes, writers and sundry artists had nothing directly to do with the toxic republic that the parlementaires were said to figure in the king's mind, it is useful to remember that parlementary texts were, in numerous instances (paradoxically, alongside certain preambles to groundbreaking or iconoclastic royal legislation), as subversive of the standing order of things as the most daring texts of the philosophes, some of whom certain magistrates frequented in the salons, academies and other crossroads

18 Cf. C. Maire's remarks on Le Paige's invocation of the "public" (178) and A. J. Lemaître's vague allusions to public opinion in his conclusion (255, 261).

19 Bidouze, *Les Parlementaires, les lettres et l'histoire au siècle des Lumières, 1715–1789* (Pau: Presses Universitaires de Pau, 2008).

of exchange. This book is an important contribution to the elaboration of a dense, comprehensive view of the "Enlightened" parlements, a perspective that the age-old historiographical dualism largely stifled. In two dozen essays, necessarily of very uneven quality and nature, ranging from deep erudition to anecdotal epitome and probing argumentation, we learn about the magistrates as historians as well as jurists, as graceful and insightful letter-writers and as tropismatic apologists, as esthetes and travelers, as polemists and conciliators, as book collectors and thinkers, as music lovers and patrons to the arts.

Many, if not all, of these undertakings offer glimpses into the formation or mobilization or refinement of the multiple and often contradictory strains that constitute parlementary ideology (or ideologies). For example, Stéphane Baudens demonstrates the persistence of an "institutional legend" that unflaggingly shaped parlementary discourse across the very long run, incarnated by the *Judicium Francorum*, "bible" of the sovereign courts, the core doctrine articulating their claims for political prerogative and legitimacy (27–28, 32–34, 36). Julien Niger presents the historicist/historiographical inscription of parlementary authority by A.-T. Hue de Miromesnil, first president of the Normandy Parlement and future keeper of the seals, who fostered a conception of a "moderate" monarchical government of the sort C. Maire summoned us to contemplate. Miromesnil's kind, poised between despotism and anarchy—not quite the future historiographical binary—was both exclusive legislator and paragon of obedience to those very laws that the crown fashioned (51). It would have been fruitful for Niger to press the first president more vigorously on the inception of the courts as "intermediary bodies between the sovereign and his subjects," in particular on the (more or less stealthy) entry onto the political stage of the "people"—vicariously, symbolically and, occasionally, directly (53). Clarisse Coulomb touches thoughtfully on an aspect of the vocation of the parlements as defenders of local liberties (73), a theme dear to F. Bidouze. In an agile chapter, Gérard Lahouati throws into relief the thick yet highly filtered culture of another inveterate letter-writer and historian, the president de Brosses of the Dijon court, a man who seems to have relished Italy as much as Burgundy, took seriously the challenge and the talent of the great philosophes and defended his court ardently, when necessary (126–33, 137–39). I would have liked for David Diop to pursue the slight traces of Jonathan Israel's "radical Enlightenment" in Montesquieu's *Dissertation sur la politique des Romains dans la religion* (1716), an opportunity not only to measure roughly the penetration of

20 See Jonathan Israel, *Radical Enlightenment: Philosophy and the Making of Modernity 1650–1750* (Oxford: Oxford University Press, 2001).

this "other" Enlightenment in elite circles, but also to see how the notions of politics took on different visages in parlement, in academy and outside (225).[20]

A sensationist thinker, educational reformer, politically ambitious magistrate deeply marked by his apprehension of history, Louis-René Caradeuc de La Chalotais, the celebrated and controversial advocate-general of the Brittany Parlement, is the object of A. J. Lemaître's essay. It is at once a stimulating and a frustrating piece: it embarks upon a reading of La Chalotais' intellectual development, but fails to articulate his epistemology with the moral imperatives of a history that opens the path to "public happiness" in part by rejecting transcendental detours and in part by embracing a utilitarianism neither defined nor contextualized. La Chalotais the intellectual (or philosophe) is not confronted with La Chalotais the magistrate—and a leading parlementary figure at a particular moment. If "history must teach the principles of a morality founded on natural law," how unfortunate not to decode this natural law, to use it as a bridge between La Chalotais' historical reflections and his economic ideas, and to ponder the extent to which it lured him to the Versailles *entresol* of Dr. Quesnay, fierce promoter of natural rights theory, embodied in physiocracy, and of La Chalotais' personal political ambitions (298–303).

Problematizing the Enlightenment

Edited by Olivier Chaline, one of the most percipient of the French school of parlementary revisionists, *Les Parlements et les Lumières* underscores once again, in a spirit of acute problematization, the central issue of the relation between the courts and their broad cultural environment (in the ambitious Geertzian sense).[21] In the bad old Manichean days, the parlements found themselves axiomatically aligned with the black hats, their genetically determined excommunication from the Enlightenment reinforced by such barbarities as the Calas, Sirven and chevalier de la Barre affairs. The framework here suffered from a double historiographical defect, for the conceptualization of the Enlightenment—the white hatted party of humanity—was no more nuanced than that of the parlements. Neither the one—an institution with certain characteristics of a movement—nor the other—a movement with certain institutional features—was as homogeneous or monolithic as often supposed; each harbored currents that eddied against the dominant tide, each betrayed tensions and contradictions that sweeping (often teleological) generalizations smothered as effectively as moving averages in a secular, upward sloping price curve obfuscated the significance of the so-called "accidents" such as subsistence crises.

21 *Les Parlements et les Lumières* (Pessac: Maison des Sciences de l'Homme d'Aquitaine, 2012).

The parlements no more embodied a coherent and consensual point of view than the Enlightenment. We have come to appreciate not merely the inconsistencies and aporias within each supposed camp, but the existence of many mansions within each of these houses.

If the Enlightenment continues to connote, in its generic public representation, a certain kind of progressivism and commitment to individual rights (corresponding to the Enlightenment project that has been under siege for the last several decades, even as it continues to epitomize for many the loftiest ideals of modernity), we now know that it was composed of many currents and tonalities, not all easy to reconcile, save when summoned collectively to resist the forces of darkness. And even the putative forces of darkness can legitimately contest their dismissal by anathema, a (politically correct) reflex that obscures much debate about their perception and appraisal of the so-called Enlightenment values and methods. Next to the unregenerate, intransigent and obtuse enemies of change and apologists of oppression emerged diverse and more nuanced voices of opposition in a multifaceted Counter-Enlightenment that merits unpacking and analysis.[22] For years, a handful of scholars have labored to crystallize the

22 The Counter-Enlightenment is hardly a fresh notion, but it calls for a much fuller and more dispassionate elaboration than it has thus far enjoyed. The term is often linked to Isaiah Berlin, borrowing it perhaps from Nietzsche, who deployed it in a somewhat narrow context, largely nineteenth-century German. For a stinging critique of Berlin's reading, see Robert E. Norton, "The Myth of the Counter-Enlightenment," *Journal of the History of Ideas* 68 (2007): 635–58. For the best recent work, thoughtful and inventive, focused on France as the fountainhead of the multilayered phenomenon, see Darrin McMahon, *Enemies of the Enlightenment: The French Counter-Enlightenment and the Making of Modernity* (Oxford: Oxford University Press, 2002). Cf. the surprisingly tame survey of J. Israel, *Enlightenment Contested* (Oxford: Oxford University Press, 2006) and the argument of Richard Wolin, *The Seduction of Unreason: The Intellectual Romance with Fascism from Nietzsche to Postmodernism* (Princeton, NJ: Princeton University Press, 2004) connecting Counter-Enlightenment with postmodernism, at once provocative and reductionist. For a recent appraisal in the aftermath of the linguistic turn and the triumph of culturalism, see Keith M. Baker and Peter H. Reill, eds., *What's Left of Enlightenment? A Postmodern Question* (Stanford, CA: Stanford University Press, 2001).

23 R. R. Palmer, *Catholics and Unbelievers in Eighteenth-Century France* (Princeton, NJ: Princeton University Press, 1939) was one of the rare mainstream precursors, cosmopolitan and open-minded, yet deeply anchored in the Enlightenment. Bernard Plongeron, "Recherches sur *l'Aufklärung* catholique en Europe occidentale, 1770–1830," *Revue d'histoire moderne et contemporaine* 16 (1969): 555–605, was the pioneer in France. More recently, Didier Masseau pursued the question in different directions: *Les Ennemis des philosophes: l'antiphilosophie au temps des Lumières* (Paris: Albin Michel, 2000). For a critical overview, see Jeffrey D. Burson, "The Crystallization of Counter-Enlightenment and Philosophe Identities: Theological Controversy and Catholic Enlightenment in Pre-Revolutionary France," *Church History* 77, no. 4 (December 2008): 955–1002.

notion of a Catholic Enlightenment.[23] Others have puzzled over how to construe and situate the Jansenist–Molinist confrontation that not only deeply discredited the church, but also raised disquieting questions about how to understand strains of what would soon be called political liberalism nurtured in deeply pious terrain or how to deny Enlightenment affinities with certain forms of Jesuit reasoning, at antipodes to fideism. Meanwhile, a "radical" Enlightenment has reminded us sharply what we always knew or suspected and denied (or sublimated in soft oppositions, say, between a High and a Low Enlightenment): that the Enlightenment engendered an array of epistemologies, anthropologies and political economies that were deeply antagonistic.

Problematizing the Magistrates as Men of (the) Enlightenment

Gradually, we have come to see the parlementary world in a somewhat analogous manner, as we have adumbrated above. Magistrates do not all march to the same drumbeat, and even those in the same procession move at divergent pace and occasionally in self-conscious disorder. Parlementaires sunder along multiple lines that are not necessarily governed by corporate constraints. Parlements as corporations or companies do not adhere mechanically to a Parisian blueprint or mobilize automatically in fronde-like blocs of antimonarchical comportment. The magistrates often struggle to reconcile (or compartmentalize) multiple identities. They have much in common and myriad differences. They are philosophical monarchists, or historical antiabsolutists or evolutive proto-libertarians; anglophiles or anglophobes; Jansensists or orthodox Catholics or deists or free thinkers of one stripe or another; they are partisans of individualism in some spheres, and advocates of proto-Durkheimian organic solidarity in others. They are attached to privileges, but not always the same ones, not always for the same reasons, not always with the same zeal. The question of the relations of robe and sword have not been definitively resolved; the elections to the estates general may not be sufficient or appropriate evidence to discredit the thesis of sword–robe fusion, but the latter needs to be revisited and the question of parlementary liminality reexamined.

Incisive and prudent at the same time, Olivier Chaline exposes the weaknesses and the blockages in the historiography and sketches fresh lines of inquiry. He enunciates both Enlightenment and magistracy in the open-ended plural. Transfixed by the etiology of the Revolution, a particularly French historiography in which the right and left happen to converge has relegated the parlements and the parlementaires of the Old Regime to culpable oblivion or to a mediocre and/or deleterious function in the life of the eighteenth century (14–15). A narrowly political history both failed to understand and then discredited the parlements. Implicitly, it seems to me, Chaline wonders whether the new political history of the parlements, given its aversion for, or indifference to, social history, will maximize the opportunity to recast the role of the magistrates and their institutions (15). In any event, the agenda here is to rethink the experience and the place of sovereign courts and their judges in the Enlightenment and, in so doing, renew our ways of apprehending the Enlightenment itself.

What are the "Lumières," asks the editor of this volume, that the parlementaires reject, and who are the magistrates in question (their position, roots, socio-professional itinerary, ideological disposition and so on)? What is esteemed "intolerable and dangerous" can cover a wide panoply of issues—from the antireligious (or anti-Jesuit) Enlightenment to the forms of contestation of the traditional hierarchies, the theories favorable to a monarchical power divested of its canonic religious justification, or the liberalization of the grain trade. The diverse ways in which parlementaires repudiate the Enlightenment "might more tellingly be seen as a mark of division within the Enlightenment than as a hostility in principle to new modes of thinking." This observation triggers a series of interrogations: how are the "choices" of the magistrates expressed and/or acted upon? To what extent are the attitudes of parlementaires driven first of all by "the indifference and conformity" specific to a milieu of jurists quintessentially conservative, fearful of whatever forges precedent or foments disorder. The historian warns against the easy temptation to "take any refusal of the Enlightenment as a sign of reactionary stupidity or lack of understanding of the sense in which history is unfolding." It is more productive, Chaline contends, to reflect on "the capacities of discernment and selection" that shape the outlook and decisions of the magistrates, a recommendation that leads him to ask what appears to me to be a cardinal question: "Are the anti-Lumières outside the Enlightenment?" (18).

In the same vein, the historian notes the profusion of ways in which magistrates can signify their adherence to certain Enlightenment precepts or institutions, without indicating the tests that would enable one to validate the engagement, for the risk here is in shifting from the Scylla of an excessively narrow and sectarian Enlightenment (despite certain universalistic claims) to the Charybdis of an infinitely plastic Enlightenment that accommodates a little of everything and ends up as a mere synonym for the sprawling eighteenth century (19–20). Chaline rehearses the range of parlementary opinion on religious matters, sometimes tied directly to politics (Gallicanism), sometimes linked to a sort of Catholic renovation; on the question of governance (from "enlightened despotism" to a limited, Montesquieuian monarchy); on norms and representations of the social structure(s) (grounded on what taxonomic foundations?); on fiscality; and on "economics," where I find the author disappointingly laconic, though I ratify his thoughtful remark on the fragility of characterizing a single model of agri-business management as "enlightened" or peculiarly parlementaire (21–23).

Chaline raises two other questions that merit attention. One concerns the manner in which law itself is conceived, nourished, modified and applied: we need to look at the ways in which the law, as uttered by the parlementaires, might have been refracted by certain of the Lumières or inflected by the (ever-nebulous) public opinion consubstantial to the efflorescence of the Enlightenment (27). But any assessment requires the long vista across centuries; it cannot be done episodically, at moments of febrility or crisis (even as the political history of the parlements is irreducible to a confrontation with Maupeou or a chronicling of remonstrances and *lits de justice*). Such a view must ask questions that most of us seem to regard as long resolved or purely technical/procedural, such as "the functioning of a sovereign court," in terms of its daily business, its sociability, its frictions, its governance and its often subterranean but significant relations with the royal council.[24] Chaline's voice is unfailingly temperate, yet unequivocally revisionist. Rather than remaining bogged down in the sterile problematic of rebellion/submission, "it is more worthwhile to ask why, during the regime of Louis XV and especially as of mid-century, royal power lost control of the courts." And to what extent the Enlightenment, in its pregnant multiplicity, conditioned the political dialectic between crown and courts.

Shades of White and Black

Points in a number of the essays in this collection drew my attention. Opening his discussion of the tension between repulsion and attraction that framed the relation between the parlementaires of Franche-Comté and the Enlightenment, Maurice Gresset takes for granted a contention that I think needs to be interrogated, but that could also have served as a lever in his inquiry: the Besançon Parlement "remains the only representative of the *comtois* people" (87). Beyond its formulaic cachet—the historian *seems* to be taking self-aggrandizing magisterial rhetoric at face value—what precisely

24 For an interesting piece of research and analysis on the judicial practices of magistrates in the Parlement of Toulouse, see Guillaume Ratel, "Between Facts and Faith. The Judicial Practices of the Conseillers of the Parlement de Toulouse (1550–1700)," doctoral dissertation, Cornell University, 2012.

does this claim signify? How did the parlement construe it and what did it signify among the faceless "people?" Presumably it bespeaks an age-old pretension, yet it could certainly resonate not only with the discursive conjuring of the court, but also with certain Enlightenment values. Did magistrates perceive, at some point in the second half of the century in particular, that the title to representation (albeit not necessarily representativeness) could tap into lively discussions that took place outside the arena of royal–parlementary pugilistics? Globally, the magistrates of Besançon were conservative—favorable both to the Jesuits and to the preservation of mortmain. Yet—for whatever it may signify—a certain number read the *Encyclopédie* and Montesquieu, and Rousseau and Voltaire penetrated into their cultural space.[25] What intrigues more is Gresset's classification scheme for demarcating light and dark. Save for liberal prejudice (should I say affinity?), I see no reason to include either as "refractory to Enlightenment" the commitment of the parlement of Dôle to safeguard at all costs the grain provisioning of the region or the decision of the Parlement of Besançon to refuse to register Turgot's edicts on the grain trade and the abolition of the guilds. The Turgot–Condorcet line of liberalism (only in selective ways heir to Gournay's conception), like the kindred, albeit more parochial, physiocratic school, has no monopoly privilege on Enlightenment. If we step outside the teleology and the ideology and, if we reject the test of being on the right side of history (or approaching its "end")[26], then there is no more reason to characterize the Besançon court for being refractory to Enlightenment in 1776 vis-à-vis Turgot than of personifying Enlightenment when it registered the even bolder, inaugural liberal measures of 1763–64 (89, 92). In the same sense, Diderot, Holbach, Galiani, Grimm, Mably, Linguet and others are no less engaged in an Enlightenment process/project for having vigorously resisted liberalization than are the clan of the *Ephémérides* for having fervently supported it.

Frédéric Pitou's more general chapter on the ideal of the perfect magistrate offers some reinforcement to this argument that underlines the infinite and delicate complexity of the physiocratic penumbra, the epistemological and existential ambiguities of political economy (the "new science") and the difficulties and dangers of Enlightenment classification. Certain magistrates "put forward an absolute refusal to the discourse of the Enlightenment." His case in point, a physiocratic militant, Guillaume-François Le Trosne, an *avocat du roi* at the présidial court of Orléans. This liberal is deeply conservative socially and

25 Cf. the avid "enlightened" book reading and collecting of a magistrate in the Parlement of Provence in the essay that Monique Cubells wrote for this volume (129–25).

26 I am alluding of course to Francis Fukuyama, *The End of History and the Last Man* (New York: Free Press, 1992).

politically; like Mirabeau and Quesnay, he avoids speculating on the implications of an unchained market individualism, on the capacity of a world built on unbounded liberty, inviolable property and unchecked competition to withstand the kinds of disorder that he believes the perfect magistrate must repress, a disorder emanating not from those he dubs "les méchants," but more or less unintentionally from the property owners to whom magistrates must imperatively provide full judicial shelter. On what side of the classic—and pernicious—white/black hat divide does one place this magistrate-*économiste*, modernizing foe of "decadence," who blames pullulating moral decay on "a new Philosophy favorable to all the passions… enemy of all duties, combating them all the way to the authority who prescribes them?" (207–8).

Normandy's magistrates share the conservative proclivities of the Franc-comtois, many of them in the devout mode of Godart de Belbeuf, Rouen's procurator-general, who evinced strong distaste for the sort of "encyclopédistes un peu mécreants"—nonbelievers but possibly also scoundrels?—who were Turgot's friends (121). There flourished in his court some magistrates far more susceptible to the allure of philosophes of all sorts, there existed masons and perhaps even some "mécréants." But the point that Olivier Chaline hammers out in his essay is that there were probably a considerable number of parlementaires who could be termed enlightened "on the condition of not reducing the notion of Enlightenment to a unique combat against tradition, prejudice, religion and the throne" (111, 115–17, 122–24). I recognize not only the pitfalls of this profession of faith, but also its immense heuristic value.

Like their comtois counterparts, the leading magistrates of the Normandy Parlement took the "general police" as their primordial daily responsibility and detected numerous ways in which certain expressions of Enlightenment could generate disorder, that is to say, undermine the administrative and moral vocation of police. Chaline is surely right in asserting that the Enlightenment "did not give form to the debate concerning, particularly in 1768, the free circulation of the grain trade [*sic*]." Contesting the position of several sister courts and of the royal government, the Rouen Parlement revealed that "a good police has priority over the interests of [grain] producers, even when the latter turned out to be magistrates" (112, 114).[27]

Enlightened Despotism Redux

Clarisse Coulomb disputes the regnant historiography that locates the influence of the Enlightenment on the magistracy exclusively "in the sense of the birth

27 See also Olivier Chaline, *Godart de Belbeuf: le parlement, le roi et les Normands* (Luneray: Bertout, 1996), 234–70.

of political liberalism battling the absolute monarchy." As we have seen, she is not the only revisionist who suggests that we need to look at the impact of the Enlightenment in a different direction, from an angle that harkens back to the days when all textbooks—even before my generation—spoke solemnly and admiringly of enlightened despotism (275). If the Parlement of Dauphiné clashed brutally with the crown over fiscal affairs in 1763, Coulomb prompts us to recall that, in that very year, it praised the king in dithyrambic terms for the gifts of liberalization. In other words, the "lumières" clearly penetrated the Palais in 1763 and showed the magistrates a new path: "no longer the road of resistance, but that of collaboration with the prince" (276). Paradoxically, inviting the parlementaires to serve as a bridge between the philosophes (or reformists) and the king, the Enlightenment was able to "reinforce the ancient duty of the magistracy which was to preserve and defend royal power." The Enlightenment thus rushed to the king's succor in his struggle against (sometimes) mutinous courts by forging a synthesis that somehow reconciled the magistrates with absolutism in the name of an unnamed notion of orderly progress or dynamic order. In her energetic argument, without ignoring the apparent incongruities and frictions involved, Coulomb identifies three influences that induced numerous magistrates to embrace a vision of an "enlightened absolute monarchy": Montesquieu, Voltaire and the theory of legal despotism of the physiocrats (276).

The last of these three strains is the least convincing, in part because of an insufficiently probing examination of the ways in which the magistrates of Grenoble read physiocracy (286–88). It may be that Coulomb is correct in rejecting Chaline's caution about narrowly (economic) interest-driven decision making. Yet even if the exuberant Dauphinois' endorsement of liberalization derived from the financial benefits anticipated by the magistrates, it still seems urgent to imagine a more capacious notion of interest that includes the symbolic as well as the material, to articulate the interests invoked by Coulomb with other interests in the province and with the ideological investments of the magistrates, yet another type of interest, which were surely more diverse than their economic stakes. A final remark: given the predicate of a natural law template for "the perfection of human laws," which the advocate-general espoused, it is not clear to me that he needed "legal despotism" to arrive at a (still physiocratically influenced) vision of an "absolute royal power in all spheres." The central point seems to me to be that the natural law paradigm constrains the absolute prince, delimiting his freedom of action as well as guaranteeing that positive law will always be in conformity with nature's prescriptions (289).[28]

28 In a wholly different context, pursuing his work on La Chalotais, A.-J. Lemaître suggests that a segment of the magistracy, in part under the influence of the Enlightenment, follows the procurator-general of the Brittany Parlement "towards enlightened absolutism" (261, 273). The historian's account of La Chalotais' conception is far

The Parlements, Maupeou and the Social Question

In another collection edited by Olivier Chaline with Yves Sassier, treating the parlements and public life, Nicolas Laurent addresses issues concerning the Dijon Parlement that are pertinent to the other courts and that echo themes already aired.[29] With perhaps some hyperbole—but it is important to verify the claim in any event—he contends that legislative and political objectives so engaged the magistrates that they appeared "to forget their judicial attributions" (143). I am not persuaded by the implicit framework of a zero-sum game in which the aggrandizement of parlementary power is either the cause or the result of the "progressive weakening of the monarchy" (145). I am struck, however, by certain dissonances in the rhythms and manifestations of royal–parlementary conflict. For example, the subsistence crisis of 1770 seems to preoccupy the court more than the explosive Brittany affair—fulsomely dramatized by political historians—that appears seamlessly to lead to the nightmare of real rather than theoretical despotism, represented by the Maupeou assault (146). Given the acuity of the provisioning problem and its complex social and cultural fallout, on the one hand, and the particular convergence of political audacity, natural disaster and commercial disarray that occasioned it, on the other hand, I think historians need to pay much more attention to it. The fiscal/constitutional fixation has obscured some of the fundamental debates, conflicts and mutations of the last decade of the reign of Louis XV and further segregated the political from the social, to the detriment of our understanding of the period.

In suggesting (without much evidence) that the Maupeou parlements were more engaged than their predecessors in the social question of the age—

too cursory: "Relying upon the theorists of natural law and the philosophes of the eighteenth century, he seems to reconcile, in the name of reason, liberty and authority, absolutism and enlightenment" (273). He goes on to insist on the quasi-Machiavellian instrumentalization of the power of the state that La Chalotais envisaged. Lemaître's essay ends unexpectedly with a far too brief yet still intriguing evocation of La Chalotais' construction of public opinion—"impartial and infallible judge." The magistrate takes the trouble to define the public he has in mind, albeit summarily: "educated individuals." Lemaître comments: "Now this public is imaginary." In this instance, the public to which the procurator-general seems to refer is the milieu of the magistrates themselves (274). The vexing question of a decisively important, but intractably elusive, opinion makes the stimulating essay in the same volume by Hervé Leuwers—by elision—less compelling than it might have been (213–14, 217, 224).

29 *Les Parlements et la vie de la cité (XVIe–XVIIIe siècle)* (Rouen: Publications de l'Université de Rouen, 2004).

subsistence—Laurent underscores another theme worth exploring: the ways in which the chancellor used the dearth and the prolonged crisis of liberalization to discredit the old parlements (as I argue in *Bread, Politics and Political Economy*). The reaction to Maupeou's "despotic" offensive, Laurent shows nicely, was not a simple black and white affair. Less promising is the absence of reflection on the relation between what he calls interests and convictions, a fragile dichotomy, as I have intimated, and an analytical lapse that traverses much of parlementary historiography, old school and new. Interests and convictions may stand in outright antagonism or in flush synergy; more commonly, they play out in permanent tension. In any case, they need to be defined categorically and scrutinized substantively, not merely labeled (154). Another Dijonnais theme that surfaces everywhere, as we have observed, is the appeal to public opinion in one form or another. Laurent exposes the Burgundian discursive ploy of expressing the magistrates' hatred of despotism through their reappropriation of the good prince's paternal role: they emphasize "their solicitude for the people." Here the people—labile concept—turn out to be "the bourgeoisie," a relatively opaque and motley social category that supposes both a certain (yet unspecified level of) fortune and education (155).

Political Justice, Fruitful Concert and Discord

Parlements et parlementaires de France, edited by Frédéric Bidouze, is another revisionist collection that makes a robust case for the rehabilitation of these sovereign courts.[30] As always, the argument reclaiming the virtues of these institutions and their members would have been stronger had the authors taken stock of their shortcomings as well. Given the roster of contributors from diverse horizons, it might have been fruitful to inventory and reflect upon any differences in assumptions, methods and manners of reasoning between French and foreign scholars, between jurists and (conventional) historians of ideas and of politics and between research focused on Paris and work dealing with the provinces. The line separating editorial plurality from unavowed dissonance is not always crystalline. In the profession of intentions and in the texts, one encounters themes now quite familiar: denunciations of the stigmatization of the parlements by the clan of promonarchist historians, ranging from writers addressing a broad public such as P. Gaxotte (normalien, Maurrasian, academician and editorialist for *Le Figaro*) to university-based figures such as R. Mousnier, J. Meyer, F. Bluche and M. Antoine; refutation of the characterization of the

30 *Parlements et parlementaires de France au XVIIIe siècle* (Paris: L'Harmattan, 2011).

magistrates as enemies of the Enlightenment; promotion of the thesis that parlementary resistance and monarchical fidelity were not incompatible engagements; adumbration of the exceptionalist claim that the parlements are a vector of a specifically French conception of liberty that is begotten in the Middle Ages or earlier, incubated during the Old Regime, resurgent after the Revolution and nurturant in the evolution of democracy; the representation of the courts, despite their alleged underlying royalism, as the first institutional mobilizers and molders of public opinion, the immensely powerful yet shadowy Enlightenment force of which they gradually lost control in a scenario that remains unwaveringly obscure (8–15).

A tonic article on parlementary constitutionalism, played out in the "beds of justice" figuring royal despotism, by F. Saint-Bonnet, a jurist, inserts the issue of political justice in a long-term perspective beginning in medieval times and culminating with the Revolution. While I resonate with this grand chronological respiration, I note that it exacts an elevated price: a strong formalistic bias, an extremely amorphous historicization and a lack of traction in the concrete experience of the politics of the eighteenth century (16–30). The following piece by Joël Félix seems designed to mitigate these liabilities by refusing to inscribe the parlementary opposition in a teleology driven by the Revolutionary dénouement and by resituating the remonstrances in the granularity of the political context that unfolds day by day, almost always dominated by fiscal concerns. No one toils more vigorously to displace the traditional binary opposition between ministry and parlement and to show the very real attention paid by numerous magistrates to the management of public finance, beyond any calculation of self-interest. Analytically, Félix modernizes the conflict between king and courts, anchoring both in plausible, albeit divergent, perceptions of the realities, emphasizing that remonstrances cannot be read as autonomous texts, and inviting reflection on the obstacles that hampered collaborative solutions between magistrates and ministers (31–47).

Like Félix, who teaches in England, British historian Julian Swann argues that the parlements seek fruitful concert with the crown. I see little utility, however, in characterizing the magistrates' posture as "conservative"—I suppose this attenuates the acuity of their clash with the king—or in pretending to explain it by reference to a supposedly regnant "mentality" (56–57). After cautioning us about taking either monarchy or magistrates at their word (56–57), by which I presume Swann calls for a close yet contextualized reading of their declarations, this is precisely what he seems to be doing two pages further into his chapter. He affirms that "the image of the monarch and the monarchy were nevertheless almost always positive." Almost always until liberalization, when the regal baker becomes a royal hoarder, a shocking metamorphosis that sullies the king before the Maupeou events (59). Following W. Doyle, Swann interprets this assault on the magistrates not as a deliberate effort (as Antoine would have it) to rid the kingdom of asphyxiating, egocentric obstructionism, but as the result of events that the (willful) king himself could not control (48–49, 59–60). As one of the major artisans of the new doxa, Swann concludes by rejecting a representation of the Parlement of Paris as practicing a policy of judicial insubordination, orchestrated in league with other courts, to combat and/or undermine royal authority. Rather, the parlements' words and acts bespeak an attempt to preserve the "professional, corporate and personal prestige" of the magistrates and "to obtain respect for the primacy of the law," in the manner of faithful monarchical conservatives. This extremely indulgent reading of royal–parlementary politics holds the king in the end responsible for refusing to take into account parlementary advice, the deplorable practices of monarchs who "stray" (62).

The rehabilitation of the parlements takes place, sometimes quite needlessly, at the expense of the king, it seems to me. Swann shows the monarch all the respect due him, as would have his magistrates, and yet he mutilates their capacity for coherent political agency. In a parallel manner, Isabelle Storez-Brancourt, a legal historian, calls forth the starkly binary classical historiographical view of crown versus court. In her commentary, she rightly stresses the "moderate" image of the parlements. Yet, in the representation of "a purely monarchical conception of political authority," while she recalls the pitfalls of tyranny denounced by its critics, she forgets to mention the portrayal of the king as a reformist and modernizer (74–75).

Far from speaking in a single voice according to the idealized version of the "union des classes," Alain J. Lemaître reminds us that certain major issues divided the parlements, in particular religion and the subsistence question, the latter understandably present in a text devoted in large measure to La Chalotais, the brilliant and extremely controversial high magistrate, a philosophe and an impassioned liberal, close to Dr. Quesnay (80, 94).[31] I regret the missed opportunity to relate La Chalotais' quasi-endorsement of enlightened despotism (supposedly reconciling liberty and authority,

31 On the "gens du roi" of which La Chalotais was an exemplar, see the rich anthology of studies edited by Caroline Le Mao, *Hommes et Gens du roi dans les parlements de France à l'époque moderne* (Pessac: Maison des Sciences de l'Homme d'Aquitaine, 2011). It contains interesting pieces by the usual suspects (Chaline, Coulomb, Bidouze and Lemaître) and by a host of other, mostly young, scholars. See also Le Mao's study of the seventeenth-century sovereign court that Montesquieu would render famous, *Parlement et parlementaires. Bordeaux au grand siècle* (Seyssel: Champ Vallon, 2007), severely criticized by Christophe Blanquie in *Annales. Histoire, Sciences Sociales*, 62nd year (2007): 118–22.

absolutism and Enlightenment) with the concept of legal despotism forged by another magistrate and intimate of Quesnay, Lemercier de la Rivière (92). Here were the makings of the "alternative [political] program" that Lemaître insists the parlementaires never managed to elaborate. Preoccupied with the role of "the public," La Chalotais offered the historian the occasion to clarify the Pavlovian concept of public opinion, present in various places throughout this collection of essays (94–95, 107, 112, 129, 134). Certainly, the public-opinion problem will not be productively addressed, let alone resolved, without a wholly fresh start. F. Bidouze has the right general idea, it seems to me, in his call for a discursive approach inscribed in social reality. But his concluding chapter is a chaotic potpourri of bits and pieces of methodology and epistemology, seasoned by endless name-dropping, rather than a reasoned guide for working out a new history of the Enlightenment parlements, "a French culture of the political" (118–36).

Self-Interest, Traditionalism and Short Memory

Avowedly influenced by Jean Egret, who had himself envisaged a book picking up the story of parlementary "opposition" at the ascendency of Louis XVI, Bailey Stone has written a study that generally fits the revisionist template in its most judicious (and sometimes equivocal) voice.[32] He vigorously rejects the vantage points from which the parlements are stigmatized as "irresponsible critics of the crown" (the standard monarchical posture), as "sponsors of an aristocratic resurgence" (the line of scholars who exaggerate, in Stone's view, the fusion of robe and sword and who assign an excessively significant role to the magistrates in the long-term gestation of the forces of revolution) (92–93), and as "politicians hypocritically mouthing popular propaganda" (a much more opaque accusation that would logically be attributed to partisans of monarchy, contemporaneously and retrospectively, and more broadly to conservatives who denounce the courts for demagogic manipulation of (mis-) information for the purpose of turning the erratic and amorphous people/public against their royal father).

Even as Stone admires most parlementary stands, he wants us to know that he does not idealize the magistrates and thus deny their weaknesses, considered more in the category of human flaws than as political or intellectual defects. He intones the familiar paradox that even as the court is increasingly aware of its dependence on the crown's authority, it criticizes

32 B. Stone, *The Parlement of Paris, 1774–1789* (Chapel Hill: University of North Carolina University Press, 1981).

royal management more or less unremittingly (62, 70). Yet, unlike certain rehabilitationists, Stone is not embarrassed to talk about the self-interest of the magistrates, though he does it in a frequently incantatory way in support of his recurrent thesis about ambivalence (180–81). "Self-interest" is supposed to account, in different guises, both for their support for certain expressions of royal authority *and* for their resistance to it; it leads them to contest administrative absolutism, including the refusal of the monarchy to inform the parlement of its financial governance, but at the same time it reinforces an outmoded parlementary conception of the needs of government. Self-interest does not preclude material self-aggrandizement, but Stone places it into relief in particular in the magistrates' defense of their professional status, located liminally between public and private vocations. Finally, if self-interest is not incompatible with principled espousal of convictions about the constitutional framework of a monarchy that is by nature and law limited and just, at the same time, it reinforces an outmoded conception of the needs of government (90–92).

I was very disappointed that Stone did not use the opportunity of the recall of the parlements to reflect on the extent to which the heritage of the 1760s and 1770s marked the magistrates. To what degree did the successive social, economic and political traumas of those years incite or constrain the magistrates to conduct an inventory of what went right and wrong, and why? To judge from this historian's reading, the parlements did not emerge deeply scarred by the Maupeou ordeal, nor from the turbulent experience of liberalization, to which it was connected in several ways. One has the impression of a keen desire to normalize as quickly as possible, despite the violent buffeting of the stanchions of an always passably imagined and imaginary "normalcy," to return to the status quo *ante-ante*: before Maupeou and before liberalization. Nevertheless, even as the kingdom still felt the aftershocks of Terray's modulated regulatory restoration, Turgot was briskly preparing the first phase of the second liberalization that necessarily posed many of the same questions that had alarmed many of the magistrates at the end of the 1760s, some of them from the early 1760s. Yet the magistrates registered the measure of September 1774, adumbrating a very different vision of society from the one to which they subscribed in very substantial majority, probably not without a vigorous debate, though Stone does not explore this critical issue. Perhaps, the registration can be explained as a gesture of propitiation toward Turgot, who had abetted their resurrection.

The student of the pre-Revolutionary Paris Parlement disposes of Turgot with dispatch, through the shortcut of a stereotype: he was a physiocrat and/or embraced the physiocratic theory that a great many magistrates reviled (126, 131, 141, 147). Did the latter see themselves in a sort of time warp, beamed back to 10 years earlier? Did the eruption of the Flour War merely confirm the archetypal dictum that history repeats itself ("nothing changes under the sun"), and that the same causes give rise to the same effects? Stone's magistrates are traditionalists. He constructs their conservatism less directly on hostility to deregulation than more positively on their espousal of a corporate (or corporative) order, the intimate relationship between the two not galvanizing his attention. Yet he dispenses with any serious sociology of this corporate order, which is not reducible to social structure, seems impervious to economic change and closely corresponds with the political order epitomized by the celebrated "chain" metaphor (9, 12, 94, 121, 123–27, 130, 163).[33]

Two of the famous six edicts of 1776 offered Stone the opportunity to explore the assumptions underlying the corporatist template, the measure transforming the labor *corvée* into a quasi-universal monetary levy on landowners and the law abolishing the guilds, both of which directly attacked the corporative framework by undermining hierarchy and subordination and fomenting "confusion" and "mixing".[34] To understand parlementary apprehension and logic, the historian would have had to unpack the various strains of ideology, psycho-reified here as "parlementary mentality" (4, 11, 60, 74).[35] Toward the same end, it would also have been fruitful to develop the striking homologies between the liberation of grain and that of work, between the dismantling of controls in the subsistence and labor markets, both based

33 Stone does not draw on an extensive bibliography in sociology and anthropology, as well as in literature and legal history, which could have helped him move beyond a rudimentary notion of social control, or upon eighteenth-century thought in the mood of Burke, for example (or the earlier writings of Seyssel, Bodin or Loyseau) in order to theorize notions of corporatism, organicism, and conservatism.

34 Under the rubric of the corvée, Stone's more interesting discussion of privilege, hierarchy and social stratification cedes quickly to a focus on humanitarian objectives, and a solicitude for the people along with a desire for their acclaim (141–42, 147, 149). The idea of a certain symmetry between the defense of privilege and the defense of popular interests is the embryo of a provocative argument that is not fleshed out (153). In the end, if the court believes that the peasants themselves were more hospitable to a labor corvée than a tax, it is still not clear why the humanitarian impulse—the paternal pretension—did not incite the magistrates to opt for a simple abolition of the levy. This reticence or hesitation (or ambivalence) has to do with Stone's appetite for an ostensibly balanced depiction of the parlement: obsessed by public order, favorable to regulation, partisans of the corporate order, attentive to private/privileged interests, defenders not only of property rights but also of popular interests, humane and so on. In this voice of what one might call "realist" rehabilitation, the critique of the monarchy sometimes seems to get lost.

35 Cf. the equally sterile concept of "popular mentality" that recurs in many of the texts that I examine here (134).

on the model of a temperate, self-restrained state and an unfettered, atomized society, consisting of individuals rather than corps, fueled by unhampered freedom, utterly refractory to a prescriptive system of social classification and to the embedding of the economic in the social fabric.[36]

Godart: Ambiguity and Anxiety, Paternalism and Regulation

The only historian of the "new" school of parlementary history to devote serious attention to the subsistence question is Olivier Chaline. His outstanding *Godart de Belbeuf: le parlement, le roi et les Normands* depicts the procurator-general of a sometimes turbulent sovereign court, fascinating figure, superficially paradoxical, but embodying qualities that loom as much less incongruous in his own time than today: paragon of the "devout Enlightenment," monarchical loyalist and exponent of a parlementary vocation that required a certain autonomy. More as a marker of prudence and a capacity to tolerate complexity than as a sign of gnawing doubt and dread of engagement, Chaline describes Godart de Belbeuf's worldview as "ambiguous." The law had to be obeyed rigorously, yet compelling circumstances justified derogation; the local authorities required strict guidelines, but should not be systematically deprived of initiative, a sine qua non for their reputation as well as their efficacy; the people were ignorant and impulsive on many matters, yet often betrayed a strategic capacity to think and act about subsistence issues and could fruitfully be heeded; the people needed to be punished pitilessly on certain occasions—the memory of the violent grain riots of 1752 at Rouen, brutally repressed, inhabited all the magistrates throughout the epoch of liberalization—and generously indulged on others (235, 252, 261–62).

Unfortunately, Chaline does not explore the hesitations or divisions that accompanied the parlement's endorsement of the royal declaration of May 1763 and its call for the authorization of exportation the following year. Despite burgeoning agitation and unrest beginning in 1766, he suggests that liberalization did not crystallize serious antagonism in the Norman court until the worrisome "*chertés*" of the last months of 1767. The first president, Miromesnil, comments ironically that the people remain "quite tranquil," but "the négociants, [various]men of distinction, and especially a very substantial number of magistrates in the parlement tremble." Alluding to 1752, he notes that "one does not get cured of fear." One of the principal destabilizing vectors in 1768, he argues, is rumor, a perilous instrument that the parlement would shortly use with astonishing recklessness. What is especially interesting about Miromesnil's observation, formulated in the midst of a growing psychosis about

36 See Kaplan, *La Fin des corporations*.

an alleged famine plot mounted by the dominant and influential against the people, habitually accused of paranoid fantasies, is their provenance: "Those who make the most of the rumors are those situated above the people, that apprehension leads them to speak indiscreetly in front of their valets."[37] Chaline dates the "abrupt turn-around in favor of regulation" to well before the riots of the end of March 1768. Godart de Belbeuf transmits the new (purportedly balanced) message to consumers, grain holders and local authorities: contrary to the (liberal) law of the land, given the emergency, the police will compel those with grain to supply markets, but the soldiers who are dispatched to prevent supplies from leaving the region to reassure the people are also there to punish the very same people harshly should they rise again in violence or pillage (237, 239–41).

L'Averdy had every reason to worry about an omnibus regulatory ordinance that was in preparation in the parlement, probably devised in consultation with the procurator-general: the former believed that it would reinforce popular prejudices and could even provoke panic terror and disorder, while the latter hinted that such action could, on the contrary, dissipate them. Chaline's appreciation is on the mark: the familiar conflict is displaced and modified in nature. It is no longer a simple opposition between consumers and the authorities: "It erupts among the authorities and risks setting the parlement against the royal power" (242). The controller-general accused Godart de Belbeuf of playing a crucial role in the parlementary *arrêt* of April 1768 that sapped the core of the liberal creed by mandating obligatory market exchange and imposing stringent restrictions on the right to trade in grain (243). The Rouen court continued to convey conspiratorial rumors that deeply offended the ministry (and presumably Louis XV himself): Chaline hypothesizes reasonably that the magistrates deployed these rumors to "turn a strong current of popular discontent against the central power in order to make sure that it does not target the parlement" (245). Godart de Belbeuf exposes himself to ministerial suspicion precisely because of his inability or unwillingness to contain the most rebellious magistrates, though, again, Chaline does not seem to have the sources required to elucidate the apparently fierce cleavages within the court (246). First President Miromesnil avows that he is unable to marshal even the most sober magistrates to support the government's position "because of their fear of the people."[38]

---

37 Miromesnil to L'Averdy, 18 Mar. 1768 and 21 Mar. 1768, Pierre Le Verdier, ed., *Correspondance politique et administrative de Armand Thomas Hue de Miromesnil, Premier Président du Parlement de Normandie*, vol. 5 (Rouen: A. Lestringant, 1899–1903), 122, 129.

38 Miromesnil to L'Averdy, 18 May 1768, in ibid., 5: 217–18.

Powerless to inflect L'Averdy's will either on the general question of regulation or on the specific issue of lowering significantly the ceiling-price at which exports are automatically stopped, the *Chambre des Vacations* drafts and publishes its (in-) famous letter of 15 October denouncing liberalization as the central cause of the social/food crisis and suggesting that the monopolists who organized and profited from the dearth enjoyed royal protection (246–47). Furious, the government is nevertheless obliged to defend its policy and its honor by reiterating that liberty is itself the best guarantee against monopoly and manipulation (248–49). The course for escalation is now set, however, as the Paris Parlement joins Rouen, not in its egregiously subversive insinuations, but in its demands for a return to a kingly kingship, to a policy of necessary and normal intervention in subsistence affairs.

In all likelihood, Godart de Belbeuf felt much less uncomfortable with his court's subsequent attack on modern philosophy in general for its fostering of libertinage, and on physiocracy in particular for its theoretical paternity of liberalization, than with the accusations tarnishing the monarch. We do not, however, obtain a clear idea of the procurator-general's influence in the court, his tendency to cede to or to resist the majority (of the moment), or the extent to which he found in the parlement a stable, hospitable ideological niche. It is likely that he agreed that "an unlimited liberty will be the ruin of the Sovereign" and that he welcomed the new controller-general Terray's return to what I have called a policy of "apprehensive paternalism," though Chaline elides the issue of his exact posture.

The historian finds much more evidence in the period extending from the second liberalization (Turgot's) to the Revolution: from Godart de Belbeuf's less equivocal relations with his subordinates in the judicial and police jurisdiction of the parlement, he draws the portrait of a sensitive and sensible leader, capable of pressing his deputies [*substituts*] to hector grain holders when it was necessary to force market supply and thereby reassure consumers, and of according them wide berth to negotiate local solutions (250–70).[39] As in other places, the local police seemed to turn to the procurator-general only when they felt under unusual pressure, and the high magistrate gave them lessons only when he viewed their actions as inappropriate. Godart de Belbeuf perceived both the advantages and the risks of the symbiosis and intermittent synergy between the people and the local judges and administrators. The procurator-general monitored the conduct of both the people and the police.

39 Chaline casts the local police on occasion as far more docile than they habitually were, especially in times of crisis (254).

"Being Reasonable in the People's Place"

His disposition not to provoke Turgot's ministry directly by sanctioning police deviation suggests that he probably showed the same restraint in the late 1760s. On the eve of the Revolution, the police, generally more inclined to favor the consumers as opposed to the grain owners, reveal a radical propensity that belies a simple model of oscillation between rigor and moderation: a proposal to assure the steady supply of markets by *laboureurs* [grain growers] by lodging troops in their farmhouses (258).[40] Here Chaline depicts Godart de Belbeuf as bent to worry about the peril of popular collective action: thus his idea of "being reasonable in the people's place" (261–62).[41] The historian prefers his protagonist to conform to his image of an ideal-type magistrate: hyper-chary, moved by a strong proclivity to try persuasion before venturing more muscular methods, adept at using the weaknesses (or strengths) of the actors (police or people) to his advantage (262–63). In action—in 1768, 1775, 1784 or 1789—the real-life procurator-general is not always able to attain this Aristotelian golden mean. When millers enter the (speculative) grain trade—this formula is increasingly pleonastic—or, more portentously, when bakers threaten to strike, Godart de Belbeuf does not hesitate to recommend draconian responses (in the case of the bakers who refuse to bake, walling the shop for six months or threatening to close it—for 10 years!) (265–69). After such a penetrating discussion, Chaline's conclusion is disappointing, for it relies on the unspoken explanatory power of a familiar, but not transparent, concept that he does not problematize:

> The subsistence question is thus the occasion for a confrontation of representations. The "moral economy," dear to consumers, is not always disdained by the procurator general and his deputies in the implementation of a good police in their jurisdiction (270).

---

40 Chaline notes shrewdly "that this is to push to an extreme the demand for visibility and transparency of the trade. It is no longer just the space of the market that is concerned, but the space of agricultural production itself that is subject to the attentive vigilance of the authorities." The historian characterizes this extension of police ambition as "revolutionary," but it was not, in fact, unprecedented. Here and elsewhere, it was part of the moral coercion to which the local authorities subjected the parlements (and their procurators-general): if the agents of legitimacy do not act promptly, the people may very well decide to serve themselves (258).

41 Here Godart de Belbeuf's "ambivalence" concerning the "people" is startlingly Manichean: on the one hand, a good people, authentically miserable, apparently prepared to count on the police for succor; on the other hand, a "seditious" people, called pejoratively "the populace," given over to "rumor" and to "violent impulse" (262). The analysis here is a bit summary and schematic.

Toulouse: From Paternalism to Liberalism—and Back

In his overview-piece entitled "Le Parlement de Toulouse et la vie économique du ressort, 1735–89," Jack Thomas briefly evokes liberalization, in particular what he labels the shift from "paternalism and repression" to liberal ideas.[42] He makes no effort to explore parlementary reasoning or motivation, beyond attributing, in reductionist manner, the philo-physiocratic ideological line of the magistrates to their heavy investment in arable land (548). The court quashes the effort of the Toulouse *capitouls* (municipality) to install a privileged corps of grain factors in 1766 as contrary to the "unlimited liberty" prescribed by the liberal legislation of 1763, an undertaking doubly baleful because it also focused suspicion on grain merchants, thereby reinforcing the prejudices of "a people blind in its judgments." Following the canonic pattern of regression under stress, the city fathers thus become people (548–49). Similarly, the court resists the attempts of the sénéschal of Rodez nearly four years later to require declarations of holdings on the part of all grain owners, another violation of the rights of liberty and property guaranteed by the liberal laws that could only stir trouble in the community (249–50).

Thomas cites a third case, an inversion of roles, at once comical and revelatory of the complex burden of parlementary responsibility. In response to budding unrest in Toulouse during the spring of 1773, when penury, price volatility and social turbulence engulfed much of the south, the *capitouls* dispatched soldiers to prevent grain from leaving the city. The first president of the Parlement himself went to the canal to block grain departures, but the historian does not indicate the extent to which he found support in the tenaciously liberal parlement. For the chief magistrate, theoretically a king's man, the urgency of assuring public order trumped doctrine, despite its scientific cachet and transformative promise. The controller-general Terray, "veritable bête noire of the Toulouse parlement," took wry pleasure in "admonishing" the court to respect the (liberal!) royal legislation that still imposed (and intoned the merits of) the free circulation of grain within the kingdom (250).

---

42 In Jacques Poumarède and J. Thomas, eds., *Les Parlements de province: Pouvoirs, justice et société du XVe au XVIIIe siècle* (Toulouse: Framespa, 1996).

43 *Toulouse et la région Midi-Pyrénées au siècle des Lumières vers 1670–1789* (Paris: Cujas, 1974). The book did not reach me in time for me to use it in *Bread, Politics and Political Economy*, though I profited from other segments of Frêche's formidable repertory of research. I knew him casually long before he launched the stunning and controversial political

Toulouse: The Regional Stakes of Liberalization; or Economics and Politics

In his immensely stimulating and erudite *Toulouse et la région Midi-Pyrénées au Siècle des Lumières*, Georges Frêche writes briefly about the Parlement of Toulouse's fervent advocacy of liberalization in the context of the complex story of the simultaneously exalting and tyrannical triumph of wheat in the course of the eighteenth century.[43] In the Toulouse region, commercially dominated by Bordeaux and Marseille, especially once the Canal du Midi was completed and road improvements made, the well-off pressed for the right to export wheat, toward the Atlantic and Mediterranean ports, for use in the realm or abroad, while the poor, including wheat cultivators, ate corn (maize).[44] Languedoc is an ideal site from which to measure both the inconstancy of royal legislation concerning the internal and external circulation of grain (passing phlegmatically from encouragement for exportation to the death penalty and back) and of enforcement (tensions between neighboring intendants, between the intendant and the ministry). Driven largely by factors that Le Roy Ladurie—not Frêche's preferred historian—would call "agro-meteorological," royal grain policy, Frêche shows, is also shaped by military, fiscal and foreign policy concerns, and by court clientelism (804–8).

The historian cites the fascinating case, straight out of the annals of the *pacte de famine*, involving the merchant and royal administrator Ribes, who managed to drain vast amounts of grain for export, regardless of the local subsistence situation, sometimes highly precarious in the second half of the 1740s, thanks to the sub rosa sponsorship of the royal financier Pâris-Duverney and the support of several influential ministers.[45] Detested and

---

career that led him to transform Montpellier and dominate the entire region. In retrospect, I recognize the *grande gueule* that was his trademark in politics, the source of much of his success as well as his acrimonious clashes: Frêche, a hulking man, was the only apprentice-researcher—maybe the only scholar, period—prepared to confront and contest Ernest Labrousse, a diminutive yet imperious man, in the colloquia on social and economic history of our common youth.

44 The construction of this canal failed to issue in the military–naval advantages eagerly entertained by Louis XIV, but proved an exceptional boon to commerce, in particular to the wholesale grain trade. See Chandra Mukerji, *Impossible Engineering: Technology and Territoriality on the Canal du Midi* (Princeton, NJ: Princeton University Press, 2009).

45 See Marc Cheynet de Beaupré, *Joseph Pâris-Duverney, financier d'Etat (1684–1770): Les sentiers du pouvoir (1684–1720)* (Paris: Honoré Champion, 2012), the first volume of what promises to be a major study of the family and of royal finance in the eighteenth century.

more or less vainly resisted by the intendant Le Nain, to whom Frêche pays homage for his public-spiritedness, "the monopolist," as Ribes was called, spurred an "intense hostility against public intervention in the grain trade" that resulted in a powerful lobby in the second half of the century "in favor of the freedom of the grain trade." The thesis requires closer investigation, but it is provocative and plausible: the figure of the monopolist is not a paranoid fantasy, but the very real product of overgovernment and corruption; in this instance, as in others, it clearly results from undergovernment and corruption, that is to say, unfettered liberty. The anger and apprehension galvanized by the "monopolist" scenario here is far more instrumental in rallying "opinion" to the liberal cause than the physiocrats, or other theorists of political economy, striking by their absence.[46] The liberal lobby, wrought (in part) by Ribes's razzias, included the Estates and the Parlement of Languedoc, the bishops, the intendants and the chambers of commerce (808–11).

Beginning in 1754, liberty of circulation is timidly proclaimed at the center, but energetically implemented in the periphery, at least in large parts of the south. Indeed, much "Toulousain" grain left the country during the following years, an export traffic that slackens after the harvest shortfalls of 1758 and 1759. In 1761, the Estates of Languedoc, the venerable regional "representative" institution, prodded by the chamber of commerce of Toulouse, called upon their deputies at Versailles to press the issue of the grain trade. After the ritual invocation of Sully, their argument focuses on how England thrived as a result of cereal exportation, significantly increasing national wealth and power, without placing its subsistence in jeopardy. Joined by the parlementaires, they argued that the king needed to proclaim himself publicly to be unequivocally and permanently in favor of an unregulated

46 The physiocratic doctrine penetrates the Parlement of Toulouse in the 1760s, but Frêche views the magistrates as men geared to practice, deeply skeptical of the utility of theorization. As an example, he cites the court's response to the effort to spur their adherence to the new agriculture: "The Parlement of Toulouse in 1756 makes fun of 'the curious speculations, of the machines' [of the agromaniacs], adding that 'the park of Versailles does not decide the fate of our countryside'" (269).

On the question of public opinion, writing at a time when one simply took it for granted, Frêche resembles nevertheless most of the historians who have written about it more self-consciously in the past four decades. Reified as an actor, in the Ribes affair, public opinion "only remembered the harmful action of the government" (811). Cf. the ministry's desire, at the end of the seventeenth century, to make "a strong impression" on a force as mysterious as it was believed to be powerful: "opinion" (805). To all historians who treat public opinion either with awe or complacency, I cite the ever-pertinent bidding, uttered, with slight variations, by *Star Wars*' protagonists Obi-Wan Kenobi, General Dodonna, Hans Solo and Luke Skywalker: "May the Force be with you."

liberty of trade, at home and abroad. In response to the laws of 1763 and 1764, Frêche reports "cries of joy" among magistrates and "proprietors" in the Toulouse region (the physiocratic figure of the entrepreneurial *fermier* does not seem to enjoy any traction in this rendering). Liberalization "reshuffled the cards" in the grain-trade game, at least in its Mediterranean play: the Toulousains were no longer dependent on Marseille, whose status as a port "reputed foreign" had enabled it to control the wholesale traffic for decades.

Frêche does not carefully examine the impact of liberalization on the economy of the Toulouse region, but it is clear that, despite the social-subsistence unrest that ripped across sections of the south like a tornado in the early 1770s, the Toulouse (liberal) establishment was deeply disinclined to envisage a return—a regression—to regulation, not even in the relatively moderate mix that the abbé Terray announced as he took charge of affairs at the very end of 1769. The new controller-general hesitated to engage in combat against the Toulouse Parlement, which clung to a defiant fictional exceptionalism in grain trade, even after the royal council changed the law of the land. The Toulousains unwittingly mimicked the posture of the abruptly orphaned consumer majority of 1763: it is not credible that the monarch, cognizant that agriculture is the sole source of national wealth—the physiocratic earmark—would abandon us. Discursively, they thus created a space for reasoned insubordination. Their quasi-legislative (usurpatory) reaffirmation of the original liberal laws of 1763–64 infuriated Terray, who had their measure quashed and asked in so doing the question that Necker and others would relentlessly rehearse: do the magistrates prefer the augmentation of the income of the rich to the subsistence capacity of the poor?

The tenor of the laws concerning the grain and flour trade,[47] and the ardor with which they are enforced, will change repeatedly during the next 15 years, until the declaration of June 1787, which Frêche describes as "the most liberal of the Old Regime." It decreed a total liberty, inside and outside of French frontiers: "Although this was called into question in 1788, it recapitulates the whole [liberal] struggle of the Old Regime, which culminates in the absolute victory of the free-exchangists." The French historian (and, later, master politician) takes immense pleasure in noting that it was "not pure coincidence" that one of the chief authors of the urtext of 1787 was Loménie de Brienne, the new controller-

47 Although Frêche devotes only a few pages to milling, he shows more interest in the question than the vast majority of historians, economic and social, rural and urban.

48 According to D. Ligou, one of the points on which the three orders concurred in 1789 in the *cahiers de doléances* was the necessity of restoring the liberty of the grain trade. *Cahiers de doléances du Tiers Etat du Pays et Jugerie de Rivière-Verdun pour les Etats Généraux de 1789* (Gap: Imprimerie Louis-Jean, 1961).

general, friend of Turgot and the abbé Morellet and the former archbishop of Toulouse during the first liberalization beginning in 1763 (812–18).[48]

Grenoble: The Identity Crisis of "the Defeated"

In her thoughtful and gracefully written *Les Pères de la patrie: la société parlementaire en Dauphiné au temps des Lumières* (Grenoble, 2006), Clarisse Coulomb inserts herself into the long-standing debate between "state worshippers" deeply inimical to the parlements and partisans of the latter, whose history she qualifies disconsolately as that of "the defeated." She finds affinity with the political-culture approach of the Anglo-American school that has renewed parlementary history, in part by distinguishing the antagonism to the administrative monarchy from the status of the absolute monarchy, the latter a system that necessarily incorporates all parlements, loyalist rather than *frondeur* (postures that may not in fact be at antipodes, according to the author) (9–11). Coulomb opens perspectives on the Parlement of Grenoble barely touched upon by her distinguished predecessor Jean Egret, though I do not believe that she has succeeded in her goal of articulating political theory and culture on the one side with social attitudes and economic investment on the other (12).[49]

The historian from Grenoble is interested in reconstituting "the political thought" of the parlement, without denying the existence of significant differences of opinion that, alas, remain lonesome outliers in the analysis (14). The force of this study resides in the intensity of its institutional focus: Coulomb is not really interested in social and economic issues in terms of their impact outside the walls of the Palais. While she places herself squarely in the "revisionist" camp, she embraces the classical points of reference: May 1763 was above all the month of an ongoing fiscal crisis, with a sort of constitutional spillover, and only incidentally the inaugural liberal moment. The Montesquieuian magistrates were locked into opposition to the crown, at least for the moment, while the economic liberals in their midst were "ready for negotiations" (359). The spring of 1764 witnessed the triumphal return of the parlement to its home in Grenoble, a political affirmation and revenge, "supported by public opinion," occasionally popular, usually educated, often effusive, characteristically considered influential, yet never really pinpointed and scrutinized (10, 339, 359, 365, 374, 387, 416, 419, 423).

---

49 Jean Egret, *Le Parlement de Dauphiné* and other works on the king, the parlementary opposition and politics in the eighteenth century that I used in *Bread, Politics*. I attended Egret's lecture course at Poitiers in 1964 where he rehearsed some of his ideas for his *Louis XV et l'opposition parlementaire*.

Given its standing as one of the most ardent and even intransigent liberal parlements, the Grenoble court merited perhaps a closer examination of its bold ideological, economic and political engagement. The magistrates who evinced a physiocratic vocation appear to have begun their pilgrimage with an early apprenticeship in agronomy. Coulomb neither makes an argument from technology to ideology nor reflects on the possible connections between economic interests and political culture (in her sense of the term) (185–87). One of her protagonists, the advocate-general Servan, seems to have been deeply convinced by the case for the freedom of the grain trade. She does not, however, look closely at the fascinating involvement of so many of the parlementaires of the Dauphiné in the liberal cause during the 1760s. The first president of the court and a counselor wrote pieces for the *Ephémérides du citoyen*, principal organ of the *économistes*, but they are not analyzed here: they espoused the physiocratic doctrine that had become a parlementary precept (286–87).

To believe that agriculture is the sole source of national wealth is not, however, a position whose ramifications can be confined strictly to the category baptized political economy. It runs over into other areas that seem to me to pose problems for the magistrates that Coulomb tends to neglect. For example, are there not significant tensions between the belief in the primacy of natural law over positive law, following the physiocratic creed, and the traditional defense of historic laws sanctuarizing the rights of Dauphiné and the fundamental laws limiting monarchy? Or between the physiocratic insistence on the necessity of a single tax confined to land bearing exclusively on proprietors and the long-term fiscal recalcitrance of the magistrates? Or between the magistrates' preference for stable social hierarchy grounded in landed property and the unpredictable dynamic energies that physiocratic competition would necessarily unleash? It is unfortunate that Coulomb did not explore the linkages between views on political economy (framed in dogma) and their broad implications for governance and for relations between the parlements and the king (the "new deal" that I map out in *Bread, Politics and Political Economy*). She evokes an "identity crisis" of the parlementaires, without wondering how it might be affected by the liberal commitment of a majority of magistrates. (And what about the resistance to this liberal hegemony within the court? (287)).

In an interesting way, this scholar tries to distance liberal engagement from a kinship with philosophy—certain liberals were manifestly not warm, say, to ideas dubbed "encyclopedist"—but she does not follow up on this line of inquiry (288). Similarly, she has a fresh outlook on the "political liberalism" of the magistrates, which could in some ways constrain or contest their economic liberalism—I'm thinking, for example, about the whole fiscal question and its implications for the relations of state to society—but the author does not articulate these two registers. Neo-Montesquieuian claims for the purchase of positive law, in part as ramparts against despotism, are not easy to reconcile with the despotism of natural law. In terms of their liberal (economic) adherence, the Dauphinais magistrates would have difficulty in projecting themselves as representatives of the people, in Frankish (or Le Paigeian) idiom. I am not persuaded that the fiscal question triggers the Grenoble parlementary embrace of grain liberalism, as Coulomb hints (in this way, the right of property takes urgent root in resistance to taxation rather than in acknowledgment of natural law and *évidence*). Here is an occasion passed over to recast the conventional framework for thinking about the parlements in the 1760s and 1770s (394–98).

Institutional Liberalism, without Political Economy and outside Social Reality

In a study devoted to parlementary thought that seems destined to intersect with my own preoccupations, Elina Lemaire manages to analyze an Enlightenment liberalism that never connects with political economy or, for that matter, with social reality. *Grande Robe et Liberté: la magistrature ancienne et les institutions libérales* is in some ways obdurately ahistorical (save perhaps in its passionate commitment to a parlementary telos): it cites endless texts of eloquence, jurisprudence, remonstrance and theory without referring to their specific conditions of production.[50] It is certainly tonic to displace the long hegemonic "individualist" reading of liberalism in favor of a plurality of readings, the most prized of which privileges an "institutional" framework.[51] This is an organic liberalism, consigned to a long gestation in a thick Burkean chrysalis before it takes on Tocquevillean wings, rather than an epistemology of individual emancipation or the autonomy of the subject. A Montesquieuian *profession de foi* permeates this book: "liberal thought is moderate thought," a structuring mantra that announces the rigidly political construction of the notion and at the same time denounces the relentless menace of its diabolical Other, despotism, without taking into account supplementary threats whose origin is not initially political (4, 13).

This book is an astute and dense examination of the crystallization of theory cast at lofty heights in the dramatic and quasi-liturgical forms

50 *Grande Robe et Liberté: la magistrature ancienne et les institutions liberales* (Paris: Presses Universitaires de France, 2010). The invocation of "robe mentalities" (7), like the decision to "allow as often as possible the *grands robins* to speak for themselves" (9), betrays a certain methodological flaccidity. Nor is the recourse to "l'air du temps" ever an auspicious sign (103).

51 It would have been interesting to work out, historically, in the eighteenth century, the thesis that the properly "French" version of liberalism is of a character "relatively authoritarian and statist" (3).

52 It is disappointing that the "rights of the people" that are a leitmotif of parlementary remonstrance are not subjected to critical scrutiny (51).

of a struggle for the affirmation of heroic, even transcendental values. Its relentlessly "meta" disposition proves frustrating for those of us who operate on the ground and in the everyday. Is the "institutional landscape" of which the author writes devoid of social landmarks? Who are "the people" whose"rights" are supposed to be respected in a genuinely liberal world, and what are those rights?[52] Do they map out on the canonic (and polemical) "formal-real" template? Are the "destructive and devouring human passions" to which the monarch is ever subject the same that are often imputed to the people, embodying another sort of danger? (14–15). Does "the sacred contract that links, in the Nation, the Sovereign and the Subjects," as the Parlement of Bordeaux put it in 1771, bear any relationship to the king's repudiation of the social contract of subsistence in 1763, and the antiliberal parlements' call for its restoration at the end of 1768? (44). Do the *grands robins* ever envision the respective rights and obligations of sovereigns, subjects and intermediary bodies in concrete terms, lodged in life experience, rather than as theoretical shrapnel? The general level of abstractness of this study is all the more surprising given Lemaire's contention that the "magistrates of the parlements were less thinkers than political actors" and that their remonstrances "cannot be correctly comprehended if they are 'decontextualized'" (109). The teleological itinerary toward Revolution invests the parlementary mission with a burgeoning radicality, but even in the incandescence of prerevolutionary politics, the courts remain somehow above the fray or rather implicated in a vaporously institutional manner.

In the atemporal universe of political and constitutional debate, does the development of capitalism make no impression? Is it possible to fathom the making of theory without historicizing the trajectory of "absolutism?" Does capitalism undermine the traditional social structure of parlementary liberalism because, in certain ways, it favors the Tocquevillean leveling that the author associates with an equality inimical to the maintenance of human society? Does the social equality or the dark subversion of the "égalisateurs modernes" derive from a political logic sheltered from social, economic and cultural change, congealed only in seismic moments such as the Revolution? (265). Is feudalism purely a matter of institutions that preserve local privilege, a nostalgic metaphor for "the old independence of the provinces," without any economic foundation, without any role in framing social relations? (256).[53] Is the passage from the exegesis of a feudal genealogy to the assertion of a "union des classes" unmediated by nondiscursive considerations, i.e.,

53 There is no effort to explain historically the possible ties between the claims of feudalism and the "despotism" of Louis XIV (96–101).

social and economic factors? (238). Does the corporate society on which many parlementary claims reside remain immobile across centuries, an instrumental and protean fiction, a device of convenience? Do the *grands robins* represent their world in the eighteenth century in ways that convey a real sense of loss or at least change when viewed against the backdrop of their foundational assumptions?

Unmade Parallels: Parlementaires and Physiocrats

At multiple junctures in this provocative analysis, I was struck by analogies, similarities and/or affinities between the theories of the *grande robe* and the assumptions/conceits of the physiocrats, none of which engaged the author: the foundational functions of property for state and society; the imbrication of property and liberty; the ways in which the dominion of property and liberty constituted a rampart against royal abuse of power; the pertinence of natural rights theory to the elaboration of a liberal anthropology; the discussion of "the necessity of subsistence" and its reverberations; the articulation of the general interest with personal interests; the balancing of the needs of the state and the respect due to (private) property; the thesis of the "powerlessness of public power" and its putative sacrality; the shared antipathy for *raison d'état*; the means of definitively limiting monarchical excesses (the curious kinship between physiocratic legal despotism, devised by a magistrate, and certain parlementary theories); the critique of political constructivism; the uses and abuses of history; the corollary of the oppressive monarch figured by the "pigeon" king unable to protect himself; the paradox of liberty as consubstantial to stateness and of the menace of equality to liberty; a second version of the paradox featuring the state as a potential threat to liberty; and the problem of forging or sustaining cohesion amidst the splintering diversity of social ranks and conditions (26–29, 35, 38–40, 55–56, 63, 68–73, 122, 180, 197–201, 203–10, 250–51).

In the same vein, I believe that Lemaire squandered opportunities, during the experiment with liberalization, to see how parlementary theory confronted and responded to shifting, intractable reality, to observe and reflect upon the deep ambivalence of the magistrates to kingly power, and to take account of the tensions between tradition and innovation in the ways in which the parlements interposed themselves between people and prince (195–96, 262–63). Finally, I do not understand why the author did not follow up some of her own leads, far from my focus on the subsistence catalyst, in order to chart out some of the deep connections—and tensions—between political liberalism (as she construes it) and economic liberalism. The latter force jolts the Enlightenment in practice as well as discourse. Thereafter, political liberalism will never have the luxury of overlooking or underestimating its presence, its potential and its perils.

Divine Law and Resistance to Injustice

Legal historian Jacques Krynen flourishes the banner of (a radical version of) parlementary rehabilitation with intelligence and elegance. His *L'Idéologie de la magistrature ancienne* is a history of ideas that extends across a vast expanse of time, in this volume from the thirteenth to the eighteenth centuries.[54] A major benefit of the long run is that it reveals connections, intersections and cumulative impacts (as well as discontinuities) that heretofore escaped us and that invest the rhetoric and strategy of the magistracy with a deeper coherence than generally supposed. The cost is a great dispersion of gaze that passes over a substantial amount of pertinent material and often wrenches the discourse from its political, social and economic referents.[55]

One particular long-run insight reminds me that the physiocrats were by no means the first to make positive law conditional upon its conformity to anterior or ontologically prior or preeminent criteria—in their case, for example, natural law and "*évidence*". Though I am uncomfortable with concepts such as "mindset" and the relentlessly apologetic tone in Krynen's book, I am impressed by his argument that "during the Enlightenment, the medieval dogma of absolute submission of positive laws to the prescriptions of the divine and natural laws is still at the core of the *forma mentis* of the high magistracy, as is the equally ancient dogma of their necessary conformity with reason, as well as with the criterion, it, too, venerable, of public utility or the common good." To make the case that these "fundamental juridico-religious conditions" determine for the magistrates if a law is just and continue "to nourish the protest argument" of the parlements, it seems to me that Krynen needs to define rigorously these fundamental conditions and examine the extent to which they remain immobile, or evolve, from the thirteenth to the eighteenth centuries. Without this analysis, it will be hard to accept the claim—beyond the precinct

54 *L'Idéologie de la magistrature ancienne* (Paris, Gallimard, 2009). Cf. the late Jacques Le Goff's thoughtful and playful idea of an ultra-long medieval period from the fifth century (or earlier) running to the end of the eighteenth century (or later). *Faut-il vraiment découper l'histoire en tranches?* (Paris: Seuil, 2014). See also his earlier, somewhat less expansive *Un long Moyen Age* (Paris: Tallandier, 2004).

55 The long-run history of ideas digested in a relatively short essay may also make glib, explanatory short-cuts irresistible, for example, the notorious "air du temps" (245) or a slight variant, "l'air philosophique du temps" (267).

of parlementary narcissism or self-representation—that the "disobedience" imputed to them derives exclusively from their resistance to "injustice," and that their reiterative refusals to register royal legislation stem from a "duty of religion and conscience" and constitute, at bottom, "so many marks of fidelity to, and not at all attacks upon, sovereign authority" (267–68).

The author does not problematize the concept of ideology that his title features: it seems to signify something like a worldview, nourished by conviction and knowledge, that articulates political beliefs, individual and collective values and a sturdy notion of justice. An unyielding commitment to the latter legitimizes the institutional ascension of the magistrates. Agents of royal power, the parlements imperceptibly (with spurts of palpable affirmation) become its rivals.

Justice as Debt and Contractualism

The legal historian gently mocks the myopia of his fellow citizens who view the "judiciarization" of social behaviors as a recent phenomenon (9–12). He seriously complicates the narrative that casts state making as the implacable process by which a central authority conquers a monopoly over justice and violence. By construing justice, first of all, as "a debt" (17–31), the author invites us implicitly to rethink and amplify the thick idea of "public debt" as a template for understanding eighteenth-century politics sufficiently ample to take account of the nourishing prince's contract with the consumer-people, the king's imperative accountability to fundamental law, his obligation to sustain the social structure embodied by the corporate chain that terminates in his hands, his personal bond with the nobility (who see him as *primus inter pares*), his commitment to the church in sundry manifestations (vicar of Christ on earth, defender of Gallicanism and so on) and, in the banal yet structuring sense of the fiscal debt, his duty to honor financial arrears of all sorts. Of course, this line of reasoning is regiocentric: the debt of justice also constrains the parlements (and other tribunals in the system), and must be integrated into this broad conception. Can the parlements, for instance, make good on the debt of justice independent of the king, *grand justicier*? Does the distinction between "justice retenue" (of which the most solemn expression is the "bed of justice," tool of royal power over the sovereign courts) and "justice déléguée" acquire a new acuity in the light and heat of chronic royal–parlementary confrontation during the eighteenth century? Is the imbrication of justice and politics utterly irreversible and necessarily deleterious?

Viewing vitriolic, Fronde-type contestation of royal power by the parlements as virtually consubstantial to their history, Krynen is patently less marked by the influence of Jansenism in parlementary political thinking than most eighteenth-century specialists (241–44). He sees a contractual lever in the parlementary defense of local (provincial) as well as royal–national constitutions. I would have liked for him to speculate on whether the parlements could countenance a "connotation pactiste" in the discursive propositions to which the king and the courts gave voice in their competition to be father to the people (261–66). Could a moral contract have purchase in the context of justice (debt) or politics (claims to legitimacy)?

Krynen hints at intellectual and cognitive (if not political) connections between the ideas of oath [*serment*] and contract [or *pacte*]. So several parlements interpret the coronation oath as a sworn pledge to the nation, implicitly recognizing the latter's right to judge its execution, a provocation that moved the king to remind them pungently that he swore an oath only to God. The magistrates construe the fundamental laws as well in contractual terms, professing that they could not be modified without the "consent of the nation." Even more audaciously, certain parlements warn the king that his failure to fulfill his obligations—the debt—released the nation from fulfilling its duties, thus breaking the contract irretrievably (271). In this sense, in my reading, the *pacte de famine* looms as a (diabolical) anticontract in which the king reneges on his solemn royal obligations, thereby legitimating the interposition of the parlements in the name of a certain justice and the forsaken/dishonored debt of the nourishing prince. Given their historic interest in notions of oath, contract and *pacte*, it is not surprising that the famine plot—*pacte de famine*—bulks large in the repertory of animadversion of several parlememts, led by Rouen, in their critique of liberalization.

Rights of the Nation and Devotion to Monarchy

The legal historian recognizes that by pretending "to incarnate the rights of the nation," after 1750 the parlements "break" with their "fundamental doctrine of the consubstantiality of the courts and royalty." I find his rationale for this rupture skimpy and hazy: a fervent, quasi-genealogical attachment—reminiscent of the rhetoric of the free-born Englishman—to the idea that

56 The historian evokes here the alleged parlementary limerence with "the movement of ideas," as if there were one cohesive intellectual mega-current—what used to be called "the party of humanity"—that marked Enlightenment thought *and* politics (279). Still, his (disputable) point that, despite an inferior education in comparison with their august ancestors, the magistrates of the eighteenth century worked to "be in phase with the philosophical and political critique" embodied by the Enlightenment, is an hypothesis that has found wide favor in the "new school" of parlementary historians, and not just those coming from the law schools.

the French have been since the Valois "the freest people in the world." The "people" in question are apparently "these noble and proud parlementaires, often of very ancient noble stock." In the end, the break turns out to be a circuitous renewal, as the ideology of the thirteenth century embraces its *aggiornamento* in the eighteenth. Krynen rejects, with some indignation, the suggestion of antirobe historians, that this discourse, recast in Enlightenment terms, merely bespeaks selfish opportunism.[56] He scoffs at their charges that the magistrates cultivated above all their "interests of corps and of class." So what, he seems to retort: this is a small price to pay for the immense service of the high magistracy which made the "royal state" a "state of the rule of law and of justice." Refusing to engage seriously the hypothesis that these parlementaires in fact sapped the foundations of monarchy, Krynen maintains that they fought till the very end for its survival against its putative mainstays, notably the ministers and other agents of "personal government" (278–79).

* * * * *

The rehabilitation of the parlements has displaced the cursor, as the French say. There is certainly far more historiographical muscle and momentum today behind the sovereign courts than in the camp of absolutism, the administrative monarchy, enlightened despotism—take your choice. Nevertheless, the "state worshippers," to borrow Clarisse Coulomb's lexicon, have not been routed—far from it—and they have surely not capitulated. Their cause simply elicits much less interest—and sympathy—than it used to, though I doubt that we can attribute this disaffection to a postmodernity that distrusts power and favors "the defeated." Yet even the revisionists contend—in most cases—that the parlements, at bottom, were monarchist, in their manner, and that they never placed into question their entanglement or even their incorporation in a royal system. Certainly, the magistrates would be the last to deny that the king, especially under assault, remained the central actor in the drama of eighteenth-century French history. The *séance de flagellation* came too late, but it was certainly worth a heap of remonstrances. Logically, then, in the next chapter I turn to the "royalist" literature of the past several decades. I also deal with some of the major policy questions of the eighteenth century, not always treated from a stereotypically royalist point of view, even in the hands of the king's ministers.

Chapter V

KINGS AND MINISTERS: POLITICS AND POLICIES, FINANCE AND SUBSISTENCE

Like the French Revolution, the trial of the king is not over. Feckless in many ways, Louis XVI also paid the price for his once beloved, later detested grandfather Louis XV, who was more kingly in his vices if not his virtues, though we don't know whether he would have faced the guillotine with such surprising equanimity. Still, it is easy to excoriate a king, especially when the monarchy declared itself absolute and of divine instauration: such pretension gave it (and him) little margin for error or for doubt. Yet Michel Antoine, foremost student of the monarchy in our time, is right to emphasize that the exercise of kingship was a "hard job". The royalist school knows, however, that it cannot count on mitigating circumstances. Thus, its proclivity to radicalize the debate in binary fashion: "monarchy or anarchy," for example. Since well before the Revolution (and thus, lest our enthusiasm for him induce us to forget, long before Tocqueville), the king was on the defensive, precisely because he was so implicated, so exposed, so (theoretically) omnicompetent and responsible for all outcomes. His advocates, from Voltaire and Jacob-Nicolas Moreau to Pierre Gaxotte and Antoine in the twentieth century, made the correct strategic decision that the best defense was offense. Hence their depiction of the king as a reformer, a modernizer and, despite his expressed horror for innovation, a trailblazer. More liberal partisans of monarchy—liberal in the American denotation of the term—ended up aligning prince and philosophes in the alchemy of Enlightened Despotism, an industrious oxymoron.

Paradoxically, though the parlementary onslaught weakened and discredited the king, it also unwittingly cast him in the role of resistant bearer of the oriflamme, not only (or not primarily) of tradition, but also of Enlightenment-vintage rationality and progress, heralded as the sole alternative to narrow-minded self-regard and reactionary obstructionism. In a certain sense, the Manichean view of the eighteenth century served the interests both of the exponents of kingship and of the parlementary path. Historiography has not yet extricated itself from this impasse, despite robust "revision" on both sides. This chapter looks at the monarch at work with his ministers on some of the principal questions of his time.

Reasoned Royal Rhapsody

"For nothing, after God, is so great as a king of France." Citing the phrase of the Renaissance poet Joachim du Bellay at the outset of his thousand-page biography of Louis XV, Michel Antoine lays his cards on the table.[1] Chartiste, archivist and scholar of rare erudition, Michel Antoine has brandished the banner of (efficacious) royalism steadfastly and dexterously in a historiography—following his point of view—that has relentlessly pilloried the king (and later kingship) in the name of values associated first with the Enlightenment and its brand of liberal, Whiggish modernization and then with the Revolution, aiming at regeneration. As Antoine presents it, this teleological exercise of sacrificial purification on the road to the foundation of a new order is, for me, redolent of René Girard's vision of scapegoating.[2] Against the swarm of (mostly) young historians who have embraced the parlementary cause in the past several decades, Antoine stands more or less alone, though he is able to draw upon a long (anti-Tocquevillean) tradition that forged a powerful and durable image of a progressive albeit somewhat authoritarian monarch ("Enlightened Despot") seeking to overcome the bloc of narcissistic, corporative obstructionism, figured by the parlements in the name of rational, reformist, state-making values. Given the force of his conviction and research, Michel Antoine has served as the major scholarly obstacle to the rehabilitation of the sovereign courts.

Antoine's chapters bear such titles as "Ligueurs et Frondeurs," an evocation of anti-monarchical mutiny deploying evocative late sixteenth- and mid-seventeenth century imagery, and "Monarchy or Anarchy," the binary either/or that frames the historian's interpretation, which I would style as Manichean with refinement. He treats the parlements more or less as they ask, as a collectivity, a "union of classes"—a posture that, in fact, he regards as usurpatory and illegal—that seeks single-mindedly to discredit the king and alienate his subjects (568). The good news, as it were, is that the courts encounter resistance, indirectly and directly, in their efforts to impose a "collective despotism": the price of their offices declines and they lose work, prestige and revenue, in part as a result of the dynamism of the intendants cast, as their

---

1 I will be discussing Michel Antoine's perfectly timed bicentennial publication, *Louis XV* (Paris: Fayard, 1989). Cf. his dense and suggestive alternative to the "political-culture" school, *Le dur métier de Roi: Etudes sur la civilisation politique de la France d'Ancien Régime* (Paris: Presses Universitaires de France, 1986), and for examples of prodigious erudition, *Le Conseil du Roi sous le règne de Louis XV* (Geneva: Droz, 1970) and *Le Gouvernement et l'Administration sous Louis XV: Dictionnaire biographique* (Paris: Editions du CNRS, 1978).

2 See René Girard, *The Scapegoat*, trans. Y. Freccero (Baltimore, MD: Johns Hopkins University Press, 1989).

rivals, idealized as peerless king's men; they face competition from provincial estates; no less portentously, they encounter division and discord within their own ranks, for Antoine rightly rejects the common stereotype of parlementary harmony (though he has trouble reconciling a quasi-conspiratorial depiction of crucial parlementary decisions taken by small cabals of agitators with the more broadly apocalyptical vision of the "political delirium that takes hold of the high magistracy around 1750"); the ministry, albeit uneven at best, contests and blocks parlementary undertakings to wrest royal sovereignty theoretically (through the subversive writings of lawyers such as the Jansenist Le Paige) and pragmatically (the attempts to "control the political, administrative and judicial action of the king," the denial of legal validity to *arrêts du conseil*, legislative vehicles of governance that number in the thousands each year) (566–71, 573–75, 580–84, 595).

Aspersing the King

The bad news resides in the implacability of the parlementary assault, their control of the entire lower-court system, their myopic obliviousness to the deep bonds that tie their fate to the crown's destiny, and their abuse of remonstrances, substantively, transformed into tools of disruption and even subversion and symbolically, through their illicit publication that disseminated doubt and disparagement. The latter tactic engages the parlements in a dangerous and ultimately fatal campaign to seek to take the king's place, as legislator and father to his people by molding and capturing "public opinion." Antoine does no better than the vast majority of his scholarly companions and adversaries in defining and mapping this concept.[3] In the case of Louis XV, these "campaigns of opinion" geared to bring the king into disrepute were all the more effective in light of his timidity, his taste for secrecy and his lack of aptitude for communication. Not even the heroic "flagellation session" of 1766 in which the monarch fulminates against parlementary "republican" insurgency and reaffirms energetically the absolutist doctrine, can redeem the king as a robust leader after a protracted phase of lethargy (589, 592–93, 595–97, 796–97, 854).

Antoine enumerates the crucial discrediting events that sullied Louis XV, including the famine plot, which he treats in perfunctory manner, as if slanderous gossip is unworthy of serious consideration and as if royal policy did not constitute one of the conditions of production of the profoundly

3 If the "conspiracy" [*conjuration*] against the Jesuits was "prepared by the manipulation of public opinion, whose jitteriness was methodically fueled by an uninterrupted campaign of disinformation, calumny and pious anathema," then the historian has to do a better job of unmasking and analyzing the operation of this public opinion (781).

defiling (I contend desacralizing) accusation that links the nourishing prince with the organization of dearth in a toxic rumor that is not confined to the "people," but involves a much broader cross section of the population. The monarchical partisan does not reflect on the possible connections between the credulousness of this public and the plausibility of segments of the famine plot narrative. It is hardly sufficient to assert that "the wind was with liberalism" in the early 1760s, not when he reports that the king regarded Quesnay as "[his] thinker," despite the hatred Choiseul nourished for him; not in light of his close ties with La Chalotais, a central figure in the Brittany affair, to which Antoine gives a certain physiocratic dimension, imputing to Louis the thought of replacing Controller-General L'Averdy, a former influential parlementaire (whom Antoine skewers—cavalierly and predictably—for his "frightening incompetence") with the chief of the *économistes* (609–10, 817, 828–29, 832, 846–48, 857, 867).

Common Ground with Parlementary Revisionism: A Narrow Political History

For all his mastery of the manuscript material, Antoine serves up an extremely orthodox framework, a circumscribed, narrowly political history, the mirror image in many ways of the agenda of the exponents of the parlementary cause. The social does not inflect this political approach, save to the extent that the "two aversions" converge, that of "high society" [*mondaine*] and of the "popular" realm [*populacière*]; the economic only when reduced drastically to equate with the fiscal/financial; and the cultural barely. Liberalization offered this historian an opportunity to rethink, not his fidelity to the king, but his way of articulating the relationship between monarch and parlements, between king and "constitution", between state and society, between capitalism and social structure and between reform and Enlightenment. The climax of Antoine's story is Maupeou's attempt to put an end "to the permanent coup d'état" exercised by the parlements, to combat the "retrograde conception" of judicial despotism and to promote the "executive management of the rule of law" in a forward-looking monarchy. The "patriotism" of the magistrates was a pretext to promote the systematic indocility and the "century of hatred" that helped make the Revolution a likely outcome. Louis XV's durable chief minister, Choiseul, "steeped in contradictions," competent in military and naval affairs, but an "illusionist" and a "schemer" who ended up fooling himself even as he encouraged both the liberals and the magistrates (to whom he rashly offered the heads of the Jesuits and the freedom of the grain trade), had to cede the helm to Maupeou and Terray who understood that monarchy required a substantive as well as a solemn reaffirmation. Rightly portrayed as not intransigently inimical to liberalization, more thoughtful and nuanced than supposed, though necessarily brutal, intrepid and unpopular, Terray emerges as a veritable "statesman" in Antoine's sometimes jaded eyes (906–7, 911, 919, 927–28, 939, 943–49, 963–64).

Paternal Love

There is no more room for the radicality that I see in Louis XV's liberal reforms, drastically recasting the relation of prince with people, in Bernard Hours' biography, *Louis XV: Un Portrait* (Paris, 2009). "Paternal love" is the fulcrum of the king's relation to his subjects, in his mind and theirs, and it is renewed time and again, despite the vicissitudes of the reign—at least in this historian's desultory decoding of the politics of the reign (682–83). There is no economic or social dimension in this work, either on markets or on the diffusion of wealth or on the destabilizing impact of money on the system of social classification. The author treats policy issues with neither keen curiosity nor explanatory fervor, save where they led to the scrambling for position among court favorites or touched on foreign policy and war. Fiscality marshals some attention, but not preoccupation with subsistence. Bertin and L'Averdy allegedly held antagonistic positions, but Hours does not set out their differences clearly beyond situating the first in a posture hostile to the accommodationist parlementary line that Choiseul fostered (468–70, 481, 490, 495, 510–12, 578). "Public opinion" looms large here, as most everywhere else on the historiographical horizon, but the historian, quite lucid about scholarly shortcomings in this domain, does not show us how its "tribunal" functioned and whom it touched (474, 476–78, 493, 517, 523, 574). Hours rehabilitates the monarch, perhaps even more decisively than Antoine, who in some ways was more interested in institutions than in men, if one can reduce kings to mere mortal status: Louis XV was not lazy, dithering, indifferent or distracted (497–98, 507–8, 513, 519–20, 591).

Hours proposes a debatable revisionist reading of Maupeou that has received considerable attention in recent times. His "coup de majesté" was not a revolution, not as "radical a rupture" as often claimed. Indeed, without lapsing into sheer casuistry, the historian sees "a certain affinity" between Maupeou's vision and the parlementarist theories of Le Paige. Following Catherine Maire's lead,[4] Hours sees in the sanctuarization of the (new) *Cour des pairs* a political counterweight to royal power, an implicit

4 Catherine Maire, *De la cause de Dieu à la cause de la Nation. Le Jansénisme au XVIIIe siècle* (Paris: Gallimard, 1998).

rejection, imposed apparently by the king himself, of the transformation of the monarchy into "an enlightened despotism in the mode of contemporary Europe," in some sense, a reversion to the pristine parlement upon which Jansenist commentators had heaped praise. Judicial rationalization and uniformization did not undermine Louis' deep conviction, Hours argues, of the necessity to maintain a parlementary system, reconfigured but recognizable, and the traditional corporate social hierarchy, both consubstantial to the monarchy (588–92).

Choiseul: Modernizing Leftist Liberal

For decades, students of the reign of Louis XV have been waiting for a deeply researched, penetrating work on Choiseul, an omnipresent yet elusive figure who played an apparently decisive role in the government during some of the stormiest moments of the epoch.[5] The idiosyncratic political biography by Guy Chaussinand-Nogaret fails, alas, to satisfy this hope.[6] Embodying a Whiggish view of French politics and history, it is a glib and perfunctory apology of the man whom the author regards, with Voltaire, as one of "the two most brilliant men of their century," at antipodes to Beaumarchais' haughty and abusive Count Almaviva with whom the author claims historians have too often associated him (125).

In his potpourri of plaudits, Chaussinand-Nogaret offers a serious look at Choiseul as a "liberal", without, however, exploring the foundations of his adherence, ideologically and/or politically. The historian's enthusiasm for liberalization is as earnest as his understanding of it is paltry. His treatment of the grain police is a caricature. He virtually ignores the royal declaration of May 1763, the decisive rupture with the past, the inaugural liberal transformation. Chaussinand-Nogaret celebrates the "great adventure" of liberalization that the chief minister shared with his controller-general L'Averdy. Given the latter's commitment to the radical reform project, Choiseul's subsequent attack upon him is enigmatic. Imperceptibly, the controller-general, described heretofore as authoritarian in temperament and faithful to his engagements, loses his nerve, reveals a timorous core and becomes hostile to the liberal cause (178, 181–83, 206). The historian idealizes Choiseul for advocating an open, experimental,

5 On the early Choiseul, see the informative work that Colin Jones rightly qualifies as quirky: Rohan Butler, *Choiseul, Father and Son 1719–1754* (Oxford: Clarendon Press, 1980). A projected second volume apparently never appeared. Much less serviceable is G. Maugras, *Le Duc et la Duchesse de Choiseul, leur vie intime, leurs amis et leur temps* (Paris: Plon, 1902).

6 *Choiseul: Naissance de la gauche* (Paris: Perrin, 1998).

quasi-global liberalism, never carefully defined, presumably in opposition to L'Averdy's more niggardly and segmented liberal perspective. While his chief minister embraced the spirit of debate consubstantial to the Enlightenment and remained ever attentive to the counsels of a sage, cosmically nebulous, yet ubiquitous public opinion, the controller-general banned discussion on fiscal affairs and eddied against the tide of the future by reinforcing the cult of secrecy in administration. Only constrictive social blinders could have enabled the author to characterize the period 1763–70 as "the seven glorious years" in anticipation of the (also highly uneven albeit exalted) "Thirty Glorious" years of recent vintage (174–75, 178, 180, 187, 227, 281, 301, 330, 332).

Chaussinand-Nogaret crafts his hero as the vector of a supposed subversion, a feared modernization and a worrisome reformism. He became suspect, not for his connection with Madame de Pompadour or his distaste for the devout, but for his proximity to mutinous magistrates and impious philosophes. The historian makes little effort to integrate this anachronistic progressivism (somehow enabling "the left to enter politics for the first time in the history of France") and this Turgoto-Neckerian desire to share responsibility with the citizenry into the narrative of an overarching appetite for revenge against England (185, 331). Rid of a seemingly schizophrenic L'Averdy, Choiseul puts in his place Maynon d'Invault, lionized as "an audacious spirit," doubtless in large part because he was totally committed to the chief minister's program. Liberalization enabled their enemies to position themselves on the side of good sense and good order, for the seven glorious (apparently!) years were not devoid of disorderly counterpoints, whose significance Chaussinand-Nogaret strains to minimize. He casts the enemy, figured notably by Maupeou, in grotesque hyperbole as "totalitarian," "a state terrorist," leading a "reactionary pack" espousing "an implacable fascism"; that is to say, he depicts his unvarnished antagonism to the Enlightenment and to the parlements. The parlements incarnated a model of English-style limited monarchy that Michel Antoine and others have distorted by refusing to recognize the innocuous character of their opposition to the crown, according to Chaussinand-Nogaret (277–80).

So Choiseul falls not because he "restored liberty to commerce" and "liberated the energies" of the dynamic elements of society, but because he did not grant "the spirit of a whole people" all the freedom it demanded; not because of the *pacte de famine*, but the *pacte de famille*, emblem of the anti-France;[7] not because he was the valorous adversary of arbitrary governance, but because he was ready to provoke revolt in "the four corners" of the

7 Chaussinand-Nogaret shrewdly notes a certain semantic homology between the formulas "*pacte de famine*" and "*pacte de famille*" that would have been worth developing.

kingdom to maintain his power; not because he was too manipulative, but insufficiently Machiavellian to avoid the (telegraphed) ambush of "the extreme right"; not because of his libertinage, but because he failed to recruit an Egeria adequately influential to counter the retrograde wiles of another nymph, Madame du Barry, the extreme right's anti-Pompadour[8] (289–92, 297, 299, 330). In contrast to the stern sobriety and obstinate demonstration of Antoine, Chaussinand-Nogaret concludes in a burst of pyrotechnic cliché that implausibly portrays the vain and sometimes quixotic Choiseul as the champion of "a return to modesty and to realism" in opposition to extravagant monarchical excesses, embodied by a regime "drowned in the mysteries of an outdated myth that made of the king a miraculous composite of Rambo, Madame Soleil [a radio soothsayer] and Apollo, and victim of the self-seeking and pitiful applause of an anachronistic and rapturous fan club" (333).

State Making and Fiscality: Culture, Politics and Economics

Financial issues are at the core of state making and relentlessly frame the debate on policy and politics till the end of the Old Regime. The grain question is inextricably linked to the financial problem. State making begins with the wrenching of a surplus of cereals, evolving from a process of brute expropriation to a chastened institutionalization called fiscality, civilized in the Eliasian sense, albeit not without persistent asperities. Royal taxes of all sorts will permit the monarchy to solidify its claims to a monopoly on the use of legitimate violence and the exercise of justice. Grain and fiscality are still deeply interwoven in the second half of the eighteenth century. The pilot sector of the economy, grain is the major source of wealth for institutions and individuals as well as the ration of survival for the bulk of the French population.

Part of the allure of the physiocratic program for the ministry in the 1760s is that it would increase government revenues without touching the tax base (and hence the system of social classification). The physiocrats, as I have argued, had a grave "people-problem" (whose acuity and urgency they denied), but they had an elites-problem as well. They maintained implicitly that a promised, almost guaranteed, beneficial outcome (generated

8 Procurator-General of the Rouen Parlement, Godart de Belbeuf attributed Choiseul's fall to "maneuvers and intrigues" orchestrated by Maupeou and Terray: the former asked the king to choose between himself and Choiseul, whom he depicted as the fierce champion of the parlements, while the latter made it clear that Choiseul's megalomaniacal foreign policy would plunge the realm further into the morass of palsying debt. See Olivier Chaline, *Godart de Belbeuf: le parlement, le roi et les Normands* (Luneray: Bertout, 1996), 418.

by liberalization) justified the extremely high social price that would be paid principally by the consumer-people in the cities and countryside, during the harrowing transition to laissez-faire. The prospect of generalized well-being, however, was not sufficient to obtain the accord of the dominant social groups to a new tax system that would not only extract more money from many of them but also shake the foundations of the traditional social hierarchy. In the short term, following the recipe of liberalization, the king and the elites could expect to enjoy the best of upshots: more money for the royal treasury without raising taxes or changing the system of assessment or levy, logistically or symbolically. The irony of the situation was that the risks of profoundly disturbing the social structure stemmed less from the physiocratic fiscal reform, which would not take place, than from the impact of the market principle, let loose by liberalization, which allocated inputs and outputs without regard to rank.

Numerous studies on financial and fiscal matters have appeared since the first edition of this book. The most thought-provoking and elegant work, in my view, is Michael Kwass' *Privilege and the Politics of Taxation*.[9] It focuses on the state's attempt to subject various privileged groups, more or less exempt from taxation, to direct fiscal levy. Without making his analysis hostage to a stifling revolutionary teleology, he shows, nevertheless, that fiscal impositions—in particular, the so-called universal levies such as the capitation and the twentieth tax–altered the relationship between the monarchy and the system of social taxonomy of which the king was putative master (arbiter and guarantor) and at the same time transformed the political culture.

Though Kwass does not resolve the nettlesome problem of making rigorous sense of the (often promiscuously reified) notion of public opinion—a persistent Achilles heel of the eighteenth-century studies—he frankly faces the Habermas challenge from which most historians flee (the connections between economic development, the crystallization of a bourgeoisie and public opinion) (9–10).[10] He shows how, in different but analogous ways, the Parlement of Rouen and the banker-philosophe-minister Jacques Necker turned repeatedly to public opinion to make their case, recast the concept of public opinion in irreversibly pluralist terms (ranging from Morellet's "educated men" to the "people" in Michelet's oceanic trope), and conceived of public opinion as a pivot in the articulation of the state and society (178, 183–4, 192, 211, 213, 239, 241, 261). I found especially astute Kwass' treatment of Necker's critique

9 Michael Kwass, *Privilege and the Politics of Taxation in Eighteenth-Century France* (Cambridge: Cambridge University Press, 2000).

10 Kwass deals with the question of opinion, *inter alia*, on pp. 8, 48, 156, 178, 183–4, 192, 211, 213, 217, 239, 241, 261. Cf. another snare, the notion of *mentalité*/mentality: 10, 12.

of political economy—the liberal chapel in particular—for failing to take into account "the effects of opinion and imagination" and his premise that public administration nurtured a necessarily dialogic rapport with public opinion, however elusive this phenomenon/representation remained (239).

Kwass rejects the culturalist conceit that the social conditions of production of ideas and attitudes are no longer analytically pertinent. Of course, he takes ideas very seriously, but not in the "air-du-temps" mode. Interests are not reducible to ideological investment, but they are inseparable from the ideas that shape them and the language that gives them expression (16). The debate that frames taxation as a form of spoliation underscores the enormous importance of the concept and institution of property in the political culture and the discourse of political economy (169, 184–85, 209). Liberty, along with property, defining leitmotifs of the Economic Enlightenment and the joint foundation of physiocracy, informed the debate over taxation that helped prepare the ground for numerous revolutions and that still jolts societies today, from European neo-liberal stalwarts to American tea-party crusaders (170, 210). Kwass points out how the fallout over fiscality contributes to a loosening of the bonds between king and people, though he refuses to see a phenomenon of the desacralization of kingship of the sort that I linked to liberalization (193, 209).

A Total Financial History?

Public opinion is at the crux of another study that targets "the fiscal question," written by Arnaud Decroix, jurist and historian.[11]An important contribution to the reinvigoration of financial history, it rehearses the dilemma of so many studies of the Old Regime, set especially in the second half of the eighteenth century, which are torn between a desire to explain its renewal and resilience on the one hand and to lay bare the ineluctability of its imminent demise, on the other hand. The failure to negotiate these tensions and escape the teleological guillotine deprives these works of the historical contingency and the intricate texture that would restitute complexity, ambiguity and a certain epistemological suspense to its argument. Ambitious in scope, Decroix's book bursts with an engaging energy and a vast erudition that is not, however, wholly mastered. Frequently, suggestive insights languish in gestation, connections begging to be made remain orphaned and the sprawling footnotes, a book in themselves, at times seems to contest, more or less inadvertently, without parsing, the reasoning they are meant to validate or explicate. He pleads

11 Arnaud Decroix, *Question fiscale et réforme financière en France (1749–1789): Logique de transparence et recherche de la confiance publique* (Aix-Marseille: Presses Universitaires d'Aix-Marseille, 2006).

for a sort of total financial history in which the political, economic and social cannot be separated from the institutional and the ideological: just as I brandish Mirabeau's affirmation that "all politics starts with a grain of wheat," so Decroix flaunts a parallel contention uttered by the economic journalist Accarias de Sérionne in which taxation ("l'impôt") takes the place of the cereal[12] (9, 16–17).

Yet, in my reading, I found that there is often a deficit of articulation between the economic and the sociopolitical, on the one hand, and between fiscality and political economy on the other hand, save through the wobbly vector of an elusive and amorphous public opinion, to which I shall return. Even if Decroix contests the primacy of the grain question, I am stunned that he pays virtually no attention to the liberalization experiment which projected self-conscious fiscal aims, albeit of secondary rank in the order of priorities, and which also entertained major political objectives—what I called "a new deal"—not remote from the "outstretched hand" [*main tendue*] that the author invokes in association, not with the radical liberal reforms, but with the surprising royal declaration of 21 November 1763 that invited the parlements to a specific sort of concertation on a major fiscal issue (231–38).

Instead of exploring and analyzing the ideas of the multitude of writers Decroix cites, he seems to weigh them, like the *poids spécifique* of a wheat harvest, in order to reckon their import.[13] He does not present a convincing case for "the monopoly" that the free-trading physiocrats "quickly imposed [...] on economic and financial matters," for their domination of "French economic culture" and for their capacity to intimidate even the great thinkers of the time (24, 377). Moreover, debate on economic and financial themes did not begin when the French "began to reason on grain" in mid-century, according to Voltaire's quip. These concerns had a protracted gestation; the Economic Enlightenment was less a profound rupture than a quite significant reorientation and quickening. Nor does the historian tell us in the end precisely why the monarchy was so inept. Apart from the personality of specific kings, what were the structural constraints inherent in kingship to which he vaguely hints? The financial question itself was already lustily politicized well before 1750 (21–25). The relation between the state,

12 V. R. Mirabeau, F. Quesnay, *Lettres sur la dépravation et la restauration de l'ordre légal*, vol. 1 (London,1769), 74.

13 See, for example, the successive treatment of Chambon, the abbé Petiot, Schmidt d'Avenstein, Goyon de la Plombanie, Graslin, Béardé de l'Abbaye, Linguet, Melon and Dutot (153–56). Or Le Trosne, Le Mercier de la Rivière, Schmidt d'Avenstein, Malesherebes, L. S. Mercier and Linguet (440–41).

embodied by the king, and the social hierarchy, also incarnated, codified and occasionally renegotiated by the king, is not scrutinized. Indeed, the social structure seems less and less pivotal as the author moves ineluctably toward the dénouement, driven by the central destabilizing force of public credit (569–70; cf. 381).

Public Opinion Summoned to Do the Heavy Lifting

To obtain credit in the various financial markets, the monarchy had to garner "a greater public confidence" and accede to the "exigency of an increased financial transparency," a formula that postulates the prior existence of a certain dose of transparency, a thesis that awaits demonstration. These two conditions, politically sine qua non, help to make the financial question, Decroix maintains, the powerful "catalyst" in the "emergence of public opinion" (28). This is the author's central concept, and at once independent and dependent variable. It has claimed a place in the historical scene for centuries, almost always as a hazy, formless vector; for want of definition and precision, it has never been able to accomplish the work that scholars have summoned it to do. Sociologists have achieved the most fecund results, moving steadily from a conceptual to a quantitative approach. In the first category, Tönnies' construction of public opinion in terms of interactivity opened exciting interpretive vistas, but made little impression on historians.[14] Several decades later, his countryman, Jürgen Habermas, aroused an astonishing response to his notion of public sphere, crystallizing what Tönnies would have styled a consensus. Habermas was at once daring and prudent and devised a coherent and complex model for the genesis, implantation and operation of the public sphere to which the vast majority of historians of the Enlightenment have paid mere lip service. With few exceptions, they have pecked at Habermas' paradigm like scavenging birds, appropriating opportunistically what seemed useful, discarding what loomed as cumbersome. The public sphere seemed to be the answer, apposite and cogent, whatever the question. Habermas seemed to save historians from the "fog" about which Tönnies had warned them. Immensely stimulating, Habermas' work may have paradoxically stifled critical reflection and innovative thinking about public opinion in the eighteenth century precisely because it seemed so elegantly to have resolved

14 See Ferdinand Tönnies, *Kritik der öffentlichen Meinung* (Berlin: Julius Springer, 1922); for a recent English version of his central theses, see *Ferdinand Tönnies on Public Opinion*, ed. and trans. Hanno Hardt and Slavko Splichal (Lanham, MD: Rowman & Littlefield, 2000).

the question and because it carried the immense prestige of the German sociologist-philosopher.[15]

Arnaud Decroix operates within the Habermasian field or rather in the patchwork periphery of more or less degraded notions derived from it. He is hardly alone: it is the place where most of us take refuge when we need to discuss public opinion.[16] General adherence to this youthful albeit canonic heritage dispenses him from either a sustained effort at a socially, culturally and politically differential set of definitions of opinion practices or an endeavor of theorization. In this manner, public opinion embodies a set of binaries that need to be deconstructed: it is at once institutional and inchoate, recurrent and ephemeral, refractory and pliable, the same and its contrary. To be more concrete, in Decroix's architecture, cause and effect are overlapping or interchangeable. For instance, either public opinion occasions a shift in the discussion of finances from the technical to the political idiom or this shift occurred—for reasons not developed—with the resultant mobilization of public opinion, eagerly responsive to the political discourse, shut out by the esoteric technical one (28, 297, 324).

Decroix deftly takes stock of the growth of private credit alongside the ever-burgeoning demand for "public credit," a more frankly political process/institution that depends on the capacity to galvanize public confidence, a variant of public opinion. Given his interest in the ways in which public opinion interacts with these two types of financing, it would have been worthwhile to explore the more broadly fashioned notion of credit, connected in myriad ways with a panoply of "opinion," cast in cultural, moral and political as well as economic terms.[17]

Public opinion intervenes frequently in Decroix's study as if it were a conventional sociocultural and political *force*, readily available to actors willing to risk its possible perverse effects in order to wager on its positive impact. Roussel

15 Jürgen Habermas, *Strukturwandel der Öffentlichkeit. Untersuchungen zu einer Kategorie der bürgerlichen Gesellschaft* (1962). Translation: *The Structural Transformation of the Public Sphere: An Inquiry into a Category of Bourgeois Society*, trans. T. Burger and F. Lawrence (Cambridge, MA: MIT Press, 1991).

16 The sprawling literature dealing with the concept of the public sphere, often only remotely related to its initial usage, rarely ponders critically its appropriation. See, however, the incisive reflections, each in a particular register, of Harold Mah, "Phantasies of the Public Sphere: Rethinking the Habermas of Historians," *Journal of Modern History* 72 (March 2000): 153–82 and Stéphane Van Damme, "Farewell Habermas? Deux décennies d'études sur l'espace public," *Les Dossiers du Grihl*, online: http://dossiersgrihl.revues.org/682; DOI: 10.4000/dossiersgrihl.682.

17 For a brilliant treatment of the notion of credit in its multiple avatars, see Clare Crowston's *Credit, Fashion, Sex: Economies of Regard in Old Regime France* (Durham, NC: Duke University Press, 2013).

de la Tour's widely commented pamphlet *Richesse de l'état* (1764) fosters the advent of public opinion and simultaneously enters into a dialogue with "that" public as a valid interlocutor of standing equal to his own and instrumentalizes it to his own, self-sanctified civic ends (289, 295). In a similar vein, the Paris-periphery tension receding discreetly into the fog, the parlements [transmuted into *the* Parlement] collectively represent public opinion, a sort of discursive Gallican golem swelled to embody more or less everyone, in the absence of the estates-general, the stilled voice of the official social and political taxonomy.[18]

The author notes "the growing part of the public in fiscal reflection" (294). Of whom is he speaking? This spectral public, in some sense, sublimates or transcends the system of social classification (juridical and/or experiential). It is a disincarnated public, intrinsically political, but asocial or unsocial, a metaphor available to the highest discursive bidder. As it becomes clear that the state must earn credit, as it were, by granting certain political concessions (a dose of transparency, for example), the author evokes in sibylline terms the "emergence of a *concept* of public opinion" [my italics], apparently to be distinguished from its social referent in lived experience (381). But the metamorphosis from concept to practice takes place imperceptibly, unproblematically: a nascent conceptual public opinion invests royal "subjects"—presto!—with a "droit de regard" on "political life" (382).[19]

The author is, of course, aware of the difficulty of apprehending and thus identifying his fugacious and impalpable public opinion. In lieu of a sociological gaze, he enumerates the observations of various commentators: the view, for example, that public opinion cannot be "popular opinion" because of the intellectual and moral infirmities of "the people" [Linguet, Schmidt d'Avenstein, Götzmann, Gin and the learnedly contemptuous Condorcet for whom a popular opinion would necessarily emanate from "the stupidest and most miserable part of the people"] (430). Decroix's sociology is not refined by his recourse to a category styled "middle class" as the (presumably low-end) conveyor of enlightened opinion (431). While a doctrine incites the physiocrats to denigrate as "mere opinion" (hence necessarily misleading) that which is not "evident," they realize, like their adversaries, that opinion "directs" the minds and actions of men and that it is thus indispensable for the sovereign to "command" it (440, 445). Short on countervailing powers to second them, the parlements see in public opinion a potentially effective check on royal authority (443).

---

18 In Decroix, at several junctures, public opinion takes on a quasi-anthropomorphic expression. For example: "Cependant, parallèlement à ce rôle accordé au Parlement, c'est le public qui serait essentiellement appelé à presenter son opinion au Monarque." [291]

19 One sees the same trajectory or glissando from discursive formulation to "a power that emerges" with purchase in the socioeconomic and political arena throughout the book. See, for instance, the extrapolation from texts of Dutot and Accarias de Serionne (417).

Unable to do the sociology, it would have been gainful for Decroix to subject the politics of manipulation of public opinion to close scrutiny. Though for me, public opinion remains an enigma, I have no doubt that in various guises it is a major influence/force/actor in eighteenth-century life. Yet, the author will have to marshal proof—demonstration is not always his central concern—that transparency is the "keyword [*maître-mot*] of the century of Enlightenment" (568). Here the historian succumbs to the weight of teleological pressure: the (narrow?) road to "democratic progress" and the representation of public opinion as a seismic modernizing juggernaut (constraining the king far more decisively and definitively than fundamental laws, the parlementary vision of a quasi-constitution and its often aggressive political disposition, natural law and the social contract binding monarch and subjects). Decroix suggests that public opinion, incarnating the Rousseauian general will and the general interest, takes the place of God in the political cosmology of the Old Regime (569). I hope that it will prove easier, and less costly, to prove the existence of the divine successor than of the deity.

It Takes Two to Govern

The intersecting axes of Antonella Alimento's study are finances and politics, which means that the core is imperatively about crown–parlementary relations.[20] She writes about them in terms of "reforms" and "crises," overused and underdefined locutions that seem locked in a generically dialectical rapport with each other throughout the course of the eighteenth century and that together frame and punctuate the politics produced by monarch and courts, each of which plays a reforming role at one point or another and provokes crises. Quite familiar with the historiography and its disputes, indebted to Michel Antoine, yet admiring numerous revisionist works on the parlements, notably in English, the Italian historian is not, however, primarily concerned with the polemics over rehabilitation/reprehension. Her working model is disarmingly simple, yet it strikes a cogent note: it takes two to govern in France, the two major albeit asymmetrically pretentious, glorious and powerful institutions, condemned to collaborate or to paralyze the state and the realm.[21] Alimento seems to evince as insatiable

20 *Réformes fiscales et crises politiques dans la France de Louis XV. De la taille tarifée au cadastre général*, trans. M. Gille (Brussels, P. I. E. Peter Lang and Comité pour l'Histoire Economique et Financière de la France, série "Economie et Histoire," vol. 3, 2008).

21 Although in the end, Alimento probably favors a sort of robust, reforming prince, she often seems to put a pox on both their houses. She notes misunderstandings, a climate of suspicion and even abuses of authority, taking various forms and bespeaking provocation and reprisal, for which they were jointly responsible (see, for example, 199). Without denying talent on the royal side, notably in what she dubs

an appetite for financial history as Marcel Marion once did; in fact, the bulk of her book focuses on a few years, basically the early 1760s, the very period shaken by the seismic liberal rupture.

Liberalization: Off the Radar

Given her interest in political economy in general and Forbonnais in particular, I was disappointed that Alimento's Richter scale did not register liberalization as an earthquake (perhaps it required close proximity with the jolting aftershocks—clearly outside the author's chronology—to take the measure of the disruptive intensity of the experience).[22] At several junctures, she remarked that the two "grandes affaires" in the post-Seven Years' War period were fiscal (taxes, debt service, conditions for borrowing and so on) and religious (the expulsion of the Jesuits), both of course engendering highly contentious confrontations between king and parlements (258, 298).

As it is now clear, even to those who have not read my work, I challenge Alimento's judgment, which remains the standard view, at least for traditional political historians, despite *Bread, Politics and Political Economy*. My argument for a deep modification of the template has not yet carried the day, regardless of some weighty endorsements.[23] Surely I would have enhanced my chances of success had I done a better job of situating the fiscal clash vis-à-vis the campaign for liberalization. The former involved a crisis that generated reforms as well as reforms that generated crises; the latter marked a dramatic reform, never before attempted and rarely imagined, which brought about

anachronistically the higher reaches of the bureaucracy, in particular the intendants of finance or commerce such as d'Ormesson or Trudaine de Montigny, she is manifestly impressed by the intellectual depth and political cunning of what she repeatedly calls the "Jansenist party," located within (say, Lambert) and around (Le Paige) the Paris court (173–77, 180, 192, 199, 267, 293–94, 300). (The "parti philo-Jésuite" remains shadowy, but apparently is capable of some sort of influence (181–82, 199).) Still, the historian characterizes numerous parlementary actions as no less than "obscurantist" or "egotistical," including resistance to certain fiscal reforms, persecution of Calas, La Barre and the philosophes in general and even opposition—not durable—to the declaration of 25 May 1763, freeing the grain trade (179, 180). She appears to deplore their invocation of natural rights to justify antagonism to royal reform projects, testimony to their traditionalism and social conservatism, two notion-epithets that require definition (181).

22 It is not propitious for my cause—nor for the clarity of Alimento's argument—that a crucial formula—liberal ideas—is rendered in French (from the Italian) as "idées libéristes" (88, 89, 139): too much "Che" and not enough Quesnay, if I might venture a rhyming remark.

23 See, for instance, Daniel Roche, *La France des Lumières* (Paris: Fayard, 1993).

cascading crises. Both took place under the auspices of the same ministers–first Bertin, portrayed as implausibly timid and apolitical (97, 100) and then L'Averdy, delineated as implausibly incompetent (324–26).[24] These ministers operated under the artful aegis of Choiseul, a shrewd and ambitious political dealer (87), who saw himself as the de facto "prime minister," embraced the parlements as allies (102, 116, 123, 217, 298, 310) even as he invested heavily in negotiating compromise and/or peace between courts and crown (63, 102, 123, 213, 217, 225, 249, 251, 261, 321), disliked and sometimes actively undermined Bertin (100–1, 203, 213), was only marginally more supportive of L'Averdy, despite the latter's parlementary roots (298) and evinced sensitivity to public opinion (258–59).[25] Politically, there is a gaping hiatus in posture between, on the one hand, the fiscal reform question, entangled in some genetic, structural sense in struggle over territorial competence, and constitutional arguments touching upon accountability and legitimacy, and on the other hand, the grain deregulation that elicited a striking chorus of assent and enthusiasm among many magistrates in all the parlements and that announced a new deal, a fresh departure in relations between king and courts, designed to supersede the chronic impasses and establish fertile ground for cooperation and mutual trust.

Fiscality and Liberty

Given her command of the Bertin agenda for the contrôle-général, Alimento might have been able to articulate the project of liberalization with the complex maneuvers undertaken to obtain a fiscal package, including the extension of current taxes such as the *vingtièmes*, the (re-)introduction of the *centième denier* and the plan for a cadastral survey to establish a new tax base, a three-pronged strategy arguably inspired by the earlier propositions of Etienne de Silhouette, briefly controller-general in 1759, and his counselor Forbonnais. Both enterprises came to procedural fruition in May 1763. Both had to pass parlementary scrutiny; Bertin expected far more difficulty with the fiscal legislation, which had been the object of fraught negotiations, was

24 Yet, Alimento contradicts herself, depicting another Bertin, capable of squabbling with a treacherous Choiseul, negotiating with refractory magistrates, and forcing parlementary registrations (103–4, 130–31, 135–38, 171, 229). And if her characterization of L'Averdy is, in the end, positive, it is in part because her expectations are quite low (inexperience, ceding the central role to d'Ormesson, not even deeply engaged in the municipal reform that we generally attribute to him) (303, 346–26).

25 In what abides as the standard operating historiographical procedure, the Italian scholar does not problematize the notion of public opinion in the eighteenth century (see also 89, 187, 193).

more pressing, certainly antagonized elite interests in multiple ways, and was burdened with short- and long-term historical asperities (political and constitutional) that no one could pretend to ignore. The liberal measures, tantamount to a veritable refoundation, harbored more sweeping ambitions, but were complementary to the fiscal reforms. For this reason, it is surprising to me that most contemporary parties to the debate did not make the connection and that historians, with some exceptions, followed this compartmentalizing tendency. On the most basic level, liberalization augured very substantial increases in revenue, which, even without changes in the fiscal mechanisms, would have commensurately enriched royal coffers. The liberal lobby in France—those who militated strenuously for the liberty of the grain trade with its panoply of dynamic outcomes–was the only group that talked systematically about economic growth as a national (and political) objective, a problematic that appeared to be beyond the purview of the fiscalists, at least for the time being.[26]

Arguably, the two undertakings were on quite distinct political and ideological tracks and, in this sense, were not destined to intersect, at least not before passage (and perhaps implementation). Probably, for this reason, and also because the fiscal story was immensely complicated and my own investigation of liberalization engulfed me, I did not look carefully at the two parallel threads. It would thus be unfair (and curmudgeonly), to reproach Antonella Alimento with not having done so. I can only note and regret that liberalization did not engage her interest. She refers to it only in passing and not in a compelling manner. Characterizing it as a device to remedy grain price stagnation, she misses its central significance, and at the same time underestimates Bertin's commitment to a certain liberal vision (139). She points to the delays in registration of the May Declaration, citing Le Paige, one of the great éminences grises of the eighteenth century, but does not attempt to account for them (179n). She wrongly attributes "the paternity" of the July edict on exportation to Trudaine de Montigny and Turgot, a reform that she links far too summarily with "the liberal current" driven by the Gournay circle (326).

Property and Political Dialogue

There are at least two themes that help bridge the fiscal and liberalization projects. One is the "right of property," paramount in the liberal argument, but invoked also by the magistrates in a way that is intriguing, even as it demands unpacking: the parlementary political culture in its most active

26 The preoccupation with "saving the country from bankruptcy" seems to preclude broader economic reflection (see, for instance, 301).

voice, "demands in the fiscal domain the right to obtain access to the factual data before being able to take a favorable stand on the projects for a tax-base land survey or an amortization scheme, in the name of the defense of the property of citizens attacked by the fiscal edicts extracted from the king's will" (180). It is in this spirit that the Rouen court contends in June 1763 that it must attentively examine the royal financial documents before being able to determine if the ministry's fiscal plans are justified "and compatible with respect for the right of property" (210). Proclaiming free registration to be "a law" on which "essentially depends the existence of the monarchy," the fervently liberal Grenoble Parlement, capable of harmonizing principles that were profoundly traditionalist and radically innovative, denounced the fiscal project as both a plot against the king in the service of "cupidity" and in witness of incompetence, and a violation of the "right of property" (233).

The second theme that taps into both fiscal and liberal narratives concerns the grounds for exchange between the king and his courts, a matter that remains rhetorically open until the *séance de flagellation* in 1766 that reasserts emphatically the claims of absolutism. The "new deal" of liberalization implies a quasi-institutionalized colloquy and comity between prince and parlements based on the uncontestable dictates of natural law, which supersedes positive law, before or after registration. Though wrenched from a "defeated" king by triumphant parlements, the law of November 1763 inaugurates a new deal of its own by establishing conditions for an obligatory dialogue, a quasi-institutionalized sharing of information and policy recommendations between monarch and courts, at least in fiscal matters (259–61, 323). The voluntary submission to nature, predicate of liberalization, also addresses the obsessive parlementary concern with the threat of royal "despotism," a leitmotif in Alimento's book. Both sides reveal acrobatic capacities for segmenting and reconciling, as these two different models of political concertation unfold almost simultaneously, one more fragile, more ontologically ephemeral than the other.

The Black History of Finance

Joël Félix clarifies many issues concerning the L'Averdy ministry in his robust monograph dealing with the financial and political troubles of an unhinged monarchy.[27] Based on much fresh archival research and a pitiless critical

27 *Finances et politique au siècle des Lumières: Le ministère L'Averdy, 1763–1768* (Paris: Comité pour l'histoire économique et financière de la France, 1999). I respect the author's rendering of his protagonist's name in this book. I maintain the spelling Laverdy, commonly used in the eighteenth century and by historians of our time, in the second edition of *Bread, Politics and Political Economy*, also published by Anthem.

evaluation of the rich, albeit often dated and/or tendentious, historiography, the study is an important contribution to a political history that I find too narrowly construed and that reinforces, paradoxically, the historiographical paradigm that he selectively assails.[28] Félix's cardinal objective, framing the book from beginning to end, is to rehabilitate the reputation and thus the work of L'Averdy. With a sometimes obsessive eagerness, he succeeds in this task, but without profiting from the opportunity to free himself of the Manichean template that opposes crown to parlements in a way that can be stifling, confining politics to religious and financial questions, played out in a hemmed-in microcosm and reified as constitutional markers that muddle as often as they clarify the underlying debate about the nature, the exercise and the legitimacy of power. In the light of his revitalized L'Averdy, irreducible to his familial and professional (magisterial) habitus, cast as a man of the Enlightenment, to whose energy and creativity the author pays vague but fervent homage, I regret that Félix did not seek to distance himself from the inherited tradition and map out a politics infused with a bolder and broader respiration.

Perfervid Apology

The focus on rehabilitation probably discouraged a more ambitious revisionist agenda. I endorse heartily Félix's argument against the "black history of finance," sometimes linked to the stigmatization of the parlements as subverters of monarchy and of all manner of reformism and his portrayal of L'Averdy as a highly competent and interesting public figure (vii–xi). I wonder, however, about the strategic and substantive value of overkill. The financial report that serves as the central basis for his reading of L'Averdy, he writes, steers one to "avoid the easy temptation to draw up the list of the good and bad controllers-general" (xi), yet he affirms that under L'Averdy's aegis, the monarchy made more daring decisions than it had since the Regency and before the Revolution (101). Setting the bar high and ceding again to the temptation to measure his hero against rivals, Félix claims that L'Averdy "implemented, in the economic

28 Concerning the historiographical critique, in my view, J. Félix is at his best, for example, when he goes after Marcel Marion, an immensely influential historian of finances and politics (ix, 34, 60–63, 172–76, 183–84, 306–17, 329–30), and at his least compelling when he situates himself rather peremptorily in the realm of "realities" or "true realities" that escaped his predecessors or when he dismisses their arguments on the self-regarding grounds that "things were much more complex" than the others imagined (419–20, 425, 442). Since I am the object of both accolades and rebukes in his book, permit me to lament the anglophilic and anglophone French historian's decision to utilize, not the full-fledged original edition in English of *Bread, Politics and Political Economy*, but the significantly abridged and poorly translated French version.

sphere, as many and far more radical measures" than Turgot (181). Unlike Terray, the anti-Turgot, narrow-minded and derivative, an authoritarian accountant without breadth of vision, L'Averdy was an original thinker (473–75). In other domains, he anticipates the achievements of the early Revolution (261, 450). The historian is frequently defensive/apologetic and rarely aggressive. The controller-general was responsible neither for the Brittany affair nor for the general economic crisis at the end of the 1760s, and his much-maligned edict for the liberation of state debts can be understood only as part of a more intrepid (and amorphous) "political program of economic government" (317, 442, 151). In his struggle to "restore the authority of Louis XV," if he "appeared at times to retreat, it was always to gather momentum and forge ahead" (345). Despite ostensible setbacks and frustrations, L'Averdy was a master politician, a reformer's reformer, the man who put an end to the "administrative chaos" that sapped financial management (404, 406, 409).

Félix characterizes L'Averdy in terms that suffer here and there from vagueness or opacity or anachronism: "liberal monarchist," "conservative liberal," "intense piety," aversion to "dogmatic activism," "partisan of moderation," possessor of unspecified "mental tools," a point of view that "went in the direction of progress," "representative of the progressive current in the parlement" (98, 99, 346, 110–12, 105, 184, 205, 464). The controller-general is a "man of the Enlightenment," but beyond his allergy to systematic thinking, the historian does not explore the ways the new, pluralistic, rapidly evolving intellectual environment marks his protagonist or the 20 men (of Jansenist spirituality and Gallican orientation) who dominated the Parlement of Paris (109, 112–13, 181, 432).[29] The Enlightenment generated new types of public opinion; Félix suggests that L'Averdy paid close attention to "public opinion" (among other reasons, to avoid conflict with the courts), but it remains, here as elsewhere, a slippery, phantom concept (202, 205, 404).[30]

29 One of my anonymous readers astutely regrets that Félix did not probe more deeply into the Jansenist habitus of which L'Averdy was a product. He was the pupil of J. B. L. Crevier at the Collège de Dormans-Beauvais, pedagogical nerve center of Parisian Jansenism. Crevier dedicated to his earnest and committed student his *Rhétorique françoise* (Paris, 1765). On the broader matter of Jansenism and political economy, see the important study by Arnaud Orain, "The Second Jansenism and the rise of French Eighteenth-Century Political Economy," *History of Political Economy* 46, no. 3 (2014): 463–490.

30 See, for example, the allusion to "…a desire, largely shared by the French, finally to undertake reforms," which offers little sociological purchase on the anchoring of this apparently widespread opinion.

Pragmatism

The historian emphasizes the minister's "pragmatic" proclivity[31] and prudential bent (201), but the trait that he celebrates as paramount in the minister's policies and politics is a disposition in favor of conciliation and compromise. A suggestive (yet not fully unpacked) leitmotif is the minister's putative double determination to reinforce royal authority and appease parlementary sensibilities at virtually every crucial juncture, the adumbration of an inchoate *troisième voie* in the standard binary historiography.[32] Partisans of the strong royal thesis (in shorthand, the Antoine school) will not be convinced by Félix's contention that the sovereign courts were public-minded rather than self-aggrandizing, by his representation of the (celebrated? infamous?) remonstrances as a soft, symbolical rather than an aggressive expression of politics, or by his exoneration of the parlements for the impasse(s) that paralyzed France, which he attributes—thoughtfully, albeit dimly—to a crisis of "the traditional justifications of the exercise of authority and of power by the monarchy" (3, 62, 169, 414, but cf. 102).[33] To shelter L'Averdy from suspicion of false consciousness or mystification, Félix needs to demonstrate that the actors themselves did not experience an apparent victory achieved by the other as a mortifying defeat, that the king and magistrates both took satisfaction in outcomes that Félix generally casts as a reinforcement—frontal or oblique—of royal sway. To escape the suspicion of casuistry, Félix needs to show why so many magistrates found it so difficult to become "king's men" in L'Averdy's labile manner, without suffering an exorbitant sense of betrayal of their parlementary moorings (78, 104–5, 121, 131, 208–9, 325, 344–45, 413, 422).[34]

---

31 Here Félix is targeting me, accused (unjustly!) of casting L'Averdy as a man of "systematic spirit." I believe that he committed himself to certain principles and policies that he pursued more or less intransigently, but such fidelity and rigor do not necessarily require the sectarian rigidity implied by the highly pejorative Enlightenment epithet of *esprit systématique*.

32 J. Félix takes a somewhat angelic élan in his depiction of L'Averdy as a fanatic of moderation: "L'Averdy was a doctrinaire only as a function of his fierce will and determination to reconcile political antagonisms in order to allow the State to accomplish the economic, fiscal and financial reform that it believed indispensable to guarantee the future of a monarchy on its last legs" (422).

33 Provocatively, J. Félix suggests that in some ways the intendants, rather than the parlementaires, can be seen as agents of the subversion of royal modernization (447). He also maintains staunchly that L'Averdy did not flinch from combating magistrates (as well as ministers) who resisted his crusade to restore royal authority (345).

34 On occasion, the controller-general reminds one of a first secretary of the Socialist Party, in the style of F. Hollande, seeking to overcome discordance and avoid confrontation through consultation, discussion and, finally, synthesis. L'Averdy's nostrum that enhances the stature of both parties without diminishing or tarnishing either could also have proved useful in the Washington of 2014.

Finance or Subsistence?

Liberalization constitutes the terrain where Félix's research bears most directly upon mine. Both of us note the connection between the liberal turn and fiscality: for me, the potential fiscal yield is an integral part of what I call the "new deal" that Louis XV proposes to parlements in particular and to the nation in general; for Félix, the link is less significant, though growth—*croissance* remains a keyword in French historiography (and politics!) in the post-Labrousse, post-Thirty Glorious era—could generate fiscal benefits (143, 158, 414). From my perspective, neither of us has probed sufficiently into the nexus between liberalization and the financial issue(s), though I have learned much from Félix's expertise in this domain.[35]

The core of our differences turns on the subsistence question, generally much less salient for Félix than for me,[36] in large measure because of his engrossing preoccupation with L'Averdy as framework, motor and gyroscope (which leads him to give primacy to exportation as the dominant problématique because this controller-general bore direct responsibility for the edict of July 1764 that granted this historically controversial trade freedom) and the absence of a significant social dimension in his conception of politics. Subsistence occasionally looms as a veritable blind spot in Félix's gaze. The enormous stakes of the subsistence question do not seem to fit into the procrustean bed of his political history that gives privilege to the financial question in the context of the canonic crown–parlement tension/opposition and to the role of personal frictions, competing ambitions and rival factions. Because it seems to me so drastically out of touch with the locus of acuity of the crisis of the late 1760s, I read with incredulity Félix's claim that "the question of the reduction of annuity purchases [*constitutions des rentes*] was at least as agitated as that of the liberty of grain." The interest rate seems to me to be a crucial concern, but during 1767–68—the years cited by Félix—it is simply less ominous and less significant in social, political and probably economic terms than the consequences of protracted dearth and sweeping deregulation (219–23).

May or July?

The radical rupture of liberalization issues from the royal declaration of May 1763 which alters the very nature of kingship in announcing a new relationship between prince and people, frees the grain trade from the

35 Though at one point Félix seems to hint that fiscal constraints weighed more heavily in determining L'Averdy's engagement in liberal reform than "principles of economic liberty to which he adhered": to attribute the controller-general's action in a context in which state debt reimbursement and preparation for the next war commanded priority would be "reductionist," he professes (186).

36 Cf. a striking exception to this dominant posture toward the end of the book where he refers to "the battle over liberalism" as "the first revolutionary event before 1789" (415).

age-old constraints that had placed it under the more or less relentless scrutiny of the authorities (the *police des grains*) and thereby legitimizes behavior heretofore treated as antisocial and criminal and ties the hands of public administrators and magistrates at all levels by forbidding them to intervene in commercial exchange or any other aspect of the provisioning process.[37] Félix pays very little attention to the grand moral and political fracture of "May" and its extreme deregulation, presumably because it did not occur under L'Averdy's watch.

He concentrates the bulk of his discussion of liberalization on the July edict, which rehearsed some of the key laissez-faire measures of May, but is best known for permitting a generous, but not unconditional, liberty to export.[38] This freedom was crucial to the liberal project, notably in its physiocratic guise, for it was the theoretical guarantor of the normative right price—*le bon prix*—that would regenerate agriculture and prepare the way for sustained prosperity. The right to export did not bear, however, the huge symbolic or pragmatic weight of the first liberal law. It mattered mightily in the global project, but the outcome of that project as it emerged from the May law—the structural metamorphosis that it presaged in social and political relations and in the construction of the everyday order—did not depend on the survival of exportation, a variable much easier to adjust, even though its most zealous exponents insisted that it had to be both perpetual and unlimited. Nevertheless, the right to export, even in the relatively cautious, partial version accorded by L'Averdy, clearly jeopardized his overriding objective of reestablishing order in the realm, even if it imperiled that order much less deeply and widely than the parlous and tentacular deregulation of May (184).[39] Moreover, the fact that liberalization required the king to repudiate the paternalist/interventionist character of monarchy and cast the prince in a new, leaner role that emphasizes less what he can do than what he cannot

37 Félix appears to miss the truly radical character of the clauses of the May declaration that he epitomizes as "free circulation" in the interior and the opening of the commerce to all comers (202; cf. 191). He still doesn't get it toward the end of his book when he writes, not about the profoundly disorganizing impact of May's radical break with the past and the disorienting deregulation that came in its wake, but about "the disastrous economic, political and social consequences of the edict of the month of July 1764" (416). As we shall see below, the practice of the trade generates disarray even when exports destined for abroad are not at stake and grave disorder persists even as export at crucial ports has been suspended. Nor was exportation the decisive issue in the debates of the extraordinary Parisian police assembly convoked in November 1768, where, incidentally, Félix inexplicably describes Sartine, lieutenant-general of police, as a liberal (432).

38 For an illustration of Félix's hyper-investment in export, see 445, 447.

39 I am not convinced, on the basis of the evidence that Félix marshals, that L'Averdy agonized over the decision to accord rights to export. And the summons to Turgot

seems to escape Félix. Yet, in many ways it starkly undermines the ambition that he places at the core of L'Averdy's mission: to reinvigorate royal authority (403, passim).

Like Félix, I am generally skeptical of linear connections because they often sacrifice complexity, ambiguity, and nuance. Yet, I believe that he errs seriously in advancing that there was no "straight line" connecting the "liberty of trade and the famine" (445). To be sure, there was grave, chronic dearth rather than famine in the 1760s (though it is not certain that the distinction had great meaning for many of the poorest consumers). I think that I have clearly demonstrated the intimate linkage between liberalization and the aggravation and proliferation of penury, between liberalization and extreme price volatility, market disorganization, panic-terror and anger among consumers, widespread uprisings and pervasive disorder.[40]

The tenacity with which L'Averdy implemented the May declaration in particular suggests not only the deep respect for royal will that Félix underscores, but also a heedful conviction of political economy that this policy corresponded to the pressing short- and long-term needs of French state and society. Given the historian's keen interest in center–periphery relations (expressed via fiscality, the enterprising municipal reform program and the irredentist claims of the Paris Parlement codified by the *union-des-classes* theory) and in the political life (and ideological stresses) within each parlement,

and Dupont to draft the legal project, or at least its preamble, does not bespeak deep ideological doubts (201–2). Surely Félix is right in insisting that L'Averdy was not a physiocrat, but why strain so hard to dilute or deny his commitment to a liberal analysis, if not a liberal vision, in terms of the grain question? I don't see him as a Teflon pragmatist (185–86). Note that the French historian makes a mistake in affirming that the authorization to export was restricted to a year: there was a price ceiling, but not a temporal limitation (203).

40 One of the symptoms of the straight line I postulate was the famine plot to which I devoted a small book cited elsewhere in this volume. "This rumor," contends Félix, "was never anything other than a (sometimes deliberately) erroneous reading of the political economy of the physiocrats, and, in a general manner, of the partisans of a far-reaching modernization of the monarchy" (448). This appraisal wholly misses the point of this deeply unsettling persuasion that touched virtually all social groups as they read their own experience of liberalization and dearth and heard about the observations and ordeals of others during the 1760s. Moreover, it can be traced back, in strikingly similar discursive and symbolic manifestations, to the end of the reign of Louis XIV (and probably earlier) and forward through the nineteenth century to the Second Empire, if not beyond (with a stunning resurgence during the terrible year of 1947). On the latter, see my *Le Pain maudit: retour sur la France des années oubliées, 1945–58* (Paris: Fayard, 2008).

I regret that he did not attempt to shed light on the shifting attitudes of the magistrates and the courts toward the liberal experiment: the swerve from an early and uneven soft consensus to a certain unity of purpose among (albeit, rarely within) the parlements; subsequently, an increasing dissonance within and among the courts; finally, quite virulent cleavages concerning not only the impact of the dramatic liberal caesura of the 1760s, but also the underlying vision on which it rested of an atomized, individualistic society, displacing the solidary and coercive corporate universe; an interest-driven, egocentric, self-adjusting capitalist economy superseding a socially embedded and regulated system of market exchange and an executive authority subservient to natural law supplanting a paternalistic and providential absolutism.

The Trauma of Deregulation

Though it resonates with our concerns today, the struggle between an embryonic liberty (exalting, vitalizing, unshackling, individualistic, innovative and subversive) and a traditional regulatory disposition (prudent, routinizing, restraining, solidary, reparative and structuring) does not fully capture the trauma of liberalization for those who were summoned to implement it. In writing *Bread, Politics and Political Economy*, I was struck by the disquiet, the dejection and the incredulity that the radical reform legislation of 1763–64 elicited in myriad local officials, a disorientation and malaise that frequently resulted in resistance, oblique or overt, interrogative or declarative, performative in one way or another and sometimes violent, symbolically and/or pragmatically. At stake, for these administrators and/or judges, was a conception of nature, of justice, of governance (central, regional and local), of the public interest and order, of community in several different senses and on multiple levels and of the monarchy itself: its attributes, levers of power, responsibilities and obligations. Many could not believe that the king could break so brutally with the social contract of subsistence: they cast their skepticism and disarray in the canonic distinction between scheming counselors and a beneficent prince led astray;[41] others suggested that their leaders were not evil but quixotic, remote and cutoff from the reality of daily life; still others sought to subject the new texts to exegeses that would afford them latitude to take actions that necessity—the *salus populi*—imposed.

I recently came upon a case that had escaped me, which seemed particularly interesting because it involved a major city, Dijon—an administrative center

41 For insights into the representation of the good king traduced by his malevolent advisers, see Yves-Marie Bercé, *Le Roi caché. Sauveurs et imposteurs: Mythes politiques populaires dans l'Europe moderne* (Paris: Fayard, 1990).

and parlementary bastion—rather than the many small towns and hamlets I had studied. If one does not find here precisely the same piquant blend of angst, anger and audacity characteristic of the renitent local officials, the episode nevertheless casts into stark relief a stunning will to disobey the central government and to test and contest its policies, and it reveals the vigorous resolution of Controller-General L'Averdy, whose commitment to liberalism turns out to be much deeper than often supposed.[42]

Dijon Dissents

The incident begins with the denunciation by the municipality of Dijon in September 1766, in the midst of rising prices, a depleting supply and a slowly crystallizing panic, of "the enormous abuse" that merchants were making of the "unlimited liberty" that the king had instituted: "On the pretext of the special protection that His Majesty has accorded them by his last edict, [the grain merchants] see themselves as empowered to buy the entire stock of grain harvested in Burgundy in order to ship it abroad, in the hope of an immense profit, and without in the least worrying if the province would thus be deprived of merchandise of first necessity."[43] The municipality chronicled the premature exhaustion of the stocks of 1765, effectuated by "foreign" buyers

42 I am grateful to Dr. Anthony Béhin, eminent neurologist and excellent historian in his free time, for the reference. The following discussion is drawn from the *Correspondance de la Mairie de Dijon, extraite des archives de cette ville*, ed. Joseph Garnier, vol. 3 (Dijon: J. E. Rabutot, 1868–70), 462–509.

43 It is a constant in times of subsistence stress, in particular when exportation is authorized as in the mid-1760s, that consumers everywhere identify *any* removal (*enlèvement*) of grain as merchandise destined to be sent to foreign countries at their expense. Trudaine de Montigny, the ardent liberal who served as a high official with special responsibility for subsistence in the 1760s, remarked on the incongruity of the uprising that occurred near St.-Brieuc to block grains scheduled to be delivered to Normandy and Artois, for the rioters claimed the right to stop exports abroad from a port that had been officially closed to exportation for over a year. "But the people do not want to hear that there was a difference between shipping abroad and sending grain to Normandy," noted the intendant of commerce, thereby underscoring one of the chronic problems faced by the authorities in attempting to manage what we would call popular representations and what they called popular prejudices. Trudaine to Miromesnil, May 1768 in Pierre Le Verdier, ed., *Correspondance politique et administrative de Armand Thomas Hue de Miromesnil, Premier Président du Parlement de Normandie*, vol. 5 (Rouen: A. Picard, 1899–1903), 200. The First President of the Rouen Parlement confirms that "the people, who suffer endlessly, groan and complain about exportation" as a sort of generic marker of excessive liberty, illicit maneuvering and monopoly. To L'Averdy, March 1768, ibid., 5:129. Officials and observers throughout the kingdom called attention to the same phenomena that Trudaine and Miromesnil adduced in the west.

(from Languedoc, Provence and Lyons), assisted by local correspondents, followed by a reasonable crop yield in 1766 that failed nevertheless to stem the *cherté* because those same traders purchased or took options (*enarrhement*) on grain still in the ground or just harvested. As proof of the gravity of the situation, the city fathers noted the "rumors" of trading maneuvers and the chilling news that repeatedly "the people ask for bread," a demand figured—significantly in the eyes of authorities—by "gatherings of women that force itself could neither contain nor dissipate."

Faced with "a famished populace" ready to take the merchants to task, the municipality insisted on the sangfroid of its methodology: "Our first concern, after having tried to allay the fears of the populace, was to verify carefully the validity of our suspicion that the merchants' abuse of the edict of July 1764 was the true cause of the evil; and our research convinced us that our conjectures were well founded." For the moment, the source of the disorder is not the policy in itself, not the reform legislation, but its abuse, its misappropriation and distortion.

The city then acted according to the standard police script, as if the other parts of the liberal code banning any public intervention did not exist: it called upon the merchants to supply the market and at the same time made purchases that it resold below the going price to nudge prices downward, a sort of surrogate *taxation populaire* that provisionally appeased consumers, but induced merchants to flee. Furious to see supplies evaporate, the "terrified" people, "especially the women," assembled, halted grain wagons and "look at us as their tyrants and executioners when we send soldiers to seize the most zealous agitators and to free the passage for the wagons."[44]

L'Averdy: Ardent Liberalism and Discreet Precaution

L'Averdy responded with a stinging rebuke, reproaching the municipality with a triple weakness: an excessive regard for public opinion (notably the "people's" view of the police), an implicit endorsement of popular "prejudices" concerning subsistence matters, along with the people's gratuitous "fears and alarms" and a deeply flawed assessment of the provisioning situation ("abundance surrounds you on all sides" and prices are moderate in Champagne, Lorraine and elsewhere; export via the Mediterranean ports has been cut off and is unlikely to be reestablished before the next harvest, an extremely sanguine appreciation that bespeaks L'Averdy's belief in the efficacy of the core liberal doctrine).

---

44 Vicomte - mayeur, échevins and syndics to controller-general, 23/9/66, ibid., 462–65.

The minister denounced the city's inexcusable trespass of the laws of 1763–64: by intervening in the workings of commerce, it "alarmed" the merchants and "destroyed their confidence." Their refractory attitude, depriving Dijon of "needed resources," was nothing less than "the fruit of sage reflection," an indulgent evaluation that could only stupefy the authorities in the field. Why should they supply you if they are not entirely free to act according to their interest? asked L'Averdy, in another formula that administrators could not help but find shocking. Your "precautions"—pressuring them to supply—will only drive them off; moreover and no less important, such actions are contrary to the law of the land, which a mayor and his city councilors are morally and juridically obliged to enforce. Transgression of the law, following the municipal logic, constitutes a self-fulfilling prophecy: "the evils that you fear can become real, if you persist in your errors; the system of forcing the merchants to furnish grain, of fixing its price, even of expressing alarm at its increase, are so many invincible obstacles to achieving the abundance that you desire."

The minister was frustrated for lack of an effective strategy, beyond exhortation and censure, to destroy "the prejudices of the people" on the one hand and to prevent the police from succumbing to them on the other. L'Averdy, the dogmatist, allowed a small space for pragmatic improvisation: in dire situations, the authorities could undertake "some precautions." Not, however, in the logic of the moral economy or any consensus based on notions of reciprocity or claims on private property. Such interventions had to be narrowly targeted, fleeting and utterly "secret" so as not to condone any cognitive regression on the part of the people. L'Averdy's bottom line remained incontrovertibly liberal: "laissés agir le commerce." When he learned shortly afterward of a municipal plan that would have constrained merchants to supply, his reaction was virulent: "It would be destructive of all commerce, it would spread alarm among the people, and far from facilitating your victualing, it would deprive you of all resources." A crisis paranoia has taken possession of the Dijon authorities: "Your fears and your prejudices spur you to envisage horrors that have no basis in reality." Liberty is a quasi-mechanical guarantee of abundance; intervention of any sort—save promptly to repress "the excesses of the people"—is a quasi-guarantee of shortage, suffering and disorder. The minister's line on the people hardened, even as his liberal conviction flourished: he became less and less sympathetic to their putative plight (for which they were in large part responsible, along with their protectors in the administration) and more and more inclined to believe that the only way to convert them was to break them.[45]

45 L'Averdy to municipality, 18/12/66 and 20/12/66, ibid., 466–70.

"Evil-Intentioned Writers" and Dijon's "Crime"

"Wounded" by the controller-general's splenetic reprimand, the municipality allowed that, if we could be "mistaken in our ideas," our "intentions are pure." That was not the case of the physiocrats, who offer a pretext for insubordination: "Some evil-intentioned writers, who have a personal interest in the affair, have turned you against us, Monseigneur." Unlike the *économistes* and the merchants, unmoored in the *terroir* (and the imaginary) of subsistence, the city fathers claimed to embody disinterest and "patriotism". After all, they ask, "what is, in fact, our crime?" They took badly the minister's hint that they were themselves responsible for popular turmoil and for market failure. They protested that they do no more than humanity and good governance dictate: we seek to "give relief to our poor citizens," to reassure "the alarmed spirits as much by our discourse as our example" and to obtain unimpeachable intelligence on the supply situation.

In the eyes of the controller-general, however, the Dijon leaders committed something resembling a crime back in September at the moment when the supply situation seemed critical. They convened 16 merchants and asked each to furnish the market in proportion to their stock. Despite the promise to allow them to set their own prices, the next day, the apparent accord fell apart: the traders seemed to understand their rights in the wake of liberalization and did not recognize the requirement to comply with an arrangement that had been imposed upon them. Faced with this provocative defection, the municipality felt obliged to convoke the merchants to the offices of the president of the *Chambre des vacations* of the Parlement, the body that represented the court during the summer pause. Apparently, only three merchants agreed; even after the menace of incarceration, very few responded to the summons to the city hall. One, deemed the most "dishonest," guilty of indiscriminate buying and hoarding—certainly evidence of a "reprehensible greed," but no longer illegal actions—went briefly to jail.

According to the city fathers, they concluded a deal ("traité") with merchants, clearly under coercion, involving this time a fixed price on the commandeered supply. Most of the traders ended up fulfilling their commitments, more or less, for a period of several months, before breaking off when the municipality refused to pay them individually for their contribution both to the marketplace and to the common reserve. Meanwhile, the merchants counterattacked, in a vehement complaint addressed to L'Averdy, which prompted his irate castigation of the municipality.

Apart from a disagreement on the base price to be used to reimburse and remunerate them, a veritable chasm of categorical incomprehension separated the two parties. Brandishing the legislative license of utter freedom to conduct business as they wished, the merchants claimed they had been illicitly bullied, even bludgeoned from the outset; whereas the city fathers, far too shrewd to be naïve about the new laws, yet deeply socialized into practices reckoned imperative for the maintenance of order and the shepherding of the populace in hard times, addressed them in a tone mingling anachronism and authoritarian effrontery, which the traders could only view with a mixture of stupefaction and resentment: "Do they see themselves as entitled to play around with impunity with the most respectable, the most solemn written conventions … in the application of the most invariable rules and principles…?" Discerning "divine justice" in the low tide that bottled up grain transport on the Saône and compromised the speculations of the traders ("punishment for their insatiable cupidity"), the city fathers, aligning themselves with the now obsolescent representation of the king as "good father to his people," hoped somehow that L'Averdy would find a way to approve or at least condone their conduct, even as they knew deep down that he would vilify and perhaps even penalize them.[46]

Conscientious Objectors

On Christmas eve, the mayor of Dijon made a strong and basically seditious political argument, even as he deployed a conventional sort of subsistence sentimentalism. He avowed, more or less frankly, that the municipality, in collaboration with "its superiors" in the parlement, violated the law but, consciously and conscientiously, in the service of a higher law, a hazardous case to make, especially at the moment that (Enlightened) absolutism is making a scientific and an economic turn and has already assimilated the moral economy and paternalism to benighted, archaic thinking:

> Moreover, your justice will never allow to be deemed as criminal, Monseigneur, whoever could not muffle the cries of misery and hunger; it will be able to fathom that, if our precautions to assure the subsistence of the people do not amount to a literal execution of the edict of July 1764, they drew upon the ancient ordinances of the kingdom, or rather upon the goodness of your heart, which is the depository and image of the tenderness of His Majesty for his peoples.

The controller-general had "inaccurate" and calumnious information propagated by our "enemies", in the service of their sordid self-interest, averred the mayor. We neither "authorized popular clamor" nor are we "in

46 Municipality to controller-general, 20/12/66, ibid., 470–80.

the bosom of abundance": quite the contrary is true. We "calmed" the people, understandably hostile to exportations that the merchant cabal continued to conduct—"immense convoys"—mostly at night, a further marker of their wicked intentions.

The mayor judged that the best defense was offense. He told the minister that his institution had prevented a major riot, thanks to its decisive, albeit quite modest, supply-side intervention. Contrary to the claims of the physiocrats and the liberal ministry, the people—at least those in the precincts of the Burgundian capital—understood their "veritable interests": how could they be expected to watch prices soar and grain flee with equanimity and confidence in their leaders? Even as we used "authority" and "force" when necessary to contain the most agitated people, the municipality maintained, correspondingly we pressed the merchants, who had "stripped Burgundy bare" in four months, to accept a contract that the parlementary magistrates concurred was the only way to spare us "a total dearth," a scarcity orchestrated and nourished by these same merchants who continued to hoard local grain that had not yet taken the export road. Neither "visionaries, impostors or rebels," the municipal administrators assured the controller-general, we know the law, new and old versions, and you must not shy away from owning up to the consequences of the grand liberal reform: the price in Dijon (3 livres 5 sous the measure) was "notoriously beyond the force of our artisans and unskilled workers, who compose half our population." Despite the promises of the "modern writers" on morally certain adjustments that would jeopardize no one, a calamitous wage lag ensued. The city fathers and L'Averdy had sharply differing priorities and preoccupations; the concluding remarks of the Dijonnais once again accentuate the fruitlessness of the dialogue of the deaf: Our"conscience"impels us to tell you the truth, they wrote, "mothers bring us their babies and tearfully demand our assistance." Given the boundless "avidity" of the merchants and the "frightening misery" of the people, can our actions really pass for "negligence of our duties?"[47]

Unobstructed Laissez-Faire

In his reply, L'Averdy avoided any discussion of sanctions against the municipality, yet demanded strict obedience: the officials had no hermeneutic license to interpret royal policy as they believed necessary, there was no higher law, no moral economy, no justification for a popular-police front. His mantra remained unchanged: "Unobstructed *laissez-faire* is the canon of commerce to which you must cede; you must oppose the prejudices of the people with

47 Municipality to controller-general, 24/12/66, ibid., 481–87.

the greatest firmness and punish with serenity the excesses to which they might have recourse." While the controller-general did not quarrel with the municipal ends of assuring the adequate victualing of the population—an ambiguous rhetorical concession—he rejected totally their means: "No motives should have led you to fail to follow rigorously the dispositions of the declaration of 1763 and the edict of 1764." Yet, you forced the merchants to furnish grain below the current price fixed by the natural forces of free competition, and you did this "against the express will of the king," strictly speaking, an act of mutiny or even treason. The Dijonnais magistrates, like their less august counterparts in the small towns and hamlets, needed urgently to accept the sea change, the profound mutation in politics and policy that liberalization wrought. There is no going back: "None of the pretexts that you have invoked to account for your conduct can justify your infraction of the law."[48]

Finding it more politic to privilege the particular over the general, the municipality indicated that it was ready to make an offer to put an end to the dispute with the merchants. But it could not help itself from stigmatizing them for failing to show public spirit or patriotism, for being liars and delinquents: "You do not know, Monseigneur, the sort of men with whom we must deal."[49] Furious at this provocation that suggested that liberty issued in libertinage and that the (abjectly naïve) ministry relinquished its ethical compass in its embrace of political economy, L'Averdy dispensed a veritable discursive flagellation to the Dijonnais, calling them to order and docility and enjoining them to revise their obsolete and (thus) dangerous ideas. He was pained to recognize in their letter "the spirit of prejudice that has for a long period shaped all your decisions." It is fanciful for you to believe that you render "a grace to the merchants in allowing them to supply your market and sell at the going price": it is their absolute right, accorded first by natural law (guaranteeing their property) and then by positive law, whose function is to ratify. Nothing can dispense you from respecting and enforcing the liberal laws of 1763–64. Pay the merchants what you owe them without further tergiversation, "let them be in full possession of the liberty that the law gives them, encourage them, stimulate them to provision the markets; be careful never to deploy authoritarian means, and habituate the people, by your example, not to give in to trivial anxieties that cause dearth when it does not really exist and which aggravates it when it does."[50]

48 L'Averdy to municipality, 28/12/66 and 15/1/67, ibid., 488–89.
49 Municipality to controller-general, 27/1/67, ibid., 490–91.
50 L'Averdy to municipality, 7/2/67, ibid., 492.

Municipal Temerity, Ministerial Fury

Perhaps because they understood the complexity of Old-Regime systems of clientage and protection, perhaps because they felt morally obliged to contest liberalization, in whose political durability they did not believe, the city fathers evinced breathtaking insolence. They denied mistreating the merchants, who once again refused to furnish the market; rejected the accusation that "prejudices" dictated their behavior; and without conscious disrespect, but with a single-mindedness worthy of the controller-general himself, they warned that "we will be compelled to act if our markets are not supplied as they should be."[51] L'Averdy responded with predictable fury, perhaps less for their temerity in itself than for the fact that the Dijonnais seemed to regard the liberal reforms as a mere epiphenomenon and to suggest that eternal verities must prevail over aberrations. The controller-general was lucid: he had enough information to determine that *he* must take measures to assure the victualing of Dijon, an engagement that presumably would pass through the merchant community rather than exceptional direct royal assistance. "I see with surprise that you persist in your initial views," he wrote to the city fathers, with the admonition that they should resist the temptation to distinguish between a good king who was for the moment blinded to the workings of truth and/or evil and misguided ministers such as himself: "The king will hold you responsible for all happenings if, against his will, you seek to establish an administration geared to contest his policies."[52]

The mayor, Rousselot, knew that he had taken things to the very limits; prodded by the intendant, who preferred the capital to Dijon, and the ministry's grain department, he visited Paris in the hopes of calming things down. Vexed at not having been kept in the loop in this protracted controversy, Amelot, the intendant, castigated him for failing to adhere to the "unlimited liberty" so ardently espoused by the controller-general. Writing to his colleagues back home, the mayor showed no lack of humor (redolent of a folksy Galiani operating outside the salon world, if such a scenario is thinkable). Nor did he lack a real acuity of mind. To escape from this Parisian trap, the mayor esteemed, he would have to mimic an Arlequin, dressed in a somewhat tattered and patched outfit that results from a brawl, but endowed with sufficient intelligence and guile to hoodwink his superiors. His narrative emphasized that the pilgrimage to the capital had not changed his view of liberalization, and once again underscored the abyss between the real and the virtual economy, between the grain equivalents of a government more oriented to Wall Street than to Main Street:

51 Municipality to controller-general, 17/2/67, ibid., 493–94.
52 L'Averdy to municipality, 26/2/67, ibid., 495.

> Here people are crazy about the story of the unlimited liberty of the grain trade, it's an enthusiasm that cannot be imagined, and one is tempted to give public festivals each time that one learns that the price of grain has risen. The surest way of successfully paying court is to exclaim loudly on the excellence of the declarations that allow the free exportation and importation of grain.

Rousselot recognized that there was no solution for the Dijonnais other than trying to extricate themselves at the lowest cost possible "without putting up too much resistance." He perceived no interest in attempting to see L'Averdy at this juncture: "We must let him explode." The intendant Amelot had to prepare the way. At the right time, Rousselot would be "ready to uphold the assault and ride out the squall."[53]

Blind Submission

The mayor's visit resulted in a ritual act of submission drafted by the municipality at the end of April 1767. Even at this moment of closure, the Dijonnais discourse does not seem devoid of irony—a hybrid parody of feudal and physiocratic idiom of deference. The submission seems quite self-consciously addressed not to the laws of 1763 and 1764, but merely to the controller-general's interpretation of them: "After all, Monseigneur, we submit blindly to that which it pleases you to order; your respectable decisions are for us the sacred laws from which we will never deviate." Magnanimous, L'Averdy accepted this submission at face value. He commissioned Amelot, unmarred by combat, to settle with the grain merchants in order to close definitively this specific chapter in the controversy. Still, more than a year from the apogee of the subsistence/socioeconomic crisis, in the midst of the proliferating disorder, especially north of the Loire, which he continued to repress vigorously, on the level of general principles, the controller-general did not budge an iota in his unwavering commitment to liberalization, though his expression no longer carried a vituperative or overbearing tone: "I recommend to you to tolerate no obstruction in the grain trade on any pretext whatsoever."[54]

Bread as Protagonist

Liberalization is a fascinating story because it thrusts into relief a host of actors from the loftiest to the humblest. Bread itself is a major protagonist. It identifies and mobilizes the other players from above and below. It

53 Rousselot to the échevins, 24/4/67, ibid., 496–97. The original French concerning L'Averdy's state of mind: "il faut lui laisser jeter son feu."

54 Municipality to controller-general, 27/4/67, ibid., 503–04; L'Averdy to municipality, 10/5/67, ibid., 509.

crystallizes a pivotal debate about the relation of state to society, somewhat more sweeping yet not grossly different from what we call regulation today. Located at the crossroads of the material and the symbolic, bread penetrates into every sphere of public and private existence. As the ration of survival of the vast majority of the population, it refuses to allow the issue of provisioning to degenerate into pure polemic: bread sounds the tocsin of reality as well as the peal of pathos. Gradually recast as a powerful *idée-force* as well as an object of daily fixation, a product of fermentation in a double sense, bread, more than chapbooks, proverbial overheard conversations, new buying experiences as consumers or any other vehicle of education or socialization, brings the people into the Enlightenment or, perhaps more plausibly and less lyrically, inflicts the Enlightenment upon the lives of the people.

Bread summons into play the people, but in the double sense to which I just referred, it also convokes the philosophes, in particular those among them who have focused on political economy. More broadly, it helps to marshal what I have called the liberal lobby, a movement of sorts, which rallied men (and occasionally women) from business (commerce, shipping, banking and so on), farming, public administration, the court, the academies, the city as well as the country and members of various elites as well as myriad upwardly mobile strivers ("wannabes" in the vernacular). If bread were figured as a genie, its bottle was an age-old sanctuary of consensus: once it leaves the bottle—or the cupboard—the bread-genie continues to feed the population even as it aliments an increasingly sharp debate about political, social, economic and cultural values and practices.

Triangle to Trapezoid

Still, at a crucial point in the drama, the stage is dominated by a triangle of actors: the king sits on his throne at the apex, while the people and the police (*sensu lato*) occupy the other two vertices. In the old configuration (before liberalization), the monarch, as nourishing prince, entered into the social contract of subsistence with the consumer-people and assigned responsibility for its execution to the police, who included most of the public administration and judicial system, from top to bottom. In repudiating the social contract, by the act of liberalization, the monarch not only abandoned the people but also forsook the police. The former, heretofore children, suddenly "emancipated" and granted peremptorily their majority, had henceforth to fend for themselves in pursuit of their daily bread, without any paternal assistance, protection or guarantee. The latter, heretofore endowed with sweeping regulatory authority to assure an orderly provisioning (in the urban context: bread in sufficient quantity, of adequate quality and at an accessible price), henceforth had its hands manacled: it could no longer intervene to lure or commandeer grain to market or to influence its price and suppress antisocial maneuvers that were now declared to be legitimate commercial methods. The maintenance of public order was somehow to be decoupled more or less completely from the (generic) *police des grains*.

It is hardly surprising that the orphaned parties inexorably drew toward each other: they had common bonds and interests and at the grassroots a shared sense of disorientation. The upper end of what I call the "police" bears upon the contrôle-général, the subsistence bureau and other segments of the ministerial proto-bureaucracy and, especially, given their role on the ground, the intendants. At approximately the same altitude, one also encounters the parlements (sometimes direct rivals of the intendants, even as they were antagonists of the government and the crown on certain occasions), in this instance as administrators and enforcers of the "grand police," regulation at the highest level of governance that shared responsibility with the royal administration for the execution (and, *a fortiori*, for the interpretation) of the law.

Though I am not sure of the pertinence of geometric imagery, let us say that in 1763–64, at the outset of liberalization, my triangle becomes, for a time, something of a trapezoid as the parlements split off from the local police. Unwontedly (and within uneven conviction), the parlements unanimously join the monarch in a new deal, a fresh departure, politically as well as economically and socially. The people and the local police—excluded as usual from the decision-making process—cling to a logic that we could style as traditionalist, conservative, safety-first, reflexively anxious. The people and the police become rapidly alienated from liberalization, as natural disasters—harvest shortfalls—aggravate the perverse policy effects of liberalization: perverse in terms of their shared view of the construction of daily order, based on an unequivocal privileging of the consumers. Enthralled by the liberal siren's song, the parlements implicitly accept, for the moment, the untoward notion that the "police," grand or ordinary, was part of the problem rather than the solution. By degrees, as a large portion of the kingdom falls prey to dearth, spiking prices, disorganization and panic, as it becomes impossible to disentangle, in causal terms, policy from accident/misfortune, the dismantling of the regulatory apparatus from the proliferation of disorder, a (growing) number of the parlements, following the lead of Rouen and Paris, revert to the logic of the police as a structuring necessity, above all in the provisioning sphere, as the triangular shape begins to reassert itself. A strong, urgent nostalgia for old-style kingship arises from the people and the police. For a prolonged period, the "apex" rebuffs the solicitations of the vertices.

The physiocrats, in the vanguard of the liberal crusade/campaign, deplore the tendency of the police to become people when under intense stress.

The symbolic and perhaps also the political turning point in the story occurs toward the end of November 1768, a month after the violent remonstrance of the Parlement of Rouen, as prices crest in the capital, with the convocation of the assembly of general police of Paris, an emergency "transversal" institution that convenes only in times of grave danger. The assembly helped to shape Galiani's celebrated *Dialogues sur le commerce des bleds*, a mordant critique of liberalization. The assembly probably also occasioned the publication in early 1769 of a poem, with an Amsterdam imprint, entitled, *La Voix du peuple, poème, au sujet de la cherté & de la diminution des grains*. Attributed to Pierre J. B. Nougaret, an Enlightenment polymath par excellence, a grub-streeter with a quasi-bourgeois habitus, it was perhaps commissioned by parlementary interests.[55]

The People as Victim

In *The Voice of the People*, the author crafts a deft and nimble polemic framed by the triangle. The people are the victims. The king is spared, with a surfeit of solicitude and deference perhaps designed to raise doubts about his true colors. After all, the crisis occurred under his government's watch and favored the cupidity of actors who tacitly operated in its (outer) orbit. The parlements, in particular the matrix-court of the capital, in some sense embody the voice of the not quite speechless people, the voice that the magistrates of Paris, in one of their representations to Louis XV, claimed was "the voice of God."

The poet advances a parsimonious conception of the people featured in his title. They are the poor, though he prefers to imagine them as toiling rather than idle. They are largely docile rather than clamorous: certainly not the rebellious people against whose leaders the Rouen Parlement did not hesitate to pronounce the death penalty in the great riot of 1752 or again in 1768. Yet there is no sign that the people of the poem are incapable of analyzing their

55 Nougaret is waiting to make the reputation of an enterprising scholar. Son of a "négociant" (of unknown scale and nature) and the daughter of a minor judicial official, he wrote scores of poems, plays, novels, histories, parodies, political polemics and various compilations. He collaborated, and then brawled with Restif de la Bretonne. A supplement to Voltaire's *La Pucelle* won Nougaret several months of prison, not enough to establish notoriety. Sundry minor administrative posts kept him alive across the Revolutionary-Napoleonic epoch. During the Restoration, he wrote a history of the United States. See Ferdinand Hoefer, *Nouvelle Biographie Générale, depuis les temps les plus reculés jusqu'à nos jours, avec les renseignements bibliographiques et l'indication des sources à consulter* (Paris: Firmin Didot frères, fils et Cie, 1853–66).

situation or recognizing their veritable interests. They live in a comfortable heteronomy vis-à-vis the prince, a relation of subordination that does not exclude asymmetrical reciprocity. These people are devoted to the terms of the customary social contract and they demand only their right not to languish or perhaps perish in the deepening privation that has engulfed them.

Evoking the "misery" of the "people," the author reminds readers of the unbearable legacy of hunger with a reference to the "Norwegian cold" that was the "fatal origin" of the famine and killing winter of 1709. A suggestion runs through the poem that the current crisis has more to do with the (malevolent) acts of men than with the caprices of the weather, a classical analogue to the supposed inconstancy of the people themselves. Following the course of reasoning of the physiocrats, agricultural production flowed from "Nature's gifts": theirs is a regular and responsible and trustworthy nature, not, in the first instance, the agent of meteorological whimsy. When the grain price rewarded cultivators correctly, as a result of unhampered circulation of which the marker in this text is exportation, France enjoyed a renewed and fortified abundance as marginal lands were reclaimed and production augmented. Yet, in the wake of liberalization, "suddenly … abundance dried up" as prices climbed vertiginously and misery mushroomed. "Can we uncover the source of our ills?" asks Nougaret rhetorically. Manifestly, it was not in the obscure physiocratic exegesis of nature, but in common-sense observation: when prices are low, grain is accessible. Penury generates high prices; in the specific case of the 1760s, it results from "an excessively free transport," for example, too much liberty.

In an allusion to the famine plot, self-consciously more prudent than the quasi-treasonous hint of the Rouen magistrates that it enjoyed royal incubation, the poet refers to "the silently spread rumors" of "sordid interests" creating "ghastly dearth" that they "fomented secretly." Could such "hard hearts" exist, he wonders, for he measures both the horror of the accusation and the danger of formulating it. Yet he cannot confidently impute these suspicions to "calumny," for the "artificial" dearth is excruciatingly real to the people and its causes do not appear to be accidental. There *may* very well be—the bard's circumspection is calculating—"infamous assassins" of boundless "knavery" ready to "double the price again" after having already "rob[bed] the subsistence of the people" to whose "sobbing and tears" they remain sublimely indifferent.

Rival Fathers

The poem has a necessary and nervous political rhythm. Feigning a certain balance, it moves from negative to positive emphases and then reiterates the polarity. For the king—"by duty as much as by justice"—does not remain inert.

He extends a "helping hand" to soften the horrors of scarcity and high prices (though the allusion to "the attentive care of the Ministry" is ambiguous), recalling the good old days when prosperity was unencumbered.[56] The lieutenant-general of police enjoys a special accolade for his success in maintaining order in the capital, largely as a result of his discreet efforts to "chase away the dearth," an apparent reference to his use of the royal grain stock managed by Malisset, signatory to the contingency supply contract vilified as the *pacte de famine*. The poem oscillates back to a scathing condemnation of luxury—a major, protean leitmotif in much Enlightenment writing—in contrast to deep misery: "one hundred delicate dishes" on one side, death on the other. Echoing the Rouen strictures, the author intimates that the flabby self-indulgence of the rich and powerful has blinded them "to the greatest evil, yes, the grain *cherté*" and "the horror of hunger." What a tragic irony when the elites manage to convince themselves—here the targets are the presumably liberal elites—that "bread is still at a low price." Isolated in "[their] palaces where voluptuousness reigns," they do not see that, physiocratic pledges to the contrary notwithstanding, wages lag terribly behind grain and bread prices. The only tragedy that moves the rich to tears, notes the writer, occurs in the theater.

Yet, the "celebrated Magistrates"—presumably Nougaret's patrons—heard the cries from below. They are attentive to the "rights" of the poor as well as to those of the rich, for rights and justice are not the appanage of the latter. The poet dares not exclude the king from the climactic panegyric. The "adored monarch"—incongruously still referred to as "Louis the Well-Beloved" in the prefatory note to the bookseller—wants the dearth to disappear—does that mean to render it less shamefully visible or to eliminate it?—and he seems ready to collaborate with the parlement(s) to assure a return to abundance in which "the artisan can once again live from his wage." Louis XV stands as ever "father to his subjects more than their Sovereign": how could the poet fail to note this decisive emblem of kingship? Yet "it seems that your voices"—those of the magistrates, guarantors of the grand police–"have fertilized the earth." Nougaret recounts how, every day, the parlementaires work toward restituting tranquility and well-being:

Voilà d'un Magistrat la plus solide gloire,
Voilà le vrai moyen d'illustrer sa mémoire.
Vous n'avez point brigué de frivoles honneurs;

56 The author or his editor/publisher inserted here a note in the text that refers, in a pell-mell manner that seems deliberate, to a quite recent measure according royal subsidies to grain imports, to the vitriolic representations of the Rouen Parlement and the vehement protestations of the Paris court and to the assembly of general police (12n).

Mais vos soins généreux ont fait tarir nos pleurs:
Ainsi que notre Roi, qu'on aime et qu'on révère,
L'auguste Parlement est du peuple le père.[57] (16)

A double paternity, two (rival) fathers? The poet implies a displacement, a sort of abdication, originally sought by the monarch himself in the liberal legislation. Symbolic parricides or heirs to a vacant seat at the head of the family table, the parlementaires have superseded the king as the effective father of a people no longer orphaned.[58]

*****

Eighteenth-century practitioners of political economy joined both the debate between monarch and parlement(s) and the debate on the nature of kingship. Often associated with the making of wealth, political economy was about governance, in the broadest sense. It was an evolving, pluralistic undertaking that one hesitates to characterize as a movement for fear of imputing to it a coherence or a consensus that its myriad cleavages belied. Sullyists and Colbertists, Christians and materialists, ultra-royalists and Lepaigistes could all claim to speak in the voice of political economy. Mirabeau, perhaps the first truly popular political economist, to judge by his astonishing book sales, detested the blasphemous encyclopedists, a number of whom also talked the language of political economy and even dined at the marquis' table.

The historiography of political economy has changed considerably during the past three quarters of a century, most notably in the United Kingdom and in the USA. In France, it is no longer in the clutches of the law schools, to which economics was consigned, or wired to the constrictive template-doxa of the (sometimes bracing) *Revue d'histoire des doctrines économiques et sociales* (whose ambition to articulate "the evolution of the facts and the evolution of ideas"

57 The unrefined prose rendition: "Here is a Magistrate's sturdiest glory/Here is the true means to render his memory illustrious/You have not solicited frivolous honors/But your generous care has dried our tears/Just as our King, whom we love and revere/The august Parlement is the father of the people."

58 See the extremely suggestive article by Arnaud Orain, evoking such durable and toxic themes as the truly pernicious ideas of physiocracy (resulting in starvation of the people), the deceiving of the monarch, and the self-indulgence of certain ministers: "To Mock and Instruct. A Cultural Opposition to Physiocracy (1760–1790)," *The European Journal of the History of Economic Thought* 22, no. 2, forthcoming.

still strikes me as a worthy unattained goal). Nor is everyone reposing in the procrustean bed of Lovejoyian history of ideas.[59] On both sides of the Atlantic (and perhaps of the Pacific too), there are signs that *ça bouge*! As we shall see in the next chapter, the study of political economy is in flowering renewal. (I do not dare write, in the venerable manner of Auguste Deschamps and Auguste Dubois, founders of *Revue d'histoire des doctrines économiques et sociales* (1908) and philo-physiocrats, that in recent times "many workers have begun to clear the ground for cultivation in this immense field.")

59 I do not have the space here to discuss the part played in the debate about how to treat economic ideas by liberals, Marxists, corporatists, Schumpeterians, Lippmannites, social Catholics, neo-Scholastics, partisans of Dogmengeschichte and so on.

Chapter VI

THE NEW HISTORIOGRAPHY OF POLITICAL ECONOMY

In recent years, the study of political economy has acquired a fresh vitality and intellectual cachet. It has (re-)emerged both as a free-standing *problématique* on its own, with an epistemological self-consciousness and reflexivity heretofore largely absent, and as a powerful lever for making sense of the rest of history, from which it has often been unyoked and even cloistered, sometimes by choice. If this estrangement seems not to have been resisted by liberals, who enjoyed a certain dominion in the subfield, it certainly was favored by the collapse of Marxism, which had begun, at least on the margins, to question the utter subordination of superstructure to infrastructure, that is to say, to reconsider the relation between things and ideas. At roughly the same time that the Soviet empire imploded, and postmodernism began to hector the complacent mainstream, in both rewarding and perverse fashions, more and more historians took the culturalist turn: a rejection of the usual methodological hierarchies and causal ontologies, a fundamental interrogation concerning the relation of texts to contexts (predicated upon an absolute refusal to reduce texts, images and myriad artifacts to the status of reflections of their time), a heightened sensitivity to the claims of language and an ambition to fathom more rigorously the linkages between ideas/words and actions/"reality."

Some of these historians began to reexamine political economy as a discursive practice and as a worldview, a reflection quickened by burgeoning ambient anxieties about the "financialization" of the economy, the profoundly unsettling impact of globalization, growing disparities between rich and poor not only between different economies, but also within manifestly wealthy societies, and a budding realization of the subterranean sway of what could be called economic ideology, lodged within a characteristically unexamined (a-)moral philosophy. If the midwife to the rebirth of political economy was cultural in spheres of Anglo-American influence, in France it was as much economic and sociological as cultural. Some of the most creative French scholars entering this field, often formally trained as economists, less frequently as sociologists, nourished their historical investigations with robust theoretical tools drawn from these disciplines and others.

Political economy was no longer necessarily (or normatively) in teleological bondage to classical/neoclassical economics. It chose new narrative trajectories. Without escaping finalist pressures, a number of researchers have placed political economy at the center of the study of the causes of the French Revolution. I have pressed for its place in a framework that pays as much attention to the construction of what we call the Old Regime as to its unraveling. Excellent scholarship has begun to show how deeply political economy pervaded, and was penetrated by, philosophy, science, religion, morality, fiction (including theater), journalism and writings on public administration. An international or global perspective has given the inquiry into political economy purchase in areas heretofore neglected, concerning colonization, war and commerce. I insist on the notion of the Economic Enlightenment to place into relief the manner in which economic concerns, *sensu lato*, permeated every aspect of this extraordinarily rich and diverse enterprise of critical thinking and interrogation of all the legacies. In this chapter, I look at *some* of the most interesting work that has appeared in recent years, once again with an emphasis on the ways it has intersected with the preoccupations of *Bread, Politics* and *Political Economy*.

Physiocrats and Policy

There are many reasons to praise John Shovlin's brisk and insightful *The Political Economy of Virtue: Luxury, Patriotism and the Origins of the French Revolution* (Ithaca, 2006); others have acquitted themselves smartly of this task.[1] While saluting his achievement, I shall focus on what is more fruitful for my purposes: the issues on which our interests intersect and on which we often differ, sometimes deeply. Like John Shovlin, I contest historians who conflate the history of eighteenth-century French political economy with physiocracy (3). For years, I have argued for according a central place in the Enlightenment to economic and political economic thought, and I have construed the Economic Enlightenment as encompassing a far broader spectrum of research and reflection than the physiocratic "sect," as their critics scornfully stigmatized them. Yet I think Shovlin opts for a doubly partial explanation of their ostensible hegemony by imputing it to a remarkable talent for self-promotion (they certainly knew how to occupy the symbolic and discursive space: after all, they appropriated as part of their franchise the very word *économiste*) and to the place they have wrenched in the "teleological" approach to a history of economic thought. He leaves out what, for me, matters most:

1 John Shovlin, *The Political Economy of Virtue: Luxury, Patriotism and the Origins of the French Revolution* (Ithaca, NY: Cornell University Press, 2006).

that the physiocrats were the only "school" that exercised a direct (and, in this instance, a profound) impact on policy.[2]

They did not take power, to be sure; but for almost a decade, they influenced decisively the way the government exercised power in a domain of enormous sensitivity and significance, and they shaped the manner in which the prince recast the very notion of kingship. Obviously, I cannot rehearse in a paragraph the case I make in *Bread, Politics*; and I do not impute to the physiocrats direct responsibility for liberalization and the dire crisis in which it resulted. Shovlin strains to show that neither of the liberalizing ministers of 1763 and 1764, Bertin and L'Averdy, was close to the *économistes*. This question seems to me to be of little importance in a ministry whose widely acknowledged leading player, Choiseul, was warmly and firmly disposed to liberalization and several of whose most influential intendants of commerce and finance and bureau chiefs—the subministerial staff of continuity and execution—were personally and intellectually close to the Gournay and/or Quesnay chapels. An avid reader of Herbert and Mirabeau, amateur agronomist and promoter of agricultural sociability and information, Bertin understood the grain question technically and commercially as well as politically. Equally telling, L'Averdy, who had to face the grave difficulties that the convergence of protracted dearth and dislocating liberalization engendered, demonstrated time and again an intransigence on the implementation of the liberal laws that one could have characterized as physiocratic in spirit—to the extent that Quesnay's school or sect (as one prefers) incarnated the liberal cause in the eyes of observers of public policy and even in the eyes of the sort of people whom Shovlin calls "ordinary" (see, for instance, 117)[3], if one is to believe Mirabeau's famously narcissistic anecdote about the risk of lapidation in the Rouen streets at the end of the 1760s for evoking name of the *économistes*.[4] In any event, patronage,

2 The Gournayians enjoyed a longer-established and more diffuse influence. On the grain issue specifically, certain of them staked out positions very close to the Quesnayians, though Forbonnais, a major and early critic of the *économistes*, entertained a rather different conception of liberty and certainly did not share the desire to move beyond the new departure staked out in the legislation of 1763–64.

3 Cf. the "ordinary members" of the reading public (142), as well as the "ordinary French elites" (5, 11) and the "ordinary people" who are said to play an increasingly significant role in the fashion regime (32n). Presumably personal shorthand, the notion seems imperceptibly to acquire an enigmatic normative charge. There is an occasional appearance of a disembodied public opinion, an even more formless entity. So, for example, how "the public viewed" the financial crisis in 1787 as "the fruit of the malign league" linking court, finance and monarchy (155); or how "the public was rightly skeptical" when the monarchy again proclaimed its commitment to regeneration in 1787 (9).

4 "I will never forget my initial surprise that the secret of getting stoned in the streets of the city of Rouen was to claim to be one of my followers," wrote Mirabeau, who

on which Shovlin insists, is much less well known and much less significant than policy, to which he pays less heed (81–82, 103–5).[5]

The problematic of the 1760s in the domain of political economy is not the "overly cozy relationship" that the *économistes*—there was no other readily identifiable group in the arena—may or may not have enjoyed with the government or some of its members. Rather, it was (primarily) the referential field in which the ministry located itself intellectually and ideologically as it embarked on a drastically new and iconoclastic governing strategy and (secondarily) how the fractions of the administration and the public capable of articulating and transmitting a point of view perceived the rupture and its consequences. On the first point, Shovlin, an elegant relativist, writes that "the Physiocrats were only one voice among many calling for the liberalization of the grain trade" (103–4). After devoting 70 printed pages to the study of the complex origins of liberalization and the multiple lineages and (sometimes rival) currents of the liberty lobby, in *Bread, Politics*, I regard his statement as literally or superficially correct. Politically and culturally, however—emblematically, Shovlin might say—I believe it is mistaken. Given its

protested that he had always been "loved by the people, showered with marks of well-earned affection." Banal élan of self-aggrandizing vanity or plausible evidence (in the postphysiocratic sense) that certain sectors of the people are familiar with the players, if not with the specifics of the doctrines, in the Great Grain Debates? On the basis of this somewhat manic testimony, I remain skeptical, albeit intrigued. "Discours de Mirabeau à la rentrée des assemblées économiques pour l'hiver 1776–77," in G. Weulersse, *Les manuscrits économiques de François Quesnay et du marquis de Mirabeau aux archives nationales* (Paris: Geuthner, 1910), 132. With the same blend of theatrical self-absorption and acute ethnographic insight, see his letter to Carl Friedrich, 21 Oct. 1770: "… the mischief is so zealous, so deft, so efficacious that there are provinces where all the people believe that the *économistes* are a sect of monopolists of which I am the chief." In *Carl Friedrichs von Baden Brieflicher Verkehr mit Mirabeau und Dupont*, ed. C. Knies, vol. 1 (Heidelberg: C. Winter, 1892), 45.

5 First, we know very little about the intersecting lines of patronage, the tensions within clientelism, and the discontinuities as well as the affinities between different sorts of patronage networks (kinship, social, intellectual, ideological, political, military, court, city, geographical, academic, religious, sexual, financial and so on). We lack a good study of Choiseul, a major figure in all the dispositions and connections in court, city and government; G. Chaussinand-Nogaret, *Choiseul (1719–1785): naissance de la gauche* (Paris: Perrin, 1998), cited by Shovlin, and discussed above, is lightweight, and often erroneous and misleading. It would be very wrong to belittle the influence, say, of the marquise de Pompadour both in the royal council and in the court and the royal apartments, yet no one can map it out and weigh its various vectors. Nevertheless, it seems to me incumbent upon the historian to make distinctions concerning the relative importance of the causes that she nourished. See Robert Muchembled, *Mystérieuse Madame de Pompadour* (Paris: Fayard, 2014).

intellectual vitality, its organizational energy, its indefatigable propaganda, a polemical trenchancy and urgency capable of overcoming, at least occasionally, the proclivity for bombast, scientism and obscurity and its singular appetite to convince and to conquer, physiocracy was unequivocally *primus* in this theater, and not *inter pares*.[6] And it was no accident that, when parlementaires and other high magistrates as well as the minor judges, police officials, procurators or subdelegates of the local administration wanted to attribute moral paternity to, and stigmatize, the chaos of the late 1760s, they referred to the "modern philosophers," the "economic philosophers" or the "économistes," all of which signified physiocrats, the members of Quesnay's group/movement.[7] Whether or not it was largely a matter of public relations—what the French today call "com"—the physiocrats successfully represented themselves as the chief bearers of the liberal torch.

How far is one willing to go in the argument concerning physiocratic clientelism? In a brilliant and intriguing article, Michel Antoine shows both the interest and the perils of "reading" meaning into patronage connections, in this instance, the close link between Quesnay and his follower La Chalotais, arch-liberal, educational reformer, perhaps the Doctor's choice for controller-general and the key figure in the Brittany affair that so aroused the king's ire. What does one make of physiocracy in this can of worms? Antoine, "En marge ou au coeur de 'l'affaire de Bretagne'? Intrigues et cabales de M. de la Chalotais," *Bibliothèque de l'Ecole des Chartes*, 128 (July–Dec. 1970): 369–408. Shovlin alleges that L'Averdy withdrew the *Journal de l'agriculture* from Dupont's hands—we don't know exactly why and in what conditions he left—and uses this information to argue for the controller-general's distance from physiocracy since henceforth the *Journal* "took an anti-Physiocratic line." Yet this anti-physiocracy, choreographed by Forbonnais, never challenged the liberal grain policy with which physiocracy was widely linked and never accepted the premise that physiocracy was a doctrinal whole, a monolith to take or to leave (104). What does one make of a gifted writer and bulimic place-seeker such as the abbé Morellet, who ate at all the tables (at several "râteliers," as Beaumarchais has Bridoison say).

6 In the same vein, it seems wholly incorrect to me to profess that the physiocrats "*began* [my emphasis] to play an important role as propagandists for the official policy on the grain trade" with the advent to the contrôle-général at the end of 1768 of Maynon d'Invau[lt], known to have closer ties to the *économistes* than his predecessors. They had written much earlier in the periodical literature, even before Dupont took over the *Journal de l'agriculture* in 1765, they had published tracts, they had ghost-written texts for the liberal parlements, three of which remained fervently committed to their program till the end, and tirelessly demanded a more uncompromising liberal line. (It thus makes no sense to affirm sweepingly that "Physiocracy enjoyed a certain official favor during this period primarily because the Physiocrats were willing to battle the parlements in defense of the official policy" (104). Cf., below, L. Charles' case for the primacy of Gournay's influence.

7 It is, of course, doubtful that the magistrates—with some exceptions—were easily able to distinguish among the dissident heirs of Gournay (Abeille, Turgot and Morellet), their more orthodox comrades (Forbonnais, Plumard and Butel-Dumont) and the Quesnay clan, very often in close alliance with the dissenting followers of Gournay.

Sweeping Transformations or Modest Solutions?

Of course, it makes tactical sense to deprecate the role of the hard-core liberal theorists and activists if you wish to depreciate the signature achievement with which they were commonly associated, and with which they themselves identified, at least until it began to fall apart. There was a palette of reforms competing for government attention in the 1760s. I agree with Shovlin on the obvious: "The royal administration did not look with equal favor on all schemes for economic reform." I challenge his assertion, however, that "those that required sweeping transformations were rejected, while more modest solutions were embraced enthusiastically" (82). The decision to pass the legislation of 1763–64 was hardly a "moderate" initiative (82). I consider liberalization to be the most radical reform enterprise before the Revolution, a stunning break with the past, a drastic "new deal." The implications—political, social moral, symbolic and perhaps also economic—were of seismic order.[8] Without fully satisfying the physiocratic program in the domain of the grain trade, which touched directly upon the main wellspring of national wealth, the main source of calories of the vast majority of consumers, and the main organizing principle of the sociopolitical order (at the broadest level, the articulation of relations between state and society, prince and people; at the most focused level, the forging of the everyday order), liberalization bore the clear marks of the physiocratic diagnosis and of certain aspects of the physiocratic ambition.[9] It is in this sense that I cannot agree that "the Physiocratic call for free trade in grain was commonplace" (112).[10]

Another incentive that might have reinforced the author's relative indifference to the grand mutation of the 1760s has to do with his long-term fixation on the Revolution and its gestational etiology. For what's the point in taking reform seriously when it depended upon a government crippled by " a stultifying prudence and conservatism," qualities (or defects) that

8 I agree that "the Physiocrats offered a comprehensive critique of all the political economic arrangements sponsored by the monarchy," but I reject the suggestion that the decision to privilege grain reform was a sort of second choice, *faute de mieux*: it was the inexorable point of departure for all the rest, the *sine qua non* (82).

9 Here I am talking about what Shovlin nimbly calls the religion rather than the theology of physiocracy. See his incisive review of Liana Vardi, *The Physiocrats and the World of the Enlightenment* (Cambridge: Cambridge University Press, 2012), in the *American Historical Review* 117 (June 2012): 941–42.

10 I have no idea, historiographically or epistemologically, what Shovlin means when he avers that "Physiocracy offers a window onto some of the central problems" that political economic writers confronted, but that "it should not be viewed as a *typical* response to those problems" (112, my emphasis). I evince the same sort of uneasiness when the author introduces the concept of "French national character" (131).

in fact encountered robust resistance in many ministries and bureaus from mid-century onward and that I am more disposed to associate collectively with Shovlin's "middling elites" (90). Apart from farming, "patriotic" political economy appeared to be in any event a largely indoor activity: as it is construed here, it seems little attracted to the marketplaces as sites of exchange and regulation, to the ateliers and boutiques as sites of production and commerce or to the streets, another ubiquitous site of popular culture.

Sublimating "interest" and the rehabilitated egocentricity that drives much of the pragmatically oriented political economy argument, the patriotic discourse—happily "modular" to accommodate pluralism if not contradiction—seems to take little stock in the way merchants and *négociants* thought about the framing issues of or for a science of commerce. If the graft upon the Gournay group of a powerful allergy to luxury is generally convincing, it would be worthwhile noting other arguments about motivation and commercial engagement that attenuate or nuance the antipathy for luxury, even in the acerbic appreciation of Plumard de Dangeul (44–48).[11] Nor am I sure that Delamare, the great police codifier, the international businessman Montaudouin, a Gournayite, the public servant and sometime trader Le Trosne, a physiocrat, or Necker, banker, merchant and antiphysiocrat, would have differed on the salience of interest as the paramount incentive for exchange and in some cases as its gyroscope.

Decentering Physiocracy and Socioeconomic Reality?

The historian further marginalizes the voice of the *économistes* by favoring the "critique of Physiocracy" that targets its putative tolerance for (or promotion of) plutocracy and embrace of values that distanced the group "from a more civic, or patriotic, rhetoric" (113). This focus wholly obscures the massive assault on physiocracy as a dangerous, even toxic political economy, estranged from or indifferent to what Shovlin might call "ordinary" realities, an ominous threat to social cohesion and political stability. It is revealing to me that Galiani and Diderot, two of the major bearers of this scathing critique of physiocracy, do not appear in the index of Shovlin's book, and a third, Necker, is treated with considerable nuance (and ambivalence) in a way that still distorts his role. Shovlin emphasizes his tie with an apology for luxury and his indifference to agriculture rather than his extreme sensitivity to social strife (very close to what we might call class struggle), his search for a sort of third way in the regulation of the grain trade and the textile industry and the refoundation

11 See Plumard's *Remarques sur les avantages et les désavantages de la France et de la Gr. Bretagne par rapport au commerce et autres sources de la puissance des États* (Leiden, 1754).

of the guilds (in the context of his broader reflection on the system of social classification) (142–50).

Shovlin's reading of (French, pre-Revolutionary) political economy in primordially moralistic terms requires a decentering of the *économistes*. His textual approach reinforces this inclination. If he had evinced more concern for the brutal realities that buffeted the bulk of French women and men in the 1760s and early 1770s, and shook the ministry, he might have been less disposed to regard the grain-and-liberty obsessed physiocrats as stark high-decibel participants in "the din of public debate on economic questions."[12] The author is interested in the trope of a "disordered" France, but not in the disorders that jolted France in the 1760s and 1770s. This incongruity—from my perspective—thrusts into relief for me an epistemological problem that seems latent throughout much of the book. Put bluntly, does discourse precede practice? Does it obviate it as an object of investigation? Is discourse, in some sense, self-sufficient and autonomous in its linguistic cocoon? Does it construct reality, independent of what I would call the social conditions of production? Cast in moral/moralizing/ moralistic terms, can political economy exist in quasi-nonreferential terms? Does it require an economy—what Shovlin occasionally refers to as the "real economy"—and a society in order to exist and shape behavior? (9, 12). Does the efflorescence of an "imaginary" (12)—a crucial conceptual tool for the author—shelter one from the asperities of social and economic reality as well as policy?

Interest(s), Language and Sundry Elites

The historian cedes to a demure postmodern temptation, for instance, in his somewhat fraught discussion of the hostility of his "middling elites" to luxury. He assures us that he did "not mean to imply that the critique [of luxury] simply articulated or expressed interests that had an entirely separate, pre-existing reality." He goes on to explain how the language of antipathy helped to create—"to bring into being"— those interests and to organize them in a way capable of imparting meaning, in this instance, militating against the

12 The social mobilizes him only at the point at which he wishes to make claims for the causes of the French Revolution. And even at this juncture, the pamphlet-driven "climate of ideas" that led to elite alienation enjoys an unproblematized ontological priority over preoccupations and perhaps even ideas that roiled large parts of the nonelite population whose cognitive functions cannot be reduced metaphorically or metonymically to a hail storm (manifestation of another kind of climate that counted) or a bread price (not a pamphlet, yet another kind of text whose conditions of production are of both a symbolic and a material order) (152–53).

crystallization of "class consciousness" that would have cast the "middling provincial elite" as "a single, unified class." Without subscribing to the Stedman Jones doctrine,[13] I am one of numerous social historians who have learned from cultural history over the years: I have no foundational quarrel with Shovlin's approach, but rather with the cursory manner in which he attempts to account for interests (largely) in terms of language. The argument for the widespread hostility to luxury would have been more cogent had he mapped out the play between language, ethos and interest(s) in several concrete, probing case studies (43).

Such a demarche might have fostered, or required, a more robust study of the reception of the scores of pamphlets that he examines. We don't really know how they were read; or, rather, the historian offers readings that he imputes, without the administration of proof, to a vast number of actors comprising a diffuse, murky and elusive category that he variously baptizes "ordinary elites" (5, 11), "middling elites" (8, 16, 38, 219), "broad middling sections of the elites" (9), "sections of the French elite" (9), "middling nobles" (9, 120, 153), "provincial elite" (25–26), and "provincial nobility" (67, 68). How does one measure the dissemination of these texts, their impact and the responses they elicited? Even if we were to obtain a sharper sense of who these readers/actors are, how do we learn whether they really shared the same values (and interests: all provincial nobles do not behave according to the Toulouse prescription[14]), and whether they all wanted the same outcomes? How do we determine whether such and such writer or actor—political economist, moralist, seigneur and so on—was representative of the group with which the historian connects him?

Neutering Market Exchange and Casting Economic Activity as Patriotic

The question of representativity, and the administration of proof, are not matters of pedantry: they go to the core of Shovlin's project. Though the dogged use of the passive voice blurs causality and agency throughout the

13 My shorthand for an argument privileging the discursive, anterior to the social, closely linked with G. Stedman Jones, *Languages of Class: Studies in English Working Class History, 1832–1982* (Cambridge: Cambridge University Press, 1983). For interesting parallels and discordances, see G. Eley, *A Crooked Line: From Cultural History to the History of Society* (Ann Arbor: University of Michigan Press, 2005).

14 My reference is to the study by Robert Forster—paradigmatic a half-century ago, today contested or highly nuanced in numerous other provinces—*The Nobility of Toulouse in the Eighteenth Century: A Social and Economic Study* (Baltimore, MD: Johns Hopkins University Press, 1960).

book, he states a part of his thesis as follows: "Through the political economic debates that played out in the public sphere, economic activity was remade as a quasi-patriotic pursuit, and economic agents—farmers, merchants, and manufacturers—came to be seen as potentially capable of civic engagement in a way they had not been before." Leave aside the question of whether this "economic activity" unfolds in the "imaginary" or in the field, what the polysemous notion "patriotic" denotes here, who performs the "remaking" and who carries out the "seeing." The "ordinary elites "were more willing to view this work or economic activity as patriotic if it seemed "vital to the national well-being." Shovlin's most imposing claim here turns on a sort of neutering or neutralizing of "market exchange," not a central lever in "beneficent" social life: "Instead, economic activity was recast as patriotic through the virtual elision of the profit motive" (12; see also 61–62, 81–82). The memory of Mandeville (curiously absent from this book) is implicitly purged, the various registers of Jansenist influence are ignored and even scholastic economics seems out of place in the intellectual lineage that leads to the stigmatization of self-interest and profit, perpetual sources of moral malaise and geysers of economic growth. I find the following statement highly contentious and never substantiated in this study: "Although *some* [my emphasis] partisans of commerce sought to represent the profit motive itself in positive terms, *more commonly* [my emphasis] champions of trade elided the egotistic dimension of economic behavior and represented merchants, farmers and entrepreneurs as driven by the desire for honor" (7).

Shovlin readily admits that "an alternative tradition" affirmed itself in the eighteenth century, privileging interest and individualism as the motors of an economy represented as an "auto-regulatory mechanism governed by the laws of the market." He maintains that such views, which he assimilates tendentiously to a liberal posture, though many of the leading anti-physiocrats shared its assumptions, "enjoyed *some traction* [my emphasis] in the old regime." I believe that he fails to marshal proof for his far-reaching lesson that relegates "such approaches" to the fringes of the "economic imaginary" (12).[15] Nor do I think that he shows that the prevailing representation of farming, trade and industry in the 1760s and 1770s was as "fields for the pursuit of honor *as much as* [my emphasis] arenas for the accumulation of profit" or that "the need to use honor to animate economic activity, including commerce," was as "widespread" a discourse as he asserts (129; see also 7, 65).

15 Cf.: "I suggest, however, that Morellet and the Physiocrats were exceptional in this respect [being 'quite well disposed toward interest']. Interest largely retained its negative associations" (128).

Boilerplate Patriotism and Alternate Reality

Even as the "science of commerce" and the "new science" seem to be less peripheral in the field of political economy than Shovlin suggests, so the concern with virtue, morality and patriotism appears to me to be embedded in a great many of their texts. They do not define political economy; the practice of (an enlightened, scientific) political economy assures their prosperity. The physiocratic contention that morality is, like everything else, subject to physical law does not mean that it loses purchase on behavior: the respect of natural law guarantees deference to it. Unless it is relentlessly problematized, however, "patriotism" risks the taint of the boilerplate. Who did not profess patriotism in the eighteenth century, and not just in the embryonic arena(s) of political economy? Vauban, Boisguilbert, Melon, then the Gournay circle and the *économiste* school styled themselves proudly as patriots, in some cases with an air of nebulous narcissism, in many others with a fervent conviction that this value of devotion to the commonweal, to the general interest and/or to the royal and national causes was a moral imperative.

In any event, the patriotism of 1700 was not the patriotism of the magistrates resisting Maupeou or of the early revolutionaries (just as the patriotism of the affiliates of the Point central des arts et métiers had little in common with Le Chapelier's version[16]) (153). The patriotic sense of work in the reconstituted agricultural academies of which Parmentier was a paragon had a different signification than when Abeille ran the Breton society three decades earlier (209, 213). I recently spent several days in the Musée Arbaud (Aix-en-Provence) reading the correspondence of the Mirabeau brothers who convey the impression of engaging in a bidding war over the relative intensity of each other's patriotic engagement.[17] Honor and virtue are also chronic leitmotifs in their exchanges, where self-interest, in the context of an underlying harmony, seems only to reinforce their foothold. In theoretical terms, economic activity found expression as "a quasi-patriotic pursuit" long before Shovlin imagines (11). And it never appears to have been as fretful about hard political economic issues as one might infer from *The Political Economy of Virtue*. Its author seems snared in a web of textuality that cannot be reduced to a mere reflection of the times (this would represent an epistemological regression to the days of a narrow-minded, hegemonic social history). Nor can one comfortably watch as the key terms of the study become imperceptibly reified into a kind of (alternate) reality whose grasp moves beyond discourse

16 See Kaplan, *La Fin des corporations* (Paris: Fayard, 2001), chaps. 13–15.

17 Just as there were several inflections of Jansensist patriotism, a Gournayian patriotism, itself subject to differentiation and so on.

to claim the central space of political deep play. The fact that the Revolution is the terminus confers a sort of unearned increment of coherence upon the analytical itinerary: we have come full circle, the *boucle* is *bouclée*.

Liberty

In the forefront of the lively "new" school of American scholars of eighteenth-century political economy, John Shovlin makes a major contribution because he raises highly important issues in a thoughtful way, rendered more compelling by a particularly graceful prose. While I am skeptical of many of his predicates and conclusions because I do not think that he has made the case, I find them nonetheless extremely stimulating. I will end by raising a final issue concerning his reading of the political economy of the Economic Enlightenment: the relative absence on his radar of the question of liberty that strikes me as the single most exhilarating, exalting and pregnant theme of the century. It is present in scores of books and hundreds of pamphlets and periodical articles. For numerous partisans of Enlightenment combats—not just those concerning political economy—liberty is the structuring aspiration of the *grand soir* of which they dream: freedom from oppression and arbitrary dominion, the affirmation of human dignity and basic rights, the prospect of self-fulfillment and individual autonomy, the opportunity to undertake initiatives and to create without constraint, the license to forge one's own place and identity, the chance to become rich as well as socially successful and so on.

Intoxicating for a whole range of actors in myriad spheres of life and activity, this vision was stressful, frightening and even apocalyptic for many others. It was possible, intellectually, to espouse one sort of liberty, and reject the others, though there was a burgeoning suspicion that, once out of the bottle, the genie could not be readily segmented or compartmentalized. In any case, I would argue that liberty, in its specifics and in its generality, constitutes a central part of the debate. Shovlin's focus on Cato the Younger and Cincinnatus rather than on Prometheus presumably reflects the preferences of the clients and protagonists of the political economy he showcases, the middling elites, who are *partout et nulle part*. In the absence of a sociology of recruitment and reception, I risk the following: this seems to be a political economy for the conservative and the anxious, preoccupied with order, imbued with a vivid consciousness of original sin (which did not prevent the Sires de Gouberville of the provincial nobility from enjoying life[18]), worried about loss of status, fearful of corruption, suspicious of change, more galvanized by the costs

18 See Madeleine Foisil, *Le Sire de Gouberville* (Paris: Aubier, 1981).

than the benefits of economic growth, even if it served ostensibly patriotic ends, more comfortable with the rigidities and solidarities of the traditional corporate milieu than with the unchartered perspectives of a free-wheeling universe where talent, money and luck generally prevail over birth, virtue and honor. The patriotic culture of the middling elites had much in common, not intellectually but psychologically and emotionally, with the moral economy of "ordinary" consumers.

A Commercial Revolution, Policy Making and Policy Mediocrity

In his splendid book, *Revolutionary Commerce: Globalization and the French Monarchy*, Paul Cheney, like John Shovlin, seeks to renew or refound (one hesitates to say regenerate in a work that deals with the Revolution) the history of economic thought.[19] His "globalizing" vantage point, his epistemological assumptions and his historiographical tastes, however, are quite different[20], and lead him frequently to a discrepant view of the ways in which economic thinking inflected the theory and the practice of power and governance and the processes of sociocultural production and reproduction, on the broadest plane, and the manner in which "commerce"—understood here in multiple senses—shaped the imagining and the writing of political economy, on a more focused register. In the paragraphs that follow, I will not pursue the comparison between these two studies, but once again comment on issues that kindle my interest or speak to my scholarly concerns. I like Cheney's cheek and his self-confident style, all the more so because they never dispense him from the obligations of argument and demonstration. In the wake of the vanishing of the agricultural and demographic revolutions (as J. Chirac might have put it, *elles ont fait pschitt*), the Chicago historian proposes that the Commercial Revolution take its place right next to the French Revolution; and I believe that he takes the full measure of the locution "Revolution" in the first instance as well as the second.

Confronted with a "Commercial Revolution" whose impact and implications they did not fully fathom, decision makers impressed Cheney neither with their percipience nor their tenacity. Less interested than Shovlin in trying to work out the specific connections between economic

19 *Revolutionary Commerce: Globalization and the French Monarchy* (Cambridge, MA: Harvard University Press, 2010).

20 Cheney's work reminds me in certain ways of Sophus Reinert's masterful *Translating Empire: Emulation and the Origins of Political Economy* (Cambridge, MA: Harvard University Press, 2011).

thought and politics, but convinced that ideas shape outcomes, he postulates an overdrawn and excessively rigid intellectual dualism that characterized the three decades before the French Revolution ("alternating between two incompatible understandings of the way forward")[21] and he is rather cavalier with policy makers, taxed with hesitancy and irresolution (6). On the latter subject, the prior question must be posed: how is policy made? In particular, how is it made once the age of political economy begins to be felt with increasing acuity in the governing spheres (and among Shovlin's various elites)?

Clearly, it is never a neat affair; I'm skeptical of the utility (or the accuracy) of describing the overall business of governing as "enlightened despotism" (5, 6). As for 30 years of policy dithering, this characterization evacuates the very notion of politics and implicitly diminishes the complexity of forging ideas-based policy. It is a bit like using a 10-year moving average to identify a severe but fugitive subsistence crisis. Viewed strictly from the perspective of 1789, it is reasonable to conclude that nothing really durable had been achieved since the 1760s. Viewed from 1763–64, however, and even more so from 1765–68, the action of the government to introduce the radical break of liberalization and implement it vigorously seems stunningly decisive, despite certain concessions that the ministry felt obliged to make in the legislation that, nevertheless, changed the very nature of monarchical representation at the summit and administrative practice at the grassroots. The first liberalization required not only immense audacity but also a delicate sort of policy feng shui that I do not think is reducible to dilly-dallying.

The originality of Cheney's enterprise resides above all in its will to defamiliarize, to insist on the primacy of the global and on the ways in which the colonial question and the Atlantic economies profoundly change the agenda (12, 18–20, *passim*). Still, apart from occasional references to the "domestic market," usually in regard to agricultural production (25, 164), and a fleeting allusion here and there to vain pre-Revolutionary efforts to modify policy, I wonder whether he does not cut himself off too sharply from metropolitan preoccupations, circa 1760–89: policy and politics, domestic economic issues (to the extent they could be sheltered from Atlantic effects), the construction of the everyday order, social cohesion, political stability and so on.[22]

21 Figured, for example, by Turgot and Necker, this Manichaeism, in my view, cannot be sustained.

22 Cheney seems to make my case, at least obliquely, in his critique of the revisionist focus on the continuity of a certain political culture (from absolutist to Jacobin theories of sovereignty): "Although undoubtedly a political failure of grand proportions, the collapse of the constitutional monarchy in fact had roots in contrasting social visions that were developed in France over the course of the preceding century in response to *les progrès*

From the Global to the Social

While Cheney is catholic in his historiographical affinities, in the spectrum of intellectual history, he veers more toward R. Chartier than K. M. Baker. He is keenly interested in the social; he looks for it in reading the texts of his protagonists—Montesquieu, Barnave and even the physiocrats. (He would have found even more matter to ponder in the "lesser" writers in the realm of political economy, morality and policy.) Social structure conditions commerce, both its practice and the ways of thinking about it; and the latter, in a subtle and sometimes more overt manner, shapes the taxonomical system and the struggle for social classification. Cheney lays his cards out at the start: "This book is an extended case for the proposition that the study of the economic thought of the Enlightenment, if approached in the correct way,[23] should retain priority for those who are interested in the relationship between ideas and social change during the long eighteenth century" (20). In the first half of the century, "the French" developed a "science of commerce, the central focus of which was reconciling a new political order founded upon commerce with the peculiarities of French government, social structure and customs" (3–4).

The author points to this Montesquieuian vocation on occasion in connection with the notion of "constitution," among whose components he identifies the social organization (25, 50, 61). He maintains that "social structure" was the long-term determinant of prosperity, though his voice here is conflated with those of Barnave and other commentators on the colonial question in the early Revolution (213).[24] Implicitly, in addressing the big question of the relation between state formation and capitalist development, subjecting the notion and exercise of absolutism to scrutiny, and arguing for the transformative impact of (early) globalization, he is casting into relief the structuring role of the social (13–16). He even uses the term/epithet/category "bourgeois" without any sense of hesitation or shame, somewhat unusual these days in the USA, though "revisionism," as it is called in Anglo-

---

du commerce" (196). The emphasis on commercial development, and its theorization, particularly in Montesquieu, who occupies almost by himself Cheney's pantheon, leads, via the dialectic of discourse/practice, to what may constitute a critique of Shovlin's accent on moral concerns: "Technical prowess and wealth [in relation to sea power, *sensu lato*] were beginning to count for more than the traditional virtues of courage and obedience" (59).

23 I don't quite know what to make of this "correct way," an uncharacteristic self-regarding norm.

24 Cf.: "Although the logic [apparently of the club Massiac, revolutionary association of French colonists residing in France] is strained, the goal is clear: some sort of compromise had to be found between the universal principles of the Revolution and the laws necessary to preserve the social structure in diverse corners of the empire" (217).

American historiographical idiom, is gradually undergoing revision (4, 7, 9, 103, 158). Generally sober in tone, Cheney cedes to a rush of optimism, perhaps, in avouching that "the science of commerce points the way out of the impasse created by the false dichotomy between 'social' and 'political' interpretations of the Revolution and its origins" (19).[25]

A Fuzzy Corporatism

I think that this integration of the social, as an object, a metaphor and an analytical prism, enriches and deepens Cheney's perspective, internally and externally, textually and contextually. I want to spar with him, however, on two points. Throughout, he treats Old-Regime France as a "fundamentally corporate society" without ever fully unpacking this rich and complex notion, not only a salient theme for Montesquieu, the subject of some of Cheney's most penetrating and luminous commentary, but also a way to fathom how French society worked (in many instances) and how various components represented themselves (176). The corporate organization was not simply a system for facilitating royal extractive practices (loans, venality) and administration (devolution of governing and judicial tasks to various elites). The corporate structure was a quasi-global stratifying apparatus that not only conferred identity and station and fixed (never wholly immutable) hierarchical arrangements, but also assured access to the king or denied it if one stood outside the "chain" that Advocate-General Séguier made famous in several of his parlementary interventions.[26] The corporate model, from the Sunday meetings of the village assemblies and the tentacular mobilization of guilds (in recruitment, in assembly, in procession, in prayer and in mourning, in struggles in the labor market, in intra- and inter-community strife and so on), to the functioning of academies, universities and a host of "companies" exercising

25 I read Cheney's brisk critique of the Cambridge School approach as a plea for the social and for "practices" (in the sense of so-called French theory: Bourdieu, de Certeau and Foucault) (11). I note his intuition that "by temporarily laying aside political economy in favor of the science of commerce," the social thought of the period will take on a very different visage. But he commits, in my view, to a sociocultural investigation even more decisively by qualifying his demarche immediately as an attempt to articulate an intellectual-history approach with research in economic history (with special attention to the rising economies of the Atlantic world), in the history of French absolutism and state formation, in the spatial organization of capitalist accumulation and in political thought during the Old Regime and the Revolution (13, 16, 18). All of these currents aliment my capacious notion of what the social comprises.

26 The chain consisted of rings representing (theoretically) each corps/corporation (or each genre) that lead eventually to the hands of the monarch. See, on Séguier's image/model and on the larger issue of corporate organization, Kaplan, *La Fin des corporations.*

various branches of public authority and to the existence of the three estates themselves (as grand social synecdoche and myth as well as manifestly dated and yet stubbornly operational taxonomy) constituted one way of integrating the social (in which space the economy played out) and the political.[27]

The Return of Feudalism

The second issue concerns the unexpected comeback of "feudalism" to which I have already alluded. It has prospered especially in the works of historians of economic ideas, one presumes, because they find it useful and perhaps also significant. On both these scores, I remain perplexed. Cheney uses the term time and again, to ends that remain obscure to me (1, 2, 4, 5, 16, 18, 60, 75, 78, 119, 139, 152–54, 156, 162, 193, 195, 199). Part of the problem arises from a lack of a clear and consistent definition. It is not, after all, a transparent notion with a historiographically consensual meaning. It has long been the object of controversy among medievalists and among modernists concerned with a whole range of political and social questions (feudalism as primarily about the fragmentation of political power or—conversely—about the gradual construction of the state, or about the defense of liberties and franchises against central or peripheral encroachments, or about the practice of war, or about the elaboration of land-based clientage systems, or about domination/subordination in a more comprehensive way, or about the exaction of dues of all sorts). Feudalism became an inherently polemical term during the Revolution when various camps instrumentalized it to serve their interests; and modernization theorists much later inherited and reappropriated the dispute to still other ends, for example, in the "transition" debates (from feudalism to capitalism), in which Marxist scholars figured prominently.

My reproach to Cheney is a lack of a clarifying archeology. He summons the word feudalism to do work that is, in fact, incumbent upon the historian to undertake. In his text, it assumes different intonations and inhabits different voices that are not always distinct, sometimes that of his protagonists, on other

27 Whereas Turgot seemed prepared to allow the equivalent of market forces in the social arena to take responsibility for the (constant) reconfiguring of the system of social classification, I believe that the physiocrats struggled much more with what they perceived as a veritable dilemma. Mirabeau, perhaps more than his brethren in the chapel, ulcerated over the question of stratification and ceded often to a historicity (not simply a genealogical conceit) that Cheney denies to the *économistes*. I am much less confident than he that, "for the sake of economic liberalism" [does this mean in order to attain economic liberalism or as a result of this liberalism?], the physiocrats were impatient to abolish "the whole system of orders, privileges and corps upon which monarchy rested" (5).

occasions his own. Often, feudalism appears to serve as a metaphor for all that is benighted, irrational, arbitrary, oppressive, grasping, devitalizing, corrupt/corrupting and obstructionist. It conveys these meanings in free-standing fashion, or as a kind of intensifier in complicity with other (putatively) negative forces such as corporatism or fiscalism or mercantilism. Or feudalism signifies a sort of imaginary that variously pollutes and misleads or persists sectorially in an obstinately perverse manner. Or it marks some sort of Rubicon, rhetorical, conceptual and/or chronological. Or it signals anomalous time lags, for example, an atemporal feudalism that functions as an arm of mass stigmatization (I'm thinking, for instance, of its association with "monopoly" or other distortions on the Whiggish road to laissez-faire).

If "feudalism," in its historicity or conceptually, is genuinely important to certain actors—Montesquieu or the physiocrats, for example—we need a more probing analysis of how they apprehend the notion and how it plays out in their history, their worldview, their vision for the future. If it is genuinely important for the historian as an analytical category, we need a sharper elucidation of its meaning(s). Cheney suggests a few, some highly suggestive, without developing them: "an intimately related set of social relations" (1); "arbitrary" government (4); a system structurally antagonistic to "the modern and commercial" (4); a particular articulation between absolutism and aristocracy (requiring some reflection on the ostensible paradox between a vigorously "absolutist state" that remains "irreducibly feudal") and between absolutism and agriculture (redolent of Galiani) (5); a symbiotic relationship between feudalism and corporate society (yet we know that urban corporate affirmation challenged feudal command) (5); the linkages between "fiscalism" (in the physiocratic sense, apparently an unequivocal expression of feudalism) and fiscality (implying state centralization and concentration that aims to annihilate feudal pretensions and assaults the so-called feudal vestiges) (153); the physiocratic amalgam (brilliantly, albeit too summarily, adumbrated by Cheney) of the idea of "feudal government," borrowed from Hume, that posits complex relationships (ever exacerbated across time) among colonial commerce, commercial privilege, extortionate fiscalism, among others, "which were compelled to work through the institutions and hierarchies of an ordered society" (156); and the "historical revisionism" of the physiocrats that demonstrates "the self-destruction of 'feudal government' in one of its most virulent form: the colonial–mercantile system" (162).

Physiocracy, Commerce and State Power

Physiocracy is important to Cheney in ways with which readers of its historiography, old and new, are not necessarily familiar. He reads and deploys parts of the doctrine with ingenuity and originality. I take issue with him on a number of points. In practical, if not theoretical, terms, the opposition of agriculture and commerce ("two opposed nations within the same territory") strikes me as hyperbolic (166). The regeneration of agriculture—the chief, immediate objective of liberalization—depends upon the drastic deregulation of internal trade, a total internal liberty being the first guarantee of the respect that nature's law requires for the inviolable right of property. It also depends upon the integration of the kingdom's trade into a national and then international market, through the play of exports (and imports), the guarantee of the *bon prix*, the "general price," the level of remuneration required to achieve sustained abundance and prosperity, via a durably enhanced investment and swelled net product. Though the doctrine of the *économistes* might disgrace trade as a sterile activity, it was crucially necessary. It was not a matter of merely tolerating it; they neither could do without it nor could they realistically farm it out to foreigners in acknowledgment of its inferior or sullied status.

This is the trade that formed the paramount issue not only of political economic debate in the 1760s, but also of policy debate and implementation, of political and social confrontation at multiple levels and of the crisis of the last years of that decade and the first years of the next. These matters do not bear directly on Cheney's problématique, but they invite nuance on the margin, even if he shifts attention to other questions and to a later period. It only makes sense, for example, to advance that "commerce thrived upon the monopolies, privileges and systems of exclusion that were anathema to the Physiocrats" if one presumes a regime of restriction, prohibition and police, as the *économistes* variously christened it; free trade—in the sense that the physiocrats espoused in the 1760s and that the monarchy largely embraced for a number of years—fundamentally alters the donnée. Moreover, the crisis and controversy of the late 1760s and early 1770s generated a robust and diverse anti-physiocratic current, absent in this book, not elided but quite reasonably relinquished. Still, when Cheney seeks a parallel voice to place against Barnave as he fulminates against the *économistes* as "fanatics, sectarians and enthusiasts," the logical candidate is not the mid-nineteenth century Tocqueville (who deserves a perpetual *rente* for the endless service he renders historians on both sides of the Atlantic), but Galiani, who used similarly scathing and evocative language to excoriate the physiocrats in 1770 ("fanatics," "Mississippians," "Jansenists," "suckers of hemorrhoidal veins" and so on) (233).[28]

---

28 See S. L. Kaplan, ed., *La Bagarre: Galiani's "Lost" Parody* (The Hague: Marinus Nijhoff, 1979); and my forthcoming piece entitled "Galiani: Grain and Governance," in S. L. Kaplan and Sophus Reinert, eds., *The Economic Turn: Recasting Political Economy in Eighteenth-Century Europe*, forthcoming. Besides Galiani, one could invoke Linguet, Grimm or perhaps even Forbonnais.

There is space only to enumerate in passing some other points of contention on physiocracy. Though I enjoy paradox and am sensitive to Derridian self-subversion, I am very dubious about the claim that the *économistes* theorized an "amplification of state power" (or "magnifi[cation] of the role of the state") or a muscular concept of enlightened despotism (164–65, 190). Legal despotism, the unfortunate denomination that Lemercier de la Rivière deployed to characterize the new liberal politics, envisaged extremely constrictive limits on the monarch's freedom of action, his ritualized claims of coproprietorship of the net product to the contrary notwithstanding. Positive law had to conform to natural law; "évidence" constrained what the king could do; indeed, it required him to abandon many of the attributes of traditional, paternalistic, interventionist kingship. Nature dictated politics; it did not preempt or obviate or sublimate them. I cannot follow Pierre Rosanvallon, endorsed by Cheney, who moves from the compelling idea of an allergy to history to its alleged corollary, the "negation of the political" (alternately put in a formula that I find doubly unfounded: "absolute despotism signals the possibility of an absolute extinction of politics") (147).[29]

The most vigorous recent argument for a physiocracy requiring robust state action is made by Bernard Herencia in his analytically suggestive, albeit somewhat strained, doctoral dissertation on Lemercier de la Rivière.[30] It is founded on what is tantamount to a theorization of the position that I have long advanced that liberalization requires a powerful, sustained dose of absolutism in order to clear away the oppressive structures of the interventionist state, precondition to the institutionalization of the laissez-faire regime; Turgot made the same point in the plausible but perhaps apocryphal demand for "six

29 See P. Rosanvallon, *Le Capitalisme utopique* (Paris: Seuil, 1979). I note in passing that the physiocrats did not, as Cheney sweepingly contends, "take sides against the parlements" (and their historicity) (148). They fostered excellent relations with the parlements and the parlementaires—legion—who initially supported the liberal cause warmly in 1763–64, and entertained quasi-intimate relations with the three parlements that passionately clung to the liberal cause even after the harrowing times at the end of the 1760s and the early 1770s. See my argument in *Bread, Politics*. Nor do I agree with the claim that Cheney imputes to the *économistes*, concerning the "primacy of subsistence arrangements as the foundation and purpose of all governments and the sacred nature of private property" (142; cf. 149: "subsistence legitimated property rights"). The physiocrats derive the sacred and sanctuarized character of property from natural law revealed by "évidence"; in practice, the right of property could prove to be inimical to subsistence arrangements, as became clear in the 1760s, and as Galiani, Mably, Linguet, Necker and Diderot all theorized.

30 Bernard Herencia, "Physiocratie et gouvernementalité: l'œuvre de Lemercier de la Rivière," doctorate in "sciences économiques," Université Paris Ouest Nanterre La Défense (2011), 285–86. Cf. Kaplan, "'Liberté sociale,' 'Economie sociale' et le Droit de Propriété comme l'Essence de l'Intérêt commun: Lemercier de la Rivière face au malaise de la Libéralisation," in *Raisonner sur les blés* (Paris: Fayard, forthcoming).

years of despotism to establish liberty" that Cheney recalls (147). Summoning Foucault for reinforcement of an ambivalent posture, Herencia envisages a state that, albeit tightly fettered by natural law, embodies nevertheless the "general interest." It is not sufficient to depict this state as "stimu[lating] economic activities for the benefit of everyone, including the monarch" by respecting natural law. That logic projects an excessively passive image of the state: "Political action relies, then, on the processes of the rationalization and the technical skill of the exercise of power, the very thing that Foucault identifies as governmentality."

Stretching a bit, I infer that rationalization and *technicité* refer to both the ground-clearing invoked above (given the capacity of the absolutist heritage to generate endless vestiges and debris even after absolutism itself in its traditional guise no longer exists) and to homeostatic and reproductive operations (taxation, public education, sanctions for violation of natural law and diverse housekeeping tasks). For me, this model issues in the shrinking and atrophying, if not the gradual withering away, of the state. Herencia does not resolve the question decisively or limpidly: "These processes must translate into a smaller State, that is a contraction of the [various] police and regulatory functions. If the question of the liberalization of the market is common to the whole physiocratic school, the specificity of Lemercier de la Rivière is to insist on the necessity of the rationalization of the governmental architecture by its disciplining," Foucault-speak for "its submission to the natural order." This is the "basis of the 'physiocratic governmentality'," writes Herencia, what he calls an instrument of a "legal-despotic regulation."

Herencia appears to hesitate: liberalizing (the economy) and rationalizing (the administration) do not necessarily result in "the diminution of state intervention." By this, however, he refers to the maintenance tasks that I mentioned above that require more government than the *économistes* were inclined to acknowledge—in particular the management of the single tax, the dissemination of education and information (which verges here on a state propaganda mission) and the operation of commerce which, in Herencia's interpretation, seems highly reminiscent of Old-Regime canon: a commerce open and free and at the same time relatively protected. In other words, as Turgot understood, it is harder for the state to disengage than the theorists imagine.

Herencia's Lemercier seems to require the state not only to secure property, the foundation of the common interest and the social bond, but also, continually, to do what the physiocrats initially hoped they could do once and for all at the beginning through the great rupture of liberalization: creating the "liberal framework allowing the shift to private initiative" in all the key spheres of economic and social activity (Herencia, 359–60). Herencia pushes the revisionist Lemercier quite far: the philosophe-administrator who embodied a certain physiocratic extremism becomes the safeguard against "an ultra-liberal conception of the Physiocrats." In other words, concludes this economist and historian of economic thought who obviously contests the vision of physiocracy as the negation of politics, "the natural order for Lemercier de la Riviere can only result from a constructivism of political power" (Herencia, 336).[31]

Economic Science as Political Rationality

Not surprisingly, politics is at the core of the recent thesis that political scientist Arnault Skornicki transformed into a book, at once perplexing and engaging, entitled *L'Economiste, la cour et la patrie.*[32] He argues vigorously against the putatively neutral or apolitical character of political economy. In any event, "it is not 'economic thought' per se that interested me," avers the author, "but its constitution as a central mode of political reason" of the eighteenth-century elites, Olympian and intermediary, central and peripheral (25). Or as he puts it later, "more autonomous vis-à-vis the economic sphere" and its pragmatic expression in textbooks on commerce or accounting, political economy "constituted a full-fledged branch of political thought" (60). Even applied to commerce, at the risk of a certain idealization, the "science of political economy" is none other than the science "of the public good" which "in no way sought to free itself from politics and morality" (103). The author takes the concept and category of politics for granted as an unproblematic given, a sort of pellucid classical canon. In the second half of the eighteenth century, "economic science" imposes itself as "a central form of political rationality," the latter notion, veritable leitmotiv, obstinately escaping a necessary definition and deconstruction (375).

At times the argument verges on a sort of political essentialism as science and politics are inextricably intertwined. Political economy cannot be seen as the rationalization of "class" interests seeking to overturn aristocratic

31 In a dissertation that mixes bursts of acumen with pockets of opacity, Alfred Steinauer comments on the shriveling of royal prerogatives demanded by the logic of natural law, on the one hand, and the desire to preserve certain regalian functions that Mirabeau, with notions of an ideal-type theocracy dancing in his head, enumerates as assuring abundance, repose (justice, order and moral behavior) and security (outward- rather than inward-looking), on the other hand. Alfred Steinhauer, "Le 'Parti' physiocratique et la formation de l'opinion publique dans la France pré-révolutionnaire (1756–1776)," doctoral thesis in political science, Université Paris I (1997), 259–62, 325. Late in his life, Mirabeau is still trying to reimagine the morphology of a monarchical-agrarian social order." Mirabeau to Butré, 8 Apr. 1779, in *Carl Friedrichs von Baden Brieflicher Verkehr mit Mirabeau und Dupont*, ed. Carl Knies, 1: 108.

32 *L'Economiste, la cour et la patrie. L'Economie politique dans la France des Lumières* (Paris: CNRS Editions, 2011).

domination—the very idea emits a folkloric perfume of yore—but a voice chanting for (and partly from within) the state, "a political discourse destined to perpetuate the absolute monarchy in tackling its internal problems" (29). The *économistes* can displace the stakes of political economy "in part against the political rationalizations" forged (brilliantly) by the Gournay circle, but they cannot and do not seek to delink economics from politics (146; cf. 374). Skornicki reads the "science of commerce" as unequivocally "a political science" (since commerce is the foundation of state power), "but it did not in the least pretend to say everything about politics." The "political and moral science" of the physiocrats was more ambitious, aspiring to cover public law, religion and myriad other domains through "a general theory of human action" (150). The representation of "the new science" as an apolitical enterprise strikes the author as incongruous. "Scientificized" physiocracy is nevertheless engaged on the political front concretely (against the politics of the court, the diplomats and the international traders) and theoretically (in response to the political philosophy of the Montesquieus and the Rousseaus as well as the parlements). "Economic government is politics considered from the economic point of view," professes the political scientist, adding more cryptically that it amounts less to a government of men than to "the administration of things," as if the two were neatly dissociable (262).[33]

Revisionist or Regnant?

Habitually, historians learn a great deal about themselves (their ethnocentric reflexes and blind spots) and their field when a scholar in a sister discipline expounds his point of view. There is much in this work that is fresh and, in a salutary sense, defamiliarizing. Skornicki induces us to think differently about staple questions, with a view toward moving beyond a strictly history-of-ideas

33 Rapidly, in passing, Skornicki evokes the exorcism of the political by contemporary scholars, such as economists like Jacques Sapir (since the eighteenth century, economics belongs to an antipolitical tradition) and historical sociologists such as P. Rosanvallon, in the wake of Tocqueville and Louis Dumont (framing the Economic Enlightenment as "warding off" politics). Instead of casting light upon this extremely interesting proposition on the "fiction of neutrality," Skornicki muddles it in a labored and bleary dialectic between embedding and disembedding (the disembedding of economic rationality being tantamount to its depoliticizaton; then, the resituating of "the manner in which political economy extricated itself from the cultural forms in which it was embedded" and the concomitant contextualizing of "the cultural and political signification of such a disembedding of market thinking [*la pensée de marché*]": another woolly notion that cries out for clarification) (11–13). On the articulation of things and people, there are insights in Bruno Latour, *Reassembling the Social: An Introduction to Actor Network Theory* (Oxford: Oxford University Press, 2005).

approach to the study of the Economic Enlightenment. At the same time, he presents as innovative or revisionist a good deal that is well known, even conventional. There is a general consensus that political economy was a state science, even if debate persists over its precise genealogy/trajectory (from political arithmetic through Colbertism, cameralism and so on), and that political and economic science converged during the Enlightenment in the direction of a more or less self-conscious social science (15–17). Scholarship of the last several decades has established that the police was less rigidly tropismatic in its regulatory behavior than had been generally assumed even as Colbertism was less Colbertist, if I can venture a shortcut, not only in its eighteenth-century life, but also during the time of the great minister. Yet it is wholly unfounded (and a mite quixotic) to imagine a continuity between, on the one hand, a supple/opportunistic Colbertism and a flexible and adaptable *police des grains*, for both of which regulation nevertheless remains the *structure structurante* and, on the other hand, what the author calls "liberalism" (79–80, 83).[34] The idea of a certain proximity between the *police des grains* and the "popular" moral economy is widely acknowledged, as is the role of the state in the formation of markets (28). Since the enormously influential work of Istvan Hont, amplified by his students, it is very hard to subscribe to a Hirschmanesque opposition between war and commerce (28–29, 44).[35] It is generally accepted that physiocrats (like most would-be reformers) were clients of, as well as counselors to, the ministry: it is a cliché to argue that they did not conquer by the (mere) effulgence of their ideas, but through an itinerary of patronage within a relation of subordination (296). No one would contest the primacy of the fiscal question for the state throughout the eighteenth century, even more acutely in the second half. And, given the work, in particular, of Roger Chartier over the past thirty-five years, no one requires the lesson that "the diffusion of ideas is never a passive 'reception,' but must be understood

34 See my arguments and cases in *Bread, Politics*; and Philippe Minard, *La Fortune de Colbert: Etat et industrie dans la France des Lumières* (Paris: Fayard, 1998). The text that Skornicki attributes to Sartine, lieutenant-general of police, was in fact written by the commissaire Lemaire (80). See Kaplan and Vincent Milliot, "La Police de Paris, une 'révolution permanente'? Du commissaire Lemaire au lieutenant de police Lenoir, les tribulations du *Mémoire sur l'administration de la police (1770–1792)*," in Brigitte Marin, ed., *La Police en Europe* (Rennes: Presses Universitaires de Rennes, 2009), 1–46. Skornicki needs to look much more closely at police attitudes toward what he calls the market, commerce, interest (and egocentricity) and so on.

35 I. Hont, *Jealousy of Trade: International Competition and the Nation-State in Historical Perspective* (Cambridge, MA: Harvard Universuty Press, 2005); and, for example, Sophus A. Reinert, *Translating Empire: Emulation and the Origins of Political Economy* (Cambridge, MA: Harvard University Press, 2011).

as an aggregate of *re-appropriations* governed by social usages capable of fashioning concepts quite differently…" (265).[36]

Airy

Quite often, the author posits, as a sort of all-purpose independent variable, an ethereal, yet hermetic, explanatory formula that invariably begs the historical question at hand. Thus, for instance, in regard to Gournay, "the current climate"—"l'air du temps"—was not unfavorable to alternative conceptions of competition (83). In relation to Quesnay, making his presence felt in the political economy arena, "l'air du temps" was no longer exclusively devoted to the science of commerce or the ennoblement of wholesale and international traders (167). Mirabeau came to write *l'Ami des hommes* in part because of a favorably disposed "air du temps" (169). This extraordinarily popular work contributed to fashion the agronomic "air du temps" so important to physiocracy, which profited from a parallel "bucolic mood of the moment" ("une humeur champêtre du temps") (275, 265). How can one account for the (relative yet surprising) success of physiocracy, notorious for "the inaccessibility of its language," in reaching beyond the learned milieu? Skornicki suggests that the "air du temps" facilitated this unlikely penetration (269). He insists on the propitious rendezvous between physiocracy's rural assets and the "air du temps" (270). Indeed, the physiocratic talent for associating rusticity and utilitarianism seemed to speak to the "air du temps" (270). Upon the ascension of Louis XVI, the "air du temps" favored Turgot's "consecration" (336). Borne by circular reasoning, the "air du temps" accounts for nothing; it cries out for explanation. This chronic failure to historicize probably fans the author's appetite for concepts; and the latter probably encourages the former.[37]

36 On the question of lesson-giving, I believe that Skornicki does himself a disservice in his merciless recourse to italics, which he deploys each time he believes that he has something especially important to say. Given the vigor of his intelligence, there is really no need for high-pressure sales tactics. Is this another sign of the conflation of voices that close reading sometimes elicits? Cf. Grimm's lampoon of the excessive use of italics by the physiocrats. *Correspondance littéraire*, 1 Nov.1767, cited by Georges Weulersse, *Le Mouvement physiocratique en France (de 1756 à 1770)*, vol. 1 (Paris: F. Alcan, 1910), 144; and Galiani's mockery of the *économiste* Baudeau, whose inveterate use of italics seemed to be meant "to prove that one was profound in the matter." *Dialogues sur le commerce des blés* (1770 edition, republished in its "Corpus des Oeuvres Philosophiques en Langue Française" series by Fayard, Paris, 1984), 23.

37 There are many other instances of the deficit of historicization. It is a bit cavalier to seek to account for the recourse to legal despotism by a sandwiched allusion between a passing reference to the "disappointments of the minister L'Averdy in the matter of the liberalization of the grain trade" and a mention of the

Concepts and Proof: Court Society

Unintentionally, Skornicki raises questions about the carrying capacity of certain concepts. He embraces with ardor the Eliasian schema of court society (within the larger framework of the civilizing process). I do not think that most historians read Elias on court society, or Foucault on madness, to learn about the specific dynamics of the relations between crown and aristocrats or about the rudiments of the *grand renfermement*, but rather to glean for insights into how to understand these practices and processes. In the case of Elias, I am one of many historians who have been influenced by the sociologist's keen perceptions. Certainly, Skornicki did not read him for the picturesque anecdotes on court life that abound in his book, but for the argument that, beyond its apparent otioseness and vacuity, the court choreographed a rational power game mobilizing intensely serious players and revealing the methods of regulation of complex individual and collective relationships.

It seems to me, however, that the political scientist asks the Eliasian concepts to do too much work, or to dispense him from doing it: brandishing a concept, whatever its cachet, is not tantamount to an exemption from the administration of proof.[38] I am not sure that "court society," in the particular

brutal, albeit tardy, *séance de flagellation* (245). The following fleeting allusion to regime instability, a recurrent notion, demands elucidation: "The politics of the physiocrats unfold in the framework of the instability of the regime…" (252). A far more frequently used concept urgently requires historicization through definition(s), contextualization and deconstruction: the idea of rationalization (29 and *passim*). The discussion of the right of property occurs at an olympian distance from the world that Mirabeau and to a lesser extent Quesnay knew intimately. One cannot be satisfied with characterizing the physiocratic conception of property as a possession "lacking in intrinsic value," representing merely "a means for the increasing of production and consumption." This is where terse becomes obscure (220). Another huge example of a lack of historicization concerns feudalism, which I shall treat below.

38 For a range of appreciations of these Eliasian concepts, see Jeroen Duindam, *Myths of Power. Norbert Elias and the Early Modern European Court* (Amsterdam: Amsterdam University Press, 1994); Daniel Gordon, *Citizens Without Sovereignty: Equality and Sociability in French Thought, 1670–1789* (Princeton, NJ: Princeton University Press, 1994); D. Gordon, "The Canonization of Norbert Elias in France: A Critical Perspective," *French Politics, Culture and Society* 20 (2002): 68–94; R. Chartier, *Cultural History, Between Practices and Representations*, trans. L. G. Cochrane (Ithaca, NY: Cornell University Press, 1988); R. Chartier, "Emmanuel Le Roy Ladurie, D. Gordon, and 'the Second Death' of Norbert Elias," *Figurations: Newsletter of the Norbert Elias Foundation* 9 (1998): 515–20; Dennis Smith, "History, Geography and Sociology. Lessons from the *Annales* school," *Theory, Culture and Society* 5 (1988):137–48; Smith, *The Rise of Historical Sociology* (Philadelphia: Temple University Press, 1991); and Smith, "The Civilizing Process and The History of Sexuality: Comparing Norbert Elias and Michel Foucault," *Theory and Society* 28 (1999): 79–100.

lilt with which Elias endowed it, is generous enough to accommodate all of the research that has been done in the past half century on politics and social and cultural relations inside and outside the court. Neither as protocol nor as arena nor as idiom does "court society" monopolize explanations of politics (in the two paramount spheres of religion and finances), of diplomacy and war making, of budgetary extortion or asphyxiation or even of the full - scale scope and practice of privilege with which it is most intimately connected. One must be singularly monomaniacal to imagine that parlementary politics is decided for the most part in the court[39]; one must be singularly sociocentric to imagine that provincial life and politics, in the parlements and in other sites of assembly and exchange, unfold in a narrowly heteronomous relationship vis-à-vis Versailles, even if we know that court society cultivated irredentist ambitions and possessed a reach beyond its formal gilded confines.[40]

I am not persuaded that political and/or economic science can be viewed/explained largely in terms of an antagonism to court society and its defects; Skornicki may very well identify too closely with his protagonists, from Gournay through Turgot, in scapegoating an ostensibly static court society that constitutes *the* bastion of resistance to change till the very end of the eighteenth century (369, 378). Both Louis XIV and Louis XV played double and triple games with court society, and achieved the "statist monopoly," each in his own way and time. Parallel political *champs* existed outside court society in the Versailles–Paris nexus. In his portrayal of the vanquishing of political fragmentation and ingrained violence and the elaboration of pacified forms of comportment, Elias may also have mislead Skornicki in his thinking both about upstream "feudalism" and the downstream "bourgeoisie".[41] On the implications of the Eliasian civilizing process for political economy and for economic practices, however, the political scientist may have underestimated the impact of the social constraint issuing (theoretically) in self-restraint that the market exercised on merchants.

39 I am thinking of John Rogister, *Louis XV and the Parlement of Paris 1737–1755* (Cambridge: Cambridge University Press, 1995).

40 See, for example, William Beik's excellent *Absolutism and Society in Seventeenth-Century France: State, Power and Provincial Aristocracy* (Cambridge: Cambridge University Press, 1985).

41 There is no sustained treatment of social structure in the book. Skornicki uses the term "bourgeoisie" (and less often the adjective "bourgeois") without (revisionist) anguish or remorse, and without (sociological) precision, occasionally in scare quotes, sometimes as mere description of a middling phenomenon, or to describe a group destined to ascend (55, 58, 73, 91, 163, 195, 260, 311, 312, 345, 395).

Deploying Foucault: Governmentality and Biopolitics

Michel Foucault's historical epistemology has marked me in many ways, but I see precious little value added in terms of clarification or interpretation in Skornicki's usage of the philosopher's concept of governmentality.[42] His definition is not luminous: "governmentality, a very malleable concept in Foucault's design, refers to a series of political mechanisms, discourses and technologies integrated into the exercise of sovereignty."[43] More specifically, albeit not more limpidly, the physiocratic notion of economic government "illustrates smartly what Foucault called *governmentality*, [a] political rationality" —the term is recurrent—"born of a long history, product of the junction between *pastoral power* and [the power of?][44] sovereignty, dating from the low Middle Ages" (212; cf. 216).

If one returns to Foucault himself, he seems engaged in a sort of political epistemology featuring a shift (apparently beginning around the epoch of the "Administrative State" in the sixteenth century, following the medieval stage called the "State of Justice"), from a governing knowledge (or a "raison gouvernementale") devised for a territorial state functioning on the basis of royal sovereignty over a physical realm to which subjects are attached to a "population-state" functioning on the basis of governmentality (apparently the government taking in charge the management of the whole of the collectivity).[45] This change—or was it a swerve?—in focus, strategy and method required recourse to an "economic knowledge" (thus Skornicki's interest), within the framework of a larger bio-regulation (or "biopolitics")

---

42 See M. Foucault, *Sécurité, territoire, population: Cours au Collège de France (1977–1978)*, ed. M. Senellart (Paris: Gallimard-Seuil, 2004), 111–13, 354–55.

43 Skornicki applies the word "technology"—a mere conceit without Foucault's aura—in a wide range or contexts… and texts: for example, Galiani's witty but deadly serious *Dialogues* are "a literary technology" aiming at a wider diffusion, beyond the microcosmic world of *mondanité* where Skornicki situates the Italian's ambitions rather than in the arena of political economy proper (315–16, 318, 323–24).

44 The French is somewhat obscure: "produit du croisement entre *le pouvoir pastoral* et de la *souveraineté…* ."

45 See M. Foucault, *Sécurité, territoire, population*. As I suggested above, while I appreciate his erudition and am dazzled by his cultivation, I read this Foucault—at many junctures particularly close to my own work—for his boldness, his unbridled freedom of reference and reflection, his sovereign indifference to disciplinary boundaries (but not to discipline!), his theoretical insight and playfulness, his bracing comparative range, his gift for making unlikely connections and so on. In a broad and durable sense, I enjoyed and profited intellectually from Foucault's effort to rethink the framing structures of the history of the Old Regime; in a narrower compass, his (re-)conceptualization, often quite derivative, did not convince me and his arguments did

touching on hygiene, health, sex and so on, as well as more strictly economic issues and of an apparatus of security (or police) to assure the life of the subjects (218).[46] Governmentality implies new ways for the state to imagine and realize wealth formation and new opportunities for actors in the population to produce riches. Here, again, Foucault beckons Skornicki, because he views this political development as embodied in a double liberalism, economic and political, with a special emphasis, crystallized, as far as one can tell, by the confrontation with physiocracy, on the intimate connection between liberty and security within the new "raison gouvernementale."

This is not the place to engage the always provocative reflection of Foucault. In terms of Skornicki's usage (appropriation?), I do not see how the evolution from territorial/law-based (passing through a phase of proto-

---

not alter my way of looking specifically at subsistence issues, the police, liberalism and liberalization, the evolution of governance, and the relations between state and society. I think that he is mistaken or unclear or imprecise about many matters (the quasi-mechanical connection between dearth and revolt (32, 43); a normative notion of dearth prevention, estranged from the realities of production and distribution, of putative facts and differential sociocultural representations (33–34, 349); the generic "peasant"-centered system of production, according to physiocratic or royal templates, requires considerable nuance (34–35); the treatment of markets and price formation is too vague (38–40, 35–52); the need to elucidate the insight concerning "dearth-as-chimera," but also the articulation of "rareté-cherté" (40–45); the historical reality of a "caesura" between a "centripetally"-oriented, rigidly Manichean and draconian "disciplinary" modality and a "centrifugally"-geared, labile, laissez-fairish "security" mechanism or arrangement (46–50, 57–59, 113), a discussion linked with notions and practices of police that require clarification (320–21, 328, 331, 334–35, 342, 348); the narrow definition of liberty, riveted to the system of security (50), counterpoised by a more buoyant notion of liberty within governmentality (361); the insufficiently luminous and historicized shift from a more or less intractable "people" to a more or less graspable, mappable and containable "population" (45, 69, 72, 359–60); an excessively cursory gloss on the articulation between micro- and macro-power (366); the supposed connections between price and the propensity to plant, an issue that remains widely debated (34, 351). To assess Foucault in these terms, however, is to look at his "thought" from the "petit bout de la lorgnette," as the French say.

46 In the Foucauldian delineation, Skornicki derives police from a "usurpation" of pastoral power from its stewardship role in the "sovereignty" stage in order to found the epoch of which "police" was the "first rationalization." Foucault construes this police as already an expression of biopolitics in its postulate of locating "the utility of the state" in "the happiness of men" (and/or vice versa?). Though the philosopher does not mention it explicitly, the nodal point of this governmentality is what he labels "the pact of subsistence," reminiscent of what I have called "the social contract of subsistence." The commentary of Foucault/Skornicki (difficult to separate) rehearses well-known analytical categories or points of reference such as the king as baker and

bureuacratization) to population/security-based kingship—a sort of elliptical modernization theory[47]—illuminates our understanding of state formation (and re-formation) and state vocation from the Renaissance to the Revolution. Nor do I see how the triad population/political–economic knowledge/security deepens our appreciation of the Economic Enlightenment and the efforts of the monarchy to retool its purchase on power, or why the word governmentality—hardly a paradigmatic permutation—enriches our comprehension more than the more modest term of policy in designating particular political or political–economic options.

---

grain as a merchandise *sui generis*. Once again, beyond the exercise of branding, I am not sure that there is much to be gained intellectually in describing the *police des grains* as situated at the crossroads "of the disciplinary and the biopolitical." Skornicki/Foucault conceives political economy (especially in its physiocratic incarnation) as "inscribed in the continuity of the biopolitical effect of the monarchy," the predicate for the thesis, to which I shall return—that "liberalism and biopolitics appear co-terminous." Finally, I am dubious about the benefit of the "reduction" of the people into the "population," heralded (by Foucault) as "an absolutely new figure [*personnage*]," the sole object of political and economic government. See A. Skornicki, "Le 'Biopouvoir': détournement des puissances vitales ou invention de la vue? L'économie politique, le pain et le peuple au XVIIIe siècle," *Labyrinthe* (22 July 2008): 3 (online) and *L'Economiste, la cour et la patrie*, 216, 218–19; M. Foucault, *Sécurité, territoire, population*, 61. Thanks to Foucault's genius and authority, biopolitcs has become a sort of conceptual growth industry in social science research. The term itself is not a neologism, as sometimes asserted. It has long and checkered history, dating back at least to the 1920s. It flowered in Nazi and philo-Nazi circles, in medicine and philosophy, before Foucault invested it with a wholly different set of meanings. For a useful bibliography, which also emphasizes the currently multivocal nature of the concept, see Laurette T. Liesen and Mary B. Walsh, "The Competing Meanings of 'Biopolitics' in Political Science: Biological and Postmodern Approaches to Politics," *Politics and the Life Sciences* 31 (2012): 2–15. See also Alfred Somit, "Review article: Biopolitics," *British Journal of Political Science* 2 (1972): 209–38 and the underhistoricized Steven A. Peterson and Alfred Somit, "Biopolitics: A preliminary history," *Journal of the History of the Behavioral Sciences* 15 (1979): 333–39. In his interesting review of Nitzan Lebovic's *The Philosophy of Life and Death: Ludwig Klages and the Rise of a Nazi Biopolitics* (London: Palgrave Macmillan, 2014), Paul Bishop suggests how Klages' anti-idealist conceptual tool-kit fit well with Foucault's critical methodology in his study of the politics of sexuality and how the German philosopher's defense of Eros, the core of his *Lebensphilosophie*, "could serve as a starting point for all manner of biopolitical persectives." *Times Literary Supplement*, 7 Nov. 2014. In Foucault's train, see Roberto Esposito, *Bìos: Biopolitics and Philosophy*, trans. Timothy Campbell (Minneapolis: Minnesota University Press, 2008) and Thomas Lemke, *Biopolitics: An Advanced Introduction* (New York: New York University Press, 2011).

47 A modernization theory that Skornicki lyrically epitomizes (elsewhere) as the shift from a (political?) focus on death to a focus on life. A. Skornicki, "Le 'Biopouvoir'."

Liberalism as a Process of Government

Foucault is both father and midwife to Skornicki's argument about liberalism, generically, and about liberalization, derivatively, though the political scientist is also tempted by a Polanyi-like notion of a disembedding of the economy with respect to politics and society in order to rationalize the behavior of both "agents on the market *and* the administration of the State"—a line of reasoning that would carry more weight if he had scrutinized the embedding process that came first and that helps to explain why liberalization constituted such a seismic shock (70).[48] I subscribe to the notion, drawn from Foucault and Polanyi—in my eyes, incontrovertible—that liberalism (I confine my scrutiny to the eighteenth century) is a state enterprise: whether one calls it a policy of rupture (as I do) or a technology of governmentality (Foucault–Skornicki), the state fosters and institutes it; it is meant to be "a process of government" (13–14, 28, 377).[49]

The rub is in the unpacking and interpreting of this predicate: what government? Government with what objectives and what instruments of action? Where I perceive a break in means and ends, Skornicki apprehends a (Weberian?) continuity. I see liberalism (as embodied in liberalization, its first policy application in French reality) as a radical rethinking of the relation of state to society, a renunciation by the king of the social contract, a global strategy for (partially) extricating the state from paralyzing impasses (political and fiscal) and structurally redefining the power of the prince according to imperious constraints imposed by natural law. Surely, liberalism/liberalization is a mode of governance, yet in a Clausewitzean manner, it is the continuation of government by other processes, by other agents and agencies. Its daring, its temerity was to imagine that drastic deregulation could issue in order, in the basic, banal and imperiously necessary everyday order, and, more ambitiously, in a veritable New Order, born of a new epistemology of power that displaced the center of gravity from state to society, founded on a new social theodicy, managed by revamped, reprogrammed and in some cases

---

48 I concur with K. Polanyi that a "market economy" unbridled from the political sphere is (historically) inconceivable, a thesis that traverses his still provocative *The Great Transformation* (New York: Farrar & Rinehart, 1944).

49 The rudiments of this argument are present in venerable work of Eli F. Heckscher, *Mercantilism,* 2 vols. (London: Allen and Unwin, 1935). Certain echoes are also in the reasoning of cameralism. See Andre Wakefield, *The Disordered Police State: German Cameralism as Science and Practice* (Chicago: University of Chicago Press, 2009) and Keith Tribe, *Governing Economy: The Reformation of German Academic Discourse* (Cambridge: Cambrige University Press, 1988).

novel institutions and rules, to a large extent sheltered from the gaze and the grasp of the government.

So, while I can agree with Skornicki, as I indicated, that "le 'libéralisme' soit d'Etat," and that it belongs to the history of power, it is only in a narrowly circumscribed (and somewhat Jesuitical) fashion that I can endorse the proposition that it cannot be understood as "hostility to the intervention of the State" (26–27; cf. 380).[50] The launching and realization of liberalization—that is, the disengagement of the state from multiple spheres of action and mediation, including the supervision and in some cases the execution of many of the responsibilities that Skornicki/Foucault subsumes under the vitalizing rubric of biopolitics—require a concentrated spurt of applied political energy that, I suppose, one could call "intervention" in the inaugural instance of the 1760s: intervention to dismantle structures of control and intervention; intervention to manacle (or emasculate) local administrators and deprive them of their richly endowed tool-kits for maintaining or restoring order; intervention to abrogate forms of judicial intervention that had criminalized practices henceforth deemed socially productive; intervention to repress disorders resulting from the refusal (or, rather, the political and legal incapacity) of local officials to intervene preemptively; intervention to protect actors who wish to engage in activities until now viewed as transgressions and aggressions; exogenous intervention to assure the movement of goods that had been previously orchestrated by endogenous intervention and entente on the local level; and so on. This is not "the dismantling of the *court society* and the system or privileges" that is one of Skornicki's consuming themes: it is a more sweeping, massively disruptive and supremely parlous wager, implicating not the 1 percent, but the other 99 percent (376). Apropos of liberalization, to which we shall return, Skornicki is right to note that "the life of political ideas was one of sometimes violent symbolical struggles" (266). A parallel commentary, articulating the social with the cultural/political,

50 In these pages, Skornicki's unself-conscious glissando from liberalism to political economy does not clarify his case. This political economy constitutes a "rival rationalization of the absolutist political order" directed against court society—an argument I questioned above (in terms of its causal relationship with state building, among other things, and its dialectical relationship with liberalism) and will not follow up here. In an abstruse formulation, Skornicki portrays court society as "the key to understanding the political significance of *the formal rationalization of economic knowledge* [his emphasis] … this rationalization that poses as [a] principle of human action monetary maximization to the exclusion of any other value, and which draws from it all the logical consequences (those of the aggregation of the interested behavior of the agents in the framework of a system of markets)."

on the even more violent social struggles of the period 1766–74, would have been worthwhile.[51]

Liberalism and the State on Steroids

Rhetorically a *tabula rasa* in many ways, liberalism/liberalization requires a more complex administrative transmutation. Turgot finds that he must create a parallel policing system, at least in Paris, once the guilds are abolished and corporate policing powers suppressed with them, even as he is obliged to use repressive power to force grain as well as human capital to be free. After having ostentatiously dismantled the state provisioning system deployed by his predecessor Terray, the same liberal minister is constrained to turn to the nefarious Leleu brothers to perform similar, strategic subsistence interventions. During the Revolution, Roland, fervent liberal, at one point minister of the interior, believes that the best thing for a government to do during a dearth is to do nothing. Yet he finds himself compelled to accommodate the vociferous public (and local administrative) demand for public supply intervention. Le Chapelier cannot ban all forms of association and impose atomized exchange without summoning force, forging espionage networks and bullying bosses as well as workers.

According to the theory and the expectations of the liberalizing engineers, the transaction costs of liberalization[52]—this initial burst of intervention—were supposed to decline rapidly as self-regulating mechanisms replaced

---

51 I wonder at several junctures about the pale presence of the people-become-population (via Foucault) in this book. Though Skornicki's voice is difficult to distinguish from the physiocrats he scrutinizes, there is an interesting discussion (217–20) that considers the morphing of people into population: "And the population permits the stripping of the people of their moral and political qualities, of their status as subjects, in order to make of them an instrument of politics and of the State." This jolting spoliation/metamorphosis merited a parsing and perhaps an integration into a larger discussion of political economy and the people. When, for example, Skornicki writes (his italics): "From the principle of the minimum of preservation [survival] to the principle of the maximum of pleasure [enjoyment], *political economy is the ultimate science of natural right [law]*." Why is there no reflection on the capacity of this science to maximize the happiness or well-being of the people/population, or at least to attenuate the misery concealed by the formulaic *principe de conservation*?

52 The cost approach, paramount in the physiocratic analysis of the economy, surfaces on the margin in Skornicki's treatment, crystallizing in a lapidary definition of liberalism that demands cliometric testing, without issuing necessarily in a consensus on the meaning of efficiency: "In the physiocratic dialect, *economic government* represents the new political rationalization proposed by 'liberalism' in introducing the principle of the least cost for the maximum of efficiency, [thus] breaking with the inflation of regulations and of surveillance induced by police and discipline" (213).

the traditional apparatus of (spasmodically exercised, but permanently authorized) intervention. The mission of this transitional intervention was to obviate intervention, even as the doctrine of liberalization delegitimized a sweeping range of interventionist modalities consubstantial to the absolutist vocation of a nourishing prince unfettered by natural law (but certainly not to the toxic logic of court society as characterized by Skornicki). The liberal desire is to move from a bloated to a lean state: the latter is to become healthier and sturdier in the end by assigning many tasks that had acquired a regalian veneer to society: not only responsibility for subsistence, but also for the fabrication of norms in other product markets, and in the labor markets, both for the attribution of status in the system of social classification and for the unbidden forging of the social bond.

In a similar vein, I can accept, in a limited, nuanced and differential way, the appreciation of "the policy of laissez-faire" as "a vector of the increase of the power of the state" (the invocation of Eric Hobsbawm as bard of the nineteenth-century Ramboesque state nourished on liberal steroids lends no particular credibility to this argument, though it allows me anachronism for anachronism) (298). To the extent that liberalization (and liberalism) free the state from costly and onerous tasks, fluidify mobility (not only upward but also downward), unleash individual creative drives, excite entrepreneurial initiative, spur capital formation, commercial exchange and industrial innovation, and generate wealth creation enhancing the state's role in the international arena, it is reasonable to view the state as strengthened.[53] But, measured against other criteria, primarily social and cultural, and perhaps also political, the state has been weakened in some important ways, fundamentally reconfigured, and represented under new auspices grounded in an alternate legitimacy. It requires a certain naiveté and utopian élan—here Skornicki's voice is constantly conflated with that of his political-economist protagonists—to imagine that liberalism, in the manner of a Hayek or an Ayn Rand, results in spontaneous order ("political economy is intrinsically a discourse of order") (379–80).[54]

53 One of Skornicki's criteria for the power of a state is its capacity to "enforce the application of the law throughout the entire territory," an endowment he associates with the efficiency and rationalization that a "free competitive market" will help to install (298). Aside from the undemonstrated connection between the undefined market institution and the law-enforcement capacity of the state, I suggest that Napoleon was probably the first "prince" to achieve a genuinely "nation"-wide execution of the law.

54 Skornicki cites the celebrated phrase of Polanyi—that a vintage Richard Posner would probably have endorsed—that "for the politician and the administrator, laissez-faire is simply a principle assuring the maintenance of law and order, at the least cost and

The stilted language makes it difficult to determine exactly what the author means when he writes of "liberal" political economy—a pleonasm, according to his own reasoning—"as a political technology for the organization of personal interests": the efficacy of Mandevillean egocentricity? The work of an underlying harmony? The state as bully-pulpit and preacher of the virtues of cupidity? The state as coordinator of (a modernized, public interest) chrematistics? Classically oriented economists even (perhaps especially) today argue that when markets become more efficient, the social demand for state intervention shrinks. (This is the sense in which Skornicki writes that "the partisans of free trade in grain desired less to limit the intervention of the state than to deliver it from a mission that they judged inefficient and even harmful" (302).) Yet was it plausible to imagine drastic deregulation, as a technology of governmentality, capable of dealing with the problems of France in the second half of the eighteenth century? The robust voluntarism of Skornicki's liberalism, according to practitioners in the 1760s, is supposed to wither away more or less rapidly. Given his assumption of the weakness ("fragility" and "instability") of the Old-Regime state, it is hard to fathom how it could marshal the resources to lurch into the liberal world that was supposed to rescue it by fortifying it (376–77, 380).

Market(s) and Governmentality

If liberalism/liberalization is a strategy or technology of state intervention, its chief instrument is the market. Given the highly controversial nature of this term/concept today, its double charge as a quasi-magical or diabolical force, the tendency of both its partisans and its critics to impute to it, by a double process of reification and anthropomorphization, qualities at once human and institutional, contingent and necessary, natural and factitious, rational and irrational, regular and histrionic and so on, it is very difficult to map and characterize it historically, free of teleological or Whiggish indenture. Concerning preliberal France, the political scientist has very little to say about *the* market (the definite article signifies something well known, important, spelled out, a specific point in a shared, cognitive compass) or about the markets (the plural instantiating elusiveness and variability as much as multiplicity). Without imputing isomorphic status, the author appears implicitly to associate Old-Regime markets—more often those linked to the likes of the Company of the Indies and the ignominious financiers than to the boundless mix of

with the least effort" (376). Plausible in the context of nineteenth-century England, this sibylline formulation, as sanguine as it is tendentious, would certainly not have galvanized much political or administrative support in eighteenth-century France.

Lilliputian and central-place grain markets—with the tarnished, obstructionist world of court society, a nebulous yet ubiquitous corporate society[55] (106–8), pervasive patrimonialization, proliferating privileges, myriad manifestations of monopoly and a malignant "feudal" heritage.

In a jumbled story line of which I recognize bits and pieces, the author conveys the liberal vision of eighteenth-century political economists as "the institutionalization of a freely competitive market"—which remains undefined—in the place of "the patrimonial and protected market"—which remains concomitantly undefined. This liberal market he represents as "the sole technology of government susceptible of perfecting the State monopoly, especially in the fiscal domain, to the detriment of the system of privileges and offices and in circumventing the parlements as well as the courtiers" (28). It is not clear to me how the liberal market will effect this generic monopoly, what this category of monopoly signifies (since it lies beyond the state's exclusive claim to the exercise of justice and violence, which seems to have nothing to do with this liberal metamorphosis) and how in particular it will realize a fiscal monopoly, the precise sense of which is not spelled out. No less cryptic is how this market will—and in what manner, with what means, to what end—bypass the parlements (which are not a monolith, which are divided along many fault lines, which contain many passionate champions of Skornicki's market, as far as one can tell, given its indeterminate nature) and the courtiers, who also bespeak many trajectories, hold divergent points of view on numerous issues, entertain disparate ambitions, and dispose of uneven talents, despite their amalgamation in the court-society concept.

Nor is it more illuminating or cogent, in the wake of Weber, to impute to numerous economists of the Enlightenment the idea of the market as "a technology of political monopolization by the State that permits the undermining of the criteria of determination of the social value peculiar to court society." Apart from the enigmatic manner in which this market-as-technology would function and apart from the opacity of the notion of monopolization, in the service, presumably, of a symbolical and political mission, together they are supposed to strike a blow against court society

55 Skornicki takes at face value the tendentious characterization of the guilds—an important segment of the corporate universe—that Clicquot and other Gournayites forged for polemical purposes. The author misses the opportunity to reflect on the meanings of what he calls "the corporative structure" (352) when he deals with Necker. He highlights his ambitious reform plans in financial and provincial administration, but ignores utterly his herculean effort to refound and re-ground the everyday corporate universe as embodied by the guilds (367).

by supplanting social capital (birth and networks) with economic capital (property, bearing a cultural message) and by prizing "productive utility" over a title or venal hereditary charge. There is a double problem with this formulation just to begin with: many members of "court society" enjoyed and represented (landed) property, in the physiocratic sense, and numerous venal office holders, practicing a segmented socioeconomic life, used their charges as a fruitful lever to engage in activities that might pass the incantatory litmus of productive utility (377). Obviously, a crass reality test has little relevance here.

In discussing the state and the market(s), the author is really in the abstract treatment of the concrete rather than J. C. Perrot's famously evocative "concrete history of abstraction."[56] Skornicki's categories have theoretical pedigree, but little purchase on the reality upon which he purports to reflect, through his protagonists and in his own voice. It is regrettable that he has not looked more closely at the actual morphology and performance of markets—notably the grain markets where he is obliged to come down to earth and approach lived experience—in order to render more intelligible the debates concerning the diffusion of so-called "free-market" (or "free trade") ideas that—once they are rigorously defined, for they cover a vast palette of inflections and are often implicitly aligned with nineteenth-century finalities—are extremely interesting because they not only percolate downward, but also often bubble up from below (82).

Under the glib banner of "liberty as government," to achieve the "institutionalization of the freely competitive market" would require much more technological precision than the "breaking down of the segmented and fragmented local markets that characterize the economy of the Old Regime," a sort of blind, nuclear strike (377). Here is where Skornicki should pay close attention to the inordinate costs and complexities of the processes of disembedding that he evoked on several occasions. Rash or audacious, this course of action—anti-archaic, anti-"feudal", modernizing—was indeed conceivable, but it needs to be seen for what it was bound to do, and in fact what it did, in the 1760s: break down the elementary structures of social cohesion

56 See J. C. Perrot, *Une histoire intellectuelle de l'économie politique (XVII*e*–XVIII*e *siècle)* (Paris: Editions de l'Ecole des Hautes Etudes en Sciences Sociales, 1992), one of the magisterial books of the past two decades, written by a formidably insightful historian, less well known outside France than he should be. See also his "Histoire des sciences, histoire concrète de l'abstraction," in R. Guesnerie and F. Hartog, eds., *Des sciences et des techniques: un débat* (Paris: Editions de l'Ecole des Hautes Etudes en Sciences Sociales, 1998), 25–37.

and political stability. In the social, psychological, demographic, economic, technological and political context of the second half of the eighteenth century, by what means could the modernizing physiocrats, or anyone else, institute a "self-regulating market"? (324).[57]

In the same spirit, a closer look at how local grain markets functioned, in the context of feeder chains and central-place drainage, would make it clear that the "moral economy of the crowd" can in fact be understood "as a refusal to enter into the market" when the market in question, transformed by liberalization, no longer represents the market with which they were familiar—the market as a regulatory bastion, as a guarantee of regular victualing, as a sanctuarized physical site of (relatively) transparent (and sometimes obligatory) exchange and as a barrier to supply hemorrhage. It did not take an "international merchant logic" to frighten consumers: the export or removal [*enlèvement*] of any grain or flour for another market—regional, metropolitan or even local—traumatized them during periods of subsistence stress (327–28).[58] That is what Galiani and Necker understood better than the *économistes*: it did not require integration in an international market or export abroad to provoke panic and resistance.

Liberalization: Grain Trade, Exports, Monopoly and "Disciplinary Technology"

The political scientist treats the actual experience of liberalization in the 1760s unevenly. Certainly, he is right to describe it, in Maussian idiom, as "a total social fact" which "violently reconfigured the symbolic forms of

57 I will leave the translation of Skornicki's explanation to someone more competent than I am: "La *rationalisation formelle* de l'économie est hypothético-déductive et repose sur l'hypothèse de la rationalité économique maximisatrice des agents, à l'exclusion de toute autre valeur. La *rationalisation matérielle* n'est pas moins neutre axiologiquement, mais intègre expérimentalement dans ses modèles *les valeurs et les passions* des agents pour mieux appréhender leurs comportements suivant une courbe probabiliste. La première vise à établir un ordre légal-rationnel administratif moderne, c'est-à-dire à parachever le monopole politique de l'Etat, en neutralisant les corporations par l'institutionnalisation d'un marché régulateur, qui requiert un ordre juridique garanti par un Etat efficace, rationalisé, gouvernant peu mais contrôlant beaucoup, suffisamment puissant pour faire appliquer la loi sur l'ensemble du territoire et à tous les sujets." Author's emphasis (324).

58 On this point, I disagree with D. Margairaz and P. Minard, "Le Marché dans son histoire," *Revue de synthèse* 127, no. 2 (2006): 247.

the French monarchy" (266, 306). His subsequent discussion of the king's engagement in the paternal role of nourishing prince is more ambiguous. Here the symbolic prevails over the pragmatic—what matters is "the popular and state representation" of the king's relationship to his subjects rather than the "political technology" actually deployed, to use the author's language, though, in crisis time, they are inextricably commingled. Nor am I sure of the pertinence of distinguishing between "an absolutist will" of the monarchy to regulate the provisioning trade and the imperious "material" obligation to do so. It is likely that Skornicki is not overly cynical in arguing that the king cared less about the people—this oceanic mass of humanity needs to be defined in the specific context of liberalization—than about the problems that they caused him, but he certainly was preoccupied with the way the people viewed him, even if he proved singularly inept at discharging this task (the famine plot persuasion that I have studied is only the most spectacular illustration) (295, 302).

But regulatory practices—the *police des grains*—cannot be understood in genealogical terms, following Foucault, as a "disciplinary technology" that, spurred by the fusing of pastoral and sovereign-state vocations, aspires to "govern souls and bodies." It must take into account the gradual transformation of the structures and practices of the provisioning trade (302–3). Skornicki needs to look more carefully at the incentives and conditions for intervention (or benign neglect), which requires that he understand the mechanisms that generate crises. For example, it is not the grain (here, wheat and wheat flour) price, reaching its peak in November 1768, which "provokes a dearth and a series of grain riots," but rather the dearth that occasions the vertiginous spike in prices (313).

The author's fixation on exportation misleads him, as it has other commentators (306, 313–14, 322, 325). It is simply not true that L'Averdy's July edict featuring export rights "will be the most violently contested" measure in the liberal repertory. The bulk of the disruption in the marketplaces results in the first instance from the radical deregulation of commercial practices introduced by the legislation of 1763; and dislocation and disorder remain acute after the government shuts down export from various key ports. "Monopoly," in the sense that it was apprehended on the ground—hoarding; the double process of trade fragmentation and concentration; buying "in the soil," on sample, and more generally outside the physical marketplaces; and a whole range of maneuvers contrived to provoke doubt, disarray and augment prices—was a more immediate source of popular and police concern than exportation. Consumers, in any event, did not view the latter narrowly as shipments abroad, but construed it as the removal of "locally raised grain" for use elsewhere, regardless of final destination. The problem in the 1760s was not nostalgia for the death sentence with which the state menaced illicit exporters in the past, but with the paralysis of local authority and the seeming indifference of the monarch at the center.[59]

Moreover, "monopoly," a phenomenon cast into relief during the experience of dearth—as much by dearths of "opinion" as by verifiable penury—is consubstantial to the grain trade itself, at every level, and in some sense to the police of that grain trade. One cannot confine "monopoly" either to the exploitation of the small players by the big or to a "totally free and uncontrolled competition"—here Skornicki relies too heavily on literary definition, bordering on the ideal-type. It can be the work of a Goliath (a *négociant*) or a David (a *blatier*). It can result from the rules themselves, draconian or merely bullying, or from police corruption or manipulation, as the liberal lobby charged, or from the timid/indulgent enforcement of rules, denounced by hard-core regulatory purists or the absence of rules and lack of administrative means, as the disoriented postliberal police will complain. Monopoly acquires new forms across the century as the shape of the trade changes, for example, with the jolting impact of the entry into play of merchant millers in metropolitan hinterlands. In the big cities, it can involve bakers as well as traders, the former on occasion disposing of more clout than the latter.[60] Like monopoly, the behavior of the police is rarely mechanical or easily typecast, and it functions not only in a negative way to "prevent" grasping merchants from "pushing up the price of grain," but also proactively and positively, by assisting them to organize their trade relations in a stable manner. In any case, it is neither mechanical nor easily identifiable or predictable (304–5).[61]

---

59 In this sense, it is unfair to impute a sort of circumspection or timorousness to Turgot for having "*limit[ed]* his arrêt of 13 September 1774 to the liberty of *internal* circulation." First emphasis is mine, second is author's (326). Turgot's measure was analogous to that of May 1763, that is to say, a radical deregulatory step.

60 Given the role of millers, bakers and factors, not to mention institutional holders of grain (religious communities, tithe-collectors, and agricultural farmers-general), the "avidity of merchants" is too narrow a horizon (327).

61 In the context of the historiography of dearth and the "police des grains" (mapping out harvest practices and calendars, grain movement in the hands of multiple actors, the range of milling options, the role of collector markets, the shifting tolerance for off-market transactions and so on), I do not see the theoretical pertinence or conceptual utility of opposing a "sovereign politics/policy of life" to a "biopower," a "*faire mourir et laisser vivre*" to a "*faire vivre et laisser mourir*." Author's emphasis (304).

Public Opinion: Protean and Elusive

Like many other scholars of political economy, Skornicki presents two other actors, said to play crucial, even decisive roles, yet portrayed frequently in imprecise and/or shadowy terms. The first is the ever-present and ineffable public opinion, here often placed in the cordon sanitaire of (scare) quotes, sometimes in conflicted italics, assertive but anxious. The signification varies from the eminently general ("enlightened" or "lettered" or patriotic) to the highly segmented (an opinion focused on agronomy, or bespeaking attitudes of the police or other administrators); it denotes a swarm of intellectually alert yet diverse individuals with no articulated connections, or a group expressing collectively a demand (for the science of commerce, as a counterweight to court society, embodied in "press, salons and academies"; for the unction of physiocratic *évidence*, as a political pressure group to keep the (future?) legal despot on the right path) or a quasi-institution (the famous "tribunal" that so many writers instrumentalized) (63, 86, 142–44, 224, 246, 249, 270, 346–47, 364, 369, 370–71). Save in his tonic discussion of Necker, Skornicki avoids the onus of definition. Necker construes public opinion at once as a (not so vulgar) vehicle of self-promotion, as a rhetorical and sociocultural construction, a language unto itself, a new political culture, an inchoate organizing "institution" with representative political functions, any powerful current of "enthusiasm," a socially differential spectrum of voices (allowing the banker-philosophe-philanthropist-political aspirant to flatter the salon milieu and larger world of *mondanité* and at the same time reserve a sheltered place for "the people" and "the popular," victims protected only by their capacity to act as a redoubtable agent/agency of opinion), an embryonic nation and perhaps—the author does not draw this out—as a nascent expression of (proto-)class consciousness from below or as a counterpoise or corrective to the exorbitant sway of property.

The Feudal Morass

The second actor to which I just referred is denoted by the formidable F-word, feudalism; it proliferates in Skornicki's book through a kind of intellectual fission that produces more heat than light (27, 29, 36, 107, 124, 131, 137, 153, 154, 159, 175, 181, 182, 185, 195, 197, 203, 204, 205, 220, 241, 256, 259, 260, 295, 311, 345, 348). It means many things, none of which is fully elucidated. It is more incarnate and institutional than public opinion, but often no less elusive and incantatory, especially in its metaphorical and "air-du-temps" usages, despite the moral authority of Tocqueville, Elias, Foucault and a number of political economists, among others. It often seems to signify what came before, an "antique" or ancient period, a tenebrous time, a stubbornly persistent epoch that yields reluctantly and rarely without some vestigial deposit, a place to which one does not or should not want to return, through a literal "retour" or a hazier "[feudal] reaction" (220, 295). Sometimes a red-herring, on other occasions it hints at various significations, often interesting, albeit undeveloped. Perhaps, the most common is feudalism as a sort of historical and emotional armature for court society, a "curialisation" of warriors who gravitate from "polyarchie" to arbitrary monarchy; or, in the same vein, a breeding ground and continuing framework for privileges, once construed as liberties, and an adumbration of a sociology that features rigid hierarchy. Inscribed in a logic of path dependence, feudalism also connotes barriers and obstructions: to capitalism, of course, and more broadly to (absolutist) state making (and implicitly to the modernizing telos that traverses the book). It carries a cultural and psychopolitical valence as an "ethos," at times attached to virile qualities such as bellicosity and conquest, and as a more or less open-ended "ideology." Even as feudalism glorifies or mourns or provokes nostalgia or chronicles the unfolding of time, it serves—now and again in the same hands—as an epithet for all seasons (the physiocrats assailing the parlements as feudal remainders). Through Quesnay, Skornicki comes closest to endowing feudalism with specific qualities, without indicating whether they map the contours of the physiocratic imaginary that engenders and legitimates their theory or are in fact anchored in a more or less objectifiable past. Quesnay contrasts the age he hopes to inaugurate with feudalism: the goal is to favor production rather than war making, the plough over the sword, an economy founded on abundance and generalized well-being rather than penury and predation.

It is striking how little has changed in the treatment of so-called feudalism in the study of the history of economic ideas, particularly physiocratic, in the past hundred years. Because it seemed to loom large both in the texts he read and between the lines, Georges Weulersse, doyen of modern scholarship on the *économistes*, writing toward the beginning of the twentieth century, made of it a major theme, without subjecting it to close examination, either as a metaphor or historical referent. He alternately described Mirabeau as a "feudal" [féodal] or a semifeudal, by "origin and temperament," by which he seemed to mean apologist for the privileges of a certain nobility and hostility to certain encroachments of the monarchy. Though feudalism offered certain "advantages", especially to the great landowners, because it divided the nation into "arbitrary despots and slaves," the *Ephémérides* pronounced its government to be "very imperfect" and even Mirabeau came to deny the existence of a "feudal constitution," moored in reality and founded on principles.[62]

62 G. Weulersse, *Le mouvement physiocratique en France (de 1756 à 1770)*, 1: 53–54, 109, 445; 2: 134–35, 536. Dated, ideologically marked, and methodologically flawed, the many

Writing toward the end of the twentieth century, Alfred Steinhauer, in his thesis in political science, rehearses many of the themes that Weulersse anticipated, with the same nonchalance, envisioning feudalism variously as a system of social organization, political control and/or administrative tutelage. Like his pioneering predecessor, the political scientist allowed his voice to become conflated with that of his witnesses, so it is often hard to distinguish between his own point of view and that of his subjects of study. The feudal system constituted an "economic aristocracy." It operated as well as a form of administration or governance, so that the first liberalization of grain production and distribution and the passage of Turgot's six edicts entailed necessarily its abolition, even as Terray, no liberal, also battled against the "feudal jurisdiction" in his rationalizing reformism. In epitome, it denoted "divine-right paternalistic absolutism." At its narrowest, feudalism is the ensemble of seigneurial dues and fees that will be replaced eventually by "'natural' private property" and at its broadest it is nothing less than a metonym for the entire Ancien Régime and its juridical structure.[63]

Historians of economic ideas will succeed in extricating themselves from this feudal morass, it seems to me, on a triple condition. First, an effort to examine closely the most recent scholarship on historical feudalism so that they can have a certain framing benchmark, a measure of the reality of feudal structures, relations, practices and so on across several centuries. Second, an inventory of the representations of feudalism in the ideology and the historiography of the post-Revolutionary world, enriched by a survey of the memory of feudalism, a scholarly undertaking that has not been fully completed and renewed. Finally, in intimate proximity with the work peculiar to intellectual historians of economic thinking, a systematic, critical analysis of the use of the word feudalism in the writings of their protagonists; the term can no longer be taken for granted, as if it were transparent and unproblematic.

Let us take two examples, the first particularly obvious to the specialists in this field. Mirabeau, as we have seen, cannot free himself, intellectually and emotionally, and probably also socially and politically, from the question

---

volumes that Weulersse devoted to physiocracy, before and after 1770, represent, nevertheless, a monumental scholarly achievement and a precious mine of information. On the question of feudalism, for example, Yves Charbit relies on him heavily. See his uninspired "The Political Failure of an Economic Theory: Physiocracy," *Population*, 57th year, no. 6 (2002): 860. In the same bent, Ambroise Saricks, *Pierre Samuel Du Pont de Nemours* (Lawrence: University of Kansas Press, 1969), 29.

63 Alfred Steinhauer, "Le parti physiocratique et la formation de l'opinion dans le France pré-révolutionnaire, 1756–1776" (thesis, political science, Université Panthéon-Sorbonne, 1997), 196, 206, 214, 232, 287, 459, 604, 667, 675, 761, 769.

of feudalism. What exactly did the question of feudalism signify to him at various points in his life? We need to understand the diverse ways in which he apprehended feudalism, how his understanding of it changed across the Quesnay years, why he could never fully move beyond it. In his correspondence, the marquis went even further than Weulersse hinted, beyond "throwing the banalities [monopolies of flour mill, bread oven and wine press] to the devil." In response to his brother, the bailli, ardent defender of (a vague yet potent) feudalism as the very foundation of the French monarchy,[64] Mirabeau charged that he "imagined a feudalism otherwise than the way it really was," which was not "well regulated, well bounded, well subordinated" and which he never would have embraced had he been the product of another habitus, say, had he been born the "son of a parlementaire." Distinguishing between a [dominant] "feudal disorder" and a [less palpable] "feudal order," the marquis suggests there is little redeeming value in the feudal mirage that engrosses his brother's mind. Yet he remained ambivalent, occasionally caught up, despite Quesnay's efforts to inoculate him, in a nostalgia for an idealized "feudal government" capable of generating social harmony.[65]

If there is obviously a great deal to do with a celebrated writer for whom feudalism constituted a defining part of his sense of self, and his perceptions of past and future, other economic authors for whom it did not bear this density also deployed the term in ways that merit investigation and interpretation. Whereas the bailli saw feudalism as a barrier against anarchy, the abbé Morellet, physiocratic fellow-traveler in the Gournay–Turgot axis, criticized, in stridently polemical manner, the abbé Galiani, reviler of physiocracy, for allegedly deriving *raison d'état* and the police of provisioning attached to it from "the times of feudal anarchy," the "state of barbarity" called "feudalism". What is at stake in this sort of quarrel, deliberately historicized?[66]

---

64 The bailli, contemptuous of the foggy and distorted worldview of urban philosophes/ reformers, did a better job in framing this question than have most historians: "… the feudal order, springing from the forests, [is] nevertheless the only [force] capable of preventing the Monarch from becoming a despot, and sinking from there to allow his people to fall into anarchy, a bit less than the type [associated with] the Republicans of Paris… [it will be seen] that the most magnificent laws were never able to sustain a true Republic for as long a time as perdures a monarchy founded on this feudal order." Bailli to Marquis de Mirabeau, 29 Dec. 1770, Musée Arbaud (Aix-en-Provence).

65 The following letters are in the Musée Arbaud: Mirabeau to Bailli, 18 Oct. 1768 (491); 11 Jan. 1771 (439); 28 Jan. 1771 (446–47). See also Steinhauer, "Le parti physiocratique et la formation de l'opinion," 175.

66 A. Morellet, *Réfutation de l'ouvrage qui a pour titre Dialogues sur le commerce des blés* (London, 1770), 250, 286. Cf. ibid., 78, 81, 141–42.

From Discourse to Practice

Henry C. Clark's study, *Compass of Society*, is situated in the new register of the history of political economy, whose ambitious and exacting objective is to connect economic thought to a host of major cultural, moral, political, social and international issues of the day.[67] Ideologically driven by a fervent liberal *parti pris*, the book, as intellectual history, avows a cautious ("common-sense") postmodernist influence, privileging a discursive approach, but forswearing any flirtation with linguistic nonreferentiality (xi). Still, one of the besetting problems of this work is the relation between the analysis of ideas and their inscription in reality. The focus on thought is often so intense that the conditions of its production and its linkages with lived experience are neglected, or taken for granted, rather than problematized and discussed.

In a debonair manner, the author slides from discourse to "the world of practice" without taking into account that context is a different kind of historical object and thus requires a significant adjustment in gaze and in method. Though Clark views Montesquieu's work as "essentially sociological" (115), he is not obliged to read it in terms of concrete, specific benchmarks anchored in the reality of a specific climate or size of state or form of government or type of mores or social structure: his inspiration is empirical, his disposition is comparative and he is interested in current events and history, but the baron de la Brède is a theorist and one does not subject each of his claims to some sort of reality check; he does not have to have a (verifiably) compelling understanding of the various ways in which the gentry shaped English public and private life in order to say something fruitfully heuristic about society and government on the other side of the channel. One cannot, however, read the correspondence involving the Conseil du commerce (or the bureau du commerce) in the same fashion (see, for example, 96).

In the same vein, I am flabbergasted by the smooth slide from representation to social reality—implicitly, this seems tantamount to the reduction of *all* reality to representation—in the reference to Abraham Du Pradel's "remarkable guide to the labor market of Paris published in 1692." Either Clark did not himself read this text—in his footnote, he notes the work "as cited by Fernand Braudel"—or he does not know what the labor market was and how it functioned, for Du Pradel has nothing to say about entry and exit, hiring and firing, disputes over placement and permission for leave, the roughness of

67 Henry C. Clark, *Compass of Society: Commerce and Absolutism in Old-Regime France* (Lanham, MD: Lexington, 2007).

exchanges, the role of informal and/or illicit institutions on the ground and so on (56, 71n).[68] Nor do merchants await Fénélon's categories before they move into action (58–64).

Was France a Low-Trust Society?

I find similar problems with the treatment of "trust," one of the major themes of this book. As a hypothesis, the putative deficit of trust might be stimulating. Yet it turns out that its definition proves to be somewhat elusive and/or protean as one moves from observer to observer, and that the temptation to extrapolate social reality from the texts proves irresistible. We take the word of the late seventeenth-century Dutch commentator Pieter de la Court and of Vincent de Gournay that Holland was a high-trust society/economy, which serves as a herald of the "wrong turn" that France would take under Louis XIV (28, 136). The further we go in pursuit of the trust factor, the more it seems to resemble Paul Krugman's "confidence fairy," both a normative vision and an assumption about behavior that is either untrue or not especially revealing. So Montesquieu, Clark's hero, the Hayek of the eighteenth century, regards the "prevalence of trust" among individuals as the sine qua non of "a thriving interdependent economy." Indeed, trust—social, economic, political and moral—is a sort of all-azimuth panacea: marker of the "characteristic virtues of a commercial people," of the faith of the "people" in its "legislative body, of "creditworthiness," of a certain collective altruism-in-serenity, of an

68 See *Le livre commode contenant les adresses de la ville de Paris et le Trésor des almanachs pour l'année bissextile 1692* [by Nicolas de Blégny] (Paris: D. Nion, 1692): this is the correct title; the one cited is truncated and misspelled. It is a fascinating text, both in its erudite introduction tracing the genealogy of the publication (the "utopian" ambitions of the father of Montaigne and of Laffemas, an early political arithmetician; the influence of Renaudot, a precocious "journalist" and of the later English address-book model; the interventions of the Parisian police authorities; the opinion of the *six grands corps*; and remedies for hernias and fevers, in the context of an (auto-)biography of the author), and in its almanac-like listing of information concerning most aspects of Parisian life, from the grand companies to the most modest artisans, from ecclesiastical, educational, financial and judicial affairs to everyday commerce (with information on guild bureaus and officers, on charitable enterprises, on the "petites écoles" of each quarter, on the availability of dancing masters and on the particular prowess of individual artisans, described in little pufferies that suggest publicity endorsements, for example, "Messieurs Loir, quay des Orphèvres, et Jacob, rue de Gesvres, sont des Orphèvres renommez pour la fabrique des Ornemens d'Eglise" (247) or "les Marchands Tapissiers renommez pour les meubles magnifiques sont entre plusieurs autres, Messieurs… (284)).

immunity from pernicious prejudice and of an international reputation for integrity (86, 122). The moral of the tale is limpid: mutual dependence and, thus, the social bond, arise from the intelligent (unfrenzied) pursuit of self-interest, as in the Dutch case (30–31).

Beyond the inference from more or less penetrating commentators (the glissando from contemporary observation to retrospective ethnography), what do we know about the judgment that France during the Old Regime was a low-trust society? On one level, it is a simple platitude, familiar to both actors at the time and to historians. Distrust was built into a world of magic and mystery, of manipulation and mendacity, of rampant inequality of rank and resources, of widespread relations of domination/subordination,[69] of concomitant upward mobility and immiseration, of a gaping abyss between the oral and the written, of clientelism and favoritism, of discrimination, of extensive violence, of suspicion of alterity (which could begin at the next village or town, even though the French were geographically more mobile than we often suppose) and of all outsiders and foreigners (*horsains*), of pervasive uncertainty and of the practice of conspiracy as a way of doing business and governing at every level (from the court and the courts to the ministries and intendancies, from the transactions of privileged companies and banks to the politics of village assemblies and guilds). The society that engendered the famine plot persuasion (or *pacte de famine*) did not have to await the Revolution to learn about the ubiquity, the efficacy and the perversity of conspiracy as a way of getting things done.[70] How could a society of chronic fear and precariousness, of recurrent dearth, where 90 per cent of the population drew the preponderance of its calories (and probably proteins) from cereals and devoted the bulk of their time to procuring their daily bread, where transportation and communication were rudimentary and unreliable, where corruption and speculation were rife, where regulation was uneven in implementation and results and where the

69 What Clark euphemistically styles "the robust give and take between rich and poor at the local level," the recourse to this euphemism bespeaking either a great naivety about social relations or a fear of evoking anachronistically the detested class struggle (325).

70 Clark refers to a scenario in which the grain trade question would be framed "as a set of mutual exercises in shrill, anti-conspiratorial unmaskings, a syndrome that would come to fore only in the French Revolution" (205). The first great unmaskings of the eighteenth century begin with the Prince de Bourbon, Madame de Prie and the Protestant court banker Samuel Bernard, but one finds traces of this sort of denunciation of conspiracy in the reign of Louis XIV. See Kaplan, "The Famine Plot Persuasion in Eighteenth-Century France," in *Transactions of the American Philosophical Society* 72, no. 3 (1982) and "Religion, Subsistence, and Social Control: The Uses of St. Genevieve," *Eighteenth-Century Studies* 13 (1979–80): 142–68.

interests of consumers and producers and of consumers and traders were habitually antagonistic—how could such a society not be awash in mistrust—local and kingdom-wide?[71]

On another level, however, the supposition of universal low trust or mistrust is unfounded. There is considerable evidence of ramifying trust relations in communities, institutions and businesses of various types. Credit linkages, upon which the economy as well as the society depended, abounded, and, even with notarial administrative mediation, within a framework of judicial sanction, they could not have occurred without a certain fabric of trust. Credit works, as a rule, because all the parties to it are invested in its success. Without a dose of trust, to limit transaction costs and compensate for information asymmetries or deficits, deals, big and small, would have been hard to conclude. Trust occurs locally, sometimes with mass consequences. Tens of thousands of Parisians obtained their daily bread, thanks to credit, the marquis subsidizing the journeyman tailor in this quite extraordinary system of quasi-mutualization. Cash-strapped, the baker turned to flour and grain merchants, commercial millers and factors in order to obtain raw materials on credit, sometimes in most-favored client relationships, predicated on trust, lubricated by bonuses in kind or rebates for fidelity and by commitments to reimbursement priority. When trust, or mutual esteem and understanding, broke down, when social capital eroded, when doubt warped confidence, credit dried up, creditors turned to consular jurisdictions or courts of lesser proximity and greater cost, for redress; or turned to symbolic or physical violence, to shame or stigmatize the other party, or punish her or him. Credit depended on trust, and trust on the broader, subtler notion of credit as reputation, as standing, as influence, as respect and as worthiness that Clare Crowston has studied so imaginatively. One can find similar structures of trust-based reciprocity in virtually all other trades and crafts, up to the highest levels of wholesale commerce, shipping and banking (family and religion facilitated networking, especially in the financial realm, serving as powerful vectors of trust or as levers to dispel mistrust, a general uneasiness, and distrust, an experience-based malaise).

I am not sure, conceptually, how useful global appraisals of high- and low-trust societies are, for in the Old Regime, and afterward, very frequently trust and mis/distrust cohabited, interacted, operated in a permanent dialogical

71 In this socio-psychological and political ecology, I think Clark is right to suggest that the king, incarnating public and private interests, imposes the social bond, though not for the reasons that he suggests, and not merely in the reign of Louis XIV (34–36).

tension.[72] Political life within guilds, confraternities, compagnonnages, village assemblies and certain municipalities was marked both by sharp strife and pronounced solidarity, in shifting tempos and portions. Public administration, at every level, elicits varying degrees of trust and mis/distrust, depending upon specific mobilizing issues, the actors involved and the circumstances. Louis XV was the well-beloved before becoming the licentious; he was the baker before becoming the grain merchant. John Law, under the Regent's protection, took the government through a cycle moving from skepticism to trust to suspicion and deep distrust, sometimes educing at the same moment diametrically opposite sentiments from different segments of society. Provisioning generated a double-bind situation: often, when the government acted (say, establishing public granaries or importing foreign cereals), it elicited mis/distrust (it was denounced for organizing hoarding and speculation); and when it failed to act, in periods of burgeoning subsistence uncertainty and stress, it aroused suspicion and disaffection for its apparent indifference to public adversity: this was as true of the Office national interprofessionnel des céréales in the early 1950s as of the controllers-general L'Averdy and Terray in the 1760s and 1770s. Nor does low-trust signify some sort of collective backwardness, as Clark sometimes seems to intimate: mistrust of the market principle, for instance (as opposed to the marketplace, in my idiom), does not necessarily bespeak superstition, prejudices and ignorance, as Condorcet would have it, but may constitute strategic thinking and/or prudent risk management and/or plausible stewardship of self-interest.

The author's stereotyping of France as a low-trust society seems to draw comfort from two other tendencies in his study. The first is a repeated reference to "national character," sometimes also known as

72 Clark opens his first chapter with these sentences, at best only one side of the story, at worst near caricature: "France in the early seventeenth century was widely perceived as, and may actually have been, what modern commentators might call a low-trust society. Peasant culture and economic practice peek at us through the centuries as fiercely mistrustful and staunchly individualistic—a time and place where 'neighbors are presumed to be hostile,' and where it was literally 'good to be bad'" (3). Collective constraints and self-conscious solidarity also marked certain aspects of peasant life. On the same page, the author cites O. Ranum who notes signs of "extreme distrust" among Parisians for their neighbors, though what he describes really is distaste and suspicion on the part of the haves for the have-nots. In any case, for each case of neighborly distrust, I can find examples of neighborly solidarity against intruders (soldiers, archers or outsiders) or against antisocial behavior on the part of a member of the community. Stereotyping facilitates generalization, but does not make for good practice, in social or cultural history.

"national identity," at least once as "national spirit." He deploys the term not only in his own voice, but also derives it from some of the texts that he scrutinizes. He does not venture a full exploration or definition of this notion, archaic and highly vulnerable in methodological terms (though he allows once that the "French national character is essentially corporatist," essentializing another descriptive category that is never fully unpacked). Perhaps, it makes sense to confer long-term, stable properties, such as low trust, to a supposed national character (42, 45, 63, 100, 133, 142–44, 155, 157). The joint preoccupation with national character and (structural or structuring) mistrust may nourish a second bent, this one somewhat more difficult to reconcile with the historian's Montesquieuian obedience: the idea that France is launched on a sort of *Sonderweg*, a path of exceptionalism. France was "a uniquely complex country" by comparison with its neighbors. The author invokes Mably's insight into "distinctive French monarchical values." He refers to "a distinctively French conception of the modernizing and commercializing monarchy" (64, 98, 101).[73]

Big Data before Its Time and the Evacuation of the Real World

Clark devotes an important chapter to the abbé Terray, who played a critical role, often obscured by the Maupeou "coup d'état" against the parlements, in the retreat from liberalization and the forging of what I call a third way in the administration of subsistence, though this is not the perspective from which the American scholar operates. He focuses on Terray's well-known *savoir/pouvoir* calculus: the conviction that modern governance will depend increasingly on the ceaseless collection and ongoing analysis of data, the fulcrum of an empirical, panoptical approach that is very different from Turgot's doctrinally driven program (the two controllers-general have only a piercing intelligence and a sympathetic megalomania in common). The historian notes in passing, in a cryptic phrase, that "in 1763–64, the French government had *mostly* freed the trade in cereals…," without taking the measure of the significance and implications of this dramatic policy swerve. When Terray replaced a resolutely liberal minister, Maynon, "the issue that arose, it should be noted, transcended its overt free-market vs. protectionist

73 The *Sonderweg* idea may also explain the author's fantasy that the French rather than the Germans exercise the dominant role in the European Community of our day (xi).

terms" (193). How does one transcend one of the foundational, structuring debates of nascent modernity? At stake, as Clark might have learned from Galiani, whom he admires, if not from the secondary literature, are the very nature of governance, the kinds of relations that will bind (or sunder) state and society, the relation of the individual (and her/his rights and interests) and the community (and its rights and interests), the reciprocal claims that each made on the other.

The kind of "transcendence" Clark evokes takes place, it seems to me, at a double cost. First, the evacuation of the real world: all of the social and much of the economic and political. From the author's treatment, one would never know that France was in dire straits in the early 1770s. Terray assumes his post in the midst of a severe social and economic crisis—not to mention the constitutional/political crisis, connected in some ways with liberalization, associated with Maupeou—that reaches its apogee in the north in 1770–71, then convulses the south, the region that most interests the author, between 1771 and 1773: harvest shortfalls, suspect grain removals, exorbitant bread prices in the context of sustained grain price volatility, chaos in many hinterland and metropolitan-collector markets, the desertion of many rural markets, cascading disorder (scores of grain, flour and bread riots, including what I call the Midi's Flour War, the background for much of Clark's discussion of the Languedoc case) and other canonic signs of popular misery and disarray (spikes of mortality and morbidity, increasing abandonment of babies, mendicancy and crime, swelling of the floating population and so on).

The second cost of transcendence resides in taking the part for the whole. Clark argues that, more crucially than the debate over liberty, at stake during Terray's tenure was a "different conception of knowledge and information" (193). I do not think that the abbé articulated a veritable epistemological position, but, as I demonstrate in *Bread, Politics*, he certainly envisaged information in a fresh way, and set about institutionalizing a tentacular data-collection system. Information was a *part* of a global strategy of "the general subsistence": I show that Terray's long-term objective was to *control* the provisioning system, from the center (the only vantage point from which a minister "sees the whole picture"), through what I call "a sort of Copernican revolution" of the *police des grains*, by crafting a third way, an alternative both to the havoc of liberty and to the babel of regulation. Clark's information informs Terray's conception of control, more fluid and less autocratic than the brutal edge of the word connotes, which has very little to do with "restoring social trust," save to the extent—Terray understood this to be a quixotic quest in the subsistence domain—that the consumer-people could once again feel confident that the government of proximity, following the lead of a renascent nourishing prince, would commit itself to assuring a market regularly supplied with merchandise of satisfactory quality—grain, flour or bread—sold at a reasonable price (193).[74]

Clark's discussion of the information question is not wholly convincing. I do not see evidence for a frantic search for data of all sorts that becomes "an end in itself." Nor is this yet the time of the NSA: I observe no indication of a reaction against a putative "systematic application of surveillance and collection of personal information." Here he appeals to public opinion, without any more rigor of definition than elsewhere in the book,[75] invoking the heightened sensitivity of "Frenchmen" or "the French" to encroachment upon their "liberties" and upon their "privacy" by nothing less than "an increasingly diligent and efficiently intrusive government" (194, 203).[76] The issue of secrecy, an archetypal Old-Regime matter, in some ways linked to the less familiar idea of privacy, merits a more attentive examination. Liberals see secrecy as an extension of the rights of property and liberty; in echo of the shared demands of the most marginal micro-grain trader (*blatier*) and the most robust (*négoçiants*), of *fermiers* of all types, they argue that grain holders cannot effectuate their socially useful "speculations" without the assurance of secrecy. The police are inclined (but *not* systematically) to regard speculations as antisocial undertakings and to impute dishonest motives to grain holders who take shelter in opaque confidentiality (coded as shiftiness or subterfuge). French women and men, at every socioeconomic and cultural level, have experience with secrecy: in the neighbor's relations with a common seigneur, in the juré's rapport with certain masters, in the police commissaire's behavior, in the decision-making process of a municipality, in the life of the court and in the very form of diplomatic and political management called the king's secret.

---

74 The recipe for trust restoration that Clark ascribes to Terray makes no sense to me in terms both of the realistic possibilities of reorganizing the provisioning trade and the regulatory apparatus: "… curtailing the actions of untrustworthy merchants [by what sort of census/inquisition and according to what criteria could one identify them, a corps of thousands?] and replacing them with government controls [which ones? after the jolting shocks of the 1760s, which inspired trust?] implemented by trustworthy agents of the Crown [selected through a purge?]" (194).

75 See pp. 78, 144, 185 ("advanced opinion" here), 194 ("the French" again), 250, 262, 266, 270–72, 283, 317, 322–24.

76 I am not at all sure that eighteenth-century taxpayers (and/or "touchy and ill-informed country folk") conceived their allergy to alleged fiscal trespass in terms of "invasions of privacy" (203).

The Realities of the Grain Trade and Its Merchants

A banal phenomenon, secrecy is almost always detestable wherever it operates, but is simply intolerable for consumers when it touches on their vital necessities. The decision to indulge it is neither mechanically a marker of modernity nor its quelling necessarily a retrograde herald. If regulators endorse, in principle, a transparent market place, they know that supply-side interventions by the government (what Clark oddly calls "the king's share of the trade," as if the historian subscribed to the famine plot persuasion) must be conducted with maximum discretion to avoid provoking disarray in the markets where it is purchased or where it is sold, and to avoid fomenting suspicion of illicit machinations covered by authorities (variations on the famine plot). The author does not look at the massive buying and reselling operations that Terray organized, many of them under the aegis of Sorin and Doumerc, who clearly apprehended secrecy as a double-edged sword. Certainly, the skepticism and the ambivalence regarding secrecy did *not* bespeak an "absence of any general legitimation of an English-style language of interests" in French political economy (and thus in "French political culture"): on the contrary, the apology and celebration of egocentricity in economic activity was at the core of the liberal project, from Boisguilbert, Mandeville and Melon to Gournay, Quesnay and Turgot–Condorcet (204–5).

This historian's handling of the grain/liberty debates is seriously flawed by his lack of understanding about how the grain and flour trade worked, who constituted its ranks and how regulators, low and high, perceived the merchants and the provisioning landscape. One can only be puzzled by his remark that Terray, facing a proliferating revolt against liberalization among the police and the people, was "finely attuned to the popular appeal of the free-trade edicts [*sic*]" (195). There was no "national market" in the eighteenth century, and it makes no sense to talk about a "national traffic in grain" (198, 205). The controller-general's "clemency" in regulation was characteristic of eighteenth-century practice, considerably more flexible than the author suggests (201, 213). Terray did not view "merchants as a class" because he knew that the grain and flour trade was a motley universe, heterogeneous in terms of social origins, degrees of education/culture, skills, capital, networks, access to information, range, business practices and so on. It is comforting for the author to imagine merchants as a class, for the actors whom he calls merchants represented a rather narrow array of traders toward the higher end of the spectrum, a poorly defined group in his hands from which it is impossible to extrapolate, as he does, to an implicitly ideal-type merchant, to a corps of traders all marching to the same drumbeat (212). Contrary to his suggestion, his merchants (and most others of all species) were infrequently members of a "royally chartered guild" (213).

Retro-projecting the neoclassical model of exchange into the grain (and utterly neglected flour) trading milieu, Clark has the chutzpah to profess to know what would be satisfying to "most of them", a claim I would not make after having studied them for four decades. He ascribes to them a coherent, shared discourse—superficially documented—of asseveration of their rights and desires and attacks on their adversaries that "sounded almost Jacobin in their debunking fervor," an affirmation as extravagant as the cryptic contention that "Terray in a sense prefigured the Jacobin regime of the *maximum*" (212). To shore up the conception of a homogeneous merchant group, a sort of "class," Clark misleads his readers by misreading Terray. The latter's decision to impose a permit system, aiming specifically at suppressing illicit exportation, peremptorily assimilated by the author to "privilege," in this instance nothing more than a red herring, affected *not* all grain merchants, but only the relatively small number, with means and vision, who engaged in coastwise trade. The vast majority of traders had merely to enroll with local authorities, as they had before 1763, the turning point in regulatory history (not 1764) (206–7).

Renewing the Field: Text, Context and Theory

On the French side, Loïc Charles is one of the leaders of the young generation of historians of economic ideas who are profoundly renewing the field with a fresh arsenal of questions and methods, drawing inventively upon philosophy, literature and anthropology as well as economics and history.[77] Our interests are both intersecting and complementary, though we have different approaches and priorities and do not pose questions in the same way. He is not as concerned as I am with articulating the tangled relations between ideas and the lived experience of social, political, psychological and economic life. He focuses on the history of economic ideas: without hewing to the internalist line, he wants to problematize the standard notion of context. His impulse is tonic in a field not renowned in France for its reflexivity; it touches on epistemological issues that remain controversial (and largely confidential in most branches of the historical profession). For his purposes, context is not an "objective" fact. The problem is not the familiar reduction of a text

77 The remarks in this section pertain exclusively to Charles' dissertation: "La liberté du commerce des grains et l'économie politique française (1750–1770)" (doctoral thesis, Université Paris 1, 1999).

to the reflection, or the expression, of some deeper reality. Rather, it is the (relative) autonomy of the eighteenth-century author and his/her capacity to make sense of the environment that he ponders. A (referential, incontestably identifiable) reality is displaced in favor of its representation: the author "is never utterly free, the context in which his work fits sends him back an image of the real world, as well as the world of ideas, which necessarily influences this work." The example he gives us is that it is less important to know if France declined between the time of Colbert and 1750, as most "reformers" believed, than to learn that they were so persuaded in order to fathom the goal of their thinking: how did the writer come to believe in this decline, did he/she follow clues encountered in reading works in English or Spanish or French, or through travels, and are his/her views widely shared by the reading public or manifestly original? Even as social historians used to deplore the cul-de-sac of political history, at the apogee of the hegemony of the *Annales E.S.C.*, so Loïc Charles laments the tendency of the standard history of economic ideas to consider that "the issues of the debate on the freedom of the grain trade were exclusively political, and that the stands taken by the reformers could, to a large degree, be studied independently of their theoretical conceptions" (5, 6).

Though he has written tellingly on the theoretical plane, clarifying substantially the thought of Gournayites and physiocrats, and their intellectual and analytical relations, Charles has perhaps contravened parts of his own embryonic epistemological doctrine in producing extremely valuable studies on the sociology of these two groups of thinkers, on their ways of working and networking, on the organization and practice of economic journalism and its periodicals and on the diffusion of ideas, among other themes.[78] He is much more interested than many of his American counterparts in the relations between ideas and policy, though he

78 Among his publications: *Le Cercle de Vincent de Gournay: savoirs économiques et pratiques administratives au milieu du XVIIIe siècle*, eds., Loïc Charles, C. Théré and F. Lefebvre (Paris: INED, 2011); *Œuvres économiques complètes de François Quesnay et autres textes*, ed. L. Charles, J. C. Perrot and C. Théré (Paris: INED, 2005); "Théorie des prix et liberté d'exportation du blé chez Quesnay: une interpretation," *Cahiers d'Economie Politique* 32 (1998): 41–65; with C. Théré, "The Writing Workshop of François Quesnay and the Making of Physiocracy (1757–1764)," *History of Political Economy* 40 (Spring 2008): 1–42; with P. Cheney, "The Colonial Machine Dismantled: Knowledge and Empire in the French Atlantic," *Past and Present* 219 (2013): 127–63.

I should add that in the thesis itself, as he grapples with epistemological issues, Charles shows that, even as he espouses certain principled positions quite strenuously (his call for the return of theory to the history of economic ideas is redolent of the plea of certain sixteenth-century historians for the return of religion to the study of the Reformation), he is a pluralist. See his interest in the social history of cultural practices,

has not yet fully theorized the complex and elusive ways in which influence operates in the Old Régime, in court and in town and country (nor has anyone else, for that matter). In what follows I comment on his doctoral thesis, which remains unpublished, an exceptional work of scholarship, unusually thoughtful and artfully crafted, which touches on some of the issues that concern me directly in *Bread, Politics*.

The Intellectual Genesis of Liberalization: Gournay before Quesnay

Building on the groundbreaking research of J. C. Perrot and Christine Théré,[79] which he has since himself enriched, Charles has contributed to the inception of a veritable re-periodization of eighteenth-century economic thought.[80] His work incites me to refine certain points in my treatment of the intellectual genesis of liberalization. I would concur that there appears to have transpired, beginning around mid-century—on this point we no longer need to rely on Voltaire's "raisonner sur les blés"—"a profound change … in the way of conceiving of the grain trade" (2).

In his story of the origins of the (re-)conceptualization of and the campaign for liberty, Charles gives precedence and a certain preference

---

manifest in his critique of both a materialist approach that sees the emergence of an economic "science" as a manifestation of the transition of France toward capitalism and a point of view stressing the constitution of political economy as a free-standing form of knowledge. Taxing both positions as teleological, Charles reproves their shared trait: "having excluded the study of the place of the economist in the society and culture of the Enlightenment" (114–15).

79 J. C. Perrot, "Nouveauté: l'économie politique et ses livres," *Histoire de l'édition française*, eds. H. J. Martin, R. Chartier and J. P. Vivet, vol. 2 (Paris: Promodis, 1984), 298–326; and his magisterial *Une histoire intellectuelle de l'économie politique, XVIIe–XVIIIe siècle*. C. Théré: "Eléments d'une sociologie des auteurs économiques de langue française (1715–1776)," *Economies et societies, Oeconomia*, série PE, no. 1 (1984): 11–33; "Political Economy and its Authors before 1789," in *From Bodin to Walras. Studies in the History of French Political Economy*, ed. G. Faccarello (London: Routledge, 1998), 1–56.

80 Of course this reperiodization is a herculean enterprise, in which many "younger" scholars such as Arnaud Orain, Sophus Reinert, Paul Cheney and John Shovlin, among others, are implicated. It is more a question of conceptualization, definition, taxonomy and analytical categorization than of chronology per se. What Orain calls "the black hole which is not" needs to be worked into the long-term scheme: the period/corpuses (not just the Great Texts) between Boisguilbert and Montesquieu, including Melon, deserve serious reconsideration, and the Jansenists, who beg for treatment (here they are for once dependent on good works). The emergence of the engineer-economists after 1770—I would put Parmentier in this category, and there are many other interesting actors—should be integrated. The noncanonic genres that traverse the entire long eighteenth century summon attention: plays, poems, tales of all sorts, *feuilles volantes* and so on.

to Gournay and his circle. He argues vigorously for the influence, heavily shaped by their perception of the English experience, of their understanding of the functioning of "the grain market (and the whole corpus of markets)" on political economy and on "public opinion" (a recurrent notion, undefined and unrefined). Yet the historian does not evaluate the validity of their view of the operation of the grain trade and, in his own voice, has very little to say about it. The idea of the grain market—in the singular, it takes on a visage that is both normative and abstract—as a quasi-template for all markets supposes a metamorphosis in the representation of grain, suddenly cast as a merchandise no different from any other, which seems to belie the pragmatism and realism with which Charles usually associates the Gournay circle (11).[81] The other factors, material and political, seem unevenly susceptible to transformation, that is, the grain could be deregulated so that its circulation was no longer obstructed and so that the conduct of dealers would become less inefficient, yet it would remain cumbersome and costly to transport; and information was likely to remain asymmetrically accessible and profitability would continue to be hostage to considerations (such as weather, variability of weights and measures, conservation vulnerabilities) that did not affect other goods such as printed calicos or furniture or pots and pans.

Nevertheless, the author's treatment of the views of the Gournay group, especially in relationship with the Quesnayites, not precisely the kindred spirits often supposed, is globally quite impressive, and invites us to rethink the historiographical heritage. Espousing a much narrower view of wealth than the Gournay circle, the physiocrats are only elliptically concerned with the grain trade; liberalization will prevent the decline of France by channeling funds into agricultural investment, to which the wealth of the nation is strictly proportional. Freedom of trade, "total and without restriction," predicated on a merciless competition, occurs at the expense of the traders, in Charles' reading of Quesnay's cramped view ("rigid" and "fragile"), fixed stringently on utilizing the *bon prix* theory "to make things return to their place in the natural order."[82] The Gournayites theorize free trade in terms of the efficient

81 Cf. the somewhat cryptic predicate: "… grain having, in virtue of its role as primary staple, a unilateral influence on the whole of the economic activity of the nation" (11).

82 The persistently intractable issue for the *économistes* remains the problem of convincing police and people (and not just *fermiers* who stand to profit handsomely) how liberty will not increase the average price of grain, while protecting the consumer from famine (292). D. Delmas and T. Demals place into relief the importance of the question: "Le 'bon prix' sans la 'cherté': la quadrature du cercle des prix chez François Quesnay," *Colloque François Quesnay* (Versailles, 1994). Philippe Steiner addresses this matter within a broader analytical framework: *La "Science nouvelle" de l'économie politique* (Paris: Presses Universitaires de France, 1998).

allocation of resources and men in time and space through a vision of the market price as a vector of information allowing producers, traders and consumers to adjust their behavior rationally in order to satisfy their variable needs, a model emphasizing their capacity to "self-organize," through the play of self-interest, and denying an ontological privilege to production.[83] Charles makes the strongest case that I have seen for the idea that, for the *économistes*, the efficiency of the market matters only incidentally, engulfed by the larger issue of economic growth, a sort of wedge issue that will induce Turgot to abandon certain of his basic Gournayian precepts by 1770 (9–10, 206, 283).[84]

The historian deploys the (sometimes idealized and heuristically demonized) example of the "enemy-model," England, to underline the specificities of Gournay's thinking, including his double interest in nourishing free trade and conquering international preeminence. In his search for the deleterious consequences of French economic administration through the English comparison, he does not reflect on why the English authorities felt so little (apparent) anxiety over the subsistence question once they declared grain an ordinary object of commerce (as Quesnay demanded). Nor does he fully work out the tension in Gournayian thinking between a more pragmatic notion of "organizing liberty" to maximize its "efficiency" (which allows place for "a certain interventionism") and the more fundamentalist espousal, extolled by the physiocrats, of the most rugged and extensive commercial competition (8, 158–59, 162, 164–65, 177).

Influence: Networks, Politics and Policy

In the end, despite the egregious theoretical deficiencies of Quesnay's theory of free trade, it progressively eclipsed that of the Gournay group as a result of "a very modern strategy of public relations [*communication*]," a line of reasoning that Charles makes one of the pillars of his study. He has done important work on the constitution of networks in the milieus of political

83 Quesnay thus displaces the study of the economic from the sphere of exchange and individual behavior—the focus of Gournay's "science of commerce"—to the realm of the production and reproduction of goods (225).

84 But not Forbonnais, who focuses on market comportment, concedes the specificity of grain as a vital commodity (claiming perhaps a special status?), rejects the definition of the *bon prix* as necessarily a high price, and even envisages "the necessity to regulate" (175, 211–19). Charles might have fruitfully enlarged his commentary on Forbonnais, on Abeille and his idealization of the *laboureur* (176), and on the role of the orphaned *négociants*, ubiquitous but not woven into a realistic grain-trade scenario (175).

economy. I agree with him that the Gournay circle weighed more heavily than the *économistes*, in terms of their personal and intellectual penetration into administrative spheres, and perhaps even that "the laws of 1763 and 1764 owe more to the principles of the Gournay group than to those of Quesnay," though this claim requires elucidation.[85] Yet the peremptory pronouncement "that physiocratic thought had no direct or indirect influence on ministerial decision-making" strikes me as overdrawn, to say the least, and not useful in the construction of his case. Even if the physiocratic intellectual presence was far more dense and vigorous after 1763–64 than before, it would be demeaning to the major players in the administration, whose modernity Charles lauds, to imagine that they were oblivious to Quesnay, Mirabeau and their followers (the indirect vector), and it would be imprudent to underestimate Quesnay's political/parlementary connections, apart from Lemercier de la Rivière and La Chalotais, and his court networks, beyond Madame de Pompadour, and to fail to take into account Mirabeau's quite astonishing range of seduction and authority in Versailles, Paris and the provinces. That said, I am not sure that the genealogy of legislation, however dramatic and significant, construed so narrowly, is a worthwhile line of inquiry.[86] In any event, Charles' analytical line leads me to believe, frequently, that he is less concerned with measuring *political* influence per se than with a broader cultural gaze that registers the relative place of various groups, such as Gournay's or Quesnay's, "in the

85 "In light of this totality of convergent facts, it is quite clear that the influence of the Gournay group on the two laws of liberalization must be completely re-evaluated" (201).

86 I understand Charles' fierce determination to render to Gournay and his circle what is theirs in the preparation of and run-up to liberalization. Yet there is a marked tendency toward overkill in this work. A plethora of voices constituted the liberal lobby, certainly many more than can be classified into the respective chapels of Gournay and Quesnay, a number of whose members, moreover, agreed on important issues, despite their underlying disjunctions. In reading the responses of L'Averdy's questionnaire to the Bureau du commerce, the deputes du commerce and others, Charles emphatically identifies the ideas of "the partisans of liberty" as "essentially" deriving from "the arguments of the Gournay group" (33–36). My reaction is two-fold: Can one persuasively precipitate out of the perfervid debates of the moment a sediment specifically attributable to Gournayites? And is this the paramount issue here? Certainly there are others, concerning, for example, the articulation of the case for exportation (following sundry scenarios) with the regulatory policy concerning not just internal circulation—the customary phrase that conceals more than it reveals—but the elementary structures and the functioning of the grain and flour trade. In the discussion over the most apposite legislative vehicle for a law dealing with grain exports, certain actors worried that an *arrêt du conseil*, relatively easy to revoke, lacked the solemnity and the durable

public debate." It is in this sense that the author intimates that the liberal laws did more to make the physiocrats—hastening their crystallization as a veritable school—than the physiocrats did to make these laws (36, 113, 194, 273–75, 322, 335, 343–45).

Articulating Internal Liberty and Exportation

On the way(s) to interpret the laws of 1763–64, Loïc Charles seems to hedge. On the one hand, he appears to argue for the primacy of the Edict of 1764, best known for its clauses concerning exportation, as a public issue, a position I contest. It is possible that the privilege that Gournay had always accorded to international commerce, reinforced by his observation of the English experience, predisposed the historian to accentuate exportation. Yet he knows full well that Gournay and many of his intellectual companions, though they did not explore the social and political implications, viewed the dismantling of controls on commercial exchange in the interior as a prerequisite for a fruitful export traffic: *inter alia*, the right to hoard—as wary consumers understood it—to constitute private storage granaries and generally to trade without impediment, in order to give full expression to the theory of "the efficiency of the market" (11, 132, 168, 185).[87] Nor is it reasonable to infer from the attacks of the Parlement of Rouen (unwontedly virulent and irreverent) and the Parlement of Paris (merely sharply refractory), along with the remonstrances of the exceptional Paris police assembly of 1768, a sort of priority of animadversion placing the Edict of 1764 in the top spot (44, 319). Rather than the chief theme of a "frontal attack" against the monarchy, export was merely a sensational metonym for a far broader evil, initiated by the Declaration of 1763, erecting liberty into the supreme value—"modern philosophy," or political economy, promoting a corrosive individualism, egotism and licentiousness—that undermined kingship as well as stable and reciprocally beneficial and binding relations between state and society. Charles fixes on exports because it was the target of liberal economic writers and framed "the editorial strategy put in place by the physiocratic

authority necessary to dissipate the uncertainties that discouraged *négociants* from engaging in traffic. Who were these traders? Where did they come from? How numerous were they? Were they deeply involved in the grain trade or occasional main-chance players? Incidentally, an *arrêt du conseil* is a less prestigious and compelling medium for a law aspiring to touch the whole realm and to perdure because it did not require parlementary registration (27).

87 I do not fathom the cryptic phrase concerning "the question of police intervention that seemed to have been definitively ended by the Edict of 1764…" (185).

school" (124, 317). Yet a great many of these texts concede the ontological priority of internal free trade, that is, the dismantling of regulatory structures, the affirmation of the inviolability of the (natural) rights of property and liberty, the desacralization of grain and bread and the attempt to rehabilitate commercial egocentricity.

On the other hand, despite his incongruous characterization of the Declaration of 1763 as "prudent," Charles seems to acknowledge its striking iconoclasm. He writes in the same paragraph: "It is a matter of the total overthrow of the traditional functioning of the grain trade; liberty is established as a principle and intervention, as benign as it might appear in the context of old habits, must be justified by irrefutable, precise, and exceptional facts." (I would argue that this exegesis allows much more latitude to authorities than the law actually accords (32).[88]) The historian seems to relativize the significance of the export phenomenon and, implicitly, the Edict of 1764, though it is difficult to distinguish his voice from that of his protagonists. He appears to consider as plausible the notion that, on one level, recourse to export after a period of abundance is a banal variable of adjustment, a traditional political–economic penchant, a simple "*toilettage* of the old laws," though he glosses over the crucial conceptual distinction: the administration construed previous export authorizations as temporary permissions, even as privileges, whereas, despite its clearly prescribed limits, the Edict is presented as a genuine break, as a harbinger of a measure that will perpetuate exportation as an incontestable right, with the intimation that it will be, at some point, devoid of restrictions (36–37, 326).

The Moral Economy and the People Problem

Liberalization foundered, to a great extent, as a result of the popular resistance that it provoked. Charles has an excellent command of the literature that he subsumes under the somewhat overstretched umbrella of the "moral economy" (20–26). He rightly rejects the mechanical/hydraulic models of hunger- (or price-)driven uprisings; the people cannot be reduced to a "stomach", as Arlette Farge evocatively underlines.[89] Yet, as the lawyer and philosophe Simon H. N. Linguet, reminds us, "the people," his volcanic protagonist, are obsessed with food (with bread, he regrets), are indeed often hungry and their stomach is nothing less than their "license" to eat, that is to make claims upon

88 Cf. his citation of Terray, which underscores the precedence, in fact and in law, of the May measure that generates "the excessive liberty in the commerce of the interior … and gives too much latitude for hoarding, monopolies and retention of grain…" (54).

89 Arlette Farge, *Dire et mal dire: l'opinion publique au XVIIIe siècle* (Paris: Seuil, 1992), 168.

state and society for their vital well-being.[90] I applaud Charles for avoiding the dual pitfalls of populism and miserabilism (say, in the flawed, albeit engaging, mode of a Camporesi[91]). Nevertheless, I do not see how one can escape the obligation to reflect on the ways in which hunger shaped the lived experience of those who were quintessentially consumers (obtaining their daily bread was the chief (pre)occupation not only of those whom the author euphemistically calls "the least favored," but also of the vast majority of the population, rural and urban) and of those who lived in contact with them as well as those who governed (26). He correctly observes, as Meuvret and Labrousse emphasized, that in the subsistence domain things were getting better in the eighteenth century (20–21), but there is no evidence that the news reached those most immediately concerned.

In a brief account of a grain revolt at Troyes in the spring of 1767, the historian holds that "one must not overestimate the role of bad harvests, nor the importance of actual exportation" (41). The previous year's harvest appears to have been good. Yet, even with price data, "agro-meteo" information and administrative reports, it is notoriously hard to weigh the reality of a harvest and its local impact. The trajectory from field to table can be tortuous, even in the best of times, as I suggest elsewhere; beyond the usual uncertainties, including the normal depletion of stocks across the harvest year, are the spread of destabilizing rumors in a volatile psychological environment and the unmeasurable effects of liberalization itself on the provisioning trade, allowing hoarding and off-market exchanges of all sorts. Actual exportation is important for us to determine, but it does not seem particularly pertinent in accounting for popular behavior (even as I think that the commonly wrought distinction between a "real dearth" and a dearth imputed to "opinion"—or an artificial dearth—is more relevant to liberal polemicists and certain public officials than to consumers in a given place). In any event, whether or not the knowledge of the existence of the 1764 Edict—there is some evidence that it was widespread—aggravated popular apprehension, consumers, in 1767 as in 1947, classified, semantically and pragmatically, any removal [*enlèvement*] of "local" grain (whatever its exact provenance) in the category called "exportation". At work here is probably also a collective sense of anger and betrayal vis-à-vis local authorities, proximate guarantors of the social contract of subsistence, manifestly transgressed (for the police, the suspected treachery led directly to the king).

90 S. N. H. Linguet, *Du pain et du bled* (London, 1774); Kaplan, *The Bakers of Paris.*

91 Piero Camporesi, *Bread of Dreams: Food and Fantasy in Early Modern Europe*, trans. D. Gentilcore (Chicago: University of Chicago Press, 1989).

It seems to me here that it would be fruitful for Charles to apply his own caution about taking into consideration "the image of world" forged by the writers. The collective representations of "the people"—the various, limited segments of them who left direct or indirect traces of the ways in which they perceived and/or constructed their world—constitute a reality certainly more powerful and as legitimate as the putatively objective one that we can reconstruct in retrospect. I am less confident than the historian about the underlying serenity of the subsistence situation in Troyes ("globally healthy"), and I would hesitate before daring to pronounce on what price was "completely bearable for the population," given the general ambience and the specific circumstances (40–41).

Like the writers of the Enlightenment and the historians of today who care about the issue, Charles is bedeviled by what I call the "people-problem."[92] Given the abyssal disproportion between their hulking ubiquity and the lack of direct testimony they bequeathed, it is extremely difficult to get at the people. I have been struck by the belief, salient in physiocracy (Mirabeau and Dupont), but not wholly absent amidst their antagonists (Galiani), that the police "become people" in situations of subsistence stress.[93] This invites us to explore and deconstruct the "people" metaphor (conveying notions of primal prejudices, primitiveness, benightedness, and so on). Charles mentions the complicity between police and people about which I have written, but surprises me by his psychological assessment, which eddies against a robust historiographical current that began with Georges Lefebvre, George Rudé and E. P. Thompson: "These actions [apparently popular price-fixing, unearthing hidden stocks, etc.] share the common trait of being based on instinctive behavior and not upon reasoning"; largely illiterate, the people "appear to act uniquely under the influence of their sometimes violent passions."[94] The author remarks that, for this reason, the philosophes and the physiocrats viewed them in the same highly negative light (15). The physiocrats and the philosophes were puzzled, worried and frightened by "the people." Why did

92 See my discussion of D. Cohen's very interesting contribution to this debate, above, in chap. 3.

93 Cf. E. P. Thompson's suggestion, in a similar vein, that paternalist magistrates became prisoners of the people as well as of their own discourse. "The Moral Economy of the English Crowd in the Eighteenth Century," *Past & Present* 50 (1971): 88. The local police in France were touched by various strains of paternalism of disparate intensities, but they rarely fit the Thompsonian paradigm.

94 Georges Lefebvre aimed squarely at the withering stigmatization of the "collective" people—still pejorative mob, not yet rehabilitated crowd—by Dr. Gustave Le Bon, an influential late nineteenth-century conservative thinker who emphasized its impulsiveness and its impermeability to logical reasoning ("Peu aptes au raisonnement,

Charles draw his psychological description from their pathological portrayal of the people? It seems inconsistent with the rest of his work.[95] In any event, if there is a case to be made for the irrationality of (certain kinds of?) collective action, it must be lodged on a very different foundation.

Public Opinion, High End

The people-problem often cohabits with the problem of public opinion in the Enlightenment, another major actor (sometimes quasi-anthropomorphized), for whose identity and role, historians have not provided a satisfactory account, as I have argued above. Public opinion looms very large in the study of Loïc Charles: though an ever-amorphous entity, it is asked to do a lot of hard labor, performing as a sort of discursive, signifying analogue from above to collective action. It appears on at least 27 pages, on one of them six times, on another four (for example, 7, 11, 114–16, 124, 135, 193–94, 200, 202, 209, 227, 275, 304–05, 316–18, 324–26, 328–29, 345, 347). Unlike many of us, he furnishes a definition at the outset, loosely congruent with Habermas,[96] but not dependent upon him, avowedly borrowed from the actors of the Enlightenment, self-explanatory in their terms, not analyzed in his: public opinion "designates the cultivated [or "well-read"] population participating by means of public usage of speech and writing in the political life of the nation" (7n). This is an interesting and rich point of departure that I wish the author had unpacked.[97] It has the merit of fixing broad but clear-cut social boundaries: when the historian invokes public opinion, he refers to an elite—

les foules sont au contraire très aptes à l'action"). Gustave Le Bon, *Psychologie des foules* (Paris: F. Alcan, 1895), 4; and Georges Lefebvre, "Foules révolutionnaires," *Annales historiques de la Révolution française*, 1934, republished in his *Etudes sur la Révolution française* (Paris: Presses Universitaires de France, 1963), 371–92. Cf., in the same lineage, the recent reflections of Sophie Wahnich, *La Longue patience du peuple. 1792. Naissance de la République* (Paris: Payot, 2008).

95 The postulate of a shared "schéma mental," or thought pattern, linking people and police, though it may be conceptually contestable or anachronistic, is untainted (60). When Charles attributes the Troyes rebellion (partly) to "individual decisions," he may be closer to what Philip Hoffman, cited above, called the capacity for "strategic thinking" among peasants than to brute instinct (41).

96 Jürgen Habermas, *The Structural Transformation of the Public Sphere. An Inquiry into a Category of Bourgeois Society*, trans. Thomas Burger with Frederick Lawrence (Cambridge, MA: Harvard University Press, 1989; first published 1962).

97 Much later, the author gives himself some conceptual cover by citing the works of Mona Ozouf, Keith Baker, Dena Goodman and J. A. W. Gunn, hovering in the spectral presence of Habermas, without subjecting their "concept[s] of public opinion" to critical examination (324n). The first three scholars on this list in particular eviscerate

presumably, in fact, to sundry albeit unnamed elites –given to regular "reading and thinking" (116).[98]

This public opinion is both demand and supply driven, it is heavily courted, especially by the physiocrats, who understand its immense power well before Necker, generally credited with its fullest instrumentalization. If the government itself seeks the support of opinion, the *économistes* aim at nothing less than to "subjugate" it, to realize a sort of public opinion putsch through their vigorous, calculated use of journalism, pamphleteering and other writings, "to take control of it in order to impose the necessary reforms upon the royal power." They seek to capture the "popularity" of the question of the freedom of the grain trade, steadfast (or burgeoning) ever since the publication of Claude-Jacques Herbert's *Essai sur la police générale des grains* in the early 1750s.[99] According to Charles, they subject the monarchy "to a media pressure that it had never before known" (317). Presumably, the parlements as

---

the social dimension from their reading of Habermas, for whom the "bourgeois" character of the public sphere (and the relation of property ownership to the expression of opinion) are crucial in its engendering and articulation. Baker is categorical in his dismissal of the "discrete sociological function" of public opinion in favor of construing it as a "political or ideological construct." K. M. Baker, "Public Opinion as Political Invention," in his *Inventing the French Revolution* (Cambridge: Cambridge University Press, 1990), 167–99. On this theme, see Harvey Chisick's thoughtful critique of the "neo-revisionist" historiographical wave of Kantian idealism that "seems to have reached a dead end," by overinvesting "in an abstract model" that proved incapable of withstanding "the incursion of the empirical reality of the historical phenomena that it is intended to explain." Chisick, "Public Opinion and Political Culture in France During the Second Half of the Eighteenth Century," *English Historical Review* 117 (Feb. 2002), 52–53, 67, 76. Noting the same sort of instrumentalization of Habermas, Dale Van Kley remarked that "If Habermas's book has successfully resisted the decline of Marxian explanation, it is mainly because historians have ignored his Marxism." Even as the Habermas influence has oriented scholarship on public opinion in the eighteenth century "away from content and in the direction of form," it has also "tended to yield a public opinion devoid of either a specific public or any particular opinions." Van Kley, "In Search of Eighteenth-Century Parisian Public Opinion," *French Historical Studies* 19 (Spring 1995), 216, 225–26. Anticipating this line in the 1780s, the percipient observer-commentator Louis-Sébastien Mercier asks "Does the public exist? What is the public? Where is it?" Mercier, *Tableau de Paris*, ed. Jean-Claude Bonnet, vol. 1 (Paris: Mercure de France, 1994), 1473.

98 Though Charles notes, modifying somewhat the framework of his own definition, that "it is completely logical to turn to seeking ways for enabling an important part of public opinion—including even the people—to attain a minimal knowledge of the theories of Quesnay." Cf. the comments of physiocrat G. F. Le Trosne on "the part of the public which is people" and is thus "singularly difficult to persuade (328).

99 If this line of reasoning is to be compelling, we urgently need a sociology of this putative popularity.

well as the crown are subjected to the dynamism and the efficacy of this public opinion because the Declaration of 1763 "is promulgated under [its] pressure" (334). In the wake of the publication of the Edict of 1764, "public opinion swears only by liberty" (323). It is all the more the regrettable that the author did not pursue this notion analytically since he identifies the physiocratic use of public opinion as "a power of a new sort," implicitly capable of changing the political landscape (345).

Rethinking the Invention of the Market Concept

Charles is at his most acute in his treatment of the notion of market—a generally teleological concept, a sort of heritage notion despite its recent origins, rarely interrogated in its assumptions or its (reified) trajectory. He argues that the liberalization debates were the midwife to the birth of the powerful idea of market in the idiom in which it would later be fathomed:

> … the modern concept of market in the sense of an abstract space where the totality of supply and demand are organized without consideration of time and space is nonexistent before the second half of the 18th century. This market is a notion constructed by French reformers to demonstrate the advantages of free trade in grain. (11, 351)

More provocative (and controversial) is his claim that "this invention" is not the product of liberal ideology. Rather, it is "a response to a practical problem," the portentous rise of British power, on land and sea, economically, politically and strategically. Charles alleges that there is no "a priori position in favor of laissez-faire" in the works of Gournay and Quesnay, a surprising claim that he needs to buttress with sustained textual analysis. Along with their collaborators, both engage in "an evolution towards more and more free-trade positions." Initially, Gournay and others close to him suggest adopting the English model of fostering exports with subsidies and inhibiting imports through tariffs. Yet by the 1760s, this posture is no longer tenable: "It is considered to be contrary to the freedom of the grain trade." The researcher insists that the "evolution" that took place was first of all "theoretical," an argument that flatters his contention that the historiography of economic thought had increasingly estranged itself from the scrutiny and the illumination of theory (351).

Echoing my conceptualization of the marketplace in opposition to (or sometimes in tension with) the "market principle," Charles contrasts the traditional vision of economic exchange (a notion of the just price, rooted in scholastic thinking, postulating a certain liberty, embedded in the normative practice called "the market of the Old Regime"—the *police des grains*—and existing "in reality only through this practice") with the "abstract representation" articulated by reformers without regard to specific transactions, a representation of a "structured concept [baptized] the Market" that can only take form as an abstraction, the sole framework in which "one can demonstrate that the most absolute liberty leads to the maximum level of well-being for the population." While the distillation of the concept of market is conventionally associated with Adam Smith, the historian contends, in fact, it occurred in France "in the context of debates over the liberty of the grain trade" (96–101).

The Fiction of the "General Market"

Charles points out astutely that the concept of "general market" is "far removed from the economic reality of the Old-Regime economy." Quesnay, Dupont and, even more compellingly, Abeille and Turgot utilize this "fiction of the general market." These thinkers made "no serious attempt to demonstrate that the grain trade functions *concretely* in the way the theory depicts it." On one level, the French scholar intimates that the theory of the general market is deployed for political reasons: "In order for the full liberalization of the grain trade to become conceivable as a rational choice of political economy, it was necessary to imagine the fiction of the market, abstract place where information and goods circulate, by the exclusive play of self-interest, as swiftly and efficiently as on the [physical] site of the marketplace." On another level, the implicit binaries fact/fiction or fabrication/truth or imaginary/real trouble Charles: the political economists craft a fiction that is nevertheless the product of a theoretical undertaking that is not inscribed outside of history or social experience. The way out of the aporia is to postulate an imbrication of positive and normative discourses, though it is not clear, in the argument too cursorily presented, whether the theoretical posture is meant to be proleptic or (merely) heuristic. So the general market "is a fiction, because it functions 'as if' the exchanges took place in the same site, and at the same time it is, in the eyes of the reformers, a concrete reality." Far from mystification, the view of these reformers is in the end ontologically "truer" than the police (or traditional) conception, confined to "appearances," because it is founded on an underlying "harmonious reality" that apparently affords abstraction traction in the world of farms and fears, property and penury, haves and have-nots. There is a brilliant analysis in embryo here, but it cries out for a much fuller elucidation and elaboration (101–5).[100]

* * * * *

100 Quite reasonably, Charles has not assigned himself the task of working out the tensions between theory and eighteenth-century reality. But the question dogs him.

Genealogical concerns preoccupy—sometimes afflict—research in the history of political economy. If one were to search for the earliest target of economic reflection, it could plausibly lead to the question of famine, an ageless horror that riveted the attention of women and men almost as far back as we can trace, even as it famously captured the dreams of Joseph in Pharaonic Egypt. A classical historical measure of good governance has been the capacity of leaders to prevent famine, or to parry it successfully. A significant part of the early, formalized literature of domestic and public economics, then of political arithmetic and political economy, deals with food (in-)security. In our time, famine has shifted definitively—or will climate change one day refute my optimism?—from a more or less universal problem to one specifically linked with underdevelopment. The political economy perspective has generated important debates on the causes of twentieth-century famines, focusing not only on agricultural production and other economic variables but also on political and social organization, ideology, international relations and a wide array of cultural factors. In the following chapter, I review some cases that commanded my attention as a result of their intrinsic interest and of the manner in which scholars have analyzed them.

Without demonstration, for example, he claims that the Gournay circle undertakes an "analysis of the functioning of the grain market"—presumably the lived and not just the imagined/ideal grain market—and that "in so doing [they] succeed in proposing a sophisticated theory of the functioning of the grain market… ." Ostensibly, the Gournayites pass from theory (analysis) and reality to a theory that explains ever more deeply and cogently the reality addressed at the outset. Yet, if Gournay, say, understood the mechanisms of the grain trade as they operated in his environment with the same command of reality that shaped Clicquot de Blervache's understanding of the functioning and management of the guilds, then he was much closer to fiction than to reality. See Simon Clicquot de Blervache, *Considérations sur le commerce* (Amsterdam, 1758) (9, 11).

Chapter VII

FAMINE, DEARTH AND FOOD (IN-)SECURITY

Probably no single issue poses the question of regulation more starkly than that of famine. An apocalyptical happening, famine places drastic strain on every system that underpins a social organization. Despite a long tradition of rejection of the naturalistic explanation, famine is characteristically the product, at least in substantial part, of grave and/or cumulative "agro-meteorological" disturbances. Famine may be simultaneously engendered or aggravated by market failure (severe exchange and distributional inefficiencies), social failure (a breakdown of cohesion), or political failure (a paralysis or abuse of power, and/or a breakdown or deficiency of regulation).

The Grim Reaper portends death the way politics (fore)shadows famine (or "merely" dearth). Culturally diverse in its performance, the Grim Reaper can in some cases actually cause the victim's death, just as politics can be plausibly called to account for the intensification and extension of famine, if not for its (technical) genesis, and for the horrors and hecatombs that follow in its wake. The irony of the Grim-Reaper motif is particularly chilling in reference to the dyad politics–famine because its central image evokes a harvester, associated in good times with the gathering of foods of first necessity, with survival if not festivity. Flourishing a scythe, the Grim Reaper harvests death rather than abundance, even as politics often dispenses indifference and mistreatment rather than succor and security.

I construe regulation, in a broad sense, as the intervention of the state, or other branches of public authority, in the name of some fundamental principles bearing upon the social bond, such as justice, equity and/or solidarity, to prevent or repair harm incurred by various members of the community as a consequence of acts committed by other members, or by outsiders, or as a result of acts considered as natural disasters (according to the formula commonly understood today). Regulation, in this sense, is the task of the institutionalized collectivity, those agents exercising power, and it takes the form of framing practices that we can call structural (upstream) because they are built-in and ongoing, though not necessarily static (such as laws, rules, and sanctions) and concomitant practices that we can style conjunctural (downstream) because they involve circumstantial action or intercession (imagine massive and fleet British assistance to starving

Ireland in 1847–48; or an efficacious and fair-minded intervention in the wake of Katrina; or a bailout to rescue individual homeowners, imprudent yet desperate, swept up in the recent mortgage convulsions; or increased and enhanced inspection of job sites to reduce the likelihood and severity of occupational accidents; or the imposition of price controls, in the mode of the Père Duchesne in 1792–93 or Richard Nixon in 1971; or the prescription of bans on certain pharmaceutical or food products because of their toxicity).

Beyond the role of the state audit agencies, there are informal regulatory mechanisms that have functioned in all kinds of societies in virtually all epochs. They are embodied by widely internalized norms and values, shared by a very large portion of the community, which shape, and in some instances, result in the spontaneous policing and penalizing of behavior deemed deviant or threatening. The characteristic example that concerns food security we have already evoked under the rubric of the moral economy in various incarnations.

Sen's Entitlements

When I wrote my thesis, I turned to the growing scholarly literature on famine, emerging from various disciplines, in search of insights into the subsistence problem in early-modern Europe. Those investigations have continued to thrive and remain a stimulating source of comprehension and points of comparison. I have looked recently at a very small sample of studies that aroused my curiosity. The most important conceptual reflection we owe to Amartya Sen; it richly merits discussion that is beyond the scope of this essay. Intellectually agile and imaginative, it moves effortlessly from commentary on Smith, Malthus and Ricardo to an approach driven by the analytical tools of contemporary economics.[1] Given the dearth of data we have for the Old Regime concerning what the economist calls entitlements

1 Adam Smith, we are reminded, argued, contrary to views widely held at all levels of Old-Regime France, that dearth has *never* arisen from "combinations" among grain traders or from any other cause but from "a real scarcity," usually the result of agro-meteorological accident, and from the devastation of war (one thinks of the South Sudan even as I write). In a way that would not have surprised a Labrousse, the moral philosopher also showed how a contraction of the labor market and a compression of wages would reduce entitlements of workers, rural and urban, amplifying their exposure to shortage. Moreover, despite the subsequent liberal instrumentalization of the iconic market champion, Smith did not cringe at the idea of intervention in a famine emergency: the question was whether it should take the form of cash assistance or direct food relief.

and the endowments that constitute them in large part (a person's original bundle of ownership and additional bundles subsequently acquired: resources an individual can mobilize using all the rights and opportunities available), given the absence of crises in France comparable to the Bengal famine of 1943, the Ethiopian famine of 1973 or the Bangladesh famine of 1974 (all of which saw a slight gain in food output during these starvation years), and given the myriad discontinuities between Old-Regime society and the worlds explored by Sen, direct parallels are less tenable and pertinent than broader intuitions about apprehending and dealing with these tragedies.

Through Sen's framing of the issues, he reminds us that observers and scholars have paid insufficient attention to the question of acquiring or establishing "command of food"; focused on the (deceptive) metric of aggregate food output in the Malthusian manner, they have failed to see that hunger and famine can prosper without a decline of food output available per capita. Food production, in Africa for example, needs to be cast as a wellspring of income and entitlement as well as a source of vital staples; in this sense, famine can be fruitfully studied, following Sen, in terms of a failure in entitlement relations. Cases of "boom" famines are most propitious for this kind of analysis: if economic expansion does not penetrate relatively deeply into the society, the ensuing uneven development penalizes a vast segment of the population's command over food due to their deteriorated position vis-à-vis groups benefitting from the boom. This problematic resonated with me keenly, as I write in the midst of a strikingly energetic and unexpected debate provoked by (the English translation of) Thomas Picketty's recent book on inequalities.[2] One can imagine the multiple implications of Sen's holistic analysis for contemporary policy for dealing with famine and durable food security, for the most part remote from the practices of Old-Regime ministries and the nostrums that their liberal critics formulated.

Entitled to Starve?

The economist acknowledged certain factors that remained outside the entitlement purview, including networks of family distribution, shared tastes and norms, morbidity and nonlegal transfers, commonly dubbed *taxation populaire* in the period from Henri IV to Napoléon III, classified as

2 *Le Capital au XXIe siècle* (Paris: Seuil, 2013). Cf. *Capital in the Twenty-First Century*, trans. A. Goldhammer (Cambridge, MA: Harvard University Press, 2014).

looting in the twentieth century, perhaps as an avatar of terrorism in the twenty-first century. There is no articulated place for a moral economy in the entitlement approach: critics have noted how Sen strips a manifestly normative term of any ethical purchase. There is no legal or moral reason for markets to satisfy subsistence needs: this postulate epitomizes the core debate in the liberalization crisis in France in the 1760s and 1770s. The law interposes itself between food availability and food entitlement. "Starvation deaths can reflect legality with a vengeance," Sen grimly noted.[3] One critic caustically observed that in his framework, people victimized by famine are not entitled to food; instead they are "entitled to starve."[4] Sen himself noted the "ambiguities in the specifications of entitlements" in what he calls precapitalist configurations, a phenomenon that deeply marks Old-Regime arrangements, customs and conflicts, especially concerning property rights and tensions between individual and collective claims.[5] It was not until the Revolution, and in the case of agricultural common lands well beyond, that France began to resolve the pervasive problem of what Sen describes as fuzzy entitlements.

In a line of reasoning that strikes a chord with the French experience, a number of scholars have contested his conception of entitlements as legal rights as excessively narrow: they invoke social, community or environmental entitlements in order to broaden the framework, without necessarily rendering it less fuzzy.[6] In a kindred vein, another researcher taxes Sen's methodological individualism that overlooks social vulnerability, and privileges more or less absolutely rational decisions to protect long-term endowments, even at the risk of exposing weaker members of the household.[7] Yet, another line of reproach, in which the "health crisis model" displaces the centrality of food entitlements or poverty, echoes historiographical debates on the Old Regime concerning the synergies between morbidity/mortality and malnutrition, or the relative weight of disease, a vector at once not wholly independent, yet

3 A. Sen, *Poverty and Famines: An Essay on Entitlement and Deprivation* (Oxford: Clarendon Press, 1981), 166. Cf. Sen, "Food, Economic and Entitlements" in Jean Drèze and A. Sen, *The Political Economy of Hunger*, vol. 1 (Oxford: Clarendon Press, 1991), 34–52.

4 J. Edkins, "Legality with a Vengeance: Famines and Humanitarian Relief in 'Complex Emergencies,'" *Journal of International Studies* 25 (1996): 550.

5 Sen, *Poverty and Famines*, 48–49.

6 M. Leach, et al., "Environmental Entitlements: A Framework for Understanding the Institutional Dynamics of Environmental Change," (1997), 16, cited by Stephen Devereux, "Sen's Entitlement Approach: Critiques and Counter-critiques," *Oxford Development Studies* 29 (2001): 253–54.

7 Devereux, "Sen's Entitlement Approach," 250.

more or less autonomous, as opposed to hunger or food deprivation per se.[8] A more broadly gauged appraisal takes Sen to task for a restrictive portrayal of famine as an economic disaster (arising from poverty and market forces) at the expense of political explanations that seem increasingly present, and germane, in twentieth-century famines—but one could make similar claims for early-modern food calamities—including such factors as war, exorbitant violations of human rights, failures or abuses of government, the use of famine/hunger as a weapon, and intentionality (the idea that famine engenders both beneficiaries and victims, consubstantial to representations of dearth/famine in France from the seventeenth to the nineteenth centuries).[9] Still, for all its limitations, the Sen thesis has deeply enriched the debate; and his subsequent work contests the reductionist charge that his perspective is narrowly economistic.

Interrogating Hunger as a Category

James Vernon has crafted another stimulating study that illuminates the problem of food shortage and insecurity from a quite different angle.[10] Focusing largely on imperial Britain from the nineteenth to the mid-twentieth centuries, he looks at the evolving understanding of hunger in a remarkably broad-ranging intellectual history that examines political as well as cultural forces and meanings at work in an arena long dominated by a certain form of materialism, however sublimated. I concur with his strong premise that hunger was "never simply a condition grounded in the material reality of the human body," a perspective that I believe was in fact shared by, among others, the *marxisant* literary scholar Piero Camporesi, who located hunger at the crossroads of the corporeal and the symbolic, between matter and the (political) imaginary.[11]

Spurning the postmodern bidding to question reality, Vernon draws nevertheless on its corrosive skepticism to interrogate hunger as a category, to explicate the genesis of its crystallization as a category, to reforge the category by freeing it from its conventional application and investing it with

8 A. de Waal, *Famine that Kills: Darfur, Sudan, 1984–1985* (Oxford: Oxford University Press, 1989), 182–83; de Waal, "A Re-assessment of Entitlement Theory in the Light of Recent Famines in Africa," *Development and Change* 21 (1990): 481.

9 Devereux, "Sen's Entitlement Approach," 256.

10 James Vernon, *Hunger: A Modern History* (Cambridge, MA: Harvard University Press, 2007).

11 Piero Camporesi, *Bread of Dreams. Food and Fantasy in Early Modern Europe*, trans. D. Gentilcore (Chicago: University of Chicago Press, 1989).

a fresh agenda of objects and questions. Given the "slipperiness of hunger as a category," the author ventures to historicize it independent, as it were, of its material causes. This task requires a deconstructive strategy that rejects reading hunger "as the result of a preexisting set of socioeconomic interests and groups competing for entitlement in a zero-sum game, with power invariably centered in the nation-state." The meanings of hunger are more diffusely situated ("in many unfamiliar places"), unbounded by the formal confines of the state, consubstantial to the "struggle to define and regulate hunger" that generates its own circuit of power, its own political constituencies, its own conception of the obligations and the scope of competence of government. The British case invites Vernon's attention to areas "long neglected in or omitted from the modern history of hunger" (which have their analogs in the much earlier French instance): critiques of colonial famine, hunger strikes and marches, the (re-)presentation of starvation in different media, the fabrication of techniques for measuring hunger, projects for nourishing populations and so on (7–9).

The story of hunger is not simply a Whiggish riff on modernization theory. In his investigation, Vernon evinces sympathy with the so-called "pessimists" who emphasize the ravages of "progress" especially amidst the laboring poor at home and the bulk of indigenous inhabitants in the colonies. The view is lodged in a more sweeping critique of classical political economy, industrialization and global/imperial capitalism (5–7). The dispute between optimists and pessimists did not play out in this way in France, though the influence of scholars of the bleak obedience such as E. P. Thompson and Karl Polanyi is evident in my work. A close reading of the representations of hunger in France remains to be written. In the eighteenth-century debates that I scrutinize, it is rarely overtly construed as either "natural" or "inevitable"; the vocation of political economy was in part to recast the very grounds of the assumptions tying hunger to sin, with sin taking expression, *inter alia*, as inveterate and even aggressive laziness (and hunger thus becoming the fault of the hungry) that required, for attenuation if not remedy, food deprivation allocated by the so-called market forces. Nor did the parties to the debate in France view hunger as structurally "beyond the government of man," though of course they differed widely, and bitterly, on what government signified in this context (2–3).

Divine and Man-Made Hunger

Vernon contends that Adam Smith liberated famine from divine causality. Much the same could be said of French liberals, though we have no thorough study of the impact of religious thinking on ideas about hunger and the way in which it shaped relations between state and society.[12] Religious practice as well as discourse comes into play here. Saint Genevieve, the patron saint of Paris, invoked and convoked to alleviate hunger and dearth/famine, survived the pedagogical onslaught of the Economic Enlightenment, both in the popular imaginary and in popular practice (and reemerged as late as the Liberation to reassure Parisians on their fate).[13] This side, too, of the history of the relation between religion and lived hunger calls for study. If one were to formulate the proposition cautiously and for heuristic purposes, it could be argued that the physiocrats (and other rabid liberals) suggested that the hungry were responsible for their hunger, to the extent that they clung—along with much of the policing apparatus—to archaic, post-Edenic prejudices favoring the crippling of the market principle and the obstruction of the circulation of commerce. They imputed this rejection of the Economic Enlightenment not to strategic thinking, even of the most rudimentary sort, but to profound ignorance, reinforced by fear (whose psychological dynamic they vigilantly avoided examining) and by an absence of leadership from the public administration. Albeit far from Vernon's analytical itinerary, this illustrates another way in which it can be maintained that hunger was not simply—or only—"a condition grounded in the material reality of the human body" (7).

By and large, French liberals could join Smith in affirming that famines were man-made, that is, the product of undue interference with what he understood as the market (11). Malthus followed Smith on the primacy of the market, though he emphasized the function of hunger as a check on the morally weak (and in this manner a natural and necessary part of the world), which occupied a far less prominent place in the writings of his Scottish colleague (11). This strain of Malthus needs to be examined much more attentively in the thinking of both French liberals and critics of untrammeled liberty. Still,

---

12 More broadly, we need searching studies of the interactions between religion and political economy. See some of the building blocks: A. Kubata, "Quesnay, disciple de Malebranche," in J. Hecht, ed., *François Quesnay et la physiocratie*, vol. 1 (Paris: INED, 1958), 69–96; Catherine Larrère, "Malebranche revisité: l'économie naturelle des Physiocrates," *XVIIIe Siècle* 26 (1994): 117–38; Michael Sonenscher, "Physiocracy as Theodicy," *History of Political Thought* 23 (2001): 326–39; Sonenscher, "French Economists and Bernese Agrarians: the marquis de Mirabeau and the economic society of Berne," *History of European Economic Ideas* 33 (2007): 411–26; P. Steiner, *La "science nouvelle" de l'économie politique*; Arnaud Orain, "The Second Jansenism and the rise of French Eighteenth-Century Political Economy," *History of Political Economy* 46, no. 3 (2014): 463–90; and the citations proposed by Yves Citton, *Portrait de l'économiste en physiocrate: Critique littéraire de l'économie politique* (Paris: L'Harmattan, 2000), 5n.

13 S. L. Kaplan, "Religion, Subsistence, and Social Control: the Uses of St. Genevieve," *Eighteenth-Century Studies* 13 (1979/80): 142–68.

the physiocrats and others were rather sanguine—for theoretical and political reasons—about the prospects of ridding France (and other enlightened places) of hunger, provided the state adopted their system. Though it was the anti-physiocrats rather than their antagonists who first adumbrated an embryonic vision of what later becomes "the social question," I do not believe that the idea that only hunger could teach people industry and assiduity was a canon of liberalism,[14] whose raw, even brutal edge I do not underestimate, but whose proto-social-Darwinism was not unchecked by scruples that one could call Christian or philanthropic (rather than humanistic). Hunger logically leads Vernon to pose penetrating questions about the emergence of the social, in the wake of Jean Baudrillard's declaration of its death, at about the time that Margaret Thatcher, epistemologically self-indulgent in her branch, proclaimed that there was no such thing as society, in a spirit suggestive of Le Chapelier's vision of the individual standing alone vis-à-vis both a clamorous market and a discreet state (14). Certainly, the debate over liberalization in France compelled all the participants to think about the highly uncertain future of the corporate order, sapped as much by its own unexpected internal dynamism as by its simultaneous yet equivocal deterioration and unraveling, and concomitantly jolted by the withering polemical assault, efficacious yet sometimes indiscriminate, from certain, but not all, precincts of the Enlightenment.

Colonial Hunger

In terms of chronology and some of the sources mined, I was especially struck by an essay entitled "Hunger in the Garden of Plenty: The Bengal Famine of 1770" by David Arnold, a specialist on South Asian history and already the author of an important study on famine.[15] The most obvious difference between acute subsistence crisis in France and in Bengal in 1769–70—apart from the sheer magnitude of the catastrophe, the unspeakable hecatombs in India—

14 Experts on mercantilism could probably trace this theme through the writings of Antoine de Montchrestien, then later find intimations in Mandeville, as well as in the broader currents of early modern European thought and practice, notably English and Dutch.

15 Arnold's piece is in Alessa Johns, ed., *Dreadful Visitations: Confronting Natural Catastrophe in the Age of Enlightenment* (New York: Routledge, 1999), 81–111. Within a broadly conceived environmental history, the study of catastrophe in past time has burgeoned in interest. See, for example, Grégory Quenet, *Les tremblements de terre aux XVIIe et XVIIIe siècles: la naissance d'un risque* (Seyssel: Champ Vallon, 2005) and "La Catastrophe, un objet d'histoire?," *Hypothèses* 2 (1999): 11–20. See also David Arnold, *Famine: Social Crisis and Historical Change* (Oxford: Blackwell, 1988), the framework for the piece discussed

arose from the colonial domination exercised by the British. The vehement protests of the supply crowns against Paris for the plundering of local grain, an outcry emanating as much from the authorities as the consumers, conveyed what might be called (metaphorically) an anticolonial rancor, but the political, cultural, ethnic and historical context was, of course, profoundly different. Reports of extreme misery struck familiar chords in both parts of the world: recourse under extreme pressure to the consumption of grasses, leaves, bark and other (ordinarily) inedible ersatz, and the recurrent rumor of people resorting to cannibalism, ultimate marker of dehumanizing desperation (84). In France, it could be said that the distinction between sustained high prices and protracted scarcity made no difference to the mass of indigent, to the extent that grain was no more or less accessible in the first instance than in the second, despite its manifest physical presence. Yet, in Bengal, beyond the quadrupling of prices, in many places rice was simply not materially available at all, the practical translation of the technical differentiation between dearth and famine (84).[16]

Famine Memory and Visions of Plenty

Potent in its short-term, quasi-contemporary impact in the eighteenth century and the first half of the nineteenth century in France, famine memory informs Indian culture even today, as perhaps it does in Ireland, another victim of English colonial-imperialism. Recurrent famine in nineteenth-century India, and mounting criticism of British rule, confirmed

here, which draws on cases from Asia, Africa, Latin America and Europe to provide a good introduction to the famine problématique. I suspect that Arnold profited from the dexterous crossing of historical and anthropological perspectives in Paul. R. Greenough, *Prosperity and Misery in Modern Bengal: The Famine of 1943–44* (New York: Oxford University Press, 1982), where cultural variables count as much as political factors in this study of a man-made calamity. Margaret Kelleher, *The Feminization of Famine: Expressions of the Inexpressible?* (Durham, NC: Duke University Press, 1997) is a pioneering exploration of the "gendering" of famine representation in writing (fiction and nonfiction) and visual imagery, primarily in nineteenth-century Ireland, and in the Bengali famine of 1943–44. More recently, Cormac Ó Gráda deftly analyzes the geneses and impacts of famine from ancient Egypt and fourteenth-century Europe to Cambodia in the 1970s and to the Niger famine of 2005 in *Famine: A Short History* (Princeton, NJ: Princeton University Press, 2009). The case studies and comparative perspective of Thomas Keneally, *Three Famines* (Sydney: Random House, 2010) are also useful.

16 Cf. the French Old-Regime formulation of this distinction: *cherté* (a situation of still spiking or already very high prices) is the beginning of *disette* (dearth). Famine is *disette consommée* (dearth pushed to its limits).

the intuition of many contemporary observers that the famine of 1770 was not a "natural" but a "man-made" disaster "and as such one of the most damning episodes in India's experience of colonial rule," along with the somewhat isomorphic Bengal famine of 1943, "directly attributed to British bungling" (86–87).[17]

Natural and man-made causal explanations clashed repeatedly in Old-Regime France. Numerous commentators, public administrators and consumers (but not zealous physiocrats) believed fervently in the (idealized/mythicized) persuasion of structural French abundance: the kingdom as a granary of such Cockaignesque fertility and productivity that only a truly horrific catastrophe—an inordinately rare happening—could occasion scarcity.[18] Therefore, they ascribed *cherté* and dearth, chronic occurrences, to "vice," to human evil: postharvest maneuvers, manipulations, speculations and hoarding—a repertory of antisocial crimes often summarized by the word "monopoly". This provided the empirical and psychological justification for a strategy of regulation and intervention, a posture that did not prevent authorities at the highest levels—civil and ecclesiastical—from seeking to preempt popular protestation and agitation by directing responsibility, in an acrobatic socio-theodicy, to the wrath of God, provoked by the sinfulness of his flock, but subject to clemency.[19] During the period 1765–70, even those

---

17 Cf. the highly imaginative and controversial study by Mike Davis entitled *Late Victorian Holocausts: El Niño Famines and the Making of the Third World* (London: Verso, 2000). It is an indictment of liberal capitalism, held responsible for millions of deaths, in connection with global climate patterns, in particular the El Niño Southern Oscillation. The toxic tandem colonialism–capitalism, according to Davis, pauperized and fragilized populations in British India and elsewhere in Asia, Africa and Latin America. Davis argues that laissez-faire policies dramatically aggravated shortages and magnified famines, and thus bore a major responsibility for veritable "holocausts." In addition to forging a damning case against the political economy that starts with Smith and Malthus, the author develops a fruitful concept of "the political ecology of famine" that has implications for both Old-Regime societies and the emergent Third World.

18 Montchrestien, among others, worried precisely that the excessive fertility of the realm would make it difficult to incite the poor to work. See *Traité de l'économie politique*, ed. François Billacois (Geneva: Droz, 1999).

19 See Kaplan, "Religion, Subsistence, and Social Control: the Uses of St. Genevieve." Cf. Arnold's remark: "Surviving sources provide no evidence that the drought and famine of 1769–1770 were seen as a form of divine retribution (94)." Yet neither the official correspondence nor the discourse of Indian leaders seems capable of sustaining a distinction between God and Nature in terms of responsibility (the human/natural/divine nexus requires a closer interrogation in terms of the relation among hapless human culpability, natural perturbation or ire and recourse to or expectation of providential intercession).

who did not subscribe to a full-fledged version of the *pacte de famine* were convinced that government-protected or backed speculators sorely aggravated subsistence disorders that in any event stemmed more from the official policy of liberalization—sweeping deregulation, redolent of the British domestic model—than from spasmodic harvest shortfalls.

Raynal's Monopoly

I have tried to tease out some angles of comparison with France that stood well outside David Arnold's purview. Yet he closes the loop, as it were, by summoning the testimony of the abbé Raynal, whose first edition of the *Histoire philosophique des deux Indes* he mistakenly places in 1772, when in fact, fatidically, it appeared first in the year of the famine, 1770.[20] Persuaded that Bengal was the richest region of India (if not of all of Asia), the Frenchman, perhaps projecting unconsciously from his experience at home, as well as from earlier travelers' texts, questioned the imputation of "a most dreadful famine in a country of all the most fertile" to drought or other meteorological disturbances. Instead of blaming the weather alone, writes Arnold, "Raynal accused the English East India Company and the 'most odious and most criminal of all monopolies' exercised by its merchants, for causing the shortage of grain and the resulting mortality" (90).

Beyond the ambient rhetoric of denunciation, Arnold does not venture to explain why Raynal took this position and deployed in particular the highly charged epithet of monopoly. Part of the answer almost certainly resides in the abbé's conversance with the French subsistence situation, past and present. As I hint above and demonstrate in *Bread, Politics and Political Economy*, monopoly is a critical concept and symbol in the debate between liberals and the so-called restricters on the advantages and the perils of a free grain trade. Often associated with speculative, venal undertaking with which the government was surreptitiously associated, monopoly became the leitmotif of the defense of liberty in the late 1760s and early 1770s and at the same time the marker of indignation and outrage of the decriers of the *pacte de famine*, the belief that the protracted subsistence period of dearth and violent disorder that reached its pinnacle at approximately the moment of the Bengal famine was the work of a monopoly commissioned by the

20 Widely associated with Raynal, the *Histoire philosophique des deux Indes* was, of course, the product of many authors, including Diderot, one of the "noneconomic" philosophes who became deeply interested in the subsistence question and the problem of regulation.

government, supported and shielded by the king himself, if one is to believe the seditious discourse of the Rouen Parlements and of many other voices across the social landscape.

Gola and Gardens, Culture and Nature

Raynal passes too rapidly through Arnold's pages, but other themes invite comparison. The latter's allusion to the transformation in the (orientalist/colonial) imaginary of nature, in particular the Fall from Eden, the blighting of the bounty of nature and the increasingly disabused nostalgia for its return, evokes the sharp debates engaged by political economists over the grain question in France where nature, for the physiocrats, furnished the philosopher's stone for governance, growth and order, while their antagonists tended to perceive it as a capricious and often vicious force of disorder and breakdown (90–91). The movement away from the idea of Bengal as an abundant garden to a land of hardship and poverty induces the British to "compensate for the apparent deficiencies of nature." (Indeed, there is an unresolved tension in Arnold's analysis between the idea that a depleted nature requires a supplement in the form of human intervention and the notion that the "savage side of nature"—figured by predatory and unpredictable tigers, analogous to Galiani's suggestion that it is the vocation of nature to run amok—has become dominant and requires muscular containment (91, 93).[21])

The Indian/colonial emblem of this sociopolitical and cultural shift—at odds with the market-driven equilibria on which domestic political economy depended—was the giant domed *gola*, or public granary, built in 1786 by the government to store grain in the event of any future famine. The *gola*, the granary of abundance, the Roman/Italian incarnation of the *annone*—all of these ideas/institutions address the fundamental question of the relation of state to society, of the obligations of a government to its subjects, notably in terms of food staples. Throughout the eighteenth century, the French debated the question of formalizing and extending the use of public granaries, already present in many cities, such as Lyon. The Academy of Sciences promoted research on the most effective models for granaries, even as scientists developed improved methods for conservation.

For liberals, the most efficient granary was the speculative hoarding of the trader. That was the case that the English government made on the

21 See Kaplan, "Galiani: Grain and Governance," in S. L. Kaplan and Sophus Reinert, eds., *The Economic Turn: Recasting Political Economy in Eighteenth-Century Europe*, forthcoming.

eve of the great Irish famine. There, the idea of venturing to domesticate nature in the service of economic and social outcomes seemed absurd and counterproductive. I would have found it interesting for Arnold to try to articulate more fully the relation between colonial decision making and British political economy in the aftermath of Hume, Ferguson and especially Smith. In the wake of Bengal's natural infirmities, revealed by the famine of 1770, the colonial authorities also fostered a project for the creation of a botanical garden near Calcutta that would introduce into India "food plants that might help to avert the kind of scarcity and loss of life caused in 1770 and again in 1784" by famine and the disease that followed. Like the *gola*, the garden cast into relief "the way in which, in an increasingly imperial-minded age, British claims to a mastery over nature were contrasted with Indians' abject subordination to it and so provided a legitimacy for empire itself." In always-ambiguously liberal Britain, the state intervened to assist nature's fragilized purchase on colonial Indian life (92–93).[22]

If the French elite continued to believe in the beneficence of nature, they also sought to find famine prophylaxis and solace in the education and propaganda projects meant to acquaint the population with an array of ersatz foods to replace or supplement scarce cereals in hard times. Men I have called subsistence scientists, such as Parmentier, renovator of milling and baking, champion of the potato and of potato bread, were in the forefront of the campaign to arm the kingdom against food insecurity, despite the liberal ideological inclinations of many of them.[23] In the somewhat demoralized liberal precincts of France in 1770, the only way in which nature could express itself fully was by a disengagement of the state. (The physiocratic magistrate and public administrator, Lemercier de la Rivière, intendant in the Antilles in the early 1760s, tried to find some middle ground for cooperation between state and nature in the colonial context that would not have been imaginable in metropolitan France.)

22 For an extremely original and stimulating study that begins in a metropolitan botanical garden and deals with the interactions between science and imperial expansion, see Richard Drayon, *Nature's Government: Science, Imperial Britain, and the "Improvement" of the World* (New Haven, CT: Yale University Press, 2000).

23 See Kaplan: *Provisioning Paris: Merchants and Millers in the Grain and Flour Trade During the Eighteenth Century* (Ithaca, NY: Cornell University Press, 1984); *The Bakers of Paris and the Bread Question, 1700–1775* (Durham, NC: Duke University Press, 1996); and "Between Habit and Necessity: The Ersatz Question in Eighteenth-Century France," *L'Histoire grande ouverte: hommages à Emmanuel Le Roy Ladurie*, ed. by A. Burguière, Joseph Goy, and M. J. Tits-Dieuaide (Paris: Fayard, 1997), 379–94.

Passivity and Revolt

Arnold calls attention to Raynal's gripping appreciation of Indian behavior in extreme subsistence stress, a view plainly informed by comparison with French/European comportment in kindred circumstances. The abbé is struck by the passivity ("gentleness" or "indolence") of the native reaction to the aggression of the famine (and implicitly, the incompetence, indifference or turpitude of those charged with governance): "Amidst this terrible distress, such a multitude of human creatures, pressed by the most urgent of all necessities, remained in an absolute inactivity and made no attempt whatever for their self-preservation." Unlike their European counterparts, they did not "revolt" or commit vengeful/punitive "massacre", they did not invest storehouses or impose a just price through intimidation or violence (*taxation populaire*). The tumultuous European subsistence scene stood at antipodes from the Bengal quiescence, which seems in Raynal's mind largely independent of colonial hegemony (and which other observers assimilated to "fatalism," "physical and moral deficiencies" or "effeminacy"): "What disorder! What fury! What atrocious acts! What crimes would ensue! How should we have seen among us Europeans, some contending for their food with their dagger in hand … trampling under foot all authority, as well as every sentiment of nature and reason" (95–96).

Raynal's remarks are doubly significant, for beyond the crude anthropological contrast between Bengal and European hunger response is a representation of French subsistence behavior, in particular for the crisis of 1765–70, which corresponds only to the most apocalyptic assessments, habitually overdrawn, molded by powerful ideological assumptions, valid in a small number of cases. This view of a tropismatically violent consumer-people is more common among the zealous defenders of liberalization, notably the physiocrats, a "sect" perhaps, but a sect first of all inscribed in the cultural universe of the Enlightenment, than among the conservative elites, who were even more worried and puzzled by the "people"/subaltern problem than the philosophes. Raynal's characterization of subsistence disorder was simply incompatible, for example, with the representation of his close friend and collaborator, Diderot, at once indulgent concerning the consumer-people's struggle for survival and disinclined to stereotype their strategies of collective action.[24] Yet there lurks an implicitly positive valence in Raynal's

24 See Kaplan, "'Isn't the Sentiment of Humanity More Sacred than the Right of Property?' Diderot's Anti-physiocracy in his *Apologie de l'abbé Galiani*," in S. L. Kaplan and Sophus Reinert, eds., *The Economic Turn: Recasting Political Economy in Eighteenth-Century Europe*, forthcoming.

proto-Le Bonian portrayal of the crowd/mob that other scholars will have to work out (or refute): an intimation that, when the stakes are basically life or death, when the suffering is manifestly unjust, disorder, if not daggers, may be an appropriate or at least an understandable reaction. In any event, even as the anti-physiocrats castigated the liberals for preferring the boosting of the income of the grain holders to the succoring of the hungry poor, so critics in Britain denounced the East India Company—"rapacious," "monopolistic," "corrupt"—for showing "more concern for its revenues than for the people's distress" (99–100).

In an interesting yet not wholly convincing concluding argument—much of James Scott's work eddies against it, though it targets, to be sure, different cultures, societies, and times—Arnold contests Raynal's views of native passivity as substantially misleading. Given the 15 years of brutal colonial exaction that aimed directly at the rural population, and the overwhelming coercive strength available for repression, he finds the paucity of overt resistance during the famine to be unsurprising. The historian cites instances, sometimes quite elliptical, that bespeak "clamorousness" and not merely resigned lamentation on the part of the peasants. They showed evidence of survival strategies, they expressed collective anger by burning *golas*, they joined gangs of bandits seeking out villages where food was believed to be stored and so on (101–3). Arnold maintains quite cogently that the famine of 1769–70 helped to transform European ideas of Bengal from an organic cornucopia into a land of blight and to shape the depiction of Bengalis as feeble and passive. I see less coherence in postulating a European "identification of Asia with nature" when the latter's savagery found expression first of all in the governance of the Company—the tiger was in the counting house, not in the countryside—and when the consumer-people, despite efforts to defy and combat, seems in the end much more nearly the victims of nature than its agents (105–6).

Bloodsucking Monopoly and Famine in Colonial Mexico

Another case of "colonial" famine shows more graphically the imprint of metropolitan ideology on governing elites and the structuring tension between liberal and regulatory dispositions.[25] The piece on which I draw is written by a young historian, Amílcar E. Challú, who is about to publish a book that I am impatient to read, entitled *The Political Economy of Hunger in Mexico*, which

25 Amílcar E. Challú, "'Their Bellies Must Be So Big!': Grain Hoarders and the Emergence of the Political Economy in Late Colonial Mexico," in Michael Rotenberg-Schwartz, with Tara Czechowski, eds., *Global Economies, Cultural Currencies of the Eighteenth Century* (Brooklyn: AMS Press, 2012), 97–119. This is a fascinating piece

argues that "a great decline in nutrition and living standards at the time of independence was intrinsically related to the inequities generated by economic growth and the expansion of markets at the expense of traditional local rights to food production." In late colonial Mexico, one of the leitmotifs of the long struggle over how best to manage a combined vision of modernization and food security is a variant on the Raynal animadversion on monopoly. As in the France of the Economic Enlightenment, whose writings influenced elite economic thought both in Mexico and in Spain, the speculating, hoarding, energetic grain trader is alternately figured as an agent of economic development and durable abundance-in-shared-prosperity, in the perspective of laissez-faire optimism, or as a manipulative parasite who abuses liberty in the service of voracious personal gain at exorbitant social cost, in the prism of regulatory pessimism (though the liberals sought to subvert this conventional binary confrontation by fashioning the distinction between the socially valuable speculator, wholesome nourisher rather than bloodsucker—image common to the Mexican and French debates—engendered by a policy of free trade, and the perverse and perverted monopolist, exclusive production of the degenerate police system itself). Shortly after "the famine of 1809 [which] reinforced criticism against grain hoarding" (107), José Joaquin Fernández de Lizardi, a *criollo* writer preoccupied with the problem of urban subsistence, captured an image of the unchained grain trader that seemed to be shared both by the consumer-people and by numerous local authorities, in the manner of the French experience:

> Girl: Oh, tata! And these monopolists are animals
> Like the weevils that eat corn, wheat, beans
> and everything?
> Tata: Yes, daughter, animals is what they are, and
> they are big […]
> Girl: Their bellies must be so big!
> Tata: Yes, they have big bellies; some as big as
> fifteen or twenty yards (97)

---

that suffers from an analysis that is insufficiently developed and sometimes tortuous; from a lack of articulation of the cultural representations of famine and dearth (not clearly distinguished), on the one hand, and the functioning of the provisioning system on the other; and from a perfunctory treatment of the political economy announced in the title. For comparative purposes, I would have liked one technical clarification. It is hard to gauge the Mexican tonality of the term *regatones*: it is translated as both wholesale merchants, professional nomenclature that does not appear to be inherently pejorative, and regraters, which, in European usage, is indeed connoted negatively and in many places pronounced an illegal activity.

Without venturing to measure the depth and range of their influence, Challú maintains that the *ilustrados*, cultivated and politically ambitious lower nobles, disseminated the liberal ideology, crystallized by Pedro de Campomanes, who obtained from the king a liberalizing measure in 1765 that provoked unspecified "great resistance and widespread rebellion." One of the leading intellectuals of the Mexican Enlightenment, José Antonio Alzate, argued for the efficacy of the market principle and the legitimacy of wholesale trading practices, a line further developed by an influential official in the viceregal administration, Ramón Posada, who maintained that the solution to chronic shortage and price volatility was free trade on the 1765 model.

Although the Campomanes reform never enjoyed full implementation in Mexico, until "the year of the famine"—1785—neither administrators nor leading thinkers considered grain hoarding to be a real or serious problem. The famine, generating unprecedented levels of grain prices and killing as much as 10% of the population even in rich agricultural districts, "split elites" into a camp espousing "government control over grain trade" and a lobby that continued to favor "unconditional free trade" (98, 102). As in France and in Bengal in 1769–70, an administrative/populist discourse fulminated against monopoly (and its manifestations such as forestalling), against cupidity, not the alleged corruption of an intrinsically beneficial application of self-interest, but its logical, necessary outcome. Certain intellectuals, in the mode of Diderot, wholly reassessed their view of the cost–benefit calculus of untrammeled liberty, and the relation between liberty and social justice.

The crowd—a "mob" for Challú, who could benefit from the immense moral-economy and collective-action literature beyond the E. P. Thompson canonic point of departure—burned down the palace and almost executed the viceroy in the wake of the closing of an important granary. Apparently far from Bengali quietude, we are not told how widespread popular rebellion became or how these rioters construed their own behavior (103). Several prominent bishops denounced hoarding and monopoly, perhaps partly in order to cover the church's own involvement in the grain trade through its tithe collection, while the unidentified "bureaucrats in the viceroyalty" espoused a "pragmatic" posture that patently favored intervention based on arguments familiar to observers of the French crisis of liberalization, in particular the reasoning that liberty degenerates inexorably into "libertinage" (104–6). The stigmatization of "monopoly" derived further credibility as a result of another "famine" in 1809. In Mexico, however, famine memory seems quite short; or at least the case against liberty is never esteemed to be definitive or irrefragable.

A resurgent postfamine liberalism drew energy from the advent of a liberal regime made possible by Napoleon: beginning in 1810, Mexico inaugurated a phase of protracted local insurrections that did not prevent the deregulation of the bakery and milling trades, in ways not spelled out (107–9).[26] Probably the most significant postfamine policy decision, symbolically as well as practically, evokes strikingly the French case, both in terms of center–periphery relations and concerning the circulation of merchandise of first necessity: local authorities no longer enjoyed authorization to prevent exports from their areas of jurisdiction (110). Challú does not work out carefully the extremely tense play between liberty and regulation, and their respective discontents: the ambivalence of authorities, especially at the center, who seem to rely upon liberty to feed the cities only as long as it fulfills that function satisfactorily (thus, for example, the volte-face of the liberal Posadas who became a "staunch traditionalist" following the famine of 1785 or the behavior of viceroys who denounced hoarders while refusing to deploy policies to control them); the capacity of local authorities to resist top-down ukases and their (limited) tolerance or (intransigent) hostility toward collective action from below; signs of a popular discourse on hunger, predation and blood-sucking *regatones*; and the evolution of actual market/provisioning structures and practices (111–14).

The Chief Cause of Famine: Bread!

One of the rare eighteenth-century thinkers who did not associate bread with either liberty or felicity was Simon Linguet, a lawyer, muckraker and pungent social commentator. His case is interesting because he contested vehemently the constrictive bread archetype, without any regard for its sacral immunities, in terms of the rational requirements for social production and reproduction. Beyond the play of paradox in which he delighted, he raised many crucial questions that others repressed or ignored concerning the logic of the "bread-centered" (*panivore*) subsistence system, its legitimizing and mystifying discourses and its perverse effects. These reflections informed Linguet's fierce campaign against the Enlightenment's self-proclaimed economists, the physiocrats, for whom grain was at the very core of the socioeconomic system and the liberty to dispose of it freely was the first principle of politics.

This Montesquieu (or perhaps this Persian) of French foodways began by exposing the overbearing ethnocentrism of hegemonic assumptions about bread—"prejudices" equally shared by the elite and popular cultures. "First, we have the idea that it is the only food suitable to our nature and that humankind would perish without it," wrote Linguet. "It is, however, a fact that the majority

26 For a more sophisticated and probing treatment of the bread question, and bakers, millers and their regulation, targeting a later period, see Robert Weis, *Bakers & Basques: A Social History of Bread in Mexico* (Albuquerque: University of New Mexico Press, 2012).

of mankind is unfamiliar with its usage," he added, echoing Voltaire, who had made the same observation without pondering its implications, "and that among those who adopted it, it produces only pernicious effects." The French needed to look beyond their navel: for Americans, who ate cassava, plantains, bananas and corn, bread was "a delicacy and not a regular food"; sustained by rice, which (claimed Linguet) was infinitely easier to cultivate, conserve and prepare than grain-wrought farinaceous foods, Asians viewed the latter as luxuries; in Africa, where people survived through hunting, fishing and fruit consumption, bread and its panoply were unknown.

A Copernican revolution away from the truth, the French had to strip away the sophistic rhetoric and see bread for what it really was: a tedious and costly compound, a nuisance in every sense that was consumed exclusively and exceptionally in a "little corner of the planet … our little Europe." Even there, "where it seems so necessary," a vast number of people were excluded from its so-called benefits: the poorest consumers of Spain who survived on chestnuts or acorns; the French who lived on a buckwheat or millet porridge or a sort of corncake; or the Germans who managed with boiled potatoes. The numbers spoke eloquently in Linguet's favor: barely 5 per cent of the world's population ate any form of bread. "There's the universal food! There's the important object of subsistence to which governments must sacrifice everything, on which all political speculations must be founded, and whose form we must attempt to give, by every violent manipulation, to all the foods with which nature bountifully endowed us [precisely] to turn us away from this one."[27]

Far from being a harbinger of democracy, bread, especially in its wheaten form, was a marker of despotism, distinction and disdain. Far from being an authentic commodity of first necessity, bread, especially wheat bread, was called into being by "luxury". To account for the "slavery" to which bread reduced (European) mankind, Linguet elaborated a sort of dependency theory, propounding that "there is no type of food that holds [men] more tightly in a state of dependence" than bread. The need to provide a regular supply of bread held the people—the poor who were the overwhelming majority—"in chains", subjected them to arbitrary power and reduced them to a contemptible status.

---

27 Simon-Nicolas-Henri Linguet, *Annales politiques, civiles et littéraires du XVIIIe siècle*, vol. 5 (Brussels, 1777–92), 431–36, and *Dissertation sur le bled et le pain* (Neufchâtel, 1779), 8–15; Voltaire, *Oeuvres complètes*, ed. L. Moland (Paris: Garnier Frères, 1877–85), 17: 348–49 and 18: 7. Cf. Darline G. S. Levy's stimulating reading of Linguet's life and thought, *The Ideas and Careers of Simon-Nicolas-Henri Linguet: A Study in Eighteenth-Century French Politics* (Urbana: University of Illinois Press, 1980).

The "bread-as-the-only possible-food" ideology justified this tyranny, and the exploitation "of the little people" by "the big." Given the enormous intrinsic difficulties of cultivating bread-making grain, conserving it, transporting it, transforming it into flour and then converting it into bread, and given the temptations to which the greedy and manipulative easily succumbed, it was inevitable for the system to fall prey to disorders, in particular "monopoly", whose victims were the "little people." The bitter irony of this subsistence system was that it engendered "the secret of perpetuating famines" that it was supposed to prevent. "Bread," implored the beggar. It was bread, however, that begot the beggar and the misery in which the majority languished. "When bread returns to assassinate you," admonished Linguet, "the image of peace and quiet, of liberty and of abundance" associated with bread will rapidly recede.

Anterior to its political ramifications, "this cruel dependence" derived from the natural and social requirements of bread production. Agriculture subjected the cultivator and then the consumer to abominable "constraints". No work was physically harder and morally more exigent than growing bread grains; no activity was less certain of resulting in success, given the risks (weather, disease and predators). In the cycle of application and vigilance, there was no repose, for once a harvest came in, another had to be prepared. And the harvest was not the end of the tale, but the beginning of a new chapter. For the grain had to be threshed, winnowed, stored, transported and (re)conditioned. Only then, after grinding, was it ready for the killing task of nocturnal bread making that fell to the bakers. And a few days after it was baked, the bread was no longer fit for eating. (Today, consumers of white "current" baguettes rightly lament that it is a matter of hours).

For Linguet, there was no rationality in this exhausting, debasing and aleatory process. It was neither in the interest of the state, which needed to develop wealth and stimulate population growth ("the plough opens the tomb of our species"), nor in the interest of consumers, for whom bread offered security no purchase, to persist in such an exorbitant and ultimately self-destructive course. It made infinitely more sense to turn to the inexhaustible supply of fish, harvestable without planting and incessant labor ("the seas are a vast countryside," which could not be turned into "a prison"), or to the production of rice, which was cheaper and easier to grow, more abundant and more certain, largely impervious to the elements, extremely durable, infinitely simpler to prepare, at least as tasty and more nourishing, in a word "the most beneficent of all foods." The truly "economic" food, rice did not have the nefarious sociopolitical consequences of bread. Linguet located the proof in the life experience of Asia, which he idealized in familiar Enlightenment terms as simple, just and sweet, devoid of the "degrading dependence" and the other criminal abuses "disguised under the name of the progress of the arts." This imagined continent is not the Asia of the abbé Raynal or of the Bengal famine or of twentieth-century China.[28]

Poison and Degeneration

In Linguet's idiom, bread was not merely a metaphor for a diseased body social. It was a veritable "poison" that menaced the health of many consumers. It was a "killing drug" whose primary ingredient was "corruption." Extremely difficult to digest, no food was "more dangerous" to the stomach nor a graver menace to the circulatory system, for bread thickened the blood and freighted its movement. The rich enjoyed a permanent antidote to the poison: they could afford to diversify their diets. Because they ate a monotonous and narrow diet built around bread, the poor stood to suffer the most. They wore their pathology on their faces, faces that betrayed systemic atrophy and premature aging in a leaden complexion.[29]

Bread induced moral as well as physical degeneration, according to Linguet's diagnosis. It led the rich on the road to decadence through self-indulgence. The *mollesse*, or flaccidity, of their loaves, fermented with enrapturing barm (brewer's yeast), delicately flavored with milk, sugar and sometimes eggs, communicated itself to their spirits and cankered them.[30] The abasement to which they reduced the poor further drained their moral capital. Flaccidity and cruelty were hardly the virtues on which to nourish an elite. Excessive refinement—an expression of the plague of luxury that so many Enlightenment "patriots" excoriated, reflected both in culinary arts

28 Linguet, *Annales politiques*, vol. 5, 443–49; *Réponse aux docteurs modernes, ou Apologie pour l'auteur de la "Théorie des loix" et des "Lettres sur cette théorie," avec la réfutation du système des philosophes économistes* (Paris, 1771), 158–90; *Du pain et du bled* (London, 1774), 9–41. Throughout his writings, Linguet played on the Rousseauian theme that practices conventionally associated with the process of civilizing in fact undermined it. (He also developed the "prison-de-la-longue-durée" image that F. Braudel would make famous two centuries later.) Parmentier's description of the onus of grain cultivation suggests that Linguet's picture was not purely polemical caricature. *Le Parfait Boulanger, ou Traité complet sur la fabrication et le commerce du pain* (Paris: Imprimerie royale, 1778), 516–22.

29 Linguet, *Du pain et du bled*, 28; *Annales politiques*, vol. 5, 431–32, 437–38 and 7: 169–70 (letter to M. Tissot, 2 Nov. 1779). See in the "Catalogue of Imaginary Books" figuring in Turgot's library a volume entitled *Dangers du pain* by S. N. H. Linguet. Anne-Robert-Jacques Turgot, *Oeuvres de Turgot et documents le concernant, avec biographie et notes*, ed. Gustave Schelle, vol. 3 (Paris: Félix Alcan, 1913–23), 683–85.

30 On the palette of *pains mollets*—soft-dough breads, usually of a pound or less, called Queen's roll, or Segovia bread, among other fantasy loaves—and the controversy they occasioned, see Kaplan, *Bakers of Paris*, 37–40, 67–68, 134–35, 544–45.

and in bread making—undermined the strength of the nation.[31] No wonder that "our *Frenchmen*, [who] attached about as much importance to an above-average chef as to a *Turenne* or a *Bossuet*, are also the greatest bread eaters in the universe." For different yet ultimately complementary reasons, virtually no one in French society (save those strategically assigned to the margins) can do without bread. "Thus," concluded the lawyer-writer, "the bakery is doubly criminal toward humankind: it increases the slavery of the poor and serves only the sensuality of the rich."[32]

On the surface, Linguet's frontal assault on the material and spiritual nucleus of French civilization seemed so outrageous that it did not have to be taken seriously. Like Rousseau, who seemed to work at not fitting in, Linguet could be dismissed as a freak of nature (even as he fought against the rule of nature imposed by the physiocrats). All the more so because Linguet himself admitted to suffering from a lifelong physical incapacity to enjoy bread, whose consumption caused him unfailingly to experience disagreeable "heartburn" and "indigestions." The argument "that renders me invincible," he boasted playfully, "is my stomach." On one level, then, his whole discourse could be interpreted as mere vengeful, psychosomatic projection, his vindictive manner of dealing with an unyielding, idiosyncratic revulsion that at bottom may have mortified him. It seemed perfectly appropriate that the leading physicians concurred that "the loss of taste for things is a sure sign of bad health, and the distaste for bread is the most unfortunate of all distastes."[33]

---

31 For a recent thoughtful treatment of the luxury question, see John Shovlin, *The Political Economy of Virtue: Luxury, Patriotism and the Origins of the French Revolution* (Ithaca, NY: Cornell University Press, 2006).

32 Linguet, *Annales politiques*, vol. 7, 165–69; *Réponse aux docteurs modernes*, 177; *Du pain et du bled*, 30–34.

33 Linguet, *Annales politiques*, vol. 7, 165; Paul-Jacques Malouin, *Description des arts du meunier, du vermicellier, et du Boulanger*, ed. Jean-Elie Bertrand (Neufchâtel: Société typographique, 1771), 3; Le Camus, "Mémoire sur le bled," *Journal économique* (Nov. 1753), 117; *Dictionnaire de Trévoux*, vol. 6 (Paris: Compagnie des libraires associés, 1771), 453. Dr. Malouin admitted that bread, "more than one thinks," provokes illnesses, especially those of the stomach. He cited an Arab philosopher who warned that "of all indigestions, the worst is the one caused by bread." Malouin, *Description des arts du meunier, du vermicellier, et du Boulanger* (Paris, 1767), 2. Cf. the story of the young man who died in a large measure as a result of his horror of bread. *Journal historique et politique des principaux événements* 14 (10 May 1774), 232–33. In the early nineteenth century, Sylvester Graham suggested that refined, wheaten white bread was the source of the "obstructions and disturbances in the stomach and bowels, and other organs of the abdomen," of the sort that may have afflicted Linguet. *Treatise on Bread and Bread-Making* (Boston: Light and Steans, 1837). Or did Linguet have an atypical clinical form of celiac disease? If so, I could imagine this tempestuous activist today at the head of a transversal movement against gluten alongside Lady Gaga, Novak Djokovic and others.

Not even the intellectuals engaged Linguet: his position was too far-fetched. The pioneer subsistence scientist, Antoine-Augustin Parmentier, merely rehearsed the claim for the merits of bread as a universal food of incomparable value, fully worth the efforts required to produce it. He considered the case to be self-evident, and he concluded in a reassuring, therapeutic tone that "wheat and bread are pernicious neither from the perspective of politics nor from those of morality and physics, as a famous philosopher has tried to show." Worried much less about Linguet's fundamental objections to the entire bread system, which he felt would exert no influence whatsoever, than about his specific critique of the perils of an unpoliced grain trade, which could reinforce the still robust regulatory camp, the minister-philosophe Turgot encouraged the *économistes* to riposte. Yet, even the most substantial of these liberal refutations, abbé Morellet's, was a superficial enterprise, largely predicated on almost frivolous raillery for Linguet's apparent extravagance (he would have us "live off fish like the Greenlanders"), his allegedly flawed anthropology (the Turks were Asians, yet they used bread) and his inability to move beyond facile paradox and uninformed reverie (he would console us with the precious knowledge that the famine produced by his system would thankfully not be "the work of monopoly"). Morellet did not take Linguet sufficiently seriously, at least on this matter, for he knew very well that it would prove very difficult to convince eighteenth-century consumers that they could not do just fine by bread alone.[34]

Not by (Conventional) Bread Alone

What distinguished the liberal phase of the eighteenth century—bitterly contested by Linguet over and above the nonpartisan issue of bread dependence—was not the state's commitment to assuring the food supply, but rather its dramatic appetite to disengage itself from its traditional paternalistic obligations. If food security were beyond the ken of the properly managed modern state, mercifully constrained by the laws of nature to stifle interventionist reflexes, it was perfectly legitimate, and indeed necessary, for the state to teach the consumer-people, orphaned by liberalization and relegated to resolve the subsistence problem on their own, to make better use

34 Antoine-Augustin Parmentier, *Mémoire sur les avantages que la province de Languedoc peut retirer de ses grains* (Paris: Imprimerie des Etats de Languedoc, 1787), 390; Louis Petit de Bachaumont, *Mémoires secrets pour servir à l'histoire de la Répubique des lettres en France depuis 1762 à nos jours,* vol. 15 (London: John Adamson, 1780–86), 109, 114 (7 Apr. 1780); André Morellet, *Théorie du paradoxe* (Amsterdam, 1775), 57–71, and *Mémoires inédits sur le XVIIIe siècle et la Révolution,* ed. P. E. Lémontey (Paris: Ladvocat, 1822), 227–30.

of the whole range of resources (rapidly catalogued by Linguet), theoretically available to them. It was no paradox, then—*pace* Linguet—that as the state groped to find its way out of the subsistence labyrinth, it paid more and more attention to the promotion of the study of dearth ersatz: substitute and alternative foodstuffs that could be used to attenuate the dislocating and debilitating effects of grain (and flour) scarcity. The vocation of this new subsistence science was, *inter alia*, to redefine the boundaries of edibility, even as the debate on political economy turned on the recasting of the relations between state and society.

Nothing better characterizes one strain of Enlightenment in the last third of the century than the desire to introduce rationality and (thus) economy—the master word of the epoch—into daily life. Far from the *encanaillement* of philosophy, this earthy preoccupation with ordinary concerns signified its exaltation, argued Parmentier, for whom the basic question of survival dominated the intellectual agenda: "Among the different objects that philosophy engages, none is more worthy of the recognition of mankind than those that concern its preservation." Even as Voltaire marveled that the fashionable women at the opera chatted about cereals (albeit unable to distinguish wheat from rye), so Parmentier summoned science to turn from the firmament to the farms: "without taking away the gratitude that we owe to the Aristotles, the Descartes and the Newtons, whose genius shed light on the universe, would not it have been desirable that one of them, instead of gliding over the most elevated heights, dropped down to consider the primary needs of his fellow men? What does it matter to the ordinary man the course by which the stars follow their path, if during this very time they die of hunger?"[35] This teleological populism masked both a genuine sense of scientific rigor, predicated on the primacy of theory over practice, and a certain contempt for the popular culture of work (idiosyncratic rules of thumb and patrimonial shop secrets).[36] At the same time, it imbued the ersatz project with a more prestigious cachet and a bolder ambition.

35 Parmentier's essay in the Besançon Prize Competition of 1772, p. 1, fonds de l'Académie de Besançon, Bibliothèque municipale de Besançon (BmB). See also Kaplan, *Bread, Politics and Political Economy*, 117–18. Cf. the noted traveler-commentator Dr. Lister, who endorsed Parmentier's conviction that food was a philosophical question *par excellence*, but phrased it in terms that explicitly deprecated the search for surrogates. *A Journey to Paris in the Year 1698 by Martin Lister*, ed. R. O. Stearns (Urbana: University of Illinois Press, 1967), 135.

36 On this question, see Parmentier's Besançon memoire, p. 3, and Kaplan, *Provisioning Paris*, chap. 9 and *The Bakers of Paris*, chaps. 1 and 2.

The older view of ersatz was mired in pessimism. Premised on a proto-Malthusian notion of structurally flawed carrying capacity, it imagined ersatz as a sort of positive rather than preventive check, emblem of desperation and failure rather than a marker of prescience and prophylaxis. Fairy tales, folk memory and administrative reports set the sepulchral tone, for ersatz was not only wretched, but also in some sense dehumanizing and/or transgressive: fashioning flour from disinterred human bones (the 1590s in Paris)[37], eating "the food of animals" (as late as the 1760s in Normandy), mixing horrid combinations of cabbage runts, boiled dirt and ferns (Brittany in the 1770s). These stories reinforced the conviction, to which certain technocrats still subscribe today, that people will eat *anything* if they are truly hungry enough, and if not, they are not authentically desperate (and thus ersatz-management became merely a problem of eliminating egregious toxicities). They also tended to support the idea that ersatz could be improvised only in the midst of great stress and that it depended upon a sort of natural or primitive wisdom on which people drew instinctively, according to the imperative need to save the species.[38] Even the physiocrat abbé Roubaud, who believed that nothing must be neglected in search for "new [forms of] subsistence" in a modern liberal world of structurally high grain prices and low wages, felt that "the Savages living near Philadelphia" were somehow closer to viable ersatz solutions than the scions of European civilization."[39]

Voltaire symbolized the shift to a more sanguine attitude about ersatz. Whereas in the *Henriade* early in the century he evoked "these starving specters" who nourished themselves on the "ashes of their fathers" that they dug up in cemeteries, almost half a century later, he cheerfully announced that "even in the most sterile year for wheat, the people have infinite resources,

---

37 Cf. the famous verse from *Jack and the Beanstalk*:
Fee-fi-fo-fum,/I smell the blood of an Englishman,
Be he live, or be he dead,/I'll grind his bones to make my bread.

38 Cf. Piero Camporesi's chilling vision of a hallucinatory world of recourse to ersatz meant to dull the anger and suffering of the people even as it acted as a nostrum of elite domination and social control. *Bread of Dreams.*

39 François Vincent, *Histoire des famines à Paris* (Paris: Editions politiques, économiques et sociales, 1946), 60; Conseil secret, Parlement de Rouen, 5 May, 19 Aug. 1768, Archives départementales (hereafter AD), Seine-Maritime, unclassified; Eugène Bonnemère, *Histoire des paysans*, vol. 3 (Paris: Chamelot, 1886), 246; C 47 and C 919, AD Puy-de-Dôme; Bibliothèque nationale de France (hereafter BNF), Coll. Joly de Fleury 1120, fols. 59–61, 92–93, 109, 176; A. Maurizio, *Histoire de l'Alimentation végétale depuis la préhistoire jusqu'à nos jours*, trans. F. Gidon (Paris: Payot, 1932), 165; H. E. Jacob, *Six Thousand Years of Bread: Its Holy and Unholy History*, trans. R. and C. Winston (Garden City, NY: Doubleday, 1944); Pierre J. A. Roubaud in *Journal de l'agriculture, du commerce, des arts et des finances* (Jan, 1772), 11.

to be found either in the chestnuts that make a nourishing bread, or in barley, or rice, or in the potato that one cultivates everywhere today with the greatest care, and from which I made the tastiest bread with one half [wheaten] flour." The Patriarch of Ferney paid implicit deference to Parmentier, who did more than anyone else to engineer this psychological and material evolution. Moral and political obligations—charity and social control—still informed Voltaire's perspective on the provision of subsistence surrogates. But in the spirit of the time (in a manner redolent of Simon Linguet), he invoked the "rights of humanity"—an expression of the equality of stomachs—that entitled people to have access to food in hard times. Nor was there any reason that "the people must always be nourished with foods that were coarse, insubstantial and poorly prepared." Neither the human condition nor the new social science decreed an iron law of food mortification. Following Parmentier's lead, other commentators emphasized that by providing ersatz that was "of pleasant taste" as well as nourishing and inexpensive, one elicited more docile behavior and more productive labor. These were the instrumental grounds on which the conversation took place among elites.[40]

Inspired by Parmentier's audacious albeit reformist project for a broad palette of ersatz opportunities (yet tantalized by Linguet's far more radical assault on tyrannical wheat culture and all its ramifying social and political derivatives), the social critic-ethnographer Louis-Sébastien Mercier moved from optimism toward utopia. "No more of those disastrous years which saw men, lying on their stomachs, grazing on the grass in the manner of animals," he reassured the French. A proliferating, and now visible, world of ersatz will free men and women from degrading dependence and misery.

> What gratitude we owe to chemists such as Parmentier and Cadet de Vaux [physicist, journalist, co-director of Parmentier's Bakery School], who, by simple and useful discoveries, will have killed the monster Famine, this child of our ignorance who dominates empires! They will have justified Providence, in showing to kings and to the people that infertility is only apparent, and that everything that grows offers to hunger a substantial nourishment; that dearth is a word that will be erased from modern languages, once we have learned how to extract from the plants that surround us their bread-like properties… .

40 Voltaire, *La Henriade*, in *Oeuvres complètes*, ed. Moland-Garnier, vol. 8, 250, and "Petit écrit sur l'arrêt du conseil du 13 septembre 1774" (Jan. 1775), in *Oeuvres complètes*, vol. 30 (Kehl: Société littéraire et typographique, 1784–89), 541; Parmentier, *Recherches sur les végétaux nourrissans, qui, dans les temps de disette, peuvent remplacer, les alimens ordinaires, avec des nouvelles observations sur la culture des pommes de terre* (Paris: Imprimerie royale, 1781), 416–17; essay number 2 in the Besançon Prize Competition of 1772, p. 5, fonds de l'Académie, BmB.

Mercier understood that food science was about politics. Chemistry could proffer not only a Cockaigne of motley ersatz—"a flowing, easy, abundant fare, at the disposition of man"—but if allowed to press to its logical end, it would be able to transform the most robust components of the ersatz panoply into the staples of a brave new world no longer dominated by the traditional grains. Concluded Mercier, breathlessly, "Our hapless political systems would be all overturned."[41]

Mainstream Ersatz

Until the second half of the century, government—at all levels—tended to focus on what we might call mainstream ersatz (as opposed to myriad "providential powders," "nutritive granulates and other Edenic concoctions"), to the extent that it was actively concerned about substitute subsistence. That meant certain lesser grains such as millet and buckwheat—the latter making a spectacular return today, because it is bereft of gluten and vaunts a delicious, nutty savor—and especially rice, though Voltaire promoted a chestnut loaf, and others pointed to familiar foods such as boiled cabbage and pumpkin, as if they were fresh discoveries with heroic vocations.[42]

Cited by Rabelais, planted in the South here and there since the sixteenth century, hailed by the police commissaire and regulatory codifier Delamare, rice was the official dearth food of choice ("good and wholesome," noted Controller-General Orry, and easy to transport). The authorities conducted myriad tests on how to use rice most effectively. The royal government chartered several companies that wished to grow rice, and financed large-scale imports at the occasion of every major dearth since the 1690s (from as far away as "Caroline" in America in 1770).[43] Throughout the century, however, rice encountered consumer resistance. "For rice, there has to be a

41 L. S. Mercier, *Tableau de Paris*, vol. 8 (Amsterdam, 1783), 140–41; vol. 6, 201; vol. 4, 124–26. Transported by enthusiasm, there are moments when Mercier takes the tonality of the providentialist abbé Pluche. For the idea that one has only to follow God's plan, see the essay number 3 (by a local cleric, Prudent de Saucifney) in the Besançon Prize Competition of 1772, p. 27, fonds de l'Académie, BmB.

42 Auguste-Philippe Herlaut, "La Disette de pain à Paris en 1709," *Mémoires de la Société de l'histoire de Paris et de l'Ile-de-France* 115 (1918): 97; Voltaire, *Dictionnaire philosophique, Oeuvres complètes*, ed. Moland-Garnier, vol. 17, 349; BNF, Coll. Joly de Fleury 1119, fols. 152–53 (5 Jan. 1739).

43 Alfred Franklin, *La Vie privée d'autrefois: Cuisine* (Paris: E. Plon, Nourrit et Cie, 1887–1901), 85; Nicolas Delamare, *Traité de la Police*, vol. 2 (Paris, 1729), 959–60; Pierre J. B. Legrand d'Aussy, *Histoire de la vie privée des François* (1783), new edition, ed. J.- B.-B de Roquefort, vol. 1 (Paris: Laurent-Beaupré, 1815), 139–42; article "Riz," Diderot,

widespread shortage to get the people to use it," related a local provincial official in Brittany. "Our peasants don't take to it at all," reported another. The poor of Auvergne preferred peas or beans, because they regarded rice as a "foreign food," underlining once again that it must be "good to think before it is good to eat," a richly suggestive formula that is commonly attributed to Claude Lévi-Strauss. During the terrible penury of 1747–48, Bordeaux consumers angrily rejected rice on the grounds that it caused various diseases, including dysentery. In 1740, a year of calamitous subsistence difficulties, observers complained reiteratively that rice recipients sold their ration in order to buy other food or drink (thereby generating a secondary market about which we know nothing). Most authorities came to believe that only a rice dish cooked for collective distribution (characteristically a soup) could successfully meet urgent needs, for the substance was too unfamiliar to be embraced unadorned and, in addition, it was long and costly to cook on an individual basis.[44]

A host of recipes circulated among officials with the deliberate goal of offering a meal for the poor "in place of Bread." The "economic rice" proposed by the curé of the Parisian parish of St. Roch, blending the

et al., *Encyclopédie* 14:306; letter to procurator general, 5 May 1739, BNF, Coll. Joly de Fleury 1120, fols. 1416; "Mémoire au sujet de ris," 1748, C 47, AD Isère; Desecherelle to Marville, 23 Sept. 1740, Bibliothèque de l'Arsenal, ms. Bastille 10277; "Mémoire sur la distribution du ris cuit," 1740 and numerous rice recipes, BNF, Coll. Joly de Fleury 1111, fols. 62–75; Conseil secret, Paris Parlement, 23 Jan. 1741, AN, Xia 8468; Assemblée de police, 21 June 174, BNF, ms. Français 11356, fol. 168; Orry to bishop of Auxerre, 25 June 1741, AN, G7 58; C 863, AD Nord; Contrôle-général to Doumerc, 1 May 1770, Archives Nationales (hereafter AN), F 12* 153; "Mémoire sur le riz, n.d., BNF, ms. Nouvelles acquisitions 22253, fols. 242–45; Trudaine de Montigny to Sartine, 13 Sept. 1768, Archives de Paris, 3 AZ 10, pièce 7; Terray to intendant of Champagne, and Malicet [*sic*] to Gaulthier, 26 June 1775, C 377, AD Marne; *Journal de Paris*, 13 Jan. 1777.

44 Subdelegate at Hennebout to intendant, 28 Feb. 1772, C 1722, AD Ille-et-Vilaine; Subdelegate at Quimper to same, C 1725, ibid.; Ruynet to intendant (Auvergne), 5 June 1770, C 917, AD Puy-de-Dôme; Pagès to same, 20 May 1770, C 913, ibid; Orry to Pallu, 13 Mar, 1741, AN, KK 1005F; Marcel Marion, "Une Famine en Guyenne," *Revue historique* 46 (May–Aug. 1891): 287; anon., "Mémoire sur la distribution de Ris cuit," Paris, 1740, BNF, Coll. Joly de Fleury 1111, fol. 72; Fontette to Terray, 11 Dec. 1770, C 1653, AD Calvados; *Révolutions de Paris* 7 (22 Aug. 1789), 3. Even as Limousins preferred chewing bark to eating intendant Turgot's rice dole because the latter was unfamiliar to them, so in recent times aid specialists in India had to treat wheat "in order to give it the look of rice because the inhabitants were disoriented by this cereal with which they were not familiar." J. Bourdon, "Psychologie de la famine," *Annales de démographie historique* (1968), 24. On the Indian anti-wheat demonstrations, see *New York Times*, 16 Apr. 1976.

exotic with the familiar (potatoes, turnips, carrots and pumpkin) won much favor, perhaps because it also contained some pieces of soup loaves: the unction of bread.[45] In large measure because it failed to overcome consumer resistance as a bread substitute in the cooked form that seemed to correspond to its nature, as Linguet had argued, rice became itself a bread, directly as a cereal-flour surrogate and secondarily as a complement to standard flours (still used, albeit sparingly, along with rye and potato in the early 1950s during the protracted post-Liberation scarcity). By forcing rice into the procrustean Eucharistic model, subsistence managers hoped it would acquire a cultural and moral legitimacy and a reassuring (placebo) palatability, both psychological and gustatory, with which no other preparation could endow it. However robust the dearth dish, served without bread, it left the consumer, particularly the poor consumer, hungry.[46]

Nothing more decisively shaped the ersatz movement in the eighteenth century than the bread Bastille to which so much of France was cognitively and emotionally confined. Simon Linguet, who languished in the other Bastille as a result of his sulfurous and iconoclastic pen, prompted little echo with his merciless assault on the irrational and degrading allegiance to bread. "But could one not substitute another food for bread?" the marquis asks in abbé Galiani's *Dialogues*, the celebrated assault on physiocracy and on the French liberalization. "The force of this habit is so overwhelming, so stunning," replies the chevalier (Galiani's voice) categorically, "that such a step would be inconceivable." Not even the indoor, or institutionalized, poor in the midst of near famine would eat the potato, contended a municipal official, "because they are accustomed to food in the form of bread." The people believed that they "would die of hunger" without their dose of bread, commented the *Encyclopédie méthodique*. With more genuine indignation than demagogy, a majority of the Paris Parlement, clear-cut antagonists of the laissez-faire program of the *économistes* by the end of the 1760s, wondered how the latter

---

45 *Journal économique* (Oct. 1752), 39–41, (Dec. 1761), 556, (Feb. 1768), 93, (Feb. 1769), 63; C 2617 and 2653, AD Calvados; article "Riz," Diderot, et al., *Encyclopédie* 14: 308; the St. Roch recipe in both C 908, AD Puy-de-Dôme and C 13, AD Aisne; *Ephémérides du Citoyen* 3 (1769), 205–10, 216–18.

46 Subdelegate at Bernay to intendant, 12 Oct. 1773, C 89, AD Orne. It was tragically believed by portions of the most vulnerable population that otherwise toxic famine foods, known to cause "horrible illnesses," surrendered their virulence by becoming a bread, a process akin to sacralization. Bertin, controller-general, to intendant of Bordeaux, 9 Nov. 1770, C 1431, AD Gironde. Partially in response to burgeoning gluten animus, the first Parisian bakery specializing in rice-based breads opened recently: Chambelland, rue Ternaux.

could possibly have conceived the "idea that the people could do without bread or replace it with artificial foods."[47]

Subsistence scientists, not all of whom sympathized with the liberal cause, did not answer unequivocally that the people could easily be liberated from the thrall of bread, but upheld that they needed to be reeducated on the question, especially when it regarded the form that cereal substitutes should take. In the struggle between science and Braudel's famous mental "prison of the long run," Parmentier found himself frequently on the defensive because he did not underestimate the strength of the adversary. He dissociated himself emphatically from "the fury" and "the mania of the day" that called for "converting everything into bread, as if, without bread, there were no food." Elsewhere, he declared that "no one has declared open war more vigorously than I against those, struck by the mania of wanting to make everything into bread, who propose to give this format everyday to substances that are not at all appropriate." It was futile to attempt to make rice into bread, "a folly especially in time of dearth"; and the chestnut, despite Voltaire's elegy, surrendered its delicious flavor when constrained to resemble a loaf. In his *Examen chymique des pommes de terre*, Parmentier aptly described the potato as "a kind of bread that nature offers us ready-made." Yet those closer to everyday popular life, such as the Paris police, discerned "grave drawbacks" in trying to make the unalloyed potato into a mass consumption good: the only viable solution was its "metamorphosis into bread," accomplished most successfully, they remarked, by Parmentier. An author himself of *Manière de faire le pain de pomme de terre, sans mélange de farine*, the chemist conceded that the potato did not command "the general esteem that it merits" until it was "ennobled through the bread-making process." And he was a keen enough observer of popular foodways and everyday psychosomatic imperatives to appreciate "that bread is necessary to certain men who would otherwise not believe themselves to be provided for if their food took another form."[48]

---

47 Kaplan, *Bakers of Paris*, 26–30; Ferdinando Galiani, *Dialogues sur le commerce des bleds*, ed. Fausto Nicolini (Milan: Riccardi, 1959), 175–76; Rattier to intendant, 20 Oct. 1769, cited by Henri Sée, "Un document sur l'assistance par le travail en 1769," *Revue d'histoire économique et sociale* 21 (1933): 136; "Jurisprudence, Police et Municipalité," *Encyclopédie méthodique*, vol. 10 (Paris: Panckoucke, 1789), 30; Representations of 22 Mar. 1769 in Jules Flammermont, ed., *Remontrances du Parlement de Paris*, vol. 3 (Paris: Imprimerie nationale, 1898), 33.

48 Parmentier, *Manière de faire le pain de pommes de terre, sans mélange de farine* (Paris: Didot jeune, 1779), 14–17; Parmentier, *Recherches sur les végétaux nourrissans*, 122, 169–70, 230–31, 449; Parmentier, *Examen chymique des pommes de terre*, 71; Edme Béguillet, *Traité des subsistances et des grains qui servent à la nourriture de l'homme* (Paris: Prault fils, 1780); and [Lemaire], *Détail sur quelques établissemens de la ville de Paris demandé par Sa Majesté Impériale la reine de Hongrie à Monsieur Lenoir* (Paris, 1780), 55–56.

Panocentrism was not tantamount to ethnocentrism in the Besançon Prize Competition of 1772 that asked authors to propose plants that could be substituted for standard fare in times of scarcity. While most of the writers yielded to the tyranny of bread much of the time, they nevertheless obeyed a prudent omnivore's instinct in their search for plant substances that could sustain their fellow citizens. Author no. 7 voiced the survivor's logic in surveying potential ersatz: "What does it matter what food one uses, provided that one can, in these sad circumstances, conserve one's strength and avoid death." The authors uncovered an astonishing range of plants, some familiar (e.g., pine kernels, beechnuts, acorns, cucumbers, apples, pumpkins and so on), most more or less esoteric, though perhaps less so to the peasants for whom they were destined than the intellectuals who promoted them (Solomon's seal, asphodel, couch grass, salsify and gratte-cul, among others). They envisaged utilizing not only the obvious components but also the unlikely parts: thorns, leaves and buds. The authors conceived of most of these substances in the form of bread, usually mixed with cereal grains (despite the limits this qualifier placed on their dearth-utility) and less frequently with potatoes, though quite often the essayists mentioned that these foodstuffs could be more simply used in stews or soups.

His fellow essayists did not cede the monopoly of the potato panegyric to Parmentier. Virtually, everyone hailed it for its versatility, abundant and regular yield, ease of cultivation, ready conservability and range of culinary preparations. Indeed, implicitly the potato had passed from the rank of surrogate to that of staple. It was fully integrated into the imaginary of the food economy, if not yet into common practice. (In counterpoint, there was surprisingly little mention of rice, in part because it was much less familiar than the potato in the Besançon region.) Another entrant hoped that the chestnut would follow the potato's trajectory, an end that could be reached rapidly if the government would agree to require and then subsidize plantations all along the roads of the realm. Still, another contestant wondered whether these newly sanctified staples could not be stocked in granaries that would become anchors of a dearth-prevention system that would not be so fully hostage to uncertainties and so dependent on improvisational foraging.

For reasons that varied from ministry to ministry (Necker marching to a different drumbeat from Turgot, for example), the royal government continued to manifest enthusiasm for ersatz research. In broad moral terms, the Enlightenment had created a climate highly favorable to alleviating—better yet, to preventing—the horrors of recurrent shortage. Subsistence science went on to flourish, despite its inability to win over the bulk of practitioners. The consumer-people both of the cities and of the countryside persisted in their mistrust of the motives of the putative do-gooders and in their resistance to the idea that ersatz served their interests. It is not surprising that Parisians hurled stones at Parmentier at several junctures during the Revolution. In the eyes of many of them, he represented, not the guarantee of survival, but the dark side of progress, a vaguely discerned scientific plot to deprive the people of the chief, everyday marker of its well-being and its basic rights.

The Wheat People vs. the Rice People

Panocentrism bespeaks deep cultural conditioning. On many levels, neither its critics nor its purveyors regarded it as an inclination that one embraced deliberately. Man was what he ate, in ways much more complex than the act of ingesting itself, ways that preceded it and moved beyond it. Bread eating was a synecdoche for larger cultural, social, economic, political and psychological processes. It involved a double operation of incorporation: the consumer incorporated bread into her body and it incorporated her into a wider universe of opportunity and obligation, of material and symbolical signification, of freedom and necessity, of order and disorder, and of norms and resistance to them. The procrustean bed of bread evolved over centuries, the product of climate, accident, evolution, religion, social organization, political power and numerous other factors. Historians, often pressed by anthropologists and archeologists, are more and more sensitive to the play of structure and agency in the working out of age-old patterns of behavior, both for survival and for many other purposes. In modern historiography, the *Annales* group, in particular Marc Bloch and Fernand Braudel, insisted on the dense and ramifying ways in which food production, exchange and consumption shaped sociocultural development; arguably they followed in the path of Homer's quest for "bread-eaters," echoed by Herodotus, a rudimentary taxonomy used from the earliest times to define ourselves and stigmatize or at least demarcate alterity. The United States used wheat to democratize Japan, in the hope of decentering and devalorizing rice, so intimately attached to imperial institutions and to a welter of cultural codes and memories, sacred and profane. In a way, this technique of domination had already been practiced by the Spanish colonists who sought to displace corn with wheat in the conquest and recivilizing of Mexico. Without following the narrative step by step, we know that the several carbohydrate cores that constitute the staples of life have fashioned our manner of living together since the dawn of time.

Quite recently, a team of social/"cross-cultural" psychologists, led by Thomas Talhelm, a young old China hand, published an intriguing empirical study that touches on the long-turn impact of staples—wheat and rice—in a manner remote from the usual historical gaze.[49] They are not directly concerned with political economy or food habits; more audacious, they contend that the rapport with wheat or rice can explain a range of fundamental characteristics that account for sweeping cultural differences. These researchers are virtually as radical as Linguet in opposing wheat and rice, and their effects on the societies that grow them and that they structure. Their investigation contends that the cultivation of rice (not nearly as easy as Linguet suggested) and the farming of wheat (not as onerous as the acerbic French philosopher indicated) generated specific dispositions that frame collective behavior. They are not only extremely durable—for centuries and centuries—but also affect those members of a given society, then or much later, who have nothing to do with producing rice or wheat (the matter of the preparation and consumption of these foods, *per se*, does not, alas, enter into play).

The point of departure is the now (quasi-) canonical contrast between Asia and the West that posits distinctive cultures: the latter culture is depicted as more given to individualism and analytical thinking (viz., an affinity for abstract categories and inhospitable to contradiction), whereas the former is said to be rooted to a much greater extent in interdependence and holistic-thinking (viz., more intuitive and more tolerant of contradiction). The authors believe that they can test this sweeping cross-cultural hypothesis in a more probing fashion by examining the opposition within a single (vast) country and ethnic group: China, where the Yangtze River demarcates the boundary between putatively self-centered northern wheat cultivators and allegedly intertwined southern rice growers, the tendencies of each group largely driven by the socio-technological requirements of their specific agriculture. For lack of competence, both in the terrain and the methodology, I will leave unexamined the governing assumptions, epistemological and cultural, articulated and unavowed, of the psychologists, including the claim that China is a "fitting natural test case" because of its unity, homogeneity and millennial dynastic persistence and the delimitation of the subject pool to students (1162 Han Chinese from six sites). From the superficial vantage point of an utter profane, the study seems elegantly designed, in particular the comparison between the "rice theory" formulated by the authors and modernization and "pathogen" theories, and the incorporation of subjects from border territories where differences between neighboring counties are less likely to be due to climate or other third variables.

49 T. Talhelm and six coauthors, "Large-scale Psychological Differences Within China Explained by Rice Versus Wheat Agriculture," *Science* 344 (9 May 2014): 603–8.

The "rice theory of culture" articulated by the authors argues that some forms of subsistence demand more functional interdependence than others: specifically, the intense labor and complex irrigation requirements of rice growing generate forms of cooperation/reciprocity absent in wheat societies, where only half as much toil is necessary for planting and harvesting and where, accordingly, self-reliance is not penalizing. In testing their subjects, Talhelm et al. used three measures, gauging "cultural thought, implicit individualism and loyalty/nepotism." For example, the triad test asks participants which of three items should be paired together (say, train, bus and tracks). People from more individualistic cultures will match train and bus, following an analytical calculus, since the items belong to the same abstract category. People from "collectivistic" cultures choose more relational (holistic) pairings (the functional linkage connecting train and tracks). Another task (the sociogram) asked subjects to draw a diagram of their social network: researchers obtain a measure of individualism (or self-inflation) from the relative size of the sketchings of self and others. In the loyalty/nepotism task, based on crafting stories of dealings with others, the psychologists predicted (correctly, according to their results) that people from the rice areas would be less likely to punish their friends than the wheat folk. To buttress the study, by extending it beyond the somewhat fragile student pool, the team looked at provincial statistics over decades containing variables that could be associated with collectivism and analytic thought: divorce rates (theoretically, lower in conflict-avoiding culture: in fact, less elevated in rice areas) and patents for inventions (theoretically, more likely in analytical thinkers: confirmed in the wheat regions) (607). For various reasons, the rice theory trumps modernization theory (increased wealth, education and capitalist practice make societies more individualistic and analytical) and the pathogen prevalence theory (a higher currency of contagious disease renders dealings with outsiders more perilous, "making those cultures more insular and collectivistic"). Positivist historians will resonate with the assertion by the authors that "the rice theory was the only model that fit the data."

Talhelm et al. conclude that China's wheat and rice zones have different cultures. The rice regions bespeak tendencies characteristic of East Asian culture: "More holistic thought, more interdependent self-construals, and lower divorce rates." The wheat areas culturally resembled the West with more analytic thought, individualism and divorce. One of the striking contentions of the study concerns the persistence of what they call "cultural thought styles" (a formula likely to trouble historians who are not still wedded to the reductionist and nebulous "mentalities" approach) across the very long run. Even as none of the student subjects in their experiment was directly involved in rice or wheat farming, "the theory is that cultures that farm rice and wheat over thousands of years pass on rice or wheat cultures, even after most people put down their plows." Simply put, "you do not need to farm rice yourself to inherit rice culture" (604–5, 607).

There is great leap from this study to Linguet's orientalist vision of wheat heteronomy as opposed to rice autonomy: obviously, they have different questions in mind and highly dissimilar approaches. They converge on one question that traverses the whole of this book and many others that I have written: the centrality of grain in the social experience, *sensu lato*. I relish the anthropologist T. M. Luhrmann's remark, in reference to the American–European conceit that we are unique, autonomous, self-motivated and self-made: "As the anthropologist Clifford Geertz observed, this is a peculiar idea."[50]

Few scholars have done more than Geertz to thicken our understanding of the notion of culture, but in its way, it too remains a peculiar idea, as it passes from discipline to discipline, from one region of the world to another, from one century to another—peculiar both in the sense of odd or strange (corresponding, I think, to Luhrmann's usage), and in the sense of singular or, as my grand-daughter might put it, "awesome," a breath-taking but still elusive and daunting concept, enthralling in the double meaning.

Though I find the study by Talhelm et al. extremely stimulating, I would not subscribe spontaneously to their conception of culture, however much various modes of cereal-determinism tempt me, now and again. Even as I am impressed by the way in which their culture affects cognitive processing, I am distressed by the apparent narrowness of its scope and contents and its apparent indifference to the symbolic dimension; and I am somewhat baffled by its relative immobility (if not immutability). The process of sempiternal transmission is not transparent; certainly the "western" case offers myriad examples of profound change across time. I appreciate the heuristically valuable psychological inflection of the idea and practice of culture, but not its lack of social differentiation.

Would some effort at historicization have engendered complementary and/or alternative perspectives, comparatively, East–West, but even within the Asian/Chinese case?[51] What do we know about the cultural capacity for compromise or adaptation or resilience or resistance during periods of intense stress, notably famine, war, economic crisis, political conflict or religious

---

50 Cited in the *International New York Times*, 5 Dec. 2014.

51 There are very few historical references in the bibliography of the study by Talhelm et al. Even an outsider such as I knows that the immense literature is in itself intimidating. Still, there are a number of recent studies, accessible to nonspecialists in Chinese history, which might have given the team of psychologists a suggestive perspective, even the books that do not privilege cultural factors. I am thinking of, for example, Pierre-Etienne Will and R. Bin Wong, *Nourish the*

friction? Does not rampant inequality have an impact on cultural behavior? Or various forms of political oppression and symbolic violence? Will not reciprocities sometimes breakdown, interwoven relations unravel? Why do we see so many instances of the communitarian moral economy in the individualistic West? The moral economy would seem, logically, to be superfluous in the rice culture, yet we know that it was widespread in Indochina in the twentieth century and probably elsewhere in Asia.

Rice culture, as Talhelm et al. evoke it, seems to be a bottom-up phenomenon. The people of the rice paddies appear to be more deeply infused with this culture than others in their province and country. Yet, they do not axiomatically have the capacity to socialize or acculturate the rest of society. How (and when) does rice culture become hegemonic? The state and the elites play a major historical role, specifically in organizing irrigation and taking measures to assure food supply, and more broadly, in a manner of governance that may not necessarily reinforce social/cultural cohesion. If, for multiple reasons—philosophical, religious and aesthetic injunction, political obligation, social control and so on—the elites prescribe the same cultural norms, presumably they derive them from experiences and sites other than the rice paddy.

Chinese time seems, to the uninitiated, to have been, at least until recently, geological in its unfolding; and this systemic tranquility, whether it signaled languorousness or patience, seems to inform the study of the psychologists. Time in Europe can move in glacial or in nervous cadence, or at some rhythm in between, depending upon the epoch. Save on the margins, it is hard to envision an individualistic Europe before the Industrial and French Revolutions. Despite an individualistic offensive that gathered some momentum in the eighteenth century, famously signaled by Marc Bloch, in Old-Regime France, the cereals agriculture that dominated the arable regions frequently imposed, for structural, geographical, juridical, political and cultural reasons, something resembling the coordination and cooperation

---

People: The State Civilian Granary System in China, 1650–1850 (Ann Arbor, MI: Center for Chinese Studies, 1991); R. Bin Wong, *China Transformed: Historical Change and the Limits of European Experience* (Ithaca, NY: Cornell University Press, 1997); Jean-Laurent Rosenthal and R. Bin Wong, *Before and Beyond Divergence: The Politics of Economic Change in China and Europe* (Cambridge, MA: Harvard University Press, 2011); and Kenneth Pomeranz, *The Making of a Hinterland: State, Society and Economy in Inland North China, 1853–1937* (Berkeley: University of California Press, 1993) and *The Great Divergence: China, Europe, and the Making of the Modern World Economy* (Princeton, NJ: Princeton University Press, 2000).

that the rice theory describes in southern China.[52] Bread dependence forged a "cultural thought style," as Talhelm et al. seem to construe it, driven by a shared preoccupation with consumption, not by shared practices of grain production, which, in any event, differed considerably from region to region.

"Famine Genocide" in Ukraine

Acute food shortage, a burning political matter at the time of the events in many (but not all) cases, has reemerged many years later in a number of instances as a contentious issue. The current upheaval in Ukraine focuses attention on a still hotly contested question: the responsibility for this Soviet-era famine called *Holodomor*, or extermination by hunger. The immediate link here to my own concerns is the claim that this tragedy was (yet another) "artificial subsistence crisis," in the Old-Regime French sense, a man-made rather than natural calamity, a Manichean metric, to be sure, but a reminder that the weather is even less a consensual scapegoat in the acrimonious ideological struggles of the twentieth century than it had been during the furious battles over the emergence of laissez-faire in the era of the Enlightenment. "Terror famine" or "Famine genocide," according to numerous commentators, the Ukrainian experience of 1932–33, like the more recent Chinese trauma, with which it shares a striking number of features, is measured in starkly demographic terms (estimates of up to 7.5 million deaths, recent research indicates), but explained in overwhelmingly political terms: rejection of outside aid, confiscation of household foodstuffs, restriction of movement of people as well as goods and, in longer perspective, the economic problems associated with coercive collectivization and the liquidation of private property—we are at antipodes from the physiocratic project—and an allegedly deliberate Soviet decision to use the famine to extirpate Ukrainian nationalism, and perhaps settle old scores with the Ukrainian anarchist insurgency.

Historians such as Robert Conquest argue that had the blueprint for industrialization been abandoned—an inadvertent message of physiocratic revenge—the famine would have been prevented.[53] Forced collectivization of agriculture engendered disorder, dislocation and desolation. Even as the

---

52 See M. Bloch, "La lutte pour l'individualisme agraire dans la France du XVIIIe siècle," *Annales d'histoire économique et sociale* 2: 329–83, 511–56.

53 R. Conquest, *The Harvest of Sorrow: Soviet Collectivization and the Terror-Famine* (Oxford: Oxford University Press, 1986).

physiocrats had proclaimed grain to be the sacred and inviolable property of its owners, to dispose of it as they desired, so the Soviets represented grain as the "sacred property" of the state. The local authorities in the late 1760s in France occasionally (and in defiance of central authority) requisitioned grain for sale at accessible prices; Soviet authorities requisitioned privately held foodstuffs to prevent Ukrainians from sustaining themselves individually and collectively. Another theme strikes a familiar chord: the exportation of 2,000,000 tons of grain during the mass starvation, complement to the refusal to import emergency supplies. The scholarly consensus today seems to be that grain stocks were sufficient to sustain everyone, if the authorities had been interested in an efficient distribution rather than in achieving political ends. The government considered the very suggestion of the existence of a famine to be a form of treason, a kind of reverse famine plot. Today, a crime in Ukraine, the famine "denial" at the time of the disaster was an objective of Soviet policy, with which many western journalists collaborated, unwittingly or not.

China: "Nutritional Fatalities" or Colossal Hecatombs

In a somewhat analogous way, the Chinese famine of 1958–62—judged today by scholars to be the most lethal in the history of that country and one of the worst anywhere—became an object of political, cultural and historical controversy. Recent works, furnishing new information and fresh analysis, have detonated a debate that the Chinese Communist Party has energetically sought to stifle as an ideological threat to its rule. Defending the Great Leap Forward as a positive achievement, linking Mao's legacy with Xi Jinping's mission, Chinese leaders sternly rebuff the proposition that one of the ghastliest episodes of the Maoist epoch claimed tens of millions of lives. As the debate on the future of China hinges in part on how one reads its recent trajectory, in the name of the doxa, quasi-negationists deny the very existence of a mass famine, clearing a space for a sort of moderate official version that allows for a mild and more or less banal cataclysm.

A recent article in *The New York Times* cites a headline in *The Global Times*, a party-run tabloid, excoriating "the big rumor that 30 million people starved to death in three years of hardship." Denouncing the distended figure as a product of flawed statistics, Sun Jingxian, a mathematician, estimated that at most 2.5 million died of "nutritional fatalities." In a work entitled *Someone Must Finally Speak the Truth*, a retired official, Yang Songlin, decries the politicization of scholarship meant to discredit Mao and the Party. He acknowledges a tragedy that may have cost up to 4 million deaths, but he insists that it resulted from weather and harvest abnormalities—nature's caprice—rather than from defective governance.[54]

The Great Leap Forward and "Fearful Conformism"

Among the striking characteristics in the Maoist frenzy to industrialize China and thus transform the ways of living and working in the countryside, is the enormous weight of the center on the periphery. In France's liberalization, the divine-right absolutist king subjected himself to the more legitimate absolutist laws of nature; instead of devolving upon local authorities, much of the power that the monarch renounced gravitated, by a sort of grand metamorphosis—the disembedding of the economic from the social—to individual agents making decisions according to the market principle, a capitalist calculus in a society that had (theoretically) become capitalist-friendly in practice as in discourse. In China, local officials who hesitated to fulfill central commands, even in the midst of ravaging famine, were purged; they operated in a climate of fear, suspicion and denunciation. In France, local administrators quite often resisted the government's will by refusing to accept the abrogation of their own authority to intervene, rectify, sanction and negotiate, and to accept the reality of the king's voluntary abdication of authority (and repudiation of obligations) that seemed woven into the very fabric of monarchy; they, too, functioned in an ambience of fear, not so much of their hierarchical superiors or administrative rivals, as of unchained grain capitalists (figured by the monopolist, the hoarder and the speculator), and of suspicion of a loosely kindred sort to the Chinese: that the central government might be in the business of making famine, in the French case for the benefit of its venal protégés. It was in part the staggering incongruity between the idealized vision of plenty espoused by the reformist prince and the practices of grain dealers under the new liberal canon that provoked such anomie among the people and their police. The French local authorities, moreover, also evinced suspicion for "Modern Philosophy," another way of talking about the theory of unlimited liberty and hallowed property, a vision that did indeed postulate a harmonious (albeit highly inegalitarian) future of abundance and sustained growth, driven of course by agriculture alone. Though the two projects differed profoundly, liberalization in France and the Great Leap Forward each sought to accelerate the conquest of Cockaigne.

---

54 *The New York Times*, 16 Oct. 2013. See the online rebuttal of the *Times*'s implicit critique of the extremely lenient, party-line point of view in *Revolution. The Voice of the Revolutionary Communist Party, USA*, 18 Nov. 2013.

Certainly, the physiocrats would have liked to achieve the "fearful conformism" that Maoist terror induced among local authorities and party cadres charged with implementing the policies of the Great Leap Forward. By its practices of collectivization and brutalization, the Chinese state liquidated the individualized peasant economy that the physiocrats were attempting, not to destroy, but to transform mightily, by allowing more freedom for the entrepreneurial fittest (*fermiers*) to take control of the most productive arable land in conjunction with the traditional proprietors (noble and bourgeois). It was widely believed that French consumers suffered in part because exportation was not only permitted but also fostered. Certainly, Chinese peasants did not profit from grain fraternally shipped to the USSR, Albania and other socialist nations in the midst of famine in order to showcase Chinese bountifulness (and burgeoning efficacy).

Terror and Tombstone

Two recent books, by Chinese journalist Yang Jisheng, and Dutch scholar Frank Dikötter, have significantly inflected the scholarly debate on the Chinese famine. Assailing mercilessly the official taboo on studying the famine, notably as a direct consequence of the Great Leap Forward, they demonstrate irrefragably the shabby hollowness of the official historiographical euphemisms: "The three years of Difficulties" or "The three years of Natural Disasters."[55] Both are written with a remarkable sobriety that serves to make their withering narratives even more telling. That self-possession does not, however, mask their sense of moral outrage, human solidarity and ideological alienation. Though they converge in the use of certain sources and in a number of important conclusions regarding the scale and intensity of the horror and some of its causes, the two books differ in genesis, conceptualization and analytical disposition.

55 Numerous westerners, by no means all Maoists, testified, often on the basis of Potemkin-style visits, sometimes merely by extrapolation from ideological assumptions, that China knew no famine between 1958 and 1962. British journalist Jasper Becker, one of the very first to make the case for a man-made killing starvation that liquidated tens of millions, recounts the observations of American journalist Anna Louise Strong, an enthusiastic supporter of Soviet socialism who had already certified that the USSR in the 1930s was famine-free, clearing China of the specter of starvation in the wake of the Great Leap Forward. Closer to my domain, Becker cites the epic press conference of François Mitterrand, after a trip to China in early 1961, heralding Mao's humanism and affirming that "there is no famine in China." *Hungry Ghosts: Mao's Secret Famine* (New York: Free Press, 1997), 45, 293.

The author of *Tombstone: The Great Chinese Famine, 1958–1962*, Yang Jisheng, born in 1940, is a former journalist for the Xinhua state news agency and member of the Communist Party, who used his leverage to begin collecting data in the (closed) provincial archives and interviewing famine survivors in the 1990s.[56] Bits and pieces of information reached him over the years that stirred him to question the official version of the famine to which he had strictly adhered: a tragic misfortune of nature. The shock of the Tiananmen Square massacre—the blood of the students cleansed his brain, he explains—galvanized him to undertake his project. That martyred ground, from each corner of which is visible the giant portrait of Mao that looms over the main entry gate into Beijing's Forbidden City, is the site of Mao's grandiose mausoleum: even as it vigilantly guides China's capitalist swerve, the current party leadership avidly cultivates its revolutionary heritage, incarnated by the Great Helmsman. Yang's unsparing book, exposing in the starkest terms the atrocities of the Great Leap Forward and the culpable stubbornness and swagger of Mao, is banned in China: it surely required great courage as well as tenacity to write and publish it.[57] If the "tombstone" in the title evokes the 36 million Chinese whom the author believes died of starvation and brutalization between 1958 and 1962, it is in particular a monument to his father, whose demise as a consequence of hunger in this very episode his son had always attributed, following the regnant propaganda line, to grievous personal mischance.

The famine struck China unevenly in spatial terms, and much of the killing took place in a six-month period at the beginning of 1960. In epitome, one can follow the story in Yang's powerful chapter on Xinyang prefecture, where one in eight inhabitants died. This district is located in Henan province in central China, the epicenter of the calamity, still marked by bitter memories of the ordeal of starvation in 1942–43 during which three to four million people died.

56 *Tombstone: The Great Chinese Famine, 1958–1962* trans. Stacy Mosher and Guo Jian; ed. Edward Friedman, Guo Jian and Stacy Mosher; intro. Edward Friedman and Roderick MacFarquhar (New York: Farrar, Strauss and Giroux, 2012). First published in Hong Kong in 2008, this edition is an abridged translation that reads smoothly and is effectively organized in an alternating rhythm of case studies and broader analytical perspectives.

57 Though a number of Chinese scholars have publicly defied political orthodoxy by characterizing the Great Leap as an unmitigated calamity and suggesting that deaths from the famine reached into the tens of millions, the semiofficial historical view remains reverent toward Mao. Yang Songlin directly reproached Yang Jisheng for undermining state legitimacy by publishing *Tombstone*. See *The New York Times*, 17 Oct. 2013 and Ernesto Verdeja, "Tombstone: The Great Chinese Famine, 1958–1962, by Yang Jisheng," *Genocide Studies and Prevention: An International Journal* 8 (2013): 72.

While the physiocratic fantasy was to see the public administration confined strictly to protecting private property, the Maoist vision was to mobilize local officials to displace landowners aggressively, and to intrude into private life, not only economically but also psychologically. The Great Leap struck the lush arable lands of Xinyang by driving peasants from their small holdings into communes in a dystopian project that aimed to dismantle the family, viewed as a contingent historical construction, in order to accelerate industrialization and bypass the West. Melted woks aided steel production, common mess (socialized feeding) enabled local leaders to govern—punish and reward—with the ladle, pseudo-science shaped the planting and irrigating practices of the new agronomy, destined to attain durable plenty.

Through the application of terror, dictated from the center, sometimes exacerbated in the periphery, the Party reallocated resources massively. Unlike French local and regional officials, who more or less systematically underestimated harvest returns in their official reports to the center in order to spare their territory from excessive fiscal plunder and threats to their vital provisioning stock, and who requisitioned privately owned supplies on occasion to meet urgent subsistence needs, their Communist counterparts in China, motivated by fear or fanaticism, announced wildly exaggerated yields ("Sputnik" harvests) to flatter their masters, and then undertook to wrest from the population whatever grain (as well other "private" food) could be found, in order to meet quotas imposed upon them by the Party hierarchy. Like the French, they engaged in anti-hoarding campaigns whose purpose, however, was not to unearth grain to feed the public, but to meet export goals (though some French administrators, like the Chinese officials, stripped the supply zones to feed the big cities, another mode of exportation). There are some signs of resistance, in Henan and elsewhere, such as refusing to relinquish all one's grain, just as some local officials here and there refused to turn over all grain reserves for disposition by the Party. Yet, there seemed to be no paucity of official zeal: the local leaders punished indocility severely, and they brutalized or murdered refractory peasants. Meanwhile, vast numbers died of starvation, or famine-linked disease, after turning to a wide-range of barely edible famine ersatz[58] and to cannibalism, numerous cases of which Yang tries to document,

58 James Scott calls attention to the service rendered by the Entomological Research Institute of China's Academy of Sciences which, in the spirit of France's great subsistence scientist and pharmacist Parmentier, but with more nutritional specificity, provided lists of the protein and fat content of many insects: dried larva of the corn borer, dried fly maggot, dried dung beetle, termites, locusts and silkworm pupae, together with recipes for their preparation. "Tyranny of the Ladle," *London Review of Books* 34 (6 Dec. 2012).

through interviews and reports, with the usual difficulties that certification of this unspeakable horror-of-last-resort involves.

Mao: Coercive Social Engineer and Murderer

Prolific scholar of modern China, born in the Netherlands in 1961, trained in Geneva and London, Frank Dikötter is the author of important studies on the idea of race, on sex and culture, on medical knowledge and eugenics, on drugs and narcotic culture and on Pre-Maoist China.[59] Clearly, he went to the provincial archives, many of them only recently opened, with a strongly articulated point of view. But he uses the vast array of material he has gathered with rigor and discernment. Dikötter esteems that previous studies of the famine suffered from their dependence upon central archives, which issued in a partial appreciation, in the double sense of the word. Working from below, he was not merely able to see how the Party functioned on the ground, but also to reconstruct a more reliable and textured understanding of the decisions taken at the summit: the damning leitmotif of the historian's argument is that Mao and the leadership were not only fully informed of what transpired in the villages, but in some sense decreed the famine, created and imposed it, and then punished the people for starving by subjecting them to political terror.

In addition to assembling the numbing catalog of violent and barbarous acts committed against millions of peasants, Dikötter is able to show how it was possible to make such a massive famine. He breaks down the *mise-en-scène*, signed Mao, following the logic of *auteur* theory: the deployment of the totalitarian apparatus of surveillance, denunciation, sanction and enforcement; the articulation of the ideology geared to boost the Great Leap Forward and the adjustments it required along the way; the diffusion of ideology through propaganda and its reappropriation at the local level; the adroit, and fiendish, manipulation of information and disinformation; the synergies between cynicism from above and opportunism from below. The Dutch historian's portrayal of Mao as Murderous Monster, ranked in the same elite class as Stalin and Hitler, is made more compelling by the mapping in precious detail of the tasks of perfervid local application and coercion (the 67,000 persons reported to have been clubbed to death in Xinyang, victims of class enemies; the torture committed in pursuit of higher grain quotas or to punish insufficiently energetic toil; the banalization of the use of starvation as a weapon and the normalization of violence, symbolic and physical). Dikötter

59 The book under discussion here is *Mao's Great Famine: The History of China's Most Devastating Catastrophe, 1958–62* (London: Bloomsbury, 2010).

puts the toll at 45 million deaths—the figure is contested as bloated not only by Party faithful but also by a number of western historians—as a result of a famine that he regards as wholly artificial, deliberately cruel, unintentionally stupid and entirely unforgiveable.[60]

War on the People

This account gives us a better grasp of the bludgeoning of rural society than its unraveling, unless one can reduce the latter entirely to the former. Did peasant communities have no collective moral, historical and kinship resources? Was the social bond particularly feeble in Pre-Maoist rural China? The apparent lapse into neo-Darwinian, individualist survival strategies seems both logical, given the context that Dikötter depicts, and implausible, in the eyes of an utter profane, unversed in the Chinese past. I would have liked to learn more about attempts at resistance, beyond individual food theft. Were the armed assaults on granaries and trains totally aberrant and thus extremely rare? Was some significant amount of collective action likely to have escaped official acknowledgment, because it was embarrassing? Could criminality—such as smuggling—have assumed the guise of resistance? The China specialist's allusions to Mao's "war on the people" and his "war against nature" were evocative for me of my French case, with all the due warnings against fallacious resemblances and specious parallels.[61] The elites in general, and, in the playing out of the liberalization project, the physiocrats in particular, had a people-problem. Though they utilized various representations of the people that created an illusory sense of familiarity, though they very often lived in proximity with various strains of "the people," they did not know how to read them, how to talk to them, how to integrate them into a changing landscape (for those of the elite who imagined a nonstatic future). Even if the authorities reduced the people to so many refractory mouths/stomachs in the midst of

60 This is not the place to inventory the praise (widespread and sometimes dithyrambic) and the criticism (occasionally pungent, but rarely aimed at the core argument) of Dikötter's book. On the agenda of reproaches: misreading of Chinese demographic patterns framing the famine experience; failure to explore (presumably for purposes of chastening comparison) pre-Maoist famines; ideological stridency; an alleged postulating of moral equivalency between Mao's Great Famine and the Shoah; putatively disdainful attitude toward other scholars.

61 Had I better command of the literature, I would be tempted to look at the French case in (distant, heuristic) comparison with the Cultural Revolution, where the goal was not industrialization but a return to the soil, a theme that resonates with Mirabeau, as well as such anti-physiocrats as F. Véron de Forbonnais and J. J. L. Graslin.

subsistence malaise, and even if the *économistes* realized that the consumer-people would inexorably pay a heavy passage price for (reluctant) entry into their brave new world, neither could conceive of a war on the people as a winning strategy, beyond very short-term (and rarely indiscriminant) repression. Their relationship with nature significantly shaped the ways in which physiocrats and their antagonists conceived their respective epistemologies of political economy. The physiocrats attributed many of the major ills of France to the relentless and counterproductive war that royalty/the state had engaged against a nature/natural order that was in fact tutelary and ontologically anterior to any positive law of the realm.[62] The anti-physiocrats did not share a unified vision of nature, but many of them had what I tremulously style a proto-Maoist intuition that it was the fate of society to combat nature tirelessly.

Famine as a Political Phenomenon

Yang Jisheng and Frank Dikötter show persuasively that the famine was not an agro-meteorological occurrence, as E. Le Roy Ladurie might say, nor a by-product of an external incident such as a war. In a far grimmer and more cynical manner than Amartya Sen imagined in theorizing the notion, the famine was a political phenomenon in Mao's China; for these authors, it was the fruit of deliberate decisions. Widely held to be the last such tragedy in French history, the famine of 1709 stemmed from the confluence of desolating weather and war; surely it had a political dimension, if only in terms of the management of the disaster, where authority had purchase, though famines before telegraphs, steamships, railroads and other tools of communication and transportation do not fit easily into Sen's framework. To the extent that they are indissociable from liberalization, the dearths of the period 1766–71—harsh penuries that are not by any reckoning tantamount to a famine—were political, manifestly aggravated, and in some occasions perhaps substantially caused, by policies that the state devised and implemented. Had they disposed of the absolutist tools of the Communist Party, the liberal ministers and intendants of Louis XV might very well have succeeded in obtaining full implementation of the radical legislation, though

62 It would be fruitful to have a study exploring the representation of nature (in terms of deep ecology) and its articulation with the natural order in physiocratic thought. Did they espouse a beneficent vision of nature, extrapolated from assumptions drawn from religion (or a generic Providence) or from physical science? In their narrative, were clearing and drainage in the service of agricultural development, for example, assaults against nature or acts of complicity with nature?

it is far from certain that it would have resulted in a highly profitable, growth-driven abundance, and would surely not have spared the kingdom from facing the cruel transitional phase, from government regulation/intervention to unfettered laissez-faire, equivocally theorized by the physiocrats, which would have generated immense human suffering. Once again, however, I must emphasize that I have not ventured to compare the incomparable: the Chinese and French experiences are deeply divergent, in nature as well as degree. There is no universal template, for famine or for dearth, yet one learns more about one's own case in looking at others, however remote. I am interested in certain (probably superficial) similarities in practices and behaviors that might help us better understand the mechanisms and agencies at work in each instance. Finally, Yang Jisheng and Frank Dikötter, each in his own manner, summon us to a solemn moral reflection on the dreadfulness of the Maoist method. Figuring, by anticipation, a capitalism that will reveal both a horrific and a creative side, physiocracy invites searching, even stringent criticism, but not the sort of moral reckoning rightly required of an amoral Mao.

Feeding the People: Economics, Politics and Ethics

Economist Alain Clément is keenly interested in the question of food security, for him as much an ethical and political as an economic preoccupation.[63] Food insecurity, in our time as in the past, bespeaks in turn the problem of poverty, most staggering in the Third World, but structurally present, often on a massive scale, in developed nations as well. Though he does not undertake to explore the etiology of poverty, he takes a post-Malthusian stand: the source of food insecurity is not "insufficient production," but "a lack of means" (301). On this point, affirms the author, "the analyses of the physiocrats and the classics are completely pertinent," though he does not show us how. The invocation of Amartya Sen in the last footnote does not compellingly close the loop; on the contrary, it casts into relief the double problem that frames Clement's book: the genealogy of economic ideas and the relation of theory to practice, of consecrated "thought" to policy.

Most commonly, writing history involves segmentation; despite the shelter (or license) accorded by disciplinary conventions, it requires constant attention to the relation of the part (e.g., demographic history) to the whole

63 A. Clément, *Nourrir le peuple, entre Etat et marché, XVIe–XIXe siècle: Contribution à l'histoire intellectuelle de l'approvisionnement alimentaire* (Paris: L'Harmattan, 1999).

(history, *tout court*). Alain Clément assigns himself an ambitious agenda: across three centuries, he means to study the "feeding of the people" in the mode of the history of economic thought, shaped by the fraught and fecund tensions between state and market. Can one seize these specific tensions without moving well beyond the confines of economic thought? Is "an intellectual history of food supply"—Clément's subtitle—conceivable without a robust articulation between the intellectual, on the one hand, and the social, economic and political on the other? Can one deal fruitfully with hunger and poverty, with the state and the market, just as representations—representations that are, moreover, necessarily socially differential? Clément himself seems to answer in the negative, for he finds himself obliged to navigate between discourse and practice, between ideas and policies, without always resisting the temptation to reduce the latter to the former, or extrapolate the latter from the former.

How Do Ideas Matter?

Ideas are for Clément both dependent and independent variables, though it is hard to refrain from imputing to them causal roles. Ideas matter, often decisively, but the historian who claims that they do must make the demonstration. Did the ideas of "nourishing minimally" and "keeping the poor poor" resonate with those who governed? (57). How? Why? Where? When? What is the evidence that "mercantilist thought succeeded in transforming a dangerous representation of a population of hungry and lazy people into a cheap and disciplined labor force…?" (31). It is more likely that so-called mercantilist thought provided rationalizations for a policy whose origins were rooted in social, cultural and economic practices and political requirements. Can mercantilist thought—either in its cosmopolitan, internationalist stage or the subsequent inward-looking, parochial phase, as Clément frames them—drawing on an Aristotelian-Thomistic "tradition," explain the crystallization of the practice of the nourishing prince who simultaneously calculates in political and moral terms? (26–27, 34). What is the relation between the theorization of food security as a political imperative, domestic and international, and its performance? (36–37).

One suspects that Clément conflates two distinct registers of reality—the representational and the social—when he postulates an abrupt expansion of the category of "poverty," heretofore limited to idle beggars, vagabonds and the disabled, henceforth to include workers unable to obtain a living wage and peasants without activity outside of agriculture (53). Put aside the matter of the official social taxonomy: does a transformation in attitude or perception occur so brusquely and, if so, why? Similarly, one must prove, not merely suppose, that the conception of labor as a commodity had actual social and economic consequences at a specific moment (57). Clément is quite brilliant in his analysis of Turgot's understanding of the market, but he takes for granted that there is quasi-universal understanding of what markets are in the Old Regime, and thus does not bother to take into account how they actually functioned (74, 92). Is the market that "commands an increasingly essential place in economic thought" the regulated social space to which the author refers or his anachronistic notion of market cast in economistic, neo-classical usage? (15–16).

Taking the Liberals at Their Word

Nourrir le peuple: Clément defines the people as the poor, but this construction remains more or less boundless because it includes a vast part of the laboring poor, urban and rural, legitimate or illicit, as well as the idle indigent, the floating population and so on. They share the status of heteronomous consumers, linked by the common onus of buying grain or bread (the peasant in this instance benefits from no relative advantage). The author does not commiserate much with them when they lose their nourishing father-prince. Perhaps he expects them to find consolation in his contention that, even as Turgot, Condorcet and the physiocrats consider that grain must be treated like any other merchandise, "the right to existence is in no way questioned by the liberals" (125, 144–45). Clément takes them at their word, despite their insistence that "one must not infringe upon the right of property in order to satisfy the vital needs of the people." Are the historian and his protagonists snared in a sort of double bind? Not if one believes in the neoclassical market paradigm: untrammeled freedom to dispose of inviolable property rekindles the appetite for profit and issues necessarily in brisk competition and exchange, which evens out grain distribution and price across space and time (45–46). Penury will not disappear definitively, but it, too, will be evened out. The French historian implicitly shares the "confidence [of the liberals] in the total liberty of trade to guarantee the food security of the people" (149). He never accounts for the asymmetrical skepticism that marks his treatment of those who are true believers in the liberal cause and those who are selective dissidents or full-fledged heretics (the absolute character of the liberal litmus rendering any such gradient difficult to operate).

One hypothesis at which the author hints is that the liberals deploy a more probing analysis of the subsistence question "from a strictly economic point of view." Do the physiocrats have a better mastery of the reality of the grain and flour trades? With a zeal that Loïc Charles might contest, Clément emphasizes their total investment in "the role of the market in food supply"—a role that he sees no need to problematize. The market is apparently the faithful reification of physiocratic theory. Yet, he says little in the discussion about *évidence*, nature and the natural order, natural right(s) and law(s), notably pertaining to property, liberty and the state/prince, or about the physiocratic conception of a sturdy, ripe grain trade (119–31).[64] Though the latter had not developed nearly as much as it could have in more favorable circumstances, the *économistes* appear to believe that the framework for an embryonic "national market"—in fact, they spoke more often of a "general market"—emerged swiftly in the wake of liberalization. Without defining a national market or presenting persuasive evidence for its existence, beyond nebulous references to improved transport and a notion of a nascent "unification" extrapolated from unspecified "conditions of commercialization," Clément sees it as a crucial indication of a modernizing current favorable to liberalism (43, 50, 73, 106, 110). Unlike their adversaries, the physiocrats rejected "popular prejudices," a highly charged battle cry that the author accepts at face value as describing a way of thinking, or not thinking (i.e., inimical to liberalization and liberalism) (119).

I believe that the *économistes* had a better understanding of the marrow of the liberal project than Clément. The latter seems to lay stress on internal and external circulation as the crucial factor in the liberal reform package of 1763–64 (109). Now the physiocrats considered exportation to be wholly necessary; it depended of course on fluid internal movement of grain. But the latter could occur only if the entire regulatory apparatus was dismantled, a matter Clément hardly addresses. As Galiani noted in the *Dialogues*, tolls [*péages*] were easier to deal with than flinty judges and subdelegates. In the same vein, a certain theoretical economic logic may suggest that transport costs are a greater barrier than police controls to the circulation of grain in the eighteenth century, but close attention to the actual workings of regulation would reveal the fragility of such an assessment (109–10).

Clément's study is driven by a strong liberal predisposition, but the map is not wholly flat or linear. "The second half of the 18th century saw the consecration of the market as a particularly efficient means of provisioning the people in subsistence goods," he writes. I presume that he construes this consecration in sectarian terms, as the triumph of liberal thinkers, rather than as a sort of broad cultural and political plebiscite enshrining "the market," a mechanism and metaphor alien to the vast majority of French women and men, and to many philosophes as well as administrators. The author evokes

64 Clément treats the question of property in his excellent discussion of Turgot and Condorcet, 145.

a "relative confidence in the virtues of the market and in the self-regulating mechanisms." He then announces the triumph of liberalism, despite the devastating defeats of both liberalizations: "Progressively the State must efface itself to make place for a system free of all rules and all constraint." Yet, Clément speaks for whom? This is likely his voice, conflated with that of the liberal standard-bearers, but it is a theoretical-normative judgment, not an historical appreciation (204–5).

Anti-Physiocracy as Archaic

The researcher is of course not oblivious to the existence of the critics of liberalism, though he barely treats them, with the exception of Necker, in whom he recognizes a latent philo-liberal seeking a safe way to give expression to the political–economic truth. So, Galiani and Mably, among others, do not share the "ambient optimism"—ambient is another notion that begs for historicization. "Their thought is considered"—the passive voice enables Clément to mask agency and responsibility—"however, more as a heritage of the past, bearer of prejudices, than as a new way of thinking, placing into question the foundations of the new economic science." So, he simply endorses the view of the losers in this great debate in the second half of the eighteenth century, for him the big winners in the long term, that is, the physiocrats and sundry liberal fellow travelers. Yet, highly sensitive to the climate, he notes a "striking change in the atmosphere" beginning in the 1780s. It is not that the liberal solution is contested or rejected, but a number of writers begin to wonder about the capacity of "the system to nourish an entire population" as well as the reasons for wanting to do so. The "difficulties of feeding the people," forcefully expressed by Malthus and Ricardo, do not, however, threaten the ultimate victory of liberalism (205). Still, it is worthwhile that Clément reminds us of what is not always obvious: that certain fundamental questions, such as provisioning the people, or the place of agriculture, or the obligations of state to society, remain at the hub of interrogation, of thinkers as well as rulers, for century after century.

AFTERWORD

We're just a freezing cold bit of rock up here in the north, but we always had one thing that the other countries didn't have. A certain equality. A certain fairness. But now we're busy wrecking it for ourselves.

—Jo Nesbø, *The Son* (2014)

While economics is about how people make choice [sic], sociology is about how they don't have any choice to make.

—Attributed to Bertrand Russell, among others.[1]

Purgatory is the promise of hope.

—Jacques Le Goff

The eminent historian R. R. Palmer, with whom I worked first as an undergraduate and then a graduate student at two different institutions, was not enamored of French historians. Yet, to judge by his affection for this aphorism, which he attributed to them, they got at least one idea right: *comparaison* was not *raison*. Palmer himself practiced comparative history brilliantly and soberly, but he warned his students tirelessly against confusing comparison with proof and exhorted us to be extremely vigilant in the use

1 This is the citation, without attribution, given by Pierre Bourdieu, *Les Structures sociales de l'économie* (Paris: Seuil, 2000). Another version, somewhat more colloquial—"Economics is all about how people make choices. Sociology is all about why they don't have any choices to make."—is attributed to J. Duesenberry, "Comment on 'An Economic Analysis of Fertility,'" in National Bureau of Economic Research, ed. *Demographic and Economic Change in Developed Countries* (Princeton: Princeton University, 1960), cited by Peter Hedström and Charlotta Stern, "Rational Choice and Sociology," announced online as appearing in *The New Palgrave Dictionary of Economics*, ed. L. Blume and S. Durlauf. Attributions to Russell, without indication of the source, can be found in many places online, including blogs by Todd Arthur Bridges and in Sergio Castrillón Orrego, "Rethinking the Performance of Management Education," *Revista Universidad EART* 43 (2007): 234. The phrase opposing economics and sociology is also attributed, without reference, to the American historian David Hackett Fisher.

of analogies, notably between past and present, always a high-risk exercise. Alert historians are allergic to reductionism, linearity and sophism, among other things, and they know that association is not causality (or intimation of guilt), that cultural genealogy is not paternity and that consumption (of ideas, for example) is simultaneously production and reappropriation, again blurring relations of etiology and even of "influence" (a lever as subtle as it is insidious). Still, historians are understandably interested in connection, redolence, continuity/discontinuity, claimed kinship, common idiom and tonality, shared referents and representations, lineage of values, constructs of identity and affinity, clues of all sorts however (apparently) remote or elliptical. Much of what we do involves not only integrating disparate elements, but also bringing them closer to each other and to us, a rapprochement that is often ventured with a view toward seeing more clearly rather than reconciling discordance or aligning with a point of view.

None of this is simple, save perhaps for journalists, especially in online and audio-visual media, who bombard us daily with extravagant and irresponsible analogies linking today's putative perfidies and/or prodigies with fascism, communism, the Holocaust, Yalta, Munich, the reign of terror, the Stasi, the Dark Ages, Athens and Sparta, the Inquisition, apartheid, the Sputnik moment, religion in all guises, oil, the American Revolution and so on.[2] For historians, endowed with a modicum of reflexivity, it is never just a matter of connecting the dots (from the Enlightenment to totalitarianism, from Robespierre to Lenin, from Dr. Quesnay to Henry George, from Simon Linguet to William Jennings Bryan, from Turgot (or Smith) to Hayek (or Ayn Rand), from Gournay to Jamie Dimon. Eighteenth-century liberalism does not lead us inexorably to Lehman Brothers, AIG, subprime mortgages and bundled securities any more than it generates and maintains durable and equitably distributed prosperity, social cohesion and harmony, political comity, ethical engagement, food security, rights to housing and health and basic human solidarities. Like Palmer, over the years, historians have made thoughtful and highly provocative, if not necessarily compelling, comparisons; most recently, one thinks of the work of Kenneth Pomeranz arguing for the fundamental similarity of the trajectories of China and Europe, which focuses

2 One of my personal favorites, the exculpatory–vituperative analogy widely practiced in the business community: Robert Benmosche, the head of superinternational insurance company AIG (the company bailed out by US taxpayers because American authorities deemed its failure a threat to the world economy) complained to the *Wall Street Journal* (10 June 2014) that the controversy over whether AIG executives should get bonuses "was intended to stir public anger, to get everybody out there with their pitchforks and their hangman nooses, and all that—sort of like what we did in the Deep South [decades ago]. And I think it was just as bad and just as wrong."

mostly on England and the lower Yangtze delta of China from the sixteenth to eighteenth centuries, but sometimes includes all of Europe, China, Japan, India and the New World.[3] The prerequisites for bold comparison in the Palmer or Pomeranz mode are probing research, critical scrutiny (of the sources, of the authorities, and of one's own hypotheses/theses), the demonstration of the plausibility and pertinence of comparisons, the administration of proof and the proportionality between claims and evidence.[4]

Closer to the domain of *Bread, Politics and Political Economy*, I think of vivid exchanges with Bronislaw Geremek, an old friend and fellow social historian, when he served in the Polish Parliament. He had helped prepare a peaceful democratic transition. Now, he turned his attention to an orderly transition to a market economy (though not perforce a market society). Persuaded that there were helpful analogies, even cues to be found in the experience of the Economic Enlightenment in France, he queried me in depth about the process I call liberalization: how to shelter the common folk (familiar to him from his own research in an earlier period) from the violent processes of social atomization and economic emancipation and socialize them into new expectations and practices, how to explain the functioning of markets (I talked with "trainers" from Rural Solidarity who toured the countryside to elucidate the selling of commodity futures), how to find the right dosage of liberty and regulation and the least costly conditions of their cohabitation and so on. An excellent historian and astute politician, Geremek was not looking for a blueprint; rather, he sought stimulation and perhaps some insight through the dialogue between present and past.

The way *not* to do this sort of comparison-for-edification is forcefully illustrated by the economist Walter Eltis in his article entitled "France's Free-Market Reforms in 1774–6 and Russia's in 1991–3: The Immediate Relevance of L'Abbé de Condillac's Analysis."[5] The research is shoddy and the analysis superficial. He has little understanding of old-regime institutions

3 *The Great Divergence: China, Europe, and the Making of the Modern World Economy* (Princeton, NJ: Princeton University Press, 2000).

4 On the hazards of ill-considered comparisons, notably the apples–oranges fallacy, see P. Krugman's denunciation of the *Financial Times*' critique of the Picketty thesis on accelerating inequality for "a series of errors that skew his findings." According to Krugman, "The alleged errors were actually the kinds of data adjustments that are normal in any research that relies on a variety of sources. And the crucial assertion that there is no clear trend toward increased concentration of wealth rested on a known fallacy, an apples-to-oranges comparison [in this instance, juxtaposing fiscal and survey data] that experts have long warned about—and that I identified in that 1992 article [cited earlier in his text]." *New York Times*, 2 June 2014.

5 *The European Journal of the History of Economic Thought* 1 (Autumn 1993): 5–19.

or social structure, even less of market organization and the functioning of the grain trade, about which he has much to say (farmers were not forbidden "to move within France"; the Rouen guild model was an outlier, not a paradigm, and monopoly was not the template for trade; it is pure fantasy, derived from liberal dogma, that the government created "vast bureaucracies" to govern the grain trade; it is even more absurd, at least on the French side, to pretend that corrupt bureaucracy in France as in Russia "threw much of the movement and trading of food and consumer goods into the hands of the semi-criminal") (6–7, 14). There is absolutely no discussion of the Russian (and "East European") cases, merely the peremptory assertion of "striking parallels" when "reform" attempts in France and Russia generated surging prices and hostile reaction from "vested interests" (16). This is a self-parodic neoclassical economic teleology spun on a modernization loom. Apart from the shared admiration of Stanley Jevons and Maurice Allais for Condillac's work, mined here as an ethnographic map to French realities rather than a doctrinal exposition of neo-physiocratic/Turgotian obedience (9–13), the most telling sign of Eltis' own liberal investment and his propensity to take liberal press releases as revealed truth is his relation of a vigorous protest against the baneful effects of Turgot's liberalization drafted by the Paris Parlement that "asked the king to revoke the laws of market economics" (7).[6] What galling royal effrontery to contest the claims of these transcendental "laws" soon to be canonized by the scientific promoters of market economics! Divine origin and absolutism subtly switched camps.

Even as he warned against rash comparison, R. R. Palmer "was adamant that historians must use their knowledge to illuminate contemporary concerns."[7] Referring to his own contributions, Palmer commented: "Let us use the revolutionary era to investigate what is most on our minds, to find out what a world is like that is divided by revolution and war." Intellectual and international comparativist historian David Armitage characterizes what Palmer did as "call[ing] the present to account at the bar of the past."[8] Given the dialogue on which it is predicated, this undertaking is implicitly reciprocal. It strikes me as extremely difficult for the historian, in the course of an investigation, to avoid summoning the past to account at the bar of the present. Armitage's metaphor is juridical. Historians are often loath to

6 According to one of Condillac's most persuasive recent interpreters, Arnaud Orain, the philosophe believed much more deeply in education and a sensationist apprenticeship to reform society than in a heroic, transformative liberalism. Personal communication.

7 David Armitage, "Unfulfilled Promises: R. R. Palmer's 'The Age of the Democratic Revolution' fifty years on," *TLS* (21 March 2014): 14.

8 Ibid., 15.

be judgmental: it is politically incorrect and inelegant. Yet, they judge all the time: in deciding on a methodological strategy, in their choice of authorities in which to have (relative) confidence, in their decision about the weight to attach to archival testimony, in their appreciation of various actors, ideas and institutions and in their positioning vis-à-vis the work of other scholars. We judge as professionals, as historians, but we also judge as citizens. It is often impossible to separate the two subject-positions, whether one is dealing with feudalism or centralization or patriarchalism, the Wars of Religion or the French Revolution, slavery or imperialism/colonization, industrialization in its early (mechanization) or later (robotization) phases, or communism, war or nuclear energy, the United Nations or *droits de l'hommisme*, humanitarianism or contraception, spying or the death penalty, globalization or gender. There are serious perils—epistemological, moral and political, *inter alia*—at both sides of the dialogue between past and present. Among other pitfalls, we need to resist projecting the present (including our own individual predilections and problems) on the past, and crafting a usable past to meet the needs of the present.

In my case, beginning with *Bread, Politics and Political Economy*, I have studied issues that engaged me as a scholar and as a member of civil society. The scholarly questions were directly shaped by my encounters at Princeton and Yale with professors and with texts, bearing positive and negative influences, generating attraction and repulsion. Concurrently, they were more diffusely, yet no less tellingly, fashioned by the combined work of my habitus and my *Bildung*, processes that involved dispositions, determinations and experiences beyond formal educational settings. My family life molded my inclinations in ways that I still cannot wholly fathom. I was a red-diaper baby with a father who went from the City College of New York ("CCNY: the Harvard of the Proletariat") to the bar through clerking instead of formal law school training, and then on to a vice-presidency of the American Labor Party by way of endless cell, union and committee meetings in various chapels of both the utopian and the pragmatic left; and my great aunts were nostalgic-messianic, vocal bundists, one of whom, the wife of a successful petty capitalist, dreamed of returning to a democratic socialist place somewhere far to the east of Brooklyn. My youth was marked by McCarthyism and the early morning visits of the FBI to chat with my father; by the arrest of my neighbor Morton Sobell, friend of the Rosenberg's, for atomic espionage; by my inability to figure out exactly what it meant to be Jewish in the 1950s in an America (even in New York City) still saturated with anti-Semitism, subtle and conspicuous, institutional and idiosyncratic—an anti-Semitism against which I was supposed to be armed by that part of my thrice weekly Hebrew School classes devoted to teaching us about "heroes" in American history (in government, the military, education and even sports, from world boxing champion "Kid" Kaplan to New York Knick basketball guard Max Zaslofsky) who were Jewish. My father accompanied me to see hotels on Long Island that refused Jewish clients, taught me to see parallels between the unending plight of African-Americans and the troubles of the Jews at numerous moments in their trajectory; took me to the courtroom where he tried cases to show me about formal justice and make sure that I understood the distinctions between justice in the judicial and social arenas. Surely, all of this, including the ambiguous revenge that admission on a scholarship to Princeton, with its quota on Jews, represented, contributed to my later interest in what we commonly call today social or sociocultural history, with its many subfields.

So, in retrospect, it seems hardly surprising that, since graduate school, I have been deeply preoccupied, in company with hosts of others, by questions turning on the construction of social order and disorder, social domination and (in-)subordination and, more broadly, the relations between state and society. I have examined these problems primarily through the study of two mass imperatives, collateral for individual survival and collective stability, food and work, Proudhon's famous "deux mamelles" of history. I have addressed these questions in the mode of investigation, not denunciation, of empathy, not indignation. Such an approach did not preclude anger and outrage, but my whole family/life experience had taught me that these powerful emotions could have neither legitimacy nor purchase unless they issued from a (more or less) deep understanding that required patience, application and a certain abnegation, psychological and intellectual preconditions for both epistemological coherence and edge.

Though I felt the pertinence and even the urgency of the issues I first began to explore more than four decades ago, in the wake of the recent quasi-apocalyptical crisis, variously called the Great Recession, the Second Great Depression, the Lesser Depression or the Global Recession, the question of regulation has acquired an especially intense resonance, far keener than, say, during Reagan–Thatcher years. Allowing for myriad definitions, some of them partially antagonistic, the notion of regulation goes back in time to the formation of the very first communities or societies. While it has intellectual and perhaps political roots deeper in the past, the modern history of the debate over regulation starts up in the Enlightenment. No other matter crystallized the problem as sharply and as passionately as the grain or provisioning trade (or more broadly the subsistence question).

The "grain trade debate," as it is conventionally albeit reductively styled, can by no means be construed narrowly as a concern of agricultural policy or a matter of the circulation of merchandise. All the engaged participants understood that the stakes were infinitely greater: that they turned on the very notion of governance, which was the way certain commentators defined political economy, the contested idiom in which many of the actors spoke and wrote. Liberals, of many different stripes, and their equally diverse critics, fought bitterly over the most fundamental matters of collective existence, of what the French dub the *vivre ensemble*: the prerogatives and the duties of the state, the relations between state and society, the claims that individuals can make on state and on society, the meaning and significance of social organization and of social cohesion, the ways to define and enforce public order, the responsibilities and the latitude of exercise of what was understood at the time as public service, the anthropology of man, the role of commerce and the systems of exchange (practices, institutions, codes, blockages, conflicts and adjudications) habitually though not exclusively associated with markets, the place of self-interest in these exchanges, the question of economic development (the regeneration of agriculture, the promotion of industry and the organization of work), the people-problem (virtually inseparable from the subsistence question and the matter of public tranquillity), the mission of police in its multiple senses, the articulation of norms and rules framing and/or governing social and economic relations, the vocation of liberty in the society of the Old Regime and the affirmation of sometimes antagonistic rights and their grounds of (alleged) legitimacy. These rubrics constitute certainly more than the tip of the regulatory iceberg, but they do not by any means account for the entirety of its sprawling, and partly concealed, mass.

Liberty was at the metonymical core of the debates, both for its exalting perspectives of freedom in a polity that was in many ways arbitrary, oppressive and vengeful, and for its pernicious implications in a society robust in some sectors, disquietingly fragile in many others. Just as relatively few persons, including many aristocrats who took their social role seriously and many Catholics who took their religion seriously, openly savored the idea of rejecting the Enlightenment, so very few actors in this elite world relished coming out against liberty, in so many ways intoxicating, if only because it was intrinsically empowering, bracingly unsettling, polysemous yet wholly located on the side of right and virtue. In the debates that were most fevered during the decade 1765–75, but that also preceded and followed it, it was easy to stigmatize the thinkers or administrators who supported one form of regulation or another ("restricteurs," "réglementaires," "prohibitifs" or "suppôts de la police," the last term stained with an accelerating pejorativization that will reach a pinnacle in the Revolution); it was immensely more difficult to vilify, and in some sense morally disqualify, those who espoused liberty.

The latter task remained challenging, but became less unnerving in the wake of the experience of liberalization, which denotes the grain liberalism that spills over subversively into many other domains, but concerns in the first instance the articulation of an intransigent conception of the social compact, of right and rights, of the legitimacy and efficacy of egocentricity as a driver of social action, of the empire of the market principle and of the limits of state intervention. At stake is not the place of a supply-and-demand-steered model for the allocation of inputs and outputs. Even police authorities viewed freedom of action and self-interest together as the soul of commerce. At question were the purposes, the design and the operation of markets, the extent of their moral and political extraterritoriality and the proper rapport between liberty and regulation, the one considered as no less decisive than the other to the public well-being, impossible to achieve without an articulation of both. The striking (iconoclastic) departure here was the postulate of the utter incompatibility of liberty and regulation: the claim that only a "total," "unlimited" liberty, premised on the absence of any administrative "hindrances" (including intrusive requirements and rules, surveillance, accountability to the public and the authorities, and state or administrative intervention) could open the way to a felicitous future Given the torpidity of French agriculture, the crippled state of commerce, the chronic recurrence of equally deleterious scarcity and excessive abundance, the obstructions that stifled development in other sectors of the economy and the political impasse of the entire system, the most ardent critics of the old regulatory regime put forward the plan for a sea change to be effectuated by a willful, unbending, transformative conception of liberty.

Liberty/liberalism is not a vestigial Lovejoyian "idea unit" or the object of a Cantabrigian contextualization. I am interested in broad sociocultural questions (from emic and etic perspectives), not properly speaking, in intellectual history or the history of ideas. The concept of liberty, inextricably linked to that of property, both lodged in nature, erupts from the crucible of the social in the 1760s and 1770s (and subsequently again and again as the grain question morphs into the social question). Without diminishing the decisive significance of its ideational and ideological formulation, this liberalism engages me as a pregnant and paradoxical *fait social total* that simultaneously emancipates (exuberantly) and subjugates (insidiously), that accentuates the autonomy of the few and the heteronomy of the many, that energizes the dynamic minority and enervates the anxious majority and that both offers the prospect of enrichment to virtually everyone (under unlikely *ceteris paribus* conditions) and generates a reality that excludes almost everyone from attaining it.

In calling the present to account at the bar of the past and the past to account at the bar of the present, I cast an ambivalent gaze on the legacy of this grain liberalism that weighs so heavily in so many domains of life today, across the entire planet. I remain well aware of its exhilarating, even heroic side: at a time of institutional asphyxiation, it believed in men, especially in individual initiative, and it cultivated a vision of progress that was not merely incantatory. Yet, this luminous side stands in stark contrast to the darker part that it largely denied, ignored or repressed. This liberty produced economic growth, as a burgeoning capitalism moves us step by step closer to the "end of history," yet it provoked permanent social and political struggle—Galiani's *bagarre* writ large—because it conflated market outcomes with social justice, because it ratified a sort of proto-social Darwinism that is chilling in so many ways.

The ultimate conceit of this liberalism is its pretension to be more or less mechanically self-regulating. The market functions according to physical, not moral, laws or political considerations, argued the physiocrats, among others, who did not doubt for an instant the irresistible reason and *évidence* of nature: exogenous control of any sort was not only unnecessary and illegitimate, but also counterproductive and thus intolerable. I am in sympathy with the numerous rereadings of Adam Smith—too plentiful to cite—that have portrayed his attitude toward public intervention and correction in the market as more supple and more adaptive than generally supposed. The liberty with which I dealt derived less from theory than practice, and the French theory with which it is so intimately associated was deeply marked by distorted, overdrawn representations of the experience of the *police des grains*. It was applied liberty, liberty unleashed in society, a society utterly unprepared for it, psychologically, politically and technologically.

This liberty, at least initially, proved to be effective, in the sense intended by its theorists. According to many of the critics of its policy consequences, this liberty quickly transformed into libertinage, in the most expansive sense of the term, a kind of liberty run amok; and then, paradoxically, into a sort of liberticide, at least in the eyes of the bulk of ordinary people who construed liberty first of all as the freedom to have ready access to grain or bread of tolerable quality. Liberalization revealed how grim, brutal and inhumane liberty could become in the hands (and minds) of those who seemed indifferent (or loftily, even scientifically resigned) to its impact on the majority of consumers, symbolically akin in *some* ways to the mythified 99% of the Occupy movement, the international protest campaign against social and economic inequality and in favor of a host of regulatory measures launched in 2011.

Echoes of that brutality persist today, even as the history of the past two centuries can be characterized as a relentless combat between a liberty that takes no prisoners in a world it construes in Manichean terms as permanently threatened by tyranny, and an equality that takes multiple forms, ranging from revolution to regulation, in an effort to check the excesses of liberty in its stewardship of "business" of all sorts (touching on issues of accountability, honesty, safety, reliability and so on) and in its distribution of resources, revenues, benefits, emoluments and other rewards. Liberty has been historically corrosive of equality, despite the symbiosis in which they were theoretically conceived. Equality can stifle liberty in certain circumstances, though it has done so very rarely in the Western European and American experiences. The asymmetries between liberty and equality remain daunting: the aggravation of inequalities documented by Thomas Picketty, the horrors of the flames of Bangladesh, the climate of indulgence in the management of Fukushima before and after the tsunami, the American Supreme Court's anthropomorphization of money as performing free speech, the proliferation of *E. coli* infections (and deaths) via barely monitored production facilities and the pathetic announcement by Arnaud Montebourg, the French economics minister, that his decree giving the state authority to block foreign takeovers of French companies marks "the end of laissez-faire" are just a few recent examples of this radical disparity.[9]

Codified, if not launched, by the French Revolution, where the debates over grain liberalism itself and its sundry ramifications were intense and bitterly divisive, the *modern* struggle between liberty and equality was in some measure anticipated and theorized, directly and obliquely, by numerous critics of the liberal current, in France and elsewhere, who deserve far more attention and more probing readings than we have given them. Generally referred to—without nuance—as antiphysiocrats, they constitute a wide range of opinion, with diverse appreciations of the liberal vision, some rather discriminating in their critique, others more sweeping and/or radical. It is a literature that casts regulation in the idiom of the Enlightenment, that is by no means aligned with a conservative *pensée unique* and that asks searching questions about governance (sometimes with Montesquieuian percipience), about social organization (reprising the Rousseauian question: how does one make of individuals a society?), about economic morality and social justice, about the nature and operation of markets, about fiscality and about economic development and what we later came to call modernization (no less promising and ambiguous than the vertiginous program of "progress" that the Enlightenment presaged).[10]

9 Montebourg's desire to impose greater "strategic" control over the "jewels" of the French economy derived directly from the ongoing effort by GE to absorb Alstom. See *Le Monde*, 16 May 2014.

10 See the forthcoming volume, edited by S. L. Kaplan and Sophus Reinert, *The Economic Turn: Recasting Political Economy in Eighteenth-Century Europe*, as well as the recent mega-conference that Arnaud Orain organized in Lyon in April 2013, "L'anti-physiocratie: Critiques et oppositions au mouvement physiocrate, de la fin des années 1750 au milieu du 19e siècle."

These questions have different inflections and often different premises, but they generally point to issues concerning the functioning and the impact of capitalism in its various guises and the ways in which states and societies deal with them. Rarely do they issue from a point of view intransigently hostile to laissez-faire practices *en bloc* or to its constituent elements. Diderot is among the more unlikely commentators of this ilk. One of the most creative and audacious thinkers of the Enlightenment, this former inmate of the Vincennes prison, victim of various forms of old-regime tyranny (and simultaneous beneficiary of protection and favors that only a conflicted system could proffer), was a passionate proponent of liberty in virtually all spheres of human activity. Indeed, for a time, he evinced a certain sympathetic interest in physiocracy. The crisis of liberalization, in particular his first-hand observations of the calamitous dearths of 1768–70, occasioned a change in his thinking. He became an acerbic critic of doctrinaire liberalism, alimented by abstraction, estranged from reality, characterized by rigidity, economically narrow-minded and socially callous. Aiming directly at the physiocrats, Diderot asked: "Isn't the sentiment of humanity more sacred than the right of property?"[11]

Espousing a sort of social humanism, the only viable, this-worldly social theodicy, he viewed the dogma of a totally inviolable right of property as "a principle of Tartars and cannibals."[12] He recognized the consumer-people's right to existence, as close to an absolute right as this philosophe was ever inclined to accord in a world that he knew to be infinitely diverse, changeable and changing. He epitomized it in a doubly subversive parable, a direct assault upon physiocratic canon and a vindication for popular sedition that closely mimics the practice of *taxation populaire*, a collective price-fixing technique often associated with the arsenal of tools of the adherents to the moral economy:

> [Imagine] a man [who] hoarded in his home a trunkful of quinine. He would only sell it to his neighbors, attacked by an epidemic fever [malarial?], at a price that was beyond their means to pay. His reasoning was that buyers abroad [akin to those purchasing grain for export in the midst of the subsistence crisis of the 1760s] were willing to pay him more. Since this quinine belonged exclusively to him, he did not owe to anyone the sacrifice of his self-interest. In this case, people would surge to his door, break it down, leave the money that they had for the quinine, which they would take away, and they would be right to do so.

11 Diderot, "Apologie de l'abbé Galiani" in *Oeuvres Politiques*, ed. P. Vernière (Paris: Garnier frères, 1963), 118.

12 Ibid., 85 and Mme d'Epinay to Galiani, 20 Jan. 1771, in *La Signora d'Epinay e l'abate Galiani: lettere inedite (1769–1772)*, ed. F. Nicolini (Bari: G. Laterza e figli, 1929), 138–41.

The consumer-people were right to do so because it seemed flagrantly true to the philosophe that self-interest, the motor of the liberal paradigm, did not work inexorably in favor of the general interest ("general utility") and that the putative underlying harmony that adjusted the multitude of particular interests to work for the social good was an illusion or a pretext. How, then, justify an act of collective violence, a usurpation of the rights of another person?

> What? Is the epidemic fever a more dangerous disease than dearth and hunger? The abbé [Morellet, physiocratic fellow-traveler] would have been well counseled by the remarks of this sturdy farmer of Sully [Henri IV's celebrated economics minister, physiocratic icon due to his interest in agriculture] who, deeply penetrated by the sacred principle of property, declared: "I have grain, but, damn me, you'll need silver teeth to eat it."[13]

Diderot's corollary to this analysis strikes me as especially pertinent: the social theodicy, the thoughtful and fruitful application of regulation, requires incessant political engagement and action. Part of his antipathy for the liberal doxa resides in his distaste for its sociopolitical quietism. The renunciation of politics and the serene passivity of Morellet and those he ardently defended worried Diderot: "For, you get yourselves involved in nothing; the sublime of your system is to stand idly by with your arms crossed; things are good on the condition that neither you, nor anyone else, does anything."[14]

---

13 Diderot, "Apologie de l'abbé Galiani," 121.

14 Ibid., 115. Cf. this perfervid warrant for a totalizing laissez-faire uttered by Roland de la Platière, a Gournayian-type figure, writer, *inspecteur des manufactures* and mordant critic of this regulatory system, when he was a Girondin minister during the early war years of the French Revolution: "Everything, the history of England and our own, the grand perspectives of Turgot and the disastrous errors of Necker, everything proves that the government has never interfered with any commerce, with any manufacture, with any enterprise without generating enormous costs, in competition with individual actors and to the detriment of everyone; that every time that it wished to become entangled with private business, make regulations concerning the way property be used, to modify property as it pleased, it did nothing less than to put barriers in the way of industry, raise the cost of labor, and the merchandise that came from it. The object of subsistence illustrates this question better than any other, precisely because it is a product of first necessity … the only thing perhaps that the Assembly can allow itself to do on the subsistence question, is to announce that *it must do nothing*, that it will suppress all barriers, that it declares the most complete liberty of the circulation of goods." [My emphasis] Letter from the minister of the interior, Roland, to the Convention, 19 November 1791, *Moniteur universel* [repr.], XIV, 517–18.

Suggesting that, in circumstances of acute subsistence stress, grain devolved to the status of a common good, the Encyclopedist likened it to the air we breathe.[15] Jacques Necker, a much neglected and generally underestimated Enlightenment figure (international banker and salon sponsor, grain speculator and philanthropist, philosophe and several times chief minister) also used the air metaphor to evoke the subsistence bind in a liberal world:

> If air had been susceptible to as uneven a sharing out as subsistence, one would have probably held in high esteem men who, by the clever disposition of tubes or conductors, would have found the means to deliver this air rapidly to the places that lacked it; but, one would have regarded as catastrophes of Society those who, by the invention and the usage of several pneumatic pumps, would have made the air scarce in one place in order to convey it to another, and who would have thus disrupted the general well-being [*Bonheur*], in favor of their self interest or convenience.[16]

The allegory could have pointed to an execrable monopoly or to a ramification of the insidious famine plot. Necker remained elusive on this matter, perhaps because he wrote just at the moment of the outbreak of the Flour War, the ruinous popular verdict on Turgot's attempt at liberalization and, unlike Diderot, he published his work forthwith. By and large, however, he was not shy about making his case against liberalization—an excessive liberty cast in a dogmatic framework—in terms quite similar to Diderot's. He argued for a distinction between property of goods of first necessity and ownership of other things. Property in grain was held in a sort of "trust"; it could be called upon in times of emergency. Like the coeditor of the *Encyclopédie*, he maintained that the exigencies of "humanity" itself demanded a conditional application of the laws and rights of property. "Social laws" were required in order to check the hegemony that the dominant exercised over the dominated. Necker's vision of the precariousness of the social order, particularly under the stress of penury and the fears and suspicions that it generated, but more generally and structurally, as a result of excessive inequality, was no less apocalyptic than Diderot's. A kind of embryonic

15 Ibid., 120–21

16 J. Necker, *Sur la Législation et le commerce des grains* (Paris: Pissot, 1776), 225. Cf. ibid. 246, where the author observes that "the people accustom themselves to view grain as one of Nature's goods, similar to the air that they breathe …." Necker also compares grain with air in his *Eloge de J. B. Colbert, discours qui a remporté le prix de l'Académie française en 1773* (Paris: J. B. Brunet, 1773), 94.

class struggle takes on a sharp relief when "proprietors" raise the price of grain/bread while refusing to raise the wage of working men [*des Hommes industrieux*]: "There emerges between these two classes of Society a sort of dark but terrible battle, where the number of wretched are countless, where the strong oppress the weak under the cover of the laws, where Property weighs down heavily with all the burden of its prerogatives upon the Man who lives from the work of his hands." As Diderot calls forth tartars and tigers, the future minster warns of "lions" menacing, if not devouring, "defenseless animals."[17]

Certainly *the* philosophe, as his friends baptized Diderot, followed Necker's contention that it was the obligation of the government to intervene to help the people acquire their daily bread, notably in hard times. A government had to be "moderate" in its general spirit and discreet in its interventions, even if Necker harbored no illusion about its capacity "to curb the excessive power of property" or to bring about "the safeguard of the weak against the powerful." Unbearably acute during times of soaring prices and penury, this problem was not merely a matter of cyclical concern. Like Galiani and his apologist Diderot, Necker emphasized that the governors had to be concerned with the problem of social cohesion every day. No task was more difficult and pressing than the forging of the "general harmony." Even if we find a way to attenuate the impact of shortage, he wondered, how can we weave a social bond connecting the have-nots with the haves:

> One would say that a small number of men, after having divided up the land, made laws of union and of guarantee against the multitude, as they might have built shelters in the woods to protect themselves against savage beasts.
>
> However, one dares say it, after having established the laws of property, justice and liberty, almost nothing has yet been done for the most numerous class of Citizens. Who cares about your laws of property? might they advance. We possess nothing. Your laws of justice? We have nothing to defend. Your laws of liberty? If we do not work tomorrow, we will die.[18]

Necker does not circumvent the political upshot of this situation. Doubtless, the state cannot directly reduce the "prodigious inequalities" that seem to get deeper and deeper (though one could perhaps imagine Necker taking

17 Necker, *Sur la Législation et le commerce des grains,* 35, 38, 87, 88, 132, 156, 166, 238, 249, 337, 361–62, 388. Cf. a rough sketch of the iron law of wages, similar to Turgot's version. Ibid., 372, 381.

18 Ibid., 91, 117, 323, 327, 338, 387, 400, 406–7, 409.

into serious consideration Picketty's relatively conservative fiscal solutions or, rather, propositions, despite the banker's general allergy to increasing taxes for fear of alienating elite opinion). Still, the soon-to-be minister solemnly remarks: "Political institutions and the laws of the administration are almost the only [forces] that defend the People." He concludes with an appeal to the prince, lucid rather than mawkish in its reference to the "tender anxiety" and the "prudence" that must necessarily accompany his enlightened and paternal inclinations, and devoid of any dramatic omen (or moral blackmail) about the possibly explosive consequences of royal inaction or indifference. "Never forget," he exhorts the monarch, that the majority are not consulted on the making of law; given the long labor required for them to earn their daily bread, they cannot participate in the Enlightenment ("elle ne participe point aux lumières qui se répandent"). As a result, "their feebleness and their abandonment beg for [or demand] your ceaseless wardship [supervision or protection]." Like the philosophe, the minister-in-the-making calls for the exercise of politics in the service of some sort of social equilibrium. Predictably, the propertied ask you only for liberty and justice as they construe it. "Those who have nothing," however, "need your humanity, your compassion, and political laws which collectively will temper the force of property." Specifically, since this is what the people think about all the time and this is all they have—paradoxically their "sole possession" is the vital minimum which they imperatively need and obsessively seek—"it is above all by the wisdom of the grain laws that you will come closest to giving them happiness and peace of mind."[19]

Born indirectly of my fascination with Fernand Braudel's reflections on the rhythms of time, especially the long run and its totalizing cortège, *Bread, Politics and Political Economy* taught me a lesson that seems equally valid 40 years later: that certain questions bearing intensely on the human condition in society are timeless.

---

19 Ibid., 407–8.

INDEX

www.ingramcontent.com/pod-product-compliance
Ingram Content Group UK Ltd.
Pitfield, Milton Keynes, MK11 3LW, UK
UKHW041830100926
8556IPUK00002B/101

9 781783 084760